CAMBRIDGE LATIN AMERICAN STUDIES

TERRA LINDA HIGH SCHOOL LIBRARY
SAN RAFAEL, CALIFORNIA

46

EARLY LATIN AMERICA

A HISTORY OF COLONIAL SPANISH AMERICA AND BRAZIL

DISCARD
Terra Linda High School Library

For a list of books in this series please turn to page 479.

EARLY LATIN AMERICA

A HISTORY OF COLONIAL SPANISH AMERICA AND BRAZIL

JAMES LOCKHART
University of California, Los Angeles
STUART B. SCHWARTZ
University of Minnesota

CAMBRIDGE UNIVERSITY PRESS
Cambridge
London New York New Rochelle
Melbourne Sydney

Published by the Press Syndicate of the University of Cambridge
The Pitt Building, Trumpington Street, Cambridge CB2 1RP
32 East 57th Street, New York, NY 10022, USA
296 Beaconsfield Parade, Middle Park, Melbourne 3206, Australia

First published 1983

Printed in the United States of America

Library of Congress Cataloging in Publication Data

Lockhart, James.

Early Latin America.

(Cambridge Latin American studies ; 46)

Bibliography: p.

1. Latin America – History – To 1830. I. Schwartz,
Stuart B. II. Title.
F1411.L792 1983 980 82–23506
ISBN 0 521 23344 5 hard covers
ISBN 0 521 29929 2 paperback

Contents

Tables, figures, and maps

TABLES

FIGURES

MAPS

Preface

Plans for this book go back to the time some years ago when, participating in a conference session on comparisons between Spanish America and Brazil in the early period, we discovered that the two of us had written nearly the same paper. Rather than comparing Spanish and Portuguese America as two separate entities, we had each treated the whole of Ibero-America as one entity, finding that the parts of Brazil tended to fall together typologically and in other ways with certain parts of Spanish America in contrast to other Spanish American areas, especially Peru and Mexico. We decided that there ought to be at least one work in English which treats within a single framework the entire area occupied by Iberians during what is usually called the colonial period.

In the years since our first commitment to the project, an additional motivation for it has grown ever more important in our minds. The spate of significant scholarly production in the field after World War II, in the period of about 1950–65, has been followed by an even more varied and voluminous outpouring. Under these conditions, frequent updating of syntheses is called for. Here, as in the matter of the two imperial zones, our aim is a unified view. Subfields have grown up – not an entirely new phenomenon in Latin American history – which hardly seem to recognize each other's existence, much less speak each other's language. In trying to combine the results of the subdisciplines, we also try to achieve a common vocabulary. Although we are not incognizant of the contribution of anthropology, sociology, linguistics, and other neighboring disciplines, and although we have developed some new terminology of our own in this book, we attempt to stay inside the boundaries of the readily intelligible across disciplines and specialties.

Intending the volume as both synthesis and introduction, we have forgone footnotes, which here tend to be irrelevant for the neophyte or general reader and unnecessary for the professional, who will quickly recognize many of the works on which we draw and the extent to which we follow or comment upon them. We do, however, provide a relatively ample selected bibliography to satisfy partially the need for a guide to further reading and to acknowledge some of our debts. Those debts go far beyond the items of the bibliography, and we wish to thank the countless individuals who have contributed through their writings to the understanding of early Latin America. Our special thanks go to William Taylor for a thoughtful reading of the manuscript.

J. L.
S. B. S.

Part I

The context

The Western Hemisphere after European contact has often been called the "New World," but the intrusive and indigenous people who created the American societies hardly seem to have seen it in that light. Rather, both groups operated within worlds already highly structured, whole bodies of social, cultural, and technological practice, which shaped and colored all they did. Their innovations were largely forced upon them, usually taking the form of extending an already-known principle into a new sphere. The Iberians in America sought and found analogies between the new experience and what was familiar to them, whether in their own society, in their relations with the Moors on their own ground, or in their contacts with the Africans outside it. And the Indians too dealt with the outsiders in terms of analogies from out of their past. The meshing of the respective backgrounds was a vital factor in quickly bringing some areas of America to the center of attention while others long remained on the margin, and it helped determine not only the rate but also the forms of development.

Since so much of what happened after the conquest can be understood and even predicted from a thorough grasp of how the societies involved were constituted immediately prior to contact, we want to discuss that topic at considerable length; what follows here in Part I, however, is meant not merely to depict something prior in time but also to describe the functioning of the two societies in any place and time period where they can be identified. Despite the remarkable growth and differentiation of Iberian society in an American setting, the overall strategy of marriages within the Iberian framework, for example, is not discernibly different in eighteenth-century Mexico, Peru, or Brazil than it was in fifteenth-century Spain and Portugal. Similarly, despite vast transformations and losses in the indigenous world, some types of indigenous sociopolitical organization persisted from ancient times through the entire colonial period and beyond, as long as the peoples who originated them could be said to exist. In dealing with Iberian and indigenous society around 1500, then, we are aiming not so much at a rounded picture of the status quo as at the description of certain organizing principles, standard procedures, and types extant both before and after contact.

1

Iberian ways

At the border of the Christian and Muslim spheres, the home of many kingdoms and several languages, turned partly to the Mediterranean, partly to the Atlantic, and partly in upon itself, early modern Iberia had more than its share of diversity. But recognizing the idiosyncrasies of each of the various Iberian kingdoms, all nevertheless shared a common cultural and historical experience. Especially they shared the general organizational patterns we will be emphasizing here, so that in the following discussion we will treat them as a unit for the most part, subsequently devoting a few pages to distinctive features of Portugal or Spain.

The city

Not very far beneath the surface of Iberian reality lay the city-state, the basic entity of Mediterranean civilization from time immemorial. Nationality was still fluid, distant, and easily undermined by dynastic change and conflict. Everywhere they went, the early modern Iberians gave more importance to provinciality and less to nationality than one might expect. Anyone from the home province was a friend, anyone from elsewhere was an outsider. Again and again political alliances and antagonisms in the New World were based on provincial origins. The province, the city, and the neighborhood were crucial reference points in helping individuals to define themselves in relation to others. Nothing but family had as strong a hold on the emotions of Iberians or was as essential to their sense of identity as regionalism, the love of what was later called the *patria chica* (home province or town).

Even more important than loyalties were the nature and structure of the provincial entity. The city proper was indissolubly integrated with a larger or smaller area around it, its territory, where many of its citizens had their holdings; people domiciled in surrounding hamlets were as much citizens of the city-province as the true urban dwellers. The percentage of the populace living within the city walls was not necessarily high, but nearly everyone with any position was located there. All organizations, whether ecclesiastical, commercial, social, or even agricultural, had their directorship and headquarters in the city. To advance in anything was to approach the city. As centers of craft production and the markets, the cities were naturally the home ground of the artisan and merchant groups, but the nobility too, both the high nobles and those only locally prominent, were urban based. Their chief residences and social ties were in the city, though their economic sinews might be flocks of sheep and estates in the country and whole rural areas might be under their dominance. This nucleation was symbolized in the municipal council, where representatives of the area's socially most prominent and economically most powerful families (these two attributes almost always went together) sat in great dignity. The Iberian city, with its traditional rights and privileges, its political-symbolic functions, and its broad command of the social and economic resources of its region's inhabitants, was a theater of action for the entire society, not merely half of an urban–rural dichotomy as may have been more nearly the case in northern Europe.

Functional groupings of society

The society inhabiting these city-provinces can be described in many ways, some more useful than others. Iberians themselves spoke much of the distinction between noble and commoner, and so much was made of nobility that a fairly large proportion of the population, people who in some countries would have been considered prosperous townsmen, asserted noble status for themselves. Much of the activity concerned with establishing nobility was superficial, a sort of subterfuge and camouflage that deceived no one, but the ideal, the well-defined role and life-style of the nobleman, was a force in life. Nobility was as much a set of attitudes as it was a matter of lineage. Whatever the medieval military origins of noble status, by the sixteenth century its avenues of approach were broader. Full economic success in almost any branch of life created nobility, and the nobles new and old all adhered to the same patterns. Mastery of the martial arts, horsemanship, and literacy were expected. There were also things a noble did not do, as important to his status as his positive attributes. The noble married a woman of high lineage (underneath which ideal much jockeying for wealth and position went on); he maintained a large establishment of relatives, retainers, and servants who filled a city house of much magnificence and spread out to care for lands and stock in the country. Though seigneurial, noblemen were not anticommercial. Through their employees they invested in every aspect of their region's economy. The goal was permanent wealth, enabling a family to "live nobly" from rents and herds without daily activity in trade. Despite the modern stereotype of the threadbare *hidalgo* (the most widespread Spanish term for a nobleman), in Iberian society there was a reasonable correspondence between wealth and nobility, both factually and ideally.

If we subsume the noble under the category "person of independent means" or estate owner (not the same as landowner, since Iberian noblemen often had numerous dependents and employees and innumerable sheep but very little land), then Iberian society's most meaningful subdivisions were those according to occupation or function. Professional people, with training for the church, the law, or medicine, were a group important beyond their numbers – all the more so in the Indies, as we will see. They were not a social class in themselves but were recruited from a broad social spectrum, starting with the nobles at the top. Though the professions were practiced most seriously, they were hardly bourgeois; they were perfectly compatible with nobility, even an added distinction, and the titles stemming from university degrees and bureaucratic office were so prized for the status they conferred that they displaced other titles and sometimes even an individual's first name. Professionals shared the attitudes and life-style of the nobility, and success in the professions or the royal employ could lead to a formal grant of noble status for those who did not have it already.

Lower ranking but still toward the upper end of the social scale were the merchants, especially those involved in long-distance wholesale trade. They were propertied and literate by definition, not nobles per se, though the most successful of them were forever merging into the nobility. They were closer to being a self-sustaining social group than the professionals and had a life-style of their own involving much geographical mobility, for lucrative trade was still almost always long-distance trade.

A large number of Iberians were the direct dependents and employees of others, their retainers, stewards, "servants." These ranged from literate, influential majordomos who had practical management of the affairs of important noblemen to hangers-on, pages, henchmen, and stableboys. Spaniards had a special word, *paniaguados* (from *pan y agua,* "bread and water"), for those who received their sustenance from a patron. Varying from noble to the lowest commoner, these retainers were in no sense a social class, but the function, the client relation to a patron or family, was quite constant.

In a prefactory economy, most manufactures were produced by artisans in shops where wares were both made and sold. Definitely plebeians, often low on the literacy scale, artisans nevertheless were trained in special skills, and their tools and materials represented capital; successful masters headed good-sized establishments of journeymen, apprentices, and slaves. Trades ran in families, and artisans as a group had much social solidarity. Shopkeepers and other people who engaged in local petty trade, as opposed to long-distance merchants, were on the same level as the artisans and had much in common with them.

Most Iberians were farmers or herdsmen. If large holders were at the top of Iberian society, agricultural small holders and workers were at the bottom. The variety of their tenure and living conditions was wide, ranging from prosperous farmers who owned their own land to migrant laborers. Many paid various rents and duties to their lords, whether noblemen, the church, or the crown. Most lived in small agricultural towns and villages, the typical Mediterranean pattern, going out to their fields in the morning and returning home at nightfall. The relatively unskilled Iberian peasant, as such, had little impact on America. It was rather those at the middle levels of agricultural life, the agricultural entrepreneurs, the skilled animal breeders and vegetable gardeners, who would help to change the face of the Western Hemisphere. The low prestige of working directly with the soil, however, would be a factor in the behavior of Iberians in the New World. Spanish and Portuguese farmers worked as hard as any in the world, but when given the opportunity to raise their social status by giving up labor in the fields, they invariably did so.

At all of these social-functional levels there were women, not as outwardly oriented as the men, but sharing the general social characteristics of their group. Although traditions of patriarchalism, the Moorish heritage, and strong concern with family honor all combined to subordinate women in some ways, Iberian women did hold and inherit property and had other rights in custom and law. Widows and spinsters sometimes asserted themselves quite actively in economic life, and although the ideal of the secluded and retiring woman was commonly held, it was often far from reality. A fact of life, however, was that fathers made marriages and arranged dowries for their daughters, or placed them in convents, purely as a matter of social-economic family strategy, aiming for husbands who would bring the family the most possible wealth and prestige.

Though Iberia is surrounded by water, central Castile is landlocked, and mariners had no place in its society. All around the edges of the peninsula, on the other hand, were semiforeign peoples who lived from the sea, the Catalonians, the Basques, the Galicians, the Portuguese. Thus there arose the double-barreled Castilian disdain for sailors and foreigners, the two being considered largely the same thing. For the Portuguese, with a long seafaring tradition, attitudes were somewhat different, but not as much as one might expect. Captaining a maritime expedition or investing in overseas trade were occupations worthy of some regard, but common sailors, fishermen, and even ship captains were without high status. People with pretensions to nobility shied away from maritime associations or cloaked them under a surface of servants, land, and other symbols of rank.

Other principles of social organization

Aside from the rather miscellaneous functional groupings, there were certain organizing principles that ran through Iberian society and affected it at every level. One of these was patriarchalism, the principle that any group, familial or otherwise, will form a hierarchy from the lowest or youngest up to one senior figure under whose protection and dominance it stands and through whom advancement is obtained. Society in a very real sense was made up of large units built around a family and an estate, with the proprietor ruling paternalistically over the direct family, many relatives, employees, and slaves, a unit that encompassed many social levels and stretched from city to countryside. If patriarchalism was most fully expressed in great family estates, other partial embodiments of it were to be seen in merchants' companies, artisans' shops, and ecclesiastical and governmental organizations.

In accordance with the nature of patriarchalism, the Iberian family was an inclusive entity, existing at several social levels at once. Ties to other families were emphasized through naming patterns, and "cousin" was as good as "brother." A rich and powerful family had poorer and less noble relatives who were taken into the fold to some extent, not to speak of orphans and slaves who adopted the family name. The practice of prominent men maintaining second relationships with women of lower class provided the basis for the acceptance of these liaisons in the New World. The illegitimate children of such unions (Spanish law recognized several levels of bastardy) usually received some recognition from the father, often taking his name and getting some support, being treated simultaneously as a servant and a relative. Thus Iberians had models for marriageless relationships with Black and Indian women and the recognition of their mulatto and mestizo children without implications of full equality.

Let us add that true to its inclusive multilineage and multilevel nature, the Iberian family practiced division of the inheritance rather than strict primogeniture. Only those who built the greatest fortunes established entails with obligatory inheritance of the eldest son; others gave the eldest preference but by custom and law left significant amounts to all legitimate children including daughters. Iberian family strategy, to be fully reduplicated in America, involved the attempt to consolidate and preserve the family's position while giving each heir a good basis in life, through several devices: arranging lucrative marriages, putting some sons into the clergy or other careers, sending daughters to nunneries, marrying close relatives, sacrificing illegitimate to legitimate heirs.

The paternalism of this system, with its mutual ties and obligations between patron and client, family head and dependents, master and retainer, cut across the strata of functional grouping or economic class. Each person or family group was tied to a patron by bonds of kinship, obligation, or interest. The system encompassed both affection and hatred and had places for people of very different characteristics. Transferred to the New World, it proved particularly adapted to the situation of a society in formation, with its typical decentralization and its need to incorporate people of divergent culture and ethnic origin.

Patriarchal organization was not the only social principle competing with that of occupational-economic groupings. In theory, society was divided into various corporations, self-contained entities which in cooperation with each other maintained the health of society and the general welfare. Different kinds of groups or social divisions had corporate status. The traditional three estates, nobility, clergy, and commoners, were in a sense corporations, each with its specific duties and privileges; together they made up the organic whole which comprised the body politic of the monarchy. There were also more specialized corporations, on the order of the artisan guilds. Each branch of society was to be a world unto itself, with the right to regulate its own practices and customs, to adjudicate disputes among its members, and to establish the standards of behavior expected of them. Theologians and political thinkers often made a great deal of the corporative ideal as the basis of Iberian society, but it was seriously undercut by the other, often more vital and pervasive principles we have mentioned. Many corporations had reality mainly as a kind of semi-institution or special-interest pressure group. The *consulado,* or merchant guild, for instance, represented some merchants but not all, and there was cutthroat competition among its own members; in general, such corporate organizations never embodied whole sectors of society. Yet the archaic, theoretical nature of corporatism as a general explanation of society should not disguise its remaining importance. Organized groups of any kind, including ecclesiastical and governmental, tended to become autonomous, self-contained bodies. Even more importantly, corporatism conditioned social expectations. The hierarchy of status rested squarely on affiliation with established categories such as "artisan" or "noble" even though they were not true "corporations," and people were correspondingly sensitive to the recognition of their rank as expressed in constantly used titles or epithets.

Ethnic groups

Christian Iberians did not live in cultural isolation. In the counterpoint of conquest and reconquest, retreat and advance through the Middle Ages, Muslims were often left under Christian rule and vice versa. In the lands of both there was also a significant Jewish minority. Relations between these ethnic groups were usually uneventful; in many ways each group formed another type of corporation. Jews living under a Christian prince, for example, had their own statutes, customs, and special obligations. Over the course of centuries, certain occupations came to be associated with specific ethnic groups, so that it was common to find Moors as artisans or gardeners, Jews as merchants and physicians, and Christians as workers of the soil or men at arms. But we must be careful not to overstate these associations, which fell far short of making early modern Iberia a caste society. Not every merchant was a Jew nor every artisan a Moor. The Moors especially were heavily concentrated in the southeastern part of the peninsula. There was considerable diversity in the types of occupation that any one group would perform, and Christian or Latin Iberian society contained the entire range within itself alone.

The Christian reconquest of Iberia was accompanied in its later stages by a growing conviction of the necessity of religious and political unity. Toleration of cultural and especially of religious diversity weakened. The fall of Granada in 1492 brought an end to Muslim political control anywhere on the peninsula, and almost immediately thereafter the Jews were forced either to convert or to leave Castile (they had been expelled from Aragon a hundred years earlier). A similar "conversion" took place in Portugal in 1498. In Spain even the Christianized Moors (*moriscos*) and intermittently the gypsies would eventually be the target of expulsion orders. Thus whereas Christian Iberians had a cosmopolitan tradition of dealing with other cultures, they were also embarked on a process of cultural and religious unification. The tensions created by the clash of these two tendencies within Iberian society were transferred along with everything else to the New World. It is well to remember, however, that diversity was the primary phenomenon and the search for orthodoxy the reaction to it.

Forced conversion created a large body of people who remained suspect in the eyes of their neighbors and of the church. Although the religion of their fathers was practiced in secret by some *conversos*, they were all nevertheless suspect, and the stigma passed from generation to generation. It became necessary to prove religious and ethnic orthodoxy (*limpieza de sangre*, "purity of blood"), that is, that one's ancestors were "Old Christians," to obtain advancement in royal service, entrance to certain schools, positions in the clergy, and many other honors and rewards. Though conversos and their descendants lived a strained double existence, they found ways within the fluidity of Iberian society of circumventing the restrictions, legitimating their status, and rising to the highest positions of government and society. Some who were caught practicing their old religion might suffer torture and death at the hands of the Inquisition, but the "New Christians" remained an integral part of Iberian society and could be found at every stage of the conquest and colonization of the New World along with their Old Christian fellows.

As a disguised minority, the New Christians had little separate impact in the New World. They concern us further in two main ways. First, their treatment, involving discrimination along genealogical lines together with much surreptitious acceptance, represented an important precedent for the treatment of non-Europeans in the New World. Second (and of secondary importance), within the Portuguese merchant corps there remained an influential, self-conscious, intermarrying community of New Christians who would later surface in America as a bone of contention between Portugal and Spain and would be prepared to ally themselves at times with northern Europeans.

Overall, the Iberians shared fully the general ethnocentricity of human groups in world history, assuming that their own language, religion, and ways were superior to those of others and looking for dominance in their relations with other peoples. But unlike some

European nations, they had deep, long-lasting, and yet recent experience with radically different linguistic, religious, and racial groups on their home ground and came to the New World equipped with expectations and mechanisms for dealing with them.

Government

Though Iberia led Europe in the evolution of strong centralized monarchies and Iberian legislation was an impressive corpus as to bulk, Iberian governments of the early modern period were very far from being activist, unitary states. Like their predecessors, their main function was to confirm and legitimize status and to adjudicate disputes, providing a framework within which social and economic forces worked themselves out quite autonomously; from those forces proceeded the system's dynamism. The government's principal powers were appointive and judicial. The prince's ambitions were to stay in "power," to find patronage for allies and dependents, and above all to collect revenue.

There were no well-oiled hierarchies of obedient civil servants at the crown's behest. Rather, government consisted of various entities largely independent of each other, under loose control, competing with each other for a domain of action that was not tightly compartmentalized. In this world of hazy jurisdictions, the crown asserted itself by acting as the arbitrator betwen competing agencies, each encouraged to watch and report on the others.

Principal among such agencies were the high courts, exercising administrative and legislative as well as judicial functions. Of all the sectors of the government, the judiciary was the most professional and the closest to being a modern-day bureaucratic hierarchy. In both Spain and Portugal an educated class of trained lawyer-bureaucrats (*letrados*) was used to consolidate royal control and carry out the business of government, staffing the high courts, the circuit judgeships, and lesser positions. Although dedicated to the business of government, these judges could be better described as royal ministers than as civil servants. And though in this one area of administration the Iberian crowns were formally pledged to modern concepts of bureaucracy, an older tradition of favoritism, nepotism, and office as property nevertheless persisted even in the courts.

The treasury was another quite separate entity; the three or four high officials in any given area were appointed directly by the crown, and they too at times carried out functions going beyond revenue collection. Both the courts and the treasury juntas were conciliar and multipurposed, as were the royal high councils.

At the local or provincial level the main organ, the municipal council, was also conciliar; it was even more separate than the others, for although appointments needed royal sanction, they were ultimately generated locally. Council members were prominent citizens rather than trained officials, and the councils, representing local interests, essentially did not belong to the royal government at all.

Various organs of the church also entered into this system, especially bishops and cathedral chapters, which not only were conciliar but competed with secular courts for jurisdiction and received their appointments formally or informally through the crown.

For the members of all these entities, and also for the secretaries and notaries who did most of the daily work of government, the concept of office holding was proprietary. Terms of office were long, often for a lifetime or indefinitely. An office belonged to the holder in many senses. It was a personal honor, often coveted for that reason as much as any other. The duties of office were given to the holder personally; he was responsible for both policy and execution and had much discretion in obeying directives. The office was his to "enjoy," a reward for services or connections and at times for actual pay by the holder to the crown, since what can be owned can be bought and sold. And as with an investment, the officeholder repaid himself through the office, from fees for his services and use of influence and other advantages the office brought. The crown lacked the resources, machinery, or will to pay truly "adequate" salaries to officials.

Counterbalancing the long-term, proprietary officials were direct representatives of the crown, often from well-known noble families, appointed for shorter terms to preside over municipal councils or to govern regions. But these functionaries shared many characteristics of other officeholders. Looking like executives, they also exercised judicial functions; in most cases the crown representatives were merely one more of the multifaceted independent bodies competing for jurisdiction, local influence, and royal favor. Only the occasional appointment of an inspector general, empowered to suspend all other officials, ever brought the system under unified control and then only briefly and sporadically.

Elements of the general populace were forever inundating government officials with litigation, trying to find a court that would favor them against rivals. And petitions for favors, ostensibly in reward for services, were rife: not only requests for office, but for the right to practice a trade; a notary's title; a coat of arms; a patent of nobility; membership in the noble orders; and on and on. On the surface, such petitions were accompanied by resounding proofs of the petitioner's good birth and service to the crown; underneath, hard bargaining and solid payments took place. For their part, officials high and low, royal and local, rained ordinances on the public, concerning everything from commerce to manner of dress. Taken literally, they might seem to regulate national life in its entirety; in fact, they were not intended literally, or so taken, but were a miscellaneous set of emergency measures, reactions to interest-group pressures, ineffectual protests against general trends, statements of consensus opinion, and so on.

Government as framework was an essential facet of society, but with its fragmentation and limited resources, it could be a prime mover only in certain restricted spheres. The ideology of the activist state had made its first appearance but could be little more than mouthing until later developments, from the eighteenth century forward, began to give it more substance.

The ecclesiastical component

The Iberian church was, needless to say, a congruent part of Iberian society. It was also, as we have seen, very nearly a part of Iberian government, which it resembled in consisting of several independent, competing bodies. The interpenetration of society, state, and church did not mean that the church dominated everything, as Anglo-Saxons have been so prone to think; rather, the relationship was interdependence, and lay groups and agencies often used the church to their own advantage.

As to governmental ties, the crown exercised practical appointive power over bishops and cathedral dignitaries and was not without influence on advancement in the regular orders themselves. It employed ecclesiastics in its councils and especially for inspections and other extraordinary missions. The crown arbitrated between ecclesiastical entities as it did between governmental ones, and ecclesiastics wrote reports to the crown as regularly and as voluminously as did royal officials.

The clergy was so thoroughly splintered that the people of the time rarely perceived it as an entity, using the word "church" only for the mystical body of all Christian believers. First there was the secular–regular distinction. The secular hierarchy, from parish priest to cathedral chapter, stood apart from the regular orders not only organizationally but socially. On the whole, the members of the orders were better educated, recruited from wealthier and nobler families than the seculars, for whom they had considerable disdain. They were also more tightly organized and better endowed, whereas parish priests had to make their way partly through their own economic activity and were under the loosest of supervision, accepting whatever assignments suited them, going wherever their private interests dictated. Though upper members of the secular clergy were usually quite well connected, even at this level the regular clergy was often preferred, so that many bishops had not advanced up the ladder of the secular hierarchy but were friars acting under dispensation.

Nor was the regular clergy a single unit. Each order was a world in itself, with its own organization, its own clientele in lay society, its own proud tradition and jealousy of others. The mendicants, to be so strong in Spanish America, stood apart from the older contemplative orders; the Jesuits, not yet in existence at the time of the discovery, would be organized on even newer principles and would stand quite outside the framework of the rest of the regular clergy. A unifying wave of reform swept through the Spanish mendicant orders at the beginning of the sixteenth century, leaving them primed for a prominent role in the New World. But differences still remained, especially between the two orders destined to be most important in Spanish America. The Franciscans, following their traditions, were given to popular action tinged with pragmatism, whereas the Dominicans, the Order of Preachers, true to the spirit of their own foundation, were more inclined to doctrinaire positions, doubts, and polemics. Controversies between the two orders along these lines were to be endemic.

As to the Inquisition, that tribunal, concerned with the orthodoxy of former or secret Jewish and Moorish elements in the Iberian population, pertained to the rest of the church only in being manned by ecclesiastics. Often attacking both secular and regular clergy, it is best seen as another of the conciliar arms of government.

In the unspecialized way so characteristic of the time, ecclesiastical organizations were involved in activities going far beyond spiritual affairs and the sacraments. Cathedral chapters and the orders operated schools at all levels, over and above ecclesiastic participation in instruction at universities and other institutions under lay auspices. A good percentage of all intellectual endeavor took place within the framework of an ecclesiastical career. Ecclesiastical organizations also ran most hospitals, though the endowment and patronage were often lay. To support themselves, church organizations had substantial assets, including both outright ownership and liens on properties held by laymen.

All these things spread the activity of ecclesiastics into the society more generally. At the same time, lay activity entered importantly into ecclesiastical spheres. Organized through some church or monastery, dedicated to some saint's image, lay brotherhoods (*cofradías, irmandades*) in fact became social clubs, giving cohesion to residential, occupational, or class groupings. In the New World they would be especially useful as vehicles for group activity by non-Iberians within an Iberian framework. In a similar way the church's sacraments became the occasion for ritual kinship (*compadrazgo, compadrio*), which could reinforce existing ties or create new ones. This practice may have become more important in America, where people coming from all over Iberia were initially in special need of cohesion, than in Iberia itself, but the institution already existed. Another important mechanism was the chaplaincy or chantry (*capellanía*). Ecclesiastical endowment was always a two-way street. The church entity received assets, the contributor received influence, renown, and other benefits. In the case of the chaplaincy, the benefits to the contributor are especially clear. The contributing family would oblige a certain yearly amount in return for a certain number of masses weekly. Not only were the masses specifically for family members, but the family retained the property from which the income came, the patron of the chaplaincy, in charge of its funds, was a family member, and the priest saying the masses was himself to belong to the family. In this way the family gained in prestige, stiffened its credit by a mortgagelike arrangement while retaining the income, and launched one of its members on an ecclesiastical career.

Indeed, such arrangements are symbolic of the fact that many clerics were in their calling as a result of the overall plan of a family for maintaining itself (to avoid having too many sons inheriting, to have a representative in various branches of life), and their career progress reflected their familial and regional origin. In a yet broader sense, clerics were so many more Iberians, with the same cultural equipment as the others, and church organizations reflected Iberian society, recruiting from its whole middle and upper range and flourishing where it flourished.

Commerce

It was once common to find statements to the effect that Iberians avoided association with business and were at heart anticommercial.

Although it is true that the Italians and especially the Genoese played an important role in the development of long-range commerce in the Iberian world, Iberians had their own merchants and their own commercial traditions. The Genoese and north Europeans supplied manufactured goods to Iberia in return for agricultural products from Castile, salt and fish from Portugal, and a certain number of luxury goods from all over the peninsula. But there were Iberians who competed or sometimes cooperated with them: Castilians of Burgos and Medina del Campo (a thoroughly commercial city with a famous fair) who took part in the wool export trade, Portuguese merchant-investors in wine and sugar, who were centered at Lisbon and Oporto, and of course the great Catalan merchant families of Barcelona.

The basic unit in the mercantile world was the "company," a form long known in the Mediterranean area. Perhaps best called a partnership, it was in principle an agreement intended to achieve some relatively immediate goal, such as the selling of a single lot of merchandise. One partner, often the larger investor, would stay at home, the other as "factor" would travel to do buying or selling. Although such arrangements lacked the permanence we associate with the modern-day company, they were not as unstable as one might think. If a venture was successful, the partners would reinvest. Familial ties kept associations alive long after the immediate goal had been attained. Often the senior partner was the father or older brother and the distant factors were his sons or younger brothers, their honesty assured by family loyalty. Even where this was lacking, merchants counted on regional origin for solidarity. In Seville the merchants of Burgos had their own combines, the Basques theirs, and so on.

The company-partnership was a flexible way of doing business. It provided a means by which all sectors of the population, not just merchants, could invest. One person might supply the capital, the other the mercantile know-how. And investment of this type had come to be made in many areas besides wholesale merchandise. Companies were formed for construction enterprises, manufacturing, shipping, and a whole range of other activities. For the New World, therefore, there existed at the time of conquest and colonization familiar, time-tested mechanisms for investing capital and financing activities both large and small in scale, both local and at long distances. Moreover, there were people with the necessary expertise, and Iberians manifested a general willingness to invest. Nobles, lawyers, artisans, and women of means were as ready as merchants to invest in anything likely to bring a profit. Such individual economic initiative was to play an important role in the occupation and exploitation of America.

Despite the pervasiveness of commercialism, Iberia was not Genoa or Holland, and the merchant was not at the very peak of the social scale. A massively successful merchant could be counted on to buy and marry his family's way into the nobility and out of commerce (a trend seen in other and more recent societies too, of course). In addition, frequent restrictive action by the crowns and the municipal councils can hardly be reconciled with a thoroughly commercial orientation. On close examination, however, such actions usually reveal themselves as consumer interest-group pressure or rational economic policy in the context of a market quantitatively more limited than in later times. We are dealing with the commercialism of the early modern period, and in this Iberia was neither more nor less than part of the Europe of its time.

Slavery

To understand Latin American slavery one must begin by comprehending that slavery was a tradition as well established in the Iberian peninsula as marriage, and the two familiar institutions were transferred to the New World in much the same way. We refrained from including the slave among the standard Iberian functional groups previously discussed not from doubt that slavery was a standard feature but because slaves are by definition outsiders, usually recent arrivals, and of different ethnic stock, religion, and language than the slaveholders. Slavery is doubtless in some sense an economic phenomenon, but it operates mainly between populations radically divided in some basic aspect, so that they view each other as beyond the pale. The Mediterranean world had far greater religious and linguistic diversity than northern Europe, and it maintained a living tradition of slavery from ancient through medieval into early modern times. On the Iberian peninsula Christians and Moors, speakers of Romance and Arabic, were enslaving each other century after century.

Such longstanding situations shape expectations, channeling relationships and roles into conventional patterns. If the Mediterranean had great diversity, it also had an overarching shared culture and ethnicity; no one seriously doubted the humanity of slaves, and over time their change of status and assimilation (as individuals) to the local society was a normal, expected thing. The slave belonged to society, merely being located at its bottom and edge; centuries of practice, parts of which were codified at times, standardized behavior to the point that the slave had what can be seen as some rights, if unimpressive ones, as well as duties. By early modern times the societies of Mediterranean countries were largely complete in themselves, with free local members carrying out all essential functions, so that they were not "slave societies" but used slaves in a secondary, mainly domestic-urban role.

Into this Mediterranean pattern, well in advance of the discovery of America, stepped a new actor: the sub-Saharan African. There were still Moorish slaves in Spain and Portugal in the early sixteenth century, but Black slaves, largely coming out of Portugal's African activities, became increasingly important, appearing as a group as early as the late fourteenth century and overshadowing Moorish slaves in Lisbon and Andalusia by the time of the discovery. Thus age-old patterns were adapted to the African in a European setting, and the entire complex was transferred wholesale to America, as a matter of course, without debate or innovation.

The role for which Blacks were stereotyped was above all domestic service, the women in housework and the men accompanying and aiding their masters. Black slaves were a prestige item; in parts of Portugal and southern Spain, owning several slaves was a practical necessity for a wealthy household's reputation. In Seville, at least, ownership of Black slaves was spread widely among the population, including Spanish artisans, who standardly increased productivity by training their slaves in their trades. Thus skilled, intensive work was within the ordinary range of Black slave activity.

Iberians were used to the idea of a Black servile element in their cities and had developed measures of control – restricted assembly, no right to bear arms, and so on – which appeared everywhere in the Indies too, however often violated. African group dancing was known and tolerated to a certain extent. Africans became Christians, practiced the sacraments, and had their own religious brotherhoods. Most importantly, Blacks, like other types of slaves before them, could be manumitted. This might take place either through the owner's last testament or during his lifetime. Very often freedom was purchased, either by the slave himself or by someone else on his behalf. Even when the motive was personal, it was more a recognition of sexual-familial ties or a reward to a deserving individual than an act with any overtones of humanitarian protest against slavery.

Iberian domestic slavery was not the only precedent for African slavery in the New World. Sugar-industry slavery was something quite different, with its own origins and continuities, as we will soon see. But these two traditions, as living ideas held by the generality of Iberian settlers and embodied in set practices, were the main cultural determinants of the shape of Latin American African slavery, rather than any activity of church or state (which in any case merely shared the same ideas) or any conscious attempt to come to terms with something new and outside the society's experience, as in the English confrontation with large-scale slavery. Large moral issues and ideological controversies in Latin America would principally concern Indians, an element newer and stranger, whereas Black slavery was unquestioned and unproblematical, and the Black himself was a familiar subordinate and collaborator, indeed in the first years of occupation was often brought from Iberia itself.

Castile

Spanish America is more properly Castilian America, held by the crown of Castile, conquered and settled by Castilian subjects. The individual experience of Castile thus becomes especially relevant. Holding the core of the peninsula, with more land and people than the two remaining major kingdoms of Portugal and Aragon, Castile was also the most landlocked, inward-turned, and ethnocentric (see Map 1, Table 1). Its great idiosyncrasy within Iberia was that through historical circumstance it had kept the legacy of the preceding centuries more alive than had the other kingdoms.

Whereas the others had completed the reconquest of their respective regions and had turned to trade and the sea, Castile stayed in face-to-face contact with Moorish principalities until the very year of the discovery of America. The ethos, if not the reality, of a constant forward advance was fully maintained. Southward migration of marginal individuals and families was a mechanism built deeply into Castilian society. For the Castilians, expansion still meant conquest of the classic kind that was practiced first by the Moors and then by the Christians in the centuries of struggle for the peninsula: permanent settlement by a good number of immigrants, formal rule and the collection of tribute, and, over time, the change of religion and the general incorporation of the new area into the homeland. Just as important was the tradition that what was conquered was to be divided among the conquerors. Great nobles, ecclesiastics, and the military or crusading orders were sometimes the primary beneficiaries, but the most significant facet of the process for the future was that all the participants above the plebeian level received some

Table 1. *Comparison of the Iberian kingdoms in the sixteenth century*

	Area (km^2)	Percentage of total area of peninsula	Inhabitants	Percentage of total population	Inhabitants/km^2
Crown of Castile	378,000	65.2	8,304,000	73.2	22.0
Crown of Aragon	100,000	17.2	1,358,000	12.0	13.6
Kingdom of Portugal	90,000	15.5	1,500,000	13.2	16.7
Kingdom of Navarre	12,000	2.1	185,000	1.6	15.4
	580,000	100.0	11,347,000	100.0	19.6

Source: J. H. Elliott, *Imperial Spain, 1469–1716* (London, 1963), p. 25. (Used with permission of St. Martin's Press.) Although Elliott feels the population figures may be somewhat inflated, and they are for late rather than early in the century, they give some indication of relative weights near the time of the American conquests.

Map 1. Iberia in the sixteenth century

share, either lands, urban property, dominion over a group of the conquered, or the right to collect revenues from them. Under various names and in various forms, there were institutional arrangements for granting these benefits to the conquerors, many of whom would make the new area their permanent home. Such institutional traditions had their effect on the evolution of what came to be called in the New World the "encomienda" (an already traditional term), Spanish America's first general framework for relationships between Iberians and Indians. The national experience created an expectation on the part of Castilians that after a conquest a general division would take place, and in America they would tolerate no other result, in the face of crown resistance or the divergent Mediterranean tradition of commercial colonization. In the fifteenth century all the Castilians' propensities were reinforced by their expansion to the Canary Islands, where conquest rather than trade was the mode, and the local inhabitants were given in encomienda to prominent settlers.

With Portugal on one side and Aragon on the other, the Basques and Galicians to the north and the Moors to the south, Castile proper hardly touched the sea. Only in the far southwest did a region of Castile participate fully in the maritime and commercial development characteristic of the coastal peoples. Here lay Seville, miles inland it is true, but on the navigable Guadalquivir and a major seaport, as well as being Castile's largest city and a thoroughly commercialized center of international trade. Cosmopolitan, much like Lisbon except that it was not a national capital, Seville too had its Genoese mercantile colony, as well as active groups of north Castilian merchants. Already involved in overseas enterprises and export of Andalusia's olives and wheat, these mercantile interests were well prepared for the business of supplying Spanish settlers in the Caribbean. And Seville, along with the ports of Huelva just to the west, teemed with sailors and ships no different from those of Portugal, both adapted to the rigors of the Atlantic. Somewhat distinct culturally from the more pastoral inland Castile and Extremadura, western Andalusia had the population, mariners, merchants, capital, and skills to carry the burden of Spanish overseas expansion in its first, or Caribbean, stage.

There is no need to go into the political-dynastic vicissitudes that naturally marked past centuries of history in a kingdom as large and diverse as that of Castile. The strong rulers at the time of the discovery, Ferdinand and Isabella, fell far short of imposing true uniformity, since the newly added crown of Aragon was still entirely separate in theory and nearly so in fact, aside from the highly individual localist institutional arrangements in parts of Castile itself. But as a result of this striving after unity and governmental strength, Ferdinand and Isabella's time at least saw the evolution of standard forms, norms for courts and administrators which could be spread easily and uniformly over Spanish America, as well as the growth of a more numerous officialdom ready to man distant posts.

Portugal

In comparison with its neighbor Castile, Portugal was a small country, with only moderate economic and demographic resources. Still, for more than three centuries the country maintained and exploited a colonial empire stretching from East Asia to Brazil. The story of this imperial success is at least in part explained by the nature of Portugal's own historical development.

Despite its small size and relatively early political unification, the sentiments of localism ran as deeply in Portugal as in the rest of Iberia. This was due in part to very real economic and geographical differences existing within the country. Portugal north of the Tagus River was a land of vineyards, small farms, and in some places a dense population pressing on available resources: a perfect breeding ground for emigrants. "Mediterranean" Portugal to the south had its own traditions, being characterized by large estates, herds of cattle and sheep, and whitewashed villages whose appearance reflected their Moorish heritage. Both regions shared, however, a long tradition as seagoing merchants and fisherfolk. In the small ports of the Algarve, Portugal's southernmost region, mariners drawing on the skills and lore of both the Atlantic and the Mediterranean sealanes developed a maritime technology that would greatly assist the process of overseas expansion. More sparsely settled than the others, this region was the center of Portugal's domestic sugar industry during the short time it flourished and the area that employed the most African slaves in agriculture.

In the fifteenth and sixteenth centuries as today, to say Portugal was to say Lisbon. Situated on the south-central coast at the mouth of the Tagus, lining one of the world's greatest natural harbors, Lisbon dominated the commercial and political life of the nation. With a history uninterrupted from the time of the Phoenicians, by 1500 Lisbon was the unquestioned capital of Portugal and one of the great cities of Europe. In Iberia its only rivals were Seville and Barcelona. Its commercial, administrative, and political functions attracted a varied urban population and made the city a cosmopolitan center. Commercial ties to northern Europe, Italy, and other parts of the Mediterranean brought many foreigners to the city, among whom, unsurprisingly, the Genoese were particularly important. Genoese sailors and maritime experts had been brought to Portugal as early as the twelfth century, and by the sixteenth the Italians were well established in Portuguese economic life. Their commercial experience and contacts played a major role in Portugal's early voyages and the creation of Portugal's seaborne empire.

Despite the emphasis of Portuguese historians on their nation's uniqueness, much of Portugal's early history was like that of the other Iberian kingdoms. Reconquest from the Moors, dynastic struggle, repopulating newly won territory, all these were general, though the tempo and absolute chronology of the processes were individual. Partly because it was a small country, Portugal's political unification was relatively easy. A dynastic conflict brought John of Aviz to the throne in 1385 with general support. His victory over the Castilian pretender established Portugal's independence (for a time) from its distrusted larger neighbor and placed an active monarch at the head of government. It also brought to power the commercial interests of Lisbon and the university-trained lawyers who legitimated the victory and who now provided administrator-bureaucrats for the new state. The early political unification of Portugal, combined with the presence of an active royal house, administrators interested in the extension of royal power, and merchants interested in profit, gave much impetus to Portuguese overseas ventures.

Portuguese expansion

In 1415 the Portuguese, with a three-century maritime tradition behind them, struck out across the Straits of Gibraltar and took the Moorish fortress town of Ceuta. This was the first step in a large-scale involvement in Africa and Asia, some knowledge of which is indispensable for understanding later events in America. Portuguese activity in Brazil was preceded by almost a century of colonial expansion, during which economic and political institutions were created and techniques for dealing with peoples of other races, religions, and cultures were developed. Much of the early history of Brazil is a direct extension of this story, and it also set patterns for the Spaniards in the Caribbean. Moreover, until the mid-seventeenth century the areas of Africa, with its gold and slaves, and Asia, with its spices, loomed larger in Portuguese imperial calculations than Brazil. This situation was far different from that of the Spaniards, since the metallic wealth of Mexico and Peru quickly made America the heart of Spain's overseas enterprise.

By the time the first settlement was established in Brazil, the Portuguese had settled and colonized the Atlantic islands of Madeira and the Azores, set up trading forts along the West African coast, established a flourishing sugar-production colony on the island of São Tomé, and rounded the Cape of Good Hope to reach the wealthy ports on the Indian Ocean.

Scholars have long argued, and still do, over the nature of Portuguese expansion and the reasons for it. The military spirit of crusade, the missionary impulse, royal interests, the search for commercial profit, and scientific curiosity all doubtless contributed in some way. Recent scholarship has underlined the economic origins of expansion, although at the same time disproving the old idea that the Portuguese were primarily in search of an alternate route to India and its spices. Instead, it appears that, even before an interest in spices developed, Africa represented an attraction in itself. Portugal was in need of grain and gold, both of which could be found in the cities of North Africa; these cities were terminals of a trans-Sahara trade which linked gold-producing West Africa to the Mediterranean world. The Black Plague, with its resultant labor shortage and rising wages, heightened the interest in new sources of wealth. But who knows what moves human beings? The belief in the kingdom of Prester John, an isolated but powerful Christian realm somewhere in Africa or Asia, which would provide an ally on Islam's flank, was in the minds of Portuguese captains or at least on their lips (after all, Christian Ethiopia did exist). And ordinary crew members doubtless believed implicitly in the morality of Christian expansion at pagan and infidel expense. For the Portuguese as for the Castilians, religion often functioned as the justification for all kinds of actions.

Once the Portuguese discovered that Ceuta did not fill their needs, they began to push down the west coast of Africa toward the sources of gold, ivory, and slaves – the traditional staples of the trans-Sahara trade. During this gradual process, which eventually led them to India, the Portuguese developed or refined a number of techniques for commercial and political operation in the lands to which they sailed. Chief among these were the commercial trading post–fort, or "factory," and the donatary captaincy.

The factory was characteristic of Portugal's contact with Africa from the early stages. As the Portuguese pushed down the coast they established a number of small trading forts, the most important of which was São Jorge de Mina (1481) in present-day Ghana. At each of these factories (*feitorias*), typically located on islands, a small fort was built and garrisoned by a few Portuguese. This gave the commercial representatives, or factors, a safe place to carry on their trade with local people, and ships arriving from Portugal could be assured of cargoes to carry back. Such trading stations had been used extensively in the Mediterranean by the Venetians, Genoese, Catalans, and others. The Portuguese "factory" at Bruges (Belgium) had operated since the 1300s, but whereas in Europe these stations were purely commercial, outside it they took on military functions as well. The factory system was an excellent way of establishing a permanent commercial presence in an area without the cost of conquest and occupation.

The purpose of the factory, of course, was trade. Portuguese trade in Africa, following various precedents including that of Italian commerce with the Slavs, was of a special kind, a barter of European trinkets and cheap cloth for slaves and natural products. Shading readily into use of force, this trade, which came to be called *resgate* ("rescue"), shaped the expectations and actions of both Portuguese and Spaniards in their commercial relations with the inhabitants of the Western Hemisphere.

When the Portuguese colonized and settled in an area, as in Madeira, the Azores, and later Brazil, the burden of the initial cost fell on the shoulders of private individuals. Noblemen were often willing to accept the cost of transporting settlers and initiating economic activities in return for extensive powers and privileges granted them by the crown. The institution used in this process was the donatary captaincy, going back to medieval precedents of lordly domain (*senhorio*), yet now used for imperial ends and, as we shall soon see, for capitalistic agricultural development. The nobleman received the hereditary title of captain and lord proprietor (*donatário*) of his area; in return for the title, economic concessions, and a certain amount of political and judicial autonomy, he agreed to administer and develop the territory. It was a form of colonization well suited to the patriarchal traditions of Iberia, and it offered noblemen an opportunity to live according to their ideals. At the same time, the donatary captaincy, like the factory, cost the crown very little at the initial and most risky stage. Whereas the factory was most associated with coastal Africa, the captaincies were first used effectively in the Atlantic islands as part of Portugal's great and successful enterprise, the commercial production of sugar.

Sugar and commercial-agricultural slavery

Sugar was the first tropical export crop of the expanding capitalist economy of western Europe. Though some sugarcane had been grown in Iberia since the days of the Moorish conquest, the sugar complex of specialized milling technology, commercial (often foreign) investment, and a coerced or enslaved labor force was originally an eastern Mediterranean development. In Cyprus and later in Sicily, estates in many ways resembling the later plantations of the New World produced sugar for the markets of Europe. The Venetians and eventually the Genoese took the initiative in financing and marketing sugar in the Mediterranean, and they were not slow in developing production in Iberia and its colonies as well. By the fifteenth century Genoese merchants were carrying on a brisk business exporting sugar produced in southern Iberia to Italy and northern Europe. Always anxious for expansion, they quickly took the occasion to invest in Portugal's overseas adventures. The Italians thus were human links in a chain which transferred the techniques of sugar production, estate management, and commercial organization from the eastern Mediterranean to the Iberian peninsula, where the industry flourished only briefly, and then on to the Atlantic colonies.

The Iberian colonization of the Atlantic island groups, the Azores, Madeira, the Canaries, and São Tomé, was accompanied, and in many ways stimulated, by the expansion of sugar agriculture. The Azores produced some sugar, but they lay too far north and eventually became a colony of Europeans growing temperate crops. Madeira was another matter. There, aided by investments from Genoese, Flemish, and other foreign merchants, the Portuguese quickly established a sugar industry which by the end of the fifteenth century was the largest single producer in the Western World.

The Portuguese in Madeira, along with the Castilians in the Canary Islands, re-created the Mediterranean complex centered on the sugar mill (*engenho, ingenio*). Capital came from foreign investors and Iberian nobles, the mills were usually owned and managed by colonists from Portugal or Spain, and the labor was provided by slaves. Because not all the colonists had the money or credit needed for setting up the expensive machinery of a sugar mill, many became cane farmers (*lavradores, labradores*), providing cane to the mill owners in return for a percentage of the sugar produced. Others specialized in the skilled crafts of production or managerial roles. The sugar mill complex, from its capital and commercial aspects to the details of its organization and operation, was fully formed on the Atlantic islands before its transfer to America.

The conjunction of the sugar industry and Portuguese expansion down the West African coast brought about some significant changes in Iberian slavery. The first large shipment of African slaves arrived in Lisbon in 1441; through the fifteenth century Portugal received some 800 or 900 slaves a year, who worked in the growing sugar industry of the Algarve in addition to filling the traditional roles of artisan and house servant. By 1551 10 percent of Lisbon's population was slave, to say nothing of those who labored in the countryside. These Africans, as we have seen, were integrated into the religious and social life of the kingdom in much the same fashion as Moorish slaves had been before them. But with the large-scale influx of Africans to the cane fields of southern Iberia, Madeira, and the Canaries, the nature of slavery began to change or at least to broaden. The long-standing urban domestic tradition was now joined by a more intense, less acculturative form of labor associated with the highly commercial, mechanized sugar estate. Slaves from afar had been important in the sugar industry's labor force starting in the eastern Mediterranean; as the Iberian industry developed, commercial-agricultural slavery came to be associated almost exclusively with Africans. The two traditions or tendencies, Iberian domestic slavery and tropical export slavery, would continue to coexist uneasily in the New World, influencing and contradicting each other, varying greatly with the requirements of local situations; but almost everything the New World Iberians attempted with African slavery would fall within one tradition or the other.

The human, financial, and technical aspects of the sugar mill complex came to full maturity in the Atlantic island phase of Iberian expansion. The final step in the process was a change in scale. The engenhos of Madeira and the Canaries were small compared to the later sugar estates of Brazil. On the island of São Tomé, however, the Portuguese were able to change this. Lying near the African coastal factories of São Jorge de Mina and Axim, the São Tomé industry was able to employ slaves on a scale previously impossible. Whereas the largest Madeiran mills used some eighty slaves, on São Tomé engenhos a hundred and fifty were not uncommon. On São Tomé the Portuguese saw how the factors of production could be increased, and profit with it. All the elements of the capitalist agricultural estate, oriented toward the production of an export crop, yet drawing on a web of noncapitalist social relationships for this end, were now present. The technology, the organization, the financial arrangements, the sources of labor supply, and even the possibilities of scale all reached full development on the islands off Africa, and when Portuguese and Spaniards moved to the other side of the Atlantic they discovered that this institution, like so many others, was readily adaptable to the situation.

Brazil and Portugal's empire

In everything Portugal's empire drew on precedents, whether those of Mediterranean maritime and mercantile expansion or those of Iberian reconquest. The trading factory, the donatary captaincy, and the sugar mill complex are simply three examples from a list which could be extended to include even the most mundane or intimate aspects of life. The Portuguese proved to be adaptable colonizers, more because of their small numbers abroad, doubtless, than because of the cultural malleability claimed for them by Freyre. They certainly had no single preconceived imperial policy. Confronted by a great variety of cultures, geographical realities, and historical circumstances, they used any appropriate technique, whether conversion, cooperation, threats, or force, to gain their objectives. However, the Portuguese did not control or aim to control vast expanses of land, at least not until the late seventeenth century. Instead, their empire was basically a series of commercial ports, coastal spheres of influence, and trade routes. In Asia the Portuguese concentrated on holding a few strategic maritime cities, pressure points of trade, and then dominating the sea-lanes. In Africa, with the partial exceptions of Angola and Mozambique, their network was primarily one of trading factories and slaving stations, involving only occasional missionary or military expeditions into the interior.

Though Brazil eventually came to be a notable exception, it too originated as a "factory" colony, and it hardly stood out from other areas during the long years of the sixteenth century when it was the least important of Portugal's overseas colonies. In the end, the nature of its indigenous inhabitants, its soil and climate, and its location relative to Europe and Africa turned Brazil into a colony of settlement and distinctive social development. Yet the techniques and mechanisms that the Portuguese had developed in a century of expansion all found employment in Brazil and one of them, the sugar complex, would be the primary dynamic force.

Christopher Columbus, Genoese

Columbus epitomizes one whole side of the European background. By now the reader will readily understand that his nationality is no isolated, incidental fact. Columbus sums up the elements of the Mediterranean-Genoese-Portuguese tradition of maritime and commercial expansion. It was people like him who maintained the continuities and transmitted the colonial techniques shaping the actions of both Portuguese and Spaniards in America. Though his career took him to many remote places, in everything his activity was typically Genoese, and he lived inside a chrysalis of Genoese and other Italian connections. Early in life he was employed in the eastern Mediterranean islands where the Italian tradition began; then he like others went west, in the employ of a Genoese mercantile firm, which led to his spending a time in Lisbon. Still operating as part of the Italian colony, he worked with his brother and married the daughter of an Italian who was donatary captain of the Portuguese island of Porto Santo next to Madeira. The activities growing out of these connections were also typical: maritime mapmaking and residence in Madeira as agent of a Genoese firm involved in sugar. This led to voyages down the West African coast as far as São Jorge de Mina, where he learned of the gold trade at first hand. Thus by the time he approached the Spaniards with his famous project, Columbus had recapitulated the entire course of Genoese-Portuguese expansion, had been imbued with its maritime, commercial, and organizational lore, and had experienced the sugar industry as well as the African trade in gold and slaves. Even when he came among Spaniards, he found sympathetic Genoese in the financial circles of the crown and among the merchant-exporters of Seville.

A carrier of the commercial-maritime tradition thus (unwittingly) offered Iberia a means and rationale for passage to America. Once the Iberians were there, reconquest patterns could begin to assert themselves. Conflicts and accommodations of the most basic nature for the creation of new societies would take place, beginning immediately after the European arrival in the Caribbean. But at this point the topic transcends the notion of context, and we will deal with it as part of the first European activity in America.

2

Indigenous ways

Though complex and varied, the heritage of the Iberians of 1500 was simple compared to that of the peoples of the western continents. Perhaps the lands we call the Americas had been occupied for a shorter time in terms of millennia, but the variety of their peoples, languages, ecologies, economies, and social-political systems was so great as to invite comparison with all of Eurasia or all of Africa. We must therefore abbreviate our treatment even more than we did with the Iberians, choosing from the vastnesses of time and topic only certain elements present at the time of contact which were crucial to the shape of things to come.

General characteristics of indigenous cultures

"Indian" is of course a misnomer for the people the Iberians encountered. Not only did the name originate in a geographical misconception on the part of the Europeans, who imagined themselves near the East Indies; far more seriously, it did not correspond to any unity perceived by the indigenous peoples. Many groups were not aware of each other, and those groups which were in contact felt only the kinds of identity dictated by affinities (where such existed) of language, religion, life-style, and political unit. Not one of the peoples had a word in its language which could be translated as "Indian"; that is, the concept of distinguishing between the inhabitants of the Western Hemisphere and human beings from the outside was unknown. Consequently, there was no tendency to unite in common resistance to European invaders; rather, each polity sought the most advantageous situation for itself alone. Any sense of a broader "Indianness" grew only slowly out of the colonial experience, and even by the nineteenth century Indian self-consciousness remained centered on specific units harking back to preconquest times.

The question then arises, did the "Indians" have important common distinctive features? Should we even continue to use the term or one like it? Surely we should, for despite their variety and their lack of self-consciousness, the peoples of the Western Hemisphere shared not only a geographical habitat but a common experience, giving them certain marked special characteristics in relation to the rest of the world's peoples. Relative isolation is the key. Of all the major ethnic-geographical branches of humanity, and certainly of all those who had agriculture, cities, and large political units, the Indians were the most isolated from the rest of mankind. Peoples, techniques, and disease strains had continued to pass back and forth over the entire great land mass of Europe-Asia-Africa for interminable centuries, on into modern times, whereas the Indian peoples, whatever sporadic contact there may have been, had for some thousands of years not been in continuous touch with the ecumene. In view of the research done in African history in recent years, it should no longer surprise anyone to know that there were multiple long-standing contacts between sub-Saharan Africa and other areas. Thus whereas a generation of European scholars liked to divide the world into "West" and "non-West," a far more real division would be "Indian" and "non-Indian." For all their differences of background and assigned status, Iberians and Africans in the New World were in some respects a single intrusive group, with some important common traits not shared by the Indians.

In a sense, the results of Indian relative isolation were superficial. Indian language, social organization, religion, and art are unique and uniquely valuable, like all things human; at the same time, it is not clear that they in any way fall outside the general range of variation for human groups of other continents. Only in the special areas of epidemiology and technology were there quite drastic, and very similar, effects of isolation from the larger mass. The larger an interacting human group is, the more disease strains and the more inventions it will generate. If humanity is divided for a long time into a larger and a smaller interacting group, when the two come together again the larger group will have more diseases to which the smaller has no immunity than vice versa; it will have developed more new machines, processes, domesticated varieties, and so on, than the smaller group. In these respects all the Indian peoples were alike. Despite differences according to climate, settlement type, and the like, Indians on both continents were to succumb in large numbers to diseases to which the incoming Europeans and Africans were already hardened. In technology, Europeans and Africans knew, for example, how to manufacture and use steel weapons, and this alone gave them ultimate military superiority in the New World, for though some Indian groups had great cities, pyramids, empires, and long-distance trade, none had iron and steel. Thus the New and Old

Worlds were alike in harboring a quite similar spread of societies, from the very small to the very large, from hunting-gathering bands to urban-centered agriculturalists, but because of some rather superficial differentials, the smaller sphere was highly vulnerable to the impact of the larger, once the two had come back into steady contact.

Thousands of years of history stretch back to the time of presumed migrations from Asia and a stage of big-game hunting across the length and breadth of both western continents; such things need not concern us directly here, any more than their counterparts in the history of the Old World. We need only a sense of the antiquity of certain kinds of developments, so as to grasp how very refined they had become and what deep roots they had. The domestication of food plants goes back millennia in the Western Hemisphere, far into the pre-Christian era, as do sedentary village life and the arts of pottery and weaving. The first millennium A.D. saw the growth of cities and large political units, as well as achievements in the arts and crafts that equaled or surpassed anything still existing when the Europeans arrived. By 1500 there had been two or three cycles of the creation and destruction of vast "empires" in Mesoamerica* and the Andes.

Whether or not certain basic innovations had been brought from outside the hemisphere has not yet been established with certainty. The important thing is that by the time of contact with Europe, everything in the Indian systems of life had undergone long processes of independent evolution and had its own strength, integrity, and rationale. This is the other side of the coin of the peculiar developmental course of the Western Hemisphere: At the same time that the area was left vulnerable to conquest and population loss, its basic modes of social, political, and economic life had an exceptionally strong flavor of their own and an ability to survive under great pressures.

Social and technological innovations in the Western Hemisphere had a tendency to center in two areas, Mesoamerica and the central Andes, and to spread from there into other regions. The variety of American geography, however, prevented the development of any neatly concentric spheres. Because of the existence of pockets of especially wet, dry, or fragmented terrain, villageless hunters and collectors could live almost within hailing distance of a great urban

*A term used by anthropologists for central and southern Mexico and Guatemala as home of an interrelated set of high cultures in pre-Columbian times.

center. But in broadest outline, a scheme of classification of the Indian peoples, possessing considerable explanatory and predictive power for the postconquest period, can be based on the principle of degree of similarity to the Mesoamerican-Andean, or central, peoples. The central people's possession of permanent intensive agriculture, stable town and village sites, strong tribute mechanisms, and dense populations puts them in many respects in the same category as most of the peoples of Europe in 1500, a category which we will abbreviate as "fully sedentary," though in truth sedentariness is only one symptom of the entire complex (see Map 2). Population density might be an even more sensitive symptomatic indicator, if we knew it with exactitude. It now appears that central Mexico and the Peruvian–Bolivian region had a population measured in the many millions and that the population density was far greater than that of other areas (see Table 2). Yet the latter point remains somewhat controversial.

Our next category is "semisedentary." These peoples also had agriculture and villages, but cultivation and settlement shifted over the course of some years from one site to another; hunting was still vital, the delivery of tribute to superiors was not as important or institutionalized, and population, though it could be very substantial, was, most would agree, far less dense than among the central groups. Such peoples were to be found all along the periphery of the territories of the fully sedentary peoples, in parts of present-day Chile, Colombia, northern Mexico, and so on, as well as in many forested or wet tropical areas where the leaching of nutrients, regrowth of brush, or difficulty of clearing made continued cultivation of a given site impractical or unadvisable. A great swath of territory northeastward from Paraguay up the coast of Brazil and on into much of the Caribbean, as well as much of eastern North America, fits into this category.

The third category is "nonsedentary." These peoples might share large components of language, religion, and world outlook with historically related more sedentary groups, as in the case of the forest Lacandones and the famous Maya of Yucatan, but their lifestyle diverged sharply, as did their potential utility to any would-be invader, whether Indian or European. Few if any of these groups were truly nomadic in the sense of migrating indefinitely, like the prehistoric big-game hunters; most American peoples of fairly recent times have operated on the basis of maintaining rights to a quite well defined territory. Within that territory, however, nonsedentary peoples migrated frequently in a seasonal cycle of hunting and

Map 2. Approximate distribution of sedentary, semisedentary, and nonsedentary peoples at the time of European contact. (In viewing this quite rough scheme it must be remembered that the three categories are a continuum with no sharp lines of division and that a great many pockets deviated widely from the surrounding dominant culture type.)

gathering. Lacking agriculture, they had camps rather than villages; small bands were the normal social unit, tribute was token or unknown, and population densities were extremely low. Such peoples existed in parts of all the major regions but above all in those areas most inhospitable to sedentary life as then known: in the driest or wettest areas, on the plains, or in the thickest forests. The dry parts

Table 2. *Estimated indigenous population of America at the time of European contact*

	Estimated population	Percentage of total American population
North America	4,400,000	7.7
Mexico	21,400,000	37.3
Central America	5,650,000	9.9
Caribbean	5,850,000	10.2
Andes	11,500,000	20.1
Lowland South America	8,500,000	14.8
Total	57,300,000	100.0

Source: William M. Denevan (ed.), *The Native Population of the Americas in 1492* (Madison, Wis., 1976), p. 291. Used with permission of the University of Wisconsin Press. Denevan emphasizes the hazards of such estimates and recognizes that their surprising magnitude, especially for peripheral areas, is still to be well established.

of the Mexican north, the Argentine plains, and much of the Amazonian far interior are such regions.

Rather than stages of human development, the three categories represent primarily adaptations to certain environments, given a prevailing technology. Within that framework, one system was as capable of maintaining itself as another, one as complex in the totality of its relationships to an environment as the next. And being adjustments to environmental variables, the three systems we speak of were part of a single continuum, partaking freely of any characteristics appropriate to a given situation, so that the mix was never exactly the same in any two places. No people was entirely sedentary, none entirely mobile. Several of the Mayan groups, whose cities, provincial governments, and tax systems seem to place them fully among the central peoples, at the same time practiced shifting rather than permanent-site agriculture and in other ways shared characteristics with the semisedentary groups. A combination of traits such as this is a bit unusual, but it is no anomaly within the multidimensional spectrum of Western Hemisphere reality.

In general, it can be said that the Europeans concentrated their activities overwhelmingly in areas with fully sedentary indigenous populations and that other peoples held attraction only insofar as they resembled the latter. The semisedentary peoples were thus of no more than secondary interest, and attempts to deal with the more mobile groups were a last resort. It naturally follows that the lands of the sedentary peoples should be the first and principal arena for the growth of Latin American society in the sixteenth century. We will then treat the central peoples first and more extensively.

Sedentary peoples

The "imperial" peoples

A correlation exists between empire and sedentariness in our sense; no peoples answer to the description of sedentary groups better than the inhabitants of central Mexico and the central Andes, the respective homes of the Aztec and Inca empires. It is vital to understand the nature of the correlation. Rather than creating sedentariness, the large tributary regimes that have been called empires fed on it; their borders stopped abruptly at the borders of sedentary life. Sedentary peoples antedated the vast agglomerates; over the centuries they had seen empires rise and fall and had experienced long periods of provincial autonomy, during which their way of life remained much the same. In general, the most spectacular large-scale phenomena of the preconquest Indian world are not as relevant to the postconquest situation as less visible mechanisms at the provincial level, mechanisms which survived the empires and which could support a European presence as well.

The distinguishing features of the sedentary peoples begin at the level of family and hamlet life. Intensive agriculture was the basis of that life; most often this meant maize cultivation, though the high-altitude Andean complex of potatoes and hardy grains was an equivalent. Permanent site agriculture meant that the local social-political unit (in central Mexico often called *calpulli,* in the Andes *ayllu*) held specific arable lands on a long-term basis, and individual families tended to retain the same plots for a lifetime or over generations. The integration of agriculture into the way of life was meaningfully symbolized by the fact that men shared fully in working the land, planting, and harvesting. Members of the group might live nucleated in a village or dispersed over the land; in either case there was a tight, stable set of connections of people with land and of the people with each other, since as far as we can tell most such groups married among themselves. Kinship ties and territoriality reinforced each other as the basis of a strong feeling of common identity. Indeed, the minimal local unit at the level of the ayllu or calpulli was in many respects a microcosm of the society, and one would be justified in making it the basis for a general discussion of the sedentary Indian world.

Nevertheless, we will here adopt a different procedure, concentrating on a level between the local hamlet and the great empire: a provincial unit on the order of size of a European county or smaller, sometimes though not always centered upon an urban nucleus. There are two reasons for our emphasis. First, the provincial unit was to be the crucial one after the Europeans came; maintaining its integrity after conquest, it dictated the size and shape of jurisdictions and provided the mechanisms that allowed a concentration of the European presence. Second and just as importantly, there were many aspects of the total complex which either did not exist in the minimal local units or, if they did, served their purpose only within the provincial context, so that in some ways the province is the smallest self-contained unit intelligible on its own terms. Though hamlet groupings must have preceded provincial groupings in time of origin, one can make a case for the primacy of the province in the minds of the people living at the time of concern to us here. Province names were quite distinctive, while calpulli and ayllu names were repeated again and again, almost like street names in American cities. Patriotism, pride, and legend tended to operate in terms of the suprahamlet unit.

The bulk of the ordinary agricultural populace received land and other rights from the hamlet and provincial authorities, and in return, through well-established procedures, they performed public duties and gave tribute, which went first through the local authorities and then to the dynastic ruler of the province. The hamlet-sized unit was broken down into wards, each of which had a headman with various duties, including tribute collection. For central Mexico we know that the headman might have jurisdiction over anywhere from five to fifty households; older accounts of the Andean situation speak of an almost clockwork system of centurions and decurions, but recent research shows that at the local level the true picture may have varied as much from place to place as in Mesoamerica. Tribute consisting of products went along a well-defined route: The commoner gave it at the appointed time to his headman; he in turn to the hamlet head, who might have some assistants for the purpose; and the hamlet leader in turn to the provincial ruler or king, or rather to the latter's substantial staff of stewards and recordkeepers. For public works – building and maintaining palaces, temples, roads, and irrigation systems, or working the lands of the lord – a system of draft rotary labor existed (in the Andes called *mita,* a term based on the word for "turn," and in central Mexico, *coatequitl,* once again "turn-work"). The duty rotated from ward to ward and hamlet to hamlet, the commoners working in their familiar units under the combined supervision of their own leaders and the ruler's men. For major projects, a large proportion of the population could be called out simultaneously. The system could also yield tribute products, that is, the rotary labor could be diverted to cutting wood, fishing, or any other economically productive activity, above all to planting and harvesting lands set aside to be worked in common or lands belonging to the dynastic ruler. In fact, in the Andes all tribute was conceived of as labor, performed by the commoner in expectation of reciprocal benefit from the ruler.

Provincial organization as it existed in central Mexico is easiest to grasp, perhaps only because it is best known. Though the provincial unit was called an *altepetl* ("water and mountain"), referring both to the people and to the entire territory, at its core was one large nucleated settlement or capital, typically containing several calpullis, as opposed to the scattered outlying hamlets, typically one calpulli each. The Spaniards were to call the former a *cabecera* ("head town"), the latter *sujetos* ("subjects"), a useful terminology which we too will follow at times. The economic specialties of the sujetos were exchanged at a public market in the cabecera. The latter contained also the palace of the dynastic ruler and the province's chief temple with its priesthood; on both counts, the area's tribute was channeled in toward the cabecera (see Figure 1).

This picture applies also to many parts of southern Mexico, but in other parts, in Guatemala, and above all in the Andean highlands, there appears to have been less nucleation of settlement. At the center was not a residential concentration so much as a ceremonial complex, with each calpulli or ayllu unit living in its own subarea. For the Andes, there is some question about the role or even the existence of markets. But the unifying force of tribute to a ruler, whether the *tlatoani* in central Mexico, the *batab* in Yucatan, or the *curaca* in the central Andes, was the same in all these situations.

Everywhere among the sedentary peoples there was the concept not only of a ruler but of a nobility, a set of interrelated lineages, the members of which stood apart from the commoners: They dressed differently, had other, lighter duties, monopolized the higher roles of government and religion, and had direct, individual control over certain lands and followers. The ruler was dynastic but rarely so by

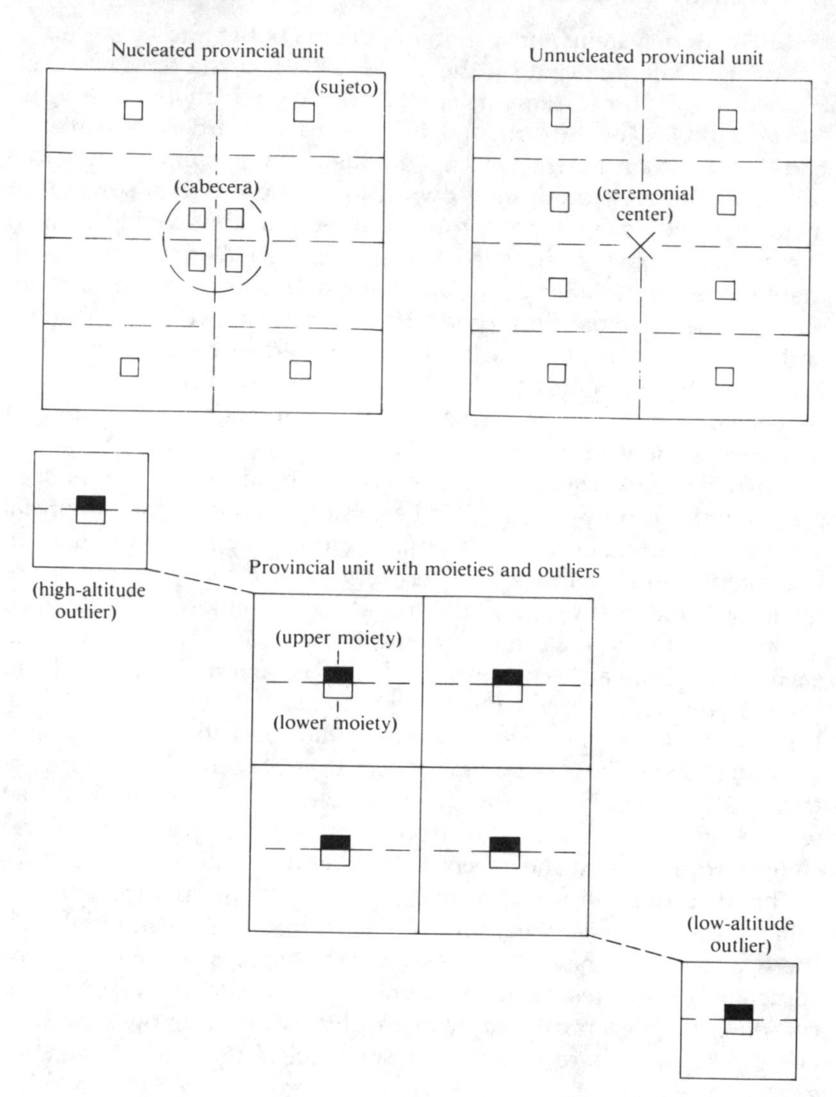

Figure 1. Schemas of some types of unit organization among sedentary peoples.

strict primogeniture in the legitimate male line as in early modern Europe; rather, the whole body of the mature nobles, a council of a kind, chose and legitimated the ruler from among various eligible members of the dynasty, whether brothers, uncles, sons, or nephews of the old ruler. These were unified societies, that is, noble and commoner spoke the same language, and the same processes and ambitions were at play in the lives of both. But by the time of the Iberian conquest, a deep-seated consciousness of the separate role, life-style, and privileges of the nobility existed in the minds of both nobles and commoners.

The two most basic constituent groups of society, then, were a tax-paying body of commoners and a directing corps of nobles. Yet they were far from constituting the whole; a prime characteristic of the sedentary societies was the degree of specialization, the number of people who were neither nobleman nor agriculturalist. In Mesoamerica and the Andes, not only were craft skills spread among the populace, but there were numerous craft specialists, as well as (at least in Mesoamerica) specialized traders and merchants, all of whom to some extent were removed from agriculture and public duties.

Most especially, though, all the sedentary societies had a class of people who were direct dependents of others, who shared neither the duties nor the rights of ordinary commoners and were not full members of the local calpulli or ayllu group. This phenomenon bears a close relation to another, the constant movement of people in and out of the hamlet and province units. Among the peoples we are discussing, the organizational units were fully stabilized in one place, but the same cannot be said of the individuals. Individuals and small family groups were continually leaving one unit and joining another for reasons very familiar to us: overcrowding at home, opportunity elsewhere, the opening of new areas, the attraction of cities. What emerges from the early central Mexican records particularly is a process somewhat like the following: A small family occupying adequate land in a calpulli would increase beyond the supporting capacity of its allotment; if the calpulli had other good land free, a new allotment might be made, but if not, some of the younger members would go elsewhere, either to another calpulli, to the special domains of the ruler or powerful nobles, or to another province altogether. In his new situation the migrant would be marginal, outside the regular framework, a foreigner whose duties and rights emanated from his new protector and master. Around the ruler, on his extensive lands, there was often thus a group of nearly calpulli size dependent upon him alone. Not all members of this group would be new to their status, but in general they were recruited from the most marginal, recent, and alien elements. Another source of dependents was conquest. Interprovincial wars often detached a calpulli, or several, from one province and attached it to another. In such a case many, or even the majority, of the inhabitants might be assigned to powerful leaders of the conquering province rather than become members of the regular calpulli-province structure. The proportion of dependents to calpulli members was higher the more recently acquired the area. In Mexico the dependents were a subclass of the ordinary commoners and were most often referred to by the same name, *macehualli;* over time they seem to have been constantly reconverging with the calpulli commoners. There was, to be sure, a special class of slaves who could be bought and sold. The origins of this group are, however, much like those of the other dependents: war captives, people in great economic necessity, orphans. Some early census records with actual listings of slaves show them mainly as having been brought as small children from the outside, carrying out functions much like those of the other dependents and eventually marrying among the local calpulli commoners.

In the Andes (which lacked actual slaves as far as we know) the dependents had a special name, *yana,* and a well-defined set of rights and obligations vis-à-vis their masters. As in Mexico, they did not hold ayllu lands or participate in community draft labor. They ranged from influential, wealthy chief stewards of lords down to the lowest menial. Although less is known of their origins than of their Mexican counterparts, in some cases at least the yana were ethnically or linguistically distinct from the main body of ayllu members. In general, the strength of this group seems related to the constant small-scale seasonal migrations demanded by the extremely varied and fragmented Andean environment, as we will have occasion to discuss later. With members of a single group holding lands far apart from each other and much traversing of the lands of others, it must often have happened that individuals took the opportunity to join other groups or that individuals and families were stranded in remote places.

Looking forward to the time when the Europeans would come, one can readily see how each of the three main social types in the sedentary societies would suit the requirements of an invading and occupying group. The basic commoner population could perform tribute labor and deliver agricultural and other products as it always had; the rulers and nobles could be intermediaries, through their traditional powers channeling labor and tribute to the conquerors; and the dependent group, already somewhat outside the normal structure, could become the conquerors' much-needed auxiliaries and personal dependents.

Landholding among the sedentary peoples is an extremely complex subject about which all too little is known, but there are a few important points to be made. First, we must distinguish between territory and land. The provincial unit was concerned primarily with territoriality or jurisdiction, with the notion that a certain area belonged in a general way to one people rather than to another. In Mexico it could happen that nobles would hold and work land in a province not their own, which caused no trouble as long as there was no challenge to sovereignty. The primary entity holding land in the sense of acreage to be cultivated was the hamlet group, the calpulli or ayllu. At this level, then, we must come to grips with the meaning of the concept of "communal" landholding. Communal it surely was, in certain basic ways. In general, only by virtue of community membership did individuals or families hold prime arable land, land which they could not alienate and which community authorities reallocated upon a family's extinction. It would be wrong, however, to set up communal landholding as something monolithic and entirely foreign to European ways. There were several important points of contact between the two systems.

First, most land among the sedentary peoples was not communally cultivated, that is, the norm was not an undivided area worked by all together but a plot held by one individual for his lifetime and worked by himself and his family. Only lands held by rulers, nobles, and priests were normally worked by the tribute payers as a group. Plots could vary greatly in size within a single community. In the Andes, reciprocal work was common, but it was individually oriented in that a person helped another work his land in return for the other's doing the same for him. Thus, despite considerable differences in the rationale, families, in effect, worked their own lands for themselves and paid taxes on the basis of them, much as in Europe.

Second, the rulers and nobles had not only personal dependents but lands which belonged specifically to themselves or their families. We have little certainty as to the exact status of such holdings, the extent to which they belonged in theory to the commonwealth, the noble house, or the noble individual. However, there is little doubt that the provincial rulers and the most powerful nobles in some manner held extensive private lands in various localities of the province, worked by their own permanent stewards and dependents, with periodic help from the mass of the commoners – a system in its essence identical to that of later Spanish American estates, except that in preconquest practice the holdings of an individual were often scattered in very small units over a large area.

Third, community control tended to be restricted to irrigated or otherwise prime arable land, leaving lands of marginal utility open to exploitation by anyone who thought it worth the effort. In Mexico at least, calpulli commoners might have "hill land" in addition to their main family plot, or "house land." The latter was inalienable, but marginal land could be and was traded or sold at the occupant's pleasure. Thus the concept of selling land or holding it on an individual basis would not be something entirely outside the experience of the sedentary peoples.

In several ways, then, the provincial units we have been discussing were a great deal like the Iberian province-municipality; both entities had a close generic resemblance to a city-state (the central Mexican provinces, indeed, were full-fledged city-states). Each contained all the principal traits and mechanisms of its respective culture, and each was quite autonomous and capable of survival on its own; with the Indian provinces it is striking that many institutions which are often thought of as imperial were deeply embedded in the local situation and not at all dependent on the empire's existence in order to function. The similarity extended to the matter of micropatriotism and separatism. As with the Iberians, every smallest province mistrusted all its neighbors and was forever inclined to split off from any larger unit of which it was, willingly or unwillingly, at the moment a part. With the Indians the feeling of provincial identity went so deep that each province felt itself a people and maintained its own cult and origin myth (however similar these might be to the corresponding phenomena among neighboring related groups).

In pointing out areas of contact between Iberian municipality and sedentary Indian province, we are of course not asserting any absolute identity. Only the central Mexican city-state was a close overall analog of the Iberian entity. Even there, aside from the deeper ethnicity and autonomy, there were aspects unmatched in the Iberian-style province. Through war and migration, some cabeceras had come to control subject hamlets scattered far outside their immediate hinterland. In some provinces there was a thoroughgoing moiety (dual) organization, in others a division into several parts. Such divergences were sometimes to cause problems for the Iberians, or, if they were not in direct conflict with Iberian goals, they might persist indefinitely into the colonial period, though ignored or misunderstood by the invaders. In the Andes such divergences were far greater, since the degree of urban nucleation was lower, moieties and double dynasties were rife, and holding scattered territories in distant ecological zones was the rule rather than the exception.

Despite the predominance of provincial organization in determining postconquest structures and procedures, some supraprovincial aspects were highly relevant. In the millennia before European conquest, the sedentary peoples had a varied experience of provincial autonomy or life in confederacies, small kingdoms, large kingdoms, and empires; there was hardly an area that had not known each of these forms at some time or other. The changes came about largely through warfare or the threat of it. Thus there had grown up over the centuries a set of expectations and standard procedures surrounding conquest and territorial expansion. The conquered province would retain its identity, the essence of its local autonomy, and even its ruling dynasty. It expected, however, to pay substantial tribute (collected internally) to the conquerors, to acknowledge the conquerors' gods (while retaining local deities), and to see pressures exerted on the choice of local rulers. By intermarriage, by taking members of the nobility of the conquered group to live among the conquerors, and by even more direct and forceful measures, the conquerors often in effect named the local ruler; as long as the imposed rulers were of the traditional dynastic line, they usually met no insurmountable obstacles in securing their subjects' allegiance and obedience. Furthermore, in the expectation of conquest, weaker and smaller groups were accustomed to bargain with expanding powers, semivoluntarily accepting their overlordship in the hope of more favorable tribute terms and greater local independence than might be their fate after military defeat. Or, war having started, they might come to terms after one serious trial of strength. All of these practices naturally bore on the behavior of the sedentary peoples when faced with the Europeans; the more remarkable thing is the extent to which their expectations matched those of the Iberians, whose conquest lore also included notions of tribute imposition, change of religion and allegiance, and manipulation of local rulers, together with at least provisional local autonomy.

But what of the great empires which held sway over so many of the sedentary peoples and their richest territories? Actually, these formidable structures differed from earlier or smaller ones principally in the scale of their activities. They grew out of the provincial world, and hence their institutions were enlargements of local institutions and their procedures were the same. They too allowed local autonomy, preserved provincial units, and cooperated with provincial dynasties, concentrating on tribute collection and interregional exchange and communication. For the Mexican sphere, the scholarly public already understands the situation quite well. Texts speak of how the Aztec empire originated as a confederation of three dominant provinces, whereas the subject provinces were under loose control and often desirous of regaining total independence, not to speak of central Mexican areas large and small which were not part of the Aztec system at all. But for the world of the Incas, we still must deal with the unrealistic picture lovingly constructed by generations of idealizers – first by the Inca nobles of Cuzco after the conquest, then by legalizing or nostalgic Spanish chroniclers, and then by writers of the earlier part of the present century. In this view, the Inca empire appeared as a vast welfare state regulating every aspect of its subjects' lives, insisting upon complete uniformity and turning the populace into little more than automatons organized in strict groups of ten and multiples of ten. The Inca empire was indeed as impressive a social-political structure as the world has seen. On analysis, however, its characteristic institutions – roads, messengers, warehouses, armies, garrisons, even houses of virgins of the sun – turn out to create a supraprovincial structure by tying together, adding to, and especially extracting from a set of provinces which continued to exist on their own terms (it becomes increasingly apparent, by the way, that the Aztecs had analogs to most of these institutions). Take the example of the Lupaca, a kingdom-empire of Aymara speakers in the highland Lake Titicaca region, near the present borders of Peru and Bolivia and in the heartland of the empire. After coming under Inca domination, the Lupaca not only retained their language, their entire internal organization, and their double dynasty of kings, but their kingdom actually expanded as they, in alliance with the Incas, subdued further neighboring groups. When the Spaniards arrived, the kingdom was still intact in this form, which it retained for quite some time even after that.

Under the Europeans the empires were to be destroyed and replaced by the invaders themselves. But even after they were gone, their precedent helped ease the way for the newly dominant group. The provinces were accustomed to delivering goods and services to outsiders; they were accustomed to having outside officials and stewards in their own territory, hastening the delivery. The European stewards and tax collectors thus stepped into a familiar slot; the parallel was so close that in Mexico the underlings of the Spanish encomenderos were called *calpixque* (stewards, literally "guarders of the house"), the Nahuatl name given previously to the tax collectors of the Aztecs. When the Spaniards settled in great centers such as Tenochtitlan-Mexico City or Cuzco, tribute went not only through familiar channels but to a familiar destination. Another feature outlasting the empires was the corps of high imperial nobility existing in both capitals; enough of them survived the conquest and occupation to maintain their cohesiveness and the substance of their traditions for some generations. Not only did they receive somewhat special treatment from the Europeans but members of the local dynasties of surrounding provinces continued to seek marriages with them, so that interprovincial dynastic politics, centered on the capitals, did not entirely disappear.

Up to this point we have been emphasizing common traits of Mesoamerica and the central Andes. Without forgetting that for both preconquest and postconquest history the two areas constitute the core of an important unity, let us now discuss some salient differences between them. It was already seen that territorial organization varied considerably between a more nucleated central Mexican type and a less nucleated Andean type with subdivisions in widely separated ecological zones. There is no sharp overall differentiation, since parts of southern Mesoamerica veered toward the unnucleated pattern, and in Guatemala it was even common for highland groups to maintain distant lowland subject areas where cacao and other special crops were grown, whereas on the Peruvian coast there were provinces and kingdoms displaying a high degree of urban nucleation. Even so, one can say that in Mexico there was a push toward a nucleated settlement with a circle of contiguous surrounding hamlets as a goal; trade or conquest would provide needed products from a distance. In the Andes, the goal was that each province and indeed, it seems, each ayllu should have a complementary set of holdings in different microclimates. Such a procedure was feasible because in the equatorial central Andean area sharp variations in altitude created vastly different zones quite close to each other, and it was necessary because no zone by itself supplied all the staples of Andean civilization. Ideally, a group would want Pacific lowlands for cotton, medium lowlands for maize, higher land for potatoes and the like, bleak highland plains for llamas and alpacas, and eastern Andean wet hill land for coca growing. This system affected every aspect of life; ultimately it was responsible for the special strength of Andean traditions of rotary labor and colonization. In the Andes society was fully sedentary, territoriality was fully developed, and yet the people were quasi-migratory. The Andean peoples had made one kind of successful adaptation to an extreme environmental challenge. The Europeans would not be willing or able to follow suit and would make their own adjustment, which included simple avoidance of the highlands as far as possible (far different from their acceptance of the more temperate and accessible central Mexican highland as a base).

Both Mesoamerica and the Andes knew maize, chiles, and cotton. In addition, each had some domesticated varieties not known to the other. The cacao grown in southern Mesoamerica was an important item of trade between that area and the central Mexican highlands, and it was to play a large role in the postconquest economy. But if the Andean region lacked this significant item, it had several others peculiar to itself: potatoes and other high altitude crops, as well as the narcotic coca, and especially the domesticated cameloids, the highland-dwelling llama and alpaca, which were important as pack animals, for meat, and for the wool that allowed the high development of Andean textiles.

In technology the two cultures were quite similar, but the Andeans had far more silver deposits in their territory (most of Mexico's silver lay to the north of sedentary settlement). Partly for this reason, the Mesoamericans did little with silver, whereas the Andeans had located deposits, mined them, developed sophisticated smelting techniques, and used the metal freely for artifacts. This aspect alone was to make Peru at first more valuable to Europeans than Mexico; in Peru there was to be utilization of indigenous techniques and trained personnel, as opposed to the new start that had to be made in Mexico. Since silver mining was to be the base of the postconquest economy, the differential location of the main deposits in respect to the bulk of the sedentary population was to have vast consequences for the general organization of the two areas in the postconquest period.

In the sphere of cultural achievements, one could write volumes comparing and contrasting Mesoamerica and the Andes. Only one striking difference need concern us here. The Mesoamerican peoples had writing systems, and the Andean peoples did not, though their *quipu* method (knotted-string calculation) was fully capable of maintaining statistics on an imperial scale. Both systems were esoteric arts known only to specialists, and being very different from European techniques, they did not long survive the conquest. Nor is it clear that Mesoamerican writing, as practiced when the Spaniards came, had either the intention or the capability of capturing running prose. Nevertheless, Mesoamerica had paper, ink, professional writers, and a veneration for writing. It is doubtless no accident that many Mesoamerican peoples adopted the European alphabet for various kinds of communication and record keeping in their own languages from the sixteenth century forward, whereas the Andeans generally did not (or at least, searches have as yet revealed little evidence that they did).

Nonimperial sedentary peoples

Though many of the peoples just described were organized in relatively small autonomous units at the time of European contact, most of them had at some point been part of quite large and stable sociopolitical structures, and it is hard not to think of them in a general way as the "empire peoples." Still, as we have been emphasizing, it was not empire, organized priesthood and religion, great stone temples and palaces, or magnificently elaborate artifacts which were important for the postcontact period but the basic social, economic, and political structure at the local level. Any group which shared this structure, or most of it, fit into the same category from a postconquest perspective. And in fact, there were sedentary peoples who for reasons not always clear to us had neither experienced an imperial phase nor built stunning physical complexes. Their way of life is not nearly as well documented as that of the Aztecs or Incas, and among the great variety of American peoples they fade imperceptibly into the semisedentary groups, but we will briefly discuss two prominent cases to give some notion of the phenomenon. First we will treat a group deeply and clearly influenced by the central people's patterns, the Chibcha of Colombia, and then a group with greater apparent affinities to the semisedentary peoples, the Arawaks of the large Caribbean islands. Somewhat comparable groups were to be found scattered in many places, particularly around the periphery of the two empire areas and in the entire region of Central America and northern South America which separated the two. Also, many of the peoples of southern Mesoamerica came close to fitting in this subcategory.

The Chibcha of present-day Colombia were located in high valleys of the eastern range of the northern Andes, constituting a population that is sometimes estimated at around a million. Both women and men participated in a permanent intensive agriculture based on maize as well as the more specifically central Andean complex, including potatoes and coca (though the cameloids were lacking). Society included dynastic rulers, nobles, and tribute-paying commoners, and though yana-like dependents do not seem to be mentioned, there were slaves. Markets were held on a regular schedule – in this the Chibcha were more like the Mesoamericans. The nature of organizational units is still a matter of some controversy. The smallest unit of which much is known was what the Spaniards were to call a partiality or captaincy, an endogamous group of perhaps several hundred or a few thousand occupying a distinct agricultural territory and led by a hereditary ruler to whom the Spaniards gave the title of captain. The members of the group largely lived scattered about the land they worked, five or six large house compounds together. The body of commoners worked lands held individually, but they also worked land for the captain and gave him cotton cloth, gold, and coca. Speaking in central Mexican terms, the captaincy seems to have fallen somewhere between the individual calpulli and the full-fledged province as to size. In any case, captaincies or combinations of them served after the conquest as the basis of encomiendas for Spaniards that were much like those of Mexico and Peru.

It was to matter little, then, that in some other respects the Chibcha were not at all comparable to the Aztecs or Incas. Although there were two large kingdoms, centered at Bogotá and Tunja, respectively, with rulers who were venerated almost in the manner of the Inca emperor, and although there were high priests and temples, allegiances shifted frequently, temples and palaces were of wood, cane, and mud, and the rulers were surrounded by only moderate concentrations of people and power. Under the high rulers were a certain number of secondary rulers, over whose selection the former exercised some control; each of the secondary rulers in turn had several captaincies in his district. A chain of tribute obligations extended from bottom to top. But in frequent warring (against less sedentary groups at lower altitudes on all sides and among the Chibcha themselves), the mid-sized groups sometimes went from one kingdom to the other or asserted independence, and, even more indicative of the instability of the larger entities, captaincies frequently switched from one secondary ruler to another. After the conquest, conflicting claims of fealty and independence were rife. Though the Spaniards were to take the royal residences of Bogotá and Tunja as the sites for their own main settlements, they would build tribute and labor arrangements mainly on the captaincies.

The Arawaks, inhabitants of the chain of large northern Caribbean islands, present a case of a sedentary people with an even less elaborate material culture or superstructure, whose way of life nevertheless supplied an adequate immediate basis of support for a substantial European presence. Having migrated from northeastern South America, they differ from the Chibcha in showing closer affinities, in their agriculture and aspects of their social structure, to the semisedentary peoples of the South American east coast. Estimates of their population have risen over the years to seven or eight million for the island of Hispaniola (to be the first center of Spanish occupation) alone. If this is correct, densities would have been comparable to those of the empire peoples. This is more than one might expect from an agricultural system which has been described by some as a shifting one of slash-and-burn; more recently, however, it has been denied that cultivation shifted and in some areas it seems that irrigation was practiced. There is room for uncertainty on both the exact nature of the agricultural practices and the exact size of the population, but we may postulate a relatively large and dense population for Hispaniola at least. As with the eastern mainland peoples, root crops, especially cassava, which were produced on fields worked into a series of large mounds, or *conucos,* were the staple; maize and other seed crops were also present.

Sizable kingdoms, with secondary rulers over subdistricts, existed, on a pattern not unlike that of the Chibcha, but the unit basic to social organization was the village, of perhaps a thousand or two thousand inhabitants, surrounded by the conucos from which it maintained itself. In the villages, or in the larger ones at any rate, were social groupings by now familiar to us: a *cacique,* or chieftain; some *nitainos,* or nobles; ordinary commoners; and dependents called *naborías* (the Spaniards were to use the words "cacique" and "naboría" for comparable types all over the Indies). The residential pattern, however, was less like that of the individual family dwellings of most fully sedentary peoples and more like the multifamily units of certain semisedentary groups. Fifty or even a hundred people would live in a single large structure of pole and thatch; the occupants were closely related to each other, and we may infer that this large cohesive unit carried out more of the functions of society, and the superordinated institutions fewer, than among the central peoples. The house of the cacique was larger than the others and his preeminence was marked by a special seat and a litter, but his revenue was limited in that he apparently did not receive tribute in kind for himself but only in time of war for the general cause. On the other hand, his people worked on conucos for him, and he had general authority in the distribution of work. This was to be a sufficient mechanism to make Spanish encomiendas viable in the postconquest period, that is, in the few years before the culmination of a devastating demographic decline, typical of what happened on European contact to all dense congregations of people in the warm lowlands of the Western Hemisphere.

Semisedentary peoples

Large areas of preconquest America were inhabited by ethnic groups who were intermediate between agriculture and a life of hunting and gathering, in many cases for clearly environmental reasons. These were predominantly forest peoples. They had villages and cultivated fields which were vital to their sustenance, but cultivation sites shifted frequently, and village sites tended to follow suit over time. From a combination of necessity, tradition, and preference, these peoples placed great emphasis on hunting and fishing as a pursuit and a source of food. Indeed, one of the most universally applicable and most crucial diagnostic traits in analysis of the American peoples is that among the fully sedentary groups both men and women devoted much of their lives to agriculture, whereas among the semisedentary peoples women had the primary responsibility for agriculture and men, though they may have helped clear the land, were primarily hunters and warriors. Although it is generally thought that this type of economy could not sustain the population density characteristic of the central peoples, recent scholarship has tended to place estimates much higher than before.

These groups were culturally rich, possessing in some variant a great deal of the technology prevalent among the empire peoples, plus much that was specifically their own. The variety among them, as to customs, details of social organization, and type of plant or animal life at the base of the diet, is kaleidoscopic. For our purposes, they are perhaps most simply defined by what they lacked relative to the fully sedentary peoples. Even at the village level, tribute paying and community rotary labor were not known, nor was there a strong chief empowered to demand levies; there might be a headman in some cases, but he was concerned more with ceremonies and war. Specialized social classes generally did not exist, neither nobles nor commoners nor dependents, though some peoples had temporary captives taken from their enemies, nor were there high priests and special temples. Though ethnicity was strong, village organization was loose and unstable; not only did the site shift from time to time, but in many cases individual constituent lineages came and went as they pleased. Supravillage confederations were fleeting, for specific defensive or offensive purposes. Above all, there was no good-sized provincial unit with strong coherence, permanence, and identification with a specific compact core territory; that is, there was no potential base for encomiendas in the usual sense. Not only was there little in the way of surplus produce, there were no mechanisms capable of delivering produce and labor to a conquering group, no intermediaries to channel it.

But if, in general, it was what the semisedentaries did not have that was to be crucial for the postcontact period, one trait which they *did* have was to be very important: Their potential to combat an invader was a great deal higher than that of the empire peoples. The bow and arrow was much more prevalent than among the central groups, and the level of proficiency was as high as might be expected among constant practitioners of war and hunting. Poisoned missiles existed among some groups, the only weapon indigenous to the hemisphere which was capable of putting combatants roughly on a par with opponents equipped in the European style. Forest terrain made ambush and retreat easy, and the fragmented nature of society meant that every tiniest unit had to be conquered separately.

Peoples answering in a general way to the above description were to be found in many parts of the hemisphere. Some were located on the edges of the central peoples. One large block was in the woodlands of eastern North America; another, even larger, was spread through the entire vast tropical rain forest region of South America, with the three main culture-and-language groups of Arawakan, Cariban, and Tupian. The Tupians especially had carried out long migrations in recent times, and on European contact branches of the family were located in Paraguay, along the main part of the coast of Brazil, and in the Amazonian basin, not to speak of pockets elsewhere. They were to have more direct interaction with Europeans, both Portuguese and Spanish, than perhaps any other comparable culture, so we may appropriately use them as our principal exemplar of a semisedentary people.

Tupian agricultural practices were standard for groups of this type, involving the technique known as slash-and-burn. Parties of men cleared a patch of land of as many of the larger trees as possible, circled the trunks of others to kill them, and then burned off the underbrush, leaving the women to plant, tend, and harvest the crops, of which the primary one was manioc. Under wet tropical conditions, fields so cleared were productive for only two or three years, after which the process was repeated elsewhere. Hunting and fishing, performed by men, was a vital activity, as usual for a semisedentary people; in this case fishing predominated, either in the Atlantic or in the extensive inland river systems. It has in fact been suggested that the tropical forest villagers were more than anything else riverine folk.

The principal social unit was a tightly knit kin group or lineage, usually dwelling together in one large house, with anywhere from thirty to sixty interrelated nuclear families. A senior male stood at the head of this entity; such power as he had emanated mainly from the fact that the other inhabitants were his junior relatives; he might have several wives or concubines, and his in-laws were obliged to help him perform certain tasks. Rather than class groupings or technical specializations, the divisions of society were by age, sex, and distinction in war. Age groups were important in the division of labor, and sex groups even more so, as we have seen. Indeed, some villages had a special men's house which constituted the community's principal means of ceremonial and social integration. Villages varied in size, being larger where resources were richer; they might contain four to eight of the large lineage houses just mentioned. As a result of constant intervillage warfare, palisades were common.

If there were groups like the island Arawaks, transitional between sedentary and semisedentary, there were also semisedentary groups veering far toward the fully mobile hunters. One could have put the Tupians themselves in such a class during their migratory phases. At the time of European arrival, a prominent group of this type were the Caribs of the Lesser Antilles, the people after whom the Caribbean is named. Originally from the mainland, they had wrested the smaller islands from the Arawaks within recent generations and were still expanding and raiding at the Arawaks' expense.

Crops were still grown, and indeed the Caribs are known for the richness of their complex of fruit trees. But they had become highly specialized as a mobile maritime people. Their large oceangoing canoes allowed long-distance voyages and warfare as well as extensive fishing. Villages were extremely small, apparently often containing only one exogamous lineage and thus comparable to a single household among the Tupians. The organization and implementation of surprise raids on other groups occupied a large part of life, so much so that Carib women were treated almost like alien captives, since that had been the origin of so many of the Caribs' women over generations: They were kept entirely separate from the men, assumed the entire burden of ordinary tasks, and even, we are told, spoke the Arawak language of the people who were such frequent victims of raids rather than the Carib of the men. The Caribs were to cause the Europeans as much trouble as any hunting people, and indeed, the Spaniards generalized the term "Carib" to mean any extremely hostile, indomitable, mobile, poison-arrow-shooting group of Indians.

In emphasizing the difference between the fully sedentary and the semisedentary peoples in their potential as a base for a European presence, we do not want to lose sight of the fact that certain kinds of interaction were in fact possible. Europeans in areas like this could at least barter for food or commandeer it; in time they could adopt the local crops as their own, as happened with manioc in both Brazil and Paraguay. The *mate* tea of the Tupian Guaraní in Paraguay even became a successful commercial crop in postconquest interregional trade. Populations were significant, if not dense, and Europeans could in one way or another impress local people directly into their service, people who were not totally unaccustomed to agricultural and other kinds of productive labor and to whom sleeping inside walls was nothing strange. Indeed, Europeans could go beyond individuals and use the social structure of the semisedentary groups to their own advantage to the extent that they were willing and able to become a part of it themselves. That the social and political institutions created on this basis should differ considerably from those arising in the lands of the empire peoples is not surprising.

Nonsedentary peoples

In the *Florentine Codex,* compiled by Franciscan friar Bernardino de Sahagún, a sixteenth-century Nahua writer of the Valley of Mexico has described the Chichimecs of the Mexican north: They live in the wilds, in the plains and forests; they have no homes but wander from place to place and sleep where night overtakes them, sometimes in a cave. Their dress is skins; their food, game and wild fruits. They have sharp eyesight and never miss a target with their arrows, no matter how small or how distant. They are lean, hard, and fleet.

That is to say, the sedentary peoples of America were fully aware of the distinction between themselves and the mobile hunters and gatherers of the hemisphere. Their attitude toward them was much like that of the similarly sedentary Europeans: part romanticizing admiration, part contempt for a group lacking the basics of civilized life as they knew it. Never does the Nahua writer use in connection with the Chichimecs the word *tlacanemiliztli* ("people-living"), or as we would doubtless say, "civilization," a term he uses with several other sedentary and semisedentary groups and which he seems to equate with possession of permanent houses, textile garments, and maize cultivation. Beneath the stereotype was the truth that the economy and organization of the hunters was very different and that they were extremely resistant to domination by sedentaries (for whom they returned the contempt), whether Indian or European. The empires could do nothing with them, and the European invaders little more; indigenous groups in areas such as the Argentine pampas or the American Great Plains maintained resistance and independence until the late nineteenth century.

Tendencies already seen among the semisedentary groups reached their culmination here. The hunters and gatherers had literally no cultivation of domestic varieties, no permanent settlements. Their efficiency in a mobile type of warfare was even greater than among the semisedentaries. Population densities were extremely low. Unless he brought his own supplies, an invader who fought his way into their territory would be faced with the threat of starvation in an empty landscape, for there were no stands of crops ready to commandeer. Though the hunting and gathering peoples put much effort and skill into gleaning what their environment offered, they had little if any surplus production and hence no mechanism for delivering such; and they had no framework of regularized productive activity. Normally they could be brought to live in one place and perform "work" only through physical constraint and mixing with other peoples.

Hunter-collectors were found in many corners of both continents. Most (not quite all) of their habitats were unpropitious for agricultural exploitation in either the sedentary or semisedentary fashion: deserts, swamps, rocky shores, infertile forested areas away from large rivers, and plains areas. The latter, which since the advent of draft animals and the plow have become the richest agricultural lands of the hemisphere, were a hostile arena for the techniques then employed. Hunter-collectors occupied much of southern South America, including the present Argentine and Uruguayan plains, the south coast of Chile, and the Chaco desert of Paraguay and Bolivia. The Mexican north was another area with many such peoples, and they held large sections of North America proper.

These peoples did not live in a vacuum but were linguistically, culturally, and technologically the cousins of the other American types. Despite the prejudices of the central Mexican writer mentioned earlier, practically all the hunters knew the principle of artificial, though portable or temporary, structures for human dwelling; their weapons were related to those of the semisedentary peoples, as were their legends, and kinship, age, and sex structured their lives in quite similar ways. Some semisedentary peoples, such as the

Ge of the inland Brazilian savannahs, had originated as hunters (and were correspondingly resistant to European conquest). In their religion and sense of emotional identification, the hunters stand with the semisedentaries as opposed to the fully sedentary peoples. The latter had cults in which a god or gods symbolized and gave unity to a province or a larger state as a whole, whereas with the former, spirits associated with individuals predominated. For the sedentaries, patriotism had a strong territorial dimension, being applied primarily to a group of people holding lands defined almost to the yard, whereas for both the other types, the equivalent was, on the one hand, identification with one's own immediate lineage and, on the other hand, with a much broader territory in the sense of a total environment or "nature." Even so, the hunters stood out in the American scene as the peoples with the smallest and most mobile functioning units, the least attractive lands, the greatest resistance potential, and the least willingness to accept change in their way of life.

We have not gone into the subtleties of Nahuatl poetry or Inca masonry, both of which we greatly admire, nor have we expatiated on Tupian and Carib cannibalism or Aztec human sacrifice (though these topics could profit from a nonsensationalist treatment of their rationale) because these aspects do not bear as directly on the shape of the future as do matters of social and economic organization. All the American peoples had art and intellectual achievements deserving our admiration and study. All had practices which would horrify Europeans and which, when the latter felt it necessary, they could quickly bring to a halt. It was the durable basic features of local life, such as crops, the organization of work, and the nature of territoriality, which put their stamp on nascent Latin American society and made it differ from one place to another.

Part II

Origins and early maturity

The course of events in the Western Hemisphere over the several centuries following contact, if taken as a whole, demonstrates that the Iberian or European factor in early Latin America was essentially uniform and that it took certain shapes or developed at a certain rate in any given region depending principally on that region's already existing attractiveness or potential. The Indian peoples and the resources of their lands were the primary determinants of regional differentiation. Or to put it another way, at any given time Europe was interested in, and technically capable of exploiting, certain New World resources more than others, and attention went to areas with such resources, no matter which group of Europeans was involved. Mexico and Peru, as we have seen, were homes of what may be called the central, fully sedentary peoples, and the same areas also contained the largest and most available deposits of the American commodity in greatest demand in the Europe of the time: precious metals. As one would expect, these two regions received the main impact of sixteenth-century European immigration, with consequent quick creation of impressive European-style social, economic, and institutional networks, whereas immigration to all other areas was small, and change was slower, until a later time.

The simplicity of this schema tends to be obscured by considerations of European nationality. Partly because of Portugal's heavy involvement in maritime enterprises on other continents, and partly because of the operation of chance, the Spaniards were the first to take on America in earnest, and hence they were the ones to occupy Mexico and Peru, the ones to build large-scale, complex structures that attained a precocious maturity well before the end of the sixteenth century. Portuguese Brazil, on the other hand, seemed to lag behind until the development of a sugar industry in the northeast after about 1580 in response to trends in Europe and Africa. Seeing this differential, commentators have sometimes spoken of Spanish action in America as strong or early as opposed to Portuguese action, which they have deemed weak or late, in every aspect from immigration to the creation of institutions. The truth is that the

Spaniards rushed into feverish founding activity only where there were sedentary Indians and mineral wealth; elsewhere their territories also languished in neglect, more indeed than the Brazilian northeast.

Our procedure in this book is to treat the main blocks of development separately; we hope the reader will be prepared to look beneath the superficial emphasis on nationality which this entails. First, we discuss in three chapters the beginnings and early maturity of Latin American society in the central areas, which all happen to have been under Spanish rule. Next, in the following two chapters we do the same for eastern seaboard tropical export society, which for reasons of precedent, geography, and markets happens to have been all Portuguese – or was until the north European powers became involved in it in the seventeenth and eighteenth centuries. Finally we devote a chapter to areas which were frankly marginal from the point of view of Europeans in America in the sixteenth and seventeenth centuries, and here, at least, the reader will see directly illustrated our contention that local conditions shape things more than European national propensities, for the fringes include areas under both Spain and Portugal, and indeed, the Brazilian south and interior make one unit together with much of Spanish American Paraguay and Argentina in contrast to either Mexico-Peru or the Brazilian northeast.

A further complicating factor is that, though the Spaniards went quite quickly and by direct routes to the central areas, their first impact was in the Caribbean. Because the island inhabitants shared only part of the characteristics of the fully sedentary peoples, structures and practices there were discernibly different from the often more elaborate or stable ones which evolved on the mainland. Nevertheless, the Caribbean experience left such an imprint on all that followed that treatment of it is an indispensable introduction to discussion of the European occupation of the central areas.

3

From islands to mainland: the Caribbean phase and subsequent conquests

In a society which has existed in unbroken continuity in the same area for some centuries, there will be strong regional distinctions and competing traditions of thought, and change is usually piecemeal and cumulative. When people are removed in large numbers to a new environment, however, things happen somewhat differently for a time. Although the newcomers will attempt to preserve as many of their patterns of thought and behavior as possible, circumstances force them to make wide-ranging adjustments in the first years of their presence in the new area, merely in order to survive and achieve their proximate goals. A set of practices and a new vocabulary crystallize very quickly, thereafter changing little for relatively long periods of time. If the new society expands quickly over a large area, as with Spanish America, there will be great uniformity in certain things such as local governmental forms, commercial arrangements, and even spoken language, despite regional variation in the new local base.

The reasons why new areas experience quick cultural-institutional crystallization followed by slow change are many and complex, though if one takes the view that human societies innovate as little as possible at any given time, the rest tends to follow. More relevant here are some of the specific mechanisms. Many new societies have revered and rewarded firstcomers. In the Spanish Indies this tendency was to take the form of a strong emphasis on *antigüedad*, or seniority. The wealthiest and most respected settlers were those who had been there longest, and newcomers readily heeded the advice of old hands on how things were to be done. Senior settlers were always the ones to lead ventures into yet newer areas, and once there, they, as governors and council members, arranged things in the way already familiar to them. Of course change continued, in every branch and on every level of life; over long stretches of time, new regional dialects and subcultures would arise. Any new area eventually becomes an old one. Meanwhile, for a matter of decades or centuries, the Caribbean tradition would be a large element in the workings of Spanish American society.

The Caribbean phase becomes even more complex because the Spaniards were not a previously immobile people occupying their first new area. Rather, they were inclined to view the Caribbean in the light of their own already established tradition of expansion, mainly "reconquest." At the same time, the initial discovery and attempts at exploitation were carried out under the direction of Genoese Columbus and his relatives and cohorts, entirely within the framework of previous Genoese-Portuguese activity in the Mediterranean and above all in Africa.

Not only Columbus and his friends but many of the Andalusian maritime people who manned his ventures, as well as the Spanish crown itself, were prepared to emulate Portuguese overseas experience, to treat America on the analogy of Africa or perhaps India. However, America was neither Africa nor India. And just as importantly, the Spanish immigrants to America insisted on operating within their own heritage. A maritime tradition of trade and exploration thus competed with, and in the end largely gave way to, the old Iberian tradition of full conquest, substantial immigration, and permanent rule – though some aspects of the Portuguese-Genoese tradition entered definitively into Spanish American life. The following pages, then, will deal with the Caribbean phase in the double light of transition and precedent.

The course of Caribbean events

First let us take a narrative glimpse at the general course of events in the Caribbean in order to have a context for a more topical analysis. No sooner had Columbus, in the name of the Castilian crown, "come upon some islands in the Atlantic," as the resentful Portuguese have tended to phrase it, than the Spaniards and the maritime organizers began to pull in different directions. The basic notion of Columbus, in line with his Genoese and Portuguese background, was to establish forts and factories manned by salaried employees, to trade with the local population for any products of value in Europe, and to continue exploration, in search of stronger and richer trading partners. The instinct of the Spaniards, on the other hand, was to concentrate first on settlement and thorough rule of the well-populated area which had already been found. As a result, 1493 saw the departure from Spain of the largest and most complete expedition yet to leave Europe, equipped with everything needed to transplant European life: people of many trades and estates, seeds, plants, and animals.

For some years the newcomers concentrated entirely on Hispaniola (today the Dominican Republic and Haiti), which apparently had the largest indigenous population of any of the islands. After a short time of trial and error, Santo Domingo, on the southeastern coast, emerged as the Spanish capital and principal seat, a role it was long to retain for the whole Caribbean. The Arawaks of Hispaniola generally offered little resistance to the mere presence of the intruders, so that the latter became established without what one could call a real conquest, and resistance took more the form of sporadic rebellion as the indigenous people came to realize the extent and permanence of the change. Columbus and others familiar with the Portuguese experience in Africa investigated the local possibilities for all the economic enterprises successful there: tropical woods, spices, slave export, sugar, and gold. Of these only gold proved immediately and decidedly viable, and even so there was one major difference between African and American gold exploitation, for whereas in Africa an outsider could acquire through trade gold which was already mined, in the Caribbean islands he must direct production himself if it was to be on a sufficient scale. This meant a thorough occupation, a systematic rechanneling of indigenous labor, and, with the success of the operation, continued strong European immigration and the consequent rise of a complex immigrant society.

This large development began to take place under the direction of a non-Spaniard who would have been much better placed on the African or East Asian coasts than as perpetual viceroy and admiral of Hispaniola and all the other new lands. Columbus turned out, of course, to be a "poor governor." Earlier we saw how the Spaniards despised sailors and foreigners; now someone who was both was supposed to rule them and command their respect. And Columbus, rather than turning full attention to Hispaniola, continued his preoccupation with Mediterranean-Genoese concerns, from further exploration to the redemption of Jerusalem from the Muslims. Soon the Spanish personnel of Hispaniola were rebelling, imposing Iberian forms on their own initiative. There was nothing for the Spanish crown to do but to appoint Spanish governors, from 1499 onward, to regularize and legitimate the process.

At home in Spain, international commercial organizations based in Seville began to transfer some of their business to the Caribbean, and as word spread through the south of Spain, the social and regional sources of emigration continued to widen. As to the crown, soon after the first reports on the islands it negotiated the treaty of Tordesillas (1494), intended by the two parties to let Portugal exploit Africa and Asia while Spain took the Western Hemisphere. It was not then known how far South America jutted to the east, so that the line drawn gave Portugal treaty rights to much of Brazil, an area which they discovered independently not many years after. (This is not to ascribe great importance to the treaty. The decisive factors were rather that Spain had its hands full with the major American centers, Brazil appeared of little worth at first, and it lay very near the Portuguese sea route to India.) In governmental affairs, a process similar to that in the islands was going on, that is, an initial inclination to accept a Mediterranean model was giving way to classic Iberian forms. In 1503 the crown formally created the Casa de Contratación (House of Trade) in Seville. Apparently it was modeled ultimately on a Genoese original and was intended to perform the actual exploitation of the American colonies in the crown's name; instead, it soon became a checkpoint, registry, and customs collecting agency for incoming and outgoing fleets. Crown governmental functions were increasingly exercised through councilors of the royal court, who by 1524 had become the Council of the Indies, organized like other royal councils.

On Hispaniola, cycles of gold mining and demography were crucial to the timing of events. Significant placer deposits, quickly located, produced enough wealth to sustain the overall Spanish venture, but they were becoming exhausted by around 1515. Through the encomienda, the Spaniards acquired sufficient labor to work the mines for a time, but so precipitous was the decline of the Indian population that exhaustion of the labor supply antedated that of the deposits. Slaving expeditions into surrounding areas were one Spanish response. There followed the full-scale occupation, in 1508–11, of Puerto Rico, Jamaica, and Cuba, where similar, though quicker, cycles immediately got under way, as well as the first venture in force to the mainland, to Tierra Firme (the area of Panama and the western Caribbean coast of Colombia), in 1509–13. By the time of the conquest of Mexico, 1519–21, the original demographic and mineral basis for a strong European presence had practically disappeared from the large Caribbean islands.

For some years yet Santo Domingo retained the aura of being the capital of the Indies. A brief boom of pearl extraction off the Venezuelan coast helped, and export of sugar and hides gave the islands a new economic base, though an extremely limited one, while the importation of African slaves began the long slow process of re-creating a demographic base. But for many decades the Caribbean was to be a backwater, important mainly for the supply and safety of fleets going back and forth between Spain and the Spanish American central areas.

Spanish city and society on Hispaniola

A closer examination of the content of Spanish society in the Indies of the conquest period must await our discussion of the central areas, about which a great deal more is known than about this area whose primary records have suffered so from buccaneers and wet tropical conditions. For the moment, let us presume only that a surprisingly broad cross section of Spanish types was present and active in the same style as in Spain itself, as far as conditions permitted. In terms of regional origin, they were overwhelmingly from the south of Spain (exclusive of the just conquered Moorish kingdom of Granada), that is, they were from the areas closest to Seville, from where ships departed and news disseminated. Much doubt remains as to whether or not the southerners were able to put a permanent imprint on the Spanish culture of the Indies in the brief time before masses of immigrants from the rest of Castile joined them. In any case, Andalusians dominated the first phase and large numbers of Extremadurans joined them starting with the arrival of Cáceres-born Governor frey Nicolás de Ovando in 1502. By the time of the occupation of the mainland, one can speak of a spread of immigrants from all areas of Castile.

The facts do suffice for us to discuss some general aspects of the Spanish city as it evolved in the Caribbean. If society in Spain was urban centered, Spanish society in the Indies was to be even more so. Before many years had gone by, so much of the Spanish population was in the city of Santo Domingo, soon a well-built urban complex with many stone buildings, that the name given to the island tended to be ignored in favor of calling the entire region after the city – a custom retained to this day in the "Dominican Republic." Congregating in urban centers in a new area, where the immigrants would otherwise be too scattered for joint social-economic or even military action, seems so natural a development that one might wonder why things are ever done any other way. At any rate, the consequence was that there could be stability, growth, and even a flourishing of the refinements of European culture at the central urban nucleus while the broader hinterland from which the city drew saw little Europeanization or underwent marked decay. While gold was running out and a more modest economic base was being found, while the bulk of the indigenous population was disappearing from disease and other ravages, Santo Domingo not only remained a strong Spanish center but received in 1508 a Castilian high-society contingent in the retinue of Columbus's son, now nominal governor, followed by the first high court, or Audiencia, in the Indies in 1511; the great gothic cathedral was built after the full demise of the original system, around 1527–40, and a university was created, formally at least, in 1538. The stability of the major foundations did not necessarily extend, however, to any smaller more specialized ones in the hinterland, especially towns or camps set up for something as ephemeral as gold mining. Some fifteen such settlements existed on Hispaniola during the boom years, only to fade away when their reason for existence was gone.

The overall functioning of the Spanish city in the Indies was the same as in Spain itself, from the role of the municipal council, or *cabildo,* composed of the locally powerful to the descending hierarchies which reached out of the city into the countryside to rule it and draw from it the city's sustenance. In the Indies there was, however, initially a new element of stark differentiation between the two spheres: The city was Spanish, the countryside was Indian, and any Spaniard in the country was there fleetingly on the city's behalf.

In one other respect the Spanish cities of the Caribbean, and after them those of all the Indies, stood apart from the Iberian originals. Urban structure, both physical and social, is one of the most marked examples of the quick establishment of a uniform procedure which Spaniards in America would follow wherever they went. And a very important one it is, for the city was the general framework of Spanish life. The first act settlers would carry out in a given area, during or even before its conquest, was to set up a Spanish city and council. Despite the fact that mining towns and ports would rarely conform to the norm and that Santo Domingo itself was not perfectly standard, the Spaniards, well before the end of the primary Caribbean phase, had hit upon a definitive plan for their cities (see Figure 2). The layout was simplicity itself: a large square in the center, a gridwork of wide, perfectly straight streets extending from there in all directions, forming square or rectangular blocks, four lots to a block, of which only a certain number in the proximity of the square were at first actually surveyed, assigned, and built on. On one side of the square would be the principal church, on another the munici-

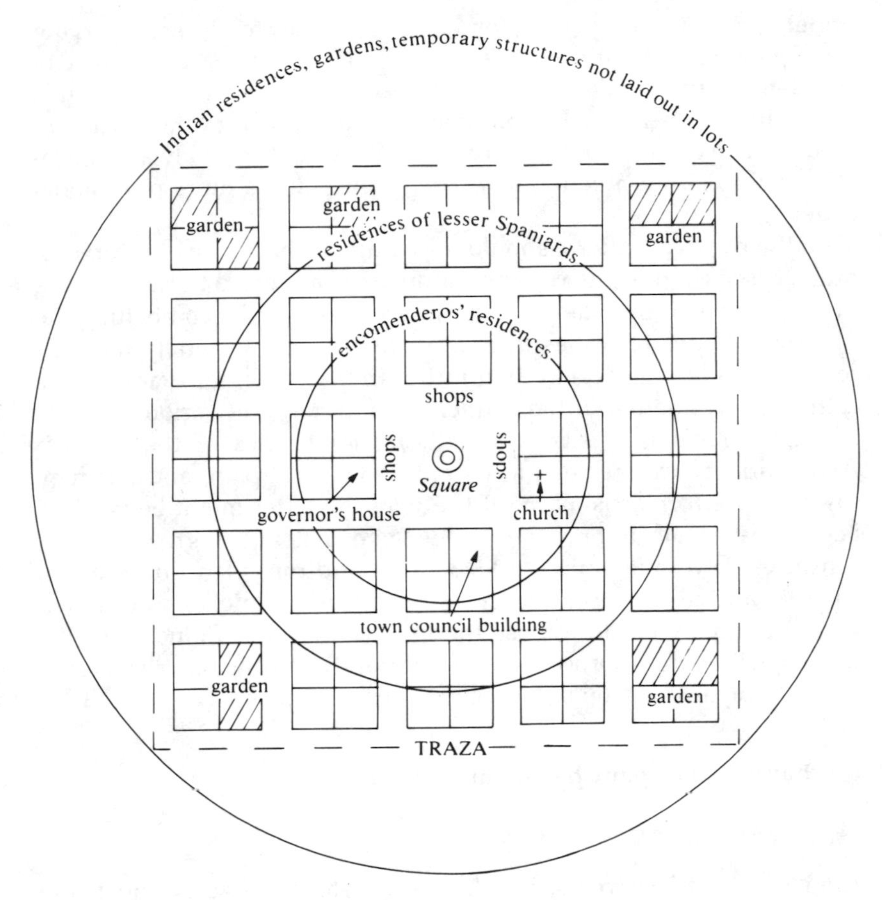

Figure 2. Layout of a Spanish city of the Indies, conquest period.

pal council building, on another the residence of the governor or governor's representative; remaining properties facing the square, as well as those nearby, held the residences of the most important local citizens (usually the encomenderos), which would be as imposing as possible, so that the center would soon be built up wall to wall. The wealthy citizens, however, rented out shops facing the street or square to merchants, artisans, notaries, and the like. If the city flourished, an arcaded gallery would shortly ring the square. Humbler Spanish settlers had their homes in an outer ring of lots, and beyond these, whole blocks were given over to gardens. This orderly complex constituted the *traza*, or "layout." After that the streets were undefined; temporary huts, or *ranchos*, mainly for Indians serving the Spaniards, dominated the scene. The Spanish American city could thus grow indefinitely through expansion of the traza while maintaining a near-total stability at the center. The overall structure would not vary or need to vary over many centuries: always nucleated, always with a better-developed center and a more provisional edge.

Just why this pattern should have arisen has been the topic of much discussion; some commentators have appealed to Renaissance ideals, others to the plan of camps used as bases for combatting the Moors of Granada. Cities in Spain proper were generally more irregular and less nucleated than in the Indies, with, for example, the cathedral on one plaza, the council on another, and various pockets of choice residential sites. But all the tendencies of the Spanish American city can be seen in its antecedent in Spain, and one may say that the former is all in all the way the latter might be if it had been created all at once on a new site instead of growing over centuries and millennia. Indeed, the gridiron plan, the central square, and the concentration of wealth and functions around it would almost seem to impose themselves in a new foundation. Yet the English were to proceed quite differently in America, as were, in part, the Spaniards' fellow Iberians, the Portuguese.

Mechanisms of Spanish–Indian interaction

The encomienda

After the first few years, for the conquest period as a whole, the primary tie between the Spaniards and the indigenous people of America was an institution which has come to be called the encomienda. Its history is most complex, since it was both governmental and private, affected all sectors of the population, spread in varying forms to greatly varying regions, and changed quickly over time. One can say of most forms that they represented a Spanish attempt to acquire Indian services or goods through the use of traditional local indigenous authority and on the basis of already existing sociopolitical units. The full-blown, classic form of the encomienda was never attained in the Caribbean, so we will need to return to the topic again, but the essential structure came into being and traditions were established which the mainland encomienda would continue unbroken.

In the first years, before the foundation of Santo Domingo, the operating presumption was that all local Spaniards were to be salaried employees of a monopoly company. Spanish discontent with such arrangements reached the point of serious rebellion in 1497. Perhaps half the Europeans on Hispaniola went off to the western side of the island, where, in a rough and ready way, they divided the Indians among themselves, each Spaniard dominating or living off one group. In 1499 Columbus, still governor, found on returning from one of his absences that the new system of *repartimientos* (as the individual shares were called) was too entrenched to abolish, so he restored calm by issuing the allotments himself, as governors after him were to continue doing. Much was left undefined and unrationalized. The grants stated more or less "I give you Cacique So-and-So and his Indians, to work for you in your properties and mines." The land itself remained in the hands of the Indians, and the village operated on the same basis as before, except that the cacique used his prerogatives to channel labor in large amounts to the purposes of the encomendero, as the grantee was called. Tribute was not mentioned in the grants, and indeed, the Arawaks of the islands had little that they could pay in tribute.

What the encomendero had, then, was an inalienable grant, held at the pleasure of the governor, of the labor of the subjects of a cacique or caciques. The grant per se gave him no land or mining rights. Such rights came through separate grants, often from the local municipal council, and on a very different basis. Land received in this way could be kept, sold, or passed on to heirs and thus in effect was private property despite certain restrictions on it. Any Spaniard, encomendero or not, might hold land, and some humble people did so, but in general there was little point in having land unless one had labor to work it and a place to sell the product. At this point the system becomes comprehensible only if we go beyond the limited encomienda grant and look at a wider, self-reinforcing circle of de facto social-economic connections. It was the wealthiest and most influential of the settlers who became encomenderos in the first place; the largest of these dominated the municipal councils; the councils in turn favored encomenderos in grants of land and mining sites, and even if they had not, no one else had the necessary labor pool, so that the encomenderos were directly or indirectly the principal miners and commercial agriculturalists. Encomienda labor, mines, and supply activities complemented each other to the ultimate benefit of the encomendero, headquartered in the nearest Spanish city, as we have tried to indicate in Figure 3.

From a very early time the word *estancia* was used for private land-

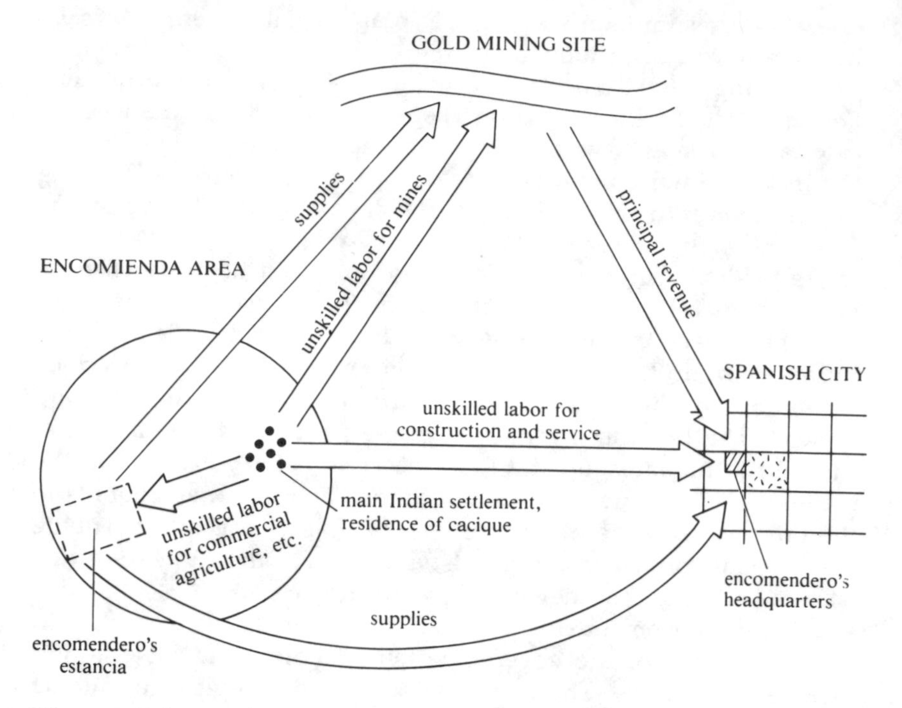

Figure 3. Schema of an encomienda on the Caribbean islands.

holdings of Spaniards and also for any agricultural enterprise undertaken there – though over time the connotation was increasingly that of the European livestock which were the item most in demand. Some estancias were on the edges of the Spanish cities, the only market other than the mines, but the pattern that most interests us here is that an encomendero would often have an estancia granted to him in the immediate vicinity of his Indians, so as to have the labor supply close at hand. Certain early directives, trying to alleviate the problems arising when a new encomendero would be appointed and would arrive to find the old encomendero still owning an estancia in his area, give the impression that this informal conjoining of estancia and encomienda was an almost universal practice.

Though the encomienda was built upon the traditional powers of the cacique, the system we have sketched put new demands on the Arawaks as to type and amount of work. There was need for direct Spanish intervention, for supervisors and auxiliaries. Of the supervisors the most frequently mentioned is the *estanciero,* who was named after the estancia which was his main responsibility, but who served the encomendero also as labor boss or even miner. He would be poorer, more recently arrived, or humbler than the man he worked for. Some encomenderos could afford Black slave aides, but the most numerous auxiliaries were Indians themselves, outside the encomienda system proper.

Naborías

The reader will remember from our discussion of preconquest Arawak society that "naboría" was the name for a permanent dependent of a noble or chieftain, not subject to general community duties and privileges. Through commandeering, voluntary adhesion, and actual assignment by the authorities, Spaniards quickly began to acquire naborías as their own personal servants. Both encomenderos and nonencomenderos did this, soon using their aides in any number of tasks requiring stability and new skills not to be expected of shifting encomienda laborers. Though the naborías bore no formal relationship to the encomienda, the system at its height could hardly have functioned without them. It is not to be imagined that all or even most of the Spaniards' naborías had had that status from birth; rather, many seem to have been encomienda Indians subtracted from their villages. The important thing is that because of the existence of this role in preconquest society, both Indians and Spaniards had well-defined expectations concerning it. Before the culmination of the demographic disaster, the naborías new and old were on their way to becoming a group apart, in cities and in association with Spanish enterprises. On the mainland this movement was to be resumed under more stable conditions. In 1514, when the Indian population had declined to a small fraction of its former size, of the remaining some 22,000 able-bodied adults, nearly half as many were naborías as encomienda Indians. Earlier the proportion of encomienda Indians would have been higher, for the naborías had been replenished from the outside, but this can serve to indicate that they were a major group, important to conquest society and even more important for the Spanish American future.

Indian slavery

Encomienda Indians were not slaves. A slave is bought and sold individually for a price; in the Latin American context he was always removed from his geographical and ethnic origins and lived in close and permanent association with Europeans. None of these things are true of the encomienda Indians, who stayed on the same lands as always and retained their group organization, even when they went in parties to work for the encomendero. In world history generally, it has been neither advantageous nor feasible for a conquering group to enslave a dense population on its home ground. Enslavement was rarely to be practiced with fully sedentary peoples of America and only under certain conditions with those who were semisedentary, so that Indian slavery was to be a marginal phenomenon, primarily used in connection with the mobile peoples of the fringe.

Until this distinction established itself firmly, however, enslavement of Indians occurred as a measure of transition and emergency even with some sedentary groups. In the Iberian heritage, nonbelievers taken in just battle could be enslaved, and there were set procedures of official branding, registry, and payment to the crown of duties on the new slaves. Indians who in any way resisted Spanish entry into their lands were thus liable to enslavement; as population and labor supply decreased on Hispaniola, Spaniards sailed to neighboring islands on what were little more than slaving expeditions, with no regard as to whether or not the people were agricultural villagers. Before long, however, full-scale Spanish occupation extended to all the areas of dense settlement, and slaving came to apply more to small isolated groups like those in the Bahamas or to truly hostile and mobile groups, among whom the Caribs of the Lesser Antilles were outstanding. The difference between Arawak and Carib was soon fully apparent to the Spaniards, who placed no settlements on the Caribs' islands and after some experience decided there was no necessity to prove their hostility in each individual case; the mere fact of a person's being a Carib was sufficient basis for legal enslavement. As the Spaniards pushed their raids and explorations past the Lesser Antilles and along the Venezuelan coast toward the west, they continued to identify the people with the Caribs and to proceed accordingly. The captors sold the new slaves to Spaniards on the large islands, to be used in gold mines or to supplement the naborías; but before many years the Indian slaves died out almost as completely as the original inhabitants.

Congregation

Let us at this point merely mention that in response to both declining population and Indian residence patterns, which were more dispersed than those of Europe, there began in the Caribbean the Spanish attempt to nucleate the Indians more highly and to reorganize their settlements on the model of Iberian towns, while respecting indigenous units where possible. Governors, priests, and encomenderos could all, for their various purposes, readily agree on the desirability of having the Indians close together and behaving more like Spaniards. Such plans and attempts were not central to the organization of the Caribbean system, and the demographic disaster brought them to a complete halt, but the notion was henceforth to be a standard part of the Spanish American cultural baggage and would appear in varying forms in different regions.

Precious metals and their role in the economy

The gold of West Africa led the Iberians to expect more of the same in the Western Hemisphere, which seemed at first a comparable area. At the same time, Iberian reconquest was associated with the idea of spoils, precious metals and jewels. Even more important than precedent, though, was the basic structure of the social and economic situation which presented itself to the Spaniards in America. Whether they were impelled by ambition or economic pressure, the immigrants' aim was to live at a standard at least as high as the European, and, since they were as ethnocentric as other peoples, they meant to live in the European fashion. Consequently, they would have to be able to import European cloth and other manufactures, as well as some staples not easy to duplicate, such as wine and olive oil. To pay for such imports, they would have to have an export with high specific value and strong, steady demand in Europe. At the time there was only one such commodity, precious metals, and of these the Caribbean offered only gold. Freight was intolerably expensive for anything bulky, ships being small, distances great, and so much of the ship's capacity needed for provisions alone. America had no Chinese silks or East Indian spices. The only at all realistic alternative was sugar production, but the Portuguese Atlantic islands were already filling the then relatively inelastic European demand, the Portuguese had the market connections, and sugar was in any case a highly capitalized and technical business, whereas the Spaniards at this point needed not only something nontechnical but something which would provide capital rather than require it.

So gold it was. Following up on the Arawaks' beginning, the Spaniards looked for and found gold on the islands, not truly major deposits but placer mines which produced very significant wealth for a time. It took little equipment and only moderate expertise to dig out sand and gravel and then pan it, and the settlers soon mastered the technique. Untouched mountain streams almost anywhere will yield at least a little of this kind of gold. After the Caribbean experience, the Spaniards would seek out and exploit placer mines wherever they went, so that each new area in turn would go through an ephemeral gold-rush phase, helping to pay the expenses of the early stages.

While it lasted, Caribbean gold mining set precedents that would carry over to other areas and even to the much more long-lasting and large-scale silver mining of the mainland. In Spanish law underground wealth was in the public domain. One consequence was that mines did not merely go to their discoverers, or to any class of miners proper, but were distributed by local political authorities to those who were already powers in the community. Another consequence was that the mines and the gold in some sense could be said to belong to the crown, which through its officials at first tried to take half the product or more, then settled on a nominal fifth, or *quinto,* long to be the most important source of royal revenue.

Elements of the international maritime tradition

Iberian commerce in the Caribbean arose as a branch of the international commerce of Seville. The reader will remember that the Genoese were the financial-commercial leaders in Seville at the end of the fifteenth century. Hence (and certainly not hindered by the role of their compatriot Columbus), they dominated the first phase of commerce between Spain and the Indies. Through loans, they supplied the capital for expeditions, individual emigrants and shipmasters, and mercantile ventures, and they themselves were very much involved in trade to the Caribbean. Since they already controlled the business of exporting Andalusian agricultural produce, they easily entered the field of provisioning the Indies, sending out junior partners and factors to sell the shipments. But before 1540 the Spaniards of the Indies were becoming self-sufficient in European foods, except for wine and olive oil. The Genoese, in any case already concentrating on European high finance, tended to drop out of the trade.

The forms and mechanisms of commerce remained the same as previously explained for Seville, but personnel shifted quickly. The successors to the Genoese in the Caribbean trade, which soon became primarily an exchange of Spanish cloth and manufactures for gold, were the north Castilian merchants who had been Seville's second commercial power; on their heels came the Andalusians proper.

Caribbean carry-overs from the Portuguese African experience were many, at times with the Genoese as the connecting link. Columbus and others immediately imagined that it might be possible, based on the African analogy, to export Indian slaves to Europe. But if mortality was disastrous among Indians when exposed to only a few Europeans, the effects were even quicker and more universal when a few Indians were immersed in a European world. As soon as this was known, Indian slaves became unsalable in Spain, precluding a transatlantic Indian slave trade. Instead, there was soon interest in bringing African slaves to the Caribbean, as auxiliaries and then over time simply to help repopulate the islands. For a time the Genoese were the intermediaries, but for the long run it is more important that the Portuguese were in control of the trade at the source and later were to use this avenue to enter the mainstream of the Spanish American import–export business.

At the end of the gold phase, around 1515, the Spaniards began to build sugar mills patterned after those on the islands off Africa, importing technicians from the Canaries as well as African slaves for the most intensive labor. In the 1540s a score of mills were in operation on Hispaniola (three of the largest run by Genoese) and production was substantial. Earlier we mentioned some reasons for the failure of the Caribbean industry to expand further at this time. That it was viable at all was largely owing to a hidden subsidy from the precious metals of the mainland; the latter paid for the arrival of goods and people on numerous ships which would have had to return to Seville in ballast if it were not for the sugar being grown and hides taken from the European livestock which nearly overran the islands after their depopulation.

The Spaniards in America abandoned the Portuguese African tradition of trading with indigenous peoples as a principal technique in favor of direct occupation, primarily because that was what the situation demanded. But still there were many echoes of the Portuguese *resgate.* The Spanish cognate *rescate* appears in many connections, with the same connotations of a trade with an indigenous non-European people, mixing barter and force or the threat of it. Slave raiding was rescate; the Spaniards were willing either to trade or to fight and were as interested in gold or pearls as in slaves. The term was also used for unofficial individual trading with any Indians, and it continued in this sense on the mainland. Above all, though, rescate was the mode of dealing with the mobile peoples. Thus before the end of the Caribbean phase the principal modes of Spanish interaction with the peoples on the fringes had been established: enslavement, barter, and intermittent raiding without full conquest.

In general, then, the Spaniards adopted many Genoese-Portuguese techniques, though as ancillary rather than as central, except in the case of international commerce, and the Genoese themselves faded out of the American picture, until by 1550 the only reminder of them was their presence among the humble mariners of the Indies.

The Spanish Caribbean heritage expressed in vocabulary

For most purposes the Caribbean island phase of the Spanish occupation of the Indies was over in less than twenty-five years after 1492, during which the Indians of the large islands had practically died out and the numbers of Spaniards involved had never been great. (In the wet tropics of America, Europeans as individuals did not fare markedly better than the Indians; the majority of any large incoming group would succumb within a couple of years – the difference was that there was an outside source for further immigration and that a European who lived past the acclimatization period had a normal life expectancy.) No more than a few thousand Spaniards had as yet come to America, and those active at any one time could often be measured in hundreds. Yet well before 1510 the major techniques and structures having to do with city life, the economic base, commerce, and mode of relationship to sedentary and nonsedentary Indians had been developed. The Spaniards would not treat the mainland as a fully new area but would operate as they had on the islands.

Perhaps the reader can get some notion of the extent and nature of the Caribbean heritage by glancing at a list of terms, not used in Spain, which became general in the Spanish of the Indies after first being adopted in the Caribbean (see Table 3). Some of the terms denote types of people, practices, artifacts, or plants characteristic of Indian cultures; others refer to Spanish practices specific to the Indies. All these words would be heard on the mainland during the conquests and for generations afterward, when the Caribbean was a backwater occasionally brought to life by the passage of the silver fleets.

Table 3. *Spanish American words from the Caribbean*

Arawak words		*Spanish words in a new or more specific sense*	
cacique	Indian ruler, chieftain	repartimiento	one's share; that is, an encomienda
naboría	permanent Indian dependent	encomienda	the word preferred by high officials for this basic social-governmental institution
guañín	gold alloy	estancia	private landholding or agricultural-pastoral enterprise in Spanish style
bohío	Indian dwelling (hut)	estanciero	humble Spaniard in charge of an estancia
duho	low seat of honor	demora	the mining season
coa	digging stick	rancho	temporary hut, usually inhabited by Indians, on the edge of a city
barbacoa	grill, anything of pointed sticks	reducción, congregación	act of nucleating and resettling Indians, and the resulting settlement
canoa	Indian boat, canoe	fundición	general melting down and assaying of precious metals before they circulated among the Spaniards
areito	Indian dancing	peso	the principal unit for reckoning money, larger than the Castilian ducat
maíz	maize	bubas	sores, syphilis
yuca	yucca		
maguey	maguey, the century plant		
batata	sweet potato		
Words of uncertain origin			
batea	pan for washing gold		
baquiano	tracker, guide; hence veteran, old hand in the Indies		
cimarrón	renegade, hence either a runaway Black person or feral livestock		
Words from the Portuguese African heritage			
rescate	(forcible) bartering with Indians		
pieza	a human unit, referring to a slave or servant		
ingenio	sugar mill		

Mechanisms of expansion and the evolution of expeditionary forms

In the Caribbean one did not speak of "conquest"; not until the mainland phase would actual campaigns and pitched battles be standard fare. Still, in this as in other aspects, mainland practices would grow out of Caribbean precedents. The idea of direct crown supervision of overseas expansion, insofar as it had ever had substance, faded rapidly in the face of the realities of the Indies. Spanish occupation of vast territories of America was to occur relay fashion, each new area becoming the base for another push forward. The essential initiative was local; local conditions determined the timing, and personnel, capital, and materials were organized locally. Because of distances and inherent tensions, each new area soon became independent of the last. The process was somewhat as follows: A senior and powerful figure or figures in a given area would propose the acquisition of a known but still unoccupied territory within reach, and the local governor would approve the venture, even helping organize it, in the hope that the new acquisition would be a part of his own jurisdiction. But no sooner would the leader of the expedition meet with success than he would write off to the crown asking for a separate governorship, which would usually be granted. (This was often the first the crown heard of either the leader or the new region.) In such a fashion Puerto Rico and Cuba became independent of Santo Domingo, then Mexico independent of Cuba, and on and on, to the far edges of the Indies.

We have already discussed in general the impetus given by the two different traditions of European expansion and more specifically the effect of mineral and population depletion in pushing the Spaniards on past the Caribbean islands toward the mainland. Certain social-political tensions among the Spaniards tended to accelerate the process even more. Two elements among the settlers were often volatile and discontent: on the one hand, some of the most senior, wealthy, and influential, who chafed to have a governorship for themselves, and, on the other hand, late-arriving Spaniards who hoped for encomiendas and were satisfied with nothing less. In effect, the former led the latter off to new areas, nudged or helped along by governors and established settlers who were happy enough to see them gone. In this connection, though the Caribbean receded from the forefront and Spanish interest went elsewhere, there was no wholesale exodus from the islands. Rather, those who had any sort of established position stayed on, as was to happen again and again as new areas were occupied. The motor of expansion was not adventure but poverty and rivalry.

Concerning the complex topic of the organization, social composition, and functioning of conquering expeditions, we need say only enough to demonstrate the continuities pointing both backward and forward. As spectacular an episode as conquest was, it had strong components of commercial capitalism and of permanent settlement. In other words, it embodied the Caribbean experience. The conquering groups transmitted the customs of their base area to the new area where they became the most senior and powerful encomenderos and imposed their ways on the new arrivals from Spain attracted by their success. Acts as transcendent and permanent as the foundation of major cities and delineation of protonational jurisdictions were carried out by the conquering groups in the ordinary course of their activities. Thus conquest was not a hiatus before settlement but an integral and vital part of settlement.

Expedition forms underwent an evolution related to other Caribbean trends. The early expeditions going out from Hispaniola to hunt for slaves and trade for gold or pearls were organized on a mercantile basis. Two or three wealthy men would make the whole investment and hire the rest. But with capital scarce and yields uncertain, increasingly the entire group would invest something and agree to share profits according to investment. By the time the Spaniards came to the mainland in force, the practice was well established that group members (except the sailors) were partners in an enterprise, expecting a share in gold or slaves or an encomienda if it came to that, rather than a salary. The entrada, or "entry" (into new lands), could serve equally well to trade, raid, or conquer, according to what was found. Thus the slave raids of the Caribbean, the great conquering expeditions of the central areas, and the later, often futile explorations in fringe areas represented different uses of the same basic organizational form. By the time of the mainland phase that form had departed from the maritime-commercial *compañía* to become more the Iberian reconquest *compaña,* or band of men, though with traces of the former still much in evidence.

The leader of a major expedition would invariably be a man of standing in the base area: usually an important encomendero, member or former member of the municipal council, senior in the area, wealthy, and an hidalgo or passing for one. Both Cortés and Pizarro fit this mold, though Cortés had somewhat more education than usual and Pizarro less. The leader would sport the title "captain," which was not a rank in a hierarchy but simply meant "leader in an expedition." He and some associates who became subsidiary captains made the largest investments, usually in ships, clothing, weapons, and horses. The ordinary members supplied their own equipment and provisions (though sometimes these were purchased on credit from the captain). The men had no connection with a royal army, received no pay, had no uniforms, no rank, and in nine cases out of ten no professional military training or experience. Only distant or posterior commentators have called them "soldiers," a term they never applied to themselves during the conquest years. They were of many types. Among the 168 men who seized the Inca emperor at Cajamarca in 1532, there were about a dozen notaries; perhaps twice that many working artisans, including smiths, tailors, and carpenters; men of merchant background; an ecclesiastic; a Black piper and crier; seamen; members of the lower nobility; people from both urban and rural backgrounds; men from all regions of Spain; in a word, a cross section of Spanish society, indistinguishable from the general stream of Spanish immigration to America in following decades. It was groups like these, accompanied by numerous naboría auxiliaries from the base area, which carried out the mainland conquests and set up a new social framework in the conquered lands.

Patterns of conquest and resistance

From the earliest years on the island of Hispaniola, the Spaniards were aware how greatly easy entry and quick control could be facilitated by capturing the cacique. The idea may have been suggested by precedents from earlier Iberian contacts with Moors and Africans. At any rate, surprise seizure of the local ruler during a friendly parley was a standard tactic. The actions of Cortés and Pizarro with the Aztec and Inca emperors were run-of-the-mill and entirely predictable. In the Caribbean the Spaniards also learned to expect that some peoples would accept Spanish overlordship voluntarily, or even aid the intruders, often in order to win advantage over traditional indigenous enemies.

Fighting was often necessary, however. Only the secondary powers in a given region would make terms; the dominant group could be counted on to resist strongly, often even after the loss of the ruler. The Spaniards entered the central areas of the mainland, with their populations mounting into the millions, their strong kingdoms, empires, and warlike traditions, in expeditions numbering usually from 200 to 500 men and invariably won decisive victories within a short time. The weaponry of the sedentary peoples could neither stop nor seriously harm someone equipped with a steel sword, steel helmet, and some sort of shield and thick clothing. Where there was at least minimal room to maneuver, groups thus equipped were irresistible against as many indigenous opponents as could be brought to bear against them, until they should tire. Here the horse proved invaluable, so much so that a horse counted as much as a person in the division of treasure, and the horsemen were always the leaders and senior, wealthier men. Fifty horsemen with lances, or even as few as twenty, could roll back or split up an Indian army, however large, at will. Horse and foot could relieve each other indefinitely. In a battle on flat ground and against sedentary peoples, victory for a mixed body of Spanish horsemen and footmen was a foregone conclusion. Indian fatalities could be in the thousands; Spanish casualties were ordinarily restricted to superficial flesh wounds, and the rare fatalities were more in the nature of accidents. In 1536–7 some 180 Spaniards holding off perhaps a hundred thousand or more besiegers for more than a year in the Inca heartland, at Cuzco, suffered one fatality, that of a man fighting without his helmet. Firearms were unimportant, too few and too slow to deal with Indian numbers. Strategy was equally unimportant, if only the Spanish leader had the prudence to keep his men out of constricted places. The high mortality rate among the conquerors was attributable primarily to disease and fighting among each other, and secondarily to loss of isolated small groups which were in highly disadvantageous positions or off their guard after initial victory. At root, then, the Europeans of the sixteenth century had a technical military advantage over the sedentary peoples of America as overwhelming and decisive as that which the Europeans of the later nineteenth century acquired over the peoples of Africa and Asia with the repeating rifle and the Gatling gun.

Courage and skill were abundantly present on the Indian side. What little anyone in their situation could do, they did. Generally they tested and double tested the results of battle before capitulation. In a confined place, through weight of numbers, Indians could and sometimes did almost literally smother the Spaniards. In a very steep or narrow place one could hurl stones down on their heads, and this the Indians quickly learned to do when there was any opportunity. In 1536, during a great general Indian rebellion in Peru, Pizarro sent out one thirty-horsemen contingent after another in relief of Cuzco; each one in turn was annihilated in mountain passes. But the Spaniards soon caught on.

Among all the sedentary peoples, the Aztecs of the Valley of

Mexico were best situated to offer resistance to Spanish conquest. Tenochtitlan, their capital, was surrounded by a great lake, accessible only by narrow causeways with removable bridges at intervals, and the city itself was tightly built up with stone and adobe walls and crisscrossed with canals. Under these conditions the Aztecs were able to pen up and force out a large party of Spaniards who were already on the island and then to resist a prolonged siege by a reinforced expedition with many Indian allies, their former enemies and subjects. Even when the Spaniards fought their way down the causeways they faced obstacles and constrictions rendering their usual procedures ineffectual, and the Aztecs were able to resupply themselves by boat. Only by drawing yet deeper on European technology and constructing large vessels equipped with artillery were the invaders able to dominate the lake and starve the city out. At the same time, the Spaniards progressively razed the buildings and filled in the canals, creating a plain on which their usual advantage was restored.

The only alternative to an ultimately futile resistance was to flee the good lands of sedentary life and take refuge in mountain or forest fastnesses. This possibility was not open to the bulk of the population and was not generally adopted for more than fleeting periods, though an Inca splinter group held out in a remote tropical forest river valley for more than a generation after the end of the conquest proper (without much effect on the general course of events). It is true that vacillation on the part of Indian leaders sometimes resulted in Spanish control earlier than would have been absolutely necessary. Both Moctezuma, the Aztec emperor, and the Inca emperor Atahualpa wavered between understandable overconfidence, curiosity, and equally understandable apprehension of a total unknown until the Spaniards were in their very presence and it was too late. But submission under these conditions was not in itself decisive. In a very short time a serious armed rebellion would almost always occur, carried out by people who were now coming to realize the full implications of a European presence; after initial successes owing to surprise and Spanish scatteration, the decision would again be the same, for the same reasons as in primary conquest. Thereafter, the sedentary peoples would never again pose a threat to Spanish occupation and dominance.

As to Indian allies of the Spaniards, for a perspective on them one needs to understand first that they often become allies precisely because of the intruders' military power and second that in the conquests their primary role was in support and logistics. Tlaxcala is a classic example. The Tlaxcalans suffered two weeks of steady defeat in hard battle before deciding that the best thing to do was to help the Spaniards against their traditional enemies, the Mexica. Something of the role of the Tlaxcalans, who accompanied the conquerors over all Mexico, can be seen in the fact that many never returned home, but instead became naborías in the vicinity of the various Spanish cities.

The double trajectory of conquest

Conquest spread outward from Hispaniola in two great, approximately simultaneous thrusts in the direction of the (at first unsuspected) central areas: one to Panama and then Peru, the other to Cuba and then Mexico. Sometimes one of the two streams would take the lead, sometimes the other. The southern thrust reached the mainland first, in Tierra Firme (that is, Mainland), from 1509 forward. Here, for the first time, were indigenous peoples whose accumulations of precious metals were large enough to allow the Spaniards to pay off their debts and conquer further immediately, without going into placer mining first, though of course they did that soon enough too. Here encomienda was first transferred to the mainland, and conquest began to assume its classic form. On the other hand, the northern thrust was the first to take one of the empire areas, the territory of the Aztecs, in 1519–21, whereas the southern thrust, held back by a detour to Nicaragua and difficult sailing conditions on the Pacific coast of South America, did not take the central lands of the Incas until 1532–3.

Hardly were the two central regions provisionally occupied when another series of expeditions, the largest and best equipped yet, went out from them as bases, sped along by the capital, antagonisms, expectations, and strong continuing Spanish immigration which the great conquests spawned. As a result, all the fully sedentary areas in America had been located and occupied by 1540, and occupation of the contiguous semisedentary areas was well under way. As the dates on Map 3 indicate, things proceeded much more slowly in the latter areas, but even there, regional capitals had generally been founded by 1550.

Despite some contact between the two major streams, all in all they were remarkably separate, resembling each other principally because they were such direct continuations of the Caribbean complex and because they met such parallel sets of conditions. Above all, Mexico had no major impact on Peru merely by virtue of some

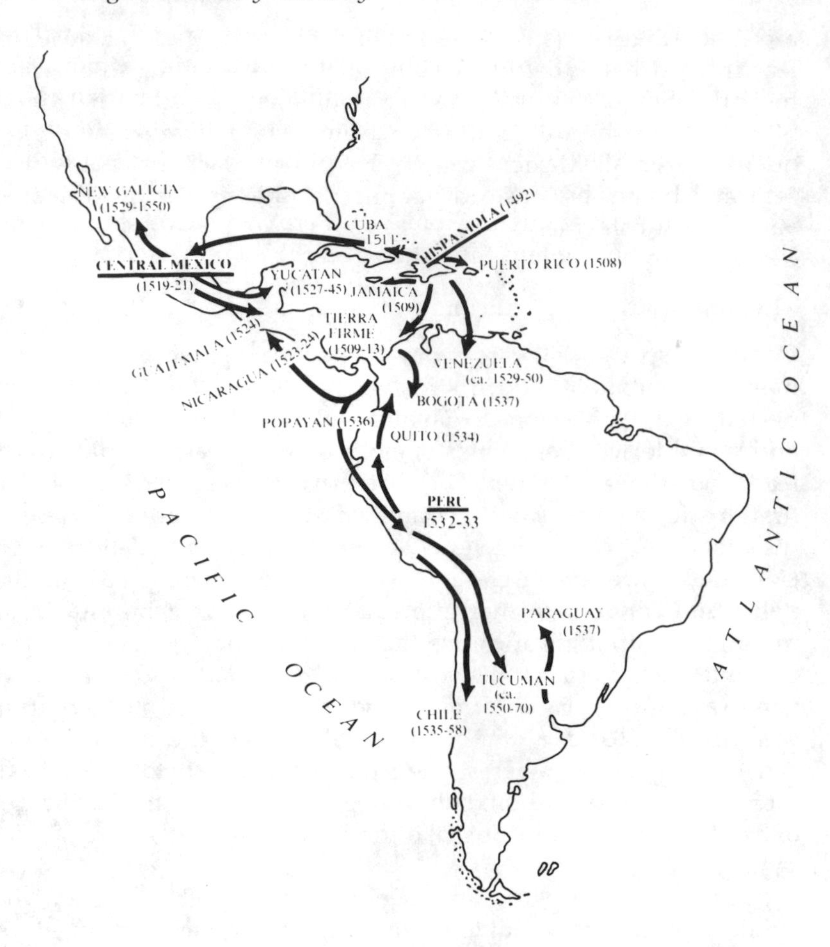

Map 3. The path of Spanish conquest.

years precedence; the Tierra Firme encomienda was the model operating in Peru, not the Mexican variant (in any case nearly identical), and Pizarro was certainly not thinking of Cortés and Moctezuma when he seized Atahualpa; he had been capturing caciques in Tierra Firme long before Mexico was heard of.

At the same time as the wave of post-Mexico–Peru thrusts into contiguous populated areas, some major expeditions went out with the same intention into regions more remote but failed to find people or resources indicating that Spaniards should occupy those regions at that time. The importance of these ventures was thus mainly negative. The most famous are: Hernando de Soto from Cuba (financed by money from the conquest of Peru) into the North American southeast in 1539–42; Gonzalo Pizarro into the Amazonian region from Quito in 1541–2; and Coronado from Mexico into the northern borderlands in 1540–2. A great expedition under don Pedro de Mendoza, though inspired by Peruvian successes, departed directly from Seville and thus bypassed the step-by-step tradition of the Indies. The Plata venture failed in its attempt to occupy the Buenos Aires region in 1535–6, proving the untenability of the pampa region in the sixteenth century, but nevertheless led to permanent settlement in Paraguay, to which we will return in a future chapter. After this, there was little more to know and even less to exploit, since by this time the Portuguese had established themselves among the remaining semisedentary peoples of the eastern coast of the southern continent, and Spanish America settled down with borders and territorial units much the same as those it has today, except that the plains areas were still largely empty of effective Spanish settlement.

4
Conquest society: central areas

The various conquests fastened on the respective Indian culture areas, which gave the approximate configurations of the larger functioning colonial units (and later to a large extent the Spanish American nations). During and immediately after conquest, a primary network of Spanish cities was created in each major area, consisting of a capital – main center of Spanish residence, commerce, and institutions for the entire area – a port, and some widely spaced cities of second rank, each with an extensive Indian hinterland divided into the encomiendas of its principal citizens. Hardly was this bare frame in existence than it was found necessary to establish some intermediate Spanish settlements along main routes; at the same time, the richest silver mining sites were being discovered and were becoming towns. In places some of the basic original cities, though existing as organizations, were still wandering about on temporary sites while the supply and mining towns were already being founded. In the first twenty or twenty-five years after Spanish impact in a given area, the entire complex would come into existence. This essentially unitary, unbroken phase we call the conquest period in a broader sense. The absolute timing varied with the time of original penetration; for the Spanish Indies as a whole one may think of the entire time up to 1560 or 1570, with the understanding that phenomena of initiation, elaboration, and conclusion occurred in different places at different times.

Corresponding to the two Indian central areas and the two main thrusts of conquest, there arose two Spanish orbits, or city networks, the Mexican (Map 4) and the Peruvian (Map 5), of which the latter was the more extended. The port of Mexico, or New Spain, was Veracruz, established in 1519 even before the conquest. Like so many ports in Spanish America, despite a crucial function and stability of a kind, it was to be in itself a poor thing, built of that ignoble material wood, inhabited by the humble, nearly deserted except when fleets put in, and hence to be moved several times over the years to come, though always within a restricted circle. Spanish concepts of the sea and mariners may have been relevant here, as

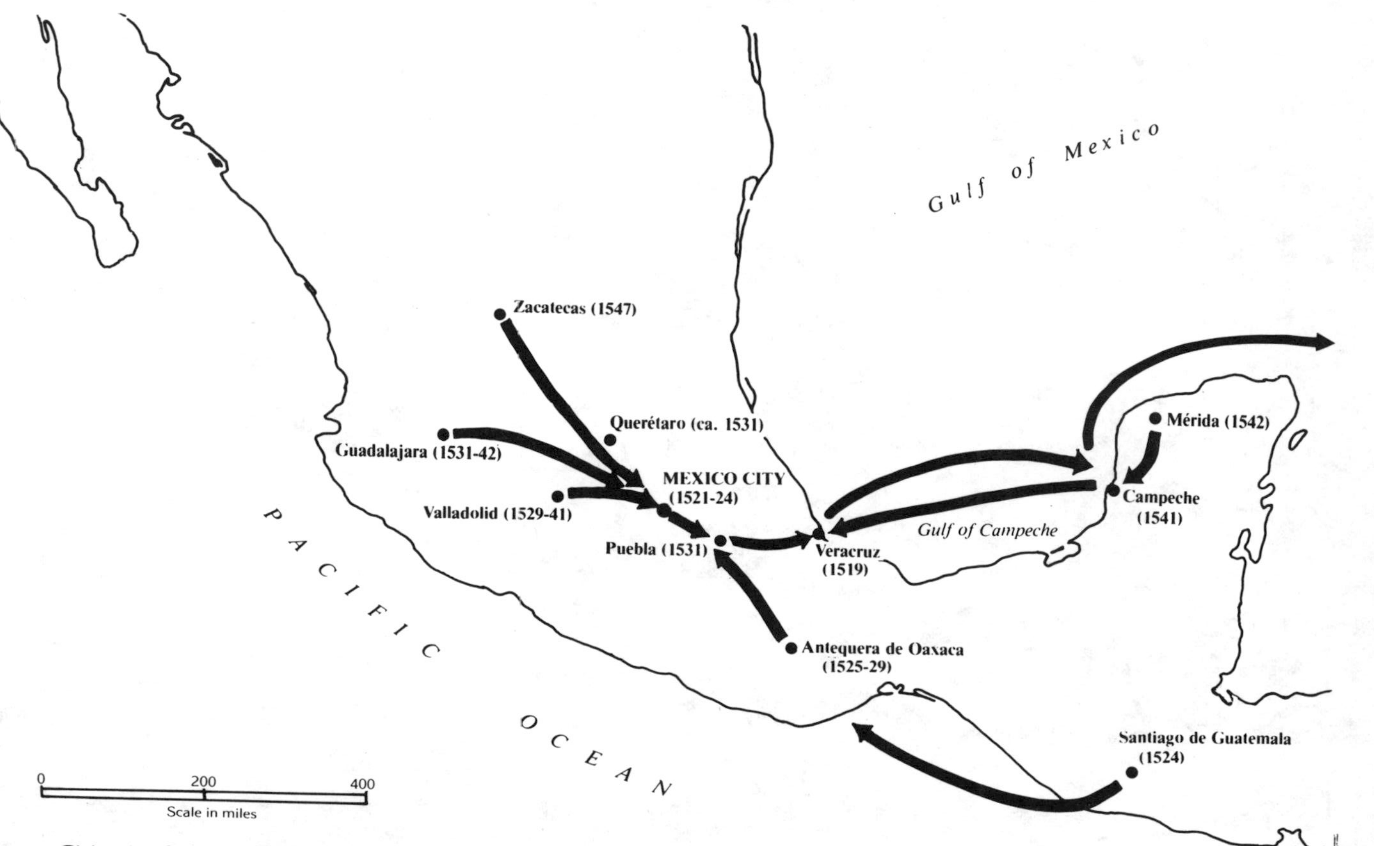

Map 4. Cities in the Mexican orbit, conquest period.

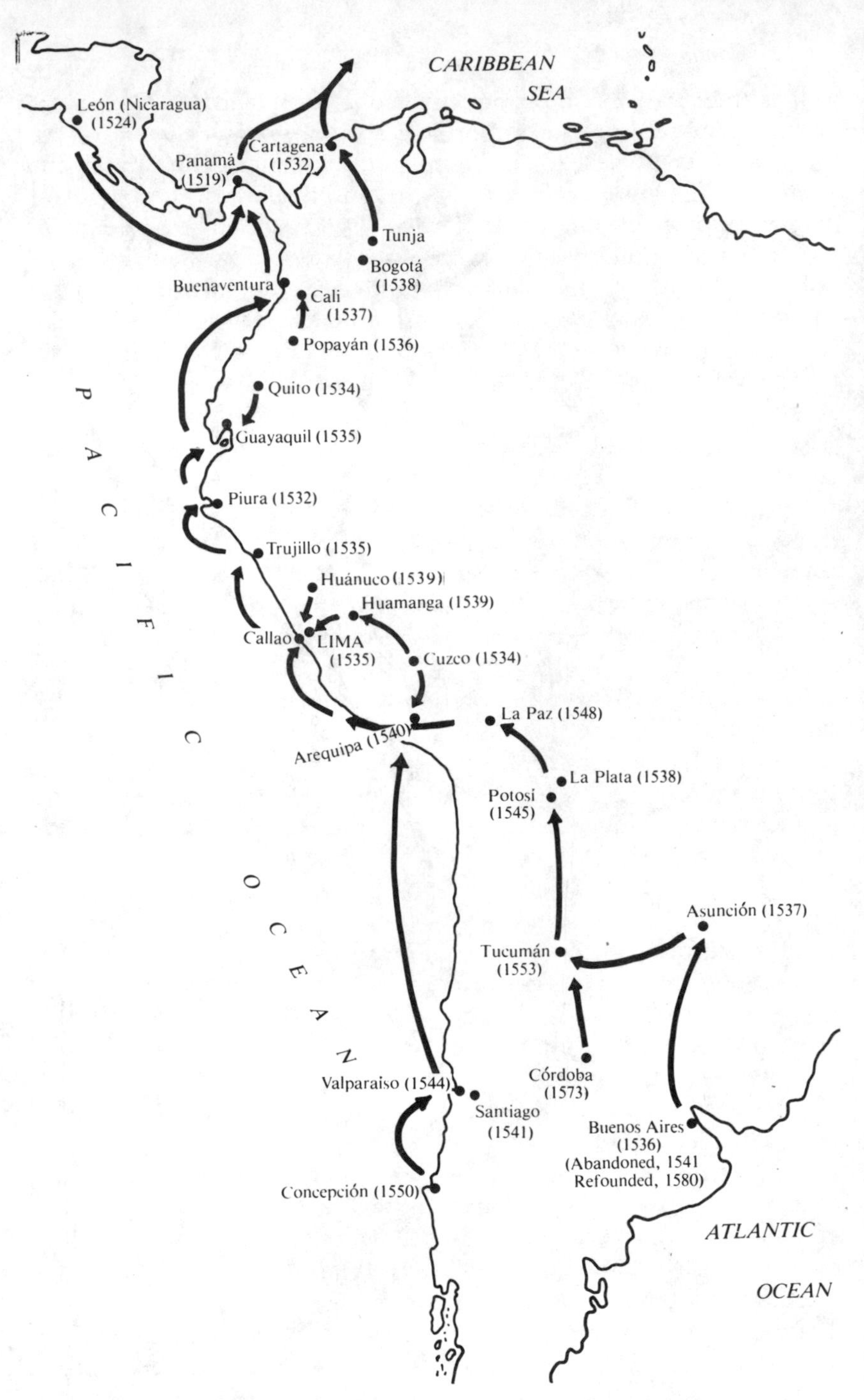

Map 5. Cities in the Peruvian orbit, conquest period.

well as their idea that a proper city should be inland, but even more to the point was the uncomfortable and dangerous climate of the wet coasts, compared to the temperate highlands. The capital, the location of the grandest encomenderos and the largest stone houses, the center of everything, was Mexico City, founded so squarely on Aztec Tenochtitlan that its main plaza was on the same site, its cathedral in the old temple compound, and the governor's palace where Moctezuma's had been. So dominant was Mexico City, like Tenochtitlan before it, that the rise of other Spanish cities in central Mexico was retarded. The important nearby basins of Toluca and Cuernavaca received no Spanish municipality at all, and only after hesitation did Valladolid become established in the Tarascan region to the west. Tlaxcala to the east had been such a prominent ally that no Spanish city was placed there; instead, a little later Puebla was founded nearby, and then not as a headquarters of encomenderos but as a way station between Mexico City and Veracruz, as well as a center for artisans, wheat farmers, and other humble Spaniards. More standard encomendero cities arose in the southern provinces, so distant and inaccessible as to be almost separate countries, and of these, Guatemala in fact became partly independent from an early time. Spanish prospecting turned up only a few relatively small silver deposits in the central region proper, hastening expansion to the north and west into the territories of less sedentary people; one of the greatest and earliest finds was at Zacatecas, far into Chichimec country.

Mesoamerica under the Spaniards thus largely replicated the organization of the area in preconquest times, except for the existence of a port leading to the outside and the increasing reliance of the economy on silver mines located in the nonsedentary north; now, as before, Tenochtitlan-Mexico City (and with it all central Mexico) was dominant, while the south remained a remote and subordinated area looking to the center.

In the Inca area too the weight of the preconquest situation was great. On reaching the Inca capital, the Spaniards had the sense of attaining a goal; in a matter of months they refounded what they called the "great city" of Cuzco as a municipality in their style, retaining not only the form of the earlier plazas and streets but many of the fine stonemasonry walls, some of which are there to this day. Nevertheless, the expectation of some that Cuzco would become the Spanish capital was frustrated. The location seemed too inaccessible, too far south, at too high an altitude. The secondary site of Jauja, far to the north, emerged as the capital-to-be, but it too immediately seemed too high and too isolated behind impassable mountain barriers, so that its citizens wanted it moved, leading to the foundation of Lima on the central coast. The rigors of the Andean interior, combined with the relative hospitality of the dry Peruvian coastal strip, thus caused the Spaniards to place their main settlement on the coastal lowland. As in other low-lying areas, the indigenous coastal population declined precipitously to very small numbers, with the result that before many years had passed the Peruvian coast was on its way to being strongly Euro-African, leaving much of the highland in relative isolation and strongly indigenous in character. The situation was in marked contrast to that of Mexico, where the main thrust of Spanish settlement went into the Indian heartland of central Mexico, and only the southeast – Yucatan, Oaxaca, Guatemala – was left in a position somewhat analogous to the Peruvian highland.

A further result of the Peruvian reorganization was that there was no strict equivalent of Veracruz; although a few miles inland, Lima was so close to the shore that its port, Callao, was no more than a suburb of the capital. And since the line of communications and transport went up the Pacific coast and past the Isthmus of Panama into the Caribbean, all the Spanish cities along the coast to the north partook to some extent of the nature of maritime entrepôts. The real equivalent of Veracruz was Panamá, through which all the goods, people, and silver of the Peru traffic passed; though the town had some of the apparatus of a capital, it was unimpressive, built of wood and shifting in site like any other Spanish American port.

As to silver mining sites, the Peruvian structure was more concentrated. Almost from the time Potosí was opened up in 1545 (a couple of years earlier than Mexican Zacatecas in absolute time and much earlier relative to the Peruvian schedule), this rich southern highland site became the dominant and almost exclusive source of Peru's silver. Spanish South America's lifeline ran from Potosí to Lima to Panamá, over great distances but in a highly unilinear fashion; the Mexican equivalent, Zacatecas–Mexico City–Veracruz, took somewhat longer to establish, and Zacatecas never approached Potosí's near-monopoly position. In addition, although Potosí was high and remote, it nevertheless lay within the sphere of the south-central highland, with its sedentary Indians, encomenderos, and Spanish cities, whereas the north Mexican mines were outside of direct reach from central Mexico. But before the end of the conquest period in the broader sense, the Spanish sectors of both Mexico and Peru had economies distributed along a line leading from silver mines to main

Spanish settlement to port, with all other areas oriented to that central artery.

Into the Spanish cities of the central areas, the moment their wealth was evident, there began to pour hundreds and then thousands of immigrants, including all the elements of Spanish civil society: the now-familiar merchants, artisans, professional people and notaries, and Spanish women. Except for the women, the immigrants were types similar to those who had carried out the conquests, and in fact the newcomers were primarily the conquerors' relatives and fellow townsmen, drawn by promises of help and tales of opportunity. Like immigrants of the nineteenth and twentieth centuries, both the conquerors and those who came after them wrote letters home, telling an attractive mixture of lies and truth about available jobs and wealth. Some of the richest of the conquerors and early migrants returned home to Spain, where their stories and ostentatious displays convinced those around them to follow their example. This transatlantic movement of nephew following uncle, townsman following townsman, continued across the entire span of the colonial period.

Along with the thickening stream of Iberian immigration came the African, consisting mainly of slaves directly from Africa, with a sprinkling of Iberian-born Blacks. They were destined for the same central areas as the Iberian settlers, for it was expensive to import slaves, and they went where there was wealth to buy them. Few in number in the conquering expeditions, they increased rapidly after the accretions of precious metals in the conquests, until in Peru at least (the wealthiest area) there may have been at times more Blacks than Spaniards. They were above all the Spaniards' auxiliaries in skilled, intensive, or permanent tasks and their intermediaries in dealing with the indigenous population. Their utter divorce from their own original context, their lower susceptibility to European diseases, and their distinctness from the indigenous population all came together to make them better adapted to these functions than the Indians themselves.

Yet with the Spaniards' massive need for auxiliaries, they drew on Indians too. In Mexico often called naborías and in Peru *yanaconas*, the Indian servants and employees of Spaniards soon became a major element in the Spanish cities and mines. Some lived with their masters, and others, not all steadily employed, lived in slight and irregular structures on the edge of town. Their movements back and forth to their home provinces represented a vital urban–rural tie and mechanism of incipient cultural change. The city now took on its definitive aspect: Spanish at the center and Indian at the edges, culturally and physically dynamic while stable in structure and location, like the entire society in which it was immersed.

Except that the greatest silver strikes lay a few years in the future, the entire new complex we have been describing had been created and was already in good functioning order when Audiencias and viceroys first came on the scene. Only two viceroyalties were established for the entire Spanish Indies, based, of course, in Mexico City (1535) and Lima (1544). Audiencias also resided in these cities, and in view of the great distances, some additional ones were created: in the Mexican orbit in Guatemala and Guadalajara, in the Peruvian in Charcas (present Bolivia, with Potosí), Quito, and Panama. The viceregal capitals became archbishoprics, and bishops were appointed for other major Spanish cities and their districts. This institutional overlay has a double significance. First, it accurately reflects the overwhelming dominance of the two central areas and their capitals. Second, the new officialdom, through its patronage and its very presence as a prominent social element, reinforced the already marked tendency of the Spaniards to concentrate numbers, wealth, and headquarters for all endeavors in a few outstanding centers. Needless to say, however, the appointment of viceroys and designation of their capitals did not create the rest of the structure but represented formal and permanent recognition of what local people had already built upon a local base.

The encomienda

In the central areas several factors worked to alter the encomienda of the Caribbean phase, giving it for a generation or two an even stronger development, then weakening and nearly destroying it in the richest, most thickly settled regions, though the institution and associated practices and structures had already set precedents for later estate forms, and in more isolated regions the encomienda itself was to endure until near the end of the colonial period. The first of the new factors was the greater strength and magnitude of provincial organizations among the central peoples. Where provincial structure was weak, there were many small encomiendas; where it was strong, there were fewer but larger ones. It was one thing for an encomendero to be granted a village or two on the Caribbean islands, another to receive a central Mexican city-state. In Mexico and Peru the holders of the larger grants had the basis for building up all-inclusive social-economic complexes which were at once commercial and seigneurial, and they hastened to take the opportunity. The mainland sedentary peoples were accustomed to the large-scale delivery of tribute products, and this quickly became a standard part of the encomienda structure. With large and increasing supplies of precious metals in the economy and Indians involved in mines and cities in large numbers, Indian products could be traded for silver and gold. As Spanish society grew, and as the silver mines and the trunk lines to them became more established, encomenderos whose holdings were distant from the mines put more emphasis on Spanish-style products for city markets in the capitals and other places along the silver routes. But the more remote an area was from those routes, the more likely that traditional tribute products and labor would retain their original importance.

If the nature of the central peoples and the silver economy tended in the first instance to strengthen the encomienda, these assets before long attracted two other forces which, working hand in hand, would soon weaken it: increased Spanish immigration and increased royal interest, with the concomitant growth in the number of royally appointed officials. A system which inflexibly, indivisibly gave so much of the wealth and power of these vast areas to a few hundred Spaniards could not survive the influx of thousands of their fellow countrymen without considerable change. Though the encomenderos employed many of the newcomers, gave hospitality to people from their home regions, and were the backbone of the clientele of merchants and artisans, they could not encompass all the expanded opportunities nor contain all the new ambitions. Humble Spaniards, including the encomenderos' own former employees, began to acquire estancias (in Peru often called *chácaras,* a term from Quechua) to raise wheat and other European varieties, as well as any livestock they could afford, for the urban market. Wealthier and better connected immigrants, whether officials, encomenderos' relatives, or simply entrepreneurs, began to build up estates which rivaled those of the encomenderos and were very similar to them, except that they received no Indian tribute and had no direct and regular access to unskilled labor. Nearly any Spaniard could get a land grant and collect some naboría-yanacona auxiliaries; if he had some capital he could hire Spanish employees, buy Black slaves, and invest in some animals and equipment. Livestock enterprises required little unskilled labor, but more complex or intensive estates demanded a regular labor supply; there thus came to be intense pressure on the encomienda's unskilled labor monopoly.

At the same time, crown officials were working in a complementary direction, though for their own purposes and in their own way. The conqueror-governors first assigned encomiendas to the men who accompanied them, giving the best to their own relatives, friends, and compatriots, or to others who were senior, wealthy, or influential. When the first governors died or were replaced – and this happened in less than a decade in the hotly contested areas of Mexico and Peru – the succeeding viceroys and governors continued to assign and reassign encomiendas. Though the strength of the senior local settlers was such that the governors could not brusquely take away encomiendas from current holders, the power to assign was very real, because of the large and increasing number of contenders for grants and because encomienda succession rights were by no means well established. Using the leverage of their appointive power and enjoying the support of many nonencomenderos, the governors were gradually able, in the face of strong, sometimes armed opposition, to alter the institution so as to be more palatable to them and to implement a good deal of the voluminous royal legislation relating to the encomienda.

This process had begun, like so much else, in the Caribbean. The governors immediately succeeding Columbus, who belonged to Spanish crusading orders, tried to shape the amorphous "repartimiento" of the settlers in the direction of what the noble orders knew in Spain as an "encomienda," a restricted and well-defined institution in which the holder performed certain governmental duties and in return received tribute which residually belonged to the crown. The new legal concept of the encomienda had taken shape by the time of the Laws of Burgos of 1513, too late to have much impact in the Caribbean, and, indeed, even mainland encomienda practices showed little of their effect at first. The concept of the limited encomienda was strengthened and reaffirmed in the New Laws of 1542; these called forth noncompliance in Mexico and actual rebellion in Peru, but throughout the 1550s and 1560s much of their content became reality. Not all parts of the newer system met with encomendero resistance. To maintain horse and arms and a substantial city residence, now among their duties, was already their practice. Nor did they object to the notion that they should hire a priest to instruct the Indians. The right of one and only one succession in the encomienda by a legitimate heir was less than the perpetuity that the encomenderos had hoped for, but it was much better than nothing, could be renegotiated, and fit in well with their set aim of finding Spanish wives and founding families at the first possible moment. And the emphasis on tribute, too, was at first fully acceptable to them, now that they had come upon peoples who could deliver precious metals and other negotiable items. Even the growing insistence on specifying a set number and type of tribute products did the encomenderos' interests little apparent harm. The corollary, however, was less acceptable to them: that in view of the tribute products, the encomendero was to lose his special rights to tribute labor in favor of short-term ad hoc allotments to the general Spanish populace according to need. It took a generation or two to achieve reasonable compliance, but with the silver economy to make it possible and other local Spanish interest groups to insist upon it, this most basic change in the encomienda system in fact did gradually take place in the central areas. Since tribute quotas were now predicated on the numbers of Indian tributaries, the population loss – close to total in lowland areas and devastating everywhere – meant among other things a reduction in tribute income, in some places to nothing.

The effect was that after a generation or two the encomenderos were merely the first among equals. They shifted their reliance to the more private and informal aspects of their estates, which began to differ from the growing number of other Spanish estates only in having had a head start. Some of the encomendero families lost their position almost entirely, but the wealthiest and strongest tended to make the adjustment, allying themselves with the new elements rather than combating them, while maintaining their social position in the cities and much of their dominance in parts of the countryside.

Such changes did not occur automatically in all regions, rather only in places characterized by that inseparable pair of phenomena, silver and strong Spanish immigration. In the isolated south of Mexico and in that part of the Peruvian highland distant from the silver mines, the older system survived: total encomendero dominance, reliance on tribute, even retention of exclusive labor rights. And as one approached the semisedentary peoples, one would find the even older emphasis on labor rather than tribute. Yet the crown officials, once a solution had been worked out for the central areas, dutifully sent the ordinances everywhere, sometimes in the hands of officials who tried to enforce them, but with no success until such time, perhaps centuries later, as a livelier economy and increased immigration reduplicated the earlier situation of the central areas. Here we see which forces were basic, which supplementary.

In its heyday, the encomienda of Peru and Mexico was at the center of the center. The forty or fifty encomenderos of a good-sized Spanish city were a dominant minority among other hundreds of immigrants.

Differentiation grew sharply. Whereas in the Caribbean it was not at all unheard of for merchants to hold encomiendas or municipal office, in the central areas one had to make a quick choice between appearing as a merchant or vying for an encomienda, for one could not do both. Even the title of *vecino*, or "citizen," was often restricted in usage to the encomenderos, and with good reason. Their large establishments, clustered in the vicinity of the square, were the backbone of the city, sheltering not only the encomenderos and their Spanish wives but relatives and semitransient compatriots from the home region in Spain, as well as Black slaves and Indian servants both permanent and temporary. The encomienda staff had grown: The larger of the encomiendas now had a chief majordomo, or skilled general business manager, and under him assistant majordomos and estancieros, who would be humble Spaniards or sometimes Blacks. A priest or friar was in many cases de facto a part of the retinue. The staff, with the aid of naborías, collected and sold the tribute products of the Indians of the encomienda and at the same time used their labor in whatever local economic activity would turn a profit, whether at the mines, on the encomendero's estancias, or in enterprises as diverse as house construction, charcoal manufacture, and commercial fishing. To the extent that was possible, the encomendero built his overall estate into a diversified, interlocking, but profit-oriented whole. To illustrate the complex at full development, we include here a schematic chart of a large encomienda-associated estate of Peru in the 1550s (see Figure 4). (Depending on the conditions, of course, encomienda estates took myriad forms and varied greatly in degree of elaborateness.) Though the encomienda per se was destined for an early demise in the central areas, the aspects of estate organization connected with it – the urban–rural structure, the staff, the respective roles of permanent and temporary labor, and the general economic orientation – would survive in estate forms of the following centuries.

Commerce and artisanry

Large-scale commerce in the central areas soon came to consist essentially of the trade of Spanish goods for American silver. By the 1540s and 1550s there were at the core of this trade transatlantic companies or combinations of merchants, based in Seville, with factors in the main Spanish American port towns (Panamá, Veracruz) and sales representatives in the capitals (Lima, Mexico City). Some groups traded to Mexico, others to Peru, others to both. The large merchants were primarily wholesalers, but they also retailed in the

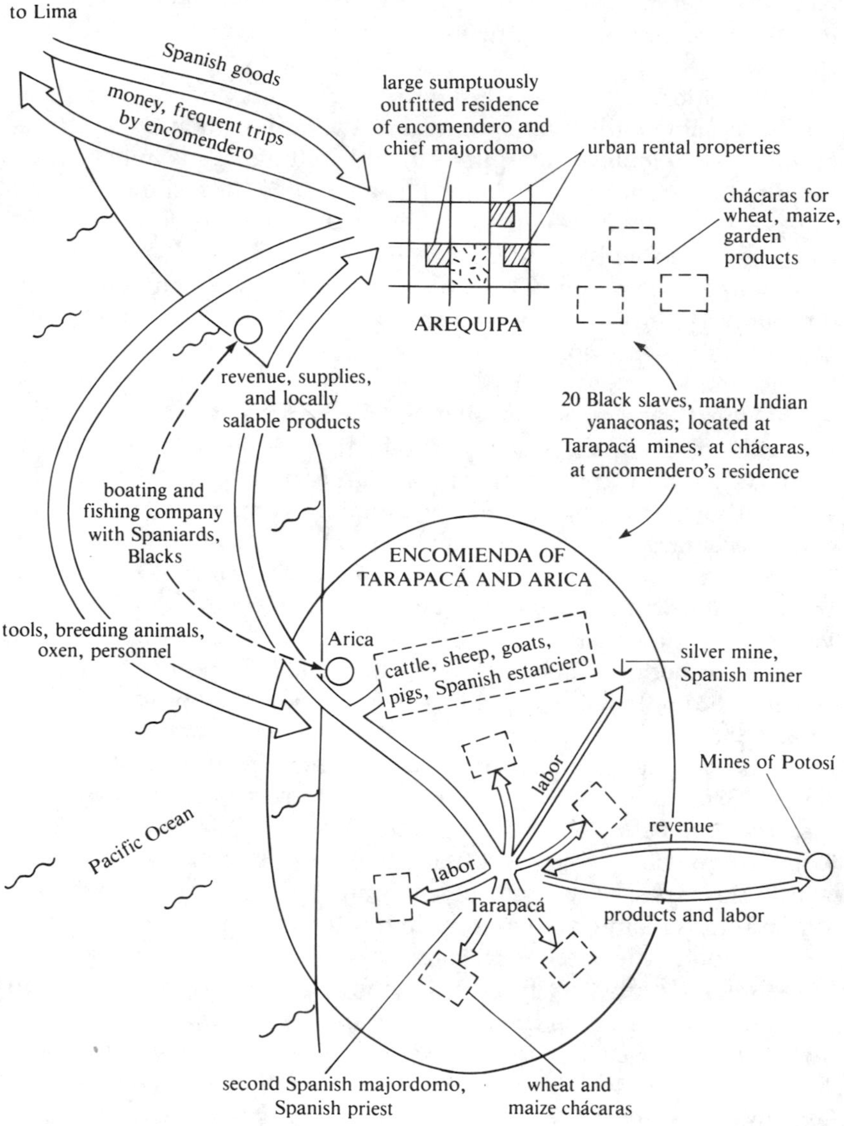

Figure 4. Schema of the estate of encomendero Jerónimo de Villegas, Peru, ca. 1550.

American capitals and, when they deemed it suitable, sent shipments on to the mines or major provincial centers along the silver route.

Continuities from the Caribbean period abounded. Company forms remained the same, networks continued to have a strong familial and regional underpinning, and shifting trends in personnel recruitment went further along the same lines. If in the Caribbean the north Castilians began to supplant the Genoese, on the mainland the Genoese had faded out almost entirely, and the Castilian merchant families, some of whose members now sought encomiendas rather than mercantile careers, had to make room for Andalusians who had previously been lowest on the commercial ladder in Seville.

The great increments of silver of the 1540s and 1550s, and the expectation of further steady production, brought some adjustments. Company arrangements grew larger in investment and scale, included more personnel, and were for a longer term. The American trade became Seville's main business, and with fleets and communications increasingly steady, the commercial networks treated the transatlantic world as one unified space. The normal course of advancement for a merchant in this trade was from American port or mine to American capital and on to Seville. Import–export merchants were only half located in America, more European-American intermediaries than settlers. America's great liquid wealth hastened the process of back migration, allowing the local representatives of Seville firms to accumulate funds of their own in short order and also making it possible for some extra-network traders to found new large companies, which forthwith took Seville for a headquarters.

But this same American silver strength caused tensions in the unified transatlantic system, tending in the long run to divide it into two sectors. The local representatives of the big combines were sometimes tempted to invest in the growing local economies even though that was not in the interest of the senior partners in Seville. And even the Seville partners were increasingly inclined to sell to local traders at the American waterfront rather than assume the expense of American facilities and the worry about grasping distant junior partners. Local companies, manned by professional merchants who lacked direct connections with the Seville networks, were built on the same principles, although the senior partner was in Mexico City or Lima and the junior one at the port or the mines. Merchants of this second rank were more inclined to take root, to marry locally, buy properties, and seek local honors. They were the first to become actively involved in supplying miners and to become mining financiers, even entrepreneurs. Thus well before the end of the first generation after conquest, forces had been set in motion which would tie import–export merchants more closely to the local society and economy and give them a more central place in it, though of all the major sectors they would remain the one with closest direct ties to Europe and Seville.

At the lowest level of Spanish commerce were petty dealers often called *tratantes,* the commercial world's equivalent of the humble estanciero. Recently arrived, little educated, of foreign extraction – always in some fashion marginal – they were not part of any larger network and dealt mainly in locally produced goods. Their specialty, indeed, was to sell Indian products to a clientele that was mainly Indian but had some buying power in silver as a result of work and residence in Spanish cities or mines. Often the products came through irregular individual trading with the Indians in the countryside (still called *rescate*), to the disgust of the encomenderos of those regions. As marginal as it was, this kind of activity was at times lucrative (especially near Potosí, where large numbers of Indians were in close proximity to a large silver supply), and it was to have an ever-growing role in the Spanish American scheme of things.

The cloth and iron the merchants imported needed reworking for the purposes of the settler population, and since there was silver to pay for it, there were Spaniards willing to perform the tasks. Within a decade after the conquest of each of the major areas, one could have books bound, jewelry set, fine costuming tailored, or mansions built, though all at astronomical prices by peninsular Spanish standards. As in the other branches of life, there was strong regional variation in degree of development. In the capitals and to a lesser extent all along the silver route, Spanish artisans practiced most of the trades known in Spain, whereas the crafts were much thinner wherever ability to pay dropped off. Even so, no Spanish city was without its blacksmith, tailor, and carpenter. Tied to a local clientele, the artisans were an integral part of local Spanish life. One aspect of their procedure was to train helpers – Black slaves when they could afford it – who greatly multiplied their productivity. In the main centers the shop of a successful artisan could contain a Spanish apprentice or two and several Black slave artisans in addition to the owner. In less wealthy areas or less flourishing shops, the helpers were likely to be Indian naboría-yanaconas – a growing trend everywhere. This shop and apprenticeship system was to be a basic mechanism in the gradual creation in the cities and mines of a class of Blacks, Indians, and persons of mixed descent who possessed skills in a European trade and were acquainted with many other facets of Hispanic culture as well.

Mining

Since the highly technical business of silver mining took many decades to reach maturity, we will reserve a fuller discussion of it for a future chapter. But even in the first generation it came to be the third pillar of a system in which import commerce supplied European goods, the mines paid for them, and the estates (mainly encomienda estates) supplied Indian labor and local products, both for the mines and for the Spanish cities whose existence and prosperity the whole worked to provide.

In the first postconquest years each of the central areas went through a significant transitional gold mining phase. In Peru it was over in a decade, but in Mexico it lasted longer and had greater ramifications, for the very good reason that indigenous accumulations of precious metals were much smaller in Mesoamerica than in Peru and major silver deposits were not discovered or developed for some time. The twentieth century sometimes loses sight of what was very well known in the sixteenth, that Mexico for all its fine cities, provinces, and people was not at first an outstandingly wealthy area in Spanish terms. This is reflected among other things in the fact that far more of the first conquerors left central Mexico for other surrounding areas, and fewer returned to Spain, than was the case with the conquerors of Peru. In Mexico it proved unfeasible, first with gold and then with silver, to base mining firmly on encomienda labor, mainly because of relative locations. The central Mexican Indians who formed such a solid basis for encomiendas were located mainly in temperate highland areas, whereas the gold deposits were in low wet areas, often at great distances. The mortality of highland Indians in wet lowlands was such that using them in gold mining would be directly destructive of encomiendas, and there was apprehension that the total disasters of the Caribbean would repeat themselves. Therefore, in both practice and law, encomienda Indians of central Mexico were not per se employed at gold mining. Instead, there was a continuation for a time of the Caribbean tradition of enslavement of hostile Indians, preferably those of remote nonencomienda regions, though there is little doubt that the central peoples were affected too. Although one basic part of the encomienda-mining nexus was thus short-circuited, the encomenderos were nevertheless prominent among those acquiring or hiring slaves and making companies for mining.

By 1540 or a little after, the Mexican cycle of gold and Indian slaves was largely over, after which Indian slavery was never again a significant factor in central Mexico. The shift to silver, beginning very early, was virtually complete by 1550. Some deposits were found in central Mexico proper, but the richest strikes were off to the north beyond sedentary territory. Here it was even more difficult to bring the encomienda to bear. The great mines of Zacatecas were first discovered and opened up with the help, participation, and investment of some encomenderos of Guadalajara, the nearest encomienda area, but the tie began to weaken almost immediately. Within a very short time the northern mining entrepreneurs no longer had a direct connection with the encomienda, and the labor force, skilled and unskilled, consisted entirely of naboría Indians from central Mexico, with a minority of skilled Blacks.

In Peru, on the other hand, the sedentary peoples and the encomienda stood in the closest relationship to the silver mining that became the economic mainstay earlier, relatively speaking, than in Mexico, because the Andean peoples had already developed sophisticated techniques of mining and refining silver ore. Already known deposits were worked in the early postconquest years, and in 1545 it was Peruvian Indians (though in Spanish employ) who discovered Potosí. Since the site was located at such a high altitude, European bellows would not bring ores to the proper heat, and the indigenous *huayra,* a smelting oven placed on ridges to take advantage of Potosí's fierce wind (and indeed it is named after the wind), was used to achieve the first boom production, with yanaconas both building the ovens and performing the smelting (all of which did not prevent a Spaniard from claiming the invention and having a huayra portrayed on his coat of arms; the Spaniards did in fact modify the huayra somewhat).

Claims in the richest ore veins went initially to large encomenderos of the Charcas region. Before long, encomienda Indians constituted the principal bulk work force; they came as part of the tribute labor obligation, which was called the mita as it had been before the conquest and would be in later times as well. Encomenderos of the Charcas region were for a time the richest people in the Indies, with annual incomes of scores of thousands of pesos. The structure was thus quite like that seen before in the Caribbean and very different from that of Mexico. And indeed, rotary draft labor by sedentary Indians coming temporarily from their home areas was to characterize Potosí for the entire long period of its productivity. Nevertheless, in other aspects trends were not unlike those in Mexico. The encomenderos soon began to retire from the direct owning and operation of mines, and a separate class of mining entrepreneurs began to arise, though this development took several decades to complete. At the same time, the encomenderos gradually lost their special labor rights, here as elsewhere. And though unskilled labor was numerically predominant, a sizable corps of yanaconas and some Blacks performed most of the skilled tasks in refining and had much in common with the mine workers of Mexico.

In both countries, silver mining towns, despite their economic centrality and the long-lasting nature of the deposits, for years remained mining camps of a type very familiar to us from other times and places: situated in remote and unfriendly environments, without regular layouts, the buildings huddled around the deposits and life characterized by transience and disorder. There were some mining experts, Basques prominent among them, but the mines attracted especially all those without established position in city or estate, so that from a social point of view the mines were marginal, the cities central. Over time this would change somewhat, and the more important mining towns would become true permanent urban entities with all that implied, but still it is meaningful that Potosí always remained a *villa,* or "town," whereas La Plata (Sucre) was a *ciudad,* or "city," and the seat of the Charcas Audiencia, even though Potosí came to be by far the larger and more active center.

Officials and practices of government

The social and economic strength of the Spanish presence in the areas of sedentary Indians soon brought about the full development of formal institutions, already alluded to, and a concomitant influx of royal officials, lawyers, notaries, and ecclesiastics. Of course these elements had been present to some extent from the beginning, and no place where Spaniards went was entirely without them, but the weight of numbers and institutional development was in the central areas; within those areas, along the silver route; and within that, in the larger cities and above all the capitals. The pattern of distribution thus followed that of everything else Spanish. And indeed, having described earlier, in dealing with the Iberian background, how governmental and ecclesiastical entities functioned in general, our concern here is to show how they fit in with other aspects of Spanish society in America.

Incentive for the grand-scale entrance of governmental agencies existed in the need to collect and protect a massive source of steady liquid revenue. The possibility came from the growing diversity and multiplicity of Spanish interests in the central areas, not only allowing but even demanding a governmental-judicial role. One governmental activity of great importance to the metropolitan-colonial tie (though not a part of Spanish America proper) was the organization of the transatlantic fleet and the provision of convoys for it, services which were paid for by taxes on ships and merchandise without inordinate protests from the shipowners and merchants who benefited. In America, leading conquerors from the beginning sought the legitimacy of a royal appointment to a governorship as an additional support against rivals. The rivals, on the other hand, clamored for royal intervention in their favor. And things continued just so in the postconquest years. The senior and the powerful, those who had encomiendas and mines, looked to government for legitimation and assured continuance of their position, whereas the many latecomers constantly appealed for favors for themselves and were only too happy to support officials in limiting and controlling the conquerors and encomenderos. Restrictions on governmental power were severe: The first viceroy of Peru, Blasco Núñez Vela, was overthrown (1544) and killed in battle (1546) for trying to enforce measures against the senior encomenderos. On the other hand, however weak the crown might be in a given area, it had the great advantage of being on the outside and unassailable, able in the long run to restore at least nominal obedience by attracting dissident Spaniards to its banner. (Let it be clear that there was no element of ideological protest or threat to the Castilian crown in settler rebelliousness, merely defense of self-interest.) By 1550 the crown, the Council of the Indies, and the high officials in America had learned not to unleash abrupt challenges to settler interests, and the settlers had learned to stay this side of open rebellion. But even though local social, economic, and demographic forces set the overall rate and course of developments, officials played a significant role in the specific allocation of encomiendas, labor, and mining rights, and in the adjudication of disputes over them.

Some insight into the role of royal officials can be obtained by looking at them as immigrants of a special kind, quite comparable to the international merchants in being at once part of the Indies and part of an international network stretching back to Spain. If the merchants, moving from one site to another in their careers, were a unifying force for the whole, the same was true of officials, who had their own mobile career patterns and ladders of promotion. It soon became the practice that a successful viceroy of New Spain would be promoted after some years to the same post in wealthier Peru and then return to high honors in Spain. A judge might be named out of Spain to a provincial American Audiencia, proceed to a high court in one of the two viceregal capitals, and possibly be advanced from there to the Council of the Indies at the Spanish royal court. Hence those involved with affairs of the Indies at court had often had firsthand experience in America, just as many large merchants of Seville had had their business beginnings there. And as returning merchants sent young relatives back to America to replace them, so it was to come to pass more than once that father and son would hold the same viceregal post over the course of years, and that the Indies veterans on the Council of the Indies would name relatives and compatriots to Audiencias where they themselves had once served.

From the beginning there were certain ties between the royal officials and the settlers, and such ties quickly multiplied. Any official would of course find in the new area some people from his home region, who would expect and receive favors from him. But sometimes judges and others were named precisely because of the urging of prominent settler interests. Even more importantly, however, the officials actively sought alliances with powerful local people. The highest officials did have fairly meaningful salaries, but these were a temporary asset. For a more secure underpinning they invested in estancias, urban real estate, and commercial endeavors. A governor, viceroy, or Audiencia judge never left Spain without merchandise to be sold in his new area, bought with the credit his appointment gave him. After the time of the conqueror-governors, high officials did not hold encomiendas; instead, they married their female relatives to the locally wealthy – encomenderos and subsequently mining entrepreneurs. Even the high and mighty viceroys arranged such marriages on occasion, but it was especially the practice of Audiencia judges and treasury officials, who were usually in one post for a longer period of time, and who standardly brought wife and children with them to America. The locals were naturally most happy to marry into these families, for prestige and in hope of special favors.

The viceroys and the Audiencias became significant social and professional nuclei. A viceroy had a secretariat, of course, but more especially he had a retinue and maintained a court. The office of viceroy had a strong connotation of high nobility. After the one disastrous experience in Peru, never again did the crown name a viceroy without the title "don"; rather, all the viceroys were authentic high nobles, close relatives of counts, dukes, and marquises, or even themselves holders of such titles. They brought with them, in addition to some dependents, other people from their own milieu, whom they would make their most trusted agents. There would be further similar figures on the scene, remaining from the previous viceroy, for the retinues had much less geographical mobility than the chief figures. The viceregal set attracted also the noblest and most powerful encomenderos and other wealthy figures, both from the capital and from other Spanish cities in the entire extended region. The two elements, the viceroy's followers and the local establishment, came together to constitute the core of Spanish American high society. The Audiencia judges figured here too, but even more important for general social evolution was the legal hierarchy that arose around the Audiencia, as an entity with much corporate and individual continuity and to which disputes of all kinds were constantly being appealed. There were the court's own notaries, secretaries, and officials in charge of relaying the written testimony to the judges. A corps of *letrados,* or university-trained lawyers, gave legal advice concerning Audiencia cases to litigants of all kinds, from encomenderos to Indian towns. At the next lower level, another corps of *procuradores,* or untitled lawyers, did most of the actual court representation. All these people together constituted an element of society in the capitals, seeking permanence whether on the basis of appointment to offices or ownership of properties. By far the largest concentration of them was in the capitals, but they also filtered out one at a time into the provinces, seeking opportunities.

Extension of direct royal representatives into areas away from the capitals was a slow process, not fully belonging to the time we are discussing, but it did begin then. From the first, governors and viceroys named short-term lieutenant governors, sometimes called *corregidores,* to represent them in all the Spanish settlements, presiding over the local municipal councils and hearing cases appealed from the alcaldes, or first-instance judges. In the early years the appointees might be local encomenderos, but before long they were outsiders, typically out of the governor's retinue. The governmental presence in Spanish cities, then, reached maturity quickly and was hardly to change until the late eighteenth century. For the Indian countryside, however, things took much longer, partly because the quasi-governmental encomienda was an autonomous, all-inclusive system, leaving little room for other kinds of Spanish authority and taxation. An entry place did exist in encomiendas which were left vacant and in those which were directly assigned to the crown, an increasing number as the encomienda was progressively weakened; in fact, some of the largest and most populous Indian provinces went to the crown from a very early time because on the one hand they were hard to divide and on the other hand the deadly competition for encomiendas would not allow such vast assets to go to any one person. The first holders of posts of this type were often little more than majordomos, on the payroll of the crown rather than of an encomendero. But soon, especially with the larger Indian units, they were acting as subgovernors, adjudicating disputes as well as collecting tributes for the crown; there were several titles for posts of this type, of which *corregidor de indios* is the best known. By 1550 in central Mexico, and perhaps twenty years later in Peru, they existed in all the areas of dense population. Often appointed from among the viceroy's personal following, they included also other disappointed candidates for encomiendas, encomenderos' relatives, and occasionally unemployed lawyers. Gradually they began to assume jurisdiction even in areas held by encomenderos. The question of corregidor jurisdiction was not settled in many areas for decades, but ultimately the encomenderos were able to reconcile themselves to it, relying on informal ties to protect their interests. The post of corregidor de indios was one of considerable honor, but as the second and even third postconquest generation came and went, the position of encomendero still had greater permanence, inherent power, and prestige.

The setup just described must be thought of as existing primarily in the wealthiest and most centrally located areas. In secondary capitals like Guatemala, Quito, or Bogotá, there was only the Audiencia, whose presiding judge doubled as governor, there were fewer supporting legal personnel, and the process of naming corregidores went much more slowly; without viceregal retinues and strong continuing immigration, there were fewer people pressing to hold such posts. In yet more remote regions, only the governor would come from the outside; other governmental functions including the treasury offices were taken over on a part-time basis by local Spaniards, either encomenderos, merchants, or notaries.

Ecclesiastics

Though they were without an incentive quite as urgent as the crown's *quinto,* or silver revenue, and though they in part appear oriented directly toward the Indian population, ecclesiastical entities and personnel also built on and reflected the growing Spanish society in America. Like all other Spanish organizations, those of an ecclesiastical nature were urban-headquartered. The archbishops were in the two viceregal capitals, the bishops in other major Spanish cities, and other high-ranking secular clergymen were in the cathedral chapters; a second level was in urban parishes in the cathedral cities or in benefices in the main church of noncathedral Spanish towns. The lowest ranking were in the countryside, instructing encomienda Indians; within the ecclesiastical hierarchy they were quite comparable to the estancieros within the encomienda staff: most recently arrived, least well trained and connected, often discontent and frequently shifting position in the hope of finding urban employment. With the mendicant orders, so prominent in the sixteenth century, the urban orientation is at first glance not so clear, since the mendicants sent their very best people into Indian towns, where in Mexico they built impressive complexes. Even so, on a closer look one sees that the best trained and most gifted figures, after a stint or two in remote areas, were located mainly in Spanish centers, as were the orders' largest churches and the concentrations of personnel, whereas rural monasteries had one or two, rarely more than three or four, friars.

And as with ordinary immigrants, seniority meant much for ecclesiastics, both individuals and organizations. Just after the completion of the conquest of central Mexico, in 1524, a party of twelve Franciscan friars arrived (whenever possible the friars matched the apostles in number). Not only were The Twelve thenceforth turned into a legend and preferred for advancement within the order, but the order as a whole predominated in central Mexico, whereas the second-arriving Dominicans mainly took areas off to the isolated south, and the third-arriving Augustinians were left with parts of the dry, less populated north. On the other hand, the ecclesiastic with Francisco Pizarro's conquering expedition in Peru was a Dominican; he became the first Peruvian bishop, on exactly the same principle by which first conquerors received encomiendas, and he brought his order into an early predominance in Peru which it never entirely lost. Likewise, the secular priest who accompanied Pedro de Valdivia to Chile became the first bishop in that country.

Seen as immigrants, ecclesiastics were rather less likely than judges or governors to be promoted outside of a given area, though some of them, especially among the lower secular clergy, returned to Spain to retire. Like governmental officials, they sometimes initially received positions because of ties of kinship or regional origin with prominent settlers, and they too often proceeded to arrange marriages of their female relatives with encomenderos, drawing themselves yet closer into the social fabric and securing powerful patrons for their organizations. Pious donations and other help from the local Spanish population gave church entities their first economic sinews, the wherewithal to increase membership, buy income properties, and build impressive urban establishments. As to the secular priests, they as individuals participated in the local economies in most of the same ways that any other Spaniard would.

Within the Spanish world, the function and activity of the clergy continued to be as it had been in Spain proper. It is the relationship to the indigenous population that we need to examine here. In one sense the rural parish, or *doctrina,* was erected directly on the Indian provincial unit, from which, like the encomienda, it took its size, shape, and structure; its local headquarters too was in the chief Indian settlement, or cabecera town, and it used the cacique's authority to help build churches and assure attendance. Nevertheless, in the first generation the parish was included within the encomienda, integrated with, dependent upon, and subordinate to it, rather than parallel. The encomienda almost always preceded the parish in time, and the original parish shapes were simply those of the encomiendas. Encomenderos contracted individually with the ecclesiastics who were to man their grants; they paid them salaries and provided them with supplies out of the tributes they and their staffs collected. The one cleric per encomienda would reside in the cabecera, where with encomienda labor and often other financial support he would begin to construct a church, hold services, administer sacraments on a regular basis, and give special schooling to certain individuals, often the children of nobles. Like other Spaniards, the clerics made use of Indian auxiliaries, including a *fiscal,* or general aide and steward, as well as some sacristans and singers. In the cabecera these might be so nearly the cleric's dependents as to be considered naborías, but they differed from that type in being in their own local community and still tied to it. The outlying districts of the encomienda-parish received only periodic visits from the cleric; the building of churches and chapels proceeded much more slowly there, and where there were Indian fiscales in such situations, they were in practical charge of things most of the time.

The procedures just described, which apply to the entire area of sedentary Indian life, by no means constitute a mission system, as Anglo-Saxons are sometimes prone to think. There was no necessity to teach civilization and agriculture to the central peoples. New settlements were not established; rather, churches were built in already existing urban-ceremonial centers. Nor was the ecclesiastical establishment a spearhead and overarching institution as it would later become in certain parts of the periphery; rather, it was an integrated part of a much larger general Spanish presence. Even in the countryside clerics were outnumbered by majordomos, Blacks, small-scale commercial farmers, tratantes, and the like. The word "mission" was unknown to sixteenth-century Spanish America, and well it might be; there were parish churches and monastery churches, some in Spanish towns and others in Indian towns. Nor were there any people called "missionaries." It would not be inappropriate to apply that word to the priests and friars who worked among the Indian people of the center, but the term actually used for them at the time is most suggestive: *doctrinero,* "person dispensing (Christian) instruction." Given the fact of conquest, the sedentary peoples by and large took conversion for granted. The question was one of learning just what a converted person should do and how much of the old could be retained. Thus the emphasis was on instruction rather than conversion, on teaching Christian duties, beliefs, and sacraments.

The structure and general method of rural ecclesiastical activity was the same whether the doctrinero was a secular priest or a member of one of the mendicant orders (who had general dispensation to do parish work among Indians in the sixteenth century). In Peru and in many other regions the two types served side by side, on an equal though not entirely friendly footing; it was only in Mexico that the friars were heavily predominant in the first generation. There were, however, some characteristic differences between the operations of the two. Secular priests were under the loosest of diocesan control, often none at all, and they at times gravitated entirely into the orbit of the encomendero-employer. One result of the overall Spanish American system was that in remote Indian towns the doctrinero was generally the best educated and socially best placed permanent Spanish resident, and a secular priest in this position could be most useful to the encomendero as manager and representative, aiding or even supplanting the majordomo.

Though ecclesiastics generally accepted the encomienda as the framework of their rural activity – the Dominicans under protest, the Franciscans somewhat more willingly, the seculars without comment – all had some reason to resent a system which rendered them in certain ways subordinate and dependent. Unlike the secular priests, each of whom faced an encomendero person to person with no other resources than his own, the orders had the corporate strength to pull away from some aspects of dependence. Their general practice of quick rotation in posts kept ties from becoming too strong in any one situation. And where conditions were propitious, the monasteries they established in the largest cabeceras had two to four friars and jointly served as many encomiendas, again weakening the reliance on any one of them.

Mexico saw the greatest flourishing of mendicant activity. Here the pragmatic Franciscans were the senior order and set the tone; the flower of mendicant manpower, fervor, and humanistic training poured into this first of the central areas to be occupied. Just as important were the powerful, nucleated Mexican city-states, whose people were accustomed to expressing their corporate glory through the construction of impressive stone temples and whose records had long customarily been put on paper. The Franciscans and other mendicants, during approximately the first two postconquest generations, carried out, with Indian help and guidance, an intense activity of study, instruction, and building, of which there remains much tangible evidence; the beautiful monastery complexes standing to this day, made with European elements but adapted to Indian numbers and outdoor ceremonialism (see Figure 5); the excellent and numerous grammars of Mesoamerican languages; the masses of documents written by Mesoamerican Indians in their own languages during colonial times, products of an Indian literacy first brought about mainly by the friars. Peru, on the other hand, saw but pale reflections of the Mexican campaign. Hardly any sixteenth-century architectural monuments remain, and they are in Spanish cities; Indian literacy in Quechua or Aymara did not become a major trend. Elsewhere, the mendicants' achievements in the conquest period were yet less. Even what they did in Mexico (and we must remember that Spanish masons with their Black apprentices participated in building the churches and that Spanish notaries had a hand in the instruction of Indian writers) was a magnificent action of cultural preservation and esthetic creation rather than the mainstream of social-cultural contact between Spaniards and Indians.

The entire official community, legal-governmental and ecclesiastic, shared the attributes of Spanish American society and was caught up in its workings, yet stood partly aside, generally directly or indirectly crown-appointed, belonging to extraregional networks. Of quite similar backgrounds, officials and ecclesiastics between them accounted for most of the university education among Span-

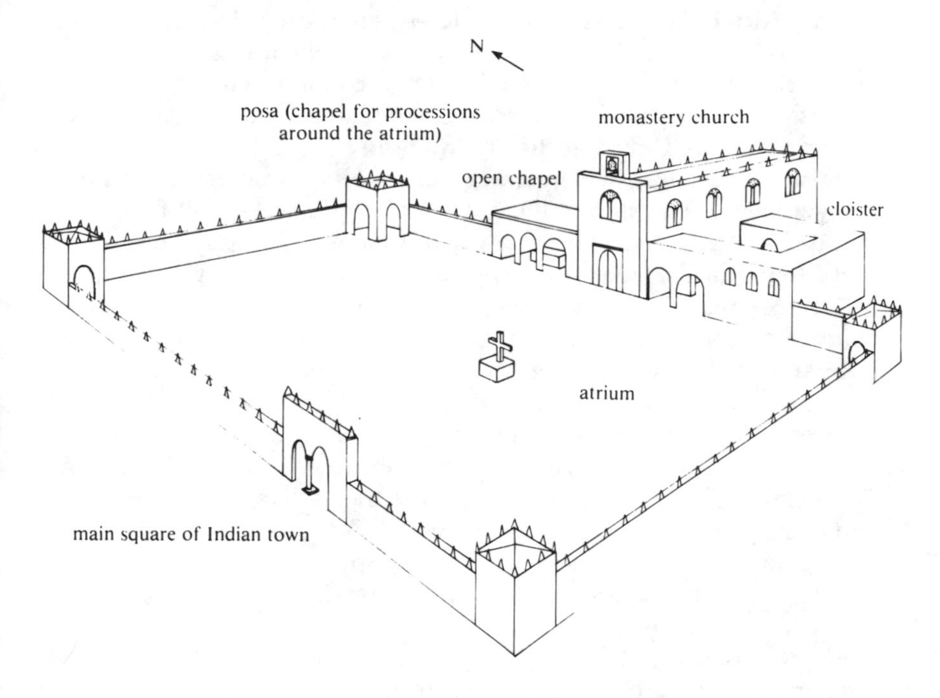

Figure 5. Layout of a monastery church, Mexican type, sixteenth century.

iards in America. All alike took part in local high society. Within this unity, there was no strong ecclesiastical–governmental dichotomy. In a given dispute, one could find the archbishop, the Franciscans, and the encomenderos on one side, the Dominicans and the Audiencia on the other. One type of opposition was endemic. The archbishop (in lesser centers the bishop), with his own court and circle, headed a hierarchy and thus was the inevitable opposite pole of the viceroy (in lesser centers the governor). Persons alienated by the viceroy ran to the archbishop, and vice versa, and so it went through the centuries, regardless of the individuals involved. The constant minor friction ensuing was neither personal irritability nor church–state conflict.

Indians

On preceding pages of this chapter we have shown in each instance the relationship of the Spanish structures in America to the Indian populations in which they were immersed, and we have also spoken of ways in which some Indians entered into those structures permanently as auxiliaries. In so doing we have already dealt with the major forces for cultural, social, and economic change in both worlds, Indian as well as Spanish. It remains to look at what was occurring in the Indian sector in and of itself, insofar as this can be done in a historical field just beginning to be explored. But before proceeding to the internal life of the Indian provinces, let us glance at the structural relationship between Indians in corporate units and those living and working among Spaniards, or to put it differently, between encomienda Indians and naboría-yanaconas, or, from another point of view, between temporary and permanent laborers in Spanish enterprises. Whereas these two elements can be viewed statically, simply as distinct groups within Indian society, yet in both pre- and postconquest times there were regular mechanisms of migration and marginalization by which one grew out of the other. The primary mode of contact between the Indians and the Spaniards, the constant temporary migrations out of the countryside to cities and mines to labor and to deliver tribute, resulted in many people being stranded or commandeered or simply staying on in the Spanish settlements. The partly acculturated permanent mine workers and urban Indians with European skills thus arose out of the corporate Indian world by the ordinary workings of the overall postconquest system (to which they were in turn essential). The first vehicle of the movement was the encomienda, but later forms of migratory labor would have the same effect, contributing to a process as basic to the evolution of Spanish America as the opposite movement of lower-ranking members of Spanish society out of the cities and into the country – also initially often in connection with the encomienda.

The most tangible and immediate effect of the Spanish presence on the Indian countryside in the central areas was, as elsewhere, demographic. Sharp, major losses took place in all regions as epidemic periodically succeeded epidemic, reducing the Indian population by the latter sixteenth century to a fraction of what it had been (the proportional loss depending on how high one estimates population at conquest). However, only in the low coastal areas, which approximated Caribbean climatic conditions, were losses on the catastrophic Caribbean scale of quick, near-total destruction. In the highlands, where both of the preconquest empires were based, though millions of lives were lost, the rate of reduction was moderate in comparison, and enough people remained to maintain the overall structure of society. Mesoamerica and the central Andes were still, relatively speaking, densely populated areas. Few if any major settlement clusters disappeared. Indigenous urban life and agriculture were both maintained much as before, and along with them language, culture, and social organization. Spanish tribute and labor demands were partly new in kind and probably greater in amount than their equivalents in preconquest times, especially in the early period when limits had not yet been set. Combined with demographic loss, these demands could represent severe disruptive pressure in given cases. In the vicinity of large Spanish settlements, such pressures could mount to the point of nearly destroying Indian corporate life and turning the residents into Spanish employees. But in general, Indian towns and provinces survived the conquest essentially intact.

In the immediate postconquest period indigenous reactions included, naturally enough, demoralization, nostalgia for what had been, and a belief that long prophesied destiny and the anger of the gods had brought about disaster, all feelings especially predominant among those who had held sway over others. But pride and self-assertiveness, in relation to the local province or subprovince, were just as characteristic. Consider a letter written from the Indian ruler of Huitzilopochco to his counterpart in Coyoacan around 1550, when both of these important central Mexican provinces had long been in encomienda, were acquiring Spanish-style municipal councils, and had seen grow up only a few miles away one of the largest concentrations of Spaniards in the Indies, Mexico City. Yet despite passing references to God, king, and Audiencia, the letter treats Huitzilopochco and Coyoacan as two sovereign preconquest states at the verge of war over a disputed border area. The insults hurled are in the grand manner of the old Nahuatl speakers, events far back into preconquest times enter into the argument, and the local officials on each side are called by preconquest titles for judges and notables. Not only did provincial units retain their vitality and identity, they took advantage of the new situation to reassert historical claims to areas which had been lost to neighbors in preceding generations. Every subgroup that had ever been independent of a head town now tried to regain that status, alleging that it had enjoyed independence "from time immemorial and before that," as one text reads.

The early postconquest situation, then, was predicated on retention of local indigenous states and regional entities, under the continued leadership of their caciques or dynastic rulers. Like the naboría-yanaconas, the caciques were vital intermediaries; unlike them, they maintained their position within the local entity, and indeed their function depended upon their doing so. Not being cut loose from their milieu, they experienced cultural change at a slower rate and in a different way than did the naborías; yet of all the people inside the corporate Indian world, they were the ones with the strongest, steadiest ties to the Spanish sector, so it was natural that they should become a focal point of early Spanish influence at the local corporate level.

On the one hand, caciques and related nobles soon began to manipulate the situation by using their traditional prerogatives to carry out activity originating in the Indian world but directed toward the Spanish economy. There were Indian nobles in both Mexico and Peru who acquired livestock, especially pigs and sheep, or grew wheat using oxen and plows, or produced cloth by Spanish methods, often with a Spanish partner or foreman but otherwise employing Indian personnel. In Peru at least, caciques sometimes rented out the services of their subjects, as laborers or porters, to individual Spaniards other than the encomendero. And along with their economic participation, nobles adopted many Spanish trappings: items of dress, horses to ride (at first with special permission from the authorities), sometimes alphabetical writing, and occasionally Spanish speech as well, though here the nobles tended to lag far behind the naborías. At this level, adopted traits were almost always an addition rather than a replacement. When don Julián de la Rosa, head of a noble house of Tlaxcala (Mexico), died in 1566, he owned among much else a horse, to be sold to pay for masses for his soul, a cloak in native style but of European domestic duck feathers, and some preconquest warrior costumes with animal devices.

On the other hand, the Spaniards manipulated the nobles, supporting their aspirations up to a point while trying to make them more responsive to Spanish needs and render their modes of operation more like Spanish ones. Spanish authorities in both main regions gave official recognition to the office of cacique and also sanctioned the caciques' retention of their personal retainers and their collection of revenues from their subjects for their own personal use. But in the early years the authorities broke or created caciques at will, choosing among the dynastic rivals those who seemed likely to be most cooperative. Within a few years there began the process of replacing the cacique with a local municipal government, manned by Indians but in the Hispanic mold, which would collect taxes, allocate labor, and maintain order in the cacique's stead. In some situations, the first step was creation of a "governor," who had many of the cacique's powers in addition to presiding over the new municipal council as it came into existence. Whereas the position of cacique was in some sense hereditary and for a lifetime tenure, that of governor was appointive and intended to rotate at shorter intervals. Almost predictably, the first governor was usually the cacique, and he usually held office indefinitely. But the trend was for the governorship to be handed about among important local nobles at fairly short intervals and for the position of cacique to lose some of its centrality. The process varied with the conditions. In some areas of strong Spanish impact, notably in central Mexico, quickly rotating governors began to take over from caciques by the end of the first generation. In the more isolated south of Mexico, caciques as such maintained themselves far better, and in highland Peru the strong hereditary cacique nearly precluded the rise of governorship.

Only in the larger head towns were caciques recognized, governors appointed, and Indian municipal councils established in the conquest generation. The local state or provincial unit of the preconquest period would normally correspond to one encomienda and one parish, with only one recognized cacique or governor and one municipal council. The latter, consisting of frequently rotating alcaldes and councilmen like its counterpart in the Spanish sector, was slower to take shape than the rest. As with the governorship, it was manned with local Indian nobles, the same persons who would have been judges, high stewards, and advisers before the conquest. Yet the Spanish definitions and expectations of the posts brought change. At any time from the conquest forward official practices and structures inside the Indian towns were a mixture of indigenous and intrusive, interpreted one way by the Indians and another by the Spaniards, with Hispanic influence only slowly gaining ground, parallel to the general slow push of Spanish life into the countryside. Change was least and slowest, often imperceptible, among officials at the hamlet level, the ward heads and petty tax collectors.

Perhaps the most obvious change was in the municipal record keeper; councils in both central areas were to have an Indian notary-secretary to keep the minutes following Spanish norms and using the European alphabet. In both areas there had already been official record keepers, and the Indians even continued to give them the older names at times, yet the change was great and abrupt, particularly for the Andeans, whose records had been on quipus rather than on paper. Hardly anything is known of the activity of the Peruvian notaries, not even when they became a standard feature if they really ever did; apparently where they existed they wrote mainly in Spanish. In Mexico, on the other hand, every sizable Indian town soon acquired, along with its council, a notary who recorded council proceedings, local trials, and many other kinds of legal transactions, in a quasi-Spanish fashion but in the local Indian language. In the large Nahuatl-speaking portion of central Mexico, writing became a self-perpetuating tradition not only for notaries attached to the town councils and churches but among some members of the upper levels of Indian society more generally.

By the 1550s Nahuatl literacy was producing a mass of writings, both current local documentation and updated histories and legends. It was an impressive phenomenon in itself, parallel to the great wave of rural church building beginning at about the same time in central Mexico, and it gives us a window onto the cultural scene that is not available outside Mesoamerica (though there is every reason to imagine comparable processes in the other central region). Before the end of the first postconquest generation Spanish nouns were pouring into Nahuatl speech by the hundreds, each one betraying an introduced item, concept, or practice. These included European plants and animals, tools and other metal artifacts, offices and occupations, legal, religious, and economic concepts, and ways of measuring and subdividing, whether time, weight, extension, or value. Indian life generally thus began, like the Indian municipalities, to be a mixture, still predominantly preconquest in mode and structure but with numerous adjustments and additions. Some of the new was superficial, some deeper going. It might mean little to call a certain day "Saturday" instead of using a traditional day sign with numerical coefficient, but to change regional markets to a seven-day cycle demanded considerable internal restructuring, even when the centers and the items traded underwent little initial change.

Sometimes parallel with the establishment of formal municipal machinery, sometimes later, the Spaniards might attempt to carry out the "congregation" or "reduction" of the Indians into more compact settlements, a policy already begun toward the end of the Caribbean period. Usually the attempt was not to create a new provincial unit but to nucleate an existing one; when such units already had well-developed urban centers, as in central Mexico, the change might entail nothing more than moving a cabecera a few hundred yards or straightening its streets. Where such centers were lacking or little developed, as in much of southern Mesoamerica and highland Peru, a more extensive reorganization might be undertaken. A first wave of congregation occurred in central Mexico toward the end of the conquest generation; the timing elsewhere is far from clear, but it seems that, as in Peru, congregation was mainly a phenomenon of the early mature period, following the principle that the greater the reorganization required the later it takes place. For a generation or more after the conquest we do not go far wrong in simply imagining that the Indians of the central areas continued to live in their original units.

The tax-paying commoners inside the Indian corporations also remained in much the same position relative to local society, although they were by no means static or entirely passive. The new disruptions, accretions, and reorganizations affected them as well as their superiors. Before long they were trying to take advantage of the general situation to lessen their ties and duties to the nobles or even to assimilate themselves more to that stratum. The nobles' personal retainers tended to try to move into the ranks of the ordinary commoners, while the commoners not only shirked some of their duties but sometimes asserted their independence by migrating to other Indian towns or undertaking small-scale Spanish-style enterprises on their own. The nobles of both major regions constantly complained of the commoners' loss of respect, saying again and again that now one could no longer tell a difference in dress or actions between the impoverished nobility and the uppity commoners. Actually, the distinction retained much of its force, and on the other hand, all of these tensions had surely been known in the preconquest period too. But just as the postconquest situation favored the traditional separatism of microgroups, so it gave greater scope to the already existing forces for mobility, physical and social, among individual Indians.

All in all, the conquest period allows us to make a quite clear distinction between a Spanish world concentrated in widely scattered cities for Spaniards and their employees, and the Indian world of semiautonomous corporations inhabiting the countryside. We should not forget, however, that where Spanish cities were superimposed on Indian ones, and they often were, from Mexico City and Cuzco on down, a corporate Indian world might continue to exist in and around the Spanish center. Thus Mexico City contained the Indian municipality of Tenochtitlan, with its governor, council, four districts, and all the characteristics of any other Indian corporation, including large areas where the inhabitants were nearly exclusively Indian. Cuzco was closely parallel, with the Indian element even more cohesive and lending its color to the entire city. In both capitals there were important remnants of the high imperial nobility, still in quite full possession of their traditional lore and still capable of attracting marriage alliances from among the dynasties of outlying Indian towns. A few imperial nobles received encomiendas and began the process of entering the Spanish world proper. The Indian corporate world in the vicinity of Spanish cities was under concerted attack in every possible dimension; yet we should not underestimate its resilience nor forget its existence within the overall early postconquest scene.

Areas of transition

Our entire discussion in this chapter has been directed to the central areas – Mesoamerica and the central Andes. Later we will devote a chapter to development in places which, in sixteenth and seventeenth century terms, were fringe areas, and some sharp distinctions will emerge. Between the poles, however, stretched a continuum of situations partaking of the developmental characteristics of the two extremes to whatever extent the basic givens were present. We have, in fact, already allowed for variation within the central areas, the pace of change and the density of European occupation being greater in proportion to the economic incentive and the degree of nucleation of the indigenous population. On the edges of the central areas lay several regions – north and central Chile, northwestern Argentina, highland Colombia, Guatemala, some parts of the near north of Mexico – where the indigenous peoples were only partially sedentary or where the sedentaries were mixed in with other peoples, or where the areas themselves were extremely remote and inaccessible (the case of highland Guatemala). Here the variation from the norm set by such a situation as the Valley of Mexico is so substantial that we can no longer speak of central areas; yet these transitional areas need to be seen in relation to the central ones. All were occupied from the center in the course of the broader conquest period; all saw during that time the permanent establishment of Spanish cities, the creation of encomiendas, and the immigration of varied elements including professional people, merchants, artisans, Spanish women, and Blacks. Central-area Indians accompanied the conquests in large numbers as naboría-yanaconas, bringing with them a whole set of Spanish – Indian relationships, and these people became a significant population element in the new regions.

The general type of the occupation, then, was the same. On the other hand, everything occurred a little later and more slowly, and all the signs of Hispanic development were weaker. Immigrants were far fewer, especially after experience made the lack of prospects apparent, and the various occupational and auxiliary groups were much less thickly represented. Marginal people, from European foreigners and the racially mixed to simple late arrivals, were a much larger proportion of Hispanic society. In this milieu, marginal social types might have greater success, and fewer distinctions were maintained. In the central areas, the solid indigenous base dictated the location and jurisdictions of Spanish cities and encomiendas with great precision. In the transitional areas, where indigenous organization was often more fluid and actual armed resistance might last longer, it was not always so clear where cities and encomiendas should be. Cities might suffer repeated false starts or go through a stage of being fortified settlements. Encomiendas usually had to be more numerous and less populous, as were the indigenous units of which they were built. Lacking silver, these areas had little leverage in the transatlantic economy, and their mercantile development suffered correspondingly. As an alternative to international trade, they sought if possible to trade with the neighboring central areas; but few of them had a product as salable as Guatemala's cacao.

Central-area influence, then, remained strong in the areas of transition, the latter being in the overall commercial and official orbit of the former. Not only did the Spaniards of such an area as Chile at first try to reshape their situation in the image of Peru, but later Peruvian trends also reverberated there, usually causing trouble because of the greatly varying conditions. Thus Chile was set up with a small number of large encomiendas, on the Peruvian plan, and only gradually evolved toward the much greater number of smaller grants necessitated by the indigenous situation. In later years directives came from Peru to abolish encomienda labor obligations and Indian slavery, that having been the general central-area solution, but under Chilean conditions neither measure could be enforced, despite endless conflict.

Phenomena of conclusion

When any strong, quick movement of creation or destruction has run its course, there comes a time of taking stock, of assessing the rights and wrongs and regularizing the new situation. For the conquest of the Indies, this process was quite complex because of the many separate areas involved, each of which went through its own cycle in turn, while at the same time the concluding phases of the older areas were felt in the newer ones; thus interconnected waves of polemicizing and lawmaking succeeded one another from the second decade of the sixteenth century well into its last quarter.

The process began in the Caribbean – early relative to the overall conquest movement but late relative to the Caribbean phase – at a time when the entire city-plus-encomiendas complex and its associated practices had reached a certain maturity and Indian population decline had become acute. Clerics, officials, and other recent arrivals, led by the Dominicans, who came on the scene in 1510, protested against the encomienda system and its effect on the Indians; they questioned the very validity of the Spanish presence in the Indies and raised alternate possibilities: Christian Indian polities entirely separate and autonomous with only clerical supervision and colonies of humble Spanish agriculturalists not reliant on an Indian base. (It was, of course, too late to test independent Indian communities, for lack of Indians, and the foredoomed Spanish small farmer experiment took place on the Venezuelan coast, a hostile fringe area already bypassed by the main developments.) The Laws of Burgos, promulgated in Spain in 1512, were the most meaningful result of the first round of ferment; they were an attempt to regulate the encomienda in a humanitarian and religious spirit, in the interest of the crown and general stability, but they addressed themselves to an institution now moribund in the Caribbean.

Further legislation of the same tendency was written for the newly conquered central areas, which, however, largely shrugged off its effect until, as we have seen, internal conditions made the laws partially applicable. The controversies over right of conquest also flared up anew and led to a nominal general suspension of Spanish military expansion in the 1550s – just after the completion of the conquests of the last known sedentary peoples.

By the second half of the century Mexico and Peru were entering their concluding phases, the first somewhat earlier because of its earlier beginning. There was a last wave of "restitution fever," a half-serious campaign to reject the conquest, make amends to the Indians, and give them back the encomienda areas if not the whole country; feeling ran highest in Peru, where the dominant Dominicans continued to be more radical and doctrinaire than Mexico's senior order, the Franciscans. In the time between the 1550s and 1570s certain Audiencia judges and other lawyers and officials began to compose systematic descriptions of how the indigenous systems functioned, making copious recommendations for proper legislation. Chronicles, often by ecclesiastics, began to be written in a similar spirit, very different from the day-to-day campaign accounts of the earlier conquest histories. Around this time the royal government instructed its local officials to carry out a thorough survey, description and population estimate of all its American domains, the famous *Relaciones Geográficas.* A series of Mexican viceroys passed laws which would stay on the books for a century and more; in Peru a single famous legislator dominated, Viceroy don Francisco de Toledo. But rather than the work of one or a few men, legislation like the Toledan was the precipitation of a general stocktaking and codification of practices evolved over several decades. At about the same time, merchants and artisans in the central areas began to formalize their guilds and write ordinances. Much of this activity is simply the solidification of conquest society; on the other hand, it was also an attempt to deal with changing conditions, and it leads to the topic of our next chapter, developments in the central areas in the mature colonial period.

5
Maturity in the Spanish Indies: central areas

After the conquest epoch the Spanish Indies experienced a long time of relative stability and slow evolution, stretching forward a century and a half or more until broken in part by a new set of developments in the late eighteenth century. We call this middle time the "mature colonial period," not implying that a given society as a whole can really be considered mature or immature but in recognition that the conditions created by the conquest had entered into a certain equilibrium. As one would expect from the regional variation we have been emphasizing, the chronology of the mature period varied according to the general type of region and even within the central areas themselves. For the capital regions and the trunk lines, one can postulate the approximate dating of 1580 to 1750, with no exact year of demarcation on either end; in more isolated areas many of the characteristic signs might appear later and remain longer.

But if the dates vary, we can discern some rather uniform hallmarks of the period as a stage of development. Demographically, it is the stage after the greatest epidemics and the most precipitous decline of the indigenous population, when slow further decline was finally succeeded by a modest upturn – a trough between the quick loss at the beginning of the colonial period and the quick gain at the end of it. For central Mexico, the trough actually coincides closely with the dates just given; for more peripheral Yucatan, there seems to be a lag of several decades; for many other areas we simply lack the data.

Socially and ethnically, the period we are discussing was the heyday of the ethnic hierarchy devised by Spaniards to span and articulate a two-sector society. The three ethnicities – European, African, and Indian – had produced mixture and the mixed types had stereotyped roles, but there was not yet the inextricable blurring that took place by the final colonial years. The majority of the intrusive population was now native-born, despite the continuation of immigration, and the indigenous population had been born under European rule in reorganized local polities. Yet despite strong economic and other ties and reciprocal influence of many kinds, the two sectors were still readily identifiable, distinct, and viable entities.

The Spanish sector, with constant accretions from racial and cultural mixture in addition to new European migration, was becoming an ever larger proportion of the whole. It was far from constituting a majority, at least in areas of sedentary Indian population, but it was large enough to increase considerably the demand for European-style items of consumption as well as the ability to produce them. The local and interregional European economy grew, becoming more diversified and partially self-contained (without at all losing its basic orientation to the export of silver). This was the time of the maturation of the hacienda, an estate form more Hispanized and more based on agriculture and land than the encomienda had been; this was the time of the flourishing of *obrajes* – mills or shops which produced textiles, usually in Spanish style, for local consumption, using Spanish or Spanish-affected technology. Similarly, local Spanish craft producers proliferated in the main centers.

As we started to say at the end of the previous chapter, laws and institutions took shape by the beginning of the mature period which were to last as long as the epoch, helping define it. The practices that had gradually evolved in commerce, navigation, and the crafts found fixed expression in merchants' and artisans' guilds and in elaborately financed, convoyed, and scheduled transatlantic fleets, all of which subsisted in much the same form until they came into crises of various kinds toward the end of the period. Likewise, the inquisitional function of the church, having been carried out by the ordinary hierarchy, came to be embodied in the autonomous Tribunal of the Inquisition. Monasteries and nunneries expanded, multiplying and hiving off to represent newly self-aware and consolidated constituencies in the local Hispanic world. Among the new organizations was one whose career, perhaps by no accident, fell together with the mature period almost perfectly: the Jesuits, who arrived in the 1570s and were expelled in the 1760s.

The middle period has sometimes been seen as a time of economic depression. Yet even if we look at the seventeenth century alone, we see ups and downs; the first third of that century was the height of the all-important silver production up to that time. After that, there were varying trends at various mining sites, with some apparent overall decline, it is true, and a corresponding decline in the overall volume of trade carried by the transatlantic fleets, if the figures can be trusted. On the other hand, the interregional Spanish economy of the Indies was, as already implied, growing along with the growth of Spanish cities and society. In such areas as Querétaro and Yucatan in Mexico, the seventeenth century was the time of the consolidation of urban society and the creation of a network of European-style estates. Likewise, monumental church construction, specifically the building of cathedrals, centers on the seventeenth century. The apparently opposite trends find their common denominator in the simple passage of time; the mere working of the silver mines entailed a gradual perfection of methods followed by the relative exhaustion of easily exploited deposits and a necessity to reorganize, hence an up, down, and gradual recouping. The same flow of time brought mixture, acculturation, and many other developments internal to the American situation which tended to increase the relative size and weight of local Spanish society and the regional Spanish economy along with it.

Another concept which has been applied to our period is that of the baroque. It is true that (allowing for any number of important exceptions) the reigning style of cultural expression was more convoluted, less spare and direct in the middle period, in both Spain and the Indies, than it had been in the first half of the sixteenth century and that there was a partial reversal of the trend in the course of the eighteenth. It is also true that society became more complex in the sense of recognizing a larger number of social-ethnic types. But there is no causal connection between the two phenomena; we are not justified in speaking of any "baroque society" as if the imported cultural trend had determined the local social configuration. The social complexity was simply the result of the ongoing interaction of the original three ethnicities. This becomes clear if we look ahead to the latter eighteenth century, when intellectual trends had gone far back in the direction of simplicity and directness, whereas ethnic groupings were reaching their all-time height of complexity.

In terms of the metropolis and dynastic affairs, much of our period coincides with what has often been called the Decline of Spain under the later Hapsburgs. Yet the dimensions of this decline are not clear, and in any case, as we have seen, many scholars are not inclined to apply the concept of decline to the middle colonial period in the Indies. Also, though the switch from Hapsburg to Bourbon dynasty took place in 1700, hardly any of the characteristics of the mature period changed until half a century later.

We are left, then, with the mature colonial period as the aftermath of conquest, nearly two centuries in which the framework set by the conquest remained the same but large-scale social and cultural transformations quietly, gradually took place.

City, government, and society

The larger cities of the mature period were the same ones as in the conquest period, still built on the grid plan with a great central square, Spanish at the center and Indian at the edges. These remained not only in the same general location but literally on the same spot where they were founded. In a view of central Lima in 1687 (see Figure 6), the street plan is the same as when it was first laid out in 1535, the site of the cathedral is that of the original church, the viceroy's palace is on the same site as Pizarro's, and across the street from it is the residence of the prominent Aliaga family, which received that lot at the time of foundation. But upon this base of bedrock stability, much growth and elaboration had taken place. The illustration hardly exaggerates the extent to which the Peruvian capital was built up, and the zone of well-ordered streets and lots had been extended outward again and again.

In a famous description of Mexico City as he saw it in 1625, the Englishman Thomas Gage remarks on the strongly built private dwellings of stone and brick as well as the magnificence of the churches, monasteries, and nunneries which proclaimed the city's greatness. The artisans' and merchants' shops, which had already been numerous in the conquest period, had now expanded to the point of extensive specialization; near the square there was a street of silversmiths, another of ironworkers, another of silk merchants, and so on. So much buying and selling took place in the central square that there was a special Alameda or park where high society could assemble and parade its coaches, horses, and well-dressed attendants of various ethnic origins.

In the course of the seventeenth century a type of development like that of Mexico City and Lima, if inevitably somewhat more modest, gradually came to be characteristic of a large number of regional centers in both spheres: in the Mesoamerican, in Puebla (almost the capital's rival at times), Guadalajara, Guatemala City, Mérida, Oaxaca, and yet others, and in South America in such places as Bogotá, Quito, Trujillo, Cuzco, and Santiago de Chile, among others. Also, secondary Spanish centers inside the orbits of full-scale cities took hold and consolidated; lacking town councils, mansions, or a bevy of churches, they formed stable communities of

1. Viceregal palace
2. Cathedral
3. Municipal council building
4. Dominican monastery
5. Franciscan monastery
6. Mercedarian monastery
7. Residence of the Aliaga family

Figure 6. Center of Lima, 1687.

fairly humble Hispanics who were closely identified with the immediate locality while on the other hand looking to a nearby dominant city. If prosperous enough or distant enough, they might start on the path toward full municipal status (as did Querétaro in north-central Mexico), but their more general importance was that of bringing Spanish nuclei into closer proximity to the Indian populace of the hinterland.

While in Mexico City, Thomas Gage saw some governmental

buildings of kinds not existing before, such as a royal mint, but primarily the situation as to governmental entities was parallel to that with other aspects of urban life: elaboration on a base of identical structure, location, and function. The Audiencia may have divided into civil and criminal subsections and its judges may have become more deeply attached to the local society and economy; the viceregal secretariats may have expanded, as well as the branches of the treasury. Yet our earlier description of governmental officials essentially holds for the mature period as well, if we presume an ongoing process of localization as ever fewer officials returned to Spain, some newly arrived officials were sons or nephews of earlier holders of the same posts, and some officials, at first mainly at lower levels, were actually themselves born in the Indies. Perhaps the principal change in the structure of government was its partial extension into the Indian countryside; about that we will have more to say later in the present chapter.

As the personnel and branches of governmental institutions proliferated, so did the directives which they issued and received. Laws, decrees, and specific orders with much of the force of general law descended yearly upon the officials of the Indies from Spain. Sometimes the legislation from the metropolis had originally been initiated and even half written by the local officials themselves or by other corporations and pressure groups in the Indies; sometimes it was the brainstorm of the crown's courtiers and councilors in Madrid, especially when it related to the perennial search for revenue. Some of it was obeyed, some protested or suspended, some ignored. On the local scene viceroys, governors, Audiencias, and lesser administrators and judges issued directives of various kinds, not infrequently conflicting with each other. The process was cumulative, for new laws did not always specifically repeal the earlier ones they replaced, and even if they did, the old ones were still in some sense on the books and in the memory of those affected. The Indies swam in law, and all the more so in the viceregal capitals, the silver mining districts, and other places touched significantly by the wealth of the international economy.

From the late sixteenth century forward, only rarely did legislation threaten basic change to the already existing and codified system embracing Spanish and Indian worlds. In the central areas, at least, there was nothing of the magnitude of the mid-sixteenth-century encomienda laws, nor the fierce resistance against them. But maneuverings and attempted adjustments went on constantly. Politics became the art of fomenting directives in one's favor, petitioning for exemption from laws in one's detriment, and above all litigating over the meaning and applicability of the law in relation to one's self or cause. Thus law and litigation were much on the minds of a wide range of people, most of all the wealthy and highly placed perhaps but also, where courts and administrators were within reach, the humble, the rural, and even Indians, both individuals and corporations. In the capitals, along the trunk lines, and also in fair-sized provincial cities, lawyers, clerks, and notaries had plenty to do.

To manipulate the mushrooming body of law, one had to keep track of it. Each administrative or judicial office kept its own cedulary, or collection of laws and orders directed to it or issued by it over the years. But this was not sufficient. On both sides of the Atlantic legal scholars were forever attempting to make compilations of Indies law, either general or for a certain region or agency. The most famous is the *Recopilación de leyes de los reinos de las Indias,* published in four volumes in Madrid in 1681, but there were many others before and after it, published and unpublished. With a large enough collection of laws, one could find precedent and justification for almost any possible interpretation or course of action.

Legal battles were a serious business, occupying the time and attention of many people, costing litigants and lobbyists vast amounts of money, often bringing grief to losers and large rewards to winners. But even in treating the mature period, the heyday of labyrinthine law, we will not expend many words on legal matters, instead taking them as a constant just as we do, for example, the family strategies which were such an integral part of everything the Iberians did. Law and governmental regulation varied, it is true, not only in being better developed in some areas than in others (for which reason we will speak more than usual of government when it comes to the silver mines) but in the actual substance of the law and timing of its enforcement. Yet on closer analysis it will usually be seen that the legal variation is a function of other factors, not a true independent variable.

Take the example of shifting obligatory Indian labor, the *repartimiento,* which we will discuss at some length later in this chapter. The repartimiento lasted much longer in some areas than in others. In a word, it disappeared quickly where there were many Spaniards competing for the labor, slowly where there were few. We prefer to limit ourselves to stating the effective reason for the development, by no means denying that in each region there were legal struggles, suspension or alteration of laws, compliance or noncompliance, and so on, though we would deny that such things were in any way the cause of the regional variation. True enough, to look at the legal aspects more closely can be instructive. In central Mexico the agricultural repartimiento was already nonfunctional, effectively dead, when laws abolished it in the early seventeenth century. This is, in fact, a perfectly normal phenomenon; as the scholar who investigated the central Mexican repartimiento wrote, Hispanic American law was standardly not so much something which shaped events as "an approximation of historical happening, or a commentary upon it."[1] In the Andes, on the other hand, the ill-informed crown tried several times, at least ostensibly, to abolish the repartimiento or mita for the silver mines of Potosí. But local conditions were not right for such a move. Most Peruvian viceroys of the seventeenth century would not even try to carry out the royal directives; one or two who made halfhearted moves saw them sabotaged by officials at Potosí; the one local official who seriously tried to act was murdered, and the Potosí mita survived until the end of the colonial period. The story would vary from region to region, time to time, industry to industry. To tell it all, in all the branches of our interest, would add greatly to the length of our presentation and possibly obscure correlations and types of causation which otherwise emerge clearly, so we will in the main leave the proliferation of law and litigation to the reader's imagination.

Progressive elaboration affected not only the organizations and physical plant of the Spanish Indies but also its people. There were ethnic types in the busy streets of Mexico City which Thomas Gage felt would be unfamiliar to an English reader and called for special explanation. Mixture had complicated the original three-category ethnic scheme of Spaniard, Black, and Indian, adding the categories of mestizo, or person of mixed Spanish and Indian descent, and mulatto, mixed Spanish and Black (until a later time, mulatto actually applied also to mixtures of Indian and Black). Cultural changes accompanied and further complicated the racial mixture, resulting in a multidimensional web which must be seen in several ways if it is to be adequately understood (see Figure 7). In the original schema the three groups stood out starkly from each other; the Spaniards and their Black intermediaries constituted the Spanish world, the Indians the Indian world. The only ambivalent aspect concerned the relative ranking of the categories. In a Spanish-devised hierarchy, Spaniards of course ranked at the top, and the principle for ranking

[1] Charles Gibson, *The Aztecs Under Spanish Rule* (Stanford, Calif., 1964), p. 235.

A. Some general configurations

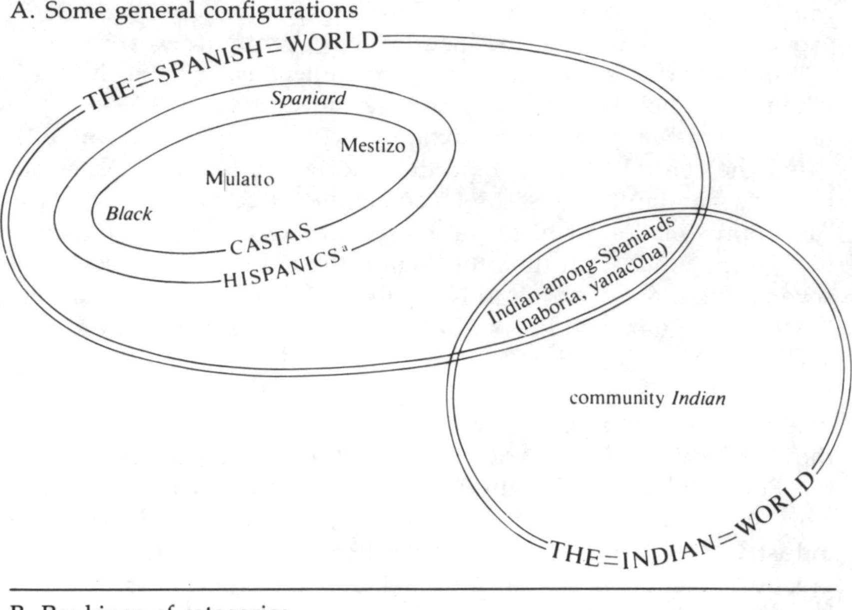

B. Rankings of categories

1. Ranking by relative position in Spanish organizations:
   - Spaniard
   - Mestizo
   - Mulatto
   - Black
   - Indian-among-Spaniards
   - Community Indian

2. Ranking by phenotype (from the Spanish point of view):
   - Spaniard
   - Mestizo
   - Indian
   - Mulatto
   - Black

[a]The term "Hispanics" is our own equivalent of the excessively ethnocentric *gente de razón*, "rational people," for non-Indians.

Figure 7. General configuration and category rankings of the Spanish American ethnic hierarchy in the mature colonial period.

the others was their degree of resemblance to Spaniards. The relative status of the two non-Spanish groupings was more equivocal. Blacks were located closer to Spaniards and acted more like them, so they ranked higher, all in all, in a social-cultural sense, whereas Indians, who looked somewhat more like Spaniards, had the edge as to phenotype; also, most Blacks were slaves, and most Indians were not, giving the latter a clear advantage in legal status. Yet in direct Black–Indian relationships it was usually the Indians who were subordinate.

The mixed types who constituted the major addition to the original ethnic scheme were Spanish speaking and belonged within the Hispanic world, though toward its edges. They were the new marginal group, assuming an ever larger role in the areas of special manual skills, petty commerce, and direct supervision of Indians. Earlier such activities had been dominated by Spanish newcomers, European foreigners, and Blacks, since those were the inhabitants of the Spanish margin in the conquest period. The principle remained the same; the intermediary functions went to those who were most recent and most ethnically distinct within the Spanish sector, but the types of people meeting such a definition had multiplied, and everything had become blurred. All the intermediary types had much in common, and they were constantly intermingling with and assimilating to each other; mestizos, mulattoes, and Blacks (in other words, everyone not considered a Spaniard or an Indian) in a sense were a single intermediary category and as such were sometimes referred to as *castas*. Blurring involved not only the facts that several ethnic types might perform the same role and that many people of each type had functions higher or lower on the scale than what was "typical" for their category; in addition an unknown and unknowable portion, especially people who were biologically mestizo, escaped their ethnic category altogether, that is, were assigned to a different one. Mestizo children who were recognized and reared by well-established Spanish parents (especially when there were no legitimate offspring) could be simply accepted as Spaniards, at a certain discount, to be sure. A common pattern was for a Spaniard to arrange the marriage of his mestizo daughter (not spoken of as such) to one of his subordinates. In fact, the acceptance of mestizos as Spaniards was so common that in the records they seem to be much rarer than they were; mestizos never did attain much corporate solidarity, and through most of the mature period the mulattoes and Blacks had a much sharper group profile.

Immigration from Spain continued to play an important role in the makeup and dynamics of society in the Indies. As with the definition of marginality, the mechanism and flavor of immigration remains constant at the same time as ethnic differences arising out of the very operation of the process complicate and change it somewhat. In the conquest period immigration was primarily a matter of Indies-based Spaniards drawing kinsmen and fellow townsmen to them; the new arrivals often had ready-made connections to help them along, but at the same time they had low initial status as juniors in a society which worshipped and rewarded seniority. Two or three generations after the conquest, however, the newcomers were no longer merely entering among those who had preceded them by a few years but were persons born in Spain functioning in a local Spanish sector comprised of members who were most often native born. In other words, where there had been only old and new, now there were what today are often called "creoles" and "peninsulares."

The important thing to keep in mind about this ethnic division within the Spanish sector is how little was made of it at the time. In the seventeenth century no one was yet called a "peninsular," and "creole" was only a derogatory nickname, except when used for Blacks born outside Africa or in the phrase *criollo de* . . . , or "native of" a given place, which could be said equally of people of any ethnicity, including Indians. Both components of the Spanish sector were equally "Spaniards," undifferentiated as to ethnic category and not very well differentiated as to function in society. The role of "Spaniard" was an essentially unitary one; the immigrant brought renewal and growth, but his striving was to join the local Spaniards already established in certain social and economic functions. One cannot say that one component was generally above or below the other. If some immigrants came as high officials and started at the top, yet even they were outsiders wanting in; far more common, in any case, was the young man starting at the bottom, the poor relative who might or might not attain success. Some became powerful merchants and entered the ranks of the older estate-owning families; others remained small farmers or traders, or less.

Both the growing numbers of ethnically mixed people native to the Indies and the continuing stream from the outside, African as well as Spanish, caused the Spanish sector in the Indies to grow constantly in size and complexity, especially at the lower and middle levels. However, though there may have been strain and blurring, the essential ethnic categorizations and rankings were still valid, and the overall framework of a two-society system, Spanish and Indian, persisted throughout the mature colonial period.

Development of the local Spanish economy

The social and ethnic expansion of the Spanish world had far-reaching economic consequences. With ever more people of Hispanic culture available to fill intermediate positions, more kinds of economic organizations could be staffed and run in the Spanish manner than before, and these same people represented an expanded local market for goods of the Spanish type. Along with the possibility of greater European-style production went the incentive for it. The basic orientation remained toward Europe; large numbers of Spaniards had poured only into those areas with assets which could be traded directly with Europe, and it was in the same places that the effects of continued race mixture and immigration were felt most quickly. The local economy remained secondary in that the ultimate object of all local Spanish activity was the acquisition of silver; there was no point in increasing meat or wheat production if the mestizos, mulattoes, and Hispanized Indians who wanted such things could not pay for them. On the other hand, with many types of products, all those who could buy European goods did so, and it was only where the need for them was combined with the inability to pay the high prices of imports that local production was viable. The markets were in the capitals, mines, and along the trunk lines, and that is where local commercial production was most intense; when more remote areas took part, it was always with production intended for the trunk line.

If Spanish growth was crucial to the local developments, what was happening in the Indian world was no less so. During the conquest period, in the central areas, vast numbers of Indians could be mobilized through their strong city-states and the well-oiled encomienda mechanism, so that some kinds of commercial production could be carried on with a maximum of unskilled and a minimum of skilled labor. By the mature period, as we have already seen, Indian numbers had fallen to a fraction of their former levels even in the most favored regions, the encomienda had lost most of its labor power, and even the Indian communities were losing some of their ability to dictate to their individual members. Spanish enterprises of all kinds were thus forced to use a higher ratio of permanent, intensive, or skilled labor. On the other side of the coin, cultural dynamism was not limited to the ethnically mixed portion of the population. Indians too acquired Spanish wants and added to the market, although for most of the mature period only urban Indians had sufficient money to count for much in the larger scheme. Whenever Indians as a group earned enough to be a significant cash market, even their traditional items of consumption would become the objects of Spanish-style enterprise. Spanish producers gradually took up coca, maize, and pulque as each became profitable in a given time and place. Some such products, cacao being a major example, spread beyond the Indians to consumption and salability among the general population.

Rural estates

The most striking single change in the local Spanish economy was the multiplication and transformation of Spanish-owned rural estates, or to say it another way, the change from encomienda to hacienda, or from estates based formally on tribute and labor rights to ones based formally on landownership. The hacienda as opposed to the encomienda is a prominent hallmark of the mature period. Remote areas retained dominant encomiendas until whatever time, sometimes as late as the approach of the nineteenth century, when the general characteristics of the mature period came to hold true for that particular region.

The factors impelling the evolution have to do with size of markets, numbers of people, and cultural attributes of segments of the population. The specific continuities and changes, however, can be expressed more tangibly in terms of land and labor (or staffing). As seen already, in the conquest period the largest and most numerous estates which channeled rural products to the Spanish cities were associated with encomiendas, but in these enterprises only the Indian tribute and labor rights were necessarily tied to the encomienda grant. Any Spaniard could apply for a piece of land, and many of those with a permanent stake in the local economy soon began to do so, whether artisans, small entrepreneurs of other kinds, long-term holders of political office, or relatives of encomenderos beginning to build independent fortunes for themselves. Long before the sixteenth century was out, the land grants of the encomenderos, especially in trunk-line situations, were a minority of the estancias (large tracts given out for stock raising), *caballerías* (areas for intense farming), and *chácaras* (a term from Quechua used in South America to mean either type of landholding, though most often the latter). As the powers of the encomienda per se diminished, and even when the encomiendas reverted to the crown, all these holdings, whether owned by encomenderos or not, remained in operation, expanding to feed the growing Hispanic population; the staple products of Hispanic enterprise were European from the beginning – meat from European animals, wheat, and other European grains, vegetables, and fruits. The properties were owned as before, the larger complexes by important city residents with majordomos seeing to actual operation, and the smaller holdings by an owner in residence who might be his own majordomo. In either case humble people at the edge of the Hispanic world provided low-level supervision as earlier, and partly Hispanized Indians, the successors to the naborías and yanaconas of the conquest period, in many cases formed a permanent skeleton crew.

Even when, by the seventeenth century, we can begin to consider the hacienda or large landed estate, selling (usually temperate) products to a local market, to have been the dominant form of agricultural enterprise in the core areas, it was anything but a closed or uniform system. In fact, in the seventeenth century there was still relatively little mention of haciendas as such; they might still be called estancias, or be left without name as amorphous entities, or be given a special combined denomination (*hacienda de labor* was a term for wheat farm, but the "hacienda" part did not yet mean what we mean by the word today, as can be seen in the common parallel form *hacienda de minas*, a silver refining plant). Their holdings were as miscellaneous as their origins. Having come into being gradually through a process of accumulation geared to the capacity of the local market rather than through any quick blanket land grabbing, they were rarely entirely contiguous. Since the early grant sites were chosen for special fertility, relative lack of competing Indian settlement, or the like, they were widely scattered. As an owner, whether encomendero or not, began accumulating, he would get further grants through relatives or puppets or buy up sites already owned by persons who were not equipped as well as he to utilize them; in either case, each site was chosen more for its own favorable qualities than for its immediate abutment on others. When the process approached its provisional conclusion, each larger hacienda would consist of a core of buildings, including some housing (an important change since the conquest period), plus a collection of estancias and caballerías, each with distinct title, usually with easy access to each other but by no means necessarily forming a solid block (see Figure 8).

Interspersed and at the edges of the area were usually smaller individual properties owned by Hispanics and substantial lands held by Indian towns. Neither type was in any special conflict with the hacienda, unless an unusually lucrative crop or market situation made it desirable to use every inch of available land intensively, which was very rarely the case. Rather, the Indians' lands fed people who were needed for hacienda work only during short periods and who would have been an economic burden to maintain full time. Likewise, the smaller properties were owned and operated by humbler Spaniards or sometimes by mestizos and mulattoes who resided in the area permanently and out of whose ranks came many of the middle-level employees of the larger estate. The piecemeal nature of hacienda holdings served the needs of the owners well.

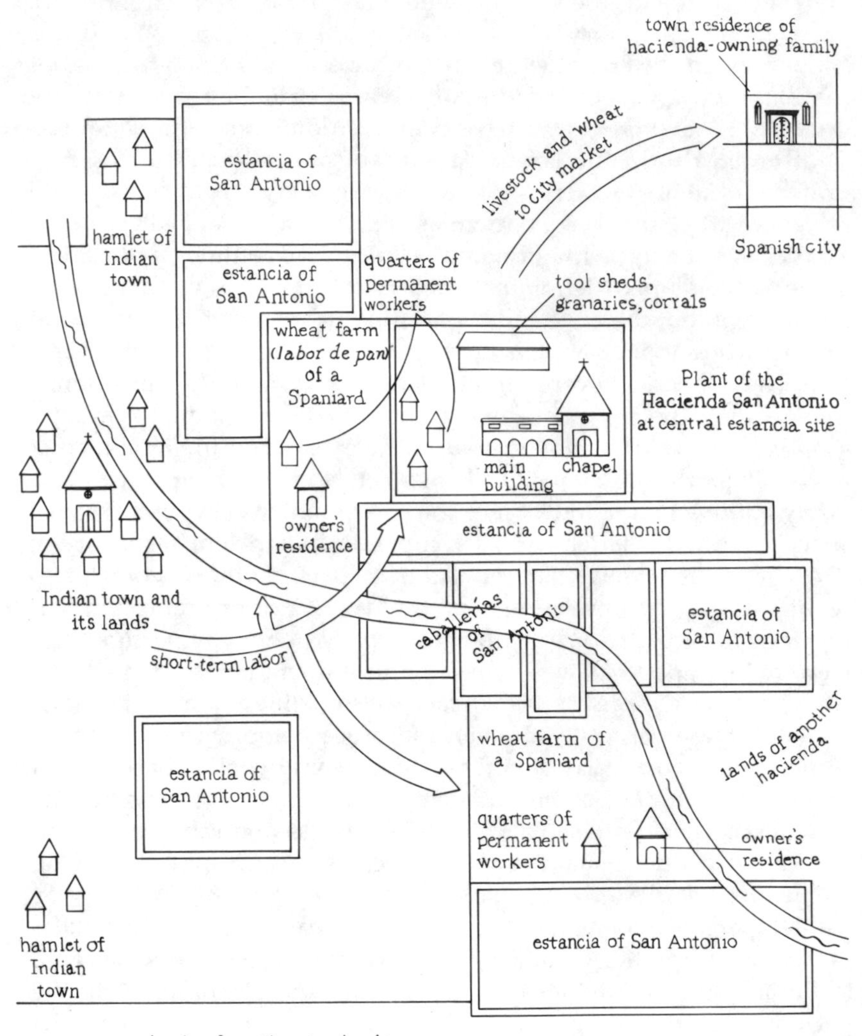

Figure 8. Schema of a central-area hacienda of the mature period: the fictitious "Hacienda San Antonio" in its context.

They had no need to treat the hodgepodges they owned as inviolable units. Rather they could sell less needed bits in bad times, trade and juggle the parts at will for a better balance, and especially they could easily distribute the various units to meet the requirements of various heirs. Dividing the inheritance by no means always meant the demise of the larger unit or of the family's fortunes, for often the most powerful heir bought the others out, or all the heirs let the most capable or oldest operate the unit as before in the interest of all.

Flux, frequent resale and subdivision, and the existence of estates of various sizes were characteristics, then, of landholding in the mature period. If the local market was weak, there might be a numerical predominance of smaller enterprises and a marked instability of ownership continuing indefinitely far into the future; the Oaxaca area is a well-known example. Nevertheless, if a certain region had a strong market situation and dense Spanish settlement, in due course it would reach a point of relative consolidation. Most of the best land would be in use, many large estates would have solidified; large owners, small owners, and Indian towns would press more tightly against each other, and informal accommodations would no longer suffice. At this stage a movement for definitive title clarification would take place. Few if any of the agglomerates had clear title to all their lands; usually there had been violations of directives that only one grant go to a person, or that grants be utilized within a certain number of years, or not sold within a set period, or used for a certain purpose. There might have been purchases from Indian individuals or corporations, which were technically invalid without specific approval by Spanish authorities, and such approval was lacking as often as not. Nothing was more common than for an owner to have expanded his activity beyond the strict area of his grant as far as needed or until he collided with competing interests. And in fact, many a family had been operating on lands for generations without any grant at all, for from the beginning the ordinary practice had been to start running one's stock, put up some sheds, and only later request a grant, perhaps when one feared that someone else might want the land.

Central Mexico, the area dominated by the great markets of Mexico City and Puebla, went through title verification, or *composición*, in two waves in the seventeenth century. Land titles, however shaky, were reviewed by the authorities; if there had been a history of peaceful possession and neighbors did not object strenuously, confirmation was forthcoming, for a fee. The process itself varied little from one place to another, but the timing depended on local conditions, occurring whenever settlement was dense enough and land values had risen high enough to justify it. Parts of northern Mexico underwent composición as late as the eighteenth century, and there were remote parts of the central areas that never experienced it through the entire colonial period.

Viewed as landholding, Spanish agricultural enterprise presents a simple straightforward evolution. At first there were few estancias, corresponding to the small Hispanic market, owned above all by the wealthiest Spaniards permanently rooted in local society; then with a larger Spanish sector, more numerous wealthy Spaniards, and a larger market, the estancias multiplied and underwent partial accretion into the larger units we call haciendas. Since markets were still much smaller and less lucrative than they would be in later centuries, the haciendas left much land in the hands of smaller owners and Indians.

When we approach the human side of estate evolution, however, complexities seem to obscure the picture entirely. A common denominator such as the estancia appears to be lacking; three periods with distinct labor procurement systems seem to follow upon each other, the stages of first the encomienda, second the repartimiento, and third informal individual labor procurement (sometimes spoken of as the hacienda stage, but this leads to confusion because the hacienda was an estate type rather than a labor recruitment system; haciendas could obtain labor in various ways, including repartimiento). Let us remember that the changing systems refer overwhelmingly to the lowest ranks of the labor force only, those doing temporary, or at least shifting and usually relatively unskilled work, who ethnically were almost always Indian. Permanent estate employees had from the beginning been taken on as individuals, usually entirely informally and certainly outside the framework of the bulk labor systems. These upper levels – the permanent laborers and the various types of supervisors and managers – present a straightforward continuity as to their role and manner of employment and equally straightforward dynamic trends: growth, in absolute numbers and in proportion of the work force of estates, corresponding to the general growth of the Hispanic world, and increasingly mixed ethnicity, corresponding to the general social trends treated earlier.

Returning to the temporary labor systems, what trends and motivations can we find in the evolution? The encomienda in its early heyday granted a lifetime monopoly on the utilization of temporary Indian labor in a given area to one Spaniard, the encomendero. The succeeding repartimiento divided temporary Indian labor ad hoc for short periods among all local Spanish entrepreneurs in rough proportion to their need. In both systems the labor was performed by the Indians as a duty or tax and was delivered to the Spaniards through the rotary labor mechanisms of the Indian corporate communities. The final mechanism is more the lack of one; temporary labor came to Spanish enterprises entirely apart from the tribute obligation, for pay and from simple economic incentive or necessity. On the face of it, the main continuity with earlier arrangements is that the temporary laborers were still mainly Indians coming from their towns at much the same times of year to perform much the same kinds of work.

Where are the lines of intelligibility in these shifts? The overall trend is toward more flexible, short-term, individual arrangements, each step being more so than the last. One can also observe that pay rose at each stage – not that it ever became high, for the temporary worker was always the lowest paid. But for encomienda labor there was usually no pay at all; for repartimiento labor, at least some pittance for self-maintenance; and for labor under individual agreement, enough to motivate the working individual to participate. In the end the movement was toward less institutionalized and more informal arrangements, with less participation of the Spanish government and the Indian corporations, but this was a zigzag trend, since the repartimiento involved the same role of the Indian governments and actually increased activity on the part of the Spanish one.

And what brought on the changes? In the full-fledged encomienda period, there was a rough balance in that the encomenderos both received most of the bulk labor and owned most of the estancias. An imbalance arose as more and more nonencomenderos became estancia owners; even if they had clear title to their land and could pay a permanent staff, they had no guaranteed access to seasonal labor. For a time the encomienda system could make the adjustments: Encomenderos diverted labor free of charge to relatives, friends, and compatriots, and in view of the great supply, they hired it out to others for very little; or nonencomenderos could circumvent the encomendero and hire labor from Indian authorities, up to a certain point. But these practices were workable only as long as encomenderos were the great majority of Spanish landowners and Indian laborers were so numerous as to be in oversupply. Both conditions reversed themselves in the course of the sixteenth century as nonencomendero landowners proliferated and Indian population plummeted. Encomenderos could no longer afford to be so generous and instead either denied short-term labor to others or charged a prohibitive price for it.

The inevitable result was subdivision: the short-term allocation of Indian labor to all Spaniards in need of it, in other words the repartimiento, or the mita as it was called in the Andean area after the indigenous rotary labor system. The more puzzling question, at first sight, is why the repartimiento system in so many areas, especially those with the strongest Spanish influx, flourished only for a relatively brief time toward the beginning of the mature period and quickly gave way to informal arrangements for most kinds of temporary labor, though it was often retained for mining, if there were mines in reach of the Indian population, and also for public works. In central Mexico it was in full force from about 1560 to 1620. Part of its unsatisfactory nature had to do with the weakness of the institutional means of enforcement. A petty, lowly paid rural official of brief tenure, appointed as judge to collect and distribute the Indians, lacked the authority and stability of the encomenderos. He might well fail to supply the expected quota of labor, or if he did supply it, he was likely to award an undue share to those in the best position to do him favors. And the Indian corporations not only had fewer workers to send than before but some of their internal mechanisms were weakening or evolving, and a good part of their constituency had become semidependents of Spaniards and managed thereby to avoid the tribute labor obligation. Spanish users of repartimiento labor not only might get a smaller quota than they expected at any given moment but their needs fluctuated in ways to which no institutional labor-supplying device could be fully adjusted. Furthermore, the system, with practically unpaid workers shifting nearly weekly in most situations, was calculated to produce callous employers and unmotivated, eternally uninitiated workers. From the beginning, employers had to hire supplemental temporary labor at times; they had much to gain by paying just a bit more, building up standing relationships with workers or intermediaries, and doing altogether without the repartimiento. The more they did so, the more they undercut it, until it collapsed. That is, it collapsed in central Mexico and some other regions. But it held on strongly, through the whole mature colonial period, in the central Andes, where Spanish penetration of the highland countryside was more restricted by the geography and where preconquest traditions of draft rotary labor were indubitably stronger than in any other indigenous culture. Guatemala too kept the repartimiento longer than central Mexico, and such tended to be the pattern for other areas remote from the trunk lines, where no numerous Hispanic population lived cheek to jowl with the Indians and subverted the system.

Haciendas of the mature period, then, had a permanent work force which, although larger than that of estates of the conquest period, was still a minority compared to shifting nonresident workers drawn at times through the repartimiento or increasingly through voluntary individual agreements. At the middle and lower levels, smaller estates of this time had the same kind of work force as larger ones. Out of the multitude of changing mechanisms emerges an additional long-term trend, that of an increasing proportion of permanent to temporary labor, which also represents an increasing Hispanization of both the labor system and the workers. It is important to remember that the pace of this development was as slow as the acculturation processes and city growth which caused it. One can imagine the trend as continuing far into the national period, finally reaching a majority of permanent workers in some regions of most intense economic activity by the late nineteenth century. The increase in permanent workers is at the expense of the temporary workers not only in the statistical sense; the permanent force was actually recruited from the temporary one, and the latter over time was becoming more like the former, not only in type of contract and remuneration but in many other ways as well. Indeed, the whole labor evolution can be conceived of in terms of changes in the proportion of elements present from the beginning and coexisting with each other.

The types of organization and the trends we have been discussing are by no means limited to agricultural estates. Close variants of these modes and trends will be found wherever Spaniards produced for a market, including in mining and textile enterprises, as will be seen. The proportion of permanent workers grows higher earlier the more technical and mechanized the enterprise is. Among the branches of agriculture, the sugar industry stood highest on the scale, and though the Spanish American mills, mainly serving a local market, could not afford a work force made up exclusively of slaves like their export-oriented counterparts in Brazil, they did have more slaves, technicians, and permanent resident workers than would have been normal for a stock and wheat hacienda. Enterprises devoted exclusively to livestock had little need of temporary workers; over time, pure stock raising tended to gravitate to the edges of the central areas, to grasslands which were in any case devoid of the sedentary Indian towns which were the principal source of temporary labor.

We are now equipped to broach a question which has occupied a great deal of the attention of historians of early Spanish America, that of the "debt peon." Only fifteen or twenty years ago, scholars felt that this debt peon (where the term came from is not clear, since it was not used during the colonial period, and *peón* by itself meant just the opposite, a temporary worker) was as central to the mature-period labor picture as the hacienda was to mature-period land tenure. Hacienda labor was thought to have been performed largely by persons resident on the estate, forced to remain there by eternally unpaid debts owed to the owner. Some scholars still hold such a view. Others, ourselves included, see only a gradual increase in the permanent force in a context of as much cheaper temporary labor as possible. There is no doubt that the permanent workers were better paid and had more side benefits than the temporary ones. They also ranked higher relative to the Hispanic world and were often in the position of giving instructions to temporary laborers. It seems to us that owners tried to minimize the number of resident workers they maintained rather than constantly grasping to hold them and get more; on the other hand, in general there was no special need for legal obligation or coercion to assure the stability of people already in a position better, at least by material criteria, than the principal alternative open to them. And even where there might be the will to hold workers, a debt obligation would not achieve that end by itself, for in the little-policed countryside they left anyway when they really wanted to, as much testimony shows. Since the need for permanent workers often coincided with profitability, many employers could satisfy that need by paying wages somewhat higher than those paid in the rest of the economy for similar work or by buying African slaves. The attempt to use debt as a holding device can be expected more in areas without a sedentary Indian population or where skilled work produced only a low profit.

Obrajes

Low profitability, in fact, was often characteristic of the next branch of the economy to be considered, textile manufacturing, which was carried on in enterprises called obrajes – the word for more or less industrial establishments of any kind but in effect appropriated almost entirely for the main exemplar of that type in the Spanish Indies. The function of the obrajes was parallel to that of the rural estates; one fed the growing local Spanish society with European-style comestibles too bulky to import, and the other clothed the same group in European-style garb it could not afford to purchase from the metropolis. Nevertheless, rural estates loomed much larger; whereas it was out of the question to bring much food across the ocean, except for wine and some condiments, clothing was much more compact and portable, and a large part of what was needed could be and was brought from Europe, constituting the largest item in Spanish exports to the Indies. Lacking Europe's large pool of trained manpower and the traditional, original materials, producers in the Indies could not possibly compete directly. They could only pick up where the ability to buy expensive European cloth left off, operating in the margin between the need for such clothing and the ability to pay for it. Upon the quality differential followed the prestige differential; everyone thought more of European cloth (*ropa de Castilla*) than of native cloth (*ropa de la tierra;* the obraje's products were called the same as the Indian textiles of the conquest period). Local textile production would thus be largely for the humble or at most for use as second-best by the better off. But obrajes had no monopoly even on this market, for craft and home production ate into it considerably. The position of the obraje was thus precarious at times and always severely limited.

Obrajes first began to appear at the very end of the conquest period, but their time of flourishing had to wait until their special constituency – the ethnically mixed, humble locally born Spaniards, and urban Indians – had grown into a substantial population element with considerable buying power. Likewise, it took a certain amount of time for the sheep population to grow from a relative rarity to a state of practical oversupply; but before the sixteenth century was out, in many places wool had become so cheap that the main expenses involved in acquiring it were shearing and transportation. By the seventeenth century the conditions were fulfilled, and the obrajes were further helped during a part of that century by some decline in transatlantic trade.

But despite these real advantages, obrajes had to face certain disadvantages not characteristic of other branches of the local economy, with results felt in labor arrangements, in the type of entrepreneur becoming involved, and in the regions where the industry was most practiced. Involving as it did a considerable amount of machinery (looms, vats, fulling mills) and a work force of necessity nearly all relatively permanent and skilled, the industry seems to imply high capital investment. Yet its return was much lower than that of enterprises connected with the international economy, and people went into it precisely hoping that they could thrive with little investment. The mainly wooden machinery could be built at relatively small expense. The more unusual measures involved labor; obrajes had to acquire permanent labor without being able to afford the all-Black slave force that would have been the expected thing for permanent, intensive, skilled work or to pay the wages the mining industry paid its workers. The obraje, far earlier than many other kinds of enterprises, had reason to try to hold on to its workers by any means available. To keep the entire establishment locked was a common enough practice, and obrajes in fact sometimes used convict labor, serving as replacements for hardly existing jails. They also frequently advanced a year's wages to a weaver and gained the legal right to hold him until his quota was filled, thus becoming one of the first types of enterprise to resort to debt as a labor-holding device (in this case abetted by locks and barred windows). In the Andean region, where the preconquest mita had sometimes involved rather long-term service, certain licensed obrajes received workers for six months or more, bending the temporary labor mechanism in the direction of permanent (something similar happened in the Andes with silver mining, as we will see). Coercion was one solution; another was to minimize the operation, keeping it extremely small, even having weaving done part time at home. The human relations could vary greatly, but all variants attempted to deal with the dilemma of requiring full-time skilled labor but being unable to pay the going rate for it.

The secondary or marginal nature of obrajes is seen also in the type of individuals owning them. The typical owner was a fairly humble person who had somehow acquired enough wealth for the investment but was neither a large estate owner, miner, nor import–export merchant. The plebeian flavor of the enterprise, however, could change in a given region if within the overall framework of the Indies economy textile production was that region's main asset; in other words, obrajes could be central and prestigious in a marginal situation. In the Quito area, with sedentary Indians but no mineral wealth, textiles to be sold in central Peru and the gold mines of Colombia were the region's principal leverage on the international economy, and consequently the best-established families there entered the business. In Querétaro, situated north of the sedentary Indian area in Mexico but otherwise extremely well located on the line from capital to mines, obrajes had both the need and the capacity to make Black slaves a substantial part of their work force, going beyond the more usual picture of a leavening of Black master weavers and bosses among a majority of Indians (of whom a large establishment might hire fifty to a hundred). Another place where obrajes seemed to transcend marginality was in Puebla. Here again many of the most prominent families were in textiles; Puebla-trained workers staffed the first obrajes all over Mexico, and even after a sixteenth-century attempt to produce silks failed, Puebla continued to make some relatively high-quality goods. But for all its success and centrality, Puebla had a special place on the Mexican scene, having been founded as a way-station and nonencomendero town.

Although any area with a considerable Spanish population was bound to have a few obrajes, the total number in the Indies must not have been too great. Quito, apparently the largest concentration, is estimated to have had some two hundred in the seventeenth century, with fewer than that in Mexico. Another area with more than its share of obrajes was Tucumán, or northwestern Argentina, which lived from supplying Potosí.

We have given so much attention to an activity of limited positive importance because its problematics illustrate those of all Spanish-style commercial production in the Indies. Whether performed in larger establishments or on a craft basis, it principally served the lower part of the local Hispanic market. Only if an item was impossible to supply from Europe, or nearly so, could locals enter the field of high quality and luxury production. Some things were altogether too bulky for import, from church towers to thirty-foot hardwood tables, so we find the building crafts very well developed by the mature period (during which most of the Indies' cathedrals were constructed) and wood carving of the highest quality being performed locally, from massive furniture to choir stalls and altarpieces. The Indies were the home of silver and came to be of inexpensive leather, and production of high-quality items of both materials proliferated. In all such branches, strongly individual local styles developed (in the face of the fact that in cathedral building, for example, architects and blueprints were often brought directly from Spain). One industry which flourished for a time was shipbuilding on the Pacific coast, on the strength of the difficulty European ships of the sixteenth and seventeenth centuries had in getting around the southern tip of South America. At first in Central America and then mainly in the Guayaquil area on the Ecuadoran coast, local yards built the ships for the crucial run between Peru and Panama. But then in the eighteenth century the time came when European ships could round the Horn easily enough, and Pacific shipbuilding went into quick decline.

While artisan production operated within this same overall framework, parts of it were quite invulnerable because they involved the necessary reworking of materials regardless of origin. Artisans proliferated wherever there were Spanish cities, until one could expect half or more of the economically active urban population to be engaged in one type of craft or another. Successful shops continued to increase productivity by the generous use of apprentices and helpers; the master-owner usually was, or passed for, Spanish, and his subordinates were usually predominantly from the castas. In the mature period many artisan guilds were formed, for social cohesion, to protect the interests of the trade as a whole, and especially to try to maintain Spanish dominance. Spanish artisans had performed a huge work of urban acculturation by training people of the other ethnicities in their crafts, but they wanted help, not competition, and as the mulattoes and others began to attain independence, those labeled Spaniards used the guilds to try to restrict the status of master and shopowner to persons in the Spanish category. But the picture was always a motley one. There is little doubt that many Spanish masters were biologically mestizo and that all the other ethnicities did manage to operate independently in the less lucrative and less prestigious trades or in smaller cities where competition was less.

The international economy

Let us turn now to the transatlantic economy which reflected itself so strongly in the local activity we have been studying, or rather, let us turn to those aspects of it that appear on the American scene, where our main interest lies. Although the international import–export sector directly employed far fewer people than the local sector throughout the mature period, it indirectly affected nearly everyone. Its structure is familiar from the conquest period – mines provided the basic economic motor, export product, and currency, while international merchants imported European goods, paying for them with the silver, which then went to Europe in return for more goods. But with time there was considerable reorganization and evolution in techniques, especially clear in mining, which we will consider first.

The silver mining industry

As was already coming to be the case in the conquest period, silver was the primary precious metal of the Indies, far outweighing gold in quantity and value produced, and there were only two great zones of silver production, the little-populated Mexican north and the high, cold south-central Andes, especially the single site of Potosí. The special distribution of the industry makes a generalizing approach to it rather difficult, but nevertheless there are some important common characteristics to be noted.

Despite an undeserved reputation for backwardness in mining techniques, the Spaniards proved to be most competent, operating on a large scale and efficiently by the standards of the time, making a large number of empirical adjustments in established methods that betray what one is tempted to call Yankee ingenuity, and even instituting one major innovation, the amalgamation process. At Potosí the mining community engineered an impressive series of reservoirs to provide needed waterpower, whereas in the arid Mexican north Spanish miners evolved what Bakewell has called the "dry technique," finding ways of reusing water and replacing waterpower with mules. Even at the end of the colonial period, when Europe had made considerable relevant scientific advances, teams of North Europeans sent to advise on mining techniques were unable to improve on Spanish American results or in most cases even to equal them.

The shafts of mines could, with time, extend some hundreds of feet in depth, and over the whole period they were becoming generally deeper and wider. There were major problems of drainage and access, solved by mule-powered whims or by adits (horizontally cut side shafts intersecting with the main one). The latter especially required large-scale investment far in advance of a return, but in view of the possible magnitude of that return, such investment was in fact forthcoming.

Not long after the discovery of any given site, the extremely rich surface deposits would give way to other ores, still rich of their kind but no longer tractable for the smelting method used up till then. The solution, found first in Mexico from the 1550s forward, then used in Peru from the 1570s on as well, was the mercury amalgamation process, which, despite the probable contribution to it of Germans and German ideas, was developed, if not literally invented, in Spanish America. The ore was pounded to a fine consistency, then mixed with mercury, and washed out after a determined period. Stamp mills, pumps, vats, and many other kinds of equipment were necessary, leading to the creation of an entity separate from the shaft operation and often located at some distance from it, near a supply of running water – the refinery. A mining camp would likely have a series of refineries along a river as its core, with the rest of the necessary elements of a Spanish settlement agglutinated to it in a somewhat chaotic, ad hoc fashion. A refinery, often called an ingenio, or mill, in Potosí and an *hacienda de minas* in Mexico, was the true headquarters of each mining enterprise, a strongly built enclosed compound which in many cases housed the owner as well as a numerous technical staff – directors of the various steps of the process – and a corps of skilled workers.

The two-part structure of the industry would have allowed for radical separation into distinct mining and refining businesses, but this rarely happened except during brief transitional periods. Rather, the refinery was the center of an estate not unlike an hacienda, varying from the latter in ways determined by silver mining's high profitability, risk, intensiveness, and technological sophistication. Close direction and technical expertise were vital; the owner often came directly out of the mining milieu, remained effective as a day-by-day supervisor rather than relying on an administrator, and resided at or near the refinery. Persons who in other branches of life would have been humble labor bosses were here more influential, better remunerated, and proportionately more numerous; the *azoguero* (mercury man) who directed the timing and mix of the amalgamation of ores was in many ways the most important person in the whole enterprise, capable of doubling or halving the profit level through his decisions. Skilled, permanent workers loomed far larger in a mining business than in a normal hacienda. Ultimately the industry tended toward *all* permanent workers, but in some situations temporary labor remained significant, as we will see, and everywhere there was the distinction between the more skilled refinery workers and the more quickly shifting, less skilled pitmen.

A silver mining operation was also like an hacienda in its integration, combining not only a refinery and shaft but, to the extent possible, support enterprises such as charcoal supply, mule breeding, and production of comestibles, each a half-separate unit, all spread over a considerable area but under unified management and with personnel circulating over the whole. But if a "normal" hacienda was in considerable flux, frequently losing or gaining parts or changing hands altogether, a mining estate was even more apt to be relatively ephemeral, corresponding to the boom-and-bust nature of the business. Nevertheless, a major silver mining site had a good measure of general stability, lasting often for several generations and becoming a full-fledged Spanish municipality. The principal mineowners at any given time, like other dominant estate owners in their respective localities, could be counted on to man the councils of the mining towns.

Considering how relatively weak and inactive government in the

Indies generally was, it may seem surprising to find the crown and its agents a major factor in the mining industry. Why should this be? Because until recently the main activities of any government were to guarantee the status of its subjects and collect revenues for itself, and the silver industry was marvelously constituted to produce revenue. In law, subterranean rights belonged to the crown, which received a share of mining production in return for delegating its rights to individuals. That share, called the *quinto,* or fifth (though it could be reduced to a tenth or less, depending on the profitability of mining in any specific locality), was the source of the bulk of surplus revenue accruing to the crown from its American possessions, along with other silver-related income from the sale of mercury and the minting of silver coins.

Until very recently, governments, lacking vast manpower and numerous tightly organized agencies, could operate successfully only within certain well-defined narrow spheres, as in customs collection. Silver production, tied down to a few restricted locations for relatively long periods of time, was admirably suited to this framework. The crown was fortunate indeed that the Indies were richer in silver than in gold, for scattered and transitory gold mining was a tax collector's nightmare. Mercury, the material vital to the amalgamation process, gave the royal government an even stronger hold. There were only two significant sources of mercury in the Spanish empire, Almadén in Spain itself and Huancavelica in Peru. With such extreme geographical concentration of the product and its quite manageable total bulk, the crown was able to make mercury a royal monopoly and sell it to the miners. Miners were thus dependent on the crown for a necessary factor of production, and at the same time government officials acquired a reliable measure of output and possible tax fraud, for there was a known standard ratio between mercury expended and silver produced at any given time and place.

When we come to the labor picture, we must make a quite sharp contrast between the Mexican and Peruvian situations. As seen before, in the conquest period it proved impossible to use the encomienda and later the repartimiento as the basis for short-term labor for the bulk of the Mexican mines, located north of the orbit of the sedentary Indian population, whereas in Peru, and at Potosí especially, these devices successively found large-scale application. Though the distances traversed were great, the mines fell within the general sphere of the highland Indians, who were already familiar with the activity, and the strong Andean rotary labor tradition included relatively long-distance movement and long-term service.

In Mexico, essentially the entire lowest component of the labor force migrated to the north permanently, losing direct connection with the central Mexican towns from whence it came. These migrants at first retained their indigenous language and even some transplanted corporate strength, settling in suburbs around the mining camps according to subethnic divisions, giving many Spanish mining practices indigenous names, and putting their stamp on the nature of work arrangements. Yet they were considered and functioned as naborías, paid as individuals, devoting full time to a Spanish activity, immersed in a Spanish context. Over the generations not only did they gain much mining expertise but they underwent strong racial mixture and acculturation, giving rise to a Spanish-speaking, mobile social type very different from the rural Indian of central Mexico.

At Potosí, the device of the repartimiento, or the short-term, ad hoc allocation of Indian draft rotary labor, was adapted to provide workers for digging, ore hauling, and the like. Because nearly all mine work demanded a certain amount of training and skill and because the distances involved were great, the term of service was extended to several months, as was the interval between terms. This was the famous mita (the word is a magnificent symbol of the continuity in Andean labor practices, for it was used first in Inca times for rotary labor, then for labor obligation under the encomienda, and finally for repartimiento labor; all such labor, in mines or not, received the denomination "mita" in Peru and surrounding regions). Denounced from the sixteenth century until today as a scourge, the mining mita remains little understood in either its mechanics or its results. Some things about its general effects on the Andean mining situation are nevertheless clear enough. The mita served as an umbilical cord between Potosí and the vast Indian countryside of Charcas and southern Peru from which the workers came. Doubtless there were many repercussions in the Indian towns and villages; but the most apparent effect was that of cutting down drastically on the rate of Hispanization of the workers. Not only did they come to the mines only once in several years, but even then they remained inside locally based units with local supervision, and the number of mita workers was so great that they colored the whole milieu. Rarely if ever did they learn to speak Spanish. In fact, their numbers at the richest mining site in the Indies made them into a major market and gave market viability to Indian products as little used by Spaniards as chuñu and coca, which in turn impelled Spaniards into the production and sale of such items and created many a fortune from what would otherwise have been marginal and unremunerative activity. The Mexican mineworkers were a market too, but not to the same extent and mainly for standard Spanish products.

In both situations a stratum of highly skilled, more strongly rooted workers, mainly associated with the refineries, stood above the less skilled, more quickly shifting diggers and carriers; in both cases there is every reason to think that the skilled were recruited primarily from among the unskilled. In both cases the refinery workers originally contained a significant component of Black slaves (as usual associated with intensive, remunerative work) who gradually receded, at least as a separate, identifiable element, in the face of the increasing mastery of Indian or mestizo specialists. In the case of Peru, we know that many mita workers stayed at Potosí voluntarily after the end of their terms of service, over the protests of the authorities of their home units; we know too that the Potosí mita allowed the forced migrants to be free a portion of the time, and that during these free periods they hired themselves out for the same tasks but at better pay. However, the difference in the two situations at the lower levels mirrored itself at the upper, for the skilled laborers at Potosí, in contact with the Indian world through the mita workers and constantly being renewed from that source, were far more Indian in culture and language than their Mexican counterparts. Nevertheless, even in the Peruvian case there was the same strong tendency for permanent, voluntary, relatively skilled workers to take over more and more of the industry's roles.

As to overall production trends, the use of amalgamation and the general maturation of the industry brought a rising curve through the late sixteenth century to a high in the first decades of the seventeenth, with Peru contributing the larger share. After that, deeper shafts, greater necessity for drainage, and related problems began to demand a larger scale of operation, more capital expenditure, and the opening of new veins, all of which took time, so that in the middle to late seventeenth century there was a decline in production, although not as steep as once thought and not closely connected with general Indian population decline, at least not in Mexico, where the number of workers involved was small and the two curves run counter to each other for most years. Another crucial factor in rising or falling production was mercury supply; whether the supply of mercury was a truly independent variable or was consciously allocated by the crown to reward high productivity and penalize low yields, in any case Mexico had to contend with low supplies in the second half of the seventeenth century, whereas

Peru, with its own source, suffered less. Then in the eighteenth century Peruvian production long continued to decline, whereas Mexican productivity revived, overtaking Peru's in a rise that corresponded to the trend of mercury production at Almadén (though the direction of the causality here is not entirely clear).

International commerce

What of the other major sector of the international economy, the merchants who traded the silver we have been speaking of for imported merchandise? At the present point in time, merchants of the middle colonial period are very little studied, and we can say all too briefly what we know or suspect about them, a good deal of it deduced from comparison of the better-known preceding and following periods. Evidently a process of localization – greater involvement in the local economy, society, and polity – was under way, resulting among other things in a greater autonomy of merchants based in the Indies and their rise in local position and prestige. By the early seventeenth century the transatlantic companies based in Seville seem to have broken in two: The Spanish-based firms sent merchandise only as far as the American ports, where other firms based in Mexico City and Lima bought up the goods for resale with the silver accumulated since the last fleet, or so it would appear from the impressionistic accounts we have of the trade fairs held on each fleet's arrival. The large merchants of the viceregal capitals still needed to maintain a high degree of liquidity, but free of the heavy hand of Seville, they had no reason to shy away from local investments.

A favored type of mercantile involvement was the almost inevitable one with the silver mining industry, source of that liquidity which was the large traders' advantage. From a quite early time merchants became the suppliers, or *aviadores,* of individual miners, advancing them goods on credit and usually also lending them coin with which to pay wages in return for a monopoly on mine supply, the highest possible prices for their goods, and often the right to see all the miner's silver through the mint. By the latter seventeenth century, when the crown had stopped selling mercury on credit and miners' needs were even greater, there had come into existence a type called the "silver merchant," or *mercader de plata,* who bought unminted silver at a discount, paying in coin. Such figures were apparently the principal financiers of the industry and likely also the ones to profit most from it. An unknown number of aviadores and silver merchants were drawn into actual mine ownership, although this seems to have been an expedient they would ordinarily rather have avoided. Presumably the silver merchants were the selfsame great importers and wholesalers of the viceregal capitals, or their agents, but even so basic a connection cannot be taken as absolutely established at present.

Another branch of commerce dominated by Indies-based firms was the import of Chinese silks through Manila, which, if not exactly a local enterprise, then at least did not involve the metropolis. Merchants of the Indies capitals diverted millions of pesos in silver to buy, through their own employees and junior partners, textiles which they sold on the American market in quite direct competition with fine cloths from Europe. Another kind of foreign trade, contraband dealing with non-Iberian Europeans, was probably becoming important, especially in areas bordering the Caribbean, but the topic is almost inherently unstudiable. The import merchants also began to take an active part in the interregional economy in ways we know little about; one way was to finance the operations of low-level governmental administrators in outlying areas. Another way was to buy in the Indies the landed property which earlier merchants had aspired to acquire in Spain, though still for the same reasons: credit stiffening, diversification, and a basis for lasting familial wealth and influence.

The merchants of the capitals now had a local institutional base in the Consulados, or merchant guilds, of Lima and Mexico City, which united most of the large importers in their membership. By this time one also finds Indies-based merchants taking over middle-level posts in branches of the royal treasury (accounting always having been their forte) and also gaining influence over other officials by acting as their bondsmen, whereas in the conquest period, mainly lower-echelon merchants or nonmerchant entrepreneurs had appeared in these roles.

Such heavy economic and political involvement brought a corresponding social change; the successful large merchant began to expect to spend the rest of his life in the Indies, marrying and establishing his family there. There too he might make the ecclesiastical endowments that topped off a family's name, establishing a chaplaincy, even donating funds for an altarpiece, chapel, or whole church. Yet such indications as we presently have tend to show that the great majority of the large import merchants were still born in Spain itself; presumably this occurred through mechanisms that are known much better for the late eighteenth century, and we will discuss them when we treat that period. International commerce had thus become half integrated into the local scene in many respects, but only half, and the local position of the large merchants had not yet reached the pinnacle it was to attain by the end of the colonial period.

Ecclesiastical matters

The secular clergy and the orders

The mature period saw the filling in of the framework of bishoprics, each centered on a major Spanish settlement, which was created during and just after the conquest. By the mid-seventeenth century the cathedrals of the viceregal capitals and some other central-area cities (such as Cuzco, La Plata, Puebla) had become great vaulted stone basilicas with imposing staffs of dignitaries; large tithe incomes, reflecting the size and prosperity of those regions' economies, supported such magnificence. Bishoprics based in cities off the trunk line, on the other hand, lagged behind in all these respects. In general, ecclesiastical entities were even more closely intertwined with the local Hispanic population than were governmental ones. Local Hispanics not only viewed church buildings as the very symbol of their corporate communities, taking a corresponding interest in church construction and decoration, but they actually entered into ecclesiastical organizations on a large scale, not only through various kinds of lay associations but as ordained clerics. From the time the first Indies-born generation came of age, prominent families standardly sent some of their sons into the church. Overall they showed a preference for the secular clergy, perhaps as less arduous for their offspring than life in one of the regular orders but surely also for important considerations having to do with general familial strategy.

Whereas the donation a family made to subsidize a son's entry into one of the orders was financially a dead loss, the funds used to set up a secular cleric could remain under family control; rather than paying cash, the family instituted a chaplaincy, promising that a yearly income from one of its properties would be paid to the son as chaplain, all under the direction of the family patriarch as patron. Moreover, the secular cleric was an economic free agent and could be useful in the management of family affairs; he could acquire and own property, which he would eventually return to the rest of the family by bequest. Small wonder then that the locally born were soon a numerical majority in the secular clergy and that when new parishes were created the seculars usually received the assignment, whereas the orders only kept the parishes they already had or at most made acquisitions on the far periphery. Just when and where the locally born became a majority among secular priests is not yet fully known, but it may have been a widespread and early phenomenon, possibly antedating the end of the sixteenth century. One hint is that by the second quarter of the seventeenth century almost a third of the bishops appointed in South America were born in the Indies, and this despite the fact that locals mainly entered at the bottom, concentrating primarily in the lesser and less well paid posts at first. From such a beginning they gradually came to dominate all positions held by seculars short of the bishoprics themselves, including the dignities of the cathedral chapters.

The mendicant orders too received local recruits, but the situation was different in two ways: The Spanish-born held their own numerically, and members born on both sides of the ocean competed for the same short-term positions as priors and provincial heads. In most branches of activity in the Indies, peninsular-born Spaniards either took marginal roles no one else wanted, or began at the bottom with relatives who had sent for them, or functioned in spheres normally dominated by them, such as transatlantic commerce or the highest levels of the official hierarchies. Only among the mendicants did they circulate in exactly the same milieu and at the same level as the locally born, with the result that two parties formed, tensions were felt, and the word *criollo,* or "creole," surfaced here earlier than in other spheres as a derogatory label for local Spaniards. By the early seventeenth century it was necessary to institute the *alternativa,* under which arrangement provincial superiors were elected first from one party and then the other in turn; the solution was not itself new, but had originated in Spain as a way of settling the regional factionalism which was rife there as well.

If the orders were in stasis as to parishes and had lost much of their early clear dominance of the ecclesiastical world, yet they too were undergoing certain kinds of growth and elaboration. The monasteries located in Spanish cities grew in architectural splendor and in number of resident friars; wherever the economy permitted urban consolidation, the orders began to subdivide and proliferate until there were many more monasteries than the original three or four belonging to the Franciscans, Dominicans, Augustinians, and perhaps Mercedarians. Convents of nuns were established and grew in size and number until they rivaled the monasteries, drawing membership almost exclusively from prominent local families who paid a substantial dowry toward the support of their daughters and the establishment. Hospitals were often associated with the new foundations, both monasteries and convents. The donations which all monastic institutions received from the Spanish populace allowed them to acquire properties as a source of income and supply; each establishment would normally come to hold one sizable rural estate and some urban rental property. Such estates were a standard part of the scene, and the more peripheral the area, the larger a proportion of total Spanish landholding they represented, but by no means did they dominate landholding in general. The false supposition of later generations that "the church" held most of the land comes from the chaplaincies; it is true that hardly an hacienda was without at least one ecclesiastical encumbrance, but as we have seen, these left the properties in lay hands, served lay ends, were paid largely to family members or dependents, and often remained under full family control.

The Jesuits

One addition of the mature period to the regular orders was of so distinct a type that it nearly represented the formation of a new ecclesiastical sector. The Jesuits, not yet having been created as an order when the conquests began, entered the Spanish Indies in force only from the 1570s onward. Sometimes greatly admired, sometimes violently opposed, often the center of propaganda battles, the Jesuits have frequently been misunderstood, seen as something without parallel, but their divergence from the rest of the ecclesiastical world was in many respects less than it appears. The most important element was time. The Jesuits were chronologically out of kilter with a basic sequence in the development of the Spanish Indies. They missed the whole conquest period, then had their epoch of foundation and great burst of energy when most other groups and institutions were in a period of slow consolidation. All this did little for their popularity with other branches of the church, which saw themselves threatened and cast in the shadow. A time differential was also important in the larger picture across centuries and nations. The mendicant orders were creations of the late Middle Ages, whereas Jesuit organization was the product of a later time with its stronger centralization and hence more international character, a time that focused even more on secular affairs; thus the Jesuits were even more distant from the tradition of the cloister than the mendicants, who themselves were not pure monastics.

Given these antecedents, Jesuit activity falls into some rather expectable patterns. Like everything else Hispanic, Jesuits concentrated in cities, especially the larger ones, with their headquarters and greatest establishments in Lima and Mexico City. An order of intellectuals and educators like the Dominicans, their bitterest rivals, the Jesuits, with their well-organized *colegios,* largely displaced the Dominicans in the secondary education of the well-to-do. The donations they attracted went to the usual ends, sumptuous churches which in some places rivaled cathedrals, and rural properties as a lasting economic base. With their organizational urges and business acumen, the Jesuits usually involved themselves in the most capital-intensive, lucrative aspects of the rural economy and ran their properties directly, thereby standing out from the other orders, whose holdings, usually leased out or left to lay majordomos to run, acquired no distinct profile among the bulk of Hispanic haciendas.

Once established in the core areas, and they were well on the way to it by the end of the sixteenth century, the Jesuits began to cast about for a field of endeavor among the Indians which would be comparable to that of the other orders; but between the mendicants and the seculars, all parishes anywhere near the center were already claimed. Like many late arrivals before and after them, the Jesuits had to move out to the margins, perforce dealing with scanty semi-sedentary or nonsedentary Indian populations; the two main fields of action were the far north of Mexico and the far southeast of Spanish South America, or "Paraguay." Sometimes seen by distant observers as some plot to create an independent state in the remote fastnesses, the peripheral establishments were chosen simply because they were still available. And though they could not operate exactly like a rural parish in the Valley of Mexico, Jesuit communities were organized on the same principles adopted by all the orders on the periphery, as their name of *reducciones* clearly betrays.

The Inquisition

Another ecclesiastical feature of the mature period was the Holy Office of the Inquisition, which, although a royal arm, had the purpose of combating religious unorthodoxy and was manned at the upper levels by churchmen. Absent from the conquest period, during which time inquisitorial functions were delegated to the bishops, the institution itself came to the Indies with the founding of two tribunals in the early 1570s in the expected places, Mexico City and Lima, followed later by a third in Cartagena on the Caribbean coast of New Granada. In the Indies, far from the large ethnic-religious minorities of Iberia and denied jurisdiction over the Indians, the Inquisition tended to lack clients. Cases of crypto-Jews and Protestant foreigners were relatively rare, as were executions: a total of some thirty for the great tribunal of Lima over about 250 years, for example. The most serious action against foreigners and Jews came in the second quarter of the seventeenth century. During the time of the union of the Spanish and Portuguese crowns (1580–1640), Portuguese merchants, starting from their position in the African slave trade, had gained a significant share of the general international commerce of the Spanish Indies. Never appreciated by their Spanish competitors, who managed to keep them largely out of the Consulado, the Portuguese were particularly vulnerable because of the large proportion of practicing Jews in their midst. As Portuguese-Spanish ties began to fray and the breaking point approached, xenophobia began to build up in the Hispanic population, most especially among Spanish merchants. In this context the Inquisition brought many of the Portuguese traders to trial, convicted them of Judaism, burned several at the stake, and confiscated large amounts of property.

For the rest, the Inquisition's stock in trade was helping to keep the peace by dealing with certain kinds of deviant behavior. A large proportion of its cases had to do with blasphemy (which often came down to settling family arguments and taming practitioners of riotous living), sorcery (mainly a matter of psychopaths), and bigamy, which was not uncommon in a world where so many males moved about in search of a living. The Inquisition also served as a desultory censor of books.

This is not the place to go into the procedures of this perhaps fascinating but much overpublicized and misconceived institution. A court with its own sovereign jurisdiction, it took its place on the social-political scene as one more independent agency along with the Audiencia, the cathedral chapter, the Jesuits, and so on, each making shifting alliances with the others and tailoring its action to gain maximum advantage for itself. The Inquisition was in no sense controversial among the Hispanic population generally; to become an inquisitor or to work on the staff was an honor as well as an assured living. There was also a network of lay agents, or *familiares,* of the Inquisition, stretching far beyond the viceregal capitals to other Spanish settlements, and to hold this position had an honorific significance not unlike sitting on the local city council.

Saints of the Indies

Sainthood, one might think, is a universal factor independent of time and place, much less of the social-economic context. Yet the fact is that those persons of colonial Spanish America who were greatly renowned for holiness in their own time and were accepted later as saints of the church concentrate in the mature period, mainly the early part of it, and tended to be located in the major Spanish settlements. They also had a strong tendency to be socially marginal – humble or female – and to stand somewhat outside the normal hierarchies. It is as though saintliness were a certain kind of reaction to a fully established situation. Often locally born, the saints also represent another facet of the maturation of local Hispanic society and its ecclesiastical component. To mention one or two of them, St. Rosa of Lima (died 1617) was born in that city of Spanish parents who had a certain position but were not rich or powerful; she never entered a convent but cultivated the spiritual life at home in an atmosphere incorporating music and flowers as well as strict ascetic practices. St. Martín de Porres (died 1639) was an illegitimate mulatto, also born in Lima, son of a prominent father and a free Black mother. Originally put to apprenticeship with a barber-surgeon, he implored his father to get him accepted into the Dominican order, which indeed occurred, although in view of his background he was and remained a lay brother rather than a fully ordained member. Fray Martín was notable for alms campaigns and benevolence to all, including abandoned children and animals.

Intellectual life

To say a few words about intellectual developments (more than a few would lead us into a potentially endless discussion of individual works and authors) is almost to continue with our ecclesiastical topic, since the various branches of the church provided a livelihood for a large proportion of all those dedicated to intellectual pursuits. The one organization most central to this whole aspect of life, however – the university – was under royal auspices. It is true that many of the universities of the Spanish Indies grew out of schools run by one of the orders, and of the more than twenty so-called universities which there eventually came to be in the Spanish Indies, those of the minor rank, the numerical majority, were mainly associated with the Jesuits or Dominicans. But the major universities, the two greatest located of course in Mexico City and Lima, with other substantial ones in one or two important secondary cities of each of the two orbits, were autonomous organizations, modeled on the universities of Spain and funded independently, though most meagerly, from the royal treasury. The incomes of the permanent chairs rarely sufficed to support their occupants, who were usually prominent ecclesiastics, judges, and other professional men. Theology, law, and (a poor third) medicine were the main curricula, for primarily the universities were professional schools, designed to train the sons of local Spaniards to be priests, lawyers, and sometimes physicians. The method and substance of instruction followed those of Spain in every detail except for the existence of some chairs in Indian languages; even these were aimed at the professional needs of priests in rural parishes.

Beyond universities and seminaries, perhaps the principal framework for intellectual activity were the entourages of the viceroys and archbishops, who acted as patrons up to a point, as did bishops, governors, and Audiencia heads in lesser centers. The larger cities had acquired theater buildings, sometimes owned by one of the orders, by the late sixteenth century; the same towns had printing presses (since the conquest period, at least in the case of Mexico City), and books of all kinds, mainly imported from Spain, were sold by the thousands every year. It appears that nearly everything published in Europe circulated quite freely in the Indies, except out-and-out Protestant tracts; ecclesiastical institutions as well as some private individuals owned impressive collections of books, tending to the religious and the orthodox because of the readers' taste and profession more than because of any pressure from the Inquisition. All the activities we have mentioned were highly concentrated in the viceregal capitals, and promising individuals from the provinces were often drawn there; the poet (and secular priest) Bernardo de Balbuena left Guadalajara for Mexico City, and when he wrote his major work *Grandeza mexicana* it was in praise of the capital rather than of the provincial town. A single tight circle, with a strong ecclesiastical and high-society flavor, used all the intellectual avenues, making them a closely knit milieu. Thus the awarding of a higher degree at the university became an event of pomp and circumstance, with a cavalcade, a ceremony at the cathedral, congratulations by the archbishop and viceroy, and much expensive feasting to be paid for by the candidate.

Within this context there soon developed the type of the Spanish American intellectual, little different to be sure from the peninsular or more general European prototype. On the economic plane, he held several part-time, lowly paid posts in some way related to intellectual activity, hoping to employ himself fully and remunerate himself adequately from the totality of them; on the intellectual plane, partly as a result of his necessarily many-faceted career, his production was equally broad, varied, and fragmented. Almost always he wrote belles lettres, history, and essays of a more technical or scientific nature.

A full exemplar is the famous don Carlos de Sigüenza y Góngora, born in Mexico City and flourishing there through the second half of the seventeenth century. A secular priest, though without a parish, he held the chair of mathematics and astrology at the University of Mexico City, was chief cosmographer (geographer-mapper-engineer) of New Spain, chaplain of a hospital, examiner of artillery, accountant of the university, chief almoner of the archbishop, and so on. His writings include: poetry; voluminous local history and Aztec antiquities, including archaeological essays; journalistic narratives of travels and current local events, some commissioned by the viceroy; treatises on mathematics and astronomy, and related almanacs. The career of don Pedro de Peralta Barnuevo, born in Lima (died 1743), is a near twin to that of Sigüenza, down to holding the chair of mathematics and being chief cosmographer of his realm (although for once he was not a cleric), and his production too falls into the identical categories.

Wide-ranging figures such as these had a characteristic facility of mind and eloquence, but their method was better designed to keep abreast than to originate. Greater depth, originality, and specialization were sometimes found among members of the orders, whose less fragmented lives were more propitious to concentration. Thus the mid-seventeenth century Nahuatl grammar of the great Jesuit linguist Horacio Carochi is hardly equaled to this day, while Sor Juana Inés de la Cruz, a Jeronymite nun, contemporary and compatriot of Sigüenza, is one of the classic poets of the Castilian language, recognized and read in many countries. (Such praise must be withheld, however, from the general run of the numerous chronicles of individual orders, often commissioned by the superiors, done superficially and in a highly partisan manner, incorporating great undigested chunks of the previous histories of the order.)

All observers have agreed that the general hallmarks of intellectual expression in the middle colonial period were exuberant intricacy, formalism, and the indirectness of allegory, allusion, conceit, or distance, rather than the relative directness and simplicity of the conquest period. The style or set of mind is often called "baroque," a posterior term applied also, and indeed primarily, to the larger trend in Spain and Europe which the writers of the Indies faithfully mirrored. Fully formed examples appeared in the Indies by the first decade of the seventeenth century and continued in evidence far into the eighteenth.

Nevertheless, the concept of the baroque does not account for all the intellectual phenomena of our epoch. The latter sixteenth century was the time of composition of some remarkable works describing the American scene in a way both more analytical and more synthetic than had been the mode of the writers of the conquest period, though still with the same straightforward vocabulary and outlook. The Jesuit José de Acosta in his *Natural and Moral History of the Indies* differentiated types of areas according to topography, organization of the Indian population, and presence of silver, not neglecting to point out when New World phenomena gave the lie to Old World lore; the Mexican conqueror's descendant Gonzalo Gómez de Cervantes surveyed every branch of his country's economy in a spirit of realism and close, acute observation; the Peruvian mestizo Garcilaso de la Vega el Inca wrote his elegant, nostalgic *Royal Commentaries* in praise of both sides of his ancestry, the conquering Spaniards as well as the conquered Incas. And such works, rather than stopping abruptly at 1600, continued to appear far into the seventeenth century, works as important as Jesuit Bernabé Cobo's histories, the judge Solórzano's survey of Indies law, and Carochi's grammar of Nahuatl.

But returning to the baroque, its mannerisms indeed dominated the belles lettres of the seventeenth and early eighteenth centuries, from the ephemera of poetic tournaments in honor of a viceroy's arrival to the poems and plays of Sor Juana Inés, which become so much a part of the international literary fashions of her era that there is, on the face of it, little in their form or content to hint that they were composed in Mexico. Outside belles lettres, the bulk of writing became, if not exactly more "scholastic" as is often asserted, then surely tending more to lean on previous authority, to memorize, allude, and quote, rather than to break new ground or improve on the authorities. And yet hardly had this tone become predominant when some writers, including ones as prominent and as "baroque" as Sor Juana Inés and Sigüenza, began to strain against it.

One might ask, as we did of international commerce, to what extent the world of the intellect, meaning here European-style scholarly and literary endeavor, was localized, and what were the trends over time. The matter has several dimensions. Institutions of higher learning existed, were a permanent and significant part of the scene, and their students were nearly all locally born. In the universities, the faculty as well was increasingly native-born (we are told that the faculty of Lima's San Marcos was entirely so by mid-seventeenth century), although the almost equally important Jesuit establishments long remained under the dominance of figures born in Spain or other European countries.

As to production in the Indies, throughout the mature period many works were being written in a broad variety of genres, a certain number of them of high excellence and lasting general interest. Some of the authors were Spaniards writing in and about the Indies, others were local Hispanics. It is notable that during the early part of the mature period much of the very best writing was done by people with deep experience of both hemispheres, so that it would be hard to say to which they belonged more: Balbuena the poet, born in Spain, growing to maturity in the Indies, then returning to Spain, and finally to the Indies again; Caviedes the caustic poet of Lima, born in Peru but educated in Spain; Ruiz de Alarcón the dramatist, born in Mexico but writing in Spain; and Garcilaso de la Vega, also growing up in his native Cuzco but living in Spain most of his life and writing there in his later years. Then by the second half of the seventeenth century the dominant writers of the Indies, like Sigüenza, Sor Juana Inés, or Peralta, were – once again with the major exception of the Jesuits – often locally born and educated, with no direct experience of the Old World.

On the other hand, if one thinks in terms of circulation among a public, it appears that the great majority of the books read and plays performed were of Spanish origin, nearly as much so at the end of the mature period as at its beginning. As with textiles, so too in writing peninsular Spanish or general European production rested on a much larger base of producers and consumers and benefited from greater time depth, so that the Indies, barely getting started, could hardly compete directly except where something tailored to a special occasion was required, whereas the Castilian product had an insuperable prestige. We have also seen that peninsular Spanish production tended to remain predominant with whatever items were easily and cheaply transportable, and nothing is more so than books, genres, styles, and general concepts.

If we look for trends in the content of writing in the Indies, the situation is complex. On the one hand there is a gradual broadening away from the local and the immediately contemporary. Conquest-period writing (though done by peninsular Spaniards) was overwhelmingly primary description of the conquest and the new local phenomena or discussion of how to deal with them. Early mature period writing still concentrated on the Indies but abstracted from the immediate scene in various ways, in search of a general assessment. This done, writers were, by the time of the "baroque," freer to engage in types of belles lettres, theology, history, or scientific endeavor that were international in scope. The later productions tend to look more derivative, but the mere involvement in such things represents a partial maturation and autonomy in local society. And side by side with works of international flavor, some baroque writers continued to cultivate local themes. What is more, they did so in a new way, consciously seeking to exalt their own areas in a spirit of local patriotism; for example, such was Sigüenza's ultimate purpose in his writings on Aztec history. Even works that appear to be set in Madrid or Athens sometimes reveal a close application to the local scene, and if the writers of the Indies generally speaking employed an international conceptual vocabulary, later scholars have not yet done the kinds of investigation that would show the special modulations and localisms which are doubtless there. But granting a local substratum in baroque writings of the Indies, it still appears that the greater originality of concept and language was in the realms of everyday life and informal or folk literature which is lost to us, except in its much-changed equivalent carried down to our own times.

All in all, Hispanic society along the Indies trunk lines showed, by the mature period, a degree of development of the framework and substance of European-style intellectual activity that would seem remarkable were it not entirely consistent with that society's wealth, comprehensiveness, stability, and progressive localization or integration of all branches of endeavor originally centered in Spain. At the same time we observe a continuing dependence and derivativeness, inevitable in so new a foundation with such excellent lines of communication to the metropolis and comparable to the situation with international commerce, where the Indies activity was but one segment of a much larger interconnected whole from which it could not be entirely separated.

The Indian world

To what extent do the trends we have observed in the various sectors of Hispanic society apply to the "Indian world," that is, to the semiautonomous indigenous provincial units which still filled the countryside of the central areas in the mature period? We must surely expect to find a somewhat different dynamic. Aside from the utterly distinct origins of the two societies, the basic principle of the organization of the Spanish Indies was the existence of the two as separate entities, and Spanish social-economic organization gave much reality to such separateness. Of course we know too, from the previous topics discussed in this very chapter, that there were strong and permanent ties between the two worlds, so strong as to lead over the centuries to a blurring which had already begun to be perceptible in the time of which we speak.

But even where the two sectors show a close relation to each other, it is often one of opposites. Hispanic society grew through various kinds of mixture, incorporation, and appropriation, each of which subtracted something from Indian society. For most of the colonial period the population of Hispanics was rising at the same time that the number of persons called Indians was falling. Although the largest part of the numerical decline of the Indian corporations was simple demographic loss, much of it was the effect of movement toward the Spanish world, in the forms of mestizo offspring, urban migration, full-time employment by Spaniards, and acculturation. A very deep tendency in the Indies was for Spanish society to grow at the expense of Indian society, resulting everywhere in the gradual long-term decline of the Indian corporations as such.

Yet the fate of a people is not quite the same as that of its corporations. The history of Indians in Spanish America (leaving aside their vast contribution to general Hispanic American culture and society) is partly the story of an ultimately declining corporate group and partly that of people making a broad series of successful adaptations to a new situation; the latter aspect has a tendency to escape the topic of Indian history per se, but it is crucial to any overall perspective. Looking at both sides of the matter, one is more inclined to speak of a gradual transformation of the indigenous population than of a decline.

At any rate, we concede as an important truth that Indian corporations over the very long run were diminishing in size of population and wealth, losing in integrity and in the amount of traditional lore preserved, becoming less central to the society as a whole. Yet in the same breath we must emphasize how very slow this process was. For the colonial period, the keynote is persistence – of functioning communities, of language, of meaningful assets, of weight in the larger scene. If we take the reorganized Spanish-style Indian municipality as our reference point, there is even a sense in which it grew as it took its full form and became more firmly established.

There is, then, some basis for including the Indian world in the same scheme of periodization as the Spaniards. Indian entities, like Spanish ones, went through a time of quick basic change in the conquest period, followed by a plateau of consolidation and slower evolution (as well as a slower rate of population loss). One can even detect in the Indian world, as we were just seeing in Hispanic intellectual developments, an early mature period somewhat distinct from the following time. In fact, the phenomenon is more striking with Indian society than with Spanish and deserves a correspondingly more prominent place in our picture of the overall trajectory of the Indian world. The early mature period is a time of absolute peak for the Spanish-style Indian corporations, the time when, despite the great population loss that had occurred, they functioned better than before or ever afterward. Taxes were collected duly, the Indian populace carried out its Christian duties regularly, the town councils had full membership rosters and met frequently, and there was a more general cultural florescence whose dimensions we do not yet fully know. Then after a certain time the Indian towns were reported to be having trouble in all these respects, and in some of them they ceased to function altogether.

The time of flourishing of the Indian communities seems to occur at the intersection of two lines of development, the rising one of the Hispanization of Indians as individuals and the falling one of corporate integrity. It took a generation or more for Indians to grasp the most necessary Hispanic legal, religious, and economic concepts and practices. During that time Indian corporate power had fallen precipitously from its preconquest heights, but the basic mechanisms were still in excellent working order, traditional internal authorities were readily obeyed, and the limited nature of the Hispanization of the bulk of individuals was itself an insulating factor. In a word, the nobles had learned what the new system required and had the authority with the commoners to implement it. Beyond this point, Hispanization of individuals continued apace, but rather than improving corporate performance it detracted, for the allegiance of those individuals was more divided and more alternate channels were open to them; they increasingly failed to obey corporate authority, or attempted to attain their ends through Spanish structures and mechanisms. Perhaps Figure 9 can help illustrate the point.

Contemporary reports hinting at the phenomenon we have been discussing come from Peru as well as Mexico, but only for the latter

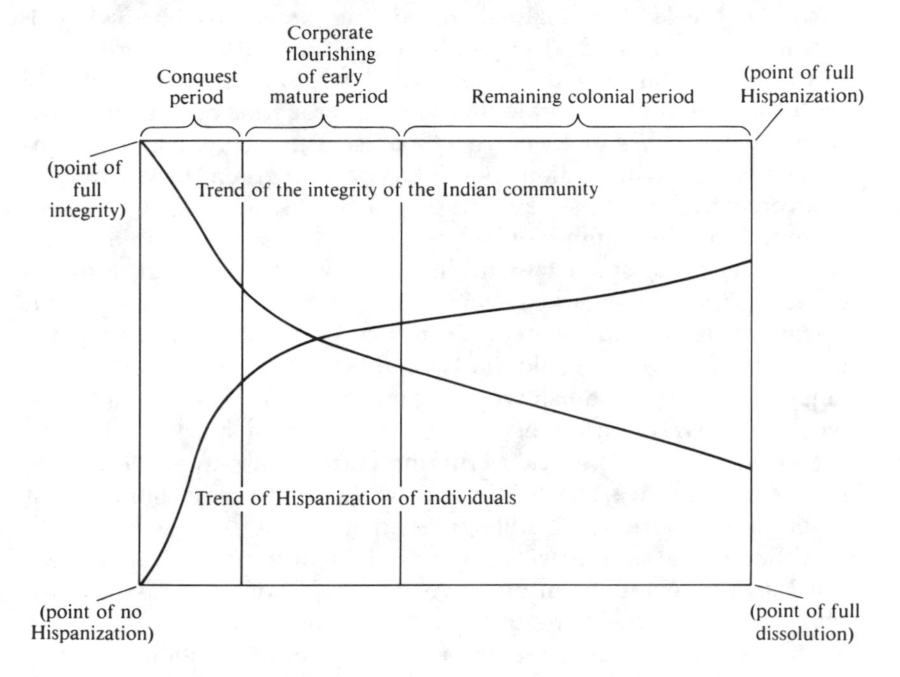

Figure 9. Indian corporate integrity, Hispanization, and periodization.

are we in a position to be at all specific about its nature and timing. For central Mexico we can place the time of corporate splendor at about 1570–1620, extendable in certain respects to about 1550–1650. Among the epoch's most lasting and visible accomplishments was the series of great monastery churches, one for each provincial unit, which were built and decorated mainly in the core of the time – under Spanish direction, it is true, but with much local impetus, funding, labor power, and craftsman participation. In this time Indian painters did masterly mural frescos and other paintings in the churches. Complex European part music flourished in the larger Indian communities, with not only many competent performers but even a few composers. The Hispanic-oriented municipal documentation in Nahuatl which this time produced is fuller, more varied, and more rounded than that of any time before or after. The greatest Nahuatl histories of the indigenous world are also from this epoch; persons of indigenous extraction who wrote for a broader public thereafter almost invariably did so in Spanish rather than in Nahuatl.

The Nahuatl language itself registers our phenomenon. Around

1550 the speakers of Nahuatl began the large-scale borrowing of Spanish nouns to name the multitudinous items the Spaniards were introducing. This period of borrowing only nouns matches closely with the period of corporate flourishing, for it ends around 1630–60, when Nahuatl began to borrow Spanish verbs, prepositions, conjunctions, and whole idioms, as it has done ever since. As surely as a fever indicates illness, such types of borrowing indicate massive bilingualism; the number of persons in the Indian communities who were in habitual contact with Hispanics and spoke Spanish in the contact situations – markets, temporary or permanent employment by non-Indians – had reached a critical mass. Henceforth many kinds of activity by Indians could and would be carried out in the Spanish language and the Spanish world, leaving the functions of the Indian world relatively narrower. Also, the Spanish-speaking Indians served as a conduit, quickly bringing current Hispanic cultural elements into the heart of the Indian world where they could spread among the majority who still spoke no Spanish.

Although the linguistic evolution is known in detail only for central Mexico's Nahuatl, in our own day one finds the same sorts of borrowings and the same bilingualism for nearly all the indigenous languages of the central areas, so that the only question is that of timing. Preliminary investigation shows that not until the beginning of the nineteenth century did Yucatecan Maya reach a stage comparable to that of Nahuatl around 1650, and such a finding is what one expects in view of the smaller proportion of Hispanics in off-the-track Yucatan. For the Andean highland too one would expect a slower rate of development, although, in view of the apparent lack of indigenous-language documents in that region, we may never know for sure.

Just as a language avenue to the Hispanic world became a part of the structure of the Indian world, so did regularized avenues for urban-directed migration come into existence, somewhat separate from the tribute and labor movements which had given them their first start. In the hinterland of Lima there was a stepped system in which migrants from the minimally Hispanized highland would move first to Indian towns in the foothills where Spanish language and ways were better known, then perhaps on to Lima's great Indian suburb the Cercado, and at last possibly into Lima proper (though most Indians in Lima were born in the Cercado itself). Likewise in Yucatan, by the latter seventeenth century there were lines of Indian towns, especially along major roads, in which each one lost migrants in the direction of Mérida, the region's Spanish center, and replaced them with new arrivals from the next town back. These movements could involve one step per generation or several steps in a single lifetime; in either case the migrants for a time kept in touch with their place of origin, and much of the movement along the system was temporary, with people retaining their roots at home.

Not only did the structure of the Indian world of the mature period contain open pipelines into the Hispanic sector; there was a strong movement in the other direction, bringing Hispanic outsiders inside the boundaries of the Indian units as full-time residents. Mainly humble people, the Hispanics worked for the haciendas which now dotted the countryside, or ran their own smaller rural enterprises, or as transporters and small traders dealt in the products of the rural economy. Rarely were they content, in the long run, to establish their sole residences at their isolated work sites; rather, they concentrated in the largest local Indian settlement and indeed usually in the largest single settlement in a set of several Indian provincial units. There, depending on the wealth of the region and their own number, they would begin to create a Spanish community within the Indian one, not formally a part of it, not represented on the Indian town council or performing Indian corporate duties, but nevertheless tending to take over the center of town, own the largest homes and employ the most people – largely Indians. In a given situation, the process might stop at one or two Spanish families living on the square of the Indian town, or it might move far in the direction of a Spanish municipality which would push the Indian world out to the edges as in the Spanish cities founded earlier.

In either case, there was a rapprochement between the resident Hispanics and the Indian nobles, together constituting the dominant group on the local scene. The nobles tended to model their economic endeavors on those of the Hispanics, and the Hispanics allied with the nobles in various ways, trying to get access to Indian labor, land, and water on better terms than would be available to them as persons relatively marginal within the Spanish sector. The alliances were often sealed by compadrazgo and other kinds of social interaction, even sometimes by intermarriage, especially when the Hispanics were mestizo or mulatto. But as important as these upper-level ties were, those maintained by the Hispanics with the many Indian commoners they employed were probably an even more significant factor in local cultural change, however hard it is to get a glimpse of interaction at that level.

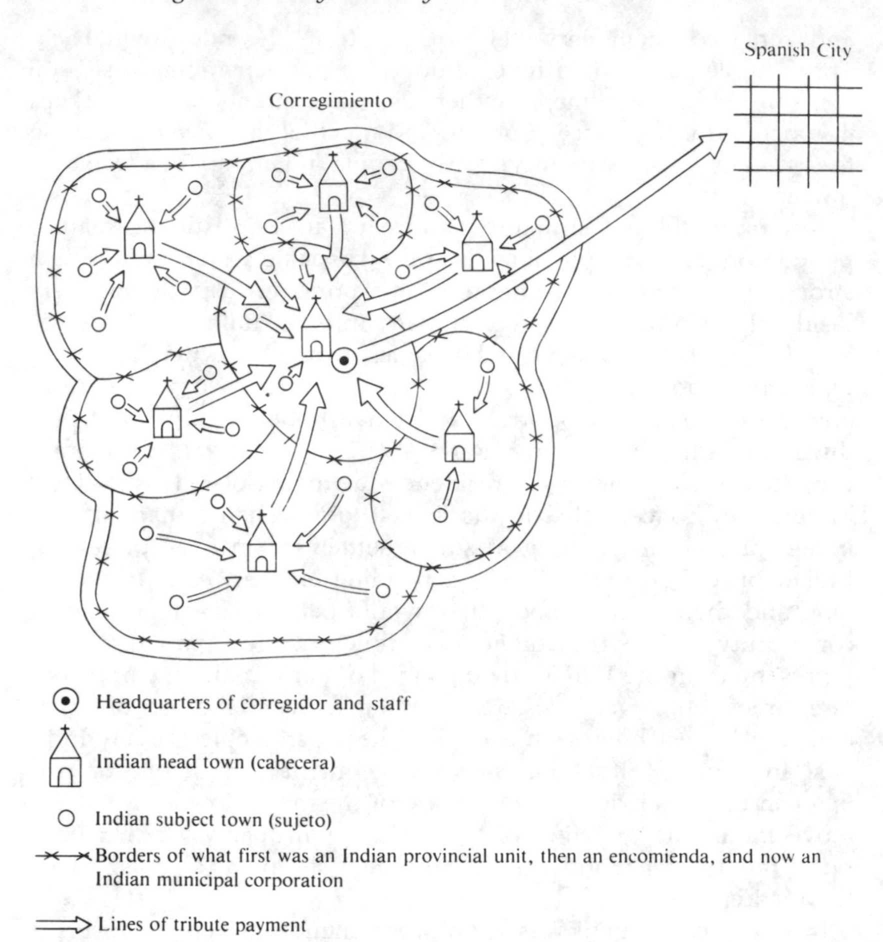

Figure 10. Schema of a corregimiento, mature colonial period.

Another facet of the gradual spilling of Hispanics out of the cities was the extension of Spanish governmental agencies into the Indian countryside. By the mature period, almost everywhere in the central areas, the hinterlands of Spanish cities were divided into *corregimientos* (see Figure 10), districts consisting of several provincial units (formerly or still encomiendas), with headquarters in the district's largest Indian town – also the center of the local Hispanic community which we were just discussing. Here the *corregidor de indios,* also often called *alcalde mayor,* held forth as magistrate, adjudicating conflicts between Indian towns or between the towns and Spaniards, or hearing appeals in serious cases which originated inside the Indian communities. He was also responsible for the collection of Indian taxes and for much of the channeling of Indian labor, which had formerly been functions of the encomenderos, and like them he acted through the Indian authorities, who carried out the original collection and recruitment. The extension of Spanish government into the country was thus minimal, since the corregidor depended on Indian corporate mechanisms rather than on any imposing staff of his own.

The corregidor himself usually served a short term of five years or less and kept one foot in the Spanish city; he was generally either a noninheriting member of the local Hispanic estate-owning families or a new arrival from Spain among the entourage of the viceroy or governor. His small staff, a few deputies, notaries, and constables, would be part of the local permanently resident Hispanic community (including the Hispanized Indian who often served as interpreter), and as such they would be knowledgable in the gradually built up practices for maintaining an equilibrium between Indian communities, humble local Spaniards, and larger city-connected estates. The predominance of local practices of accommodation and maneuver was accentuated by the fact that the corregidor's principal deputy, also usually a local, would be in full charge during his chief's frequent long absences in the city. At the same time, when an Indian town fell too much in arrears on its tax and labor obligations, the officials of the corregimiento did not hesitate to jail the leading Indian town council members until the obligation was met. But if a corregidor tried to turn the screws too tight, some of the Indian communities most affected were likely to appeal to higher authorities in the Spanish city (an art at which they were past masters), refuse obedience, or even briefly take up arms in protest against the offending corregidor and the alleged unjust action, but rarely if ever against Spanish rule in general.

The corregimiento being as limited as it was, Indian corporations not only performed the primary tax collection and rotary labor procurement, they also kept the peace internally and ran their own day-to-day affairs with little outside interference, as long as there was no head-on conflict with Spanish requirements and interests. The situation was favorable for the long retention of various kinds of pre-Hispanic organization, including moieties, which were rife in Peru and not uncommon in central Mexico; in several Mexican cases, double organization persisted far into the mature period or even to independence, with two separate councils in the same territory. Lower municipal office, at the level of ward head and the like, remained most unchanged, often retaining even the preconquest titles. At the upper levels too the preconquest heritage made itself felt; in fact, a good deal of what the Spaniards reported as municipal decline was rather the partial reassertion of older ways of doing things. In Peru, those holding office of any kind took to themselves the traditional prerogatives of the nobility whether they were of the dynastic group or not. In Mexico the new principles of an appointed rather than a hereditary governor and of relatively quick rotation of all municipal offices became standard, but in other ways the prevailing system of the middle and late colonial period looked more pre-Hispanic. Indian municipalities gradually tended to drop the corps of councilmen, who were the heart of a Spanish municipality but had no close preconquest equivalent. The ruling body consisted of the governor, alcaldes, and the fiscal, or steward of the church (despite his formally being in a different hierarchy), with the aid of all those who had previously held those offices and likely would again; very little attention was paid to whether a person was "in office" at the moment or not.

Over the long run the postconquest situation was conducive to changes in some of the most basic aspects of indigenous sociopolitical organization, but by no means all such change was Hispanization; much of it continued trends which existed in preconquest times and could be expressed more fully now that there was no interregional warfare and conquest, no killing and exiling of dynastic rivals, and on the other hand the homogeneous Spanish system extending over large areas allowed for the relatively free and unregulated movement of individuals. In Mexico one clear trend was for fragments of the *altepetl* (the city-state or large provincial unit) to attain greater independence. Each larger unit had come into existence in part through conquests, and among the constituent groups there had always been a subcurrent of separatism, which now had little to stop it. The smaller settlements in the larger whole began to acquire councils or at least alcaldes of their own, build churches rivaling those in the unit capitals, and in many cases secure entire independence of obligations to the head town, becoming such themselves. In the conquest period the Spaniards depended greatly on the encomienda and the power of the larger unit which sustained it, and they could not have permitted such a development. But as they came to rely less on the corporations in general, as they came to use a smaller proportion of temporary Indian labor, and as that labor came to them more individually and informally, the size of Indian units became a matter of relative indifference to them.

In the Andes, the larger entities are less well understood. We do know that they were normally not geographically contiguous and that the Spaniards, following their own concepts of territoriality, over time tended to respect only the geographical core of the unit, attempting to reassign the more distant parts to the units which neighbored them. The more diffuse Andean settlement pattern also brought on a more serious attempt by Spanish authorities to reorganize it. In central Mexico, resettlement was a movement of very limited thrust and consequences; a wave of it occurred in the early mature period primarily to remedy the fact that some subunits had suffered too much population loss to be viable. The most common solution was simply to collapse the unit in upon its largest existing settlement, which neither created new units nor changed the general structure. In Peru, however, a large-scale campaign got under way in the late sixteenth century, aimed at a drastic concentration of the Indians into a much smaller number of settlements (which here as in many other places were called reducciones). And indeed, the movement had a major impact, at least in the one area where it has been thoroughly studied, the corregimiento of Huarochirí near Lima; in areas farther from the viceregal capital such campaigns may have been later and weaker. At any rate, the campaign in Huarochirí reduced a hundred settlements to seventeen; it is true that they were not all on new sites and that the number of settlements immediately began to rise again as the Indians moved back in the direction of their older patterns, but even so, the Indian units had been severely shaken up.

Reducción was one of several factors tending to change the nature of the Andean ayllu. The smallest organized sociopolitical unit, the ayllu was comparable to the central Mexican calpulli; each in its culture area was the building block of larger units, the basic holder of land and performer of public duties. The Andean reducciones kept their constituent ayllus distinct, but the latter were thrown in close contact with each other and often put at an uncomfortable distance from their lands or even forced to exchange lands. The greatest challenge to the traditional form of the ayllu, however, came from the widespread migration of Indians across the countryside. Movement of individuals had always been a prominent feature of Andean structure, with its complementary microclimates included in the same units, and many people must have been stranded in foreign units in preconquest times. The pervasiveness of movement may have had something to do with the origin of the half-incorporated, half-outside *yana,* who were such a numerous and well-defined group in the Andes. In the colonial period the amount of migration seems to have increased; some of it was related to economic opportunities offered by the Spanish world, though some of it may have been inspired by the very nature of the ayllu. From the conquest period on, the Mexican local unit, the calpulli, quite readily extended membership, lands, and duties to newcomers if they would settle permanently. The Andean unit was far more hermetic and accepted only those born into it, preferably on both sides of the family. When a person was in economic straits, he could change his position by moving to a new community, where he would not receive lands but neither would he have to pay taxes or do repartimiento labor. Not only the migrant himself but his descendants as well would remain outside the ayllu in the new location. Over the centuries the proportion of *forasteros,* as the outsiders were called, increased greatly, whereas the proportion of ayllu members performing public obligations correspondingly decreased. The migrants were usually male, and the ayllus to which they came would be overbalanced in favor of females because of outmigration there too, so that frequent marriage outside the ayllu was inevitable. The ayllu thus gradually, reluctantly moved in the direction of being the basically residential organization that the Mexican calpulli had been all along.

Everywhere the standard practices of the Hispanic economy were infiltrating the Indian world. In Peru, private landholding by nobles and others; the use of money to pay for commodities and labor; the commercial production of goods for the Hispanic world; the bequeathing of individual property through testaments – all these things stood alongside the ayllu's more communal landholding and reciprocal, rotary labor traditions. It is as though there were two sectors, not always at peace with each other, in the Indian communities, one consisting of nobles, officeholders, skilled persons, forasteros, and resident Hispanics, who all leaned toward Hispanic practices, and the second sector being the residue of ayllu members holding lands by communal right and performing mita labor.

In Mexican Indian towns one sees all the same types of Hispanic activity, even more pronounced, but there is no well-defined split between two subsectors because the activities were carried on so generally. Indeed, many of the practices were not so much Hispanic as common to early modern Iberia and Mesoamerica, which already had markets, commercial specialists, and something very nearly approaching a currency, aside from apparently being acquainted with the principle of individual sale and purchase of plots of land. Members of the Mexican Indian community took part in interregional transport and commerce along with marginal Hispanics. To get a more specific notion of the nature of this kind of intertwining, let us consider the case of one Juan Fabián, a well-to-do Indian commoner living in the Coyoacan region near Mexico City in the early seventeenth century. He had several scattered plots of land, some from the community and some individually purchased. He owed money to some Spaniards, but on the other hand there were Spaniards who owed money to him. His main enterprise was an orchard of indigenous fruit trees where he sometimes employed various local people in addition to the help he demanded (but did not always get) from his relatives. He owned a few horses and mules and rented others from Spaniards; his son-in-law, from a provincial unit other than Juan Fabián's own, took the packtrain into the surrounding area with fruit to be sold.

People like these are living symbols of how elements which were originally introduced from the outside became integrated inside Indian patterns of thought and behavior to form stable associations of traits, all of which the Indian community identified with, not questioning which was indigenous, which Spanish, which a combination. On examination, nearly everything usually turns out to have been the latter: Indian at the root and altered in some way at the surface, like the provincial units themselves. (If something appears entirely Spanish, most often the Indians have taken it as the equivalent of something they already had.) Such integration is seen in the great Indian writings of the early mature period, in the Peruvian historian and commentator Huaman Poma de Ayala as well as the Mexicans Tezozomoc of Mexico City-Tenochtitlan and Chimalpain of Amecameca. All exalted the Spanish God and king as well as their own indigenous subgroups, for which they sought advantage within the Spanish system.

It is true that Indians sometimes consciously kept some of their patterns distinct from Spanish equivalents, the two being in direct competition. In regions where there were relatively fewer Spaniards, separate religious systems could long persist; in the early seventeenth century Andean highlanders still maintained indigenous state religions with priests, sacrifices, and support from public sources. In the Mayan areas too, preconquest sacred writings were preserved, put into alphabetical form, and even recopied and brought up to date far into the colonial period.

Still, one cannot help being impressed with the Indian world's capacity to achieve the stable integration of outside elements without losing its equilibrium. For Mexico we begin to know enough to be able to give a quite balanced picture of the phenomenon in its many dimensions. The pulque drinking so decried (and exaggerated) by Spanish priests was no wild excess brought on by demoralization or Spanish influence but a patterned behavior gradually evolving from the more communal and ritual toward the more private and individual; pulque production and sale played an important part in the development of a rural money economy and interregional commerce within the Indian world. Homicide in Indian towns followed much the same patterns as in world history generally; in the places where the most Spaniards were, some original strong corporate taboos gradually ceded to behavior models more like the Spanish ones. Indian corporations were still concerned with their autonomy, their borders, and the level of their obligations to outsiders, much as in preconquest times; constant litigation in Spanish courts and highly limited, localized uprisings replaced warfare and diplomacy as the means of asserting those concerns. In linguistic evolution, the Spanish words that poured into Nahuatl by no means meant decay or loss of the language's individuality or expressiveness; Nahuatl no more became Spanish than English became French in the time of the Normans. Many cultural elements which were quite purely Spanish on introduction were soon so naturalized that the Indians began to use them to differentiate their own microunits. Much of the clothing Indians wore was European in type, but since Indian style was more conservative than the Spanish mode, before long their standard garb looked "Indian," and the process began by which each provincial unit had some special characteristic of its dress which would distinguish it from its neighbors. Just so all the Indian towns produced documents in Nahuatl following essentially Spanish models, but each locality evolved its own slightly different wordings and thereby asserted its individuality.

We have only hints of how the generality of the Indian populace viewed the Hispanic American situation of the mature colonial period. As far as one can grasp it, that view emphasized the autonomy of the local unit. There was pride in all that belonged to the unit, whether Hispanic or indigenous in origin, and hostility to all potentially grasping outsiders, whether Indians or Spaniards. The folk legends of the small Indian town of Sula near Mexico City, vintage ca. 1700, can serve to illustrate. In the tale of Sula, Christianity equates with sedentary life, whereas pagan religion is equated with the preagricultural stage of nomadic wandering. The town's mythic founder pair have Christian as well as indigenous names; the Aztecs too are seen as Christian. The local church (the building, that is, for no priest is mentioned) is the very embodiment of Sula's independent existence, and the ethnic pair, in another guise, is responsible for choosing Santiago as the patron saint. In the key episode, an army representing all outside threats attempts to enter and appropriate the town's land; the force is Aztec (Sula denies ever having been subject to the Aztec empire) but is led by a postconquest Spanish estate owner. To turn back the intruders, the people of Sula use both Spanish and indigenous means. On the one hand they show the Aztecs their papers of true title from the Spanish authorities, invoking the Christian deity, and on the other hand their leader turns himself into a totemic quail-serpent to frighten them. Thoroughly deterred, the outsiders depart and go to settle in Mexico City-Tenochtitlan, leaving Sula with the lands and sovereign rule which it has enjoyed ever since.

The New Granadan gold complex

In the chapter on society in the conquest period we spoke briefly of how several transitional areas bordering the central ones shared many, but not all, of the core-area characteristics; they remained in large part oriented to the center and moved in somewhat the same evolutionary direction with a considerable time lag. This continued to hold true in the main during the entire mature period, but some regional distinctions in type of development call for a rather eclectic treatment on our part. Looking to the south, Chile and northwestern Argentina show a standard evolution, still held tightly within the Peruvian orbit and living from supply of Potosí or the trunk line; we will have occasion to say a few more words about these regions when we discuss the far fringes which were appended to them. Looking to the north, transitional areas lying just north of central Mexico were overwhelmed by the silver mining economy of which we have already spoken. As to the regions at the southern end of Mesoamerica, with their strongly organized and mainly sedentary peoples, they went hand in hand with central Mexico, if usually slower by fifty or a hundred years, in important aspects of estate formation, labor organization, nucleation, and general cultural change.

Guatemala, despite being the most distant of the southern Mesoamerican regions and headquarters of an Audiencia, was originally as fully in the Mexican orbit as less remote Yucatan, each with its Mayan peoples, each with its single fair-sized Spanish municipality, and the indigenous cacao which Guatemala sold to central Mexico was comparable to the indigenous cotton cloth which Yucatan sent to the same destination. By the end of the sixteenth century, however, Guatemala encountered serious cacao production problems. Cultivation was still in indigenous hands, the crop being channeled after harvest through the encomienda, so that epidemics and Indian population loss were crippling to the industry; probably the blight that has made cacao growing so migratory a phenomenon in later centuries was already making itself felt here as well. In any case, the great Mexico-directed cacao boom came to an end, and by the seventeenth century Guatemala was thrown into an unwanted independence, trying to find some asset directly valuable in transatlantic commerce. Indigo was the most nearly viable of the various products tried, but success even there was minimal, because of distance from the Caribbean coast and because the real time of textile dye exports had not yet come. In many aspects Guatemala was still simply a backwater of the Mexican system.

Among all the transitional areas there grew up only one complex which stood quite independent of the two major ones, with its own distinct leverage in international trade, and that was in New Granada (Colombia), the location of the longest-lasting, most significant gold deposits in Spanish America. In the conquest period, nearly every time the Spaniards entered a new region, from the Caribbean beginnings forward, a transitory gold rush phase would ensue, paying off the conquerors' debts, rewarding them, and helping capitalize further ventures. In areas without silver, there was need and incentive to push the potential of gold mining to the limit, and in Chile it continued as a significant element in the economy to the end of the sixteenth century; but only in New Granada was it the steady economic underpinning of Spanish life through the entire mature period and beyond.

The New Granadan complex had many of the same constituent parts as the Mexican and Peruvian ones: a mining district (in the northwestern part of the area); a set of Spanish cities with Indian hinterlands, partly distinct from the mining district proper, helping supply the mines and being sustained by their profits; and outlets to the sea, both the Pacific, merging with the Peruvian system, and the Caribbean, with a completely independent port at Cartagena. Yet one cannot speak of a trunk line. Though Bogotá with its Audiencia was the capital and most important city, it did not predominate over other Spanish settlements to the extent that Lima or Mexico City did in their spheres; not all roads led to Bogotá, nor was it the most important market for the produce of other settlements, nor did its companies dominate their commerce; and though some intermarrying occurred between the prominent of Bogotá and those of other New Granadan cities, there was nothing like the familial networks extending along the great trunk lines.

Reasons for the difference exist at several levels. The nature of the gold mining industry was one factor making for diffuseness; despite the existence of a few stable vein mines, the principal activity was placer mining along riverbeds, at sites which were highly scattered, inaccessible, and frequently moving. The product, gold dust, circulated nearly as freely as currency, so there was no need to rely on a mint at a central location, and governmental taxes were easy to avoid; it has been estimated that as little as a third of production ever paid the royal quinto, even though the percent demanded was greatly reduced. Another factor for fragmentation was the extremely difficult geography of the region, cut up as it was by mountains and river valleys into several distinct units very hard to connect with each other. But after all, in Brazil at a later time placer gold was to create the great capital of Rio de Janeiro; and no geographical challenge could be much more forbidding than the Peruvian one. Ultimately, the New Granadan complex simply lacked the nucleating force of sufficiently vast wealth.

Placer gold mining took place in hot, wet, low-lying localities of the kind where the indigenous population regularly fell nearly to the disappearing point not long after European entry, so that Indian labor was only used transitionally. By the mature period, the indigenous people of the lowlands were nearly gone, whereas the highland peoples, more like the sedentaries of Peru, still persisted and served encomenderos but no longer worked on a large scale in the mines; the primary labor force there consisted of African slaves.

In placer mining the basic unit was not the plant, as in the silver industry, but the *cuadrilla,* or gang, which might vary from ten workers to a hundred according to the wealth of the owner. A Spanish overseer skilled in mining techniques would be in charge, although operating to a large extent through an intermediary called the *capitán de cuadrilla,* or "gang captain," himself a Black, who disciplined the workers, distributed food, and even collected the gold from the individual producers. If the gang was small, the overseer himself might be the owner, but with larger gangs he would be only a steward; the owner, who might maintain several separate gangs, would live in the nearest fairly large town. The councils of towns in the mining area proper – some of them ephemeral foundations and others surviving through shifts of site – tended to be dominated by the *señores de cuadrilla,* or gang owners. Thus under quite unusual conditions the Spaniards of the gold mining district went far toward establishing a standard urban–rural estate structure.

For the slave workers life was reported to be strenuous, food bad, and mortality high, but even so they retained some small part of what they produced. One result was that here, as happened also in the silver industry, they were a significant market for petty Hispanic traders; another effect was that in each generation a few were able to purchase their freedom, so that the proportion of freedmen (many of them mulattoes) grew bit by bit, until by the time of independence they outnumbered slaves and loomed large in the area's general population, taking over the more skilled mining work and tertiary supervision, as well as becoming petty prospectors and miners on their own.

The larger, more stable cities of New Granada were not mining settlements per se but were dominated by the usual partly merging types of estate owners, merchants, and members of the official hierarchies; these cities still drew on surrounding Indian hinterlands, though in the final analysis investment and commerce had to do mainly with the mines. Popayán, the best studied of these towns, showed many of the characteristics of a central-area city: numerous shops and mercantile firms, some of them operating directly in transatlantic commerce; continued strong immigration from Spain, with the more important merchants gradually entering the local estate-owning circles; a growing number of ecclesiastical establishments and clerics, especially secular priests, who were increasingly of local families, so that by the end of the seventeenth century the cathedral chapter was locally born in its entirety.

On the other hand, many developments appear retarded in respect to the center: the encomienda in Popayán's jurisdiction remained important and even retained labor power; the title "don" came into general use for the locally prominent only generations after the same thing had occurred in Lima and Mexico City; indeed, not until after the mid-seventeenth century did the locally dominant group show normal signs of consolidation (such as exclusive exercise of high municipal office and tight intermarriage), and even then not all the signs endured into the following century.

6

Brazilian beginnings

The patterns of Brazil's early colonization are in many ways parallel to those encountered in the peripheries of Spanish America, as will be seen in Chapter 8. The semisedentary nature of the Indian inhabitants, the apparent lack of precious metals, and the basically extractive nature of the economy, geared to exploiting local products like dyewood, all exerted an influence. But the Portuguese had their own previous traditions of expansion in Africa and the Atlantic islands, which were brought to bear in the colonization of Brazil. In fact, a major distinguishing factor of Brazilian colonization that set it apart from Spanish America was the continuing simultaneous Portuguese effort in Asia. For Spain, America was the chief target of colonial expansion; for Portugal, it was not. This fact helps to explain much of the Brazilian colony's early history when considered in conjunction with the local conditions that confronted the Portuguese.

The dyewood phase

The Portuguese maritime thrust toward Asia gained considerable momentum toward the close of the fifteenth century. When Vasco da Gama finally reached India in 1498, the way lay open for circum-Africa commerce with the East. A second expedition set sail for India in 1500 under the command of Pedro Alvares Cabral. On the outward voyage, swinging wide around the hump of West Africa, Cabral made a landfall on an unknown coast. Contact was established with the local inhabitants, a little trade and exploration took place, and then the fleet's secretary composed a report which Cabral dispatched back to Lisbon while he himself with the other ships continued on to India. Cabral called his discovery "Land of the Holy Cross" (Santa Cruz), a name that was soon replaced in practice by "Brazil" because of the many dyewood, or brazilwood, trees that grew along the coast. Although some Portuguese authors have argued that their vessels had already secretly discovered this coast, it seems clear from the tone of surprise and wonderment in the letter of 1500 that such contacts, if they ever took place, had made no impact even on Portuguese mariners.

Brazil received little royal attention for the next thirty years. The crown at this time was simply too preoccupied with the riches of India to pay much attention to a seemingly savage land whose only attractions were exotic birds and dyewood trees. Unwilling to invest royal resources of manpower and capital on a large scale, the crown turned to private individuals who were prepared to do so in return for the rights of exploitation. A monopoly contract for dyewood cuttings was granted to a group of New Christian investors on condition that they explore the coast, provide some defense, and, of course, surrender a percentage of the profit to the crown. So long as wealth was not immediately apparent, both Iberian crowns seemed willing to make wide concessions to private individuals in order to have them assume the burden of explorations, although residual royal control was always maintained in theory. The system of private initiatives and royal contracts had been employed by the Portuguese in Africa, and in many ways the techniques of the dyewood trade paralleled those previously used to extract gold, ivory, and slaves from West Africa. Small forts or trading stations were established at suitable landing sites, often islands, and a few men under a *feitor*, or manager, stayed behind to staff them. During their stay, the Portuguese would induce local Indians to cut dyewood trees and deliver the logs to the fort in return for trinkets and European trade goods. Arriving ships could thus be sure of finding cargoes of dyewood logs waiting at the trade forts. In the beginning, then, Portuguese contact with Brazil was limited to a series of *feitorias* (factories) analogous to those on the African coast; in the course of the sixteenth century, however, a number of internal pressures and external threats forced the Portuguese to initiate colonization and settlement.

Of immediate concern was the foreign threat, always more to be reckoned with on the eastern seaboard than elsewhere in Ibero-America. Soon after Cabral's landfall, Spanish vessels began to visit the Brazilian coast during their voyages of exploration. The southern coast of Brazil became a frequent stopping place for ships heading toward the Río de la Plata. Even more serious was the presence of the French. Small privately owned ships sailing from ports in Normandy and Brittany began to appear on the coast as early as 1504. Financed by merchants and lacking royal support, these ships were primarily engaged in the dyewood trade. Brazilwood produced a reddish-purple dye that was highly prized by European tapestry and cloth makers, so that the French were no less anxious than the

Portuguese to exploit the Brazilian forests. The French court had never really accepted the claim of Spain and Portugal to the world beyond Europe, and French merchants and sailors were even less inclined to recognize Iberian pretensions. One said bitterly that the whole world was not large enough for the Portuguese, complaining that "as soon as they have sailed along a coast they claim possession of it and consider it a conquest."

The competition was fierce. Both sides made trade agreements and alliances with Indian groups while raiding the forts and shipping of their rivals. From the point of view of Portugal, which claimed Brazil for itself, the French were interlopers, little better than pirates. Diplomatic complaints to the French court had little effect because of the private nature of the French presence, and the Portuguese turned to organized military activity. A number of naval expeditions cleared the coast of French shipping, but after each sweep, the French returned. By 1530 it was clear that Portugal was faced with a choice: take possession of Brazil in some more permanent way or lose this land to active European rivals.

In that year another naval expedition was dispatched with instructions to clear the French from the coast and continue explorations. In addition, this large fleet also carried the men and materials needed to establish a permanent settlement. The commander, Martim Afonso de Sousa, received extensive judicial and administrative powers to carry out the colonizing aims of the expedition. After cruising along the coast and capturing a number of French vessels, Martim Afonso established a town at São Vicente in 1532. It was Brazil's first.

From donatary captaincies to royal government

Even while the Martim Afonso expedition was under way, the Portuguese crown was formulating plans for a permanent and stable colonial occupation able to resist foreign encroachment and exploit Brazil's potential. News of the exploits of Cortés and the wealth of Mexico was probably not lost on the court at Lisbon, and in Brazil there had long been rumors of emerald mountains and silver mines lying somewhere in the unknown interior (*sertão*). Martim Afonso himself had sent an *entrada* of eighty men to search for treasure rumored to be in the interior, but without success. Both the apparent possibilities and the reality of the dyewood trade called for decisive action, but Portugal was still too preoccupied with Asia to commit royal resources on a large scale to Brazil. Once again, the solution was to depend on private initiative and interest, stimulated by state action and the guarantee of royal law and military force.

The Portuguese crown characteristically turned to a time-tested set of institutional arrangements developed in the two previous centuries. As we have seen, these had already been modified and used to carry out settlement on the Atlantic islands of Madeira and the Azores. The main feature was the hereditary seigneury or donatary captaincy, under which lordship over extensive territories on the Brazilian coast was granted out between 1533 and 1535. The gentlemen who received the grants or donations (*donatários*) were given broad powers of jurisdiction, taxation, and other administrative and fiscal privileges usually reserved in Portugal to the highest nobility. Whereas in some ways the seigneury was an archaic form that seemed to move in a direction contrary to royal centralization, these grants were not "feudal" in either law or practice. They were made as a reward for services rendered and were not dependent upon the usual feudal obligations of vassal to lord. Moreover, their purpose was economic development. Although some donataries wished to use the grants to support a noble life-style and a few had the pretensions of "feudal" lords, such attitudes were strongly opposed by both the local colonists and the crown.

Fifteen donatary captaincies were created, dividing the Brazilian coast into strips of territory of varying length (see Map 6). No one knew what lay in the interior, but in theory the boundaries of each captaincy extended to the line of Tordesillas that divided the lands held by Spain from those claimed by Portugal. The donatários or captains could establish towns, appoint officers, and distribute land to settlers. Moreover, since the whole purpose of the donatary captaincies in Brazil was to stimulate settlement and encourage economic development, the crown offered certain financial benefits to the potential recipients of the grants. Each was to receive ten leagues of coast as his own property, control over the Indian slave trade, a percentage of the dyewood trade, and monopoly control over mills and other capital improvements. The form of the donatary captaincy came directly from Portugal's medieval experience, but it was now adapted to meet the needs of colonial expansion.

Among the key powers of the lord proprietors and most important as a means of stimulating colonization was the right to distribute *sesmarias,* or land grants. In medieval Portugal reclaimed lands and those captured from the Moors had been redistributed by the crown by means of sesmarias. The crown usually appointed an individual to distribute the lands, and the recipients were obliged to

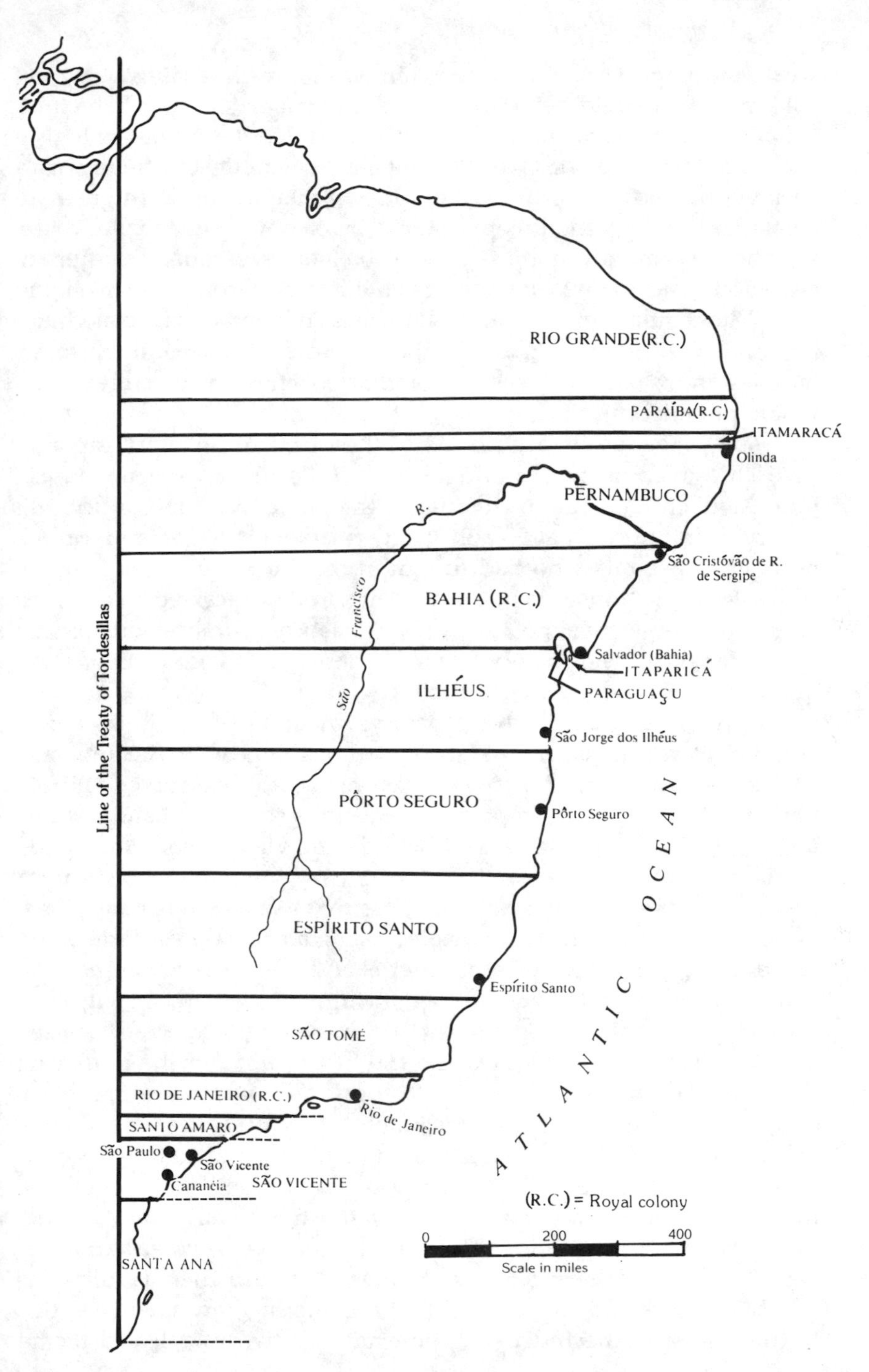

Map 6. The captaincies of Brazil, late sixteenth century.

work and improve them. Here again was an institution from Portugal's past that could be adapted to the Brazilian situation. The lord proprietors, by receiving the right to hand out sesmarias, had a means to attract colonists and to initiate settlement. But there was a curious paradox here. Whereas the sesmarias in Portugal had created a class of small copyholders or peasants, in Brazil, where land was seemingly endlessly available, the sesmarias were often enormous and in the long run resulted in a system of great holdings. The regulations that only as much land could be given as could be used were ignored, and by the late seventeenth century some families in Brazil held sesmarias that together were larger than whole provinces in Portugal.

Despite the various attractions of the Brazilian donatary captaincies, the great magnates and nobles of Portugal were not much interested. Instead, the recipients of the grants were minor *fidalgos,* gentry from the court at Lisbon, a few royal bureaucrats, and a good number of persons who had fought in the Portuguese conquests in India. Martim Afonso de Sousa and his brother received two grants each, but they were almost the only donatários with previous Brazilian experience. The majority lacked the expertise, connections, or financial resources to make their captaincies a success. The four northernmost captaincies were never settled, and four others failed because of mismanagement and poor relations with the Indians. Within twenty years the crown was moved to take direct control. The era of the donatary captaincies was thus short-lived and has the aura of failure, yet during this period a number of social and economic patterns were established that continued long after direct royal control had been established. For that reason let us pause for a moment to examine some examples of captaincies that succeeded or failed and to take note of the patterns and processes set in motion.

In reality a precolonization stage of unplanned and uncontrolled contact preceded the captaincies and in some places made subsequent settlement possible. During the first years after the European discovery of Brazil, sailors and others had jumped ship, been stranded, or put ashore as punishment or for other reasons. Cabral himself had left two penal exiles among the Indians to become versed in their language. At various places along the coast these transfrontiersmen had settled among the tribes, taken wives, and raised *mestiço* (or as they were also called in Brazil, *mameluco*) families. Trusted by the Indians and integrated into their families by marriage and blood, these men became intermediaries between the Portuguese and the Indians. Wherever they had established themselves, the chances for trade and subsequent settlement were good. At the Bay of All Saints, Diogo Alvares, called Caramurú, lived among his large family and was greatly respected by both Indians and Portuguese. The settlement of São Paulo was made possible by João Ramalho, a Portuguese castaway and longtime resident of the area. On the southern coast Portuguese ships came to depend on the mysterious *bacharel* (lawyer) of Cananea who for some crime or misadventure had resided on the coast in exile for many years. Martim Afonso's nearby town of São Vicente was placed, in fact, at a site where a few Portuguese had already settled among the local Indians.

Martim Afonso de Sousa and his brother received the four southernmost captaincies. Colonization efforts centered on São Vicente, the area of coastline near the town of that name, and on the subsequently more important port of Santos. Settlement concentrated around these tiny coastal enclaves, but eventually, in order to secure an adequate food supply, a town was established on the inland plateau at the Indian village of Piratininga. This town was later to become the city of São Paulo. Much of the success of the captaincy depended on the relatively good relations established with the Tupiniquin tribes of the coast and plateau. Without European women, the colonists married the mixed-blood descendants of the castaways and often took Indian women as wives and concubines. These interpersonal ties created a firm basis of alliance between the Portuguese and the Tupiniquin, as did the military aid given to them against their Indian enemies.

Perhaps just as important to São Vicente's success was its sound economic base. The area had very little dyewood, but Martim Afonso's connections in Lisbon were excellent. He was able to convince both Portuguese and foreign merchants to invest in the captaincy's development, and before long a number of sugar mills were operating near the coast. Martim Afonso himself was part owner of the largest mill. It was eventually acquired by the Schetz merchant family based in Antwerp. Other non-Portuguese also invested, and some took residence in the colony. Economically, São Vicente looked much like Madeira: a Portuguese overseas venture financed to a large extent with foreign capital in order to produce sugar for the European market. São Vicente was eventually surpassed as a sugar producer by the captaincies of the northeast, but in the sixteenth century it was one of the few successes of the captaincy system.

Captaincies that failed are also instructive. Porto Seguro was given to a wealthy gentleman of Viana do Castelo in the north of Portugal. He sold his properties and set sail for Brazil with family, retainers, and a good number of colonists from the densely populated province of Minho as well as many Spaniards from neighboring Galicia. Mostly poor fisherfolk, they tended to re-create the fishing villages of the Iberian Atlantic coast in the colony they established. The fact that many married couples came may help explain their consistently poor relations with the Indians, since there was little intermarriage. A few sugar mills were constructed, but the colony was ripped apart by internal dissension; the donatário himself was denounced to the Inquisition for heresy and sent back to Portugal in chains. There was a similar failure in the neighboring captaincy of Ilhéus, which had possibilities as a sugar producer. There the constant attacks by Aimoré Indians made life precarious and kept the colonists limited to a narrow strip of coastline. Eventually, the donatary captain sold his rights to a Florentine merchant resident in Lisbon.

The captaincy of Bahia should have succeeded. The area of the Bay of All Saints had long been a favorite stopping place for the dyewood cutters, and Caramurú, along with a few other Portuguese and many of their mixed offspring, had excellent relations with the local Tupinambá peoples of the coast. The donatary captain, an old veteran of campaigns in India named Francisco Pereira Coutinho, tried to develop his seigneury by bringing his family and other colonists, distributing sesmarias for farms, and encouraging the construction of sugar mills. But Pereira Coutinho proved to be a poor administrator and some of the colonists, ignoring the admonitions of Caramurú, began to encroach on Indian lands. Factions developed, and soon the donatary and his backers were forced to flee the captaincy. Relations with the Indians continued to deteriorate. When Pereira Coutinho tried to return, his ship met with disaster in the Bay of All Saints and he, along with most of his followers, was killed by the Tupinambá. The fast-talking Caramurú escaped.

Of all the donatary captaincies, Pernambuco enjoyed the most success. Its donatary, Duarte Coelho Pereira, came from obscure origins, but after twenty years of military and diplomatic service in India and a fortunate marriage into the distinguished Albuquerque family he was rewarded with one of the Brazilian grants. In 1535 he set sail for Pernambuco along with his wife, her brother, and a large contingent of colonists, many of whom were from Viana do Castelo in the overcrowded province of Minho. Towns were founded at Igaraçú and Olinda and sesmarias were distributed to the colonists. Pernambuco had long been a major area of dyewood loading, visited by both French and Portuguese ships, and dyewood had provided the captaincy its first economic activity, but Duarte Coelho was not willing to let matters rest on brazilwood alone. He used his financial connections in Lisbon to secure backing for a number of sugar mills, and by 1542 at least one was in operation. In the same year he requested and received permission to bring African slaves to labor in the sugar industry.

A major part of Pernambuco's success is explained by the normalization of relations with the Indians. The French and their Indian allies remained hostile, and fighting continued until 1560, but an alliance was formed with the Tabajaras. The donatary's brother-in-law, Jeronimo de Albuquerque, married the daughter of a principal Indian leader after a Pocahontas-style rescue. He eventually fathered eight legitimate children, plus five mameluco children by other women. This created a familial tie between the donatary's kin and a major Indian group, a tie which was extended by other such unions, and in general, Duarte Coelho seems to have sponsored miscegenation. Thus, unlike other captaincies, Pernambuco could depend on Indian allies, supplies of food, and occasionally workers. Less dependent on Europe for labor, Duarte Coelho could refuse to accept the penal exiles whom Portugal sometimes sent out as colonists. When he returned to Portugal in 1554 to manage his affairs, his wife, Beatris de Albuquerque, remained in Brazil as donatary until her son reached majority. By 1585 Pernambuco was a thriving plantation colony with more than sixty sugar engenhos in operation, by far the most prosperous region of Brazil.

But Pernambuco was an exception. The captaincies had generally failed as a tool of colonization. The mere attempt of one small, already overcommitted country to establish so many colonies simultaneously invited disaster; though encouraged by the open coastline, it subverted the more natural one-area-at-a-time process of Spanish expansion, in which each successful foundation provided capital, experience, and people for the next. In fact, the overall result of the captaincy experiment was not exactly failure but the establishment of the very small number of viable settlements which the situation of the time could bear. Even when successful the captaincies were bound to be transitional, because of their ambiguous nature and the conflicting goals of crown, donataries, and colonists. The broad seigneurial powers of the donataries recalled a bygone age in Europe, yet the captaincies were clearly designed for development and the donataries viewed their domains as profit-making enterprises.

Development really depended on the colonists and the role that they would play in the new land. Whereas the donataries wished to re-create *senhorios,* albeit for capitalistic ends, the colonists were not at all willing to see the disadvantages of Portugal reborn in Brazil. They had not left the crowded fields of Minho or the rocky slopes of Beira to play the same roles in Brazil that they had played at home. The incessant squabbling in almost all the captaincies, including Pernambuco, between the donatary with his kinsmen and retainers on one side and the colonists on the other demonstrated the latter's rejection of the roles and positions designed for them in the captaincy system. To the colonists, Brazil represented social mobility through the acquisition of land and through it opportunities to live "nobly," surrounded by family and dependents. But the colonists, like the donataries, realized that success depended on integration into the commercial structure of Europe and that this could be achieved only by exporting dyewood or the new crop, sugar. Dyewood was by law a monopoly of the crown and the donataries or their contractors. Sugar offered the hope of success, wealth, and status, but for this crop land alone was worthless. One needed capital or credit and most of all labor. We shall see shortly that the search for workers became the major theme of sixteenth-century Brazil, with far-reaching social implications for the colony's subsequent development.

Both the widespread failures and the few successes of the captaincy system caused Portugal to attempt some other form of government in Brazil. The foreign threat had not disappeared and relations with the Indians in many places were poor, and in general the donatary captaincies had been unable to create stable and profitable colonies. At the same time, the growing sugar industry of São Vicente and Pernambuco demonstrated to the crown that the possibilities for profit in Brazil far exceeded the simple trading fort stage of exploitation so long employed in Africa. Then, too, the Portuguese were not unaware of the Spanish discovery of the great silver mines of Potosí in 1545, which once again raised the possibility that similar mineral wealth might be found in Brazil.

Reacting to these circumstances, the crown sent out in 1549 a large expedition under the direction of Tomé de Sousa, who was appointed governor-general of Brazil. With him came a royal treasurer, a chief magistrate, and other officials, as well as artisans, soldiers, colonists, and penal exiles. Also in the expedition were six Jesuits, the first of the regular orders in Brazil. The crown directed de Sousa to establish his capital at the Bay of All Saints, which was centrally located, had potential as a sugar-producing area, and was unencumbered by donatarial privilege because of the death of the incumbent. A new city, Salvador, was created as the royal capital, placing Brazil under centralized control. The governor-general was granted wide administrative powers, some of which were in conflict with those previously given to the donataries. The captaincies could not be abolished legally, and the crown simply imposed centralized royal government upon the existing system. A few donataries like Duarte Coelho fought ardently to protect their rights. The crown, in fact, did not recapture full control from the descendants of some of the donataries until the eighteenth century, and proprietary captaincies, although more limited in scope and smaller in scale, were even given out anew in the seventeenth century. But the general trend was for increasing state control at the expense of private colonizing initiative and prerogatives. In many ways the process paralleled developments in Spanish America. After a period of royal concessions to private individuals and the formation of a colonial society with a somewhat autonomous economic base, the Iberian crowns began to limit the centrifugal tendencies created by this situation. What had been ceded in the period of conquest and discovery to stimulate private initiative and participation now was recalled as the American colonies gained the potential to be steady producers of revenue.

With royal government firmly established in Brazil, Tomé de Sousa and his successors, notably the vigorous and ruthless Mem de Sá (governor-general, 1558–74), increased the level of centralization, expanded bureaucratic and fiscal control, and stimulated economic development. Defense was still a matter of royal concern, for by the 1550s the French were back on the coast in force. This time they established a colony in Guanabara Bay, and although Antarctic France, as it was called, was often torn by factionalism between Catholics and Huguenots, the Portuguese perceived its very existence as a threat to Brazil. They were correct. In the early 1560s an alliance of the French with a confederation of Indian groups placed all of southern Brazil in jeopardy. After considerable fighting, the Portuguese destroyed the French colony (1565–7) and established their own city in Guanabara Bay, São Sebastião do Rio de Janeiro. It became seat of a second royal captaincy under the governorship of Salvador de Sá, Mem de Sá's nephew. For many years it was a poorer version of Bahia or Olinda, much under the influence of the Sá family. These events, coupled with a series of short and destructive military campaigns against the Indians around Bahia, secured the center of Portuguese population.

Centralization was greatly furthered by close collaboration between the royal government and the Jesuit order. The Jesuit effort in sixteenth-century Brazil was extraordinary in its effects and pervasiveness. The Jesuits received encouragement and financial support from royal officials and often served as advisers and confessors to the most important people in the colony. Here (as elsewhere outside the central areas) the order directed its primary efforts toward conversion of the Indians, and as a result, the church in early Brazil was a missionary church to a large extent, with the role of the bishops and the diocesan clergy severely limited. Yet if in many ways the Brazilian church was like the church in Spanish American fringe areas, in some respects the Jesuit role in Brazil paralleled that of the Franciscans in Mexico as the first and most important of the regular orders in the colony; the Brazilian Jesuits maintained their predominant position through most of the colonial period.

They were never very many in number. In 1574 there were only 110 Jesuit priests in all of Brazil, but they made up in quality and activity what they lacked in numbers. The order had just been founded in 1540, and the first members to arrive in Brazil in 1549 were men of conviction, fervor, and ability. Father Manoel da Nóbrega, who led the group that arrived with Tomé de Sousa, immediately set to work converting Indians and thundering out against the sexual license and moral laxity of the colonists. At the same time he became an ardent advocate of the colony, and his letters were filled with phrases such as "anyone who wishes to live in an earthly paradise must come to Brazil" and "never did I see a Flemish tapestry as beautiful as this land." Such advocacy was appreciated by a royal government that was seeking to colonize. In fact, Nóbrega and his secretary, Father Jośe de Anchieta, worked closely with royal officials. They were very much responsible for the creation of the town of São Paulo in 1557 and for pacifying the Indians in the south. Jesuit colleges (schools) were established in all the important coastal towns and each was usually supported by the crown, often by means of sesmarias granted to them. Brazilian education to a large extent remained a Jesuit enterprise for the next three centuries.

Royal support of the Jesuit effort was supplemented and far exceeded by the Jesuits' own economic activities. Unlike the Franciscans, the Jesuits had no vow of poverty, and they quickly turned to agriculture and stock raising to support their activities in Brazil. Their engenhos and ranches were often the largest and best run. Such economic success coupled with their position against Indian slavery made them the target of constant complaint and occasionally of threatened violence. Nevertheless, their close ties to royal officials and local governors often placed the Jesuits at the fulcrum of politics as well as religious life in the early colony.

For thirty-five years the Jesuits had the Brazilian colony nearly to themselves. When the Franciscans and the Carmelites arrived in the 1580s, they were forced to accommodate themselves to a situation and forms already created by the Jesuits. The Franciscan monasteries, often beautifully built, were sometimes located in smaller rural communities. The Carmelites and the Benedictines raised beautiful churches and engaged in agriculture and ranching to some extent. These other orders, especially the Franciscans, also embarked on a missionary campaign and by the seventeenth century were extremely important in the Maranhão, but they generally lacked the degree of royal support enjoyed by the Jesuits. As far as religious life was concerned, the sixteenth century was the Jesuit century.

By the decade of the 1570s the major features of Portuguese Brazil had taken shape. Royal government had been established, supplanting the earlier phase of private initiative to some extent, but the area of bureaucratic control was limited to a narrow band along the coast and the area surrounding the small towns and cities. The interior remained for the most part unknown, still a realm of mythical treasures and real danger from still independent Indian groups. Entradas of prospectors and slavers or missionaries occasionally penetrated deeply into the sertão, or backlands, but effective control in these areas did not exist. There were no wealthy empires or groups of sedentary Indians upon whom to levy tribute in the Brazilian interior and hence little to attract the majority of colonists. What Brazil offered to most was easy access to land and through the profits to be made in sugar the possibility of wealth and social mobility. Settlement concentrated on the seacoast, where the climate and land were right for sugar and where transportation was inexpensive. The sugar mills constantly needed supplies from Portugal and the sugar was destined for European markets. By the last decades of the sixteenth century Brazil no longer resembled the "factory" colonies of West Africa or Asia and had become a colony of settlement, but of a particular kind: a tropical plantation colony capitalized from Europe and created on the periphery of Europe's economy to supply a growing market. Socially, the colony was marked by a high degree of differentiation between the Portuguese colonists or officials and the Indian and African slaves and laborers. To comprehend the formation of Brazilian society, it is necessary to understand the transformation of Portuguese-Indian relations and the eventual large-scale dependence on African slaves, topics to which we now turn.

Indian and African labor in Brazil

At the time of the Portuguese arrival on the coast, much of it was occupied by Tupian-speaking peoples who lived in semisedentary villages of 400 to 800 people divided into large lineage units occupying from four to eight long houses. They raised the South American staple crop, manioc, hunted, fished, and gathered various forest products. The men devoted much of their attention to warfare against their Tupian neighbors and against peoples of different tongues whom the Tupians and later the Portuguese collectively called Tapuyas (savages), probably because they did not practice agriculture. Among Tupian groups like the Tupinambá of Bahia and Rio de Janeiro or the Tupiniquin of Porto Seguro and São Vicente, warfare helped structure the society, since a man's status depended on his ability to kill and capture enemies and to present them for feasts of ritual cannibalism. The economy was very much part of the broader social system. Each lineage satisfied its own needs, and in the environment of coastal Brazil this was not at all difficult. There was little concern for surplus. Portuguese officials found such attitudes to be "barbaric" and "uncivilized," and they were often aghast at the seeming idleness of the men and their lack of concern about material possessions and surplus. Later, colonists would cite these very attitudes as justification for enslaving Indians in order to teach them the ways of civilized man.

But in the early years there were not many problems caused by the great distance between Tupians and Portuguese concepts of economy. During the first thirty years of contact, relations were primarily those of barter. The Portuguese (and the French) needed the Indians to help drag dyewood logs to the trade forts and stations on the coast and to supply foodstuffs. In return for labor, logs, and manioc, the Europeans offered cheap trade goods, trinkets, cloth, and occasionally axes and iron. None of this was very disruptive to Indian life. Tree felling was a traditional male activity which could be organized on a village basis, and so long as the village had enough to eat there was no reluctance to barter with the surplus.

With the advent of the captaincy system in the 1530s, the nature of Portuguese–Indian relations began to change radically. The donataries and the colonists wanted Indian services, commodities, and labor on a far more intensive and continual basis than had the dyewood cutters. Towns were being built and there were many more people to feed. But most of all, the labor demands of the sugar industry were enormous. Barter was no longer able to satisfy the increasing European demands, and the Portuguese turned increasingly to the enslavement of Indians.

The older interpretation of the failure of the barter system in the 1530s is based on the assumption that both Portuguese and Indians acted as "economic men," making rational decisions in response to objective market conditions. It holds that no longer satisfied with trinkets, Indians increasingly demanded more expensive goods and firearms, thereby driving up the cost of labor. Moreover, the competition between dyewood cutters and colonists for Indian labor also gave the Indians a distinct economic advantage. This situation then impelled the Portuguese to turn to slavery.

This interpretation, while correct in its outline of the shift from barter to slavery, probably overemphasizes the effect of the market on Indian reactions. The Indian economy was primarily one of use, not exchange, and was very much subordinate to other considerations such as lineage responsibilities. Semisedentary Tupians (and even more so the nonagricultural Tapuyas) showed little desire to accumulate more and more material goods. Once a man had one iron ax, he did not need another until it wore out. In fact, too many possessions made movement for the village difficult. The acquisition of more goods would have meant a shift to a more sedentary life, which probably would not have been compatible with Tupian agriculture. Perhaps even more important was the transformation in the kind of labor now demanded of the Indians. The day-to-day, backbreaking work of sugar agriculture differed vastly from the intermittent demands of tree felling, which was, after all, a traditional male activity. Agriculture was not; it was women's work and the Tupian warriors refused to do it, especially since it left no time for warfare and ceremony. Above all, it brought the Tupians out of their own society to be immersed in a Portuguese context. Portuguese officials described the situation in the classic terms of colonialism: The "natives" were lazy, undependable, and irrational because they would not respond to economic incentives. To "civilize" them and teach them how to act like Europeans, the colonists argued, they had to be enslaved.

Barter did not disappear at once. The Portuguese still needed food supplied by the Indians and were willing to pay or trade for it. During the building of Salvador, the workers and colonists often ate bread made with manioc flour acquired from the Indians. The needs for food and for plantation workers came into conflict. Slave raiding to acquire workers drove Indian villages away and thereby deprived the colonists, and especially the coastal towns, of an important supplier of food. To resolve the conflict, royal governors began to distinguish between the "good" Indians and "bad" Indians; the former accepted Christianity and Portuguese control and were willing to work or supply food and services. They could not be enslaved. The latter resisted conversion, ran away, and continued their old habits of warfare and cannibalism. Their enslavement was just. The colonists often acted, however, as if the distinctions were meaningless, and as sugar became increasingly important, the sugar planters tended to pay less and less attention to the niceties of royal law.

By the 1540s there were three simultaneous and often apparently conflicting Indian policies being followed by various Portuguese groups or institutions. The crown, urged by the Jesuits, sought to integrate the Indians peacefully into colonial society by conversion and acceptance of European norms of behavior including wage labor. The colonists were not averse to this, but they argued that the only way it could be accomplished was by enslavement. The Jesuits, and later the other orders, disagreed. They believed that Indians could be maintained in their villages under ecclesiastic supervision and thereby be not only instructed in Christianity but also convinced to grow food or occasionally supply labor for the colony. In a sense, the Jesuits wanted to create an Indian peasantry as opposed to the slavery favored by the colonists. In the sugar-growing regions the colonists eventually won out. The Jesuit villages (*aldeas*) lasted the longest in peripheral regions like the Amazon and the southern borderlands of Brazil, where the demands of intensive agriculture were absent. Royal laws beginning in 1570 and repeated in 1595 and 1609 prohibited Indian slavery, but loopholes could always be found. One of the most effective was the "ransoming" of captives. Entradas would go into the sertão to "ransom" Indians who had been captured and bound up by their enemies (*indios da corda*) in preparation for ritual execution. In return for this rescue, the Indians were forced to labor as slaves for the Portuguese. The possible abuses of this system are obvious. Indians were illegally enslaved, and the level of intertribal warfare increased as groups tried to satisfy the demands of the Portuguese.

Despite increasing royal support, the Jesuits were also forced by Brazilian conditions to modify their policies. By the 1560s they had abandoned the idea of carrying out conversion in the original Indian villages. Instead, Indians were brought to live in aldeas, which were supposed to replicate the Indian villages but were under Jesuit auspices and were much more akin to European communities in plan and organization. By prohibiting warfare, ritual cannibalism, polygamy, and cross-cousin marriage and not always respecting indigenous sociopolitical units, the Jesuits struck at some of the fundamental aspects of Indian society. So, despite the protection from enslavement that the aldeas offered, many Indians chose flight or even working on engenhos rather than the regulated life of the aldeas. The Jesuits were, however, ardent and able missionaries. Instruction was given in a simplified form of Tupí called the *lingua geral*, and grammars and catechisms were prepared in it by the clerics. Efforts were made to teach European trades as well as religion, and a modicum of self-government was also allowed in the aldea, although always under the paternal eye of the Jesuits. By the 1570s the idea of a full-scale Indian peasantry at the base of the colony's society no longer seemed feasible, and the Jesuits justified their continued control as serving more limited and practical purposes: supplying freemen (*forros*) to work for the colonists under wage labor conditions and Jesuit scrutiny and organizing auxiliaries for defense against hostile Indians and foreign interlopers. In some ways the Jesuit aldeas were an attempt to create a settled population where none had existed before, in order to supply necessary commodities and labor. They were parallel in this to the congregations of Spanish America, both being attempts to fix and concentrate the population and bring it under closer European control and at the same time to fill the ranks of Indian workers decimated by warfare, disease, and flight. They bore especially close resemblance to the kind of congregations often called "missions," which appeared where the indigenous population was less than sedentary and the Spanish population was thin; both types were alike in not being squarely based on already existing indigenous units and social mechanisms. In Spanish America the mission type of organization everywhere proved unable to stand up very long to a denser European presence, and so it was in Brazil too. Wherever the aldeas were close to zones of intensive export agriculture with its larger Portuguese populations and its demand for workers and land, there was no avoiding attrition, land loss, and epidemic disease. By the seventeenth century, the coastal aldeas were miserable little places with a few Indian families and a lonely priest or two.

The age of Indian labor in the core area of Brazil lasted for about sixty years (1540–1600). During most of this period the majority of workers in Brazil were free and slave Indians. On the plantations the distinctions between ransomed, enslaved, and free (forro) Indians were blurred. Portuguese wills sometimes bequeathed free Indians just as if they were property, and forros often did not receive their wages. In any case, treatment differed very little. In the sixteenth century the word "Indian" was often replaced by such terms as *gentio* (gentile) and *negro da terra* (native Black). Both terms reflected Portuguese perceptions of the Indians, and since "negro" was already strongly associated with "slave" in the Portuguese vocabulary, the use of this phrase also indicates a lack of distinction between slave and forro. As the number of engenhos grew, so too did the demand for laborers. Indians were brought in from the sertão and were also shipped from captaincy to captaincy. The whole Indian population of coastal Brazil was put under pressure, and each group was faced with the alternatives of fight, flight, or accommodation.

Indian labor provided the basis for the colony's growth and the first expansion of the sugar industry, but it had serious drawbacks from the Portuguese point of view. As we have seen, the Indians were resistant to agricultural labor; they fled at every opportunity, and they lacked the skills most highly prized in the sugar industry. Moreover, as elsewhere in the Americas, and especially in the lowland areas, they were highly susceptible to European diseases. In the 1560s smallpox and then measles ravaged the whole Brazilian coast. The Indians died in vast numbers. Whole villages disappeared. A third of all the Indians in Jesuit aldeas died, and at the engenhos the situation was just as bad. Slaving and resgate expeditions went farther and farther into the interior to fill the gaps, but replacement became more and more difficult. Faced with various kinds of Indian resistance, the high mortality rate, diminishing numbers, and increasing Jesuit opposition to slavery, the colonists began to turn to another labor source: the Atlantic slave trade.

In Chapter 1 we discussed how in the fifteenth century agricultural labor was added to household servitude in the traditions of Iberian slavery in connection with the development of the sugar engenho complex in Iberia and the Atlantic islands. By the time of Cabral's landing in Brazil, Portugal had been carrying African slaves to Iberia and Madeira for almost sixty years and had developed techniques and institutions to handle this trade. These included the trading forts at Axim and São Jorge da Mina and a customs house and registry in Lisbon (Casa dos Escravos). It is not surprising then that the Portuguese would seek to use African labor also in Brazil as it began to develop as a sugar colony. It might seem more surprising that the transition to African labor was so slow, but the timing was dictated by the initially small ability of the struggling sugar industry to pay for large numbers of expensive imported slaves.

The first Black slaves in Brazil undoubtedly arrived as body servants or sailors in the early expeditions, and their presence has remained unrecorded. The donatary captains received permission to bring a few dozen Africans for work on the engenhos. In the 1540s Duarte Coelho in Pernambuco, Pero de Gois in the captaincy of São Tomé (Rio de Janeiro), and others petitioned for the right to import Africans. A few were brought, but it was really in the period after 1560 that the Atlantic slave trade began to supply large numbers of Africans to the expanding export economy of Brazil. In the mid-1580s Pernambuco had sixty-six engenhos and some two thousand African slaves. If we estimate about a hundred slaves per engenho, we can see that Indians at that time still made up two-thirds of the mills' work force. Then in the following decades the transition gained momentum, leading eventually to an overwhelming predominance of African slaves in the sugar industry.

Assessing the overall reasons for the turn to African labor in the sugar industry, we have on the one hand the strong factor of precedent in Iberia and off Africa and on the other the proven and increasing difficulties with Indian labor which we have already enumerated. All over the world there has been a tendency to prefer the total outsider as a slave because he is cut loose from his own society and entirely without independent connection to the new land, hence less able to escape and resist, more open to learning new skills. In this case, the skills were not all new, for many of the Africans came from societies where intensive agriculture was common and where ironworking, cattle raising, and other arts useful in the engenhos were practiced. In the end, one must return to emphasis on the mortality differential. Although many Africans died in the terrible conditions of the slave ships or in the first year after arrival in Brazil, those who survived the acclimatization period were far less likely to succumb to Old World diseases than were the Indians. Maintaining an Indian population base in a hot lowland where there were many Europeans and an intense economic activity proved impossible anywhere in the Western Hemisphere.

The result of all this was that the advantages of using Africans ultimately outweighed the high costs of transportation. From an early time planters felt that the investment of time and money in training an African in the specialized skills of sugar making was more likely to be rewarded than it was with an Indian. The few existing engenho slave lists from sixteenth-century Brazil show a picture familiar from Spanish America, usually recording the Africans as skilled laborers, artisans, or even managers among a body of

Indian workers without special skills. Africans were enslaved, mistreated, and even when free suffered considerable social and economic disability, but they were part of the Old World tradition brought to America, auxiliaries in the creation of the colony, and generally they enjoyed much higher effective status than the Indians, just as in the Spanish Indies.

In view of all these factors, the productivity of Indian labor was held to be very low in comparison to that of African; one African was thought to be able to do the work of three or four Indians. This was true in Mexico and Peru as well as Brazil. Such perceptions were strongly reflected in slave prices. An Indian slave in sixteenth-century Brazil was generally valued at one-third the price of an African. Even among free laborers, Indians were invariably paid less than Africans or Brazilian-born Blacks. Again, the same differential existed all over Spanish America. But a major difference arose between northeastern Brazil and either the Spanish American central areas, where the Indian majority persisted as a base, or the Ibero-American fringe, where Indians were often scarce or not adaptable to European purposes but the settlers could not afford the alternative of African slaves. In northeastern Brazil, as in the New Granada gold mining district but on a much grander scale, the Europeans found themselves with a profitable export industry which could afford to make the transition to use of Africans not only as skilled labor and intermediaries but as the majority work force and base of the industry, here as field hands doing every task that the cultivation of sugar demanded. The same was to happen wherever lowland tropical export became viable in the New World.

By the early decades of the seventeenth century, the transition to African labor in the plantation zones of coastal Brazil was complete. The influx of large numbers of Africans changed the nature of the population and culture of colonial Brazil in ways that we will discuss subsequently; in fact, the point at which Africans were a majority in the labor force and a significant population component marks the end of Brazil's beginning phase. Indian slavery or other forms of Indian labor survived in those parts of Brazil like São Paulo and the Amazon that were marginal to the dominant economy and were too poor to make the importation of Africans possible. In the sugar-growing regions of the coast, Indians had provided large numbers of workers, "cheap labor," at a crucial time when the industry lacked capital. The results for the Indians were disastrous, but for the sugar industry, the Indians had made possible rapid expansion at less cost, playing the same transitional role as in other low-altitude regions such as the Caribbean islands and the New Granadan gold district. By 1600 the predominant social and economic patterns were laid down; Africans had replaced Indians as slaves, and Brazil had become the world's leading producer of sugar. In the northeast, the phase of existence as a fringe, with the typical fringe area complex of barter in natural products, armed hostilities, missions, Indian slavery, few Europeans and Africans, and relative governmental neglect, had come to an end.

7
Brazil in the sugar age

By the early seventeenth century two kinds of society existed in Brazil. On the flourishing northeastern coast sugar mills had been established, ports serving the sugar trade had developed, and the area's Portuguese population was growing fast. Here the institutions and social forms of Portugal had been transferred with relative success, and a full-blown European-style settler colony had been created. As a result, the Brazilian northeast was beginning to parallel the Spanish American central areas of the mature period in many ways, although there were some profound differences as well. The economic basis of the northeast after the late sixteenth century was the bulk agricultural export sugar, rather than silver as in Mexico or Peru, and despite the efforts of the Jesuits to convince the Brazilian Indians to do intensive labor, or those of the colonists to force them to, a sedentary Indian labor force was simply lacking. The Indian base of the central areas of Spanish America was absent in Brazil, and the attention of the government was directed to stimulating and taxing the sugar trade, rather than collecting labor and tribute from the indigenous population. But export agriculture did create a viable basis for the growth of the northeast, and by 1600 a population of about 100,000, including large numbers of European women and some 30,000 Black slaves, sure signs of a region's wealth, were concentrated at the ports and sugar mills (see Map 7).

The failure of the Portuguese to create a dependable Indian labor force, coupled with population loss from epidemic disease and flight, made the significance of African workers all the greater. Faced with a growing demand for sugar in Europe, Portuguese planters increased the level of slave importation, so that rather than an auxiliary labor force as in most of Spanish America, Africans and their descendants became the majority of the population. This development of an agricultural export economy characterized by African slave labor and a Euro-African cultural fusion foreshadowed what would take place in the Caribbean and certain coastal areas of Spanish America in the eighteenth century.

Despite the strong European cultural and institutional overlay in

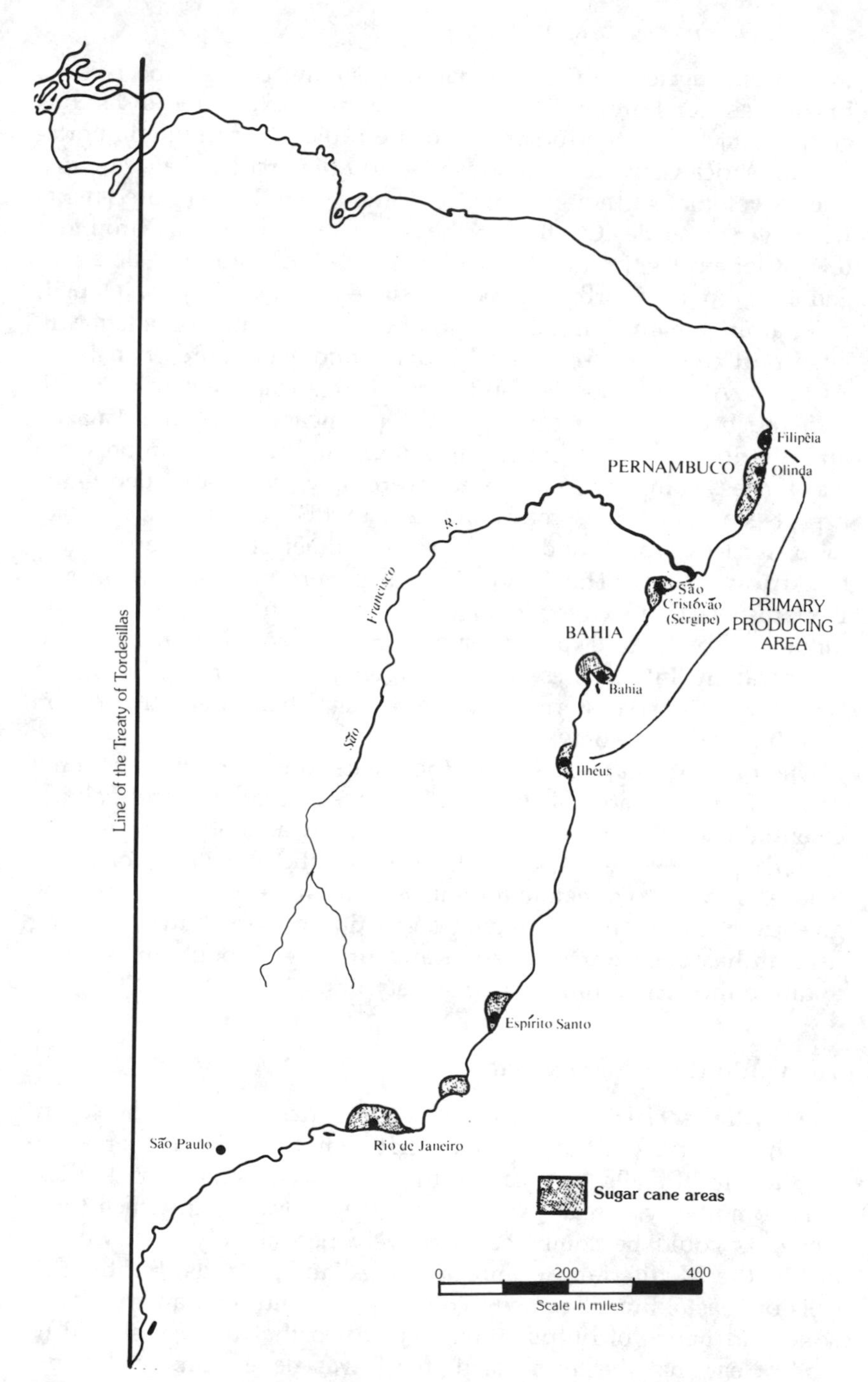

Map 7. The sugar-producing area of Brazil.

the coastal agricultural areas that formed the core of the colony, Brazil was not Europe. The early missionary effort, the disastrous early contact with the Indians, and the rapidly expanding importation of Africans created relationships and hierarchies that were distinctly colonial, although always drawing on Iberian precedents whenever possible. On the northeastern sugar coast and around a few other port cities like Rio de Janeiro to the south and Belém or São Luiz to the north, an Iberian slave-based society developed, maintaining many European forms but resting on a population in large part composed of coerced Indians and even more of enslaved Africans. Although located on the coast, this was the core of Brazil.

In the backlands, or sertão, of the northeast, along the Amazon and its tributaries, and in the south of Brazil, the European presence was far less complete. These areas were only secondarily tied to the export economy of the coast, and they tended to attract fewer colonists, far less capital, and only a small number of European women or African slaves. The hand of royal government was weak and Iberian institutions were attenuated. Here society remained far more influenced by Indian ways in material culture, social interaction, and organization. Life in these now peripheral areas remained as it had been on the northeastern coast before sugar had pulled that region into the world economy.

The present chapter is concerned with the new sugar-oriented Brazil. The international context of European economy and politics, essential enough for an understanding of any area of Latin America, is perhaps even more so in the case of the Brazilian northeast, whose life was so dependent on its agricultural exports, and we will give external matters consideration in due course. But proceeding here as has been our inclination and practice throughout, we will examine the local economy and society first.

The world that sugar created

The central social institution of colonial Brazilian life in the seventeenth century was the engenho, that complex of land, coerced labor, technical skills, and capital that produced Brazil's primary export commodity, sugar. As we have seen, the way in which these elements could be combined effectively had already been worked out in the Mediterranean and on the Atlantic islands, but the rich soils of coastal Brazil seemed to offer opportunities for an increase in scale and hence of output unknown up to that time. It should be made clear that the term "plantation" was never employed to describe the unit of production in the sugar industry. Instead, Iberians used the word "engenho" (Sp. *ingenio,* related to Eng. "engine"), which strictly speaking meant only the mill itself but came to represent the whole operation, including houses, slaves, land, and animals. The term "engenho" evokes images of the rural seigneur, of patriarchal dominance, of country estates, servants, and slaves, set among green cane fields and palms on the horizon. Although much of the image is true, there is also a heavy coating of romanticism that must be peeled away if we are to understand the nature of the engenho and its effects on the development of Brazilian society.

Let us begin with sugarcane itself, for the nature of the crop and its product, sugar, determined much of the engenho's structure. Although there were regional variations, the process described here was basically the same throughout the Americas. The first crop usually took some fifteen to eighteen months to mature, but thereafter for the next three or four years the same field would yield a new crop every nine months or so without replanting. The harvest, or *safra* (Sp. *zafra*), began at the end of July and continued for eight or nine months. During this period the engenho was alive with activity. Slaves cut the cane and loaded it onto oxcarts that were then driven to the mill. There another crew of slaves produced sugar from the cane under the direction of technicians and with the help of artisans who might be either slave or free. The process was difficult and complicated. First the cane was passed through vertical roller presses, which were usually powered on the big engenhos by waterwheels, and on the smaller ones by oxen. The syrup pressed from the cane was then passed through a series of kettles where it was boiled and clarified until finally it was sufficiently clean to make sugar. The liquid was poured into conical molds, which were then set on long rows of planks in a special drying shed. After further drainage, which required three weeks or a month, the molds could be opened, showing the crystallized sugar to have formed in its characteristic "sugar loaf." The best grade had the least impurities and was therefore white in color. Brown sugar (*muscavado*) sold for less, and the inferior grades were often used to make rum. The sugar was then dried, crated in large chests, and taken by boat or oxcart to Salvador, Recife, or some smaller port for shipment to Europe.

As one can see, sugar was a special crop in that it demanded not only agriculture but also highly technical processing. The need to process sugarcane at the point of origin meant that each engenho was a combination of agricultural and industrial enterprise, needing large amounts of capital and credit, the specialized skills of blacksmiths, carpenters, coopers, and masons, and the technical know-how of men who understood the intricacies of the sugar-making process. Moreover, the labor demands of cane cultivation and sugar production were great and terrible. During the harvest, the engenho operated eighteen to twenty hours a day, and many observers remarked that the heat and fires of the cauldrons called up images of scenes of hell.

The average mill had some sixty to eighty slaves, but a few large ones had more than two hundred. Although conditions might vary from engenho to engenho according to the personalities of owners or overseers, sugar imposed its own realities. In general, no matter what the intentions of the planters, the arduous working conditions, climate, and problems of food, housing, and care produced very high rates of disease and mortality. In a single year an engenho expected to lose between 5 and 10 percent of its slaves. Father Cardim, a Jesuit observer, wrote simply in the 1580s that "the work is great and many die." But as contemporaries put it, from the bitter captivity of the slaves came the sweet sugar, and for the slave-owning sugar planters, profit and status were to be gained from the enterprise. To be called *senhor de engenho* (millowner) in colonial Brazil was to be respected and obeyed; it was a title that brought with it power and prestige. The Portuguese crown never created a Brazilian nobility of dukes and counts, but the title "senhor de engenho" often fulfilled the same function.

Given the nature of the economy, it is not surprising that the sugar planters came to exercise considerable political, social, and economic power. Their interests were favored by a royal policy which provided tax incentives and some protection from foreclosure on debts. Unlike Spanish America, where rural estates were not central to the international economy, Brazil depended overwhelmingly on agricultural export, and the senhores de engenho were continually favored.

As a group, the planters' origins were not particularly distinguished. The first mills had been established not only by the donataries but by people of more humble origins. Although some of the titled nobility of Portugal owned land and sugar mills in Brazil, few ever set foot on their properties. They remained content to collect the profits from such overseas activities and to depend on agents and overseers in Brazil. Some fidalgos (noblemen) received awards of land for their services in the conquest of the coast, as did others who came in the retinue of governors after 1549, but many of those who obtained sesmarias in the sugar regions were commoners able through arms or influence to obtain the land, credit, and capital necessary to begin sugar planting.

It was not long before the senhores de engenho began to exhibit certain group characteristics and a distinctive life-style. First of all, the Brazilian planters were not an absentee class. The proximity of engenhos to the coastal towns and the long harvest season permitted and demanded their presence on the rural estates. Thus the planter families tended to live on the engenhos. The focus of life was the big house (*casa grande*), which was substantial in the sixteenth and seventeenth centuries but often not at all as magnificent as it was to become later on. Adjoining the planter's residence was usually a chapel, although most did not have resident chaplains. Gracious hospitality, rounds of visits, and conspicuous consumption became a way of life. "In Pernambuco one finds more vanity than in Lisbon," said Father Cardim. The engenhos he visited were so filled with food and luxury that the planters "appeared to be counts," which, of course, they were not. Often this style of life did not reflect the planters' real financial position, for one or two bad harvests could bring ruin. There were, in fact, a great many failures and a constant circulation of people into and out of the planter class, a fact often ignored because of the continued success of some families.

The planters set the tone of the society. For them and nearly everyone else the dominant social form continued to be the patriarchal family, a transplantation of the Iberian ideal. The engenho, or *fazenda* (like "hacienda" in Spanish, a term that was used for any large agricultural estate), provided the setting for this family-oriented social grouping so desired by the colonists. In Brazil, although the traditional distinctions between high- and lowborn were maintained, other criteria also emerged to mark status. Married men and heads of households held a privileged position and were often accorded rights of citizenship or local offices denied to others. This favoritism underlined the important role played by the family in the settlement of Brazil and its social formation. The "family," of course, included distant relatives, godchildren, and various dependents. Some slaves, especially house servants or children born in the big house, might also be included in the patriarchal grouping. Such arrangements did not mean that all were treated equally within the group or that class and color distinctions were ignored, but the extended family groupings did cut across class lines. The world of rural Brazil was dominated by these groups.

Eventually, the small number of planter clans became linked by marriage and partnership into a web of closely woven patriarchal families, sometimes allied and sometimes hostile, but sharing similar attitudes and behavior. The dominant place of men, the often suppressed role of women (at least in theory), the constant concern with family "honor," and the virtually unrestricted power of the patriarch over family, slaves, and property have reminded many authors of the situation of medieval times. However, whereas some relationships and social patterns may have resembled those of feudal Europe, there were great differences as well. Although African slavery had been known in medieval Europe, it became the dominant mode of production only in America, and it created social forms and patterns on a scale previously unknown. Also, if the planters resembled counts, they also acted a good deal like accountants. The engenhos were not medieval manors. They were complicated business enterprises, and although prestige was important in the minds of the planters, calculations of profit and loss were even more so. Up to the 1620s, when sugar prices in Europe were soaring, fortunes could be made; but as we shall see shortly, the boom began to slow and sugar became a less sure way to wealth.

The investment in capital stock (land, buildings, equipment, animals, etc.) was very large and constituted at least two-thirds of the operating costs. Labor, both salaried employees and slaves, made up the rest. (Some economists would list the slave costs with the capital as well.) Annual profit might run from 7 to 10 percent, but in terms of total capital invested, the return was closer to 3 or 4 percent. This is a small margin of profit by modern standards, but planters were limited by many factors beyond their control, including the supply of slaves, the vagaries of the weather, and the limitations of existing technology. The conspicuous consumption of the senhores de engenho and their elevated social position often disguised a rather tenuous financial position. Little wonder that turnover was high among the planter class. Adverse conditions in one or another sector would drive those with little capital or credit to ruin, and the engenho would become *fogo morto* (the fire out, or inoperative). It would then be placed on the auction block or be taken over by merchant creditors and within a few years would begin again under the ownership of another hopeful, anxious to try his luck.

Given the obvious hazards involved in sugar production, it is not surprising to find that a form of sharecropping developed to diffuse the risks. A distinctive aspect of the sugar economy's organization in Brazil, setting it apart from sugar-producing regions of Spanish America and the non-Iberian Caribbean, was the existence of a whole class of sugarcane cultivators, called *lavradores de cana*. For the most part they were whites who lacked enough capital or credit to set up their own engenhos and instead grew sugarcane which they brought to be processed at a nearby mill. Their contracts and arrangements with the engenho owners were complex and varied. Many were tenants or sharecroppers who did not own land but rented or leased it from an engenho. Their cane was "captive," in that they were bound to process it at the mill that provided the land, usually paying three-fifths of the sugar produced from their cane as a fee or rent. Millowners preferred to rent their best lands to wealthier lavradores who had the slaves, oxen, and equipment necessary to take on the contract *a terço*, that is, at a third, surrendering one-third of their sugar as rent after a fifty–fifty division had been made between the senhor de engenho and the lavrador. The length of the lease and the division of the sugar produced could vary considerably. Nine years was common, but fifty-year leases were not unknown. It seems that during hard times, leases and the percentage division of the sugar favored the lavradores, since planters were anxious to have them share the risks and expenses of production. The lavradores de cana in the strongest position were those who owned their own land and could thus bargain each year with a number of mills for the best division of sugar and the loan of slaves or oxen.

The variety of ownership and contractual arrangements among the lavradores indicates that they were not a homogeneous social or economic group. Most were Portuguese or Brazilian-born whites, although by the eighteenth century some free people of color also began to appear within their ranks. Lavradores de cana with noble status or with high positions in militia regiments could be found along with merchants who might own a cane farm as part of their many interests. Priests might own a cane farm as a supplementary income, and widows could also be found as cane growers. Along with the wealthier and more socially prominent people who held cane farms were many social nobodies who owned a few acres and labored in the fields themselves alongside family and slaves, something the more prominent and wealthy lavradores would never do. Indeed, the contrasting levels of wealth and social prominence among the cane growers must be emphasized, for there were a few who could boast of more than 200 acres and thirty or forty slaves, whereas many more lavradores had only a few acres and slaves. Invariably, however, this was a slave-owning group, averaging six to ten slaves per lavrador.

In a sense the lavradores de cana were protoplanters, people of the same social origins as the sugar-mill owners who hoped by the avenue of cane farming to acquire their own engenho someday. For many this was to be an unrealized dream, but the very hope of such upward mobility was an important force in attracting people to cane farming and as such was encouraged by the engenho owners, who needed the services of the lavradores even though they might eventually become competitors. The relationship between the senhores de engenho and the lavradores de cana was, in fact, one of both conflict and cooperation. The millowners tried to hold patriarchal sway over their lavradores and take advantage of them in economic terms, but they needed them as well. Lavradores resented their dependence on the senhores, but on major issues affecting the sugar industry or in their hostility toward merchant creditors, the lavradores sided with the millowners. All in all, the social niche of the lavradores de cana was a favorable and "honorable" one, ranking just below that of senhor de engenho, and a cane farmer who "made it" could hope for political and social positions as well as wealth.

The existence of the lavradores de cana had many implications for the social and economic patterns of colonial Brazil. In the early stages of sugar's expansion, the burden and risks were more widely shared than in other regions. An average engenho might have three or four lavradores, and a larger mill as many as twenty-five. They and their families were an important segment of the population and made the countryside a patchwork of lands and leases far more complex than the mythical image of the single dominant planter surrounded by a sea of slaves. The engenhos were the commercial and productive core, to be sure, but they were highly dependent on the cane of the lavradores, supplies and credit provided by the merchants, and loans from religious institutions. The lavradores were a slave-owning class and even at the end of the colonial period when their numbers had apparently decreased, they still controlled a significant proportion of the slaves. A census made in Bahia in 1816 showed that about one-third of the slaves employed directly in sugar agriculture were owned by the cane growers. Whereas their slaves were mostly field hands and not subjected to the all-night labor within the mills, on the other hand, most of the cane farmers could not afford many slaves devoted to domestic service or the sort of paternalism associated with the image of the great "plantations." In terms of the conditions of labor there is little reason to believe that the existence of small units improved the lot of slaves, but from a social viewpoint it made a great difference. Many slaves lived in relatively small groups of five or ten fellow slaves in constant contact with a Portuguese or Brazilian-born white lavrador and his family, and often they also interacted with the other small farmers and artisans who inhabited the sugar regions. This is a far cry from the old image of enormous "plantations" with hundreds of slaves virtually out of touch with the dominant European culture. By the early eighteenth century in the center of the sugar-growing and slave region of Bahia, free people made up about half the rural population. They provided the context of Iberian social and cultural forms to which the traditions of Africa were constantly molded.

The free rural population included not only the sugar planters and lavradores de cana but many other social groups as well. In the seventeenth century, free people of color and some poor whites lived on the margins of the engenhos. Given a small plot of land, they were allowed to remain in return for services as herdsmen, woodcutters, and foodstuff suppliers. Relatively few in this period, their numbers greatly expanded in the eighteenth century as the population of mulattoes and free Blacks rose from natural increase and slave manumissions, and they filled the social levels occupied by mestizos and Hispanized Indians in many Spanish American areas. Even more central to the sugar-mill operations were the various skilled artisans, technicians, and managerial personnel (overseers, foremen, administrators) who worked for wages. A large engenho, like Sergipe do Conde in Bahia (see Figure 11), often paid as much as 25 percent of its annual expenses in salaries for the services of these individuals. Carpenters, masons, overseers, sugar-making specialists, lawyers, a chaplain, and a physician or barber-surgeon all figured on the payroll of a large mill. Such an engenho might have fifteen to twenty resident employees during the safra, and although skilled slaves were often used as replacements, few engenhos could entirely dispense with the costs of free labor.

It is important, then, to remember that Brazilian society in the seventeenth century, even on the engenhos, was not simply divided into planters and slaves. The social structure was always more complex than that. At the same time, we must recognize the pervasive role that slavery and slaveholding had on all other social and economic forms. Free artisans existed, but in a situation where slaves could sometimes exercise the same crafts, wages were depressed and the guild system very weak. So long as planters had an adequate supply of slaves, any kind of free peasantry was also at a disadvantage.

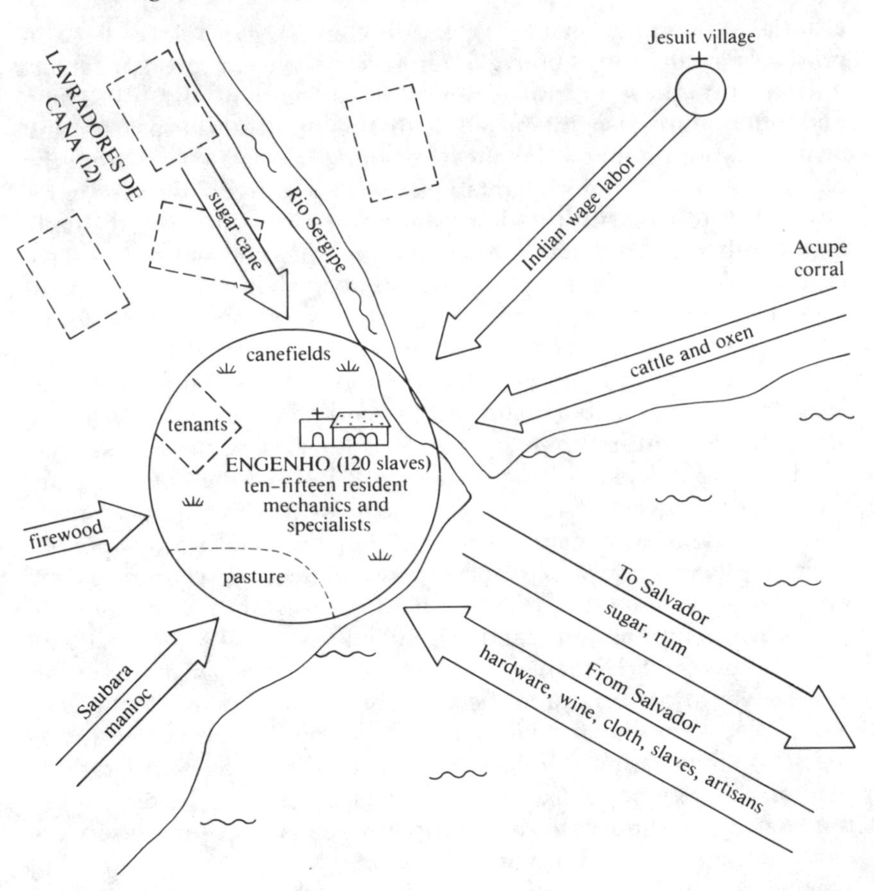

Figure 11. Engenho Sergipe, ca. 1600.

Slavery also influenced social organization and production in Brazil's other agricultural activities. Sugar was not the country's only source of income in the seventeenth century, although it probably made up 90 percent of the total value of exports. Small amounts of ginger, cotton, and specialized products such as whale oil also made their way to Europe along with the traditional dyewood, but the largest alternate export items were tobacco and hides. Grown in Pernambuco and Bahia in areas not well suited to sugar cultivation, tobacco became particularly important as the century advanced. Although slaves were used in its production as with sugar, the size of holdings and of operations was generally smaller. Tobacco in Brazil was not exactly a "poor man's crop" as is sometimes said, but it did attract a class of growers less wealthy in general than did sugar production.

Tobacco was also crucial because it had two principal markets. The better grade was sent to Europe, where it filled pipes and snuffboxes. The lesser grades, smeared with molasses to produce a pleasant aroma and taste, were used for trade on the African coast. By the eighteenth century, Brazilian tobacco had become a major item in the slave trade needed to supply the fields and mines of Brazil, giving Brazilian (especially Bahian) merchants a comparative advantage in that trade. In a sense tobacco became a necessary means by which sugar production and gold mining were carried out.

The sugar industry was also in large part responsible for the growth of another major activity in colonial Brazil – cattle ranching. The engenhos needed constant supplies of oxen for the carts and mills, as well as tallow for candles and meat for employees and slaves. Most engenhos maintained some pasturage for their own oxen, but cattle were raised mainly on marginal lands which would not support sugar or other valuable export crops. Like horses, goats, sheep, pigs, and chickens, cattle had been introduced into Brazil in the early sixteenth century and had multiplied rapidly. Forced out of the zones of sugar production near the coast, the cattle herds began to develop on a large scale in the best-watered areas of the arid sertão between Pernambuco and Bahia. By 1590, in the region known as Sergipe de El-Rey, ranchers and cowboys had pushed their herds far along the São Francisco River and with the help of the royal government had subdued Indian resistance. In 1594 there were some forty-seven corrals on the São Francisco, and by 1640 there were more than two thousand. Eventually the herds moved north into Piauí and Maranhão, rapidly expanding as the demands of the export sector grew and mining created a new market in the eighteenth century. By the beginning of that century the northeast alone had more than 1.3 million head.

In many cases the owners of the engenhos or other members of their families also became the ranchers. Sesmarias in the sertão were quite large, sometimes exceeding a hundred thousand acres, and by the close of the seventeenth century there were landholdings in the backlands larger than whole provinces of Portugal. Great ranching families might run more than twenty thousand head on their lands. Such potentates were the exception, and one thousand to three thousand head was more usual, but in general the cattle-ranching zones did tend to be divided into large estates, sparsely populated by cowboys, their helpers, and a few fieldhands, and dominated by great ranching families with close ties to the planter elite of the coast. Although productivity was low in the arid sertão and profits were reduced, the ranchers exercised virtually complete authority so far from the centers of government.

Some Indians were employed on the ranches, but the cattle-raising areas of the interior were predominantly populated by mixed bloods (*caboclos, mestiços*) and poor whites; in Brazil, as in many places in Spanish America, the mixed-blood population did the bulk of ranching work. The freedom of movement, the life on horseback, was apparently appealing to those whose social position on the coast was marginal at best. Although some cattle products (hides, tallow, and eventually jerked beef) were exported, the ranches were principally oriented toward the internal markets created by the engenhos and coastal ports. Herds were periodically driven over long trails to fair towns on the perimeters of the sugar-growing zones, where they were sold as beef and transport animals. Meat supply in the cities was carried out through a municipal monopoly on slaughtering.

A final aspect of cattle ranching to be mentioned is the important role it played in the penetration of the interior in the seventeenth century. By pushing their herds into the sertão, cowhands and cattle barons opened the vast Brazilian interior to settlement. But we must keep in mind that cattle raising was an extensive activity. Many acres of scrub were needed to raise one animal, and the need for labor was very limited, since one cowboy and his family could manage many head of cattle. Thus although the frontier was opened, the population of the interior was small and very thinly dispersed over a vast territory. The export-oriented coast was still the core of colonial Brazil.

Scattered around the engenhos in marginal lands, along the interior roadways, and in areas not favorable to export crops, subsistence crops were grown. The Portuguese adopted the Indian staple manioc and it became the staff of life, prepared as a coarse flour and made into bread or mixed with beans. Manioc farming was a humble occupation and those who engaged in it tended to be poor mestizos, mulattoes, and free Blacks, sometimes ex-slaves. Their *roças,* or farms, were small units and their tenure was often insecure, dependent on the whim of large landowners. Although some growers consumed most of their crop, much roça production was commercial. We should not lose sight of the fact that the large slave population of the engenhos and the inhabitants of the cities also had to be fed. Some engenhos grew their own food or maintained separate manioc farms for that purpose, but others bought food from independent roças. Manioc was grown not only by small farmers but also by entrepreneurs on a fairly large scale.

Two aspects of the situation need to be understood. First, Brazil's export sector exerted a considerable influence over all aspects of the economy, including the provision of primary foodstuffs. Throughout the colonial era, the desire to profit from export crops caused shortages of basic foods. As early as the 1630s the government issued decrees ordering certain regions to grow only food crops, and eventually laws insisted that every slaveowner and shipowner in the slave trade supply enough food for his slaves. The delicate balance between the export crops and the needed foodstuffs had to be maintained by such governmental adjustments to avoid famines. Second, we can note that slavery played an important role and was often the dominant form of labor even in the area of "subsistence" agriculture. In reality, the export economy and slavery cannot be separated from any other aspect of Brazilian society and economy in this period, and it is to the central institution of slavery that we now turn.

The African and slavery

The northeast of Brazil became the first fully developed plantation zone in the Americas and the first to rest so heavily on Black slavery. As European demand for sugar grew, so too did the tide of importation of African slaves to Brazil. Our introductory chapters on Iberian and Indian social patterns might well have been followed by a chapter on Africa, since in many places in the New World, Africans and Afro-Americans strongly influenced cultural and, at times, social forms. We have chosen not to add such a chapter first because in many kinds of situations the Africans became so enmeshed in the Iberian sector that their separate contribution is very hard to discern compared to that of Indians and Iberians, and secondly because of the difficulty in generalizing about African cultures. It is true that many Africans transported to the New World came from "West Africa," but that is an amorphous geographical term which has often been used loosely to include parts of central and southwestern Africa. Even within smaller and more precisely defined regions of Africa there existed wide cultural and linguistic differences. As a result, African slaves in the New World most often had to use the matrix of Iberian culture as a basis for interchange among themselves. Such a situation was sometimes purposely furthered by slaveowners, who selected Africans of various groups and regions in order to stimulate cooperation and lessen the chance of rebellion.

On the other hand, it must also be recognized that African societies widely shared certain notions and values, such as the importance of lineage and clan, concepts of kingship, the relation of people to their gods through the intervention of ancestors, and the relation of the spiritual world to good and bad or sickness and health in the present world. Such things are difficult for the historian to document in a specific situation, but if they are kept in mind it is possible to understand how Africans from widely divergent backgrounds were able to create an Afro-American culture that grew not only from the slave experience but from African traditions as well.

We have already seen how in areas of intense Spanish-Indian contact, Blacks, whether free or slave, became auxiliaries in the Spanish conquest and the creation of Spanish society. Brazil serves as an example of the tropical plantation colonies where society and economy were solidly based on Black slavery and where a majority of the population was of African or Afro-American origin. In such situations Africans took over the roles played by both Africans and Indians in the Spanish central areas, with drastic qualitative and quantitative effects on the overall structure and the general position of Africans in society. Although there were regional differences between Brazil, the Caribbean islands, and the coasts of Venezuela and Colombia, all these areas of dense African population and plantation slavery demonstrate many similar demographic, social, and ethnic patterns. (Even the Mexican, Central American, and Peruvian coasts evince certain parallels.)

Estimates vary widely, but between 1550 and 1800 Brazil probably received about two and half million African slaves. During the seventeenth century perhaps four or five thousand a year reached the colony from Portuguese slaving ports in West Africa and Angola. The slave trade was a constant and central feature of slavery in Brazil. As in most of the plantation zones of Spanish America and the Caribbean, in Brazil the slave population suffered from a natural rate of decline; the number of deaths always exceeded the number of births. Demographers are unsure of the exact reasons for this situation, although mistreatment, high rates of infant mortality, the tropical environment, a disrupted family life, and manumission, especially of women and children, all contributed to it. Given this situation, it is easy to understand the crucial role of the Atlantic slave trade. The engenhos were in constant need of replacements for the labor force, and thus the trade to Brazil was large and continual, expanding or contracting to adjust to the needs of the Brazilian economy. But there was a deadly paradox. Because newly arrived Africans often suffered very high mortality rates in Brazil and because the slavers tended to ship almost twice as many men as women, the slave trade continued to introduce a sexual imbalance and a susceptible population, factors that probably contributed as much to the continuing net loss as all the others just listed. Slave demography and the slave trade in Brazil became a vicious circle.

In the seventeenth century the majority of slaves labored in agriculture, although slaves could be found doing almost every kind of work. The slave population was not an undifferentiated mass of laborers. There were actually a series of hierarchies that structured the slave population. From the slaveowners' view, the most difficult to manage were the "barbaric" newly arrived Africans (*boçal* in Port.; *bozal* in Sp.). Although slaveowners supposedly preferred slaves from certain regions or peoples, in fact availability in the marketplace was never so great as to allow these preferences to operate freely, and slave prices indicate that age and sex had far more to do with value than did specific African origins. Once the slaves had learned Portuguese and had at least outwardly adopted Christianity, they were considered *ladinos,* or acculturated, and were generally thought of as more dependable. Of course, Black slaves born in Brazil (*crioulos*) did not have to overcome problems of cultural adjustment to the same extent, nor were they as susceptible to disease in Brazil as were the African-born. Finally, mulatto slaves had some Portuguese admixture in addition to the advantage of being Brazilian-born. Slaveowners thus considered them to be especially intelligent or skillful but at the same time crafty and untrustworthy.

This hierarchy based on color and place of birth was paralleled and intersected by another based on occupation. Field hands made up the great majority of the slave population. On the engenhos there were also those skilled in the special tasks of sugar making, as well as those who served as drivers or low-level managers. The house slaves were a somewhat privileged group, usually mulattoes and crioulos, but they made up only some 5 percent of the total slave population. Finally, those who had artisan skills were highly valued on the engenhos and in the cities as well.

In general, then, the more skilled, the more ladino, and the lighter in color a slave, the higher he or she stood in the slave hierarchy according to Portuguese standards. The slaves themselves surely had their own criteria of rank and position, about which we know little. Still, it is important to point out that certain Portuguese categorizations were adopted by the slaves themselves.

Distinctions between Blacks and mulattoes were recognized as well as those between the various African "nations." Slavery was not only an economic system but a life-style that in tropical America formed and defined the society. It should not be surprising that slaves as well as masters came to be influenced by the ideas that underwrote slavery.

The slave-based plantation societies like Brazil contained two social formations, neither of which could be really separate from the other. The slaves had their own life, customs, and beliefs, which they were able to maintain somewhat apart from the dominant Portuguese culture, but neither side was free of the influence of the other. The slaves adopted European material goods, language, and Christianity, even if only outwardly. The slaveowners, living in close proximity to their slaves, came to know the cuisine, music, language, and healing practices of Africa, learning these from nursemaids, playmates, and mistresses. The result was a society that functioned at a number of levels, dominated by European forms, yet heavily influenced by the Africans and Afro-Brazilians who formed its base.

On the engenhos life for the slaves was usually hard and short. Labor conditions during the safra were terrible. Despite the efforts of the church, the presence of twice as many men as women made family life difficult, as did the intervention of masters who took Black or mulatto women for themselves or who broke up families by sales. Housing and clothing was minimal and even food was often in short supply. Slaves were sometimes left to shift for themselves, growing their own food in their "spare" time. Royal legislation forcing planters to provide sufficient food for their slaves was frequently ignored because planters refused to give up any land that could produce an export crop in order to supply their slaves.

Although the lack of care for slaves who were among other things an expensive investment seems senseless, we must understand this brutality within the economic context. Slaveowners estimated that a slave could produce on the average about three-quarters of a ton of sugar a year. At the prices of the period, this meant in effect that a slave would produce in two or three years an amount of sugar equal to the slave's original purchase price and the cost of maintenance. Thus if the slave lived only five or six years, the investment of the planter would be doubled, and a new and vigorous replacement could be bought. No wonder there was little incentive to improve conditions or to foster a higher birthrate among slaves. Children, after all, would have to be supported for twelve or fourteen years before they became productive. The basic theory of slave management seems to have been: "Work them hard, make a profit, buy another." Of course, there were critics of such inhumanity. A few Jesuits and secular priests wrote treatises against abuses, and the crown sometimes stepped in to stop particularly sadistic actions. But, in general, slave management was left to the slaveowners and the slaves had little recourse.

Although the physical and familial life of plantation slaves suffered from the economic and demographic realities of the colony, the previous Iberian traditions of domestic slavery based on Roman law, church doctrine, and patriarchalism did create certain opportunities for slaves. The cultural life of the slave quarters remained relatively unimpeded so long as Catholicism was at least nominally accepted. In fact, the plantation system may have concentrated enough people of the same ethnic background in one place so that the language and traditions of certain African groups were maintained, but, of course, always in contact with Iberian culture. How much of the social or institutional structure of Africa was preserved is a matter of conjecture.

The Iberian traditions of slavery also provided some opportunity for slaves to gain access to freedom. Manumission was a constant feature of slavery in Brazil. Women were twice as likely to be freed as men, and children reared in the household, especially if mulatto, also had a better chance of gaining freedom. Slaveowners would sometimes free faithful or favored slaves, some of them their own children, in wills or at baptisms. Just as important were manumissions granted in return for compensation. Through their own efforts or those of family and friends, slaves bought their own freedom. Often manumissions were conditional and called for further service or other obligations. The mixture of economic motivations and religious or cultural sentiments is just as complex in the manumission process as in other aspects of Brazilian slavery. In any case, manumissions continued and slowly created a class of freedmen, former slaves who began to fill certain intermediate occupations and roles in Brazilian life. Society was divided not only into slave and free but also according to color and occupation (see Figure 12). The group of free people of color was still relatively small in the seventeenth century, but continuing manumissions and natural increase caused their ranks to swell in the following century, and we will have reason to discuss them further.

Manumission was only one means of achieving freedom. As the numbers of slaves grew, so too did the number of runaways. In the

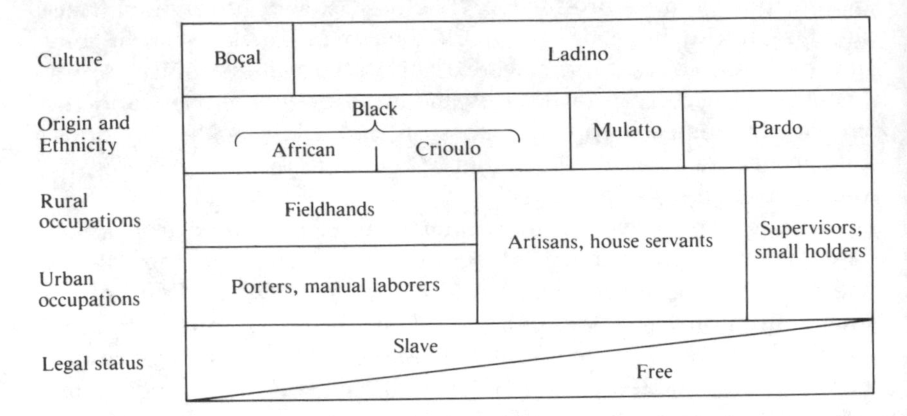

Figure 12. Approximate correspondences of culture, ethnicity, occupation, and legal status of Blacks and mulattoes in colonial Brazil. (To read the chart, imagine individuals situated along the upper horizontal line; if perpendicular lines are imagined below each, that individual should normally share all the qualities specified in the succeeding intersected spaces.)

plantation zones slave resistance became a constant aspect of the slave regime. In Brazil, with its tropical climate and vegetation, runaways were an endemic problem. Engenho owners hired Indian trackers or professional slave catchers to hunt down the escapees, but despite such measures runaway slaves would often band together to form independent hamlets (*mocambos* or *quilombos,* words of African origin, in Brazil; *palenques* in Spanish America). The majority were small in size and located not too far from the colonists' fields and towns, which they raided for food, cattle, and arms. Colonial authorities organized military expeditions against the quilombos (usually using Indian troops), but when a village was destroyed a few survivors always seemed to escape and a new community would spring up, soon to be joined by additional newly escaped slaves. The runaway communities became a constant feature of the Brazilian slave regime. Today there are more than a hundred and fifty place or town names derived from the words "mocambo" or "quilombo."

Although most quilombos were short-lived, a few were more successful. In the region north of Bahia and south of Pernambuco called Alagoas, a large quilombo developed at Palmares. Beginning in the early part of the century, it greatly expanded during the disruption of the engenhos caused by the battles with the Dutch. Although some authors claim it contained more than twenty thousand inhabitants (a certain exaggeration since this would have made it the largest city in Brazil), its inhabitants did number in the thousands. Resisting both the Portuguese and the Dutch, Palmares lasted for almost a century and was not destroyed until 1694.

The runaway communities are also interesting from another perspective. They provided Africans and Afro-Americans with opportunities to create social and cultural forms independent of European norms. The usual result was a fusion of African and European patterns, but in those communities that were very isolated (Surinam) or very large (Palmares), African traditions of religion and kinship survived, if in a somewhat modified form. The term "quilombo" is itself evidence of the cultural transference. In Angola, *kilombos* were military villages of various groups called Imbangala who, lacking the traditional ties of lineage and family, had adapted this military institution as a way of creating social bonds between previously unrelated peoples. What better means to integrate the escaped slaves of such disparate ethnic origins? The last leader of Palmares against the Portuguese was a man called Ganga Zumbi. In the Angolan kilombos, the priest responsible for the spiritual defense of the community was the *nganga a nzumbi*. Obviously, then, the forms of Africa were surviving in the New World. But just as Brazil was not Portugal, neither was it Africa. Adaptation, development, and modification were just as characteristic of Afro-American culture as they were of the general colonial culture.

Merchants and commerce

The patterns of Iberian commercial life described in Chapter 1 generally held true in seventeenth-century Ibero-America. In northeastern Brazil, where the export economy predominated, merchants played a central role in linking the countryside to the city and the engenhos to the markets of Europe. By 1600 foreigners – Italians, Flemings, Germans – were no longer as important as they had been fifty years before, and their position was increasingly assumed by Portuguese businessmen. In fact, during the seventeenth century, Portuguese merchants with long experience in multicontinental commerce with Africa, Asia, and South America began to penetrate the Spanish empire as well. During the sixty years (1580–1640) when Spain and Portugal were jointly ruled, Portuguese merchants obtained the contract to supply the Spanish Indies with slaves, and in Lima, Cartegena, and other American ports, as well as in Seville itself, the Portuguese began to expand their legal and illegal trade. Spanish competitors resented this commercial penetration, and the fact that many of the

Portuguese merchants were New Christians eventually led, as seen in Chapter 5, to repression of their activities by the Inquisition. Still, the ability of Portuguese merchants to penetrate the Spanish commercial system testifies to their vitality and broad interests.

Mercantile activities were not uniform in scale or type. Portugal had few great merchant-bankers who were able to assume state contracts, lend money to the crown, and at the same time engage in large-scale international commerce. Far more important for Brazil were those who carried on large-volume import–export trade with the colony, usually shipping out wine, copper, iron, and cloth and importing sugar, tobacco, or hides. These wholesale merchants often owned shares in the ships as well as the cargoes, and the profits they made were likely to be invested in real estate or marriages into the nobility.

The mechanisms of commerce were highly reminiscent of those we have seen in Spanish America. "Companies" were really partnerships created for limited purposes and periods. Partners were bound by contract only for the specific goal or transaction, and a man might be involved in many such arrangements at the same time. The idea of the "firm" did not yet really exist. The merchant in Lisbon or Oporto would depend on his partner in a colonial port, or he would need the services of an agent. Often younger relatives, nephews, cousins, or brothers-in-law might be set up in a colonial port to serve as correspondent. There they would remain five or ten years, learning the tricks of the trade firsthand before returning to Portugal. This type of commerce, based on *sociedades*, or short-term partnerships, and usually in the hands of commission agents, continued to characterize much of Brazilian trade through the next century, by which time more permanent arrangements were well established in other European systems. Francisco Pinheiro (1695–1760), a Lisbon merchant doing extensive business with Africa and Brazil, often formed partnerships with foreign merchants in Lisbon while depending on trusted representatives in Brazilian ports to carry out his sales. These agents included his brother, brother-in-law, nephews, and a countryman from his hometown. They worked for him for a 6 percent commission and probably initiated their own ventures at the same time. Pinheiro usually made about 20 percent profit on his Brazilian trading, although returns in the slave trade were, like the risks, considerably higher.

The agents of European-based merchants like Pinheiro often considered their stay in the tropics a kind of exile and pined for return home, but by the mid-seventeenth century wealthy merchants with multiple interests had taken up residence in Brazil and had begun to modify the social patterns in the colony. We can see the process in individual lives. Francisco Fernandes do Sim emigrated from the island of Madeira to Bahia; by the 1620s he was shipping cargoes of sugar to Portugal. His operations expanded, and he became one of the wealthiest men in the colony, acquiring engenhos, ranches, and cane fields while continuing his commercial interests. He married the daughter of a sugar planter and then later arranged the marriage of his own daughter to a senior military officer, with whom he then formed a partnership in a cane farm. As with merchants in Spanish America, Fernandes do Sim sought to gild his financial success with social recognition and the assumption of attitudes characteristic of the traditional nobility. He became a member of prestigious lay brotherhoods and made a very large bequest to the charitable brotherhood of the Misericórdia, serving an unprecedented five terms as its senior officer. His story of commercial success indicates the pattern that many followed, although usually with less luck and skill.

We do not yet have sufficient research on merchants in the eighteenth century to know if the process of merchant success and absorption went on then as before, but we suspect that it did. It seems clear that the flow of young men coming from Portugal to work as commercial agents continued and perhaps intensified, so that by the end of the colonial era the word "merchant" was almost synonymous with Portuguese-born. The export orientation of the Brazilian economy meant that the ties of merchants with the metropolis remained strong.

The Iberians generally made a distinction between the wholesale export merchant and the shopkeeper. The former was not excluded from honors and social recognition and might hope for a noble marriage or a grant of nobility. The shopkeeper (*mercador da loja*) had little chance to rise, for his was considered a base occupation. The great export merchants, often called businessmen (*homem de negocio*) or town house merchants (*mercador de sobrado*), belonged to the higher classification. In Brazil these men usually invested their mercantile profit in land and eventually became sugar planters or lavradores de cana as well as merchants. Thus over time they tended to melt into the planter class and as families they eventually become indistinguishable from them. This social amalgamation should not, however disguise the fact that at any specific time there were often conflicting interests between the mercantile and agricultural sectors of the Brazilian sugar economy.

To some extent this conflict was born of another merchant function. No banks existed in this period, so that those in need of capital or credit had to depend on private individuals or on various religious institutions for loans. The wealthy and socially prominent planters often secured funds from religious institutions, such as the Santa Casa da Misericórdia brotherhood, to which many belonged, or from a local convent. The convent of Desterro in Bahia was a popular source of credit. At one point in 1732 it had twenty cases in the courts concerning debts owed it from such loans. Planters and lavradores who did not have access to low-interest loans from religious institutions were forced to borrow from merchants who lent money or advanced credit for slaves, oxen, and equipment against mortgages of the engenhos and cane fields themselves. A poor harvest, a European war, or a fall in sugar prices could result in default. Debt collection was a major source of disputes between merchants and planters and a principal way in which merchants became the owners of agricultural properties. Without much success, planters sought a moratorium on debt payment, but by 1668 at least their engenhos, with their slaves, buildings, machinery, and land were declared indissoluble units, not subject to being auctioned piecemeal to settle debts. This was a great privilege, for it often enabled them to continue operation even when debts mounted. A second point of contention involved the fair price of sugar in Brazil. By the end of the seventeenth century, when a fleet system had been established, the state was forced to intervene and to decree a just price, determined by a committee made up of planters, merchants, and royal judges.

Although much of what we have said here about merchants and commerce in Brazil would apply in Spanish America as well, there were also significant differences. From the beginning, Portugal, a small nation, had depended on the ships of other nations to carry on much of the Brazil trade. The Portuguese crown established monopolies over certain goods and trades, like the spices of India, but for the bulk agricultural commodities, like sugar, trade was open to all, even foreigners, so long as they sailed under Portuguese license and paid the appropriate duties. In the sixteenth century the Dutch were major carriers in the Brazil trade, and ships from England, Italy, or even Poland were not unknown in Brazilian ports. This commercial system was quite different from the Spanish concept of a closed empire, limited to Spanish shipping funneled through the single port of Seville. The differences were largely the result of the different levels of human and material resources that could be mustered by Castile and Portugal. During the sixty-year period when Spain and Portugal were jointly ruled, the imposition of the Spanish "closed" system on Portugal's trade became a major source of friction between the two nations and one of the reasons for Portugal's eventual rebellion in 1640.

New Christians

One of the disabilities under which merchants operated in the Portuguese world was the assumption that anyone who was involved in commerce was of Jewish origin. Actually, not all merchants were "New Christians," nor were all New Christians merchants, but the stereotype was deeply ingrained in the Iberian mentality. The distinction between "Old Christians," or those with no Jewish ancestors, and New Christians created still another system of ranking used to place individuals and groups within their proper social category, and since New Christians played an important part in seventeenth-century Brazil, we will outline their role here. For a variety of reasons the Portuguese-Jewish converts and their descendants remained a vital force in Portuguese and Brazilian life after the importance of the *conversos* in Spain and its dominions had begun to wane. It was often hard to separate the "Portuguese" from the "Spanish" conversos because of considerable family ties across frontiers, the mass movement of many conversos from Spain to Portugal in 1492, and a large-scale movement back into Spain and Spanish America during the Iberian union (1580–1640). In this period the word "Portuguese" became in the Spanish empire an epithet, a synonym for "Jew," despite the fact that Catholic Portuguese greatly resented the term and felt it unjust.

The reasons for cohesion among the Portuguese New Christians can be found in their specific history. Unlike Spain, where Jews had been faced with attempts at conversion and proselytization for a hundred years prior to their expulsion or conversion in 1492, the Jews in Portugal had all been forced to convert in 1497. Plunged almost overnight into a new religion, there was no inner tension within the community over who was a willing Christian and who was not. All shared the same fate, and whereas some came to accept the new faith and others did not, the theological controversies that had plagued the Jewish communities of Spain were, for the most part, absent in Portugal.

Forced conversion eliminated religious distinctions, at least officially, but it did not obliterate the differences of custom, thought, and attitude that had existed between the Christian and the Jewish communities. Discrimination against Jews was now continued as discrimination against New Christians, regardless of the depth of their adherence to Christianity. The stigma carried from generation to generation, and a man whose family knew nothing of Judaism might still find a New Christian grandmother given as the reason for his exclusion from office, position, or honors. What were supposedly religious distinctions and discriminations became ethnic, supported by the code of "purity of blood" (*limpeça de sangue*). A profound faith in Christianity did not free an individual from the weight of his origins, and so both crypto-Jews and those who had not the slightest attachment to Judaism were defined together, by the society in general as a subgroup to be watched and by the crown as a target for periodic extortion. This too created a sense of cohesion.

The Inquisition was not established in Portugal until 1537, and although it was subsequently at times even more harsh than its Spanish counterpart, for the first forty years after forced conversion Portuguese New Christians could breathe somewhat easier. These forty years coincided, of course, with the period of Brazil's early beginnings. New Christians became involved with the Brazilian enterprise from the start, and then after 1537 many came to Brazil either to avoid the Inquisition or because of sentences of deportation and penal exile. If Brazil offered certain kinds of social mobility to Portuguese in general, its attractions were multiplied for the New Christians. It is curious to note that the Jesuits and the New Christians spoke of Brazil in almost exactly the same words as "their enterprise." In Brazil, the New Christians often held offices in civil and even ecclesiastical government that were barred to them in Europe. They became planters and cane farmers as well as artisans and merchants, filling a wide range of social positions. The discriminatory laws still existed and were sometimes enforced, and there was still social stigma associated with Jewish ancestors, but in Brazil these proved to be a surmountable barrier in the sixteenth and seventeenth centuries.

New Christian importance in the colony may be one explanation why the Inquisition was not permanently established in Brazil during the Iberian union. There were inquisitorial visits in 1591–3 and 1618 to Bahia and Pernambuco and to Pará in 1763–9. Bishops had inquisitorial powers and sometimes used them, but, in general, the persecution of New Christians in Brazil was much less constant or effective than that in Spanish America or even in Portugal itself. Some New Christians, like the senhor de engenho Antônio Lopes

Ulhoa, the so-called "Count-Duke of Brazil," achieved important if informal political influence. But perhaps more important was the wide range of opportunities afforded to this New Christian population as a whole. Many passed into Spanish America during the Iberian union and had great success despite being resented on both religious and economic grounds; with the separation of Spain and Portugal in 1640, however, a series of autos-de-fe in Lima, Mexico, and Cartegena seriously damaged the position of New Christian Portuguese merchants in the Spanish Indies.

The early seventeenth-century Dutch occupation of northeast Brazil and the policy of religious toleration there created a new situation for the New Christians. They were now geographically divided. Those in Dutch Brazil who were secret Jews now came out openly and were soon joined by co-religionists from Holland. The New Christians in Portuguese-held Brazil were divided in their sympathies according to their real religious feelings, although the rest of the inhabitants tended to view all New Christians as potential collaborators with the Dutch. Those who had thrown in with the Dutch fought actively in the war and were allowed to leave with their Dutch allies as part of the surrender terms. Some went to Surinam or the Caribbean islands and a few went to New Amsterdam (New York).

After 1660 the New Christians as a group never again played a significant role in Brazilian history, although they certainly did not disappear entirely from the colony. Even in the 1720s New Christians were being prosecuted by the Inquisition in Rio de Janeiro and Minas Gerais, but their importance had greatly diminished, and under the watchful eye of the church and their neighbors, cultural and religious distinctiveness slowly faded. They became an indistinguishable, although still socially disadvantaged, segment of Brazilian society.

Cities and towns

Historians have long relegated the urban centers of Brazil to a secondary position and have pointed to the agricultural orientation of the economy and the way in which planters dominated the social hierarchy as proof of the rural basis of colonial Brazil. This is a generalization that is only partially true and in some ways is very misleading. The cities can, in fact, be seen as extensions of the countryside, and ports were created to facilitate the flow of agricultural goods from the colony, but town and countryside were not separate entities.

Because of the coastal location of the engenhos, most of the population lived, at least in the seventeenth century, no more than two or three days' journey from an urban center, and the interchange of goods, services, and people between rural and urban areas was constant. Moreover, the cities and towns were important as administrative and institutional centers, providing the framework of government and religious life for the colony as a whole. In institutional and juridical terms, the colony was defined by its cities and towns.

Like the Spaniards, the Portuguese were city dwellers, with long Roman and Moorish traditions of urbanism in their own past. But in the New World certain realities called forth responses that made the cities and the urban network of Brazil unlike those of Mexico or Peru. The lack of a large settled Indian population, the tropical ecology, and an economy based on agricultural exports helped to determine the placement, organization, and functions of the Brazilian cities. In many ways, it is more appropriate to compare the cities and towns of Brazil with those of a region like Venezuela than with cities in the densely populated highlands of central Mexico or the Andes. The extractive or agricultural economy of the coast, the loosely defined network of towns, and the opening of the interior by cattlemen in search of new grazing lands are but a few of the parallels between Brazil and Venezuela, and they underline the fact that the variations between the Iberian colonies depended not so much on the national differences between Spaniards and Portuguese as they did on the various social and economic bases of colonization.

As we have seen, the first permanent settlements were really trade forts and factories for the brazilwood commerce. Although there was some shifting of town locations from one spot to another after 1530, that date can be taken as the beginning of effective urbanism in Brazil. The major cities created in the sixteenth century were almost invariably coastal ports. Olinda (1537), Salvador (1549), Santos (1545), Vitória (1551), and Rio de Janeiro (1565) were all established on the shoreline to facilitate contact with Europe, a fact that also made defense from pirates and European rivals a major problem and expense. Secondary settlements tended to be river towns or smaller coastal ports where water transport made contact with the larger cities possible. Of all the important settlements of the sixteenth and seventeenth centuries, only São Paulo and the surrounding towns of the Paulista plateau were inland, and it should be remembered that in this period São Paulo was a relatively insignificant place.

Between 1532 and 1650 some six cities and thirty-one towns (*vilas*) were established in Brazil, the majority of them within fifty miles of the coast. The first group of towns founded extended from Pernambuco southward to São Vicente, but after 1580 a second wave was established in the north and along the Amazon – towns like Natal (1599), São Luiz (1612), Belém (1616), and Gurupá (1639). This northward expansion reflected the increasing Portuguese control of the coast and the success of Portuguese arms against Indians and European rivals including the French. It was not until the eighteenth century, however, that the urban network began to spread into the interior; for the first two centuries Brazil's population and its cities remained, in the words of Frei Vicente do Salvador, Brazil's first historian, "like crabs on the beach."

The coastal cities served a variety of functions by concentrating human and economic resources. Within the cities were located the principal civil and ecclesiastical institutions, the courts, the royal treasury, the governor and his staff. The merchant community with their shops and warehouses resided principally in the major port cities, as did the lawyers and notaries needed to facilitate business. Artisans of various trades provided their skills to both the urban populations and the nearby plantations in the countryside.

Each port city and its hinterland formed a distinct unit somewhat separated from the others. This separateness was one of the distinguishing features of Brazilian towns. The urban network, the linkage of transportation, communication, and political contact, was never very well developed. Each coastal port was oriented toward Portugal rather than toward its sisters, a result of export monoculture and, to some extent, a situation sponsored by the crown, which hoped to keep each captaincy directly dependent on Lisbon. Secondary towns were slow to appear, and when they did they were very secondary indeed. In the plantation zone, this is partially explained by the settlement aspects of the sugar mills themselves. During the harvest season these large estates might have some two to three hundred individuals working within their boundaries, and an engenho often provided many of the services of a small town. As we have seen, artisans could be found there, barber-surgeons, too, and often a chapel and a priest. Thus, the rural population was concentrated around the engenhos, and the secondary towns that developed often did so to serve the interests and needs of the sugar estates. Noticeably reduced were the small agricultural peasant towns of the southern Mediterranean world. In an economy dominated by large estates and a society built on slave labor, there was little room for them. Free small farmers existed on the margins of the plantations and provided services and subsistence crops, but they were widely dispersed and, in this period, few in number. Although there were always a few exceptions, this situation generally held true until the opening of the mining zone of Minas Gerais in the early eighteenth century, when a patchwork of hastily built mining camps eventually developed into a series of cities and towns linked to each other.

The slow pace of royal colonization and the foundation of most of the towns by individual donataries resulted in little uniformity of layout or plan in the earliest Brazilian towns and cities, but there were certain regularities, imposed by tradition and similar local conditions. A few cities like Salvador and Rio de Janeiro had a modified regular plan, but in general most responded to topography and economic function rather than to royal ordinances of town planning or to preconceived layouts, at least in this period. The fact that port facilities were so important to the city's life usually meant that important government buildings and a large square might be located right at the water's edge (as in Lisbon), but at the same time, the need for defense against a threat from the sea often led to the placing of cities on hilly locations and the subsequent development of an upper and a lower city. As a rule of thumb, churches were placed either at the major squares or on high points within the city. Even today, the pattern can be seen in a sleepy colonial town like Olinda or in modern Rio de Janeiro, where churches still command the heights.

A visitor to Brazil from Spanish America in the late sixteenth century might have been struck by the lack of a dominant central plaza in the urban centers. Brazilian cities had large "squares," but there were many of these *praças,* usually one in front of any large building, and the square in front of the Jesuit College might be just as impressive and just as important as that before the governor's palace or the town hall. A commons, or *rocio,* such as existed in Portugal could be found in some Brazilian towns. Originally designed as municipal pasturage, the rocios, like the one in Rio de Janeiro, eventually evolved into town squares. The praças served as meeting places, markets, scenes for public ceremonies, bullfights, and other such activities. In one, usually that before the principal governmental buildings, a pillory and a gallows were erected. Here criminals were punished, proclamations read, and the presence of government generally made known to the populace.

Public buildings for civil or religious purposes were the cities' largest and finest. The original constructions of the sixteenth century had been modest buildings of pounded earth floors and thatched roofs, but suitable building stone and tile was brought from Europe as ships' ballast, and by the 1570s and 1580s impressive churches and governmental buildings were being raised in the major coastal ports. Many of these were replaced or rebuilt in the mid-seventeenth century during the height of the sugar boom, when funds were available through taxes and wealthy individuals were inclined to demonstrate their religiosity by endowments for church construction. The colleges of the Jesuits and the churches and monasteries of the Franciscans were particularly noteworthy examples of European-style architecture in Brazil.

The houses of the Brazilian city were almost entirely a Portuguese transplant. The vast majority were one or two stories high, although in Recife, which was occupied by the Dutch (1630–54), three- and four-level dwellings like the canal houses of Amsterdam could also be found. In the early days of the sixteenth century much construction was made of *taipa* (a sort of adobe), but the classic city dwelling was a house of *pedra e cal* (stone and mortar), often whitewashed or painted in a pastel hue and usually roofed with tile. The frontage of the city house was often narrow and unimpressive, but the dwellings were deep and could contain many rooms, a patio, and quarters for slaves and servants. The balconies and verandas so popular in rural construction were infrequent in the city. Windows were usually shuttered with some sort of grating, and since iron was in short supply and very expensive, wood lattices were in general use. The houses reflected the inward orientation of the family and the patriarchal domination of private life. Women, especially those of the upper class, were very often secluded and the pastime of watching life through a latticed window was often one of their few opportunities of contact with the society at large.

In a sense, the houses defined the streets. Each dwelling opened directly to the street. Pavement and leveling were slow to develop, and a sewage system was virtually nonexistent. Because of the lack of plan and the response to topography, streets were often winding and narrow. Although horses and carriages could be used in some cities, urban transport was usually on foot or in hammocks and sedan chairs carried by slaves. In fact, slave porters were the principal means of moving people and goods in all the Brazilian cities until the nineteenth century.

Cities were organized internally into neighborhoods according to traditional boundaries, time of incorporation into the municipality, or sometimes governmental action. The most common neighborhoods were formed by ecclesiastical divisions, centered on the parish church. Here people came into contact on a continual basis, heard vespers, witnessed marriages, baptisms, and funerals, celebrated the festival of the patron saint, and organized a variety of civil and religious activities. We should bear in mind that in this period the church was involved in social services and many other aspects of daily life that are now part of secular government, thus taking part in the administrative process. The parish formed the core of the *bairro,* or neighborhood, the basic unit of the city.

Informal groupings also emerged around other focal points of urban life. Since running water was absent in the houses, the city's fountains became centers of daily activity where slaves, servants, and the city's poor met each day to gossip, converse, and exchange information on prices, love affairs, and politics. The fountains became like the parish churches, physical meeting grounds or forums for neighborhood activities, and as such, the basis of identification within the community. The markets of urban Brazil played a somewhat familiar role as a place for interchange on a continual basis, but we simply do not know enough about their internal organization, or regularity, to say much beyond that. It is clear, however, that in the colonial cities women, both slave and free, dominated the sale of perishable items and circulated throughout the city, setting up their portable stands in different neighborhoods as the opportunity arose.

Finally, there were the taverns that multiplied at a rapid rate in the colonial cities and sprang up at crossroads and way stations in the countryside. By 1650 Salvador alone had more than two hundred. The favorite drink at these places was a rum called *cachaça,* but drinking was not the only activity. The taverns served as meeting places for the urban poor, slaves, and freedmen. Buying and selling, often of contraband goods, took place there, as did the exchange of information. Constant attempts of town councils to limit or suppress the taverns because of the violence that resulted from drinking and the supposed antisocial behavior that went on there met with little success.

It is difficult to say much about the patterns of residence in the early Brazilian cities. Rich and poor seemed to live in great proximity, although the wealthy and powerful tended to locate their houses closer to the city center. The dockside areas were the scene of much business and many shops, and retail merchants often lived above their place of business. As in Europe, there was also some tendency for skills to concentrate in certain parts of town, and a street of merchants or an artisan trade was not uncommon. Urban property in the major centers was expensive and usually in short supply. Renting was a common practice, and many religious institutions derived considerable income from the urban properties they rented out to private individuals.

All of these things – the house types, the parish organization, the fountains, the markets, the taverns, the residence patterns – had close parallels in most Spanish American cities. With a few minor adjustments (for example, in full-scale Spanish American cities streets were normally wide and straight), what has been said here is applicable to the Spanish Indies as well; we have fleshed out the Brazilian urban setting a bit because it has been relatively ignored in the past.

The Brazilian city is distinguished, however, by the absence of its wealthiest and most prominent citizens for much of the year. The sugar planters and ranchers whose families formed the colony's social elite often preferred to reside on their estates and manage operations during the eight- to nine-month sugar harvest. Some authors have made a great deal of this "rural dominance" of Brazil's social and economic life, but we should remember that city and countryside, rather than polar opposites, were part of an integrated unit. Planters usually maintained a city residence and continually called on the services of merchant-bankers, lawyers, notaries, and other city dwellers. The strong bonds that existed between city and country are underlined by the fact that planters and ranchers were willing, and until the late seventeenth century usually anxious, to assume positions in municipal government.

The social fabric

A view of life in the Brazilian cities reveals that a complex society had developed by the seventeenth century, quite similar to that of the Spanish American central areas but with some important special characteristics due to the nature of the economy and the predominant role of African slaves within it. The full range of social ranks and institutions had been transposed to the coastal regions of the northeast, although as in Spanish America the relative weight of some groups was quite different than it was in Europe. Since few members of the traditional Portuguese nobility resided in the colony, the sugar planters became an aristocracy with pretensions to noble status, despite their often rather humble origins. At the other end of the scale, there were very few Portuguese peasants, both because the young men who had left the plow at home had no intention of taking it up again in America and because in the export-crop-slavery economy there was at first little room for them.

The flow of immigration from Portugal continually brought people in at all social levels. The tide of immigration was stimulated both by flush times in the sugar industry, which, like gold in the following century, created opportunities for the newly arrived, and by bad times, when crisis and instability for planters opened doors for the immigrants willing to take the risk. Whatever the cause, the human connection with Portugal was always strong. A study of Bahia in the period 1680–1740 shows that nearly all the merchants and two-thirds of the artisans were European-born. Even the ranks of the local aristocrats, the planters and cattlemen, were penetrated by recent arrivals. About one-third of the sugar planters were born in Europe and another third were first-generation Brazilians, the sons of Portuguese fathers. This situation reflected the boom and bust history of the sugar industry and the fact that there were always eager immigrants willing to try their luck in export agriculture when the opportunity presented itself.

Little distinction seems to have been made between European and Brazilian-born Portuguese until the eighteenth century. The Portuguese population circulated freely between colony and metropolis. Salvador Correia de Sá, whose family dominated life in Rio de Janeiro for more than a century, was born in Spain, came to Brazil in his youth, married the granddaughter of the Spanish governor of Paraguay, became governor of Rio de Janeiro as his father had been, returned to Portugal, led an expedition to Angola, came back to Rio as governor, and eventually returned to Lisbon, where he served on the Overseas Council until his death. Another example is Matias de Albuquerque, brother of the donatary of Pernambuco and captain-major of the captaincy in the 1620s, a leader of its defense in the 1630s and a major figure in the peninsular campaigns of Portugal against Spain in the 1640s.

The word *mazombo* existed to describe a Brazilian-born white, but it was rarely used. As in Spanish America, the earliest manifestations of self-identification and colonial resentment against the European-born appeared within the religious orders, especially the Franciscans and the Jesuits, where the preference shown Europeans drew complaint. Eventually, the Franciscans instituted the *alternativa* between European and Brazilian-born superiors just as had been done in Peru.

Immigration from Portugal came at various social levels. Governors, royal judges, merchants, and lawyers held high and middle status; further down the social scale were artisans, soldiers, and mariners. Many came with the intention of spending a few years and then returning home, but as with other immigrants, more remained than intended to. Like African slaves, but for quite different reasons, the majority of the Portuguese immigrants were men, and it was often marriage to local women that eventually linked them to the colony. A marriage alliance with some nobleman in Portugal or his relative in the colony was the arrangement preferred by Brazilian planters, but they were willing to marry their daughters to an immigrant merchant or lawyer when a royal judge or the governor's nephew was not available. Marriage to a European-born Portuguese at least reduced the risk that there might be an Indian or a mulatto in the family tree, a curious but understandable concern since many of the elite families could themselves find non-European forebears if they had cared to look. For much of the seventeenth century it had been a common practice to send marriageable daughters to convents in Portugal in order to avoid the risk of an unfortunate liaison. This practice diminished after the creation of the colony's first convent in Bahia in the 1670s and the establishment of others in the major cities during the following fifty years. In 1734 the crown prohibited the sending of women from the colony to Portugal.

A large part of the immigrant stream had been made up of humble tradesmen and artisans who turned to their crafts in Brazil. They constituted the majority of the artisans in the Brazilian cities and formed a sort of self-employed working-class elite. The classic institutions of Portuguese artisans – the guilds, the religious brotherhoods organized by craft, and the artisan representatives elected to municipal government – were much attenuated in Brazil and lacked the depth and importance of their European models. Whereas in Portugal the status of "master" was conferred by examination by the guild, in Brazil it was simply a title based on experience and reputation. Although the titles of master, apprentice, and journeyman existed in the colony, they did not have the same formal significance as those titles in Portugal. To some extent, slavery was responsible. In Brazil, where white artisans used slaves as workers, the traditional guild functions of regulation, quality control, and standard setting were less important. Politically, the artisans had little power. "People's judges" were elected by the artisan representatives to sit with municipal councils, but their role in Brazilian towns was restricted by the planters and merchants who dominated these bodies. In Salvador such representation existed only between 1641 and 1713 when, because of a tax riot in the city, the artisan representatives were removed from government. In short, the artisan situation demonstrates how in the transfer of European traditions the reality of the colony could cause profound changes. The institutions and patterns of Europe were there, but some lacked the depth and complexity they had once had.

Given the importance of religion in everyday life, organizations like the lay brotherhoods can provide a glimpse of Portuguese society and the search for status and recognition within it. Certain groups or professions tended to concentrate in particular brotherhoods, although there was regional variation in their preferences. The Third Order of St. Francis in Bahia was a favorite of the aristocratic planters, who used its prohibitions against New Christians as a way of keeping the merchants out. They, in turn, preferred the Third Order of the Carmelites. In Recife, however, merchants so controlled the Franciscan Third Order that planters were required to pay double the usual entrance fee in order to be admitted as brothers. The artisans, too, had their favorite confraternities, less prestigious than those of the planters and great merchants but providing some corporate identity.

One brotherhood in particular is especially useful as a social gauge because of its distinguished position and its curious internal organization. The Santa Casa da Misericórdia (Holy House of Mercy) was a charitable lay brotherhood that offered a variety of social services, from a hospital and orphanage to a burial society. Branches existed in every major Portuguese city in Europe and overseas, and membership was greatly valued as a symbol of prestige. In Bahia the organization maintained a medieval distinction between brothers of upper or "noble" standing and those of "mechanic" or lesser condition. In either case, anyone descended from Black or Jewish ancestors or married to such a person was excluded. Thus the fifteen or twenty men admitted each year represented the elite of Bahian society. The "noble" brothers fell into two categories. The principal families of sugar planters and cattlemen were always represented and tended to control the senior governing positions within the brotherhood. They were joined by a second group of professionals: royal officials, lawyers, priests, and some merchants. The brothers of lesser condition were primarily white artisans, shopkeepers, and minor officials. Occasionally, someone admitted at the lower level gained enough wealth or prestige to be promoted, but such mobility was rare and was possible only for minor officials, soldiers, and semiprofessionals, not for artisans. The best they could hope for was a higher status for their sons.

The role of immigrants in the Bahian Misericórdia reflects their continued importance in colonial society. More than half the membership in the colonial period was European-born, but their relative numbers differed at the two levels. Among the "noble" brothers only a slight majority were immigrants, but at the lower level the ratio of immigrants to native-born was six to one. These figures reflect the existence of a set of aristocratic colonial families at the top of society, controlling its institutions but always permeated and joined by recently arrived Portuguese. For the immigrants to be accepted fully, their ties to local society had to be firm. All the Portuguese High Court judges admitted to the Misericórdia, for example, were married to Brazilian women. Over time, merchants and royal functionaries increasingly rose to positions of prominence within the Misericórdia and within society in general, but the traditional families never ceded their position and always found ways to incorporate new blood into their ranks.

The early years of settlement had produced a considerable number of unions between the Portuguese and Indian women, resulting in mestiço or mameluco children. These had been accepted into European society, but as the colony developed, such unions became much rarer in the central areas, and the acceptance of mestiços as Portuguese became less common. There were always some Indians and mestiços in the coastal cities and around the engenhos, but by the mid-seventeenth century their numbers were small, and as a social category they were being absorbed into a growing Afro-Portuguese mixed population whose variations of crossing were increasingly referred to as *pardos*, much as in late colonial Venezuela. Within the Brazilian colony free Blacks and pardos had no legal corporate identity and were assumed to be, juridically at least, full members of society. This did not mean that there was no discrimination against them, for indeed they were often subjected to "exemplary" punishments by zealous governors or to exclusion from honors and offices, but at the same time this discrimination represented a reaction to some social mobility on the part of the pardos as a group.

In the interstices of society, in marginal occupations that called for few capital resources, in rural areas as small farmers, and in cities and towns as wage workers, street vendors, tavernkeepers, or artisans, people of color began to gain a place fully within local Iberian society. There were a few great success stories like that of Luís Cardoso, a former slave who had worked in the shop of a German merchant of Recife in the 1680s, learned the trade, bought his freedom, and eventually became an international merchant himself; at the end of his career he bequeathed his fortune to his favorite brotherhood just as any other respectable merchant would have done. Far more common were the minor successes and small gains, as people of color found niches within the economy and sought to participate fully in the society. In this period perhaps only 5 or 10 percent of the artisans were free Blacks or pardos, but the employment of many slaves and free persons of color in the trades was creating a tradition of skills.

Manifestations of pardo and Black participation in society could be seen everywhere. There were militia regiments for Blacks and others for mulattoes. There were lay brotherhoods organized by color and churches raised by them. Our Lady of the Rosary was especially favored as a patroness of the Black population. The fact that many of these brotherhoods and churches date from the late seventeenth century is probably an index of the growing size and importance of this segment of the population in that period. Although the Blacks and pardos participated in colonial life and hoped for some improvement of their status, their criteria of organization and differentiation were not all shared with the whites. A good deal of African culture was maintained within the Portuguese institutions adopted by the Blacks. In the brotherhoods religious syncretism took place, and distinctions based on African ethnic origins were sometimes preserved. Place of birth mattered, too, and distinctions between Brazilian-born crioulos and Africans were made. At one point a pardo militia regiment complained because its officers were too dark, and in another instance crioulos sought to have Africans banned from their troop. The acceptance of distinctions based on color and place of birth of Blacks and pardos is evidence of ongoing absorption and fusion within Brazilian society. The process of social fusion was accompanied, of course, by a biological one as intermarriage and sexual unions resulted in ever-increasing numbers of people with mixed backgrounds. By the end of the following century this mixed population would constitute the majority of the free people of the colony.

Cultural matters

There is no need to discuss in great detail the central elements of Brazilian cultural and intellectual life, at least among its elite, because it was in so many ways similar to that of Spanish America, which we examined in Chapter 5. The same characteristics of "baroque" culture, allegory, effusion, and exuberant intricacy encapsuled within a fervent Catholic piety were all present in Brazil as well, although architectural styles always had a certain individuality and a separate rate of change and the literature too had its own inner consistencies. We could point out innumerable similarities, but we wish instead to emphasize here some of the differences that gave culture in Brazil its special texture and form.

We can begin with the church for, as in Spanish America, intellectual life was often an extension of it. Immediately the differences appear. The church in Brazil never developed the richness or institutional strength that it had in the central Spanish colonies. The regular orders remained strong even after the initial conquest phase, and they did not give ground easily to the secular clergy. Rather than latecomers as in Mexico, the Jesuits were involved in the colony's formation almost from the outset, and they were often favored by royal governors. By the mid-seventeenth century the missionary function of the regular clergy in the central coastal zones was, like the Indian population itself, greatly reduced, but the orders remained powerful. This situation is partly explained by the slow development of the diocesan structure in the colony. Even granting the different rhythm of growth, Brazil by 1700 had only one archepiscopal see, at Salvador, with two suffragan bishoprics at Rio de Janeiro and Pernambuco, in comparison with the five archbishoprics and more than twenty-five bishoprics that existed in the Spanish Indies. On the other hand, the situation was not without parallel in Spanish America, for there too the regular orders long remained dominant in the peripheral areas, which were in so many ways comparable to Brazil.

Through the operation of royal patronage, the Portuguese crown had much to say about the structure of the ecclesiastical hierarchy. Bishops nominated by the Overseas Council in Lisbon were invariably Portuguese, but wars, politics, and mortality in the tropics often left the episcopal sees vacant, and in the absence of the bishop, the local cathedral chapter, usually made up of Brazilian-born clerics, controlled religious matters. Even within the hierarchy, the role of the regulars was predominant, with members of the orders chosen about half the time as bishops in the seventeenth century, increasing to about two-thirds of the appointments in the following century. (Friars long continued to be made bishops in peripheral areas of Spanish America as well.) We know virtually nothing about the parish priests and their social origins, but one suspects that they were increasingly Brazilian-born.

The church in Brazil reflected the economic conditions, size, and complexity of the population. All the institutions were eventually created, churches built, monasteries and convents erected, but the pace was slower than in quickly developing Mexico or Peru, the amount of pious donations smaller, and the overall position of the church hierarchy not quite so central in the scheme of things. Not unlike the Dominicans in Oaxaca or the Franciscans and Jesuits in northern Mexico, the ecclesiastical foundations in Brazil depended on sugar plantations and cattle ranches, and to some extent on urban properties, to produce the income necessary for their operations. The Jesuits and Benedictines were especially large land- and slaveholders. The ecclesiastics were fully integrated into society, and because they were, they were subject, on certain issues, to the same pressures experienced by any other interest group.

From the early days of settlement, the church assumed the same roles as in Spanish America. Missionary activity, especially that of the Jesuits and Franciscans, was impressive, and Indian grammars, plays written for purposes of conversion, and other such literary activities accompanied these efforts. The letters and other writings of some early Jesuits reveal a remarkable talent of observation, as well as literary style and political acumen. Eventually, the ecclesiastical establishment took over the task of general education; the Jesuit colleges in Salvador, Olinda, and Rio de Janeiro became the centers of learning where most native-born Europeans received their basic education. What intellectual life existed in the colony took place principally within the shadow of these religious establishments. Art and music were partially religious expressions, and it is not surprising that the majority of writers in the colony were clerics.

Two central facts in the cultural history of Brazil set it quite apart from Spanish America. Neither a university nor a printing press was established in Brazil until the nineteenth century. The reasons for this situation are varied, but there seems to have been a conscious royal intent to ensure the continuing intellectual dependence of the colony on the mother country. In a sense, this policy was simply a further example of the concept of integration in which Brazil and Portugal were part of a single system, whether it be in terms of bureaucratic appointments, intellectual pursuits, or royal taxes. Whatever the intentions of such a policy, the results for Brazil were marked. Any Brazilian who wished to pursue a university degree, enter the royal magistracy, or study canon law or medicine had to travel to Portugal, normally to the university at Coimbra. More than three thousand Brazilians studied there during the colonial era. Any Brazilian who wished to publish a book or pamphlet had to seek a publisher in Lisbon or some other Portuguese city, where the text would be reviewed by the censors. Such dependence on Portugal meant that Brazilian intellectuals constantly moved within the orbit of the mother country, often knew it personally, and viewed themselves as part of a broader, more inclusive tradition.

It makes little sense to speak of Portuguese versus Brazilian authors in this period because there was little to separate them. Authors were either Portuguese by birth, educated in Portugal, or at least wrote for a basically Portuguese readership. The two most celebrated authors of seventeenth-century Brazil demonstrate the fusion clearly. The satirical poet Gregório de Mattos was born in Brazil but educated in the law at Coimbra. The great Jesuit preacher, essayist, and missionary Father Antônio Vieira was born in Portugal but reared in Brazil, where he joined the Jesuit order and received his early education. We are speaking of an integrated whole, and although Brazilian themes or subjects and a certain amount of pride in local things can be seen in some colonial authors, in many ways this was not greatly different from the profound regionalism found in Iberian writers in the Peninsula. Vieira and Mattos are also good examples of another pattern. Vieira was a cleric and Mattos a university-trained letrado, and these two groups, along with a few New Christians, made up the majority of intellectuals associated with the colony.

In quantitative terms, the literary production of Brazil was not large, and it tended to be even more fragmented and dispersed than in Spanish America because there were no universities to serve as intellectual focal points. All the genres of the period were produced: honorific and satiric poetry, baroque descriptions of pious or public celebrations, tracts on morality, promotional literature, histories and descriptions of the colony motivated by interest and curiosity. Some of the works we now think of as classics of colonial Brazilian literature, like the first history of the colony, written in 1627 by the Franciscan Frei Vicente do Salvador, or the penetrating description of Brazil in the form of a series of dialogues penned by the New Christian Ambrósio Fernandes Brandão, were not published until the nineteenth century. In truth, the literary production of Brazil in the period before 1750 seems meager unless we keep in mind the small size of the literate population and an imperial system in which the colony was intellectually an extension of the mother country.

If there is one figure who represents the integrated nature of the Portuguese world and the intellectual contacts between Brazil and Portugal, it is the remarkable Father Antônio Vieira. Born in Lisbon of relatively humble forebears, including a mulatto grandmother, he came to Brazil in 1614 at the age of six along with his father, a minor official in the High Court at Bahia. Educated at the local Jesuit College, Vieira entered the order in 1623 hoping to dedicate himself to missionary work, to which end he studied Tupí and one of the principal Angolan languages. He taught humanities for a while, and by the time he was ordained a priest in 1634 he was already well known as a writer and pulpit orator of great ability. Unstinting in his criticism of moral and political folly, his fame grew, and he was sent to Lisbon in 1641. The king, Dom João IV, liked him, and Vieira became his confidant, adviser on Brazilian matters, and court preacher. Vieira's sermons, later collected and published in many volumes, were the talk of Lisbon, and long lines formed outside the churches where he was to preach. He was sent on diplomatic missions and he drew up position papers for the government. He believed that Portugal had a messianic destiny to unite Christendom, but he also held that discrimination against New Christians should cease and that they should be encouraged to settle in Portugal and invest their capital in state-sponsored companies. A Brazil Company was established in 1649 under his urgings, but his advocacy of unpopular causes and liberal social views earned him many enemies. In 1652 he left Lisbon for the mission field of Maranhão in northern Brazil, where he spent most of the next nine years as a missionary and critic of the exploitation of the Indians. He and other Jesuits were expelled by the irate colonists, and he returned once again to Portugal where, after changes at court, the Inquisition now pursued him for his messianism and his defense of the New Christians. Although convicted, his sentence was light, and the old battler went to Rome to plead his case and to fight against the Inquisition. Although he could not get the policy against New Christians changed, he did, in fact, obtain a suspension of the Holy Office in Portugal for the period 1674–81 and a papal bull exempting him personally from its authority. He finally returned in 1681 to Bahia, where he lived the remainder of his life, serving in various capacities as a Jesuit administrator and continuing as an ardent fighter for the cause of the Indians.

Vieira was another man who was fully at home on both sides of the Atlantic. His career included long stays in Portugal and in its American colonies, and although he, like most Brazilian-born whites, always considered himself a Portuguese, he had deep personal feelings and attachments to Brazil, which included a sugar planter brother in a high colonial position and a sister married to a judge on the Bahian High Court. A great prose stylist, his works were avidly read in his own lifetime, although his advanced social views were atypical of the general currents of thought in Portugal and its colonies. Vieira was a clerical humanist and did not dabble in belles lettres or science. In this he was like some of the great Spanish American Jesuits; yet it does seem that in general a less diffuse pattern of activity was characteristic of the Luso-Brazilians. Vieira's great strength was a clarity and profundity of thought presented in a magnificent prose style, not variety. Although his ability and life were far from ordinary, Vieira, at the same time, symbolized some basic patterns of the Brazilian intellectual milieu in the seventeenth century.

Government and society

One sign of Brazil's maturity as a colony was the development of a full range of social and political institutions. Royal government had been initiated in 1549 with the creation of a colonial capital at Salvador and the arrival of senior administrators, and by 1630 a well-developed system of royally appointed officials had replaced the previous donatarial appointments in almost all the Brazilian captaincies. We could outline in some detail the structure of government and the function of the various offices, but this would provide only half the story. The royally appointed officials had to operate in an environment dominated by powerful planter and donatarial families. These families, as well as locally based groups like the Jesuits, sought close ties to the royal officials, but at the same time the crown's officers found that their success often depended on the cooperation and support of local groups and institutions.

At the municipal level political life centered on the senate or town council (*senado da câmara*), the equivalent of the Spanish American cabildo. In our discussion of the cabildo we limited ourselves to the barest description of its social composition and role; however, as with some other facets of urban life, we will go into greater detail for Brazil in view of previous neglect of the importance of cities in the Brazilian structure. And as with those other urban matters, nearly all that is said here, changing a title or two, is applicable to Spanish American city councils.

The Brazilian câmara was usually composed of three or four councilmen, one or two judges, a city attorney, and some minor officials without a vote in council. Voting members of the câmara were selected by a complicated system of indirect election, with eligibility usually limited to "homens bons," that is, men of property and background untainted by any association with trade, manual labor, or religious or ethnic "impurity." In the frontier situation of early Brazil these ideals had been difficult to achieve, and examples of New Christians, men married to mulattoes, or even some who had lost their ears as punishment for crimes in Portugal could be found on the town councils. Also, ordinances prohibiting consecutive terms or limiting relatives from serving together were also ignored in Brazil, the excuse always being that there were not enough qualified men to hold municipal office. As the colony grew and the size of the European population increased, these deviances disappeared, one sign among others of the colony's relative maturity. At the same time, new violations of the traditional restrictions became characteristic of the later seventeenth century as large-scale merchants began to compete for and achieve municipal office. This, too, was a sign of maturity, as well as an indication of changes in the economy and society of Europe itself.

Unlike Portugal, where artisan representation was a permanent and important characteristic of the town councils, the Brazilian senates were usually without such members or used them solely for matters of craft and trade licensing and regulation. (Spanish American councils lacked them entirely.) In the early years of colonization, artisans had been few, and even by the mid-seventeenth century their numbers in the cities were small. Salvador, the largest city, had only seventy registered artisans in 1648. The lack of people in the so-called mechanical offices in Brazilian cities was due to two related causes. First, the demand for many skills on the sugar plantations tended to draw men in these trades to the countryside. Second, and most important, many of the mechanical occupations were filled by slaves, a situation that tended to depress artisan wages and to lower artisan status. Various attempts to place artisan representatives on Brazilian town councils were in general short-lived and ill fated. At best, artisan representatives were given some voice in the control of the city's economic life, but in general their social betters considered them intrusive and disruptive of the decorum of the senate.

The câmaras attempted to regulate almost all aspects of city life, and since municipal jurisdiction often extended over the surrounding countryside, the hand of the councils was felt there as well. Taxation, sanitation, food supply, prices and wages, and social services were all frequently on the agenda. A single month might find the câmara of Salvador fixing the price of sugar, organizing an expedition to hunt down runaway slaves, assigning the salt monopoly contract, and limiting the number of taverns. Obviously, there was little in colonial life that the câmara did not feel was its concern.

In fact, the senates often sought to extend their authority into matters that were considered royal or ecclesiastical prerogatives. The câmaras acted with relative independence in towns where royal governance was weak or lax. Town councils petitioned the crown directly on many matters and some even maintained attorneys in Portugal to plead their interests. Câmaras squabbled incessantly with royal governors and magistrates over matters of precedence, taxation, and jurisdiction. In São Paulo, Belém, and Rio de Janeiro, the strongest municipal sentiments were generated by the question of Indian enslavement. Various royal prohibitions against Indian slavery in the seventeenth century were adamantly opposed by the colonists, and in all these cities governors and Jesuits who were associated with antislavery legislation were arrested or expelled by the town council.

Although it seems clear that the senate sought to promote the welfare of the city in general and was watchful of policies or situations that might injure the commonweal, it also appears that the câmaras tended to represent most actively the interests of the dominant groups in the colony. In Salvador, where the list of councilmen is rather complete, the membership of the câmara was drawn particularly from the sugar planters, cane farmers, and cattle barons. Membership was never exclusively the privilege of one group, but relatives by blood and marriage and the same family names appear year after year. If this was the case in a large city with a high degree of social differentiation, it was probably even more pronounced in small towns where the number of possible councilmen was few. Certainly, few men of mixed racial background held municipal office, and we have already seen the rather tenuous nature of artisan representation in Brazil. In such a situation it was natural for the câmara to define the common good as that which benefited the dominant economic groups from which the councilmen were drawn. Thus, the câmaras of São Paulo and Belém fought ardently to protect the right to send out slaving and exploratory expeditions; and for the town councils of Olinda and Salvador, a moratorium on debts incurred by sugar planters and opposition to a monopoly trade company were major concerns.

Much of the situation described here began to change in the middle decades of the seventeenth century. Planters elected to office in the coastal cities sought increasingly to be excused from service. To some extent this was due to the increasing influence of the mercantile class of the cities, as merchants began to assume social status and compete for municipal office. In some places tension ran high, and a short-lived "civil war" broke out in Pernambuco in 1710 between the planter-dominated town of Olinda and the mercantile port of nearby Recife. Rural interests were not in all cases forced into retreat, however. Planters and ranchers began to see control of newly developing agricultural towns like Campos (in the captaincy of Rio de Janeiro) or Cachoeira and São Francisco (in Bahia) as more immediately beneficial to their interests than participation in the politics of the coastal ports. Moreover, royal intervention in municipal government increased decidedly in the late seventeenth century. In 1696 royal magistrates (*juizes de fora*) were created to preside over the more important town councils and to oversee their elections. Certain tax collection rights were taken from the municipalities and assumed by the royal treasury, and in general the senates began to lose control of some of their traditional privileges.

Above the municipal governing bodies stood the structures of royal government. The Portuguese empire in America was divided into two separate colonies, each with its own administration. The original State of Brazil was the larger of the two. In 1621 its northern areas were constituted a separate State of Maranhão. The division lasted until the two were reunited in 1774. In the State of Brazil, the governor-general (later called the viceroy) and his staff resided in Salvador. He was supported by the usual subordinate treasury, military, and judicial officers. After 1609 a high court of appeals, or *Relação,* similar to the Spanish American Audiencias, staffed by ten letrado judges, also sat in the colonial capital. In each of the captaincies there were subordinate governors with political and military responsibilities supported by treasury and justice officers. In theory, the structure was centralized and symmetrical, but in reality these principles were never achieved. The governor-general in Salvador found it impossible to control the governors in the various captaincies and, in fact, the crown encouraged all officials to communicate directly with Lisbon.

Even in Portugal itself colonial government was never fully centralized. A number of councils had control over colonial matters. There was an Overseas Council (Conselho Ultramarino) after 1642, which replaced earlier less permanent boards, but judicial matters and appointments were the concern of the Board of Justice (Desembargo do Paço) and ecclesiastical matters as well as moral subjects were handled by the Board of Conscience (Mesa da Consciência). All of this had some parallels in Spain, but we can say in general that the Portuguese colonial system was never as administratively centralized as its Spanish counterpart; at the same time, the continual contact of officials with the metropolis and the weakness of centralization within the colony itself necessitated a constant reference and communication to Portugal. This close contact of colonial government with the mother country was paralleled, as we have seen, in the cultural sphere and the circulation of individuals. During this period, although the Brazilian colony reached a kind of maturity, it did not at the same time approach the degree of self-sufficiency attained by the central areas of the Spanish empire.

Much of what we have said about royal officials in the Spanish empire holds equally true in Brazil. Officials were often participants in the local society and economy, because such activity offered advantages to them and because their offices and powers attracted colonial families or groups to them. The governors who came to Brazil were usually nobles of military background who hoped to profit from their term in Brazil, and they usually came surrounded by relatives, retainers, and supporters, all of whom wanted lands, offices, state contracts, or other favors that the governor could provide. There was nothing extraordinary in this arrangement, for the governor's ability to take care of himself and his supporters within reason was considered one of the perquisites that attracted the best men to serve. There was hardly a governor who did not use his office for personal gain or for that of his retinue, and few who remained aloof from local ties. At the lower levels of government, offices were given as rewards for service, bought and sold, and sometimes inherited, and there is no doubt that they were looked upon as fee-earning occupations.

In this regard, the performance of the university-trained letrados who made up the corps of royal judges is especially interesting. In the early days of the colony individual magistrates had been sent from Portugal, but with the growth of the Brazilian population and economy, a high court of appeals staffed with ten judges, or *desembargadores,* was created at Salvador, with subordinate royal magistrates in each captaincy. The powers of the high court were extensive; like the Spanish American Audiencias, the court had administrative and conciliar functions, and its judges were used in a variety of capacities. These magistrates were professional bureaucrats in the sense that they were employed fully in the crown's service and were part of a well-organized system with required training, entrance examinations, periodic promotions, performance reviews, regular career patterns, and carefully defined standards of behavior designed to foster their professionalism and care for royal interests. Service in one's home area was prohibited, no judge was allowed to marry without special license or carry on business within his jurisdiction, and all contacts with local society were discouraged. The judicial bureaucrats were supposedly free from local or personal interests and thus fully responsive to the directives of the crown and their own desires for career advancement. This was the theory; reality was another matter.

The crown attempted to raise the magistrates above the temptations of local society by paying substantial salaries, giving the judges considerable privileges and honors, promising future promotions, and sometimes granting entrance into the knightly orders or even awarding noble status. These were great attractions to the judges, most of whom were of middling backgrounds, the sons of minor officials, merchants, or letrados who had seen the law and royal service as a way to get ahead. By the time of their appointment to the court they had usually served in a number of minor posts in Portugal, West Africa, or Brazil itself and were well-seasoned and experienced men. But there the plan broke down. The authority and status of the magistrates made them all the more desirable as business partners, sons-in-law, or godparents, as far as the colonial elite were concerned. The judges were, after all, "men of flesh and blood," and they often took advantage of their position for economic or social gain. They became involved in business, owned sugar mills, and served as godparents for the children of wealthy friends. Despite the prohibitions, between 1609 and 1751 about 20 percent of the 168 judges who served on the Relação married local women, and at least 10 judges were Brazilian-born. They became fully enmeshed in colonial life and thus responded not only to their career goals as judges but to other considerations as well. If such behavior was common among the highest judges in the colony, the desembargadores, it was even more prevalent among the lesser magistrates in the captaincies.

From the viewpoint of Lisbon, violations of the regulations separating bureaucrats from society were not seen with favor, but so long as they were not excessive, the crown was lenient if royal interests were not threatened. The Brazilian elite sometimes complained about the excesses of a particular judge, but most wanted to create their own links to the bureaucrats or send their sons to Coimbra where they, too, could enter royal service and perhaps return to the colony with a judge's gown. The magistrates often became intermediaries between the colonists and the crown and through their personal interests and local ties provided a dynamic element within the formal organization of government. The power of the family and of personal relations in Iberian life remained strong even in the most bureaucratic and professionalized aspects of government.

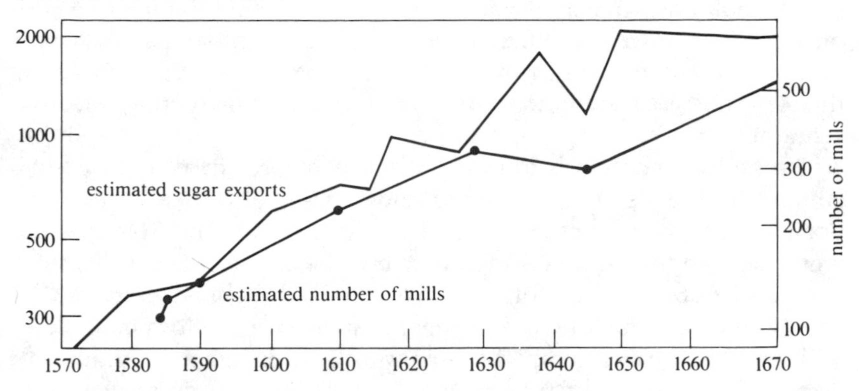

Figure 13. Brazilian sugar, 1570–1670: exports and number of mills. (*Source:* Adapted from Frédéric Mauro, *Portugal et l'Atlantique* [Paris, 1960] but adjusted downward from 1.2 million to 600,000 *arrobas* for 1600. A Portuguese arroba equals about 32 pounds.)

The international context

Having now discussed the way in which the major Brazilian exports were produced, the labor system, and major features of the society, we can turn to the international political and economic context of the colony's development. The international context would be important for any of the American colonies, but it was especially crucial for a colony like Brazil, so oriented toward export of bulk commodities. To a large extent the fortunes of Brazil in this period could be seen in the secular trend of sugar production, sugar prices, and engenho construction. Production in the 1560s and 1570s had been only a few thousand tons a year, but the number of mills and the total production increased annually. By 1600 Brazil produced more than ten thousand tons a year.

The high quality and large quantity of Brazilian sugars drove other production centers from the market. Madeira and São Tomé could no longer compete. The price of sugar seemed to keep pace with expanding production until the 1620s. Then, for a number of reasons, including resumption of the Dutch-Iberian conflict, overproduction, and financial problems in Europe, the sugar industry began to experience real difficulties. By 1640 Brazil was still the world's leading sugar producer, but the industry was beset by problems of an insecure labor supply, fluctuating market conditions, and political difficulties (see Figure 13). The Portuguese crown took an increasingly active role in protecting the sugar economy. A fleet system (at first under a government-sponsored company) was tentatively begun in 1647 and regularized by the end of the century. But such initiatives could not remedy the colony's economic problems.

The political context is important in this regard. In 1580 the Spanish and Portuguese empires came under the joint rule of Philip II of Spain when the Portuguese Aviz dynasty died out. The two empires were kept administratively distinct, but the union did create problems and opportunities for both crowns. With Spanish urging, the Portuguese administrative and legal systems were reformed. There was some Spanish attempt to penetrate the Portuguese commercial system in the south Atlantic as well, which met stiff resistance from the Portuguese. In fact, as we have seen, much of the penetration went in the other direction, and until the 1620s the Portuguese derived great benefit from the Iberian connection. Portuguese slavers received contracts to provide slaves to Spanish America, where the prices were higher than in Brazil. The slavers also found that their access to iron from northern Spain now gave them further trading advantages on the African coast. An active and mostly illegal trade sprang up between Brazil and Buenos Aires, and many Portuguese from Brazil moved up into Potosí and Lima. Peruvian silver became common in Brazil. Meanwhile, in the Amazon and the southern interior of South America, Brazilian frontiersmen and slave hunters moved beyond the line that separated the two empires and established claims and a presence in what was supposed to be Spanish territory.

The Iberian union also had its costs to Portugal, which became apparent after 1621. Portugal, a small country, had always needed and permitted a certain amount of foreign participation in the colonization and commerce of its empire. The Dutch were especially important in this regard as shippers of Brazilian produce, and Amsterdam long had been a major market for sugar and spices. The Spanish theory of commercial empire was far more exclusive. As difficulties between Spain and its rebellious subjects in the Netherlands intensified, the Portuguese were forced to sever their ties with the Dutch. The response in Holland was to attack the Portuguese possessions. The Dutch West India Company, formed in 1621, launched an attack against Bahia in 1624, but held it for only a year. In 1630, however, the Dutch seized Pernambuco, Brazil's most productive sugar captaincy, and shortly thereafter all of northeastern Brazil from south of the São Francisco River to São Luiz in Maranhão came under their control. Cut off from their supply of tropical products, the Dutch had gone to the source and tried to create their own plantation colony. Eventually they also seized African slaving ports, recognizing that a constant supply of slaves was essential to success.

For a quarter of a century (1620–54) the Dutch maintained their hold on the Brazilian northeast from their capital in Pernambuco. Recife, formerly only a port facility for Olinda, was transformed into a busy city along the lines of Amsterdam, with canals and tall town houses. Under the enlightened governorship of Johan Maurits, count of Nassau, the colony throve. Nassau was accompanied by an entourage of artists, scientists, architects, and engineers, who were to record, analyze, and build. Science and the arts were patronized, but Nassau's real task was to reestablish the sugar economy on a firm foundation. The Dutch had capital, but they needed the Portuguese to continue to produce the sugar. Portuguese and some Dutch planters were financed by the Dutch West India Company in order to encourage trade. Under Nassau, a policy of religious toleration was enforced, allowing Calvinists, Catholics, and even the Jews to practice their religion openly, as we have seen.

In social terms, the period of Dutch control was a historical parenthesis with few lasting traces. The Dutch had basically imposed their control over an existing colony that had already achieved a certain level of social and institutional development, so that whatever the Dutch introduced was a thin overlay. In effect, the Dutch controlled political and economic life, but the Luso-Brazilians made up the majority of the free rural population. Perhaps this explains the lack of a lasting Dutch social or cultural impact on Brazilian life.

In 1640 the situation was altered when Portugal rebelled against Spain and declared its independence. Negotiations between Portugal and Holland, both now enemies of Spain, did not convince the Dutch to leave Brazil, but a truce was arranged in the colony. This lasted but a short while, and in 1645 the Luso-Brazilians in Dutch Brazil, led by some of those planters most heavily in debt to the West India Company, revolted. The war lasted until 1654, when the Dutch were finally expelled from Recife.

The password of the rebels of 1645 had been "sugar," a fitting symbol of the economic reasons for the rebellion. The war against the Dutch in Brazil had consequences from which the Brazilian sugar economy never recovered. The fighting destroyed many engenhos and often disrupted the harvests. Dutch attacks against Bahia in 1624, 1638, and 1648 caused widespread destruction of fields and mills. In Pernambuco and Paraíba both sides sometimes engaged in a scorched-earth policy. The shortages caused by these tactics drove up the price of sugar in Europe, but the disruption of maritime commerce made sugar worthless in Brazil. While the price of sugar rose in Europe, it fell in Brazil. Even after the war the sugar industry could not recapture the flush times of the early decades of the century. In Pernambuco the dislocation of the population, destruction of the war, and shortages all hindered recovery. With the engenhos producing less, the crown was forced to keep taxes high, and this resulted in less capital available for expansion in the sugar industry. Bahia and Rio de Janeiro took up some of the slack, but they were faced with drought, plague, and other natural disasters.

A final and perhaps crucial result of the expulsion of the Dutch was the growth of foreign competition to the Brazilian sugar industry in the 1650s. By that decade, the Dutch and English had set up sugar plantation colonies like Surinam and Barbados in the Caribbean. The techniques of sugar production were carried from Brazil by the Dutch and the New Christian Portuguese who had been forced to leave. The northern Europeans had better capital resources, an expanding merchant fleet, and a long tradition of being the major market for sugar. Soon they were producing large amounts. The increased production caused the price of sugar to fall throughout most of the next two centuries. There were periods of recovery (1665–80, 1698–1710), but in general foreign competition and a secular downward trend of prices meant that sugar could no longer provide Brazil with a sure economic foundation. A general European and Atlantic depression in 1680 hit many of the small producers in Brazil very hard; there is evidence that larger engenhos expanded at the expense of small planters in such periods.

By the end of the century tobacco and hides joined sugar as important Brazilian exports, but they, too, suffered from the general problems of the Portuguese economy. Brazil had long since replaced India and Africa as the most important element in the Portuguese empire, and as the value of Brazilian products declined, Portugal's economic difficulties increased. Currency was devalued and the government ordered increased exploration for valuable minerals in hopes of finding some new way to meet Portugal's needs. The discovery of gold in Brazil at the close of the century seemed an answer to Portugal's prayers.

8

The fringes

In the preceding chapters we have frequently spoken of the central areas of Ibero-America. Now it is time to concentrate on the fringe or margin. Since the margin must be defined in terms of the center, let us briefly sum up the salient central-area characteristics. The first set of central or core areas, Mexico and Peru, both chanced to fall inside the Spanish sphere. Their root assets were rich silver deposits and dense, sedentary Indian populations having intensive agriculture and highly developed tribute and labor mechanisms. This combination quickly attracted large numbers of European immigrants, who within a generation created a stable network of cities, plus estates, mines, and international commercial enterprises, all of which in turn brought on the early creation of an impressive ecclesiastical and governmental overlay. Here, through successive waves of immigrants attracted by the opportunities for wealth, there soon arose local societies containing most of the constituent groups of the full Iberian original, including European women and practitioners of a wide variety of European occupations, all interacting with each other in ways approximating the European norms. Here too, in close association with the Spaniards, were the concentrations of Black slaves always found where the returns on investment were the highest. The central areas maintained close communications with the Spanish metropolis. As late as 1560 or 1570, the overall picture was a simple one. Mexico and Peru were the core, and all else, including Brazil, was the fringe, characterized by a straightforward inversion of characteristics: no sedentary Indians, no silver, no full stream of immigration, late and gradual development, and so on (see Map 8).

The transformation of northeastern Brazil after about 1580 into something immediately recognizable as a central area complicates matters, but it also throws further light on the concept and the process. Earliness is not a necessary concomitant of centrality, nor does it have to do with questions of European nationality, Spanish versus Portuguese. The northeast had been a fringe like any other, and then it became central (see Map 9). The categorization of a region as "fringe" or "center" is not static but dynamic. When an asset of

Map 8. Ibero-American center and fringe, ca. 1550.

major interest to Europeans is seen to exist in a given region, that region begins to take on the characteristics of centrality. The asset need not be precious metals, it can be sugar or presumably anything else for which Europeans develop a steady and urgent desire. In the pre-1580 configuration, the central areas were the Western Hemisphere's primary locus of urbanism, permanent agriculture, large political units, and long-distance commerce for the indigenous world as well as for the transplanted European. The case of Brazil breaks that pattern and shows that Ibero-American centrality is es-

Map 9. Ibero-American center and fringe, ca. 1650.

sentially Eurocentric: The crucial components are assets of interest to Europe and the large numbers of European immigrants attracted thereby. The wealth and the numbers then create a relatively full, complex, European-style society, economy, and polity, even without a sedentary Indian base. The centrality of the society so created is demonstrated by the fact that surrounding areas orient to it, try to supply it and copy it.

Ibero-America's fringe, then, was no permanent desert devoid of potential but that portion of the hemisphere in which Iberians at any given time were not very interested. The fringe was far more varied than the center. Topography and climate reflected themselves more directly in social-economic life; above all, the greatly varying indigenous peoples caused the Europeans to adopt different courses. There are two quite distinct sets of developments, dependent on whether the Indians of a region were semisedentary or nonsedentary. Of perhaps equal power as a differentiating factor was the degree of proximity or accessibility to one of the central areas. Nevertheless, we will attempt to name some traits common to the fringes before proceeding to a panoramic description of them.

A fringe area had no major export asset, although the Iberians there would typically try to export natural products collected by the indigenous population, then acquired through barter (rescate). The first generation of Europeans coming into the area would be relatively humble, marginal, and nearly all male; European society and all its structures would remain truncated, less differentiated, more diffuse or fragmented. The area would be relatively isolated from others, outside the main international networks, and neglected by the royal government. Cities and other European settlements would tend to be unstable. In view of the great divergence of the indigenous population from European modes of organization, the central-area forms of interaction tended to yield to ones which either took the Indians entirely out of their society, altered the basic organization of that society, or left it entirely separate as a threat and intractable element. These forms were: Indian slavery, missions, and prolonged wars. Correspondingly, one expects a relatively large and lasting role of the regular orders in a fringe area, as well as some sort of long-lasting military mobilization on the part of local Europeans. In the original central areas decisive conquest was quickly followed by demilitarization and a long period of consolidation. On the fringe one cannot easily distinguish conquest period from mature period. Everything begins gradually; basic structural changes go on, but (unless there is abrupt intervention from the outside) they occur so slowly that fringe-area traits have an archaic flavor. Nearly all the characteristics we have enumerated here were present in the central areas at the very beginning, and for many Spanish fringes we can add the long-persisting encomienda to the list.

Surveying Ibero-America outside the core areas, one is struck by the higher degree of interpenetration of indigenous and European societies, sometimes to the point where the two-society model seems entirely inapplicable. Social, cultural, and biological fusion were widespread. With fewer European women, settlers of the second generation were often heavily mestizo, which did not prevent their assuming high local status in the absence of any alternative. Most importantly, in these regions Indian culture penetrated deeply into the European. Although Paraguay or the Amazon might have versions of many institutions and forms found in the central areas, these were transformed into something very different from the originals. But even at the outset, we must make one important qualification. This interpenetration of which we speak is seen primarily where the indigenous peoples were more or less semisedentary, or if they were less than that, then they were at least in tropical forest areas where stable economic relations were possible. In open country where the Indians were highly mobile hunters, frankly and fully nonsedentary, there was less direct contact between the two societies as societies than in any other kind of Ibero-American situation, and what little Iberian presence there was might draw on Europe and the central areas almost entirely. The situation was almost the same in the few places where Iberians faced temperate-forest peoples. On the other hand, steady or constantly recurring armed hostility, continuing into the eighteenth century and beyond, was seen primarily in just these situations, whereas in tropical semisedentary areas the fighting eventually died down or became intermittent.

The southeastern fringe: the Río de la Plata and southern Brazil

Across the expanse of plateau, plains, and forests drained by the great system of the Paraná, Paraguay, and Uruguay rivers, the Spaniards and the Portuguese encountered similar kinds of environments, economic potentials, and Indian peoples. Their responses, therefore, were similar also. Some of these lands eventually became part of Brazil, others the territory of the republics of Uruguay, Paraguay, and Argentina, but only after three hundred years of trade, warfare, and diplomacy was definitive possession of the "debatable lands" achieved. Among the reasons for the longevity of the debate over control of the various parts of the southeastern fringe was the interconnectedness of the area and the basic similarity of the societies on either side of the Spanish and Portuguese imperial boundaries.

The macroregion the two nations shared was far from internally uniform. Rather, it contained three different subsystems, in each of which both Portuguese and Spaniards in some way participated (see Map 10). First there was the area of the semisedentary Tupians, of whom we have heard before, stretching north and east from Paraguay far up the Brazilian coast. Here the Spaniards of Asunción and

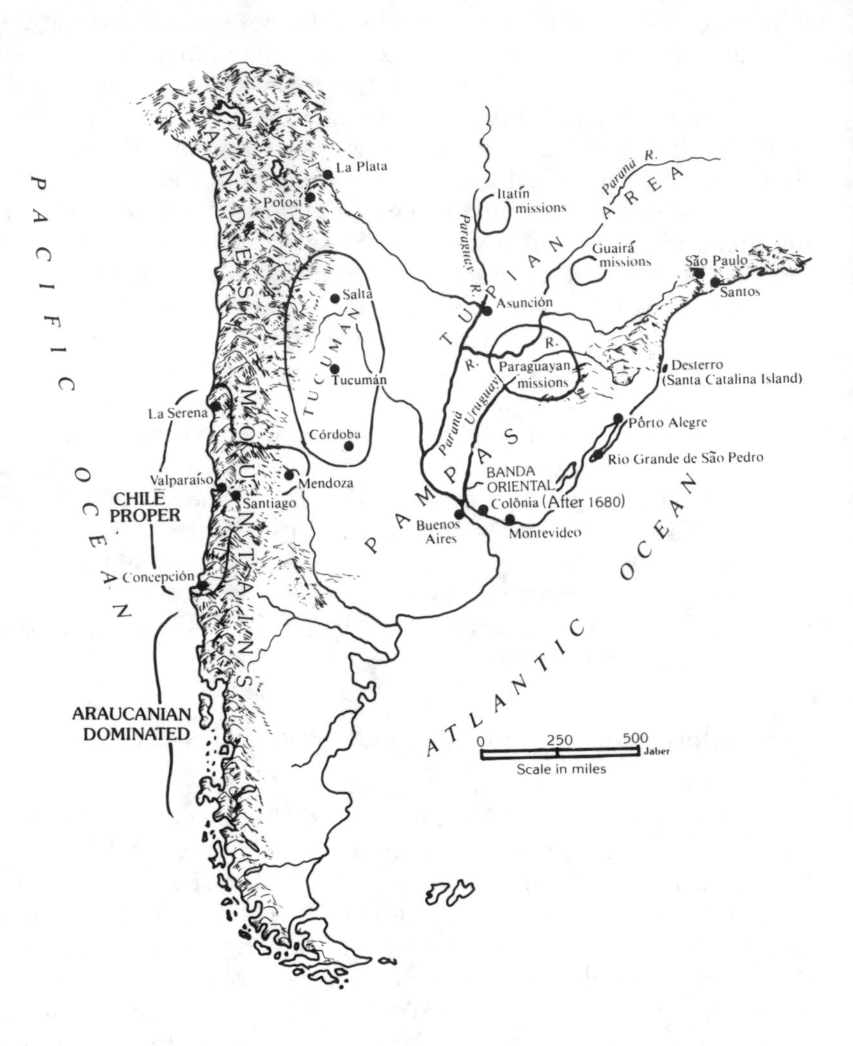

Map 10. The Plata region, southern Brazil, and Chile in the middle colonial period.

the Portuguese of São Paulo developed societies which embodied the fusion of European and indigenous culture perhaps better than any others in the hemisphere, and the Spanish Jesuits built on a Tupian base one of the most famous mission complexes in the history of Ibero-America. The second area included northwestern Argentina, or Tucumán, whose indigenous population was somewhere between semi- and fully sedentary, having been considerably affected by the neighboring central Andeans. Here the Spaniards proceeded more on the model of the central areas, in a modest way, and oriented their economy toward the supply of Potosí. There came to be a sort of surreptitious and secondary trunk line leading from Buenos Aires through Tucumán to the silver mines, with the Portuguese playing an important part in its formation. And third, there were the great plains, from southern Argentina into Brazil, nearly empty, with little apparent potential to attract Europeans and mobile indigenous hunters to deter them. Gradually herds of wild cattle grew up here, and a scattered population of mestizos began to hunt and utilize them, some of the products going toward Tucumán and Upper Peru, and others toward markets in Brazil.

The Tupian area

Many fringe areas were first opened up by misguided Europeans who were seeking the makings of new central areas. So it was with the Plata region. In fact, the first major European thrust was entirely off the mark, directed at one of the least hospitable segments of the vast Platine region.

Both the Spaniards and the Portuguese had explored along the south Atlantic coast of South America in the early sixteenth century. Early small-scale attempts to take control of the area near the mouth of the great La Plata river system had come to little. Then in the 1530s the news of great wealth in Peru jolted Spain and caused the Spaniards to depart from their general practice of step-by-step expansion. In 1535 a great expedition, larger by far than those that conquered Mexico or Peru, sailed from Spain and early in the following year founded the city of Buenos Aires at the mouth of the Plata. Despite the name (*plata* meaning "silver") and the hopes for another Potosí, there were no quick riches to be found on the Argentine plains; instead, the expedition found only some nonsedentary Indians whose mobility and lack of agricultural base made it extremely difficult for the Spaniards to conquer or rule them, or even find food. Under Indian attack and torn by internal dissent over how to respond, Buenos Aires underwent a siege in which many of the garrison died from starvation or disease. Finally, finding the situation hopeless, the survivors abandoned Buenos Aires and retreated up the river to an advance post at what is today Asunción, Paraguay. The advantage of this locale over the mouth of the Plata was the presence of semisedentary Indians living in villages and growing crops which could provide the Spaniards with a subsistence base. About 350 Europeans, including some Portuguese, Germans, and Italians, began the Spanish colony of Paraguay.

Thus in the sixteenth century the presently poor region of Paraguay, because of its more numerous and settled Indian population, offered the Spaniards a foothold, whereas what is today the rich area of Argentina was untenable. Still, even in the sixteenth century, Paraguay was poor in potential compared with Peru or Mexico, or even with Guatemala or Chile, and this poverty would be reflected in a different type of European occupation and social evolution.

The Indians who inhabited the region near Asunción and eastward from the Paraná River were the Guaraní, a branch of the Tupian villagers who were spread through much of South America east of the Andes. Their social organization, the important role of women in agriculture, and their lack of a well-defined political organization or class hierarchy have all been discussed in Chapters 2 and 6. To the west, in the Chaco desert, lived nomadic hunters, warlike people such as the Guaycuru, who were the traditional enemies of the Guaraní. As we might expect, the Spaniards chose to settle among the most sedentary, and therefore controllable, Indian population in the area. But Guaraní organization, unlike that of the central Andes, was not constituted in such a way that the Spaniards could simply leave it intact, extracting labor or tribute through local headmen; to achieve that end, a more direct Spanish intervention in Indian society was required. It is the form of that penetration that produced in Paraguay a distinctive social result.

During the first twenty years of contact the Spaniards and Guaraní formed a sort of alliance. The Spaniards gave the Indians valuable aid against their enemies, and in return the Europeans were integrated into Guaraní society as headmen. They were given presents of women and food as part of that process, and what they were not given they took. Kinship rules played a role in the Spaniards' new position, since the relatives of the women taken as concubines (or more rarely as wives) performed labor services as part of their familial obligations. Since women did the basic sedentary work in Guaraní society, the more women a Spaniard had in his household, the more access to labor he had. Some contemporary observers compared life in Asunción to Muhammad's paradise, because each Spaniard lived in the midst of so many women. The priests thundered against what seemed to be such carnal excess, failing to understand that the marital-sexual irregularities gave the settlers an indispensable structural tie to the Indian population and its resources. In the central areas the

Spaniards had worked through the large provincial unit with its cacique; here they took the lineage or household as the basis, no other solid unit existing, and became the heads themselves in the absence of a strong cacique. A similar arrangement appeared in southern Brazil and some other fringe areas.

In fact, it was out of the lineage that the Paraguayan encomienda grew. At first it was not clear how the encomienda could be applied to the Paraguayan situation. The Portuguese of Brazil, also facing mainly Tupians, did not use it at all. In Paraguay there were two pressures toward adapting the institution: first, the desire of the settlers to have the same rewards as the conquerors of Peru, and second, the aim of the authorities to have a uniform legal structure for all Spanish territories. On the informal level, the Spaniards began to consider as "encomiendas" their collections of concubines, servants, and Indian in-laws performing services, the whole group tending to become close dependents like the yanaconas of Peru. There was little agricultural surplus to be extracted from the Indian communities, no mines existed, and the Indians had no mechanism of tribute delivery, so that their obligations were primarily satisfied by personal service in the home or fields of the encomendero. Without intermediaries, the Guaraní of these encomiendas were in direct and continuous contact with their encomenderos. The two "worlds" were far more integrated here than in the central areas. In Paraguay there was really only one structure with Spaniards at the upper levels and Indians at the lower. Without much currency in the economy, with limited access to imported goods, Paraguay lacked the two quite distinct economies of the central areas; instead it had only one basically subsistence economy in which both Spaniards and Indians participated.

Given these conditions, a remarkable cultural transformation took place, altering Spanish society and civilization substantially. There were few Spanish artisans, a minimal number of Blacks (at least in the sixteenth century), and hardly any European women. The "Spaniards," in fact, were often mestizos, the sons of unions between the encomendero and his following, but hardly any distinction was made between them and persons born of two European parents. In an area of such small Spanish population, anyone with some Spanish admixture was accepted into the group. This was especially true for women, and a great premium was placed on brides with at least some claim to European descent. Spaniards and mestizos adopted the food, customs, and even language of the Guaraní. Here the basic Spanish estate form, the encomienda, and the cellular unit of Spanish society, the family, were more indigenous than European. But at the same time, direct Spanish contact with an Indian population of only moderate size eventually produced a pattern of Indian acculturation comparable to that of other areas. Hispanic ideals and methods gradually worked themselves thoroughly into the Indian population through the same channels by which Indian influence reached the Spaniards.

After a twenty-year delay, the encomienda was instituted formally in Paraguay (1556). The already existing informal arrangements received recognition under the name of *encomienda originaria;* to them were added more distant encomiendas, superficially much more akin to those in the central areas. About a hundred thousand Indians living in the country around Asunción were divided into grants of relatively small size (about thirty to ninety tributaries in each). This type of arrangement received the name of *encomienda mitaya,* after the Peruvian mita; as in a central area, it was based on already existing indigenous settlements, where the Indians continued to live, providing labor to the encomendero on a temporary basis. But these encomiendas differed from those in Peru not only in their tiny size, corresponding to the size of functioning indigenous units. There was also a lack of usable surplus to be given as tribute, and the Guaraní had no tradition of draft rotary labor, much less on a migratory basis. Small wonder that many of the rotating laborers were women and that the kinship analogy continued to play an important role. The two types of encomienda existed side by side, the mitaya feeding into the originaria. Sometimes Indians were moved permanently from the mitaya to encomendero households to make up for losses in the population of the originaria. The province was evolving toward the familiar setup of a Spanish city drawing on an Indian hinterland.

Demographic decline affected the Indian population of Paraguay as it did Indian groups everywhere; for this and other reasons the encomiendas over time shrank in size until finally, by the late eighteenth century, there were hardly any Indians left in them. Nevertheless, the encomienda in Paraguay demonstrated great longevity, as it did in nearly all areas outside the immediate center (that is, where the encomienda had been introduced at all). The very wealth potential of the central-area encomienda had created bitter competition for it, and the large immigration there had supplied numerous competitors. On the other hand, the mining industry lessened necessity for reliance on that particular form. Under these conditions, the crown could effectively limit the encomienda. In Peru and central Mexico, after great debates over Indian control, much legislation, and even some civil wars, by the beginning of the seventeenth century the principle of direct governmental jurisdiction over the Indian population had been established, and the encomienda had largely ceased to be a viable institution. But in the fringe areas, there were neither immigrants to fight over the encomienda nor governmental officials to regulate it. On the one hand it brought such little profit that it was hardly worth fighting over, and on the other hand there was no visible economic alternative to it. Although encomiendas in these areas were in many senses weak and sometimes so small as to appear meaningless, the institution nevertheless remained alive much longer. Not only in Paraguay, but in Chile and Venezuela as well, the encomienda continued as an active if declining institution until the middle or late eighteenth century, still representing a cheap and easy way of maintaining some control over the Indian population with very little expense to the royal treasury. Despite desultory attempts to enforce central-area encomienda regulations, the crown left the Paraguayan encomienda largely in the hands of the encomenderos.

No matter how adapted to the local situation, independent, or even Indianized an Iberian regional subsociety seemed to become, its members were never content to stay on the fringe if they could possibly avoid it. The Paraguayan Spaniards had searched feverishly for mineral wealth in the first generation. As the Peruvian economy continued to surge, they looked for ways to participate in it. They played a considerable role in the establishment of Tucumán as a supply area for Potosí and in the refounding of Buenos Aires as a Peru-oriented port. Above all they looked for local products they might sell in the direction of Peru. With hides, Paraguay could not compete on an equal basis with Tucumán; its tobacco had only moderate sales; its one great success was *yerba mate,* used to make a tea which is still popular today in southern South America. Finding a ready and expanding market, the Paraguayans developed the business as best they could. By the seventeenth and eighteenth centuries the crop had generated some capital in the economy, and local Spaniards began to invest in a small way in Black slaves as workers. Other corresponding social changes, about which very little is known, began to take place. The economy and social-ethnic composition of Paraguay seemed on the brink of transformation beyond what was characteristic of the fringe. In the end, Paraguay's isolation proved too much to overcome. Still, by 1800, some 15 percent of Paraguay's population was Black or mulatto.

The market for yerba mate was finite, and possibilities for the Paraguayan Spaniards were limited further by restrictive royal legislation incited by competing economic interests. More serious than restrictions was the direct competition of the Spanish Jesuits of the Paraguayan region, for Paraguay came to be a major center of Jesuit mission activity. Coming from the direction of Peru, the Jesuits began from the late sixteenth century to acquire a base of colegios and estates in Tucumán. In the first decade of the seventeenth century they constituted a province called Paraguay (including Tucumán). Looking about for a field in which to establish missions, they found that the nomads of the pampas of the Chaco were not good material, and they soon began to concentrate on that portion of the semisedentary Guaraní which had not yet been absorbed by the Spaniards of Asunción.

In 1607 the Jesuits started developing missions to the east of Asunción, mainly in the northeastern projection of present-day Argentina which is called Misiones. At their height there were thirty establishments, with a population probably well in excess of a hundred thousand. Coming out of the long tradition of congregaciones and reducciones (the contemporary term for them, as we have seen before), the Paraguayan missions were like the aldeas of Brazil and the Franciscan and Jesuit missions of the Mexican north in their attempt to concentrate the Indians, reorganize their units, and make them more sedentary. The form of Indian governance in the missions was patterned on the central-area Hispanic-style Indian municipality, as it was everywhere the Spaniards went. Here, however, the Jesuits came into control of the largest block of semisedentary Indians left unexploited by secular Iberians in the entire Spanish and Portuguese sphere and could work in greater isolation from central areas and export economies than any other mission complex. As a consequence, the Jesuits achieved an unusual degree of success over a time span of more than a century and a half. Here the Jesuits could give free rein to their propensities for thorough organization. In addition, because of the lack of a strong Spanish civil and governmental presence in the area, the Jesuits and their charges took over some functions usually appropriated by other organs. For example, they undertook military defense on behalf of themselves and the Spanish crown, a role carried out in other fringe regions, when necessary, by presidios and a paid Hispanic soldiery.

Yet another result of the large semisedentary population to which the Jesuits fell heir was an unusually bitter rivalry with the lay Iberians of surrounding regions, the Spaniards of Asunción and the

Portuguese of São Paulo, both of whom wanted their part of the rich prize even if they had not anticipated the Jesuits in its exploitation. We will speak more of the Portuguese–Jesuit strife in a moment. As to the Asunción Spaniards, in the history of Paraguay, the seventeenth and eighteenth centuries are plagued by conflicts, and at times virtual civil war, between settlers and Jesuits over the issue of Indian control. The settlers had seen the utility of concentrating the Indians and had established several new settlements, bringing together various encomienda units, with, in some cases, majordomos taking an active hand in the name of the encomendero. Now the Jesuits had done all the spadework for them in additional areas, and they wanted access through encomienda obligation to this new source of labor. But the Jesuits resisted any such claim and rejected the notion of an encomienda labor obligation even in Paraguay proper, thereby striking at the base of the Spaniards' economy. In addition, the Jesuits were just as assiduous as the settlers in growing and selling yerba mate, and their district apparently being especially propitious for the plant, they cut deeply into the Paraguayan Spaniards' market. Yet despite the particularly virulent conflict, the role of the regular orders in Paraguay was simply a well-developed instance of a phenomenon widespread on the Ibero-American fringe.

Let us turn now to Portuguese activity among the southern Tupians. We have already seen in Chapter 6 how the Portuguese at first attempted to create a sugar-exporting colony on the southern coast of Brazil at São Vicente. But despite some early success, the region was soon surpassed by the thriving sugar zones farther north, with a better climate, more coastal lands, and greater proximity to the market. The Portuguese shifted their southern base to the town of São Paulo, originally a Jesuit mission, located on a plateau some fifty miles up from the coast. But even being the headquarters amounted to little in the south, for by the end of the sixteenth century the town still had a population of only 1,500 to 2,000 people. Small, isolated, lacking minerals or exotic crops to export to Europe, and blessed with a temperate climate, São Paulo might seem at first glance to have been just the place (if there was such a place in the sixteenth century) to re-create a European-style peasant community in the New World, with small farmers growing subsistence crops in a social and cultural environment replicating the forms of Portugal. "As pretty as Evora" or "here is another Portugal" were the comments made by early observers of the village in the open country of the Paulista plateau. But appearances were deceiving.

Like the Spaniards in Paraguay, the Portuguese had been able to establish themselves as allies of one Indian group, the Tupiniquin, against their rivals the Tupinambá and the Tamoio to the north and the Guaraní (Carijos) to the south. São Paulo, in fact, had been established to control these loyal Indian allies and to provide access to the vital resource of Indian captives, needed at first on the coastal plantations. The "cooperation" between the Portuguese and their Indian allies produced predictable results. The Portuguese came to depend heavily on the labor of Indian slaves and forros (see Chapter 6), Indians who were legally free but attached to Portuguese households – a situation similar to that of the members of the encomienda originaria in Paraguay. With few Portuguese women attracted to the area, the daughters of Portuguese and Indians were preferred as brides. Concubinage seems to have been the rule, and the surviving wills speak continually of illegitimate mameluco (mestizo) children. The long-term result of the process was a considerable fusion of Portuguese, other Europeans (there were always a good number of Spaniards, Flemings, and others in São Paulo), and Indians.

Colonists and Jesuits (who unlike the situation in Paraguay were in São Paulo from the start) lived in a sea of Indians. The usual Indian population decline took place here too, especially during the plagues of the 1560s, but these losses were partially compensated by the arrival of new Indian captives brought in by slaving expeditions. Even after the legal abolition of Indian slavery in 1570, justification could always be found in the "just war" loophole, and, in fact, many Indians were held in São Paulo under the title of *administrados*, or persons under the "temporary" tutelage of the Portuguese. The rights of these free Indians did not seem to differ greatly from those of the slaves, and both were passed along in wills like other forms of property. Some Paulistas held hundreds of Indians, using them as laborers and servants but also calling on their services as allies and armed retainers. Even at the close of the sixteenth century the majority of São Paulo's population was Indian, and their impact was felt in almost every aspect of life.

Despite its isolation, dependence on subsistence agriculture, and propitious topography and climate, São Paulo did not become a European-style peasant community. The large number of subordinate Indians, the easy access to land, and the patriarchal ideal to which the Portuguese colonists were firmly attached all created conditions favoring the creation of a different kind of society. Although the social gradations of noble and commoner were transposed from Portugal, the small number of immigrants, the general poverty of the place, the need for anyone with a special skill or craft to practice it, the necessity of military cooperation against hostile Indians, all tended to level the differences between Europeans. Moreover, hardly any distinction was made between mamelucos and Portuguese, and so long as a man owned property, was married, and headed a household, he could claim what counted locally as "noble" status. Established on their estates, or fazendas, surrounded by their families, bastards, retainers, slaves, and administrados, the Paulistas lived an American version of the Iberian patriarchal ideal. Poor in material goods (a piece of linen or a real bed was an extraordinary luxury), the Paulistas counted their wealth in their followings. "Rich in archers" or "potent in bowmen" were common descriptions of the most powerful citizens. The existence of the Indians and the distinction between them and persons of European descent created a social hierarchy and way of life ensuring that São Paulo would not become a Portuguese peasant community.

Through most of the colonial period São Paulo remained poor and backward, compared with the towns of the northeast. The important families were firmly established on their fazendas, although many maintained a second residence in the town or at least participated in urban life during the five yearly religious processions or in the sessions of the municipal council. Such occasional and intermittent residence left São Paulo a humble place without a town hall until 1575, of taipa (a kind of adobe, as the reader may remember), its churches rudimentary. Although eventually some products were exported to Rio de Janeiro and the northeast or occasionally to Buenos Aires, for the most part the economy remained sluggish. Barter played an important role in the early years, and payments in kind were common even among the Europeans. Artisans were few, as were notaries. Contracts were often oral, and many other aspects of Iberian life were attenuated by the poverty and isolation of the milieu.

The Paulistas were not so enamored of patriarchal life that they were content to remain isolated and poor, and thus they turned their ambitions to the interior, "seeking their fortune in the sertão," as the wills often put it. The rumors of gold and emeralds in the interior and the decline of the local Indian population by the 1580s led to a series of almost yearly expeditions. Following the course of the Tiete and Paranaiba rivers westward or striking into the plains of the south, mobile columns, led by Portuguese and mamelucos but composed mainly of Indian "allies," sought Indian slaves and mineral wealth. Organized into quasi-military companies called *bandeiras* ("banners"), the participants (*bandeirantes*) often spent months and sometimes years in the sertão. Their hardships were great and their accomplishments formidable. In the forest the Indian background of the Paulistas was invaluable; they dressed, spoke, ate, and lived more or less like the Indians they led and those they hunted. The town of São Paulo itself was often half deserted as the Paulistas went off to seek their fortune, preferring, as one governor put it, "to spend many years in the sertão searching for someone to work [for them] rather than to serve someone else for a single day." Those who remained at home often financed one of the bandeirantes, providing him with arms or supplies in return for a share of the profits to be made in Indian captives or minerals. In many ways the bandeiras were like the entradas of conquest and discovery in Spanish America, privately organized and financed, sharing the profits among members and investors, depending considerably on the reputation of the leader and the size of his following. Here is another example of a phenomenon which appeared fleetingly in the center becoming a long-lasting fixture and archaic survival on the fringe.

After raiding the villages in the vicinity of São Paulo and the scattered groups to the south, the Paulistas began to look covetously at the Spanish Jesuit mission province of Guairá in eastern Paraguay. Raids on Guairá began around 1609, and a major bandeira went out in 1628 under the great pathfinder and Indian slaver Antônio Raposo Tavares. Thousands of Indians were taken as captives over the vehement protests of the Jesuit fathers, who got little support from the Spanish colonists in Paraguay. Only in 1639, when the Spanish crown finally allowed the Jesuits to arm the Guaraní with firearms, were the bandeirantes held at bay, at least temporarily. The missions of Guairá were destroyed and the other mission fields severely restricted by these attacks. Much of the present territory of Brazil would have remained under Spanish control had it not been for the depredations of the Paulistas beyond the Line of Tordesillas.

The raids on the Paraguayan missions did not cease in 1640, but they did begin to decline in size and intensity. The reasons were to be found not only in increasing Spanish and Jesuit resistance but also in the reopening of the Atlantic slave trade by the Portuguese with their recapture of Angola from the Dutch in 1648. Despite their patriarchal life-style, the Paulistas had never been able to use all their Indian captives in the fields around São Paulo. Many had been sold to the sugar planters of Bahia, Pernambuco, and especially Rio de Janeiro, and indeed, sale was likely the primary object of making the captures, Indian slaves being São Paulo's only equivalent of Paraguay's yerba mate as something of considerable interest in more developed regions. During the Iberian union, the Portuguese had supplied African slaves to Spanish America as well as to their own colony, Brazil. The drain of this trade, added to the disruption of the supply of Africans to Brazil caused by the war with the Dutch in the south Atlantic, created a renewed market for Indian slaves. But by 1650, with the routes to Africa opened again, the demand for Indians declined and there was less incentive to enslave them.

The bandeiras continued, but the emphasis now shifted to the search for mineral wealth. Raposo Tavares, commissioned by the crown to open a route to Peru, led a column (1648 to 1652) which crossed the Chaco, skirted the Andes, and eventually followed the river systems to the mouth of the Amazon: a tremendous feat but one with little result. The search for minerals intensified in the 1670s, a time when Portugal was entering a financial crisis and sorely needed new sources of wealth. Expeditions were still often privately organized, but increasingly the Portuguese government began to make use of the Paulistas' backwoods skills. At various times bandeiras were commissioned to search for mines, defeat hostile Indian groups in Bahia and Ceará, and destroy the community of renegade Blacks at Palmares in the northeast. Although royal governors admired the Paulistas in some ways, they often complained of their arrogance, independence, and uncouthness. Eventually, in the early 1690s, a series of gold strikes was made in the area that is presently the state of Minas Gerais. Unlike earlier finds, these proved to be rich, and by 1700 a great rush was on.

We will discuss the mining boom and accompanying social changes later, but it should be pointed out here that São Paulo could not help being affected by this development. The connection with Minas Gerais gave a new importance to the captaincy of São Paulo and a new life to the town, officially raised to the status of city in 1711. Royal government became tighter, partly because of the mining connection and partly because of the border warfare with the Spaniards in the south. More important, Minas Gerais needed supplies which the Paulistas could provide, and the availability of this market created new opportunities for the local economy. Indian slavery was definitively abolished in 1758, and Blacks began to arrive in a steady flow after the discovery of the mines. The availability of new markets began to transform agriculture, and as new secondary towns were founded, a growing rural agricultural population was forming. By the end of the century the semi-Indian, unstructured character of São Paulo was rapidly becoming a thing of the past.

Despite some obvious differences, such as the two separate nationalities involved, the presence or absence of the encomienda, and the relative strength and role of the Jesuits, Spanish Paraguay and southern Brazil were much alike in the early and middle colonial period. The nature of Tupian culture, the presence of few Europeans among many Indians, the lack of a dynamic economy, all worked to produce similar results, including widespread miscegenation, the full acceptance of mestizos, and the adoption of Indian customs. The Paraguayan encomienda originaria bore a very close resemblance to the Paulista household of lord, family, slaves, and freemen; the main difference was that the Paulistas lived farther from the greatest concentration of Indians and had to travel about to enslave them.

Isolation and the lack of firm governmental control created in both Paraguay and São Paulo roughhewn local aristocracies harboring strongly independent and regionalist sentiments. In both places local government, Indian policy, and many other matters were considered the exclusive prerogatives of the residents. The Paulistas expelled the Jesuits on a number of occasions and frequently engaged in family feuds with little concern for central authority. On more than one occasion, royally appointed officials in Asunción were displaced by local vote, and in São Paulo royal circuit judges were threatened or attacked when they interfered in local affairs. Not surprisingly, meddling with Indian affairs provoked the strongest reactions in both places. Asunción was in turmoil over that issue in the 1640s, and later a serious civil disturbance (the Comunero Revolt, 1724–35) took place over this and related matters. Although formally a part of their respective colonial empires, the Tupian-based regions were too poor and too isolated to merit strong central control.

The regionwide uniform development found on the southern fringe and the deep penetration of Indian ways into the Iberian culture of the area are nowhere more apparent than in the matter of language. Even today Paraguay is a bilingual nation in which Guaraní is understood at all levels of society, and in the colonial period a similar situation existed in some areas of northern Argentina as well. In São Paulo, Tupí was widely spoken in the sixteenth century and remained current until the mid-eighteenth. In Paraguay as in São Paulo, the Europeans and their descendants, surrounded by servants, slaves, concubines, and allies, spoke the Indian languages as a matter of necessity and convenience. By the seventeenth century, children in São Paulo had to be sent to school to learn Portuguese. When the famous Paulista bandeirante Domingos Jorge Velho came to Pernambuco, he spoke Portuguese so poorly that his interview with the local bishop had to be conducted through an interpreter.

Tucumán and Buenos Aires

A separate jurisdiction with its own Spanish governor, Tucumán, or northwestern Argentina, was transitional between Peru and Paraguay in many senses: It was located between them, had an Indian population sharing some of the characteristics of both, and its subsequent Hispanic development was intermediary between the two. Several indigenous ethnic groups inhabited the area; like those of Paraguay, they were scattered, living in very small units which shifted on occasion, but they had also come under central Andean influence. Some grew maize and other central-area crops, and each unit had a leader strong enough to be considered a cacique by the Spaniards. To the members of the first Spanish entradas coming from Peru in the 1530s and 1540s, Tucumán seemed a hostile and politically fragmented region lacking silver, and they hastily retreated.

Then through the second half of the sixteenth century other Spanish settlers returned to the region, often relatively marginal persons with more modest and realistic aspirations. They began creating cities and encomiendas on the Peruvian model, and by the last quarter of the century, after a time of Indian fighting and shifting Spanish settlement, they had attained relative stability and established a network of cities with hinterlands, including Córdoba, Tucumán proper, and Salta. The Asunción Spaniards also had a hand, founding such towns in the Tucumán region as Santa Fe and Corrientes. Yet even if the overall plan is reminiscent of a central area, the inner reality was much like that of Paraguay. Encomenderos found that their Indians were not accustomed to tribute and that each encomendero had to collect and subdue his own Indians, congregate them in villages, and give them direct supervision and training before they were worth much to him.

What eventually put Tucumán in an altogether different category from Paraguay was its potential for supplying the growing needs of Potosí. Not only was Tucumán close at hand, but with its open country and temperate climate it was just the place to raise European livestock or crops, for which the highlands surrounding Potosí were not propitious. The Spaniards of the region took every advantage of the situation, going beyond cattle and hides to large-scale mule breeding, obrajes for woolens, and various types of artisan production, especially of leather items. By the late seventeenth century, we are told, some forty thousand mules a year were being sold at the great fair of Salta, destined for Peruvian markets.

As a result, Tucumán was more in touch with central-area developments of all kinds than was Paraguay. Its society was more differentiated, mestizos were more subordinated. Places such as Córdoba and Tucumán had many of the features of a central-area city; one might compare them to New Granada's Popayán. But in estate development Tucumán did not keep pace with Peru or Mexico. Despite population loss, soon reducing the number of Indians in encomienda (over 60 percent between 1582, when there were more than 27,000, and 1607) and culminating in a figure of less than 2,500 by 1719, the encomienda remained the base for economic activity through most of the seventeenth century at least, disappearing entirely only in the eighteenth. Town councils remained dominated by encomenderos, who maintained networks of enterprises involved in all the area's main economic activities, with the labor of their Indians as a common denominator, much as in Peru in the conquest period. Every encomendero had a majordomo and some had several, with far more elaborate staffing than the occasional steward found in Paraguay. Yet in lasting so long and in relying on the directly supervised work of relatively small numbers of Indians, the encomienda of Tucumán was a close cousin of the Paraguayan institution.

Interregional trade in local products was never as profitable anywhere in Ibero-America as direct participation in the international economy, and all the Iberians of the Plata region understood that fact very well. It was to further international commerce that the Spaniards of Asunción reestablished Buenos Aires in 1580, facilitating the development of what one might call a secondary or backdoor trunk line leading toward Potosí. Given the maritime technology of the time, the Spanish commercial route past Panama to Peru and Potosí was highly rational. It was shorter than alternatives, more secure, and since it was combined with the Mexico route more economical; with its entrepôt and opportunity for reprovisioning, it also allowed for larger cargoes than relatively small, slow ships could otherwise have carried. But for African slave supply the route defied geography, particularly for slaves from the Congo and Angola, and for Portuguese merchants in Brazil it represented the purest kind of obstacle and exclusion. The Portuguese thus hastened to use the new port for trade to Potosí, in both European goods and Black slaves, sometimes with grudging official Spanish permission, sometimes as contraband – for which tiny, isolated, unpoliced Buenos Aires was an ideal setting.

In the late sixteenth and early seventeenth centuries silver from Potosí was traded at Buenos Aires for slaves, ironware, sugar, and luxury items, most of which was transported northward to Potosí. This trade flourished during the 1580–1640 period of Iberian union, and the Portuguese who dominated commerce in the south Atlantic were its major agents. The creation of an inland customs house at Córdoba in 1620 greatly restricted legal trade on the southern route, but contraband continued. Though a Spanish port, Buenos Aires was dominated in its early years by its community of resident Portuguese merchants, who also penetrated into Tucumán and as far as Potosí (thereby furthering the mercantile development of Tucumán, with Paraguay once again left to the side). Buenos Aires was, in effect, a Portuguese "factory" for trade with Peru. In 1648 Father Antônio Vieira, the great Portuguese Jesuit, suggested that the Portuguese abandon Pernambuco to the Dutch and integrate Buenos Aires into Brazil. While modern Brazilian and Argentine nationalists would find such a suggestion unthinkable, Vieira's plan simply underlined the basic unity that existed between the Spanish and the Portuguese parts of the region.

Finally, the plains of Argentina, Uruguay, and southern Brazil were a third aspect of the Plata region shared by Spaniards and Portuguese alike. Of vast future significance, they were the margin of the margin in the middle colonial period, nearly devoid of Iberian people, who were dissuaded by the scattering of Indian warrior-hunters to be found there and the lack of economic incentive in terms of markets and techniques then existing. The one resource which the plains began to develop was an unwitting Iberian introduction, wild cattle escaped from the settlements (*ganado cimarrón*), which eventually formed great herds running across the whole expanse or at least the northern half of it. Marginalized mestizo freebooters, from both Spanish and Portuguese communities, followed the herds, hunting and slaughtering them for the tallow and hides. Next to nothing is known of the exact timing and mechanisms of this movement, but out of it came, by the end of the colonial period, a distinct subculture: that of the gauchos of southern Brazil and the Argentine–Uruguayan pampas.

The Amazonian fringe

Beyond the centers of European control on the Brazilian coast or central Peru, far from the cathedrals and governmental palaces of Quito, Lima, or Salvador lay the enormous stretches of rain forest,

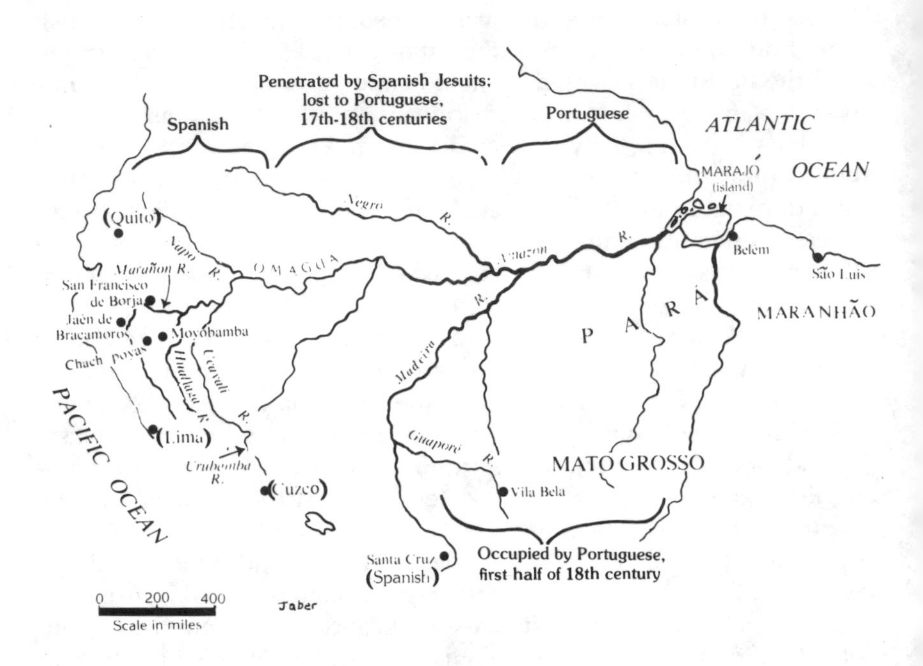

Map 11. Amazonia in colonial times.

savannah, and floodplain that comprised the Amazon basin (see Map 11). Here, as in other areas peripheral to the centers of colonial life, a loose and distinctive society grew in response to local realities, and although some of the forms and terminology of the more stable areas were present, their function and content were often not at all the same.

The Amazon region was not undifferentiated "jungle" but a series of environments, each of which supported Indian peoples at different levels of social organization, population density, and economy. We should not impose upon the past our image of the present-day Indians of Amazonia as small, scattered bands of simple hunters living in the most inaccessible places. What we see today is often the result of processes set in motion since the arrival of the Europeans. Whole peoples have disappeared, others have fled or been moved far from their original locations, and among some, deculturation has taken place as agriculture or pottery were abandoned in the struggle to survive in less benign environments.

The fringes

In Amazonia the rivers are the veins and arteries of life, their waters the essential lifeblood. Along the streams a floodplain, or *varzea,* teems with life and supports a wide variety of plants, animals, and fish. Seasonal flooding of the varzea made agriculture there feasible in preconquest times, in many places supporting large populations. The earliest Europeans who penetrated the region, like those who accompanied Francisco de Orellana down the length of the Amazon River in the 1540s, recorded many villages along the riverbanks and noted that the canoes of the Spaniards sometimes traveled whole days within sight of Indian dwellings along the banks. Although scholars long believed that such statements were exaggeration or pure imaginings, recent scholarship tends to corroborate the early descriptions. The varzea of rivers like the Solimões supported large and more importantly, dense indigenous populations. Orellana reported a rich "province" of the Omagua, a Tupí-speaking people who lived from agriculture and exploitation of the rich sources of protein represented by fish, manatee, and thousands of turtles which they raised in pens as a source of meat and eggs, a common practice among the riverine peoples. Food from river and forest supported levels of material life and social organization not usually associated with the Amazon region. The Omagua grew cotton for clothing and knew pottery. They lived in large villages and had apparently developed a political system including multivillage chiefdoms. At the time of first contact they may have numbered as many as a hundred thousand individuals. And the Omagua were not alone. Other areas of dense population (perhaps nine to ten people per square kilometer) could be found on Marajó island at the mouth of the Amazon, along the Brazilian coast, and on the savannahs of the *llanos de Mojos* in northern Bolivia, an area where large ridged fields were constructed to take advantage of seasonal inundations (some evidence of this technique of creating raised fields has also been found in Venezuela, Ecuador, and the Maya areas of Campeche and Chiapas).

The dense forests between the rivers of Amazonia were, however, the region's most extensive habitat. Here agriculture was more difficult, and the dispersed nature of the wildlife meant constant movement for those who hunted it. In this environment groups were small, seminomadic, and only marginally involved in agriculture. Even at elevations above 700 meters, on the eastern slopes of the Andes in the so-called *ceja de la montaña* ("eyebrow of the forest"), Indian groups were small and widely dispersed. Peoples like the Campa of eastern Peru and the Jívaro of eastern Ecuador had successfully resisted the Inca incursions in precolonial times, and the

Spaniards who were to follow also found these nomads particularly difficult to subdue or control and even more to the point, rarely worth the attention of conquerors or royal administrators.

In general terms, then, the Amazon basin contained a variety of environments, some of which supported dense populations. Whereas much of the forest area was sparsely inhabited, rivers, savannahs, and coasts provided excellent conditions for human settlement. The Indian population of Amazonia reached possibly as much as six or seven million at the time of contact, before disease, warfare, and slave raiding took their toll.

The Spaniards in western Amazonia

Spanish penetration of the Amazon basin began as a natural extension of the conquest of the Andean highlands. The Incas had known the peoples who lived to the east of the Andes and had, in fact, included their territory, Antisuyo, as one of the four divisions of the Inca empire. But in truth, despite some trade and recruitment of forest Indians as mercenaries, penetration was slight. The forest peoples, or *chunchos* as the Incas called them, could not be easily subdued. The Spaniards, following rumors of cinnamon forests and golden kingdoms, entered the montaña along the river courses which formed the natural means of transportation. Moving down the Urubamba River in southern Peru, the Ucayali in central Peru, the Napo in Ecuador, and other rivers, they penetrated the forests of the eastern Andean slopes where, as the Spanish chronicler Cieza de León said, "the clouds are so thick and gloomy that even the sky cannot be seen."

When easily obtainable wealth and golden kingdoms proved to be chimerical and were replaced by the reality of heat, humidity, insects, and intractable Indians, the Spaniards tried to organize the area along more standard lines. Towns were founded: Chachapoyas (1538), Moyobamba (1549), San Francisco de Borja (1615). But without a settled Indian population to provide labor or tribute, such ventures often met with limited or no success. The Indians had to be enslaved or coerced to search for gold, loss of population through disease was as quick and serious as in other wet lowlands, and the "chunchos" often proved as indomitable to the Spaniards as they had been to the Incas. The town of San Juan de Jaén de Bracamoros on the Marañón River provides a disheartening example. Founded in 1549, its site was changed four times by 1608, and its surrounding Indian population fell from 20,000 to 1,500 in the same period of time.

In a few places where gold was discovered in the streams, boomtowns sprang into existence, swelled with miners, and then collapsed. San Juan del Oro was founded by Black miners and gold hunters, who in return for their discovery received special privileges and titles as "mulatos señores." In 1570 San Juan had 3,000 inhabitants and an official mita allotment to supply Indian labor, but the mines soon played out, and by 1583 only 1,500 people were left. By the first years of the seventeenth century only a few thatch huts remained to mark the once flourishing site of San Juan. Similar tales could be told of other towns that dotted the interior of the continent from southern Colombia to northern Bolivia. Obviously, under such conditions it was difficult to create and impose the institutions of settlement and control that had been used in Mexico or the central Andes.

Only those tropical areas that became integrated into the larger economy by supplying lowland products to the centers of population met with some success. The coca leaf, a narcotic plant, had long been an important item in highland Andean culture. The Spaniards set up labor-intensive haciendas, called *cocales,* to produce this crop for Indian consumption in the silver mining areas. The Indian coca workers, many of whom were brought down from the highlands, died in great numbers despite careful work regulations. Still, a town like Paucartambo, in the montaña east of Cuzco, could thrive on its export of 1.5 million pounds of leaves to the mines of Potosí in the early seventeenth century. Regions that supplied coca, sugar, salt, or other such products to the colonial core areas survived as reasonable facsimiles of the Iberian central areas, but of course they were in good part colonies and extensions of the center.

In much of the montaña there was neither gold nor the possibility of encomiendas or profitable commercial agriculture. Once the situation was understood, few Spaniards ventured to the area, and there was no question of bringing many Spanish women and Black slaves. Population decline continued among the forest Indians, and those who survived continued to be difficult to control. The Jívaro destroyed a number of towns in eastern Ecuador in 1599, and a series of expeditions sent in the seventeenth century to subdue them met with small success. Such Indian labor as the settlers could secure was put to collecting forest products like wild cotton or, in the eighteenth century, chinchona bark, the source of quinine. The economy remained extractive, government was weak, and social relations were determined to a large extent by the environment.

In Amazonia, the Spaniards, like the Portuguese, attempted to apply their standard procedures. The institutions and techniques of conquest were all present, the municipalities, the encomiendas, the governmental structure, but in the montaña environment their content and functions were often transformed. In areas like Mainas, opened up in 1616, a town named San Francisco de Borja was created and the expedition's members received encomiendas, but as in Paraguay, these soon became little more than groups of Indians used for personal service, whose status more closely resembled that of naboría-yanaconas or even slaves.

The Portuguese in Amazonia

Portuguese penetration of Amazonia began in the early seventeenth century in an attempt to keep out the English, French, and Dutch. Belém at the mouth of the Amazon was established in 1616, and Maranhão, including all of northern Brazil, was created in 1621 as a separate jurisdiction dependent directly on Lisbon. Settlement was slow. In 1672 the whole region, including the coastal centers of São Luiz and Belém, had only about eight hundred Europeans. Those who came from the northeastern centers of Bahia and Pernambuco hoped to re-enact the success of the sugar industry, but the shortage of labor created by warfare, slaving, and disease, plus the difficulties of transport, kept sugar production and profits at low levels. After 1680, the Portuguese began to exploit the forest products, or *drogas do sertão,* wild cotton, cacao, sarsaparilla, wild clove, and other such commodities. The rush to exploit these products proved disastrous to the engenhos, aside from soon depleting the "drogas" available near the center of population.

Until the late eighteenth century, when political or diplomatic goals and commercial expansion began to transform the Amazon, the Portuguese Amazonian captaincies of Pará and Maranhão were, like their Spanish counterparts to the west, poor and loosely organized settlements in which local conditions carried far more weight in the shaping of life than did the policies of councils or governors. Belém and São Luiz were towns with few noble buildings and hardly any of the luxuries to be found in Salvador and Olinda. Barter continued as the primary means of exchange among both Portuguese and Indians, and coins were always in short supply. Wages were paid in measures of cotton cloth because of the shortage of currency and because of the reluctance of Indians to enter the cash economy. The settlements were few and widely scattered along the river system. Moreover, as in Spanish Amazonia, they tended to be ephemeral because of the underlying instability of the indigenous peoples and the extractive nature of the economy, which quickly depleted the placer gold or natural products of a region. These small communities often depended on Indians for skills normally provided by European artisans in more developed regions.

In the Amazon the Portuguese and Spaniards alike adapted themselves to an indigenous cultural milieu. The Europeans acquired not only the forest lore of the Indians but much of their material culture as well. The hammock and the canoe were indispensable articles of life, and manioc (*mandioca,* Port.; *yuca,* Sp.) was the common fare of both Europeans and Indians. The Portuguese, faced with a myriad of languages in Amazonia, fell back on Tupí as a means of communication. The lingua geral, as we have seen a simplified and homogenized form of Tupí, was the principal tongue of interethnic contacts at all levels, and most of the Portuguese and half-caste caboclos were completely bilingual. In fact, the lingua geral remained the common speech of Pará at least until the 1750s, when the government began making strong efforts to encourage the use of Portuguese. Of course, some elements of European life, like roofing tile and the steel axe, were stubbornly retained by the Portuguese and sometimes, especially in the latter case, also used by the Indians, who greatly valued the new weapons and tools.

But influences moved in both directions. The Christian religion, imposed or adopted wherever the Iberians penetrated, was in turn penetrated by Indian beliefs. Even today, the folklore and traditions of the Amazonian caboclos or mestizos draw heavily on the legends and beliefs of their Indian ancestors. This cultural mixing went parallel with racial interaction; many Europeans took Indian women as mistresses or more rarely as wives. Like many a fringe region, Amazonia became culturally and racially mixed, with European forms and practices as an imposed ideal but often considerably modified by local physical and historical realities. This fusion did not mean, however, that relationships between Europeans and Indians ran smoothly or justly.

To understand life in colonial Amazonia, we must turn to two final topics: labor and the missions of the regular orders, for in them are to be found the themes that structure the region's history.

In Amazonia Indian labor was the key to success for the colonists. Land was there in abundance, but labor was needed to exploit it, and since African slaves were drawn off by the profitable plantation and mining zones, the few Europeans present turned toward the

Indians. The Portuguese, as we have noted, did not use the encomienda, although in the State of Maranhão there were always those who advocated its use. The Portuguese turned instead to a variety of other means by which Indians could be induced or coerced to work for Europeans. Indian slavery was officially prohibited in 1570, but loopholes could always be found, and Indians who resisted missionaries or who practiced cannibalism could be enslaved even after the prohibitory law.

More important were the *tropas de resgate*, Portuguese-led, often state-sponsored expeditions to "rescue" (*resgatear*) Indians who had been captured by their Indian enemies and who were theoretically in danger of being executed. (Here we find the word "resgate," the same as Spanish "rescate," associated once again with a variant form of barter or forced trade.) In return for their supposed rescue, the Indians were forced to serve the Portuguese for a specified term (five to ten years was common); in practice, they became slaves. Indian villages along the rivers discovered that the only way to avoid war was to supply slaves to the expeditionaries, who then brought them back to Belém or São Luiz to be distributed by the town councils to the settlers. It has been observed that the demands of the Portuguese for labor and their injection of trade goods into the Amazon basin brought on increased conflicts among the indigenous groups. The peacefulness seen along the rivers in the sixteenth century was replaced in the following century by internecine warfare.

The slaving and resgate operations of the Portuguese colonists were a perfect example of the way in which local conditions, rather than imperial policy, determined the shape of life in places like the Amazon region. The colonists were constantly faced with a labor shortage, caused by their own actions and by epidemics which struck the Amazonian Indians repeatedly. Smallpox alone, to say nothing of other diseases, caused enormous losses in 1621, 1644, 1662, 1696, and 1724. As each epidemic depleted the labor pool, the colonists reached farther into the interior in search of replacements. Following the epidemic of 1724, a bloody campaign was carried out against the Manao, a large indigenous group on the Rio Negro, in an attempt to secure more captives. The crown and the clergy, unable to halt these expeditions, compromised with the colonists. After 1688 tropas de resgate were allowed only under state regulation and control, with royal officials and Jesuits organizing the operations and overseeing the distribution of goods and captives. What the crown could not stop, it now taxed. This situation continued until the mid-eighteenth century and was perhaps the best an imperial government could hope for in a remote area where the population was small, the territory enormous, the economy uncertain, and the lines of communication and administration tenuous at best.

Throughout Amazonia, and indeed in general wherever there was little to attract a European population, the regular orders played a major role. In Mexico or the central Andes the mendicants were challenged by the secular clergy as soon as the conquest had been consummated and Spanish society firmly established. In Amazonia, Paraguay, and many other such regions, the regulars remained in place and in power much longer because the areas remained poor, sparsely populated, and in need of the abilities of the religious to congregate the often widely dispersed population and make their services available. Although the colonists often opposed this approach to settlement and control, it was their very weakness which gave the orders a role, and in view of the situation, the orders could usually depend on the backing of the crown in addition, at least until the mid-eighteenth century.

Mission activity in Amazonia began in earnest in the seventeenth century. In the Spanish areas of the west, as in Paraguay, the Jesuits were the most important order. By 1700 some seventy-five pueblos of Indians were under their control in the province of Mainas. Despite occasional rebellions against the fathers and serious epidemics like that of 1680, which killed some sixty thousand people, the missions prospered. This was especially true after the arrival of Father Samuel Fritz, a Bohemian, who in 1686 established a mission among the Omagua in the middle reaches of the Amazon and by so doing extended Spain's territorial claims against the westward movement of the Portuguese. In both empires, missions often served the interests of the crown in opening difficult regions, defining and holding frontiers, and "pacifying" undependable Indian populations. At the same time, because of their control and protection of the Indians, the religious and their villages were thoroughly detested by the colonists.

The Portuguese mission field in the State of Maranhão provides an excellent and prolonged example of the tensions and conflicts that arose between settlers, the crown, and missionary clergy. The Franciscans had opened activities among the Indians of northern Brazil in the early seventeenth century, but the Jesuits under the forceful leadership of Father Antônio Vieira became the predominant order after 1655. Antislaving legislation promulgated in that year led to rioting and the temporary expulsion of the Jesuits from Belém, but the settlers' success was short-lived and the Jesuits soon returned. A compromise was reached in the 1680s with the publication of the *Regimen of Missions* (1686), which laid out the rules for Indian control. Only Jesuits or Franciscans would be allowed to live in the Indian villages, but the villages would supply Indians to the colonists under a system akin to the repartimiento in Spanish America. Slaving and resgate expeditions continued, allowed and to some extent even sponsored by conniving royal officials. When the Jesuits proved unwilling to bend their scruples, other orders like the more worldly Carmelites were chosen to open new missions, as they did on the Rio Negro in the early eighteenth century. But in general, none of the orders escaped the jealousy of the colonists. In the Amazon, all wealth depended on Indians who could serve as paddlers, gatherers, partisans, or field hands, and the missionaries stood in the path of free access to Indian labor.

Venezuela: A Caribbean variant

In the first years of the sixteenth century the lands lying along the northern coast of South America fell fully within the Spanish Caribbean sphere. They were the object of the first explorations beyond the islands, then they were raided for gold and Indian slaves as the islands came into their time of troubles, and in the 1520s the pearls of Cubagua off the Venezuelan coast seemed the Caribbean's last hope of major wealth, until their quick exhaustion. But as the full force of the Spanish thrust shifted to Mexico and Peru, the mainland facing the Caribbean began to diverge from the islands. Both were marginalized, but in different manners. The large islands had Spanish cities, the residue of a Spanish population, even an Audiencia. If they no longer operated directly in international commerce, they nevertheless had the business of provisioning the silver fleets which passed through; as north European depredations grew more serious, several of the Spanish settlements of the large islands became fortified ports, receiving subsidies from royal revenues in the central areas. The internal constitution and dynamics of the Spanish societies of Cuba, Hispaniola, and Puerto Rico are still largely unstudied, but one can conjecture that they were somewhat like the more provincial parts of the central areas, though frequent contact with the outside may have made them more cosmopolitan, and they had a much larger Hispanic-African component and much smaller Indian one. Their basic situation was like that of Brazil, in that their climate and location made tropical export their main economic potential, but unlike Brazil they had lost their Indians too quickly to serve as a capitalizing factor in a transition to African slavery, and indeed the whole process had antedated the time of bulk export from non-European areas. When in the seventeenth century the north European involvement in the Caribbean expanded beyond attacks to the development of a sugar industry on the smaller islands (more of this in a later chapter), the Spanish island societies could participate only indirectly and on a small scale.

Venezuela's situation was quite different. On the one hand, it was farther away from the fleet's stopover places than were the islands, and there had never been even an ephemeral moment when it had been so much the center of attention as to acquire the framework of a full-scale Hispanic society. Yet the size and diversity of the region meant a longer continuation of explorations and experimentation. Indian population dropped drastically, as everywhere, but with a larger area, less Spanish-Indian contact, and several sections of the territory which were not lowlands, the country retained an Indian base, especially in the inland portion. Thus parts of Venezuela came to share features similar to those of a fringe area like Paraguay, whereas in other parts there was enough contact with main-line commerce and government to create social patterns more like those of the central areas. Large enough to absorb the Caribbean demographic and economic decline, Venezuela in the middle colonial period, with its incipient plantation economy on the coast, was foreshadowing later Caribbean developments.

Before the arrival of Columbus there were perhaps as many as fifty thousand Indians along the coast and in the coastal valleys of Venezuela, plus others in the zone extending for several hundred miles toward the interior of the continent and known simply as *tierra adentro* (see Map 12). European contact was made first on both ends of the Caribbean coastline, and in neither case was there any quick movement toward the establishment of encomiendas. For one thing, the indigenous population was as little suited for the standard form of the institution as were the Guaraní of Paraguay. For another, there was no understanding of the encomienda among the Germans who received extensive rights to the western part of the little-known province from Charles V in 1528, an outstanding example of the principle "foreigners to the margins." During the short time before the experiment collapsed, the German governors were only interested in carrying out the entradas and slave raids typical of the fringe in the conquest period (and later too, in some places); they

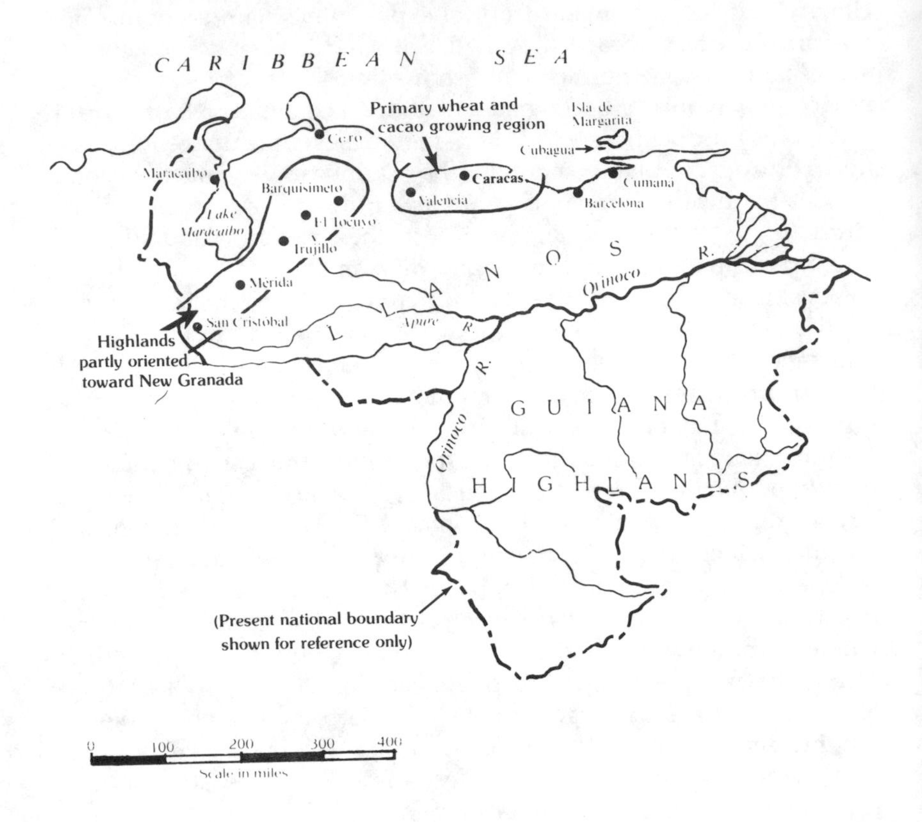

Map 12. Colonial Venezuela.

used Indians as porters for their El Dorado expeditions and sold them as slaves to Panama and Santo Domingo. Along the eastern coast, those Indians not subjected to strenuous efforts in the pearl fisheries were also likely to be sold into distant slavery.

By the 1560s and 1570s the Spanish conquest had reached the center of the Venezuelan coast. Having finally given up on expeditions, gold, and pearls, seeing that the local climate was good for wheat, which could be sold to provision the silver fleet at Cartagena (wheat did not flourish on the islands), and somewhat influenced by more than half a century's development in Indian legislation, the settlers were now prepared to turn to the encomienda and systematic use of native labor. The interim period before the encomienda has a close parallel in Paraguay, but here it was even longer. On the edges of the province, where the dictates of the European economic system were only occasionally heard, Indian slavery continued well into the seventeenth century.

In the central valleys – the area of present-day Barquisimeto, Valencia, and Caracas – where the concentrations of Indians were denser and larger (although resistance was more marked), it proved profitable to form encomiendas, but only on the basis of personal service, or rather the obligation to give a specified amount of labor to the encomendero. Like the regulations set out at nearly the same time in Paraguay, the Venezuelan encomienda required that each Indian labor one month of every three in the encomendero's fields. Despite being made illegal by the New Laws of 1542, in Venezuela personal-service encomiendas were not converted to the tribute-collecting type common in New Spain and Peru until 1687.

The administrative history of the province during the second half of the sixteenth century and much of the seventeenth reads as a record of official unconcern and local autonomy, punctuated by sporadic attempts to force compliance with the policy of payments in tribute. In 1621 one zealous magistrate who tried to force the encomenderos to conform to the royal dictate was imprisoned by the cabildo for his efforts – although not overlooked by the crown, this act of insubordination was also not rigorously punished, and the whole episode had no effect whatsoever on the encomenderos' command of native labor. In the Andean regions, in the jurisdictions of the town of Mérida and San Cristóbal, where the Indians were numerous and royal authority closer at hand – in this case the Audiencia of New Granada – the regime of personal service was terminated, at least nominally, in 1620. But on the highland plains and coastal valleys of the original province of Venezuela, not even explicit legislation (royal decrees of 1633 and 1672) could force the change to payment in kind instead of Indian labor. Appeals and delays continued even after the legislation of 1687, and the transition to tribute collection was probably still incomplete in 1718, when the crown declared that from that time forward all encomiendas would revert to royal possession as they fell vacant. Thus as in Paraguay and Chile, the encomienda of Venezuela persisted into the eighteenth century. It was also like the Paraguayan in its lateness to take shape, the small size of grants, and the use of the labor of women.

Originally the Venezuelan encomienda, like the Paraguayan, had little superstructure, and majordomos were rare. But as the interregional economy grew, the encomenderos succeeded in building up conglomerates of diverse units tied together by the same labor base and the same management, becoming more like their fellows in Tucumán. They owned wheat farms, cacao groves, and herds of cattle, with wheat as the most important encomienda-linked enterprise until the abolition of encomienda labor in 1687. Despite the commercial orientation and the growing profitability, families were able to hold on to the same grants generation after generation, circulating the encomendero position among close relatives, because immigration and internal growth were still too small to generate seriously competing interests outside the dominant group.

In the coastal regions encomienda labor gave way to African slave labor earlier, perhaps as early as the third decade of the seventeenth century, especially in the cacao plantation economy. Cacao increasingly took over from wheat as the main source of external income. The cacao tree was indigenous, apparently known in Venezuela itself at the time of the conquest, and at first the business even had something of the flavor of a typical fringe-area collection of natural products for sale. The principal original market was Mexico, so that the basic orientation was the usual one of supplying a central area. But cacao was beginning to gain a following not only among American Spaniards but in Europe itself, and the Spanish American cacao business, from having been extractive, was becoming an intensive European-style operation, not only here but in faraway Guayaquil (on the Ecuadorian coast) as well. Thus the Venezuelans were being drawn bit by bit, in a process whose timing is still little understood, into the rising slave-labor, tropical-export complex of the eastern seaboard.

Caracas became the province's foremost settlement because within its jurisdiction were included both cool highlands where wheat could be grown for sale in Cartagena and hot, well-watered coastal valleys where the profits and credits from wheat sales were used to purchase slaves at Cartagena and build cacao plantations. As the first of the coastal towns to enter the Caribbean-Atlantic market, Caracas by the mid-seventeenth century was the administrative center of the province and the residence of a strong cacao planter oligarchy which had no peer on the Caribbean coast and which would last until the wars of independence (Simón Bolívar was its most illustrious son). Caracas began to resemble a provincial capital in the central areas. Its social hierarchy was well defined, mestizos played only a minor role, and living in Caracas proper was a highly valued attribute for those who pretended to upper-class status. Later immigrants, like the Canary Islanders who began to arrive in the 1680s, sometimes came to hold dominant roles in lesser towns like Valencia but never in conservative and stable Caracas.

Yet it had taken a very long time for local Spaniards even to decide where to locate the capital, and the region remained unintegrated. The Venezuelan settlements were largely unconnected and independent of one another throughout the colonial period and for most of the nineteenth century, with only the slowest penetration from the principal towns to the surrounding hinterland. In the west, the chain of settlements that began in the Andes and terminated at Maracaibo developed an interdependence based on their character as points along a trade route. The Caribbean towns were different, and there was no such growing together, apart from an insignificant exchange of salt and dried fish for wheat. Although eastern Venezuela was the first landfall after the Atlantic crossing, once the early pearl boom had passed, eastern Venezuela had nothing to offer to the hyperactive commerce passing right in front of its doorstep. On the interior plains of Venezuela, a gradual development comparable to that of the Argentine pampas was taking place – the interconnected spread of wild or nearly wild cattle and a scattered group of cowhands of mixed ethnicity. We know as little of the formation of this group as in the Argentine case, but by the end of the colonial period they had become the principal inhabitants of the plains, with a subculture nearly as distinct as that of the Argentine gauchos.

Frontiers

Up to this point we have been concentrating on areas populated by quite sedentary indigenous peoples who were tied to shifting tropical agriculture or at least to riverine pursuits and who were in possession of assets of possible use to the Europeans, so that there was a basis for some form of social and economic interaction between the two. Now we propose to discuss developments in places that might be better termed frontiers than fringes. Here the Iberians faced indigenous groups who offered them an absolute minimum of economic incentive and who at the same time were better able, for various reasons, to resist invasion or even to counterattack.

The most widely spread such peoples were the fully nonsedentary inhabitants of the open country, small bands of highly efficient hunters and fighters who moved frequently in search of game and other bounty. Despite the large distances covered by some of these groups in the course of their normal pursuits, one hesitates to call them nomads, for they all considered a certain territory their own, and many had well-defined annual migration routes. But nomadic they certainly were in the sense of being forever on the move and having no settlements that were more than seasonal shelters or camps. As we saw in Chapter 2, commonalities between nonsedentary society and European society hardly existed, nor were there any already existing organizational modes or economic activities that the Europeans could bend to their own purposes without transformation and deep shock to the indigenous system. Very little strictly societal interaction was possible. Messianistic movements, which can be seen as the reaction of a society which feels its very existence threatened, appeared with greater frequency among nonsedentaries in contact with Europeans than among groups of any other kind.

A situation comparable to that of the people of the dry flatlands was that of the inhabitants of temperate forests. Even if more given to agriculture and settled life, they had nothing the Iberians wanted, and they were highly fragmented, able to resist anything but the full-scale occupation that never came.

In the territories of the tropical semisedentaries, some central-area forms such as the encomienda or the plantation appeared (though greatly changed) alongside other more archaic or idiosyncratic forms – Indian slavery, missions, prolonged wars. On the frontiers only the latter modes were possible. Central-area forms were simply not present: no encomienda at all, no hinterlands feeding into a city, not even, unless other factors were involved, Iberian municipalities. Even the well-tried fringe-area device of rescate failed among the indigenous peoples of the frontiers, for they had no tropical exotica to barter for trinkets. Indeed, the Europeans were sometimes reduced to trying to achieve the pacifying side effects of barter through outright gifts to the Indians. The other side of rescate, however – raiding for Indian slaves – was a standard feature and marked characteristic of the frontier, often being the only element of the entire regional complex through which local Iberians exercised any leverage on the economies of richer regions. Since here indigenous and intrusive societies were colliding more than meeting, the acculturation that occurred between them was not the deep everyday influence exerted elsewhere but an over-the-fence introduction of discrete items or techniques. The Indians might adopt new weapons, the horse as a new means of transportation, new items of consumption, but they became not a whit more sedentary or organized along European lines. If structural changes took place, such as the larger confederations and stronger leaders that appeared among these peoples when under long-lasting pressure or attack, these were responses, latent in indigenous culture, to an outside force, rather than results of European influence as such. In the other direction, indigenous influence on European culture was less in this kind of situation than in any other, though the intruders did acquire much specific lore on how to deal with nonsedentary and forest Indians.

In surveying a broad variety of Ibero-American regions we have seen that formal institutions generally reflected the local Iberian society and economy, being strong where it was well developed, weak where it was not. On the semisedentary fringe, institutions of most kinds, particularly the royal government and the hierarchy of the secular clergy, were weak, with far less manpower, revenue, and influence than in central areas (regular orders also had fewer personnel than in the center but greater relative weight locally). On the frontier, the trend was partially reversed. The expenditure of men and money was small, to be sure, but relatively speaking the role of institutions – missions, forts with paid soldiers – was dominant in a way it was nowhere else, because there was hardly anything to attract Iberian migrants, so that the Iberian civil population was extremely diffuse, humble and thin, sometimes almost to the vanishing point. Part of the reason for an Iberian presence was strategic: fear of competing European powers, need to defend against any incursions of the Indians into economically more developed areas, and the politics of the regular orders, each seeking a field of action for itself. As a result, subsidies came in from branches of government based in more central areas, channeled to individuals on the scene through the frontier institutions, so that the latter were able to play, on a small scale, the usual role of cities as a market of goods and labor.

If we now look about Ibero-America for instances of the phenomenon we have been discussing on the abstract plane, the first thing that strikes us is that, though elements of the composite are in evidence, the whole in its pure form nowhere appears. In fact, if an area had nothing to offer but plains and plains Indians or temperate forests and their inhabitants, Europeans would leave it strictly alone until the advent of the worldwide economic-technological changes of the late eighteenth and early nineteenth centuries – a statement almost as true for English America as for Ibero-America. The relatively untouched peoples of the southern Argentine pampas are perhaps the best example of what would happen in the absence of other factors; or one could include the North American forests and great plains as well, since if the Spaniards had thought them worth occupying they would have done so.

For the process of Iberian confrontation with peoples of such areas to get under way in the early or middle part of the colonial period, such peoples had to be in relative propinquity to an area of more intensive Iberian development. The frontier aspects would then be colored and altered by the nature of the more established neighbor to which the fringe area was attached, so that both must be seen together. This is the procedure we will follow in discussing Ibero-America's two most pronounced frontiers, at the extremes of the Spanish Indies: the north of Mexico and the south of Chile. (No region of Brazil seems to have undergone a closely comparable process, largely because its indigenous peoples were overwhelmingly semisedentary or riverine.)

The north Mexican frontier

The peoples of central Mexico, as we saw in Chapter 2, had long recognized a distinction between themselves and the less sedentary inhabitants of the arid plateaus and mountains to the north, whom they called Chichimecs, or barbarians. "Chichimec" territory began surprisingly near to that of the sedentaries (see Map 13). The Lerma River, arising only a few miles from Mexico City, has been taken as generally marking the boundary between the two cultural traditions, and even the great basin of the Bajío, which today seems so much a part of central Mexico, belonged mainly to the Chichimecs. In the conquest period, the normal course of outward expansion soon brought the Spaniards as far as Guadalajara (first established on a temporary site in 1531), which began to take shape as a quite standard encomendero city. But a hint of the future occurred among some transitional peoples just to the north, especially the Caxcanes, who had agriculture and caciques but also shared many traits with the nonsedentaries. Already seemingly conquered, having been distributed in encomiendas, in 1541–2 they rose in a rebellion so serious that outside help was required to quell it, and the Spaniards endowed the conflict with the name of the "Mixtón War." At about the same time Spanish expeditions of discovery, most prominently that of Coronado, proved that thin populations, mobile and hostile, extended indefinitely far to the north.

The whole of north Mexico might have become an ultrafringe, like southern Argentina, with the Iberian presence limited to a few mestizos hunting wild cattle, had it not been for the great silver strikes starting in the late 1540s, quickly turning the north into the ultimate source of Spanish Mexico's wealth, bringing in both Hispanics and sedentary Indians, creating a complex of towns, mines, and support

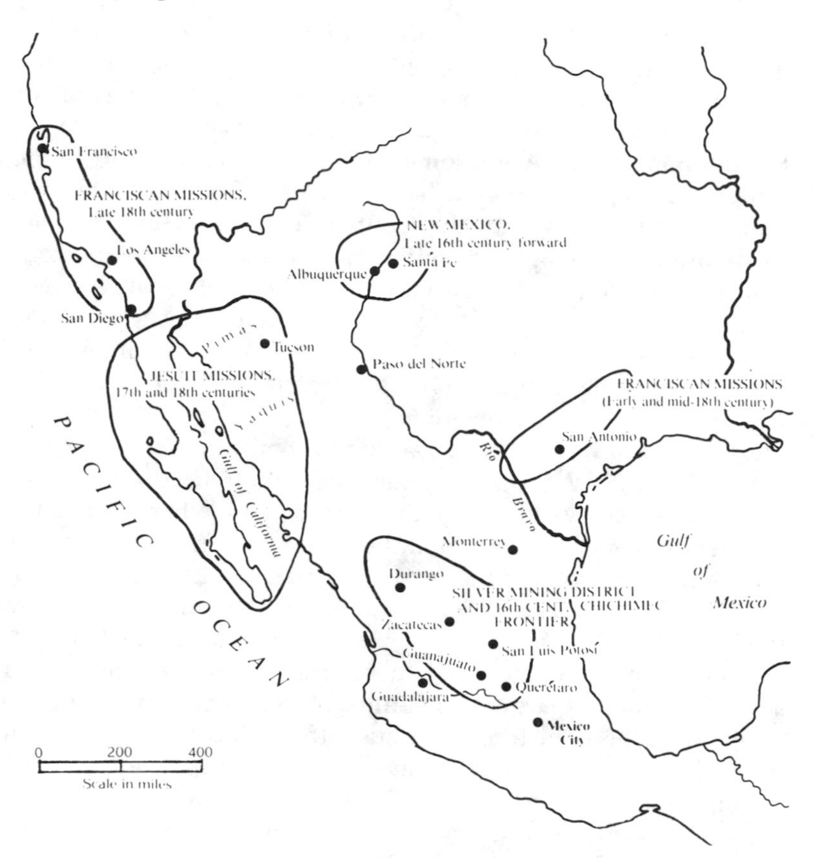

Map 13. Northern Mexico in the colonial period.

enterprises that was in one sense a part of central Mexico, and a very important part indeed (see Chapter 5).

As a result of the development and continued expansion of the north Mexican silver mining district, the Spaniards were brought face to face with peoples whom they would just as soon have ignored. The stark juxtaposition of hunter-warrior peoples and the most technical branch of the international economy made the evolution of the north a very complex process. Since discoveries of new deposits continued ever farther north, and since the market represented by the growing Mexican economy made livestock and other enterprises viable farther and farther out, the frontier advanced over the centuries, or to put it in a way perhaps more relevant to our immediate interests, the fringe receded. Through the second half of the sixteenth century a set of institutions and practices grew up which would characterize the north Mexican frontier permanently, but the locus gradually changed from Querétaro and Zacatecas to Nuevo León and Sonora and then to the Californias and Texas. Furthermore, there were some features of the original Zacatecas-centered configurations that had to do specifically with the mining industry rather than with the frontier. Thus an easily passable cart road with frequent Spanish settlements as way stations and convoys guarded by mounted men going back and forth regularly were not sights to be seen where there were no markets for supplies or silver bars to bring back. We must abstract a bit from the mining scene to isolate the lasting institutions of the frontier.

The Spanish military techniques which so quickly subdued central Mexico or Peru were not at all suited to combating the peoples of the north. The "Chichimecs" included many unrelated ethnic groups, some of which were more agricultural than others, but all were excellent bowmen, skilled in ambuscades and sneak attacks, able to break off contact at any moment. The first Spanish expedient, entradas with ad hoc recruits, had little effect; the Indians would evade them and then harass the weary Spaniards on their way home. After a few decades of contact the Chichimecs became even more formidable. They formed larger, if fleeting, confederations, what the Spaniards called the "Chichimec League"; they adopted the horse; strong messianistic leaders arose, some of whom had been among the Spaniards and understood their strengths and weaknesses.

One Spanish response made use of indigenous auxiliaries, not only for logistics and relief as in the central areas but to take the brunt of the fighting. The Otomí, already a buffer population in preconquest times, were particularly successful; their caciques were rewarded with titles, authority, and economic concessions; they even founded some new Indian municipalities in the southern part of the Chichimec area. And the military tactics of the Spaniards changed, with more emphasis on small-group combat and mobility and a new role for firearms; single-shot muskets had been nearly useless against an enemy without number, but they proved more suited to dealing with opponents who appeared in handfuls and were hard to lay one's hands on.

The most essential part of the Spanish military response to the Chichimecs was the creation of a paid, standing soldiery housed in fixed installations – forts or presidios. In the great conquests of the previous generation there had been no such thing, and the Spaniards did not come to it easily. The force was still far from truly professional. At first the captains were great men of the region as they had traditionally been, here concerned with security for their own self-interest. When the frontier later moved beyond the area of a strong Spanish civil presence, more professional military officers finally began to appear, spending the middle years of a career at various frontier assignments. The soldiers were marginal Hispanics, just one step from the kind of late arrivals, transients, and potential troublemakers who had been hustled out of the central areas in the conquest period on this or that hopeless entrada into the wilds. By the mid-eighteenth century, half of the presidio forces were castas or Hispanized Indians. The men did receive pay from the viceregal government, but hardly enough to live on, and they had to provide their own horses, weapons, and armor. Near the presidios where a dozen or two of them might be stationed, along the roads, or sometimes attached to a mission or a small town, they would often acquire lands and try to get into the supply business, perhaps entering civil life fully after a period. Above all, they lived from selling as slaves the Chichimecs they captured, for after some debate, selling Chichimecs into a twenty-year term of slavery was allowed; most were destined for central Mexico or at least some place far distant from their point of origin. The presidios of the Zacatecas environs gradually became unnecessary, but by 1723 there were nineteen such garrisons on the northern frontier, manned by more than a thousand men.

Presidios were important not only for military purposes but as the nucleus of subsequent civilian settlements. Indeed, ways of making the north Mexican peoples sedentary were the other main branch of the frontier complex. One such tool was the foundation of some transplanted Indian towns peopled by sedentaries from the center, of whom the Tlaxcalans are the most frequently mentioned; but these were relatively few and in any case before long were caught up in the area's growing Spanish world. The primary instrument was the mission, the creation of new, more concentrated Indian settlements under the auspices of one of the regular orders, the better to disseminate Christianity, European culture, and sedentary life. Growing out of the earlier congregaciones, no different in their general procedures from the missions we have mentioned in other parts of Ibero-America, those of the north were nevertheless new on the Mexican scene; standing in sharp contrast to the central Mexican monasteries, which were tailored so closely to already existing towns, they had to reorganize Indian structures and ways even more drastically than did the missions of Paraguay or the Brazilian coast. In fact, the orders obtained their greatest successes among those northern peoples with the most elements of sedentary culture.

Central Mexico was still important as an ideal to be achieved and a standard from which to depart. Indigenous "governors" and alcaldes were imposed in the mission communities just as in the center, whether the local people understood initially or not. Mission establishments were an adaptation of the center's rural monasteries. In the center, a compact cloister, serving only the needs of the religious and their immediate dependents, hugged the side of the church, facing onto a great open atrium where the numerous population could congregate. As one moves north the cloister grows larger, containing shops, storehouses, and people being trained new skills, whereas the atrium withers, since there is no multitude, no existing community in need of it. Finally the cloister walls expand to enclose the entire new community, church, conventual building, shops, Indian residences and all, defending it against a hostile outside; in some Texas establishments the enclosure becomes so large that livestock could graze inside it during prolonged seasons of Apache attack (see Figure 14). As in the center, the Franciscans were at first the most important order; by 1600 they had twenty-five establishments in the north. The Jesuits began to develop an active northern mission field during the seventeenth century, concentrating their activities in Sonora, Arizona, and the western coastal regions, that is, in areas the Franciscans had left them free. Receiving governmental subsidies like the presidios often attached to them, the northern missions gradually transcended their original purpose of helping to make the silver mining district secure. One can see an evolution in the sequence of events from central Mexico, where the orders got started only after the conquest, to the mining areas, where they came in simultaneously with Spanish civil occupation, to the far north, where they began to precede it. As they did so, they were carried by Christian zeal, to be sure, but also by the microimperialism and rivalries of the individual orders, attempting to expand from a central Mexican base. They also received blessings and monies from a government desirous of claiming distant areas through occupancy by its nationals and rendering lands farther south more secure, even when the economic incentive was insufficient to attract many individual Spaniards.

But in fact, in the specific Mexican situation, lay Spaniards were never far behind. The large and active Hispanic society of the center was constantly marginalizing the ethnically mixed, recent immigrants, and others; the near north had its great mines to attract

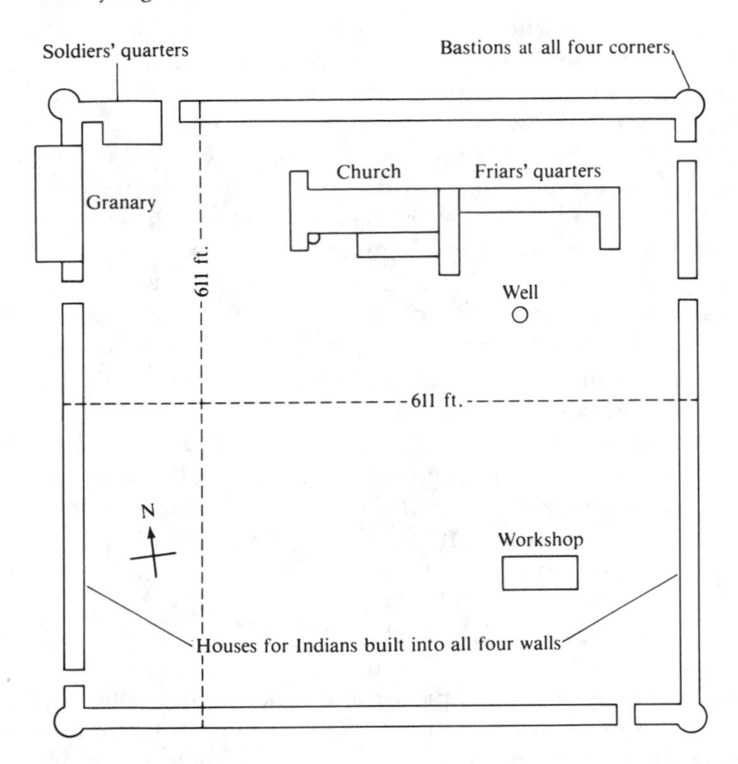

Figure 14. Plan of a mission at San Antonio, Texas. (Mission San José y San Miguel de Aguayo, built ca. 1749–82. Note particularly the fortification, the size of the space enclosed, the inclusion of all facilities and stores, and the lack of a separate cloister. Compare with Figure 5. *Source:* Adapted from Marion A. Habig, O.F.M., *The Alamo Chain of Missions* [Chicago, 1968], p. 101.)

them, and the far north always held out the hope of new strikes. Mining-camp supply gave haciendas a strong original impetus. European livestock quickly spread into the near north, almost by themselves, as they multiplied and filled a vacant ecological niche, if some contemporary accounts are to be believed. Then with the center growing over the decades and centuries as a market for Spanish-style products, interregional commerce in livestock and their derivatives became viable over ever greater distances. In a repeating cycle, stock enterprises would begin to flourish in a certain region until, as the market expanded, more intensive activities would partially displace them, and the livestock would go farther north. A center for raising sheep and cattle in the seventeenth century, the Querétaro region became an area of wheat farms in the following century, when in far northern Coahuila livestock was still predominant.

Northern ranching gradually extended toward what is now the American Southwest; the techniques of ranching, the equipment, the terminology, and the way of life that one associates with the American cowboy are almost entirely drawn from Spanish American precedents. In areas not yet in market contact with the center, the ranches tended to belong predominantly to the orders – at the end of the colonial era the various Franciscan missions owned more than 400,000 head of cattle on the northern frontier, whereas lay rural estates were poor, few, and owned by humble people, though in no part of the Mexican north was there the radical diffusion of the more isolated Argentine plains, where estates were entirely lacking. As an area came within the social-economic orbit of the center, lay estates would increase in importance. The basic organization was not unlike that of an hacienda of the center, except that the bottom level, temporary workers from Indian towns, was largely missing. Cowboys, or *vaqueros,* were, as everywhere in Latin America, ethnically mixed and Europeanized, essentially at the same level as tertiary supervisors in central areas, and, in fact, in Mexico the first name for them was "estanciero," the same name given to the labor bosses and tribute collectors of the conquest-period encomienda. With poor, dry land and no press of competitors, viable estates of the north tended to grow to vast proportions. The holdings of the Marqueses de Aguayo in Coahuila and Nuevo León included hundreds of thousands of acres; the products went back toward Mexico City, where the owning family became a prominent part of high society. Huge estates were better able to outlast the area's droughts and to organize their own defense against Apaches, Comanches, and others who with the horse, some access to firearms through trade, and centuries of practice, were able to hold their own better and raid over even larger distances than their predecessors, the Chichimecs of the near north. In almost every respect, the great ranching enterprises of north Mexico foreshadowed developments in other plains areas of Ibero-America as the latter gradually gained access to markets.

An apparent anomaly on the frontier was New Mexico, because of the nature of its indigenous inhabitants; in fact, the Spaniards gave it that name because it was the closest thing they had seen in the north to the sedentary center. Already in 1542 Coronado's expedition had revealed the existence here of Indians with a settled agriculture and villages (from which they were dubbed the Pueblos). Thus at the end of the sixteenth century, late in the broader scheme of things but early for the Mexican north, a privately organized expedition leapfrogged hundreds of miles of uncontrolled territory and carried out a quick conquest. Encomiendas, hardly seen north of the Lerma, were distributed, the Indian towns were nominally reorganized, and by the 1630s the settlers and the Franciscans were squabbling over control of the Indians and access to their labor. Santa Fe, founded 1609, lacked any impressive urban development, but it was intended as a provincial capital city, sitting in the midst of an Indian hinterland. Once again, as in the Plata region, whenever there was a choice between settling among nomads and among agriculturalists, the Spaniards invariably chose the latter.

But central Mexico was not to be duplicated so easily in the north. On all sides were less sedentary peoples, and like the Caxcanes farther south, the Pueblos shared much with them despite their settled civilization. There was nothing to attract new Hispanic immigrants. By 1680 the province had only 170 able-bodied Spaniards and mestizos to face more than 6,000 Pueblo warriors who rose in a great rebellion in that year. Under messianic leaders, the Pueblos actually forced the Spaniards to abandon the province and retreat southward. It would be another twelve years before they returned and regained control. By the end of the colonial period Hispanic society in New Mexico would have somewhat greater maturity and density than in other parts of the extreme north but would stand out from the others less than earlier.

Thus in the Mexican north a pure and classic situation of missions, presidios, and nonsedentaries nowhere obtained. Perhaps the nearest approach to it occurred in the Californias of the eighteenth century with their Jesuit and Franciscan missions, but even here the Hispanic civil element soon encroached. Mining and ranching interests were too close, and the flat country made communication with central Mexico easy. Spanish settlements of the north were far more Hispanic than Indian, as they were on any nonsedentary fringe, and most Indian elements they contained came from the sedentaries who migrated along with them. Direct cultural influence of the northern indigenous peoples is hardly to be detected. It is most suggestive that around Zacatecas in the early days there were separate suburbs for Tlaxcalans, Indians of the Valley of Mexico, and Tarascans of Michoacán, but none for Chichimecs. Being in relatively close touch with the center kept the Spanish community of the north from developing a radically deviant culture. Each area might have its own variants of the Spanish-Mexican cuisine, its own local language usage, and all of the northern regions were a bit archaic compared with Mexico City, but there was nothing as distinctive as the culture of the Argentine gaucho. As to the nonsedentaries, wherever the Spanish-central Mexican intrusion took on full force, as it did in the heart of the mining district, they eventually disappeared with little trace except in rugged pockets of land not part of the main development. In missions or as slaves, the nonsedentaries either died out from disease or became indistinguishable from other Hispanized Indians. As long as they maintained their own societies apart from the Spaniards, and many groups did so throughout the far north, they took what they chose of Spanish culture, from horses and weapons to (with the Apache) running sheep and using Spanish as a lingua franca. But they put it all to their own uses, and as long as they continued a separate existence, the inner core of their society and culture changed little. To this day the surviving languages of the far Mexican north and the American Southwest show less European influence on their vocabulary and structure than central Mexico's Nahuatl did in 1550 or 1560.

Chile and the Araucanian frontier

Central and southern Chile were the land of the Araucanians, a people in many essentials like the semisedentary tropical villagers of Brazil and Paraguay, but much affected by central Andean influence and inhabiting a more temperate area, with a climate of the Mediterranean type in the north and a colder, wetter climate in the heavily forested south. All the Araucanians had maize as well as the specific central Andean crops, and even the llama. But beyond this they diverged from each other in ways, corresponding to the climatic differences and relative distance from the central Andes, which reflected themselves in entirely different patterns of development in the two areas after the Spanish conquest.

The so-called Picunche of the north practiced irrigation and knew many of the skills of the central Andeans, including metallurgy. They lived in settlements, apparently entirely autonomous, of up to a dozen lineages under one hereditary ruler whom the Spaniards on arrival immediately considered a cacique. The mita may not have existed, but there were well-developed forms of reciprocal labor. The so-called Mapuche, mainly south of the Bío-Bío River, were distinct in several basic respects. They used slash-and-burn agricultural techniques, with women doing most of the planting and harvesting while men hunted. Settlement patterns were even more diffuse than among the northern Araucanians; without caciques, they lived in units constituting single lineages with a kinship head, the nuclear families dwelling in scattered houses and frequently splitting off from the lineage.

A major Spanish expedition in 1535–7 under Diego de Almagro, coming from Peru, discovered that Chile was not comparable and went back. Even so, the Spaniards at first seemed to take Chile for a poorly endowed central area. In a second entrada from Peru in 1541, Pedro de Valdivia and his men, accompanied by Peruvian yanaconas, carried out what appeared to be a quick, decisive conquest. In the expectation of further immigration, a string of cities was founded including the capital of Santiago and others both north and south, some far into Mapuche territory. Large encomiendas were distributed and the usual gold-rush phase with encomienda labor got under way. An Indian rebellion, not entirely unlike postconquest phenomena in the central areas, shook the Spanish settlements in the 1550s. The Spanish cities went through a stage of existence as palisades, Indian fighting took many casualties, and no flood of new immigrants arrived.

At last the Spaniards began to grasp the specific Chilean realities. In the center and north there grew up a Hispanic society reminiscent of such transitional areas as Tucumán or Popayán; the Bío-Bío became a static frontier with some characteristics comparable to those of the far Mexican north, and the Mapuche of the south remained mainly unsubdued throughout the entire colonial period. The Spaniards of the Picunche region soon found that they had to reduce the size of encomiendas to correspond to existing local units and to emphasize labor over tribute. In that form, the Chilean encomienda proved, as in Tucumán and Paraguay, viable and long-lasting despite population decline. As in Tucumán, the encomienda provided labor for a set of related enterprises by the encomendero, from stock raising to obrajes, and just as there, the Indians were drawn ever closer and more fully into full-time, specialized work for the encomendero, becoming hardly distinguishable from the Peruvian yanaconas, especially numerous in Chile, who had carried out such functions at first.

Chile's placer gold mining turned out to be rather more than the usual ephemeral rush. By 1569 the Spaniards had collected more than seven million pesos' worth of gold. Before it went into permanent decline at the end of the sixteenth century, the gold industry had supported the evolution of a very humble, marginal local Hispanic population – there were foreigners and even a free Black or two among Chile's early encomenderos – into a quite well-developed

Hispanic nucleus, including some import merchants, professional people, artisans, Spanish women, and even considerable numbers of Blacks, of whom there were twenty thousand in 1600. In 1609 an Audiencia was established. Mestizos filled many of the middle and lower Hispanic roles, but this was no minimally differentiated society like that of early Spanish Paraguay. Though not as well placed to supply Potosí as was Tucumán, Chile was in closer touch by the sea route with Lima, which, if it had less urgent needs, was potentially an even stronger market. Through the seventeenth century the Peruvian market for Chile's livestock products was growing, and finally the stage was reached, starting with the earthquake there in 1687, when Lima seriously demanded wheat as well. In response, estate development took a familiar turn, with the diversification of ownership, a gradual diminishing of reliance on the encomienda proper, the consolidation of haciendas, and the growth of secondary Hispanic settlements in the countryside related to the estate economy. Until the reorientation of the late eighteenth century, central Chile had doubtless the most developed Hispanic subsociety south of Peru.

Meanwhile, things in the southern part of Chile had gone in very different directions. The southern settlements had fallen far behind in the course of the sixteenth century; then in 1598 the Mapuche unleashed a general rebellion that destroyed almost every Spanish settlement south of the Bío-Bío, with repercussions in the south-center as well. The river now became a real frontier, beyond which the Araucanians were in control. As in the Mexican north, the traditional means of combating Indians proved inadequate. The early central-area indigenous rebellions were put down by ad hoc forces consisting of encomenderos and their followers, fulfilling their legal obligation of defense and serving their own self-interest. The long-lasting nature of Araucanian resistance and the geographical distance between the rebels and the defenders made the method inadequate. As in Mexico, the solution was a paid standing force in permanent installations. A string of forts was created, manned by a frontier army of two thousand men, and by 1601 a yearly governmental subsidy was coming from the Peruvian treasury to support the garrisons. Like the Mexican soldiers, these were marginal Hispanics, many of them Peruvian and Chilean mestizos. And much as in Mexico again, their pay was hardly sufficient for their needs, so that they organized *malocas,* or slave raids, and sold the captives in the direction of Hispanic Chile or even Peru, all of which was fully legal from 1608 to 1674.

Like the Chichimecs, the Mapuche quickly adopted Spanish

horses and some Spanish weapons. With the help of mestizo renegades, they made gunpowder to use in captured firearms. They abandoned their traditional massed battles for guerrilla tactics; they developed a sixteen-foot pike for use against Spanish cavalry and a mounted infantry of bowmen who rode double on horses and dismounted to support the cavalry. They even adopted the Spanish crop wheat because it had a shorter growing season than maize and was thus less exposed to the burnt-earth tactics of the Spaniards. Just as importantly, out of the tradition of strong war leaders grew larger political configurations, and in a sense an "Araucanian nation" was created by the incessant warfare.

By the eighteenth century the Araucanians not only were holding their own in south Chile but were crossing the Andes to trade and raid on the Argentine pampa. Not until the late nineteenth century did the national governments of Chile and Argentina finally break Indian resistance in the southern part of their territories, partly because new technological advances like the repeating rifle, telegraph, and barbed wire enabled them to regain the advantage these peoples had neutralized in the sixteenth and seventeenth centuries, and partly because growth and the same technological advances brought the Ibero-Americans to the point of having something profitable to do with the territories. The story was the same in North America; it is not simple coincidence that the final conquest of the Indians in the temperate countries of the United States, Chile, and Argentina occurred at roughly the same time.

Returning to the Mexican comparison, certain notable aspects of the Mexican complex were absent in Chile. Chilean missions remained largely plans, abortive attempts, and outright failures in which the religious were massacred. Central Chile was too settled, southern Chile too unsettled, and the orders in South America had already committed their limited manpower elsewhere. Nor did the advancing Mexican frontier have a Chilean parallel. Southern Chile was farther removed from a major trunk line than was northern Mexico; the dynamism of central Chile was secondary and relatively weak, and in any case the wet forested south was no place for more livestock, wheat, and vineyards. It is not that the Spaniards absolutely lacked the capacity to occupy the Mapuche territory. One can easily imagine the sequence of events had a second Potosí been discovered there in the sixteenth century. In some ways Spanish interests were well enough served by the situation as it was. The viceregal government of Peru felt the need of a safety valve, a place to send the unruly or overambitious Spaniards and mestizos who previously had gone on entradas, and at the same time it needed posts and emoluments to give to supporters. The subsidy, which long hovered around 200,000 pesos annually, was a minor expense, hardly what two or three Peruvian mining or commercial firms might gross, but translated into Chilean terms it was a major asset, turning the frontier into a market for agrarian products just when the gold had played out. The central Chilean economy, based on intensive use of a relatively small body of laborers, among them an ever-diminishing number of Indians, received the captive Mapuche gratefully (for as usual the individual removed from his social context was cooperative). The ongoing wars were certainly a drain when they drew the encomenderos and others into emergency situations or when raids and unrest spread north of the Bío-Bío, yet it would be hard to say whether the military frontier retarded or hastened the growth of Hispanic Chilean society.

Some comparative aspects

If the Western Hemisphere had been somehow sealed off from the rest of the world except for the presence of a considerable number of Iberians, one would expect that most of them would have concentrated in the areas of the sedentary peoples, forming two-sector societies; that some would have lived among the semisedentaries, where interpenetration would have ruled, and that a few would have battled eternally against the nomadic peoples. But the outer world and the international economy made themselves felt strongly, so that the archetypal quality of a situation such as that in early Paraguay – extensive cultural interaction between a few Spaniards and a semisedentary population – could assert itself only in maximal isolation. Depending on their proximity to central areas and the demand for their assets in the relatively active central-area economies, the fringe areas were drawn either more or less into the broader network and affected in their internal structure. In areas of strongest interest, an invasion of people coming from the center, both Hispanic and indigenous, could bring engulfment and transformation, as in the near north of Mexico; the same thing was to happen again in eighteenth-century Brazil during the Minas Gerais gold rush. The relative degree of impact of the center was the main reason for the cultural distinctiveness of the isolated Platine gaucho as compared with the north Mexican vaquero or charro. The irrelevance of temperate forest products to the needs of the central areas is an important reason why not only in southern Chile, but also in Florida there was a static, garrisoned, subsidized frontier, even though the native peoples were essentially semisedentary.

Perhaps we can use the encomienda as a means to illustrate both the sameness and the variety of the fringe, for even though the institution fails to appear at all in the Portuguese sphere, the experience with it covers the full gamut of regional types. On the fighting frontier and among any fully nonsedentary peoples, there could be no encomienda, though the Spaniards usually did not neglect to give it some brief try. The fringe-area encomienda is primarily that of the warm-country semisedentaries. Whereas the central-area encomienda was large, quickly established, depending heavily on a cacique, and including the delivery of tribute in kind as well as draft labor, the fringe-area encomienda was small and slow to take shape; also, it relied less on intermediary Indian authority and emphasized labor rather than tribute, often the labor of women. All these things directly reflected the nature of indigenous society in both cases. As to differences having to do more with the relative number of local Spaniards and the amount of liquid wealth in the economy, central-area encomiendas had an impressive staff of majordomos, estancieros, and Black slaves, and they branched out from the encomienda proper into many commercial enterprises. As a result, they produced great incomes for the fortunate few at the top of Hispanic society who held them, but in the conditions of stiff competition, the specific institution of the encomienda became obsolete within three generations or less, losing its labor power first. Fringe-area encomiendas lacked superstructure, had few ancillary enterprises, produced little income, and were held by a broader segment of the local Hispanic population; there being little competition over them and no alternative, they lasted many generations, far into the eighteenth century, complete with labor benefits in many cases. These things were generally true in Paraguay, Venezuela, Tucumán, and Chile, not to speak of other transitional areas and peripheral central-area districts (such as Yucatan) whose economies and populations shared some of the characteristics. But the central areas did represent a differentiating factor. In regions closer to a central area, the conquerors, coming directly from the center and knowing its well-developed encomienda structure, attempted to impose the full standard form from the very beginning, only gradually making the required adjustments to the indigenous system. This distinguishes Tucumán and Chile, for example, from Paraguay and Venezuela. The closer regions had a better market and over time were able to develop extensive ancillary enterprises like those of the central areas in the conquest period; again Tucumán and Chile were in the lead, but Venezuela too, with its sea access to Mexico and Cartagena, developed encomienda-based enterprise networks in advance of isolated Paraguay.

This same sort of comparison could potentially be carried out for agencies of government, mercantile firms, livestock enterprises, missions, familial organization, and a host of other topics, including the Portuguese areas in the framework of analysis; but the same principles will be found to operate in all cases, and the same infinite regional variety and flavor will be seen as well.

Part III

Reorientations

In our presentation to this point we have tried to give some notion of the state of things in Ibero-America up to about the middle of the eighteenth century. A few important matters occurring before 1750 (notably the great Brazilian gold rush) have been reserved for later treatment because they lead into the final period, whereas on the other hand some of the situations we have described remained unaltered until the end of the colonial period and beyond. But a quite sharp break occurs in a number of dimensions in the second half of the eighteenth century, and we take ca. 1750–60 as the approximate demarcation point of two periods in preference to the temptingly round date of 1700, when Spain experienced a major dynastic change. Concentrating as we do in this book on structures and evolutionary trends in the Indies themselves, we have had little occasion to speak of metropolitan dynasties. At the beginning of the sixteenth century Ferdinand and Isabella, the monarchs who brought Spain a relative political unity, witnessed the initial Caribbean phase of the Indies enterprise, but before the great mainland conquests they had been succeeded by Charles I, a Hapsburg whose affiliations in the Netherlands, Germany, and Italy made him Holy Roman Emperor (whence he is usually known as Charles V). In a sense Charles's central and north European interests outweighed his Spanish ones, yet in another sense Spain with its Indies was for a while Europe's dominant power. Under Charles's son Philip II, who ruled until nearly the end of the sixteenth century, the imperial title was lost, but much of the strong Spanish role in the rest of Europe remained. Then through the seventeenth century Spain's position in and relative to the rest of Europe weakened even further; concurrently, internal political and economic problems became acute, and the succeeding members of the dynasty seemed lesser than their predecessors. Finally, at the end of the seventeenth century, the Hapsburg line was extinguished. In 1700 a scion of the French Bourbons attained the throne, though not without dispute, establishing a Bourbon line which ruled Spain through the time of Latin American independence.

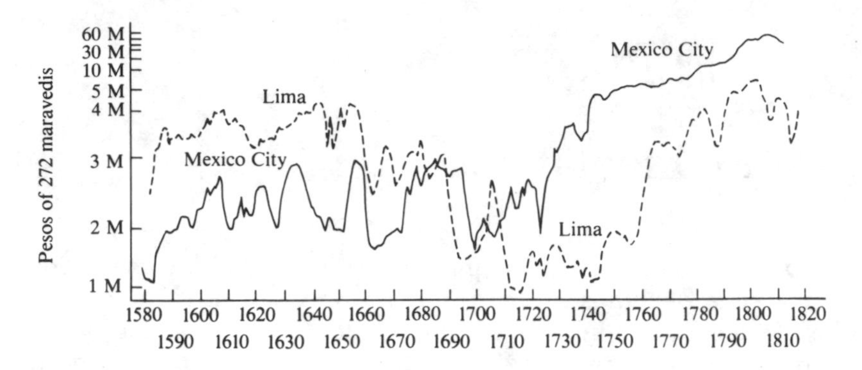

Figure 15. Income of the royal treasuries of Mexico City and Lima, 1580–1820. (*Source:* From John J. TePaske and Herbert S. Klein, "The Seventeenth-Century Crisis in New Spain: Myth or Reality?" *Past and Present* 90 [1981]:116–35. Note that if it were not for the progressive downward adjustment, the lines would rise even more sharply in the late eighteenth century.)

The change in dynasties, however, was not matched by changes in more basic respects. During long wars of succession, Spain was inert and under foreign dominance at least as much as in the seventeenth century, the time of its supposed decline. How great and all-embracing that decline was is a matter of continuing controversy; for one counterexample, Spain notably strengthened its naval defenses in the Caribbean in the decades before the turn of the century. In the Indies the picture is extremely mixed, vigor in some sectors, areas, and industries being matched by stagnation or worse in others. At any rate, there is no observable change in the pace or direction of developments around 1700.

It is later in the century that the marked changes occur. Significant demographic, commercial, and industrial resurgence took place in Spain, especially in the north and east, and the country regained some military, naval, and governmental strength. The new developments, and their analogs in the Indies, were to a large extent simultaneous with the rule of Charles III (1759–88), as were the partially parallel trends in Portugal and Portuguese America with the rule of Portuguese minister Pombal (1750–77). In the Indies, the new period of the late eighteenth century is seen most easily in dramatic quantitative upswings: demographic growth of a different order than before, including the Indian sector, in most regions for which reliable information is available; vast growth in production and trade related to the international economy, not only in now traditional precious metals but even more in newer bulk exports; steady price rises

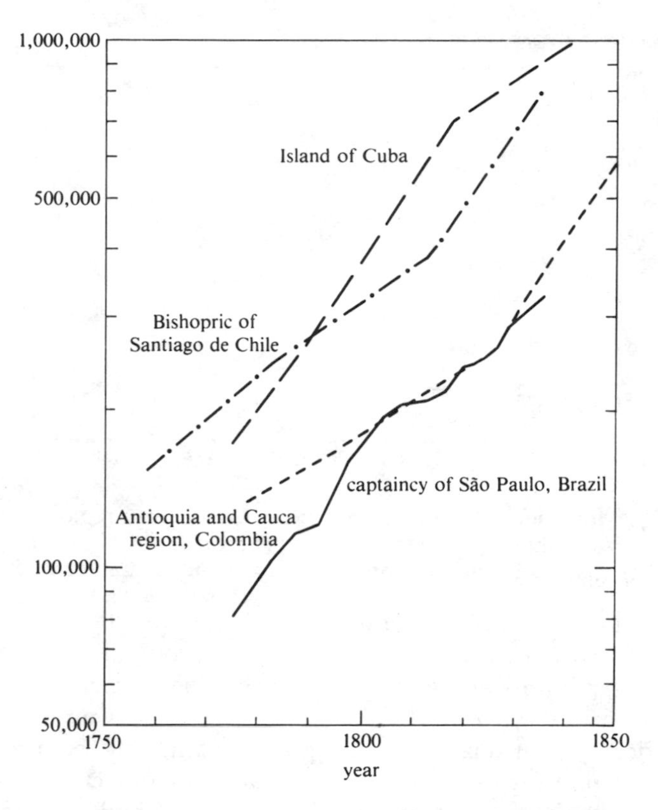

Figure 16. Examples of sharply rising population trends in the late colonial period. [From Nicolás Sánchez-Albornoz, *The Population of Latin America* (Berkeley, 1974). Used with permission of the University of California Press.]

which began to supplant the older pattern of fluctuations in prices against a background of long-term stability (see Figures 15, 16, and 17). Not quite so decisively demonstrable, not quite so sharply pinpointed in time, there were also occurring shifts of emphasis and reorganizations which drastically and permanently altered the picture of Latin American center and fringe and also changed the institutional picture considerably: the development of the eastern seaboard regions, favorably placed for bulk export to Europe; the changing of sea routes, hence rerouting of trunk lines; the creation of new viceroyalties in the growth regions; the addition of a military and the subtraction of the Jesuits, and much more. Some of these trends had been evolving for decades, but they took on strength or precipitated in the latter eighteenth century.

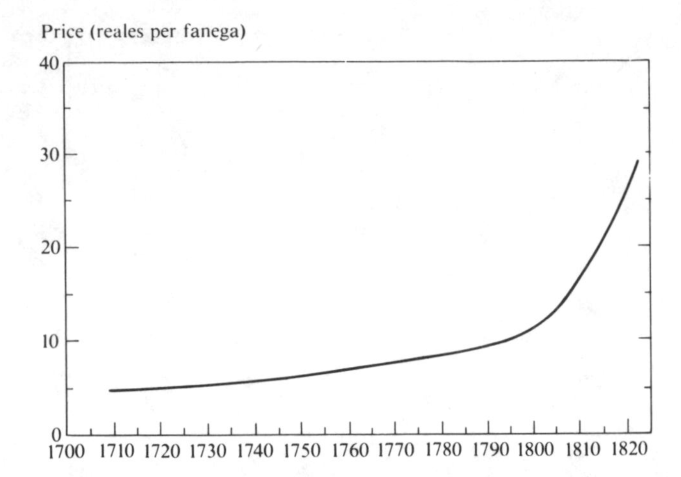

Figure 17. Movement of maize prices in the Guadalajara region, 1700–1825. [From Eric Van Young, *Hacienda and Market in Eighteenth-Century Mexico* (Berkeley, 1981). Used with permission of the University of California Press.]

As to the causes of the new phase, many clearly lie in Europe, which itself underwent demographic and economic growth at exactly the same time and experienced technological changes in industry and navigation as well. The combined result was that Europe demanded greater quantities of a greater variety of Ibero-American items and had greater amounts of cheaper manufactured goods to give in return. Larger, faster ships meant that bulkier items could pay the freight in both directions across the Atlantic and that the original trade and communication routes needed reexamination. Yet some important aspects of change may have been primarily internal. The indigenous peoples appear to have begun to make the adjustment to Old World diseases at last, as epidemics declined in frequency and virulence, and all population elements increased, even in areas apparently little touched by the new economic growth. The entire Ibero-American system was coming to a new stage as the cycle beginning with the conquest drew to a close. But the resolution of these matters will require much future debate and research, and this is not the place for any full discussion, particularly of the European end of it, which we are treating only as its effects were felt on the Ibero-American scene.

Hardly two generations after the great reorientation of the late eighteenth century came another, in one sense highly secondary and bringing little change, in another sense as significant as the first, namely, the attainment of political independence from Spain and Portugal. Coming on the heels of the slightly earlier wave of change or realignment in demography, economy, and organization, the second movement appears in some sense as the consequence of the first. The same ambiguity attaches to the causes of both. Again Europe provides the more obvious and tangible explanatory elements. The European renovation stemmed primarily from the north; not only did the technology, organizational principles, and other key ideas originate there, but the nations of that area had become both the primary recipients of New World exports and the primary producers of what the New World received in return. Ibero-America now looked to northern Europe in almost every dimension of outside interest except that of politics, and Spain and Portugal had no indispensable role in the ties so established. On the other hand, and with even more reason than in the earlier case, one can point to internal Ibero-American developments. So far in the history of the world, all distant colonies have sooner or later, peacefully or forcefully, asserted their independence of the founding country. Now that the postconquest regional societies had become progressively more localized and autonomous, each distinct from the other within the larger cultural sameness, perhaps they were ripe for political independence regardless of external conditions.

Of our final three chapters, then, we will devote two to the eighteenth-century quiet revolution in the Spanish and Portuguese territories, respectively, and the third, by way of epilogue, to some considerations on the independence movements. To provide a needed background for our subsequent discussions, let us first glance at the activities of the non-Iberian Europeans in the Caribbean, which, though not fitting entirely into our essentially Spanish-Portuguese field of vision, do reflect the timing and nature of the reorientation as strikingly as the Iberian areas, thereby demonstrating again the supranational unity of trends in the larger region.

From the sixteenth century, English, French, and Dutch ships intruded into Spanish American waters to raid or sometimes to smuggle, in either case mainly attempting to profit in some way from the main-line silver trade. Since navigational difficulties long kept them out of the Pacific, they concentrated on the Caribbean sea-lanes through which the silver of Peru and Mexico passed. By the late sixteenth century, English raids were becoming serious, with Sir Francis Drake briefly in control of Santo Domingo and Cartagena.

In the seventeenth century north European pressures mounted

and began to broaden in nature. The Dutch captured the entire silver fleet off Havana in the 1620s, and in the same decade, in the Lesser Antilles, the English began permanent settlement oriented toward tropical export. Foreign interference with the trunk line brought stiff and usually effective resistance from the Spaniards, who protected their vital interests in the fleets, major ports, and well-settled areas but put up only token opposition to what the foreigners might care to do in such fringe dependencies as Venezuela and no opposition beyond words in places where there was no Spanish presence at all. There was in fact hardly any Spanish presence on the smaller islands of the Caribbean. The small islands were nearly devoid of potential in the terms discussed in previous chapters, and in view of the stagnation of the economies of the major islands, there too large sections, including western Hispaniola, or Haiti, had been left practically empty except for wild cattle and pigs.

Thus as the northern Europeans began to evince a serious desire to have their own colonial dependencies and to produce tropical goods for themselves – one manifestation of which we have already seen, the Dutch intervention in Brazil – they found the Lesser Antilles not only close and propitious in climate but as good as unoccupied. By 1650 the English and French had settled on several of the Leeward and Windward islands, above all English Barbados. Emphasis was on production of a variety of tropical crops by estates or individuals, using European indentured servants for labor. The settlements took root, but the overall plan soon evolved in the direction of something closer to the precedent of the Portuguese Atlantic islands and Brazil. The reader will remember that the Portuguese expelled the Dutch from Brazil at about midcentury. With their Brazilian experience and African slave-trading posts, the Dutch brought the whole sugar complex to the Caribbean. The transition to African slave labor was quick, and by the late seventeenth century Barbados, Guadeloupe, and other English and French islands were receiving a substantial portion of all Africans imported into the New World, were producing thousands of tons of sugar for the ever-growing European market, and were cutting deeply into Brazil's share of it. In 1655 an English expedition, having failed to seize Santo Domingo, went on to take Jamaica, the least settled of the larger Spanish islands, and the area remained permanently in English hands, though for a time it lagged behind Barbados.

In addition to the rising sugar colonies, which were independent enterprises and part of a campaign of the north European nations to become more self-contained, the traditional kind of activity, parasitic on the Spanish system, also continued, evolved, and grew in scope. The more or less state-sponsored transatlantic marauders gave way to highly unofficial and irregular forces based in the Caribbean itself. These "buccaneers" arose from communities of renegades and outcasts – runaway bond servants from the French and English islands, shipwrecked sailors, and others of whose origins we know nothing – who lived from hunting cattle, then selling smoked meat and hides to supply ships. In a way they were comparable to the "gauchos" of the Plata as marginal members of European society going out beyond that society's effective borders, and in both cases cattle escaped from Iberian settlements were among the resources they tried to exploit. But the transfrontiermen of the Caribbean were placed in a much more tempting environment, and almost from the beginning they were also raiders and pirates.

Though they seemed to care little for nationality and included some Spanish speakers, often mulattoes or Blacks, among their number, most of the buccaneers were of English and French origin, and they began to group themselves roughly by nation, finally in some sense even serving national purposes. In the second half of the seventeenth century there were French-dominated pirate bases in present Haiti and on the nearby island of Tortuga. English buccaneers came to use Jamaica as a base, whereupon the English government tried to manipulate them as a military force, giving their leaders official position. Up to the 1680s, in the most cinematic portion of Latin American history, the buccaneers time and again raided Spanish Caribbean ports and once crossed over to take the city of Panamá on the far side of the isthmus.

But by 1700 the age of buccaneering was over. A strong, if selective, Spanish defense was one reason, despite the scorn formerly heaped on it by north European historians; even more important was the French and English realization that sugar export and peaceful trade (or smuggling) with Spanish America were the wave of the future. Haiti became a formal French colony under the name of Saint-Domingue, and Jamaica turned to sugar production in the style of Barbados. In the eighteenth century the English and French possessions became the world's greatest producers of sugar. The rise in levels of production went on over the entire century, accelerating in the second half to figures several times as large as the already impressive amounts of the first decades. The same trends held true in slave importation; some have estimated that more Africans were brought to America in the last fifty years of the eighteenth century than in the previous 250 years, and probably more than 60 percent of these went to the Caribbean. Jamaica eclipsed Barbados, then Saint-Domingue surpassed Jamaica in turn; throughout the history of the highly mechanized sugar industry it has been hard for established growing areas to take advantage of technological advances and increase in scale (though the older areas usually do not literally fade away). Toward the end of the eighteenth century Jamaica was producing on the order of 60,000 tons of sugar annually and had a slave population of some 250,000; Saint-Domingue was approaching 80,000 tons and 500,000 slaves.

The French and English islands thus came to be comparable in some respects to the Ibero-American central areas: They generated great wealth in the international economy; they pulled in large numbers of Africans and Europeans; they turned the North Atlantic colonies of the northern powers into partial dependencies and supply areas; and they were at the very heart of north European interest in the Western Hemisphere. The Caribbean islands were pawns in one European war after another, with the Spaniards on the margins of the conflicts but always affected in one way or another. (The large Spanish islands were cut off from the main sugar export developments by their very nature and purpose, but when the English occupied Havana in 1762, thinking they might stay, they set up large up-to-date sugar plantations, brought in thousands of slaves, and set Cuba on the same road as the other islands. It was not until the nineteenth century, however, when slave labor became impossible in the north European possessions, that Cuba would have its turn as the world's largest sugar producer.)

But for all their wealth and importance, the Caribbean sugar islands did not develop societies like those of prosperous Ibero-American areas. The units were too small, the societies were too specialized, often not even self-sufficient in food supplies, and they lacked the temporal depth to have acquired autonomy of various kinds; communications with the European metropolis were altogether too good, so that the local element tended to be overwhelmed in almost every respect. Nearly the entire European population was quasi-transient and profits were spent in Europe rather than on the islands. The African population, on the other hand, had a far greater numerical predominance than in any other situation we have seen, even that of northeastern Brazil, reaching levels of 80 and 90 percent of the total. As a result, the culture of the slave population apparently contained more African elements than European; the runaway problem was even greater than in Brazil, and no island was without its renegade communities, some of which were never put down. Actual rebellion was a not infrequent occurrence, and the only successful large-scale slave rebellion of the whole colonial period in "Latin America" took place in 1791 in Haiti, against the French.

Set up as an independent system or systems with Caribbean production, North American and African supply, and north European home markets and sources of capital, the sugar network nevertheless came into close connection with the Spanish Indies through the need of cash to pay for slaves and supplies. To get the money, the north Europeans traded illegally in their own manufactured goods – the same goods that otherwise would have come through Spanish ports and intermediaries – with the Spanish Americans. The true extent and nature of this trade may never be known, but in this way the north Europeans acquired a good share of the silver of Mexico and Peru (aside from what they got through the formal indirect channels), and smuggling was so institutionalized in the Caribbean that it hardly deserved the name. Some of the contact with the Spaniards occurred through the African slave trade. The Portuguese monopoly of slave supply disintegrated with that country's independence in 1640, after which the Dutch, then the French from 1702, then the English for a while, successively had the monopoly; after 1750 individual licenses were instituted. All the slave suppliers used the occasion for additional trade in goods, which at times even received partial official sanction.

The Caribbean thus saw a huge expansion of bulk tropical production and export in the eighteenth century, especially in the second half, under north European auspices, and the concomitant creation of a complex and dense, if highly unbalanced, local Eurafrican society. It is within this context that the late colonial flourishing of Venezuela and the Plata region must be seen, all three cases being variants of a single phenomenon. At the same time, through legal and illegal avenues having to do with the sugar complex, the north Europeans (increasingly the English) were gaining more direct access to trade with the Spanish American territories, partially bypassing Spain and making the transition toward the total dominance of that trade which they would achieve in the nineteenth century.

9

Late colonial times in the Spanish Indies

By the last fifty or sixty years of the colonial period in Spanish America, the dynamic tendencies described in Chapter 5 had been in operation for so long that they had brought about transformations altering the nature of the entire system, giving it yet more autonomy and rendering the original ethnic hierarchy inoperable. Spanish America was thus spontaneously approaching the end of a first great colonial cycle. But because of changes in Europe, these trends were not allowed to play themselves out undisturbed. Rather, new techniques, demands, and ideas coming from Bourbon Spain and ultimately from northern Europe hit the New World with greater impact than anything else since the conquest. Outside factors hastened some developments, slowed or reversed others, and turned the regional balance nearly upside down. External elements became so much a part of the fabric of the Indies that, however desirable for clarity of understanding, it is impossible to talk long of internal evolution without considering outside influence. Nor is the external aspect unaffected by the internal; many of the imperial reforms of the Bourbons are straightforward reactions to the situation in the Indies.

Our procedure in this chapter, then, will be to move gradually from the more internal to the more external, halting frequently to observe reactions and interrelationships. Only after getting a preliminary understanding of all the different factors and how they mesh will one begin to grasp the overall situation and its dialectic.

Society: elaboration, fusion, and growth

The most nearly universal social process affecting the Indies was the intermixture of its constituent cultural and biological groups, which went on according to an internal rhythm without regard to changes in techniques, ideas, or policies, wherever they might have originated. Since the ethnic hierarchy of the middle colonial period recognized mixture and allowed cultural attributes to be considered in assigning categories, the scheme was doomed from the beginning to phase itself out in due time. By the later eighteenth century, in many areas, the time had come, and the system entered into crisis – not necessarily a true general crisis of social organization but at least one in the manner of labeling and categorizing society's members. As the mixed groupings – mestizos and mulattoes – increased in number and as time passed since the inception of mixture, the range of people in these categories grew wider, and contemporaries began to discern subtypes. The original process repeated itself; new and more refined categories gained some currency. For example, whereas once the term "mulatto" had covered all people of mixed African descent, the late period saw the introduction of the category "zambo" for persons who were half Indian, half African, leaving "mulatto" narrowed to those who were Spanish and African. Special terms arose for finer distinctions along the Spanish-African continuum; "pardo" was popular for the more Spanish end of the scale. But at the very moment we mention this late proliferation of categories, we must hasten to say that their use was extremely varied and limited; they never attained the status of the original set. The five categories of the ethnic hierarchy of the mature period and the stereotypes they embodied were the same all over Spanish America, and they had legal implications, being used for census and tax purposes. The later categories had no such status; though some of them may appear at times in baptismal registers, they are rarely to be seen in census summaries or tribute calculations, nor are individuals so denominated in notarial or other legal documents. The terminology and the time of introduction of individual terms varied greatly from one country to another. If "pardo" in most places meant the upper end of the broad mulatto grouping, in others it could mean the opposite, and on the Caribbean coast of South America it became the general category for the large population group of mixed African and Spanish descent, many doubtless with some Indian affiliation as well, so that there it replaced "mulatto" as a census designation. "Zambo" also varied hugely in significance from place to place. Some of the terms give the impression of nicknames invented in parlor games or gossip sessions. *Tente en el aire* (literally, "suspend yourself in the air") is a term supposedly referring to persons of very complex genealogies who fell between certain already overrefined categories, whereas *salta atrás* ("leap backwards") allegedly described a person whose line had been approaching the Spanish category until it lost ground through marriage to a person with discernible African admixture in the immediately previous generation.

If there was no unanimity on the proliferating categories, there were even greater problems in deciding which individual fit into which category. The late colonial ethnic terms were, at least on the face of it, genealogical, requiring precise knowledge of an individual's ancestry on both sides for two generations, if not more in some cases. Yet prevailing among the humble people being classified was an especially high rate of illegitimacy, concealment of parentage, lack of well-defined surnames, and other factors making elaborate family trees, such as those on which the prominent prided themselves, quite out of the question. Popular usage seems to have assigned individuals to categories mainly according to how they looked and acted.

Another possibility in late colonial practice was for people to change their nominal category to adjust to their changing social-economic status. This fluidity is hard to pin down in the records, but in Valparaíso, Chile, between 1777 and 1778 about half the heads of household appearing in censuses changed their ethnic designation at least once. Label switching may have been hastened by a royal decree of 1776 making cross-category marriages open to challenge by the parents of the pair. A category switch by one partner could make the marriage appear beyond question; thus though the rate of exogamy appears very high in late colonial records, in actuality it was doubtless higher yet. Despite the mass switching, the category definitions remained important to both the authorities and the individuals involved, and the latter at the time of bearing a given label would generally indeed display behavior and status consonant with that category's stereotype.

But for many purposes, the ethnic hierarchy had become unworkable, so that however much contemporaries may have chatted about it or told gaping outsiders of its complexities (most of the rigid descriptions we have of the late colonial scheme come from foreign travelers), they paid less attention to it. Instead, they reverted to simplicity, treating all the intermediary types as one under the heading "castas," a word already heard in the middle colonial period and now becoming the predominant way of designating the totality of all who were not considered either Spaniards or Indians. On the individual level, simple nonlabeling was an increasingly popular solution.

Something analogous was happening with some of the distinctions of title which had been so important in the early and middle colonial period. At the time of the conquest, "don" had been a rare and resounding title restricted to a few persons closely connected with the high nobility of Spain. In the central areas, it was extended in the second and third generation to encomendero families, and by mid-seventeenth century it was being used by most people in the professions or who were prominent in any other way, whether through wealth, family connections, or office. Even many merchants were "don," though those directly from Spain often lacked the title, since peninsular usage evolved at a slightly different rate. During all this time "don" and the feminine equivalent, "doña," had been used with great consistency except in borderline cases. Generally speaking, one was either "don" or not, from birth to death, and was so styled on all conceivable occasions in both speech and writing. In the late period the "don" spread so far that nearly any Hispanic with an established position, for example a master artisan, was accorded it. Even at this point it was used quite consistently, and there were some people at the lower end of the Spanish world without it, but it no longer corresponded to basic distinctions in society. As a result it meant less; it was no longer used in signatures, a true stylistic revolution. It could also be acquired, under certain conditions, by a simple rise in status. Whereas with Spanish Americans of the sixteenth and seventeenth centuries we lose a great deal if we do not reproduce their names today with or without "don," exactly as they appeared during their lifetimes, we are not incorrect in ignoring the title when referring today to people living from about 1750 or 1760 onward. The chronology of this evolution, however, applies only to main-line Spanish American areas; the more remote a place was, the slower its use of "don" changed, and in upper California, for example, even at the very eve of independence few local Hispanics were called "don."

Just as the late period tried, ultimately unsuccessfully, to define ethnic groupings more sharply, it saw too the attempt of the Spaniards as a corporate group to spell out more restrictions on the rise of individuals from the other groupings into higher functions, against the irreversible movement gaining strong momentum now that the numbers of those of mixed descent had grown so vastly and their culture in the course of generations had become so Hispanic. Ordinances may have come into being to prevent anyone with even partially African bloodlines from attending a university, but that could not keep medicine, the lowest ranking of the three professional fields (behind theology and law), from being notably infiltrated by mulattoes. The restrictions in artisans' guilds also grew tighter, yet the crafts were the very domain of the castas. There were many ways around such restrictions, of which the most unanswerable was an individual's acceptance by the public into the Spanish category despite various kinds of admixture in his genealogy. Impossible though it may be to quantify, those who have worked most closely with the records of late colonial society are satisfied that a very large proportion of lower-ranking Spaniards were, in purely biological terms, mestizos and other mixtures.

As confusing as late colonial social trends may appear, they grow naturally out of what came before and obey a simple dialectic. Continuing mixture brought continuing recognition, until at last the complexity became unmanageable and there was a reversion to simplicity. Continuing fusion brought the attempt to restore the earlier situation through legal restriction. Underneath it all was the fact that massive cultural and biological mixture had transformed the original ethnic picture. The people of mixed heritage, having once been secondary auxiliaries in a picture dominated by the primary ethnic groups, had expanded vastly; in some places they had become a majority or were on the way to being one. Not only were they supplanting Blacks in intermediary roles – new importation of African slaves had nearly ceased in many of the more established parts of Spanish America well before independence – but, since there were too many of them by now for their traditional functions, they spilled over in both directions, on the one hand pressing into the Spanish grouping and aspiring to higher positions and, on the other, taking over functions traditionally in the Indian domain. It is significant that the great demographic losses of the early part of the colonial period affected primarily Indians, whereas the resurgence of the late colonial period occurred on the basis of a population already heavily mixed and becoming more so at a rapid rate (see Figure 18).

The most basic new trends, then, had to do with the middle ranges of the social spectrum, but there was one noteworthy development at the top as well. Across the colonial period "Spaniard" had been a single category, in law and in ordinary speech, referring to the essentially unitary grouping of ethnic Spaniards, whether born in Spain or the New World. Whatever rivalries there may have been between locals and outsiders on the personal level, the two were so closely meshed by blood, marriage, and function that they made up a single sector and shared a common designation. In our discussions until now, whenever we have said "Spaniard" we have meant the whole grouping. And in truth, the two elements continued to be one in many ways until the very end of the colonial epoch. Yet a new distinction and subgrouping did grow up, parallel in some ways to the finer categories among the mixed elements. Not only were the lower reaches of the local Spaniards by this time

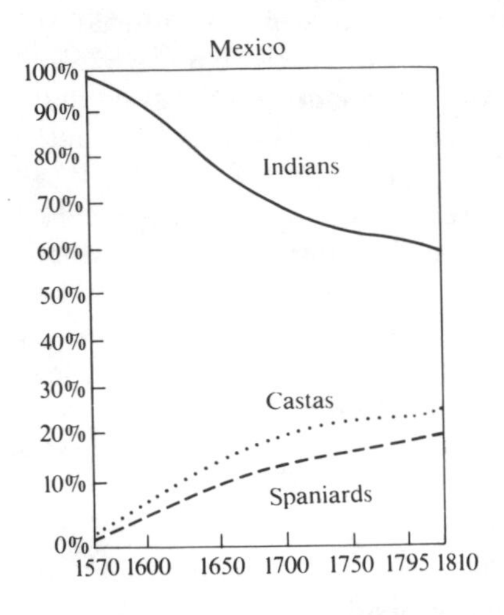

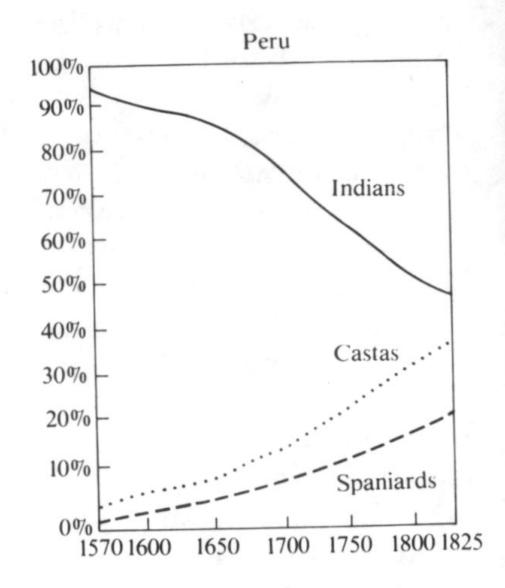

Figure 18. Changing ratios of ethnic categories through the colonial period in Mexico and Peru. (*Sources:* [Mexico] Gonzalo Aguirre Beltrán, *La población negra de México* [México, 1972], pp. 197–241. [Peru] Noble David Cook, "La población indígena en el Perú colonial," *Anuario del Instituto de Investigaciones Históricas* [Rosario, Argentina] 8 [1965]: 97, slightly adjusted in view of J. R. Fisher, *Government and Society in Colonial Peru* [London, 1970] [see Table 5, this volume].)

discernibly mixed biologically, they all, including the highest ranking, were strongly localized in culture, speech, and outlook. New arrivals from Spain stood out ever more strongly against them, all the more because Europe itself was changing quickly. As a result, usage in speech began to split the outsiders off from the locals; the distinction had few purely legal implications, but it does begin to appear in many late colonial censuses. Both types were still Spaniards; the locals, as the great majority and point of reference, were the "Spaniards" (*españoles*) pure and simple, and the immigrants were "European Spaniards" or "peninsular Spaniards," terms often shortened to "Europeans" and "peninsulars." At last, then, in the final colonial years, there came to be a public distinction corresponding to the one which today's popular mind tends to conceive as between "creoles" and "peninsulars" and mistakenly extends across the entire three colonial centuries. It is no coincidence that the basic term for the locals in their ordinary lives was "Spaniard," not "creole," which even at this late time continued to have a pejorative flavor derived from its original use to designate Black slaves. As was already coming to be the case in the middle colonial period, it could apply to locally born people of any ethnicity, and it was still most often used together with a specification of one's place of birth (that is, *criollo de Michoacán,* "born and raised in Michoacán," which could be said of an Indian, mestizo, or mulatto as well as a Spaniard). Occasionally the locals began to turn the word around (the same process as with our "Yankee") and apply it to themselves en masse in the context of political sloganeering, or on some rare occasion a humble individual from the provinces might be designated *español criollo,* but even so, individuals still did not call themselves "creoles" in the course of their daily affairs, nor does the word appear in legal documents, censuses, baptismal and marriage registers, and the like. Still and all, we today need a word to designate the locally born Spaniards, the "españoles" of that time, so we will continue to use "creole," hoping that the reader will remain conscious that it is a partial anachronism.

As to the Indians, no new subcategories are reported, and in many ways the trajectory of this grouping stands in contrast to that of all the others. In fact, this was realized at the time, and there are census summaries from widely scattered regions which list the Indians in one column and all other categories in a second. Among sedentary Indians of the old central areas, the concept "Indian" may have been closer to acceptance than at any time in the past, since many were bilingual and the colonial centuries had worn down the microethnicities a little, bringing some awareness of a common broader ethnic tie in contrast to the Hispanic and Hispanized. But this is not to say that the category presented no problem. In the cities, in areas such as the north of Mexico where most of the population was transplanted, and in places such as central Chile where a relatively small Indian population was drawn into steady face-to-face contact with the Hispanics, there were many "Indians" who spoke Spanish, understood Hispanic skills and ways, were removed from indigenous culture and corporations, and were in most respects indistinguishable from the castas. Such people chafed under the tribute obligation and many other things implied by Indian status. In the final decades of the colonial period, in some areas outside the zones of sedentary Indian settlement, the individualized, Hispanized Indians were marrying non-Indians with such frequency that the category as such was headed for local obsolescence. Wherever highly acculturated Indians formed a sizable population block, they had the potential of being a volatile element, for they had outgrown the connotations of the category to which they were born.

Creole consolidation and metropolitan reaction

In a previous chapter we have seen how in the course of the mature colonial period the locally born Spaniards had gradually taken over more and more functions in the economy, church, government, and intellectual life of the Indies. It happened gradually, not as some quasi-nationalistic attempt to displace the foreign-born but as part of the maturation of local society. To some degree it was the result of the fact that, though many centuries of tradition may have given peninsular Spaniards more solid preparation for various kinds of specialized activities than the provincial Americans, precious few peninsulars were willing to go so far and do without so much unless they had no other alternative. By the last third of the eighteenth century the process had reached a tentative culmination, at least in the longer established regions. Only those roles and posts which were markedly international, involving transatlantic ties, were still held mainly by peninsulars; the locally born predominated in all the rest.

Let us survey the situation for a moment. "Creole" families and individuals owned most of the rural estates and other productive units functioning in the regional and interregional Hispanic economies. They provided nearly all the parish priests, the great bulk of the members of cathedral chapters, and equally impressive majorities in the mendicant orders. As secretaries and petty administrators they dominated the lower reaches of the imperial government, not to speak of the cabildos, which had long been principally theirs. Late colonial viceroys brought far fewer people with them as staff and retinue than had their predecessors in the earlier period, again giving the locals more play. And it was not only at the lower levels of government that the creoles advanced; in the third quarter of the eighteenth century they held overwhelming majorities in the Audiencias of Lima and Mexico City, the Audiencia having been by all accounts the most substantial organ of government throughout the mature period, while the special position of the high courts in the viceregal capitals needs no underlining. Other Audiencias throughout Spanish America also experienced creole majorities at various times. When a serious militia came to be created, very close to the time of which we are speaking, creoles officered it and even penetrated the regular army detachments stationed in various parts of the Indies.

Nor was the creole record a mere list of miscellaneous advances. In each area there were dominant creole families, some of them sporting surnames going back to the conquest, which through a broad strategy embracing all their various assets and family members sought to create great unified complexes touching every aspect of economic and institutional life (not a new aim, of course, but something the prominent had striven for and achieved to various degrees ever since the days of the encomenderos). The most fully developed and best understood networks are those centered in Lima and Mexico City. By a careful allocation of roles among its members, manipulating marriages and inheritance and using economic leverage, a great family would hope to end up with one senior member in charge of its large hacienda or collection of haciendas, another on the Audiencia, one on the cathedral chapter, one in the militia, and so on, with the females married to men of allied similar families who were in yet other complementary positions or businesses. A fully successful family of this kind often bought a title of high nobility, marquis or the like, and established an entail to keep the family assets together. Although there were some extremely powerful families with all the essential characteristics of success which for whatever reason never sought this final outer recognition, the granting of high noble titles picked up noticeably in the late period. The great families did not live in perfect harmony with each other; rather, there were often factional and even intrafamilial disputes fought in a vast arena covering every local institution and every branch of the economy. But such families did constitute a group which was tightly intermarried (ties often extending across whole countries) and had broadly the same outlook and interests.

The viceroys were still peninsular; so, usually, were archbishops, and even at the creole high-water mark on the great Audiencias, at least a few of the judges were always from Spain. Yet they were hardly able to dominate the creole sea in which they swam. Officials had always formed local social and economic ties and did so all the more now that local society was so well developed. Even fewer officials coming from Spain ever returned than had been the case earlier; Audiencia judges rarely, high ecclesiastics hardly ever (although this trend was partially reversed at the very end of the colonial period). In the eyes of the metropolitan government, there was little difference between a creole judge and one who was *radicado* (rooted or settled), with marriage ties to the same families we have just been discussing and with similar economic interests as well. And though the viceroys still served limited terms before moving on, some of the officials sent to inspect their activities claimed that hardly had a viceroy reached the city limits of his capital than he received such gifts, flattery, and promises of alliances that he became a local forthwith. In his court and among his advisers, the same prominent families once again loomed large.

Aside from the very tip of the imperial bureaucracy, the major sector in which the creoles had made less than stunning progress was, naturally enough, the international economy, especially export–import commerce. As had been true all through the conquest and mature colonial periods, peninsulars mainly manned the largest commercial firms at the upper levels. How was this continued peninsular dominance of commerce possible? Surely, one would think, the creole sons of a big merchant would inherit the business. We still do not know all the reasons why this did not happen, but some aspects of the process are clear enough. Although the great merchants were still born in Spain, they were American-based and permanently committed to local society. As they had gradually become more locally rooted and it became ever more obvious that international commerce was the greatest steady money producer in the Indies, their local status had risen until by the end of the colonial period it was very high indeed. They were present at the most aristocratic functions, frequently made marriage alliances with the local great families, and some of the richest of them bought titles of high nobility even while continuing in commerce. There were counts who were members of the Consulado of Mexico City. At the same time, such families shared a tendency, seen also in Europe, England, and North America, to move away from direct and exclusive involvement in commerce over a generation or two, in favor of liberal professions, landowning, and more emphasis on gentility. Almost any large merchant would in the course of his career buy an hacienda, or a set of them, partly to improve his credit position and diversify, partly to have something lasting to leave to his heirs, for grand-scale commerce was as risky as it was lucrative.

A large merchant would have arrived in the Indies already a young man, probably coming to join an established relative or fellow townsman, and would marry, if at all, only years later, after having established himself. When he came to die, his creole son would still be a stripling or less, surely not the person to manage a great commercial firm. This son would probably inherit the landed property and the noble title if there was one and would marry into another great local family. With the typical Hispanic division of the inheritance, the merchant's daughter would receive a good part of the commercial assets as her portion. The key figure was the merchant's peninsular nephew. Once on his way to success, the merchant would send to his Spanish hometown for an unattached young relative who would help him in his business and be initiated in all its secrets (in fact, he often sent for several, of whom only one might work out). On the merchant's death, management of the business, in which he was probably by this time a substantial partner, would fall to the nephew. He also might very well marry the merchant's creole daughter, his own cousin, ending up with the lion's share of the commercial part of the inheritance. This pattern of succession, common enough among all Spanish immigrants, had become a social convention among import merchants. (Of course it need not and could not be carried out in its archetypal purity; any young man from home would do; he could marry the daughter of an allied merchant rather than his own cousin, etc.) In Mexico the same small north Castilian towns supplied younger relatives to merchants based in Mexico City in one generation after another; there were firms which carried on this kind of succession for a hundred years. The peninsular in these cases did not have to start from scratch and rise merely by his own industry. Rather, he entered the local system with great advantages of kinship, common regional origin, and even age compared with the locally born heirs.

Thus the international commercial sector could be dominated by peninsulars and yet be a part of local society, since the merchants were rooted in it by permanent residence, property ownership, the acquisition of local honors and offices, and above all by the constant merging with upper-level creoles through marriage. Seen from the local perspective, each great family had its own merchant in-laws who in a sense were its satellites, serving the family's interests in the one sector where it was not directly represented. On the other hand, the absorption of wealthy immigrants into locally prominent families had been such a common procedure for so long that the great families often had only one line going back to the sixteenth century, having been penetrated repeatedly by wealthy outsiders. At any rate, the commanding position of the great local families was reinforced by the alliances; and we must not forget that at least a few of the largest merchants were creoles who had followed after their fathers despite the prevailing pattern (the unusually long survival of a merchant or the absence of a qualified nephew could easily bring this about).

As to the other main branch of the international economy, silver mining, this activity was more rooted in the local situation and its personnel were correspondingly of local origin to a higher degree – almost entirely so at the level of laborers and technicians. Owners and operators were divided between creoles and peninsulars without a clear predominance. Large merchants had always had a strong interest in the mines as the source of the specie by which they lived, and as time went on, major investment becoming ever more important to mining success, merchants (who as we just saw were usually peninsulars) were among the owners of some of the most lucrative mines, though never to the exclusion of creoles. In the late period the great mineowners of Guanajuato, then Mexico's richest site, are said to have been nearly all creoles.

Added up, the position of the creoles, especially of the most powerful families in the wealthiest and best established regions, was beginning to transcend what one would ordinarily expect in a country considered to be the colony of another. As the situation reached a peak at about the onset of the late colonial period, the metropolis finally reacted, seeking to reverse the trend in at least some of its aspects. The effects were most dramatic in the matter of recruitment to high governmental office, especially the royal Audiencias, where creoles had been gradually increasing their hold since the seventeenth century. Around 1770, in the early part of the reign of Charles III, the Audiencia of Mexico City was overwhelmingly creole. There were eight creoles to three peninsulars, and even these had been in Mexico so long they were almost native. But by appointing Spaniards born to fill nearly all vacancies as they occurred, the royal government reversed the proportions within ten years, so that there were ten peninsulars to four creoles. In the Lima Audiencia creoles were heavily predominant from 1740 forward, but the same process took place there as well; a creole majority of thirteen to two peninsulars as late as 1765 faded through the 1770s, giving way to a peninsular majority in the 1780s and 1790s and finally a fully reversed situation of twelve peninsulars to three creoles by 1800. With the lesser Audiencias, things were not quite so clear, since some of them neither saw such devastating creole majorities as did Lima and Mexico City nor did they experience such marked replacement campaigns. But generally, the creoles had come to hold most of the most sought-after judgeships by about 1750–70 and then lost that position in the course of the late colonial period, although there was a partial resurgence in the very last years before independence. In addition, the late Bourbons, as we will see later on, created new administrative posts and new agencies of various kinds, nearly all to be manned or at least headed by peninsulars, associates of the peninsular officials who initiated the changes.

To what extent all this altered the overall creole situation is questionable. The depth of the personnel changes was not great. Creoles remained in most subordinate posts and also still dominated most of the older agencies of government. It does not appear that there were social and economic reversals corresponding to those in governmental recruitment, though it is true that mercantile firms based on the other side of the Atlantic, on the strength of the Industrial Revolution, seem to have regained some of the ground they had lost since the sixteenth century, and European goods presented new challenges to goods produced locally. In the governmental sphere, it is instructive to look beyond the categories "creole" and "peninsular" to matters that were of more immediate concern to contemporaries. From the point of view of both metropolitan officials and local interests, the underlying issue was whether the judges were to be primarily bureaucrats in a far-flung imperial system or whether they were to identify their interests with the locality where they served. The government's campaign was not so much against creoles in general as against those born in their own districts. A judge from Santo Domingo serving in Mexico City was as much an outsider as one from Madrid. The true distinction was between outsiders and insiders; creoles from elsewhere together with newly arrived peninsulars constituted the outsiders, and locally born creoles and peninsulars long resident, with strong local ties, were the insiders. The campaigns surely cut deeply into the direct representation of the locally born, but there are many hints that indirect ties may have actually grown at the same time. Creole influence was not easily reduced.

The traditional complex: haciendas, Indians, and silver mining

Since the sixteenth century the support system of Spanish American cities had consisted of Spanish-run rural estates and the Indian towns of the hinterlands, together supplying the cities' local needs, plus the silver mining industry, providing them economic leverage on Europe. In the old central areas, the system was still essentially intact in the late colonial period, but there had been many adjustments to the times.

Spanish estates of the late period were strongly affected by the general changes in the size and nature of the population. The greater numbers meant a greater demand for food products, but that was only a part of the change. The growth was disproportionately among the Spaniards and castas, who were the most urban and affluent groups and hence the most powerful market. The Spanish staple, wheat, flourished accordingly; this relatively intensive crop began to push other crops off the best lands in areas near markets, partially displacing stock raising toward more distant places and drier sites (a process which, it is true, had begun much earlier near the largest cities). Needing irrigation and milling, wheat demanded a fairly high degree of capital investment, and the participation of the mercantile element in agricultural marketing, financing, and ownership increased. Growing Hispanization and market participation also affected the Indians, who by the late colonial period were enough a part of the regional economy and in possession of enough currency to represent a significant market, not to speak of their increase in numbers in some places. Not only did Indians now use more Spanish-style products; it was even more important that they had money with which to buy their own traditional products. By the late colonial period, it was no longer true that Spanish rural enterprises concentrated almost exclusively on Spanish products, Indian enterprises on indigenous products. As the markets arose, Spanish estates made maize one of their commercial crops, and in Mexico by the latter eighteenth century there were great haciendas, owned by some of the noblest families of the capital, devoted primarily to producing pulque for sale to humble people in Mexico City and environs (the analogous phenomenon in Peru, Spanish coca estancias, far antedates the period of which we are speaking, because of the precocious buying power of the Indians involved in the Peruvian silver industry). The case of Guadalajara illustrates the basic trend; in late colonial times the city's population increased sharply, meat and cereal prices rose steadily for the first time, and consumption rose too, though with a highly meaningful differential; wheat increased seven- or eightfold while maize only doubled and meat held steady.

There had always been certain families and individuals owning multiple landed properties, but in the late period, in both Mexico and Peru, it became a standard phenomenon for the largest owners, whether the newly wealthy in mines and commerce or the long-established families, to possess whole strings or sets of haciendas, each still with its separate staff, type of land use, and saint's name or toponym to identify it – by no means usually contiguous holdings but rather in complementary distribution. To manage such complexes there arose the type of the estate administrator, inserted between the owner and the majordomos of individual haciendas; he was part businessman, but socially and by education he stood very nearly at the large owners' level and sometimes joined that group by the end of his career.

If the transformation of the population had large effects on the markets of rural estates, the implications for their staffing and labor arrangements were equally great. The hacienda form, with its concentration of responsibility, skills, and remuneration at the upper levels, came into being and was best adapted to a situation where those fully endowed with the dominant culture, the owning group, were a minority, a somewhat larger group of humble or ethnically mixed people took the intermediary roles, and a majority only beginning to be introduced to Hispanic ways supplied short-term labor without entering fully into the life of the estate and the Hispanic economy. Before the end of the colonial period the situation had changed drastically in all three respects, but especially at the middle levels, which, as we said earlier, had become overpopulated. There were by now far too many mestizos, mulattoes, and thoroughly Hispanized Indians to occupy the roles of technicians and foremen for which they were culturally equipped and for which, almost as importantly, they were socially stereotyped. It is true that the quotient of skilled and permanent personnel had been rising all through the colonial period, not only because of the changes in type of demand and product but because of the simple increase in numbers of persons apt and motivated for such positions. Yet the Spanish American market was still far from being able to support rural enterprises in which supervisors and skilled resident personnel would have been the majority.

What was to come of the "excess" of mestizos and other humble Hispanic people in the rural areas? One alternative was for them to attempt to run their own properties, commercially oriented and producing much the same things as the haciendas if on a much smaller scale. Called "ranchos" in late colonial Mexico and by other names in other places, such modest rural properties were a prominent feature of the late period. As all through the colonial period, ranchos were quite compatible with haciendas. They were oriented to lesser and more local markets or sold their products at times of plenty when prices were low, whereas haciendas aimed at the large cities and times of scarcity and higher prices. The rancheros were intertwined with the hacienda personnel, often spending portions of their time as majordomos, stock watchers, or muleteers in the service of nearby haciendas. It is hard to say whether independent ranchos increased in general in the late colonial epoch or not. The growth of secondary Hispanic centers in the city hinterlands, representing considerable markets, was in their favor. But the overall upswing was not. Whenever a given region's market and investment situation improved sharply, as happened in the Mexican area of León, near the booming mines of Guanajuato, many modest properties would become consolidated into large ones, whether through the success of rancheros or, more often, through large-scale acquisitions by the already wealthy.

Under the new conditions, a very strong pattern was for the owner of a large hacienda to exploit directly only the best of its lands, growing there only the most profitable crops and perhaps investing considerable capital there, while he leased and rented out much of the rest to the same sorts of people who would once have been estate foremen and skilled workers. Some might be the former owners of the largish sections which they now worked under long-term lease, but even more characteristic of the late period were tenants on quite small plots, held often without formal contract, the rent for which they might pay in money, a share of the crop, labor, or all three. By the end of the colonial period, many haciendas from Mexico to Chile had large contingents of Hispanic or Hispanized sharecroppers and tenants on them, available as a labor reserve and often drawn on in times of work peaks in addition to or instead of Indian villagers.

Changes also affected the lowest level of the estate labor force; as occurred with social groupings, here too merging of various kinds went on, so that the difference between permanent and temporary laborers lessened. In central Mexico, where the situation is best studied, we know that some Indians who possessed less than the average amount of land in their own towns were spending not just a few weeks at harvest and planting time working for haciendas but whole months, often the majority of their work year. Clearly such people gained skills and customs that in an earlier age would have been exclusive to permanent workers. Yet there were also continuities from the past. These workers hired on for a week or two at a time, so that, in contrast to the true permanent workers, they shifted sites frequently, and they were paid at the bottom of the scale. In many cases intermediaries, Indians from the same towns as themselves, entitled "gang captains," procured them, collected their pay for them, and even kept them together as a unit while working at the hacienda, all relics from the earlier more formalized systems of encomienda and repartimiento. In the Andean highland, on the other hand, it appears – though our knowledge is limited to little more than category names and numbers – that among the permanent resident workers on haciendas were some who lacked the expected cultural profile and differed little from village Indians in life-style or type of work performed (though even these tended to be geographically displaced and divorced from village units).

In talking of estates we have thus approached the topic of the shape of the Indian world in the late colonial period; the ever more thorough interpenetration of Indian towns and estates, of which we have just mentioned some examples, was one important part of the picture. The central Mexican gang captains were natives and prominent residents of Indian towns, yet they were also fully integrated into the Hispanic estate system. The rancheros were Hispanic, yet they normally made nearby large Indian towns their headquarters and by this time had turned the centers of many such towns into typical Hispanic complexes. And so it was not only with estates but with every aspect of the interrelations between Hispanic and Indian worlds; the Hispanics had approached closer to the Indian sector, and the Indians were reaching out to more participation in the Hispanic or general sector.

One of the phenomena most commented upon was the large-scale entry of mestizos and other castas into the Indian towns to live, work, and hold lands, not as members of the community, but still competing, intermarrying, displacing. Some of the larger indigenous towns of central Mexico came to have more non-Indian than Indian inhabitants. Even in the heartland of the relatively isolated central Andean highland, the Cuzco region, the proportion of persons in non-Indian categories increased to more than 17 percent by 1786, growing especially quickly in parts of the countryside dominated by Indian towns rather than by haciendas. In both Mexico and Peru the old nobility of many of the larger Indian entities had mastered the Spanish language and culture, had intermarried extensively with local Spaniards and mestizos, and now owned and operated properties little different from Spanish haciendas and ranchos. In Mexico, indeed, some of the "cacique" group ("cacique" now simply meaning, in that context, any wealthy and prominent person rooted in an Indian community) were losing indigenous language and identity and finding a place among the provincial Hispanics.

The increased employment of Indians by Spaniards and their greater activity in interregional trade and transportation by no means brought them any general prosperity, but it did mean that more money circulated among them; they became a better market both because they had more Hispanic-style needs and because they were better able to pay to satisfy them. In view of this situation some local trading patterns gradually reversed themselves. Originally, the efforts made by nearly all corregidores de indios to remunerate themselves through participation in the local economy had one thing in common: They were attempts to funnel local products, whether coming from Indians or from Spanish estates, toward the cities. After a time corregidores began to involve themselves also in the sale of some indigenous products from other regions, such as cacao, to their own constituents, and by the late period their most characteristic activity was the sale of items coming out of the countrywide general economy – mules, oxen, textiles, tools, and other things – to the Indians of their districts. The corregidores would often oblige Indians to buy stipulated amounts as part of their general obligation to the government, a practice which even had official approval in many times and places; since these short-term and nearly unpaid local administrators in the search for profit did not fail to press too hard on this weak, marginal, nascent market, the institution of forced sale (*reparto de mercancías*) was one of the most universally unpopular features of colonial times, denounced on all sides from that day to this. The reputation is not entirely undeserved, but even so it is significant that the later period, not the earlier, was the time of the flourishing of the "reparto." Exactly the same trend is to be observed in the economic activities of caciques, at least in the Peruvian case, where they still retained much of their power and influence in the late colonial epoch. In the sixteenth century they are seen hiring their subjects to Spanish employers or selling local products in the direction of mines and cities; by the late period they too were selling products from cities and other regions to their subjects. Spanish estates too, though still primarily oriented toward city markets, began to show more interest in selling goods from the outside to their workers or paying them in such goods, which amounted to nearly the same thing.

All these developments put strains on the Indian corporations, at least in their by now traditional form. In some transitional areas, the "Indian world" almost ceased to exist as a separate entity, the best-known example being the disruption of the Colombian *resguardos*, or reserves, by the massive invasion of Hispanics. In the central areas too, some Indian town governments were vestigial, marginal to settlements which were now Hispanic at the core. Nevertheless, it is clear that the picture of Indian corporate decadence in the late colonial period has been overdrawn. Even in central Mexico, where the Indians faced the greatest concentration of Spaniards and Hispanic structures, and indeed even within sight of Mexico City, there were Indian municipalities functioning as they had for some generations now, adjudicating local disputes, authenticating land titles, keeping

Nahuatl records. Some of the corporations had suffered the loss of formerly dependent towns and hamlets, which now insisted on and won independent municipal status for themselves, resulting in smaller entities and a less complex structure. To us, however, this development represents Indian vitality, the traditional microethnicity carried to new extremes under conditions which allowed it, for the Spaniards, who had once depended on the full provincial unit to operate encomiendas, large parishes, and labor systems and hence would not countenance its partition, no longer needed it. Persons labeled "Indian" and speaking Nahuatl were still the majority even in the Valley of Mexico itself. In the more isolated south of Mexico the corporations were even more solid; in Oaxaca at least they retained most of the arable land, including much of the best of it, and strong, wealthy *cacicazgos* still existed. In the Andes too the caciques or curacas not only still existed but still exercised much authority. The most recent research on the great Tupac Amaru uprising in the Andean highlands in the 1780s (we will have more to say on the topic later) shows that small local ethnic entities asserted themselves mightily, the strong sense of independence and rivalry among the groups in many cases being the deciding factor in whether or not they supported the revolt.

In the core of the old central areas, the changes in estates and Indian towns which we have been discussing here coincide in a general way with the late colonial period, but they had been coming on gradually for a long time, like the ethnic and cultural fusion that caused them, so they cannot be seen as beginning in any fixed period of a decade or two. Nor were they by any means uniform, in the sense that Audiencia recruitment policy, for example, had the same general chronology all across Spanish America. Whereas the hacienda was evolving beyond its classic form in some areas, impelled by new markets and an excess of intermediary personnel, other more remote areas lacked either impetus and had as yet hardly even attained the classic hacienda of the mature colonial period. In general, growth and greater integration characterized both the estate system and the Indian sector (of the old central areas), but this did not necessarily bring benefits to the individuals affected. Rather, the intermediary types often saw their status depressed as a result of their having become too numerous. As to the Indians, growth in populations and markets meant among other things rising land values and pressures on the land, factors which had been of relatively little concern in the mature colonial period, and as the Indians' traditional crops and activities became more profitable, they had to face the competition of well-organized and well-financed Hispanic enterprises in what had been to an extent their own niche of the economy.

The late colonial export economy became increasingly diversified; as we will see, startling growth took place in some eastward-facing areas exporting nonmetallic products. Yet in Mexico and the central Andes, silver continued to play much the same role as in the previous centuries. It also continued to be mined in the same general locations and by somewhat further evolved versions of the same techniques. The rhythm of production followed the general late colonial upswing closely. From the early decades of the eighteenth century until past 1800, annual silver production rates rose steadily, with the most marked increase in the last third of that period.

Both internal and external factors had their part in the expansion. Internally, the mines profited from the ballooning double trend of the late period, population growth and increased Hispanization. There were more people available of the type apt for permanent and technical work in a Hispanic framework, so that the mines both had a more plentiful supply of labor of the type they especially needed and had to pay less for it (though as ever, mine workers were relatively among the highest paid in the economy). Given the nature and depth of deposits and the veins already mined out, silver mining did best when practiced on a large scale. As we have seen earlier, conditions had already been forcing participants into larger, more cooperative operations in the seventeenth century. By the late eighteenth, the scale was at an all-time peak. The famous Valenciana at Guanajuato was 635 yards deep, and the shaft was 32 yards in circumference. A big mine might require up to a thousand mules and horses to power its machinery. More men were employed – more than three thousand at the Valenciana. Refineries had also grown larger. Vast and long-term investment was required for the greatest mines, and by the end of the period consortia of miners and merchant financiers, with considerable staying power, were the dominant mode. Some financiers, in Mexico at least, operated what amounted to true investment banks. Mining techniques, still primarily empirical and in the hands of persons trained by experience, nevertheless were by now highly sophisticated in their way. The one apparently major technical innovation of the later period also seems to have come about through experimenting at the local level: the large-scale use of gunpowder for blasting, which was especially important in constructing great shafts and drainage adits.

Silver mining had always been the royal government's darling, so it is no surprise to find heavy governmental involvement in mining in the late colonial period. It was the late Bourbons who did the most, so that the major thrust of official activity coincides exactly with the production heights. Mining success and governmental encouragement fed on each other, so that both contributed to the ultimate result. Which was primary or contributed the most can hardly be settled, though it seems worth remembering that the expansion was part and parcel of a general social-economic trend on both sides of the Atlantic and that the royal government had a long history of encouraging mainly things which were already doing well on their own. In any case, the government gave substantial tax concessions to the largest mining investors. Perhaps the most significant development was the great increase in mercury supplies, especially from Almadén in Spain, and the crown's reduction of prices, eventually to half their former amount. With more and cheaper mercury, mines with marginal ores could be worked profitably. Bourbon actions such as these were timely and apparently successful, but they were no different in kind from measures taken in previous centuries. The results of newer steps the government took were more dubious. Many consider that the attempts to establish direct governmental financing of mining were a failure. New-wave Age of Enlightenment mining experts and techniques brought in from Europe led to little. The Born system of refining produced less than ordinary amalgamation; foreign pumping machinery failed. In general, the new European methods required excessive fixed investment and lavish use of materials in short supply; in a word, they were not well adapted to the local situation. It is true that, in part as a result of such efforts, miners began to adopt a more methodical outlook, and in Mexico a mining academy was founded and took hold.

Although the preceding discussion applies in a general way to both Mexico and Peru, Mexico benefited more from the trends. Its upswing in production began around 1700, Peru's some decades later, and at the late colonial peaks Mexico far outstripped Peru, having by then quadrupled its production since the beginning of the eighteenth century. In fact, in the late period Mexico was moving more quickly than Peru in general; its possession of an Atlantic coast was more to its advantage now than earlier, its population growth was more marked, and there had been greater cultural interaction between Hispanic and Indian sectors, in large part simply because of the country's more tractable geography. One very specific strain on the Andean system, the direct result of Peru's lack of access to the Atlantic, was its split in two in the late 1770s; Charcas (Bolivia) with Potosí and most of the other silver mines went to the new Viceroyalty of Río de la Plata, and their production was routed through Buenos Aires rather than Lima. We know far less about the details of the Peruvian economy than about the Mexican, but there must have been a time of financial disruption as the well-established Lima merchant community gradually became alienated from the Upper Peruvian silver industry. One of Lima's answers was to develop silver production in lower Peruvian sites, which enjoyed considerable success, outdoing Potosí by the final years of the colonial period; yet the two halves together nowhere near equaled the Mexican performance.

Both major mining industries had evolved toward a majority of skilled permanent workers, but the old differential persisted. In Mexico, practically the whole labor force consisted of mine workers by trade, many of them of the second generation or more. With proceeding race mixture, most of them by this time were, as well as we can tell, mestizos and mulattoes. The remaining laborers who were still identified as Indians were quite highly Hispanized. A folk notion had even grown up that Indians were unskillful miners, people having forgotten who the original mine workers were despite the clear line of direct descent. In the Upper Peru of the late period, on the other hand, though perhaps three-fourths of the force were voluntary wage workers, one-fourth were still coming through the mita system, and many of the others may have been mita workers in their off spells; the proportion of Indians and the retention of indigenous culture in the whole force was much greater than in Mexico.

The east coast revolution

As already seen, during the late colonial reorientation the Atlantic seaboard areas experienced growth and consolidation, since they profited most from navigational improvements and were best placed for the bulk exports to Europe which were now becoming increasingly viable. Some former fringe areas now took on many of the characteristics of centrality and even displaced the old central areas to an extent, particularly in the case of Peru (see Map 14, Table 4).

The most spectacular change of this type in the Spanish American sphere occurred in the Plata region. Having long been the farthest fringe and poorest dependency within the Peruvian orbit, it now found itself, because of transportation improvements, sitting on a

Map 14. Ibero-American "center" and fringe, late colonial period. (By the late period there had come to be so many independent centers that one can no longer use the term "center" in quite the same sense. Compare Maps 8 and 9.)

route between the Upper Peruvian silver mines and Europe which was better than the old established route through Panama and Lima. (Let it not be thought that there was any particular change in outlook or that the old route was irrational. For a time of slow, small ships half full of provisions, the Panama route, with its shorter stretches and opportunity for reprovisioning, was optimum, in addition to being easier to defend against foreigners on the Pacific side.

Table 4. *Estimated populations of Spanish American regions, ca. 1800*

	Estimated Population	Subtotal	Percentage of total population	
Mexico	5,837,000		46.4	
Central America	1,160,000		9.2	
		6,997,000		55.6
Caribbean islands		550,000		4.4
New Granada	1,100,000		8.7	
Venezuela	780,000		6.2	
		1,880,000		14.9
Quito	500,000		4.0	
Peru	1,100,000		8.7	
Charcas	560,000		4.5	
Chile	550,000		4.4	
		2,710,000		21.6
Buenos Aires & Tucumán	310,000		2.5	
Paraguay	100,000		.8	
Uruguay	30,000		.2	
		440,000		3.5
		12,577,000		100.0

Source: Compilation of numerous counts and estimates of the time made by Professor Robert N. Burr of UCLA and his student Karl F. Graeber.

On the other hand, in the late eighteenth century ships were not yet so large and fast that the route from Upper Peru out to the Pacific and around the Horn was markedly preferable to the one through Buenos Aires, as it was to become in the course of the nineteenth century.) In addition, the vast herds of wild cattle (ganado cimarrón) that covered the Argentine, Uruguayan, and southern Brazilian plains, having long been rightly considered next to worthless, were now becoming an asset in export, at first for their hides alone. The growing Europe of the Industrial Revolution needed more leather not only for shoes and saddles but for the moving parts of machines. Leather export was shifting from a marginal position, with hides hardly more than ballast for returning ships, toward being a motor of the economy. By the 1770s Buenos Aires was exporting 150,000 hides a year. Both the British (the main consumers of the hides) and the Portuguese showed an appreciation of the area's growing attractiveness by increasing their activities in the vicinity. The same factors which improved transportation and changed the nature of exports also gave non-Iberian European powers the ability and motivation to intervene in remote places they had ignored before. Buenos Aires had been a small, poor port and presidio town, far off the main routes except for an appreciable traffic in slaves from southern Africa toward Potosí. As the advantages of the Platine commercial route became ever clearer after the mid-eighteenth century, Spanish merchants and firms began to establish themselves there to import and export, either through individually registered ships that began to be allowed or through contraband. By the mid-1770s the town was still no marvel, but it did contain an extensive, active, and well-connected merchant community.

In 1776, cognizant of all this, the crown created the Viceroyalty of the Río de la Plata with Buenos Aires as the capital, hoping at once to derive more revenue from the booming economy beginning to form and to provide better protection from menacing foreigners. The arrangement reversed the traditional balance of the region, giving primacy to the insignificant port over the better developed northwestern interior. But the greatest act of reorganization, already alluded to, was the inclusion of Upper Peru and its silver mines in the new viceroyalty, a reorientation affecting the entire continent by making Buenos Aires rather than Lima the main outlet for Potosí's silver.

Buenos Aires now began to undergo the same process of consolidation that Mexico City and Lima had experienced in the sixteenth century, for the emergence of major new export resources in an area invariably favored the formation of a tight network centered on a single dominant city. Not only did Buenos Aires now receive a viceroy, Audiencia, merchants' Consulado (after a time), and in general most of the governmental and institutional trappings of the other viceregal capitals, but (unlike Bogotá, which nominally had the same status) the city continued its already quick population growth, rising to well over forty thousand by the eve of independence. Migrants from the interior met another stream of immigration coming from Spain. The merchants of Buenos Aires began to become the creditors and suppliers of their colleagues in the interior, and the interior began to find in the capital a market as powerful as, if different in kind from, the one in the Upper Peruvian mining district.

Yet in many ways the newness of the situation, the recent emergence from peripheral status, left strong traces. The merchants of Buenos Aires, like their counterparts in Mexico City, were mainly from northern Spain, and like them, most were permanently committed to local society, but they maintained much closer contacts with Spanish firms, of which they were in some cases mere representatives. On the other hand, they were much more dominant in local society than were the Mexico City merchants; there was no complex set of competing, long-established economic interests, no great creole families with extensive landed estates. The peninsular merchants themselves dominated the municipal council of Buenos Aires, which was very far indeed from being the case in Mexico City or Lima. The lack of a creole establishment showed itself also in a thorough peninsular predominance in governmental and ecclesiastical office and even in some of the crafts. Buenos Aires received no university but sent its sons to the one at inland Córdoba or even farther to Upper Peru, a sad situation for a capital city.

Unlike the merchants of Mexico City, those of Buenos Aires did not acquire titles of high nobility, nor did they buy up sets of haciendas, there being no haciendas to buy. The interior had rural estates comparable to those, say, of the near north of Mexico, but in the pampa region, as on the rest of the far periphery, estate development had been minimal. As everywhere, prestige and influence accrued to those involved in that part of the economy with the largest steady income, in this case commerce along the silver route. Though hides were the most dynamic aspect of the export economy, silver outweighed them in value until the very end of the colonial period, at first several times over. The people involved with hides and rural estates were on the lower end of the social scale. Owners of the small rural enterprises around Buenos Aires were much like majordomos in more developed areas; the population working directly with the cattle on the plains was, as we have seen earlier, sparse and mobile, of the type later called "gaucho" – Spanish speakers, racially mixed, not unlike the mestizo cowherds on many Spanish American plains, though more localized in dress, speech, and customs because of the great isolation of the region before the late eighteenth century.

The hide industry was long primarily concerned with the hunting of wild cattle, either on unowned lands, sometimes with a special permit, or on large tracts called estancias and belonging to private individuals but differing in no other way from open plain. With the depletion in herds and continuing rise in values, a transition began by the early viceregal epoch in the direction of a more standard type of herding, breeding, and estate formation. Before the end of the colonial period exports were running over a million hides yearly, and a new dimension had been added in the shipping of salted beef to Europe and the Caribbean. As the silver economy faltered in the last colonial years and the rural component grew, the merchants of Buenos Aires at last began to take a more direct hand in the estancias, purchasing, managing, and developing them. In a movement continuing into the national period and not reaching its climax until the middle or late nineteenth century, the full set of phenomena of consolidation came into existence: a closely intermarried set of great local families, often descended from late colonial merchants, resided in Buenos Aires, dominated political office, and owned fully elaborated great estates in the countryside, where a large part of the population looked to them as patrons – all without giving up involvement in the export of the products. After much struggle Buenos Aires was to gain a clear ascendancy over all the interior provinces. In the end, then, though far into the national period, the Argentine situation came to bear a close resemblance to what had existed in Mexico and Peru far earlier.

The other major episode of growth and consolidation on the Spanish American mainland occurred in Venezuela. We have already looked briefly at the explosion of tropical export on the Caribbean islands, mainly those possessed by north European nations. Although outclassed in sugar production by lack of access to the foreign markets, topography, and other factors, Venezuela did enjoy a Caribbean coast, and its coastal range was suitable for various export crops. As seen in Chapter 8, the expansion there began in the seventeenth century, typically oriented toward more central parts of the Indies. Having at first sent wheat to Cartagena for fleet supply, the Venezuelan Spaniards increasingly relied on exporting cacao to its traditional market, central Mexico. On the basis of this trade, the Venezuelans were able to convert from the sparse labor provided by small encomiendas to the use of African slaves. Caracas became a reasonable urban entity, estates took mature form, and there arose a set of urban-based, landholding, cacao-exporting families, a mixture of locally born Spaniards and new immigrants – all of this far earlier than the equivalent in Buenos Aires. As cacao came to be a salable commodity not only in Mexico but in Europe, the crown gave a monopoly concession on Venezuelan trade to an association of Basques, the Caracas Company, under which further advances were made. Unhappy local interests, petitioning endlessly and sometimes using violent protest, finally broke the company's monopoly, and growth continued as well as diversification of tropical export, accelerating most, like nearly everything else in the Indies, in the last

Table 5. *Estimated ethnic composition of some Spanish American populations at the end of the colonial period*

	% Spaniards	% Castas	% Indians
Mexico (1793)	18.0	21.0	61.0
Peru (1795)	12.6	29.2	58.2
Central Venezuela (1800–9)	25.0	52.0[a]	13.0
City of Buenos Aires (1810)	66.0	33.0[a]	1.0
Cuba (1792)	49.0	51.0[a]	–

[a]Exclusively pardo, mulatto, and Black. The estimates for Mexico's castas include 11% mestizo, 10% mulatto and Black; for Peru's castas, 21.9% mestizo, 7.3% mulatto and Black.
Source: Mexico: Gonzalo Aguirre Beltrán, *La población negra de México* (México, 1972), p. 234. Peru: J. R. Fisher, *Government and Society in Colonial Peru* (London, 1970), p. 253. Venezuela: John V. Lombardi, *People and Places of Colonial Venezuela* (Bloomington, Ind., 1976), p. 68. Buenos Aires: Lyman L. Johnson and Susan Migden Socolow, "Population and Space in Eighteenth-Century Buenos Aires," in David. J. Robinson (ed.), *Social Fabric and Spatial Structure in Colonial Latin America* (Ann Arbor, Mich., 1979), p. 345. Cuba: Verena Martínez-Alier, *Marriage, Class and Colour in Nineteenth-Century Cuba* (Cambridge, 1974), p. 3.

years of the eighteenth century. By that time Caracas was not only approximately equal in size and institutional development to coeval Buenos Aires; it had a stable urban-agrarian hinterland network of towns, villages, and estates which Buenos Aires lacked. In 1777 Venezuela was made a captaincy general independent of all other jurisdictions; in 1786 it received an Audiencia, based of course in Caracas, and in 1793 a merchants' Consulado. Caracas did not become the capital of a viceroyalty, largely no doubt because it lacked the silver flowing through Buenos Aires; and though it had interior plains with numerous cattle and a mixed population of plainsmen not unlike the Plata region, the export of hides and meat seems not to have flourished to the same extent, perhaps because of inaccessibility to the coast.

Both Venezuela and the Platine littoral had, by independence, a population makeup markedly distinct from that of the old central regions (see Table 5). Indians as a separate category were the smallest of the ethnic groups; the population was mainly a conglomerate of Spanish and African, even in Buenos Aires, which was able through its new prosperity to bring in a large number of African slaves in the late colonial years. The proportions varied, it is true; in Buenos Aires about two-thirds of the population counted as Spanish and nearly all the rest as Black or mulatto, whereas the African element in Venezuela, which had been present longer and in a more basic function, was far more heavily represented. People of at least partly African descent made up perhaps 60 percent of the population countrywide, and the largest single census category was "pardo," apparently meaning a Hispanized person of mixed African ancestry. There were many more pardos than slaves or free persons labeled Black, so the process of absorption and acculturation was far advanced. It is noteworthy that these two areas we are discussing, where the two basic demographic building blocks were European and African, were among the first to go over to using the census category "white" (*blanco*) instead of "Spaniard" in the late colonial period.

Cuba, the largest Hispanic concentration in the Antilles, was growing even further apart from mainland Spanish America and becoming, in chronology and nature of trends, more a part of the multinational world of the Caribbean islands. Nevertheless, it deserves at least some mention in the present context. Cuba did not participate in the main thrust of the English and French sugar boom of the later eighteenth century, the whole point of that development being for the principal consumer countries to produce for themselves. The population of Cuba retained a far larger European element than that of the French and English possessions. The principal export crop, not notably flourishing, we are told, was tobacco, grown on quite small properties, and there were also cattle ranches. Havana, astride the sea routes, was an important port as well as an urban society with some pretensions and complexity, containing among other things a contingent of acculturated Blacks and mulattoes. From the 1760s forward Cuba's sea trade with both Mexico and Spain began to rise sharply, in part because it was the first area to experience the new policy of free trade within the empire. In the last decades of the eighteenth century its diversified exports began to veer in the direction of tropical crops. Coffee took the lead in the 1790s, the same time when it was becoming important in Venezuela and Brazil, and sugar, with up-to-date operations modeled on the French and English industry, followed just behind, fueled by the loss of French production after the Haitian slave revolution. The two industries were soon the largest users of slaves on the island, and slave importation picked up correspondingly. By the end of the colonial period elsewhere, Cuba's population was quite evenly balanced between European and African, with about twice as many slaves as free Blacks and mulattoes. The constituent parts, then, were much like Venezuela's. However, the proportions varied and the trends were very different, since the heights of the Cuban sugar industry were yet to come, Cuba was to retain colonial status for many decades, and it would continue to experience waves of both slave importation and new immigration from Spain.

Intellectual trends in the Age of Enlightenment

As discussed earlier, in the mature colonial period the Spanish Indies had developed a home-grown Hispanic intellectual establishment centered on universities and certain branches of the church, yet at the same time intellectual life remained under strong influence from the metropolis as to content. Little changed in these respects in the eighteenth century; there continued to be local personnel and organizations, and the modes, at least on the face of it, continued to be dictated from the outside. In Europe the dominant mode, an emphasis on reason, science, practicality, and simple clarity of expression, had been emanating mainly from France over the whole century, finding an excellent conduit into Spain in the French Bourbon dynasty which ascended to the throne in 1700, so that Enlightenment manifestations are not entirely confined to the late colonial period in the narrower sense. Even before that, a militant spirit of antischolasticism and antiobscurantism had begun to win out in the Spanish American universities, where dissertations regularly berated Aristotle and all untested authority. But much of the new wave does concentrate in the last decades of the eighteenth century. It was then that in nearly all the Hispanic-American local capitals discussion groups called "economic societies of friends of the country" sprang up to study the local scene scientifically and apply that knowledge to furthering the local economy. It was then that it became de rigueur for leading intellectuals to establish encyclopedic journals, containing a little of everything but emphasizing scientific examinations of local crops, industries, diseases, geographical features, and the like, with an eye to practical application.

Both of these characteristic phenomena were based on Spanish models and they in turn on French originals. Enlightenment ideas and writings circulated quite freely over the whole Spanish empire, but at the hands of the intellectuals of Spain they took on a specific flavor and emphasis which was transferred to Spanish America as well: A pro-scientific attitude was not construed as antireligious, and at least until the immediate preindependence years, it was the practical rather than the ideological aspects that fascinated most Spanish and Spanish American intellectuals. Many of the most important figures in Spanish American thought continued to be churchmen, as in previous centuries. José Antonio Alzate, late colonial Mexico's leading journalist, was a secular priest. All in all, Spanish American intellectuals were recruited from the same general circles and had the same types of careers as in the previous epoch. One notable extension was the increased participation of physicians, medicine being at least potentially more scientific than law or theology. Alzate's Peruvian equivalent, Hipólito Unanue, editor of, and principal contributor to, the review *Mercurio Peruano* in the 1790s, was a physician and professor of medicine. There may have been an element of social rise in this trend. As we have seen, medicine had been the lowest ranking of the three major professions, practiced by persons of correspondingly more modest origins, sometimes even ethnically mixed; it is noteworthy that several of the physician-intellectuals of the later period were mulattoes or otherwise said to have been not pure Spanish. Whether the status of medicine really improved in general, as it did in fact in the course of the nineteenth and twentieth centuries, may be doubted; in preindependence Mexico City, at least, physicians still fell far behind lawyers and priests in family connections. In general, the social range of those actively engaged in intellectual pursuits had not expanded in any pronounced fashion, though it is true that schoolmasters were finding pupils at lower levels of society and farther into the countryside than earlier.

Throughout the early centuries a substantial part of intellectual production in the Indies had been carried out by people coming from the outside in various capacities, usually Spanish-born, though some of the Jesuits were Italian, Austrian, or German. Such penetration continued now as before, but a new element was added: Foreigners or foreign-inspired Spaniards were sent not to occupy positions in the Indies but to carry out expeditions, visitations, and inspections to determine physical features, measure and report on the society and economy, or study the flora and fauna. From the French-Spanish expedition of the 1730s and 1740s to measure an arc of the meridian at the equator in the Quito region to the German Alexander von Humboldt's extensive fact-gathering travels in the early nineteenth century, foreign investigators were frequently on the Spanish American scene, bringing locals into close contact with the very latest in Europe.

It might thus appear that localism had suffered a setback. Surely powerful new trends and conventions from the outside shaped intellectual life, foreigners were more in evidence, and the new outlook was strongly cosmopolitan and universal. Yet the Spanish Americans knew how to turn the European Enlightenment in their own direction. Although they occasionally devoted some time to astronomy or mathematics, practically all of their activity and writing was concerned with scrutinizing some aspect of the very local scene. One could say that absorption with the society of the Indies had increased greatly since the days of the exotic dramas of Sor Juana Inés, or that it had returned to the emphasis of the sixteenth century in a different guise. One aspect of eighteenth-century European thought was a preromantic extolling of simple and distant peoples, and the Spanish American intellectuals made this coincide with an antiquarian Indianism even stronger than that of Sigüenza y Góngora, with definite overtones of patriotism. Intellectuals still scraped together an existence from odd employments in church, university, government, and professions, and as earlier they prided themselves on a great variety of production, including the more literary and occasional as well as the more scientific. Titles such as "Reflections on the Smallpox" betray something of the mixed nature of much of the writing, very much in the earlier tradition, which is not to deny the very real contributions in the Enlightenment vein made by late colonial intellectuals throughout Spanish America (and it was indeed almost throughout, not only in Mexico and Peru; Venezuela, Argentina, Chile, New Granada, Guatemala, and Cuba also had their gazetteers and societies of friends of the country, including some stellar figures). The deeper one looks, the more it appears that the Enlightenment gave only coloration and impetus to a new Spanish American self-study and self-assessment whose time was coming as a result of the attained maturity of the local societies regardless of the intellectual fashions of Europe. At any rate, it does seem that intellectual production picked up momentum at just the time when a general upswing was occurring in other aspects of Spanish American life, from the economy to the size of the population, so that to some extent at least it can be seen as emerging from general forces operating within local society.

The "Bourbon reforms"

The intellectual trends we have been discussing were not without their implications for the operation of the imperial government; in fact, many observers have seen the new intellectual climate as the primary explanation of the wave of governmental changes instigated by the Bourbon kings, especially in the latter eighteenth century. The connection is surely a real one; not only were the ideas of the French Enlightenment highly relevant to the operation of government, but in Spain some of the best-known writers on the economy and politics actually served as royal ministers.

In line with its emphasis on clarity in reasoning, the Enlightenment preferred unity and uniformity over multitudinous distinctions. In governmental matters this meant holding up the ideal of a unitary state not hampered by the existence of independent corporations. Such thinking could easily lead to notions of equality of all citizens with government as their servant, but if kept within a monarchical framework, as was decidedly the case in Spain, it led rather to the ideal of a strong king issuing orders along very clear lines of authority for the general good of the realm. Enlightenment concern for efficiency pointed in the same direction, preferring one man for a given assignment over a slow-moving council, and a responsible, removable, salaried official over a proprietary one who held office for life or near it and was deeply involved in his local milieu. Ideas such as these were all directly counter to the way Hispanic government and society had always been constituted, and they would indeed imply drastic change if taken seriously. Equally radical, in principle, was the belief that the enlightened despot at the head of his unified government should go beyond the roles of legitimation, adjudication, defense, and tax collection to take a far more active part in life in general, especially the economy, not only by encouraging those branches of industry and trade that most needed it but by creating new agencies and even directly undertaking large-scale production and commerce.

But from general ideas to specific governmental actions is a large step. Without at all denying the palpable influence of the international climate of opinion, we are more concerned to show that the series of measures known collectively as the Bourbon reforms also obeyed other imperatives, factors often more potent in determining the reforms' timing and nature than the Enlightenment slogans under which they were sometimes propounded. Many of the ideas most frequently expressed in connection with the reforms had become common coin in Spain by the 1740s and earlier, but it was not until later, when Bourbon rule had become fully consolidated and acclimated and, above all, general growth and evolution on both sides of the Atlantic had made the measures desirable and somewhat feasible, that the bulk of them came to pass.

In the package of Bourbon reforms were many important items which, though perhaps compatible with, were by no means dependent on, Enlightenment thinking: They implied no particular change in attitude since earlier times but were much the same as what any government would have done under the circumstances. We have already reviewed one important late Bourbon policy, the preference of peninsular-born Spaniards over creoles for Audiencia posts. This campaign could be seen as an Enlightenment government's attempt to acquire more responsive, less localized bureaucrats. But surely we do better to view it as a response to a gradually growing creole dominance at just the point where predominance became a devastating majority. As to the nature of the new appointments, they look a great deal like eternal-Hispanic patronage politics. And if the royal government showed new energy, it was not only because of the concept of a more activist state but because of such circumstances as the economic and demographic resurgence of the northeastern part of the Peninsula in the latter eighteenth century.

The same is true, to an extent, of the Bourbons' far-reaching reorganization of jurisdictions, again mainly post-1760. This aspect of the reforms can be seen as an Enlightenment quest for units more efficient than those remaining from Hapsburg times. But it was the situation, more than governmental attitudes, which had changed. The sixteenth-century viceroyalties were established atop major new export resources already being developed by local Spaniards, leaving other Spanish American areas dependent on them; but as some of these areas, in turn, in the late eighteenth century, evolved major new export potential, the Bourbons made them too into independent units, of the same type as earlier – viceroyalties, captaincies general, Audiencia districts, as we have already seen in the cases of the Plata region and Venezuela. One other new jurisdiction carved out of Spanish South America was the viceroyalty of New Granada, including present Colombia (the capital being Bogotá) and Ecuador, plus Venezuela and Panama at times. First created in 1717, quickly abolished, and then created anew in 1739, it was somewhat different from the others not only in being carried out by the early Bourbons but also in not fastening on any marked new economic flourishing, either then or later. Caribbean defense was a consideration, however, and there was a certain geopolitical basis for the measure: The northern areas were growing ever more distinct from Peru, being oriented increasingly to the Atlantic and the gold mines of Antioquia and the Chocó, and they presented insuperable communications problems which had become ever more obvious over the decades and centuries. (Such problems had been plain enough from the start; the Pizarros had decided by 1540 that Quito should be governed independently of the rest of Greater Peru.)

Other forms of jurisdictional change looked newer, at least on the surface, such as the French-inspired intendancy reform, which we will deal with in the following section. Indeed, many Bourbon reforms were not merely influenced in some general way by Enlightenment doctrine but were specifically patterned on French models. The Bourbons gradually converted from conciliar government to reliance on ministers and ministries. In Hapsburg days the "crown," as far as Spanish America was concerned, was in effect the Council of the Indies, composed in large part of senior judges like those on the Audiencias, which received and evaluated materials, made preliminary decisions, and passed them on to the king for an approval that was often pro forma. Never set up for speed or incisiveness, the system became ever more cumbersome as time passed. In 1714 the Bourbons created four ministries to assume many of the duties of the old royal councils of Spain. The new Ministry of Marine and the Indies partially displaced the Council of the Indies, leaving it mainly in charge of litigation and other matters concerning individuals. Under Charles III the ministry was divided in two, and later yet it disappeared in favor of a *junta de estado,* or cabinet of ministers, for the whole Spanish empire including Spain, which was organized topically by specialty rather than geographically. Thus the conciliar principle got its due after all at the highest level, but even so the ministerial system favored somewhat quicker, more uniform and incisive decisions in matters of the Indies than had been the case in Hapsburg times.

Another area with the unmistakable stamp of French influence was Bourbon policy toward the church. The French were renowned for an insistence on the relative autonomy of the national church in respect to the pope (the very doctrine being called Gallicanism), and the French crown had long since drastically reduced special ecclesiastical status or privilege. After tentative moves in this direction by the early Bourbons, a serious drive began under Charles III to achieve a new kind of royal ascendancy. In the system as it had existed until then, the crown had presided over the various ecclesiastical corporations, each largely self-ruling except in looking to the crown for confirmation of appointments and adjudication of internal disputes, whereas on the other hand the crown used the branches of the church as a counterweight to the almost equally independent organs of the secular government. Now the crown, at least in the plans of some of Charles III's most influential advisers, was to reduce ecclesiastics to the same status in civil and criminal law as any other subjects, and church property too would enjoy no special exemptions. The church would be rationalized, putting its many autonomous bodies directly under the hierarchy and the hierarchy directly under royal orders, and at the same time the crown would rely more on more responsive army officers and other secular officials for special missions, inspections, and the like.

Predictably, the regalist program for the church proved very hard to enforce. Much of it, even after having been written up as legislation, was never promulgated. Other measures took highly diluted form, and the overall effect on the position of the church relative to either society or government was absolutely minimal, though it is fair to say that the clerics themselves were more sincerely alarmed than they had been by the constant jurisdictional bickering with viceroys, governors, Audiencias, and each other which had been endemic to the system from the conquest forward.

The one truly decisive, spectacular action which the regime of Charles III carried out in church matters was the expulsion of the Jesuits from Spain and the empire in 1767, together with expropriation of all their properties, which were administered for a time by state agencies and then auctioned off. Again, the French and international precedent was an important factor. The Gallicanists in the French church considered the internationalist Jesuits their archenemy, and French secular intellectuals also fastened on them as a symbol of church obscurantism and excess (an ironical choice in the sense that the Jesuits often led the ecclesiastical sector in embodying such Enlightenment virtues as reason, scientific investigation, efficiency, and attention to practical matters). The controversy over the order became pan-European in scope. Jesuit expulsion from Portugal in 1759 and France in 1764 set off a wave in which the Spanish action was only one episode.

The expulsion did, however, make sense in purely Spanish and Spanish American terms. It was not true, as some claimed, that the Jesuits were trying to build a state within a state in such out-of-the-way places as Paraguay; they had merely established their missions in the only vacuums other orders had left them, which were located naturally enough on the far fringe. Nor were they probably guilty of any of the intrigues against the Spanish government of which some accused them; rather, the Spanish Jesuits had repeatedly served the interests of Spanish crown and nationality very well, inside the order as well as in their outward posture. On the other hand, they were indubitably the most international segment of the Spanish church, in both orientation and composition, and if the crown wanted an appropriate target for regalist action, the Jesuits were well suited. At the same time, for all their success, the Jesuits were vulnerable. In Spanish America they had a lower proportion of creole members than the mendicant orders, plus a large concentration of non-Spanish foreigners, especially on the periphery. Their late arrival and organizational idiosyncrasies set them apart from all the rest of the Spanish American church. Despite their large, well-run estates, their closeness to the highest governmental officials, and the partisans and prestige they enjoyed, they were the least rooted major ecclesiastical organization in the society of the Indies and the least popular with other ecclesiastics. With their expulsion, the crown was able to demonstrate its power and the seriousness of its intentions toward the church without undue alienation of the general population or even of most churchmen. When the more than two thousand Jesuits left Spanish America, momentary unrest was the limit of the protest, and many clerics including some bishops openly favored the move. The effects on education and mission activity were certainly felt, especially in Paraguay, but in general it seems that the loss was not as much of a jolt as one would have expected.

In somewhat the same direction as the action against the Jesuits was the crown policy in the latter eighteenth century favoring replacement of the mendicant orders by secular priests in rural parishes. From the crown's point of view, the motivation in both cases was to reduce the role of agencies felt to be too independent and unresponsive. Much more was involved than the crown, however; the policy resulted in numerous turnovers only in the better developed areas where there was a large backlog of secular priests desiring the relatively lucrative benefices of such regions, and hence social pressures favored the change. In peripheral areas the orders largely proceeded as before, no one wishing to replace them.

Another important measure of the Bourbons relating to the church came so late that it is almost a phenomenon of preindependence rather than the colonial period. Having in the later years of the eighteenth century decreed the forced sale of church properties in metropolitan Spain, where direct church ownership of land was massive, the crown in 1804 proceeded to order the same for the Indies. The situation in Spanish America, however, was quite different. Jesuit properties, already expropriated, had constituted the largest block of directly owned rural church holdings. In Mexico at least, where the matter is best studied, church entities had less rural land and more urban real estate than had been the expectation, and their greatest assets by far were in liens on lay properties and funds from donations. Individual lay patrons of chaplaincies and other pious foundations still existed, paying a percentage each year on certain of their own property so encumbered, but with the passage of time a larger amount of the assets had come to be held by ecclesiastical tribunals for pious works, which lent them out at interest, mainly for agriculture and small to medium commerce. The 1804 law of Consolidation called in directly owned properties, the capital from lay patrons, and the amounts lent out to lay individuals. The total impact on the intertwined local lay-clerical economy could have been great, but as usual full enforcement of the law was not forthcoming. Many properties and funds remained untouched, installment payments were permitted on those affected, and the whole campaign soon came to a halt with the effects of the Napoleonic wars and local uprisings (on the other hand, the 5 percent annual compensatory payments for funds expropriated also ceased). Overall, it is judged that the effect on the church, landholding, and the economy was not great, except for the loss of income by lower clergy who often subsisted mainly on chaplaincies.

The intendancy reform

In the field of civil administration the Bourbons' most striking reform was the introduction of intendants, provincial administrators with broader powers than any who had preceded them. Again the inspiration came specifically from France, where over the seventeenth and eighteenth centuries officials called intendants had come to be the principal representatives of the crown in the provinces, important in extending central power and reducing provincial autonomy. The early Bourbons, faced with the rich variety and provincial independence of Spain, soon began to introduce the intendancy system, with the help of French advisers. By midcentury the new arrangement was well established in the Peninsula. Its transfer to Spanish America began in Cuba in 1764 in the aftermath of the British occupation of Havana. After much discussion, delay, and transitional measures, the full system was introduced into the viceroyalty of La Plata in 1782 and then extended in 1784 to Peru, in 1786 to Mexico, and by 1790 to most of the major Spanish American jurisdictions.

The essence of the change was that it placed a well-salaried official with a reasonable staff and general cognizance in each important provincial city, giving it for the first time a really serious central governmental presence, somewhat comparable to what had long existed in the capitals. In a city of the importance even of, say, Puebla in Mexico or Cuzco in Peru, the only direct representative of royal administration and justice had been a *corregidor* (also sometimes called *alcalde mayor*) with an almost nominal salary, holding office for a short term, sometimes a member of a prominent local family, sometimes out of the viceroy's entourage, but in any case not a true counterweight to the local municipal council over which he presided. Rather, his function was ceremonial and judicial (serving as an intermediate court of appeal for local cases), and much of his effort ordinarily went into paying his debts and trying to improve his social-economic position. In contrast, the intendant had general charge of administration, finance, the military, and justice (though at some times and places there was doubt about the latter). He received an annual salary on the order of five thousand pesos or more, several times that of most corregidores, and though he too could be replaced at any time, the term of an intendant might extend for ten years and beyond, barring illness, disgrace, or quick promotion. And whereas corregidores were often creole, the great bulk of the intendants (there were some prominent exceptions) were peninsulars appointed directly from Spain, just as were the judges who were being appointed to Audiencias in the same years. A very large proportion of them were military officers, sometimes of very high birth, or professional administrators; few were men of the law. In fact, the intendant was very much like a little viceroy in his own area. Though nominally subordinate to a viceroy in some ways, the intendant had a separate appointment from the crown, communicated directly with the crown ministries, and in general managed to fight off viceregal dominance, as governors and captains general had in the past. Many intendants were soon immersed in the sort of disputes over jurisdiction and power which had always been characteristic of Hispanic government, on the one hand against the local muncipal councils and bishops and on the other against the viceroys and Audiencias, all of whom they in one way or another partially displaced.

Having such a relatively powerful official on the provincial scene not only caused conflict, it also made some new types of governmental activity practicable. For example, census taking was an obsession of all Enlightenment governments, but it was not until the age of the intendants that one sees truly systematic aggregated population counts in Spanish America. The intendants' presence stimulated as well as antagonized the municipal councils. But perhaps the greatest effect was on the royal treasury and tax collection. The Bourbons took many measures to try to reduce tax farming, rationalize taxes, and make the treasury a functioning unit directly responsible to the administrative branch rather than a varied collection of independent and uncoordinated officials. Especially in provincial towns, with revenue low and viceregal regulation distant, the treasury officials had often been part-time, almost honorary employees, mainly involved with their own entrepreneurial or commercial activity in the local economy. Wherever intendants were introduced, they regularly brought tax revenue to a substantially higher level; although these levels were not usually maintained, and one could in any case attribute both increase and decline to the age's general growth and war crises, yet clearly there was a difference.

A higher degree of centralization seems to have been a primary aim of the Bourbon government in establishing the intendancies. In a sense they achieved their aim, successfully establishing officials in remote places who were in close contact with the crown, more responsible to it than to viceroys or Audiencias. The other side of the coin was that provincial officials were freer of any other restraint than before. One way to achieve independence is to be subservient to an authority at a great distance, as Spaniards had understood ever since the conquest, when the leader of each successful expedition wanted to be directly under the crown and free of the governor of the area from which he came. Thus at its root the intendancy reform had a large element of decentralization, and it can be seen as a precedent for the federalism of postindependence times. Although the reform was surely a product of Enlightenment thinking in the metropolis and had a specifically French coloration, it also corresponded to basic trends and structures in Spanish America, elements to which it owed its relative success. From an internal Hispanic American point of view, the intendancy reform was a response to growth and maturation in the provincial Hispanic societies to the point where they represented wealth and consolidation comparable to that which had existed in whole viceroyalties in the sixteenth century, and hence needed, and could remunerate, a somewhat corresponding institutional structure. Few intendancies were entirely new units; many were based on the district of a Spanish city which had started as an encomendero headquarters and soon became the seat of a bishopric, such as Valladolid and Guadalajara in Mexico or Arequipa and Trujillo in Peru. Or the entity might be the district of a major, long-lasting mining center, such as Zacatecas, Guanajuato, or Potosí. In either case the unit had its own distinct center, which became the intendant's headquarters, in addition to, by this time, a well-knit hinterland. The intendancy units not only existed before attaining their late-eighteenth-century institutional capping; most of them were to continue to exist after independence as states of the new nations. In other ways, too, older patterns were in evidence. Traditional Hispanic patronage considerations largely governed the appointments of intendants. José de Gálvez, the minister of the Indies most active in bringing about the intendancy reform, may have denounced the inefficiency and corruption of locally born officials and wanted more faithful servants of the crown, but what he in fact did was to appoint numbers of people surnamed Gálvez to the new posts and related offices and, having exhausted relatives, to fall back on people from Málaga, his hometown, and other business associates and protégés.

One purpose of the intendancy reform was to try to improve the quality of local administration of the Indians in the countryside, until then in the hands of the *corregidores de indios.* The establishment of intendancies in and of itself did nothing to replace the petty rural administrators. There were only twelve intendancies in all Mexico, eight in La Plata, and eight in Peru; all Paraguay was a single intendancy. The corregimientos de indios, on the other hand, dotted the countryside and numbered in the hundreds. The solution here was to attempt to replace the corregidores de indios, who had usually been named by the viceroys or governors, with *subdelegados* in the same districts, named by and responsible to the intendants. But the success attained in the case of the intendants was not to be repeated with their subordinates. Intendants were based directly on strong, nucleated, and growing Hispanic provincial societies, and their meaningful salaries gave them a certain independence of action, whereas subdelegados were based on Indian communities which, though their power of survival is impressive, were at a low ebb as corporations, and resources did not exist to pay the numerous subdelegados truly remunerative salaries – such salaries would have quickly eaten up the additional revenues the intendants were producing. A major underlying problem with the subdelegacies was that they had little authority over, and could collect little revenue from, the Hispanic subcommunities that had infiltrated and in many cases come to dominate the Indian towns.

As mentioned earlier, the chief means by which corregidores de indios, by the late colonial period, remunerated themselves was not through salaries which ran less than the nominal pay of hacienda majordomos, but through the reparto de mercancías, or the obligatory purchase of merchandise by the Indians from the corregidor. By the 1760s this practice had aroused a storm of criticism and indeed, rightly or wrongly, many blamed highland Peru's Tupac Amaru revolt of the early 1780s on Indian resentment of it. The topic has generated an entrenched mythology, but what is known about the actual operation of repartos is very little. They are sometimes portrayed as the fobbing off of silk hose and books in Latin onto poor people who could never use such things. Yet in the Cuzco region, for example, the main items of trade were apparently mules and textiles made in highland obrajes. In general it appears that the problem was not that the Indians did not want such goods or that they absolutely lacked means to pay for them but that the corregidores charged more than comparable things would have cost in the mainstream Hispanic economy, and the general run of the goods suffered greatly in comparison with those circulating there. Unfortunate as this is, it is the more or less expectable result of market forces. The rural Indians were at the uncomfortable point of having entered the interregional market but still existing at the very edge of it, representing a far less attractive opportunity for merchants than the supply of Spanish cities and mines.

Ordinarily it was the lesser merchants who became involved with corregidores and repartos. As it happens, however, the setup is best studied for one of the few areas where the rural Indian economy produced an item of great value in late-eighteenth-century export commerce and hence attracted the participation of some of the largest merchants along with the small. The area was Mexico's Oaxaca region (outside the central valleys), the product cochineal. Though the case is unusual in a way, perhaps it can illustrate some general procedures and at the same time emphasize how closely practices were adjusted to each idiosyncratic milieu. In Oaxaca, then, a corregidor de indios would make an agreement with a merchant, often of Mexico City, in such a way that the merchant would be responsible for paying the royal treasury the revenues the corregidor owed the crown; he also paid the corregidor's other debts and supplied the goods which went to the Indians – mules, oxen, lines of credit on general merchandise. In return he received a large portion of the cochineal in which the Indians paid their debts (as well as their tributes). Despite the fact that cochineal was Mexico's second most valuable export after silver, the industry was originally indigenous and moreover its cactus and insect culture did not occupy the best lands, so that here a major export industry remained largely Indian at the productive base, and the corregidor-merchant alliance served to tap it. Since the merchant invested so much in these ventures, he often reserved the right to appoint as the corregidor's chief lieutenant a junior partner of his own, who was the true operator of the corregimiento. The merchant and his representative might also run a general store in the locality, which would have the status of a near monopoly.

Since the elimination of repartos in the hope of obtaining a freer local commerce, with better results for both Indians and Spaniards, was the main thrust of the creation of subdelegacies, abolition of the practice was a prominent part of the enabling legislation. Less prominent was mention of any other form of remuneration that would replace repartos as the administrators' main source of income. The right to retain a small percentage of the tribute collected was the only gesture toward a salary for the subdelegados. The failure – actually the inability – to provide a minimally adequate salary had several results, all of them counter to the intentions of the reform. On the one hand, it became difficult to attract qualified candidates, and the merchants who had guaranteed the administrators were slower to come forth, leaving some posts unoccupied for a time. In some places rural commercial activity slacked off, because merchants felt that such ventures were not worth the risk without guaranteed debt collection and monopoly concessions. Even in Oaxaca, where free trade in the Indian countryside should have worked if it was going to work anywhere, cochineal production fell off in the time of the subdelegados (admittedly, there were many other factors contributing to the decline). On the other hand, many of those involved at all levels quickly became convinced that there was no alternative to repartos if there was to continue to be any Spanish administration among rural Indians at all. Many subdelegados, in both Peru and Mexico, returned to the practices of the prereform era, sometimes surreptitiously, sometimes with the tacit approval of superiors. Among high-level policy makers too there was soon a party openly favoring the revival of repartos; with viceroys and ministers on their side and highly contradictory legislation continuing to appear, the subdelegados were increasingly indistinguishable from their predecessors, the corregidores de indios. Like them, they were mainly creoles or peninsulars seeking permanent local connections. Though it goes quite unnoticed, under the subdelegados the already existing trend to devote ever more attention to the affairs of the rural Hispanics went on unabated.

The creation of a military

The sixteenth-century conquest, as we saw much earlier, was not the work of a professional or standing military. In the aftermath of conquest there arose what were called "soldiers," but these still lacked a steady connection to a permanent organization. Rather, they were candidates for expeditions into still unconquered territory, and the very name "soldier" came to mean, especially in South America, neither more nor less than Hispanic transient or vagrant. Through the whole mature colonial period, Spanish America in general had no need for a well-developed military organization. The central areas were relatively pacific except for intermittent localized disturbances, and although wealthy and attractive, they were beyond the effective reach of other European powers. Such military development as occurred was concentrated in the few areas of need and vulnerability. One area requiring a military presence was at the frontier of Hispanic society and nonsedentary Indians, where, as we saw in Chapter 8, presidios and a paid soldiery were standard phenomena (though the soldiers were still first cousins of the marginalized transients of the immediate postconquest period); northern Mexico and southern Chile are the prime examples. A second requirement was maritime defense, for if the non-Spanish Europeans could not take Mexico and Peru, they could prey on the sea-lanes and raid ports on the trunk lines, hoping for bonanzas of silver. The strongest military organization relating to the Indies in the sixteenth and seventeenth centuries was that of the fleet convoys, but these hardly pertained to Spanish America proper. Included in the system, however, were fortifications and garrisons at strategic ports such as Veracruz, Havana, and Cartagena. Beyond ports and frontiers there were viceregal guards, more gentlemen, courtiers, and errand runners than soldiers, and a militia which was almost entirely fictional beyond its function of giving high-sounding military titles to certain merchants or miners who felt the need of such social bolstering and were willing to pay for it.

In the eighteenth century all this began to change, with the pace accelerating, as we have by now come to expect, in the latter part. The threat became greater than before, and there was more to defend, for former fringes now had gained value to both Spaniards and outsiders. Not all the measures taken were strictly military. The new civil jurisdictions established in newly flourishing areas, first among them the Plata viceroyalty, were partially motivated, as we have seen, by defense considerations. In less settled areas, where the economic potential was insufficient to attract a Hispanic population but foreign marauders were beginning to show interest, new funds and impetus went into combined campaigns of missions, presidios, and modest new civil foundations, all partially subsidized from central-area royal treasuries. An important locus of such activity was the far north of Mexico, set on a quasi-military footing as the "Internal Provinces." The last decades of the eighteenth century and the nineteenth up to independence were the great age of the Upper California missions, established by the Franciscans after the Jesuits had been expelled, with a scattering of presidios among them and, at first, an extremely scanty and dispersed Hispanic population.

In strictly military matters (as in some others) the shocking British occupation of Havana in 1762–64 served as the catalyst. The royal government set about establishing a truly effective military organization, in the style of late eighteenth-century Europe, for all of the main Spanish possessions in America. Since Spain could not send vast armies, a core of regular army units, manned at first largely with peninsular Spaniards, was established, as well as a more numerous militia, more disciplined and better outfitted than in earlier times, recruited from the local population and trained and stiffened by the regulars. In the late colonial period the two great old viceroyalties each had a standing army on the order of two thousand to six thousand men and a supposedly active militia of twenty thousand and upward, and units of the same type, though smaller, existed in all the Hispanic American jurisdictions.

The actual number of militiamen varied greatly. Despite the acquisition of weapons and uniforms and the duty of drilling regularly, some units remained determinedly fictional, especially beneath the officer's level. Just before independence, the Peruvian militia totaled, on paper, more than seventy thousand, of which figure some knowledgable officials estimated that only a third or less could ever be mobilized. Aside from the questionable status of units at any given time, general policy toward the militia underwent considerable evolution. No sooner did the Bourbon government get its new militia established than it began to have second thoughts. One consideration was the apparent near uselessness of many units. Another was that strong reliance on locals went against the exactly contemporaneous Bourbon drive to reduce creole influence. The peninsular army officers who arrived to carry out the reorganization, and those who succeeded them, were surely among the most paranoic, culturally restricted, and ethnocentric lot ever to reach Spanish American shores. They held the paradoxical position that the locals were both totally ineffective and capable of the most dangerous revolts. At any rate, policy veered toward deemphasizing the militia; one viceroy of Mexico came close to dismantling it there. But such steps could not be carried out constantly because the men and funds for greatly increased regular units were not available. And the regular units themselves, rather than being peninsular bastions, moved with the years from peninsular majorities to a mere token peninsular presence except in the officer corps.

By now, unlike the earlier centuries, one can speak of a clear-cut distinction between officers and enlisted men. The peninsular officers were often career professionals from quite high-ranking Spanish families, and creole officers came from roughly comparable strata, though not as many of them were committed to a lifetime military career. Before long, though peninsulars retained dominance of the senior ranks, creoles came to be well represented among the officers of the regular units, in some times and places a minority, in others about half, and in others an actual majority. In the militia a large majority of the officers were creole, although peninsular merchants too continued a tradition of participation. Depending on local conditions, the military would appeal more to locally prominent families in one place, less in another. Although the military hardly became an avenue comparable in importance to the church, it was used by the great families and families seeking to rise in roughly the same way that the church or the law was used.

Enlisted men were another matter; except for some elite units, they were humble people, not usually career men but often forced into service by various means, including the emptying of jails. As such, they were highly prone to desertion. Remarkably, they were practically all members of the Spanish world – poor Spaniards (some peninsular, many creole), mestizos, mulattoes, members of all the castas, but *not* Indians. They were uniformly from the strata that provided society's low-level supervisors, petty tradesmen, artisans, and skilled permanent workers. Indians were literally not eligible for military service even in the militia, and this recruitment precept was not one of the many so frequently violated but is borne out in detailed company rosters in region after region. Indians were excluded even from military censuses. It is true that there were special militia units of sedentary Indians at frontiers bordering hostile nonsedentary Indians, a new form of a traditional function that had existed almost since the conquest period. And in Peru, though Indians there too were ineligible for the militia, numerous auxiliary companies of Indians, whose status is as yet not well understood, were formed in times of emergency. If in general the Indian element was negligible, the mulatto and Black element was prominent; in coastal regions especially, there were whole pardo companies, often with pardo officers up to captain rank. The army, then, was an instrument of Hispanic society, with much the same constituent elements and manner of operation as other Hispanic organizations such as haciendas, mines, or obrajes (minus any temporary Indian workers). Persons at each level cooperated with their immediate superiors not out of loyalty to an imperial government or any Spanish American patriotism but because they were obeying the same kinds of people who ordinarily gave them instructions and rewards in their daily doings outside the military – in the case of the militia, often literally the same people. As to emotional motivation, there was at most a feeling of identification with the home municipality and environs.

Bourbon policy advocated the maximum use of career army officers in administrative office at the expense of lawyers and clerics. We have seen that most of the intendants were career army men, as were most of the late-period viceroys. The rationale of the policy was largely that army men and the army were likely to carry out orders from the imperial center more quickly, energetically, and without question. Yet following the age-old Hispanic pattern, the army did not fail to become a corporation or set of corporations in its own right, competing with the older ones in the traditional way and also tied to the others as in the traditional system through familial and other bonds. That such corporatism was exactly counter to the whole thrust of the Bourbon reforms did not hinder its rise. The royal government even had to grant the military corporate privileges of the usual kind, the *fuero militar* through which military personnel including militiamen were exempted from other jurisdictions and tried in their own courts when accused of a crime. Having made these concessions, the crown immediately issued new restrictions, especially among the militia. In truth, the special status did not amount to a great deal anyway, since this weak, new jurisdiction often lost out to older, stronger ones on matters of importance, and the apparent separateness was half canceled by the multiple interlockings of the society and economy.

All in all, the military effort seems to have had the desired effect of deterring major attacks by foreign European powers, and the one that the English aimed at Buenos Aires just before independence was successfully repelled. Defense was, however, exceedingly expensive. Military expenditures became the largest item in the viceregal budgets; over and above the millions of pesos spent on defense in the old central areas, vast subsidies went to the periphery as well. The voracious Bourbon appetite for revenues, at the root of so many of the general reforms, was brought on above all by the need to increase military expenditures against a greatly increased foreign threat. On the other hand, the measures taken were similar to those in the air all over Europe at a time when professional standing armies of the type to be characteristic of the following centuries were first being created. The story of the Bourbon military is a particularly good example of the interaction of all the major late colonial developments. The early Industrial Revolution allowed the northern European nations to become formidable economic and naval powers with the ability and desire to threaten the Spanish Indies; the internal growth of the Indies heightened that desirability yet more. The Bourbons' establishment of a full-scale military, if principally motivated by the foreign threat, was also part of their general thrust in the direction of better controlling and de-creolizing the Indies internally. Yet the population trends of the late colonial period blunted the Bourbon drive and put an indelible local stamp on the Spanish American military.

Economic reforms and their implications

In the interrelated set of late Bourbon reforms, the economic element was pervasive. If getting more revenue for defense was a crucial theme, making the economy grow so that it would produce more revenue was an even more basic aspiration of the government. To encourage local economic growth was one of the prime instructions given the intendants and also part of the rationale for creating the office in the first place. We have seen that the Bourbons used tax reductions, lower mercury prices, the reorganization of financing with more state participation, and technical aid in the attempt to encourage the silver mining industry, being apparently successful in some of these endeavors, unsuccessful in others, but always with the aim of increasing revenue. Just as with the mining industry, so more generally the Bourbons tried a wide variety of measures. Some implied the more active intervention of the state in the economy. State monopolies were expanded from silver mining's mercury to gunpowder, rum, and tobacco processing. The latter especially became a far-flung enterprise, responsible for erecting some of the finest-looking buildings in the empire as its factories, though many have judged that direct governmental operation held back what would otherwise have been an even more thriving export business.

As with mining, there was an element of attempt to stimulate the economy in the Bourbons' tax policies in general. The government involved itself more directly in collection, and at the same time it reduced and simplified taxes, especially customs. In part, the intention was to cut into the motivation of Spanish Americans to avoid taxes through contraband dealings, but there was also the simple hope that overall volume would increase if production and commerce were taxed less and that receipts would go up despite smaller percentages of yield. This in fact happened in the final decades of the eighteenth century in many geographical areas and branches of the economy of the Indies, although one could argue forever over whether or not Bourbon tax policy had anything to do with it.

The largest item in the Bourbon economic reforms was just the opposite of more active state intervention: the gradual dismantling of the system of convoyed fleets, set trade routes, and a few designated ports in favor of more flexible, wide-open trade and navigation across the entire Spanish empire, Spain itself as well as the American possessions. The original system had been well adapted to the situation of the sixteenth century and much of the seventeenth, when the Indies were characterized by a strong distinction between a few rich central areas with all the assets of interest to international trade and many peripheral areas which were not realistic participants in transatlantic commerce either as producers or consumers but rather were oriented toward the Spanish American center. For defense, the routes were optimal. The primary threat was by individual raiders and pirates who could bag loners or stragglers but were helpless against large fleets of armed merchantmen convoyed by warships. Notwithstanding the one great disaster against the Dutch in the early seventeenth century, the fleets in their time were generally sufficient to face any force likely to be sent against them, and above all, they were an effective deterrent. Despite unwieldiness, inevitable irregularities caused by organizational difficulties, expense, and wartime emergencies, the fleets seemed worth it overall.

As we have seen, these things were changing with time, and by the later eighteenth century conditions were almost diametrically opposed to those of the sixteenth century. First, technological, demographic, and economic growth in northern Europe had resulted in, among other things, the overwhelming naval superiority of the northern powers, especially of Britain; that Spain made some serious efforts to improve its navy in the course of the eighteenth century could not alter that basic fact. Pirates and privateers were fading in importance, and the British navy could easily have taken the most formidable fleet eighteenth-century Spain could possibly have assembled. Individually licensed ships were now a better defense gamble than a fleet whenever hostilities with Britain or France were impending, and, in fact, a series of multinational conflicts affecting Spain stretched from the time of the Bourbons' ascent to the throne all the way to Spanish American independence. Secondly, the destination of people and goods going to the Indies was no longer so exclusively Mexico City and Lima; now former fringes like Venezuela and the Plata region were beginning an upswing, and transitional areas such as Guatemala and New Granada also loomed larger than formerly. Thirdly, by about 1700 the larger merchantmen could round Cape Horn with considerable security and were capacious and swift enough to carry substantial cargo as well as supplies for the crew.

As a result, the fleet system collapsed. Generally speaking, across the century there were no fleets in times of war or threat of war. Their place was taken by individually licensed Spanish ships and even ships of friendly and neutral nations. After a first spell of war, during which there were no sailings, the fleets were partially reinstituted in the period after 1715, but a new interruption came by 1740. After that time the fleet to Panama, with goods for Peru, never revived; by midcentury Panama was in a deep depression, to last far into the national period, and it lost the Audiencia that had been based there. The Mexico fleet did revive from the 1750s forward, but never with regularity. Nor did the creation of the viceroyalty of La Plata lead to a new fleet in that direction, nor was the traffic around the Horn organized in fleets. Finally in 1789, the government abandoned the fleets even for Mexico.

Hand in hand with the last phases of the fleet system's demise went the most famous of the late Bourbon economic reforms, *comercio libre*, "free trade" within the empire. Although foreign nationals were not included, individual Spanish ships were allowed to go from any Spanish or Spanish American port to any other without necessity of special license. As with the fleet system, the change occurred gradually. In the course of the mature colonial period the single Spanish port through which all the Indies trade passed, Seville, had switched much of its actual activity to nearby Cádiz because the latter was closer to the seaside, an ever more important factor as larger ships were unable to mount the Guadalquivir River to Seville itself. By the early eighteenth century Cádiz had primacy, but this change was of little moment; a single Seville-Cádiz mercantile community still handled all trade with Spanish America. In the Indies only Veracruz and Portobello (Panama), with ancillary ports in the Caribbean such as Havana and Cartagena, were fully authorized destinations of ships in transatlantic trade. With the establishment of the Caracas Company, trade to Venezuela became somewhat permissible and regularized, and the same was gradually happening with trade to Buenos Aires even prior to the establishment of the viceroyalty.

Extensions of trade and navigation in the first half of the eighteenth century were ad hoc concessions to specific local conditions. Actual introduction of free trade on principle began, as did so much else in the way of reform, in Cuba immediately after the English occupation. Since the area had already been lost once and seemed of no special value, perhaps the crown felt that there was nothing more to lose. In 1765 trade was opened up between Cuba (along with some other Spanish Caribbean island ports) and Spain; on the Spanish side not only Cádiz but eight other ports could participate. Cuba's volume of trade increased vastly, and the experiment seemed successful. In following years the same arrangements were permitted in some other peripheral American ports; in 1778 comercio libre was extended to thirteen ports in Spain and twenty-two in the Indies. Only Venezuela and Mexico were excepted, in the former case apparently because of the vestiges of the Caracas Company and in the latter because New Spain's trade was by far the most valuable of any region's, nothing to tamper with lightly. But for New Spain too Spanish ports other than Cádiz gradually received shipping allotments, and in 1789 free trade became uniform for all Spanish American possessions.

Free trade as an administrative reform has often been given almost the entire credit for the great general late colonial upswing in Spanish America. But what would "free trade" have accomplished in 1650, 1700, or 1730? It was the gathering force of changes in European technology and markets from the 1750s forward and the simultaneous cumulative internal growth in the Indies that made free trade viable and determined its chronology. The measure surely was timely and made good sense on both sides of the Atlantic, giving free scope not only to the former fringe areas of the Indies but to eastern and northern Spain, which were now leading the Spanish economy. In the time between 1778 and 1796, when major new wars interrupted colonial trade, the value of exports from Spain to the Indies increased fourfold. Moreover, Spain's share of trade seemed to increase; by the official figures, exports of Spanish origin increased from under 40 percent in 1778 to more than 60 percent in

1794. Even under free trade, however, Cádiz did not crumble but kept 76 percent of the total exports over the period 1778–96. One may also ask whether the rise in volume and increased exportation from the northeast of Spain would not have been much the same even if Cádiz had not lost its status as the exclusive port.

As to effects on the society and economy of the Indies, it is said that with more goods available, prices fell. Free trade may have reduced contraband trading with foreigners in peacetime, though it surely never eliminated it. In any case, commerce on the old Spanish American periphery and in some of the provinces of the old center not only flourished but gained greater independence of the formerly dominant capitals of Mexico City and Lima. In the years 1793 to 1795 new Consulados were sanctioned and organized in several cities other than the original two, namely in Caracas, Guatemala City, Buenos Aires, Havana, Cartagena, Santiago de Chile, and even in two towns of Mexico proper, Veracruz and Guadalajara. Nor were these purely institutional events; each foundation represented a newly mature independent mercantile community chary of Mexico City and Lima. In Mexico the great wholesale merchants of the capital, the *almaceneros* ("warehouse men"), could no longer buy up the entirety of the goods imported, now that the volume had increased so markedly; instead of being the sole distributors to merchants of the provinces, they had to stand by and see Veracruz merchants and others both importing directly from Spain and redistributing to the rest of the country. But what the merchants of the new Spanish American Consulados gained in independence from the older ones, they often lost in increased dependence on Spain. Spanish shippers now supplied goods on credit. In the case of Buenos Aires and Veracruz, some locally based merchants were deeply in debt to their Spanish-based counterparts, and others were their actual factors and junior partners. Thus something of the old structure of metropolitan-based transatlantic companies, so characteristic of the sixteenth century, revived in a different form at the end of the colonial period.

We must not think, however, that the mercantile communities of Mexico City and Lima faded away under the onslaught. The almaceneros of Mexico City continued to dominate the commerce of the capital, by far the country's principal market even then, and still maintained junior partners and dependent client firms in all parts of the country, as well as keeping up their pattern of diversified investment in agriculture and mining. And even the merchants of Lima survived quite handsomely, despite their protestations of having been utterly ruined by the creation of the Plata viceroyalty. Spanish exports to Peru in the late eighteenth century were regularly far larger than those to the Plata region. Thus, despite the elaborate machinery established to channel silver from, and goods to, Upper Peru through Buenos Aires and despite the apparent advantages of that route in terms of eighteenth-century conditions, Lima merchants must somehow have remained important suppliers and financiers for the Upper Peruvian mining industry, and they must have thereby reaped a good share of the silver, in addition to benefiting from the newly developed mines in Peru proper. Although the established commercial centers lost their exclusive status, they seem to have maintained a certain dominance, and such diminution as occurred seems to have been more in percentile terms than in absolute amount.

Much the same may yet prove to be true of the effect on local manufactures. Again, the loud public complaints of local producers have given a picture of the ruination of obrajes and artisan shops, unable to survive in a market flooded with cheap, high-quality European goods. It is certainly true that the structure of the situation changed to the disadvantage of local production to the extent that both northern Europe and Spain itself were now mass-producing and sending to the Indies goods, above all textiles, which were by no means luxury items but competed for the lower part of the local Hispanic market, the traditional domain of local producers. Real competition between metropolitan and colonial producers now came into existence for the first time, and it was also at this time that the metropolitan government began to manifest a serious classical mercantilism, issuing taxes and regulations designed to discourage those manufactures in the Indies which would cut into the markets of items manufactured in Spain. Yet, as always, enforcement and compliance were spotty, and if there were new factors hurting the locals, there were also new factors helping them. The absolute growth of the Spanish American population was greatly in their favor, and even more so was the nature of that growth, heavily weighted toward the racially mixed and humble Hispanics – the traditional primary consumers of the products of local Spanish enterprise. The constant interruptions of transatlantic trade by war favored the locals again. If we look at one of the most important local industries of the Spanish Indies, the cotton textile obrajes of Puebla, we find that from a modest start in the late seventeenth century they grew to over 1,100 looms in 1793 and nearly 1,200 in 1804. From 1785 to 1805 the volume of Puebla textiles sent to Mexico City generally increased, almost equaling the total volume of European textiles entering the Mexican capital during that time. Effects must have varied with the local conditions. If the market was at seaside and the local producers in the interior, as with Buenos Aires and the Córdoba-Tucumán region, doubtless the locals could suffer greatly.

Scholars often speculate on whether the Bourbon reforms were a success or a failure. Since independence followed so close on their heels, it is legitimate to see them as in some sense a resounding failure. They did come together with a time of great economic growth and increased revenues, but there are many other and more basic explanations for that result than the reforms per se. Success or failure, the Bourbon reforms were largely reactive, a part of the situation rather than its primary cause. They recognized important changes that had taken place in both Europe and America, in techniques, markets, and populations, and they served as a transition toward the yet fuller recognition of those factors that would occur as the national period began.

10

Brazil in the age of gold and absolutism

We have just seen that in Spanish America a readily discernible "late colonial period" stretched from about 1760 to independence, a time marked by strong upswings and sharp reorientations in a great many dimensions. Does Brazil show a close parallel, as we would expect in view of the many cross-regional and cross-national affinities previously described? In point of fact, the parallels are not extremely close. One major boom, accompanied by important demographic and jurisdictional shifts, did indeed occur in Brazil, but it took place in the first half of the eighteenth century, not the second. Further, it had nothing to do with new European demands for bulk products but was, instead, a result of the late development of mining for precious metals (in this case gold), the economic mainstay in Spanish America ever since the conquest period. It is true that in the later eighteenth century, starting perhaps a few years earlier than in Spanish America, Brazil underwent a series of organizational reforms quite comparable in nature and even in scope to the reforms of the late Bourbons, but in the Brazilian case the measures failed to coincide so closely with economic growth; rather, a decided slump occurred when gold production proved nearly as ephemeral in Brazil as it had in most of Spanish America. Nor was there any marked growth in agricultural exports until the last few years of the century. In the seventeenth century Brazil's sugar had already led the trend toward eastern seaboard bulk export to Europe. In the late eighteenth, sugar production was precisely the activity which was expanding so astronomically on the French and English Caribbean islands, so that Brazil's competing industry was hard put to maintain itself at all, much less grow, until the Haitian revolution wrecked French production in the 1790s. It took time for alternative tropical exports, of which coffee was to be the greatest, to get started and find a market; the coffee industry, as in other countries, was not to come to maturity until far into the nineteenth century.

Nevertheless, if we construe the Brazilian late colonial period as the time from the discovery of gold in the interior around 1695 until the arrival of the Portuguese court, fleeing Napoleon's armies, in 1808, then we can say that during this time Brazil experienced great territorial and demographic expansion and a considerable shift in its center of balance, not only in social and economic terms but in the moving of the capital from Bahia to Rio de Janeiro. Moreover, although Brazilian economic growth was slow in the second half of the eighteenth century, the country was growing in importance within the far-flung Lusitanian world, encompassing Portugal, Africa, the Far East, and America. By 1750 it was clear that Brazil had become the keystone of the Portuguese empire, and as such it figured most prominently in Portugal's attempt to ensure its survival, whether against European rivals like Spain or in relation to allies like England. Ironically, Brazil's increasing importance in the Portuguese colonial equation was matched by a growing impulse toward absolutism and centralism on the part of the crown, first under João V (1705–50) and then under José I (1750–77) and his minister, the Marquis of Pombal, placing Brazil and Portugal on the road to conflict, although few realized it at the time.

Minas Gerais

Undoubtedly the most significant event in eighteenth-century Brazil was the discovery of mineral wealth in the interior (see Map 15). Expeditions from São Paulo had traversed the south-central interior throughout the seventeenth century, and although some gold had been found, it was not until 1693–5 that the Paulistas made a number of major strikes. Paulista attempts to keep these finds a secret and exclusively theirs soon failed, and once the word was out a gold rush was on. "From cities, towns, plantations, and backwoods of Brazil go whites, browns, and blacks" wrote one observer as a flood of gold seekers set out from the coast for the mine fields. They were soon joined by an annual tide of some four thousand immigrants from Portugal; most of them were young bachelors from the overcrowded northern province of Minho, a fact that was to have a profound impact on the architectural, religious, and social development of the mining zone. This great tide of men (the number of women immigrants was small), although of all ranks and conditions, was heavily weighted toward peasants and others of lower status. The mining region could be reached by a number of routes. At first the most popular route was from São Paulo along the Paraíba River, a journey of two months. An easier but longer trip could be made

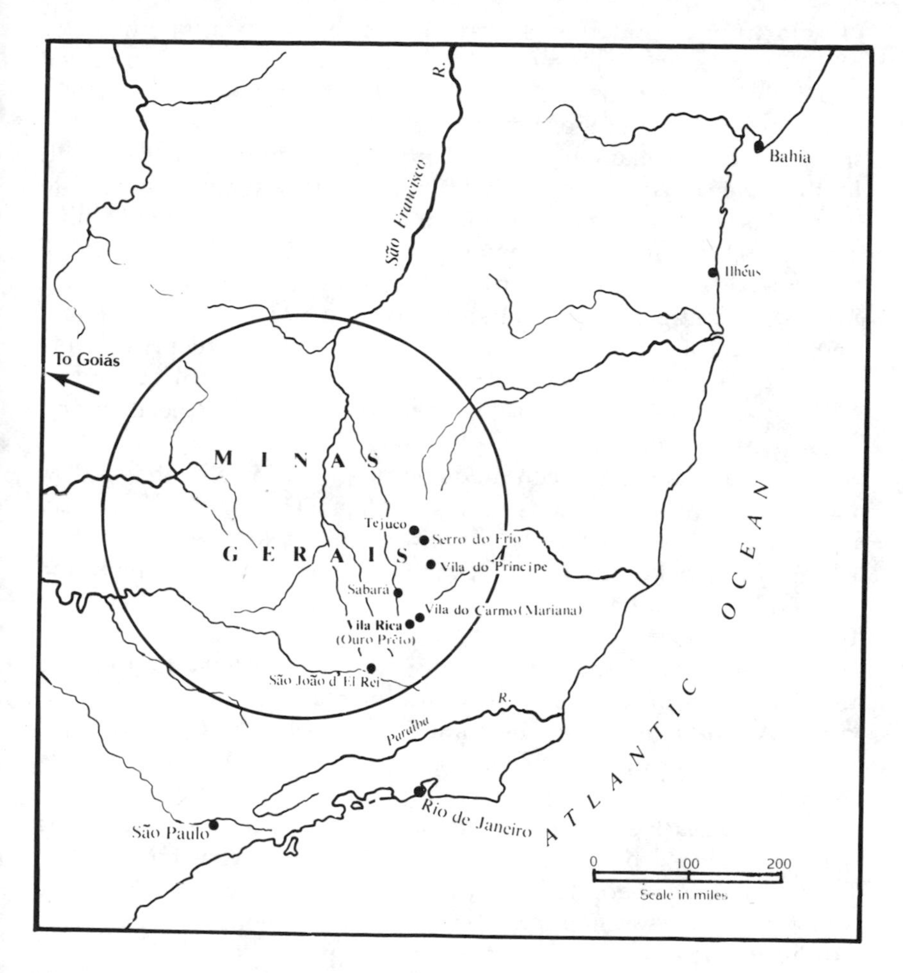

Map 15. The Minas Gerais gold mining region.

from Bahia up the São Francisco River. Eventually, a road was opened from the coast at Rio de Janeiro over the mountains; this difficult but shorter route became the main access to the mines and the chief direction of gold export. Rio de Janeiro's rise to predominance on the Brazilian coast was largely the result of its proximity to the mines.

The rapid movement of such large numbers of people created problems for the country and the crown. In order to prevent the ruin of export agriculture on the coast and to control the smuggling of gold from the interior, a system of passports, checkpoints, and other controls was imposed, but to little effect. The rush continued and little could stem it. As in the California rush of 1849, it was often those who sold the shovels or the bread and cheese who made the fortunes, for many miners became rich and then poor overnight. In the haste to find the gold, little attention was given at first to foodstuffs and other necessities, and famines resulted. Eventually, after 1720, mixed farming developed alongside mining because of the expense of importing food. A joke of the time was that the king needed all that gold in taxes because he had no farm of his own and had to buy his food. Everything was expensive, and prices were measured in drams of gold. A coat sold for 12, a cheese for 2, and an ox for 100. The miners paid dearly for the things they needed, and what they needed most of all was slaves.

The gold strikes had been made in a region sparsely inhabited by mobile and hostile Indians. Thus, unlike Peru, where sedentary peoples could be mobilized through the mita system of draft rotary labor, in this major mining district the Portuguese turned instead to African slavery, the form of labor that had already characterized Brazil for two centuries and was typical of gold mining in Spanish America as well. Black slaves went with their masters into the gold mining region or were sold from the plantations and towns of the coast. As the demand in the mines increased, a brisk direct trade quickly developed, sometimes causing labor shortages in other regions and driving up the price of slaves throughout the colony. Having had no Black slaves at all in 1693, by 1720 Minas was receiving some 5,000 to 6,000 a year, and the total was well over 35,000. In truth there were two great population movements into the mining zones: a voluntary European immigration from the coast and especially from northern Portugal and a forced Black immigration from the coast and Africa, mostly from the Bight of Benin (modern Ghana and Nigeria). By 1775 Minas Gerais had 300,000 inhabitants, or 20 percent of the population of Brazil, half of them slaves. The gold strikes had changed the economic and demographic configurations of Brazil.

Turbulence was typical of the early phase of a mining region, and it took a decade and a civil war before some sort of order could be imposed on Minas. The population was mobile and volatile, towns were little more than groups of miners' shacks, and there was virtually no effective governmental authority. In this raucous atmosphere it was inevitable that grievances would be settled by resort to force. The Paulistas, although outnumbered, still considered the whole region to be their domain, and they lorded it over the "tenderfeet" (*pes-rapados* or *emboabas*) from Portugal, even calling them *vos*, a form of address used by masters to their slaves. A civil war was not long in coming. In this War of the Emboabas (1708–9) the Portuguese immigrants and their allies from the northeastern captaincies finally ended the pretensions of the Paulistas. Casualties were not many but feelings ran deep. In the end, the crown took advantage of its position as a mediator to bring peace and impose a bureaucratic and administrative structure.

The apparent defeat of the Paulistas may have had other results as well. Intrepid woodsmen and daring prospectors, the Paulistas were actually only itinerant miners; their techniques were crude and their tendency was to move on to the next stream as soon as the washings began to play out. Minas Gerais could have become another flash in the pan like early Hispaniola. But in Minas Gerais the heavy secondary wave of Portuguese immigration, the imposition of royal government, the use of more advanced methods of gold extraction, and the relative proximity to the coast meant that this region would develop a permanency and take on the social and cultural patterns of the central areas of colonial society.

The Paulistas were never eliminated from Minas Gerais, but their power was gone. Many turned instead to lands farther westward, making gold strikes at Cuiabá (1718) in Goiás and at Vila Bela (1734) in Mato Grosso; these, more like the other gold-mining fringes, flourished briefly and then declined, hampered by the necessity of a seven-month canoe trip through hostile Indians and difficult terrain as the only means of communication with the coast. Although the emboabas and their allies seemed to have gained the upper hand, the real victor was the colonial state. Town councils were created at Riberão do Carmo (present-day Mariana), Vila Rica do Ouro Preto, and Sabará. Four *comarcas*, or administrative divisions, were established, each with its royal officials, and by 1720 Minas Gerais was a separate and tightly controlled captaincy.

The government's primary concern was the collection of the royal fifth (*quinto*) of all the gold produced; as in Spanish territories, the crown was entitled to this tax because it retained all subsoil rights and in theory simply allowed private individuals to mine on its behalf. Royal officials controlled the distribution of claims under a complex system (formulated in 1702 as a new mining code) in which the size of claims depended on the number of slaves a miner owned. From the point of view of crown revenues, the real difficulty lay in the geography of the mining region and the type of mining done. In Minas Gerais and the western captaincies, as in Spanish New Granada, the mines were usually hundreds of miles from the nearest government officers, isolated and difficult to control. Gold mining in Brazil consisted primarily of panning for alluvial gold in streams by prospectors equipped with only a pan and shovel or using only a few slaves. More complicated sluices and excavations (*catas*) were less common, and there was very little use of the more permanent, and thus more easily controlled, pit and gallery mining. Under these conditions, miners found many ways to avoid taxes, and contraband was a chronic problem.

Throughout the eighteenth century the crown tried some dozen different methods of taxing gold production. The first law, requiring miners to bring their gold to smelting houses on the coast, was simply impossible to enforce. In 1710 a royal plan to tax each slave in the mining zone was submitted to representatives of the town councils of the mining region. This junta and those that followed were as close as Brazil ever came to an estates general, and their convocation was a clear indication of the lack of royal power at this date. Little wonder that the plan was rejected and an alternate and less onerous system was negotiated. By 1720 the crown felt secure enough to establish smelting houses in the four principal towns of the captaincy, bringing on a violent tax revolt in Ouro Preto, which was, however, forcefully suppressed by the Count of Assumar, the royal governor. Further adjustments were made in the 1720s by negotiation between royal officials and the miners, but nothing seemed to produce the required amounts of revenue. The inhabitants of Minas were considered to be restive and independent-minded, and many royal officials felt that nothing could make them pay the proper amount. In 1735 a direct head tax on each slave in the mines was proclaimed, plus a 5 percent tax on all merchant income. A representative junta was again called to discuss the measure, and although they at first rejected it, enough pressure was finally brought to bring about acceptance. The convocation of a junta had been simply a way of masking royal intervention. By the 1730s the crown's control of Minas Gerais was firm and the outcome was inevitable. Royal administrators like Martinho de Mendonça, who had been sent to institute the head tax, felt that the loyalty of the Mineiros was questionable and that any concession was a risk. As he put it: "When the sovereign is certain that his will is useful to the people, consultation with them is a mere formality . . . furthermore, no government, no matter how dependent it may be on the vote and consent of the people, cedes the right to vote on public matters to its colonies and conquests."

This increasingly stringent and restrictive governmental attitude was even more apparent in the diamond mining zone. Diamonds had been discovered in the Serro do Frio comarca in the 1720s. Since the value of the jewels was so vulnerable to oversupply, the crown tried to limit production, but because of the ease with which diamonds could be hidden and smuggled, ever stronger measures were needed. In 1734 a diamond district was demarcated under the control of an intendant, and all mining or prospecting in it was prohibited except under the monopoly license of the crown. Two companies of Portuguese dragoons were formed to patrol the area and arrest illegal prospectors; at one point all free Blacks and mulattoes were expelled from the district because of their supposed illegal activities. Although the royal contract system never eliminated all the contraband activity by prospectors and escaped slaves, it did demonstrate the extremes to which the Portuguese crown would go.

The behavior of the Portuguese government in connection with the Brazilian gold and diamond mining district belies the false comparison that has sometimes been made between the supposedly activist policy of Spain in its American colonies and the seeming laxity of the Portuguese crown in Brazil. Such comparisons have usually been made by persons whose perspective is Spanish American; without considering the wide variations and differing pace of developments within Spanish America itself, they always tend to see Mexico or Peru as the model and Brazil as somehow pathological. Although the Portuguese crown did play a less active role in the comparatively decentralized economy of the agricultural regions, the same is true of the Spanish royal government. With the discovery of gold and diamonds, however, Lisbon demonstrated that it could be as active, forceful, and sometimes callous as Madrid. Governors like the Count of Assumar or Gomes Freire de Andrada were intelligent and energetic administrators, every bit the match of any Spanish counterparts. The major Brazilian mining region eventually drew the viceregal capital to it and started the move toward a thicker institutional web in all respects, just as had happened in Peru and Mexico in the sixteenth century. As we have emphasized elsewhere, the differences in Iberian colonial government were not so much due to national character as to the nature of the local environment, indigenous population, and economic potential. When there was large-scale mineral wealth to be had, Spain and Portugal responded in a similar fashion.

The social and economic history of Minas Gerais can best be understood against the background of the rise and fall of gold produc-

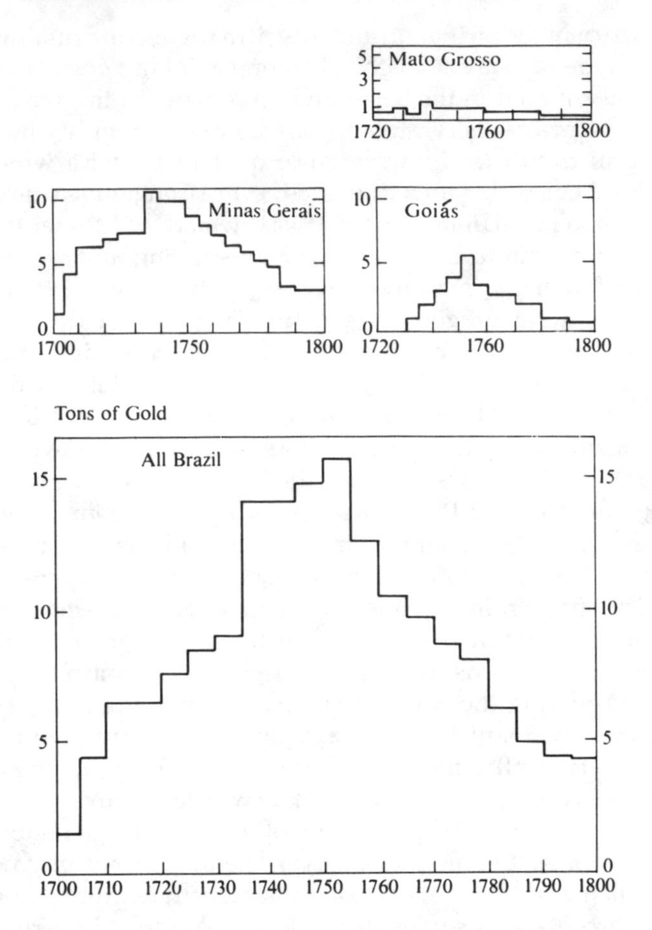

Figure 19. Brazilian gold production in the eighteenth century. (*Source:* Virgilio Noya Pinto, *O ouro brasileiro e o comércio anglo-português* [São Paulo, 1972], p. 122.)

tion. As Figure 19 demonstrates, gold production grew rapidly, reaching more than ten tons annually in the decade of the 1730s and more than fifteen tons in the 1750s. Then after 1760 production began to decline sharply. As it did so, Minas society adjusted to the change. Subsistence farming became more important, and the population shifted from the old mining centers in search of new ways to make a living. We will deal with these readjustments subsequently, but at this point let us examine some of the distinctive features of Minas Gerais society during Brazil's age of gold.

Society in Minas Gerais was more urban than in most parts of

Brazil. The early mining camps developed haphazardly into urban centers, the mud and thatch houses slowly replaced by stone and tile. Since the towns were established near the major mining sites, population was naturally concentrated in and around them. By the 1740s Vila Rica had more than fifteen thousand inhabitants. Minas took on a particularly urban atmosphere, and the towns provided the dominant forms and institutions of life. The câmaras exercised control over each town and its surrounding *termo,* regulating, licensing, and taxing. Artisans, many of them former slaves or their descendants, flourished, but the guild organizations were weak and subject to the price and quality controls of the câmaras. In and around the towns the population depended on the many stores (*lojas*) and shops and stalls (*vendas*) for supplies. By 1733 Vila Rica had 350 of these in its jurisdiction. As in other parts of Brazil, the petty commerce of the vendas was often in the hands of women and sometimes of slaves, either acting on their own or as agents for their owners. The more heavily capitalized lojas were in the hands of free men.

The curious religious history of the mining zone also had its effects on the style and organization of local society. Alleged moral excesses, smuggling, and other activities had led the crown to prohibit members of the religious orders from the mining areas in the early days of the rush. Thus, unlike the rest of Brazil, where the regular orders had provided the structure and style of religious life, in Minas Gerais they played almost no role at all. Instead, secular clergy of the ecclesiastical hierarchy molded the Mineiro church, and this fact, along with the heavy direct immigration from northern Portugal, meant that the church in Minas would in some ways be more conservative and more "Portuguese" than in other areas of Brazil. This was especially so after 1745 when a separate bishopric was created in Ribeirão do Carmo.

The lay brotherhoods (*irmandades*) that had existed in the coastal areas (as indeed throughout the Catholic world) experienced a rapid flowering in Minas Gerais. The upper-ranking Portuguese would usually build a small church and form a brotherhood dedicated to the Most Holy Sacrament (Santissimo Sacramento); other groups would at first often maintain a chapel in this same church, but as soon as possible would seek to raise their own. The brotherhoods and their little churches proliferated in the towns, organized mostly around race and estate rather than profession as in Portugal. There were exclusively white brotherhoods like the Third Order of São Francisco. Our Lady of the Rosary was usually the patroness of the Black irmandades, and the Brazilian-born Blacks often chose Our

Lady of Mercies as the protector of their organizations. Sponsored by the church hierarchy, the brotherhoods, organized for prayer, charitable works, burial societies, or social services, provided the context of religious life. Their competition to honor themselves and their respective saints led to the construction of jewel-like baroque chapels and stimulated the work of goldsmiths, artists, architects, musicians, and composers, many of whom were mulattoes. In both Spanish and Portuguese America one can speak of a "mining town baroque," involving extremely elaborate ornamentation and gilding of relatively small structures. Religion permeated the life of Minas Gerais and presents us with images of people, often fully armed, kneeling in the streets for the Angelus bells. After the creation of a seminary in Mariana in the mid-eighteenth century, the clergy became increasingly native to the region, linked to the principal families. Little wonder, then, that later movements for independence in this region rarely took on any anticlerical tinge.

Going beyond the institutions of government and church, perhaps the crucial characteristics of Mineiro social development were its fluidity, the rapidity of its evolution, the large number of slaves, and the shortage of Portuguese women in the early years. Illegal unions were the rule, usually between white men and slave or free women of color. Even as late as 1804 only a third of the household heads of Vila Rica were married within the church. Despite the attempts of both clergy and crown to force the miners to settle down by limiting office to married men and by sponsoring an early age for marriage, stability was slow to come.

As a result of the demographic realities and the social fluidity prior to 1720, the mulatto population grew rapidly. Rates of manumission were high, especially for children, which can probably be ascribed mainly to two factors: the desire of men, in the absence of legitimate heirs, to free their children by slave mothers and the ability of slaves to accumulate sufficient gold to purchase their own or their families' freedom. Free people of color, especially mulattoes, became a large and somewhat threatening segment of the population. Laws were passed to exclude mulattoes from municipal offices, but these were at times ignored. Mulattoes also occupied many middle-level posts as skilled craftsmen, artisans, musicians, and shopkeepers, and some acquired property and wealth. Royal governors in Minas sometimes expressed stereotyped racist views in their attempts to limit the freedom and position of the mulattoes and free Blacks. Efforts were made both to restrict manumissions and to prohibit mulattoes from inheriting property. As one governor, Lourenço de Almeida, put it: "Mulattoes being unstable and rebellious are pernicious in all Brazil; in Minas they are far worse because they are rich, and experience shows us that wealth in these people leads them to commit grave errors, chief among them being disobedience to the laws." Although similar attitudes could be found throughout Brazil, they were especially intense in Minas because mulattoes were so securely in place as an indispensable part of the social hierarchy. Just as in Spanish America, the more their position bettered, the more criticism and countermeasures they evoked. By the 1740s there were as many mulattoes as whites in Minas Gerais.

The situation of the mulattoes in Minas was, of course, made possible by the general social and demographic structure which rested so firmly on the basis of African slavery in Minas as in other parts of Brazil. Thousands of Africans were brought each year to work in the mines and fields, with preference given to those from the Mina coast, perhaps because of the knowledge they already had about mining for gold. Slaves constituted more than half the population in the towns and performed every sort of labor. Conditions were harsh, and ten to twelve years was estimated to be the effective working life of a slave in the mines. Slaves fled in large numbers, forming quilombos whose raiding and depredations increased the instability of remote areas and sometimes threatened the major towns. From the beginning, the society and culture of Minas was built on gold and slaves.

By the 1760s the gold began to play out, but the patterns of life were already well established. Stimulated by the strong local market of boom times, mixed fazendas of ranching, mining, and farming had developed, in contrast to the coast, and local food and craft products were available in the towns. As elsewhere, life was dominated by the white elites, here miners and farmers, plus an active state bureaucracy. Mulattoes had won a special place, but as elsewhere they suffered restrictions and discrimination. The social pyramid rested once again on slave labor. As gold declined, the diversified economy of Minas was able to absorb much of the shock rather well. What was left was a residue of towns, churches, artisans, music, art, and other forms of cultural life that made Minas a singular place in Portuguese America.

The impact of gold

If Potosí in its time had affected all South America, the impact of the Brazilian gold rush too reached far beyond Minas Gerais, producing important short- and long-term effects on both Brazil and Portugal. The Brazilian sugar industry, which had suffered disruption and decline in the 1640s and had made a slow recovery in the decades thereafter, received a major blow in the general depression that struck the Atlantic world in the 1680s. By 1688 the price of sugar had dropped to about one-third its level at the end of the Luso-Dutch war in 1654. The gold strike looked for a while as though it might cause the permanent collapse of coastal export agriculture. The rise in slave prices and the shortage of workers caused by new demand in the mining zones, the dislocation of the population, and a general inflationary trend brought many planters to the brink of ruin. "God has given gold to Brazil in order to punish it," warned one royal governor. Sugar production fluctuated wildly between 1700 and 1713, and an internal restructuring of the industry took place, as some planters sold out to others who could afford the rising costs. But with governmental regulation of the supply of slaves, the institution of a regular fleet system, and peace in Europe after 1713, export agriculture held on. Although sugar was no longer the most profitable activity in Brazil, it remained the leader in volume. In no decade did the value of gold exceed the value of Brazilian agricultural exports.

Although gold did not destroy Brazilian agriculture, it did have detrimental effects on the mother country. Portugal had maintained its colonial system by using the revenues generated by the sale and taxation of its colonial products to buy the manufactured goods needed in the metropolis and the colonies. The decline in the value of colonial products in the seventeenth century resulted in Portugal's inability to get the currency it needed. This deficiency, coupled with wars against the Dutch and the Spanish, taking away the traditional sources of silver and creating a large national debt, led to serious fiscal problems. Portugal devalued its currency throughout the century in an attempt to cope with the situation, and by 1670 it was also moving toward the development of light industries to meet its own and its colonial needs. With the discovery of Brazilian gold, all this changed abruptly. Portugal now had all the cash it needed – or so it seemed – to supply itself and its overseas possessions. This situation and pressures from the Portuguese wine interests led in 1703 to a commercial treaty with England (Methuen Treaty) which granted preferential treatment to Portuguese wines in England in return for corresponding advantages given to English woolens. The move toward the creation of national industries in Portugal was aborted. Portugal would continue to depend on other European nations, primarily England, to supply what its colonies needed, paying for everything with Brazilian gold. The gold flowed into and out of Portugal at a rapid rate, leaving only new palaces, some beautiful churches, and a fleeting sense of euphoria. By the 1760s, when the stream of gold began to slow, it was apparent that Portugal was even weaker than it had been a half century before. The actions of Portugal's authoritarian prime minister, the Marquis of Pombal, to resurrect the Portuguese economy and combat the growing dependence on England were responses to the long-term consequences of Brazil's golden age.

The export economies of sugar and gold mining stimulated the growth of other economic activities and consequently the opening of new regions to settlement or at least occupation. To feed the population concentrations of the coastal engenhos and the gold mining towns, commercial agriculture often developed on their peripheries. Mule teams moved the gold down to coastal ports from Minas Gerais and returned with goods needed in the mines. Towns like Sorocaba in the interior of São Paulo became famous for the trade fair of mules, which were distributed all over Brazil. A typical scene of the eighteenth century was the muleteer (*tropeiro*) with his train of thirty or forty pack mules, moving along fixed routes, stopping at little way stations, carrying on the internal trade of the colony.

The demand for livestock as food, transport, and power also resulted in the expansion and opening of new areas. We have already discussed the early development of cattle ranching in the northeast as an extension of the sugar economy. This process continued, moving into new areas of the arid sertão of the interior. The number of ranches (fazendas) grew over the century. Large herds of 400 to 500 cattle were driven hundreds of miles to fairs in Bahia and Pernambuco or sometimes all the way to Minas Gerais. The sertão society which supported this activity developed its own peculiarities. We can use the captaincy of Piauí, opened in the 1690s, as an example of the "society of leather." By 1772 the captaincy had 578 ranches, some of incredible size (one was twice the size of Lebanon). The great ranches often left much of their land unused and refused to sell or rent it in order to assure themselves of sufficient pasturage and an adequate labor supply. The 26,000 inhabitants were widely dispersed over the vast territory, concentrated in little groups on the fazendas, which were in turn located around the scattered water holes. Piauí had seven towns, all of them ramshackle and poor. It was a rural society. The population itself was mostly people of color, Blacks and caboclos. There was little here to attract whites from

Portugal, and those who came from the coast were often fleeing debt or the recruiting officer. Levels of miscegenation were high. Despite what some historians have argued, slaves did much of the labor on the ranches alongside free people of color. Apparently, there was enough profit in cattle ranching to make the use of slaves worthwhile. A common pattern in the vast expanse was to make slaves and free workers practically their own supervisors as vaqueiros and farmers. Placed at a distant corral, a slave family or two were left to care for the stock somewhat independently, and were sometimes allowed to keep a portion of the yearly increase in calves as an incentive to good service.

Loosely structured and free of much government control, the society of the sertão developed its own characteristics. The *fazendeiros* exercised broad social and political power over slaves and *agregados* (retainers, attached workers, the word was used also in Spanish America). The horse become the center of life, the means of making a living as well as a symbol of manly prowess. Materially poor, the people lived in leather – household goods, clothes, tools, saddles, window coverings, all were made of leather – a logical result of an economy based on livestock ranching in a society that was relatively isolated from its markets. A similar society and economy spread with ranching northward into Maranhão and westward into Goiás. By the 1780s the northeast had joined the Plata region in exporting large quantities of leather to Europe.

A somewhat different ranching tradition developed in the far south of Brazil in the area known as Rio Grande de São Pedro (today called Rio Grande do Sul). An extension of the pampa of Argentina and Uruguay, the plains here were well watered and fertile, quite unlike the sertão of the northeast. Ranching developed in competition with agriculture, becoming the dominant activity only at the very close of the colonial period. As in the nearby Plata region, the cattle industry in Rio Grande began with the hunting of feral herds, descendants of stock introduced by the Jesuit missionaries in the seventeenth century. Cattle hunters (*gauchos*), as in Argentina, had made a living from hunting cattle for hides and smuggling across the Luso-Spanish frontier. In order to protect the Portuguese outpost on the La Plata at Colonia (in present Uruguay, opposite Buenos Aires), the crown moved to control the southern area. In 1737 occupation began in earnest. Settlers were of a variety of types. The fertile plains, unclaimed herds, and a temperate climate drew colonists from other captaincies. In addition, the crown sent couples from the overpopulated Azores to settle in Rio Grande. Finally, toward the end of the century, fortified towns peopled by militia-colonists were also established at various points. By 1780 Rio Grande had a population of 18,000, about 60 percent white. Although the Rio Grande in its early period was not dominated by a slave-based economy, slaves were there in significant numbers, making up between 25 and 30 percent of the population. They were used in small groups, mostly in wheat agriculture. Another social reality in Rio Grande was the relatively small number of mestizos and mulattoes, perhaps a result of considerable settlement by couples rather than single men.

Although much has been made of the gaucho tradition of Rio Grande, it developed alongside other activities. Both ranches (called *estancias* here as in Argentina) and farms existed in the region. Rio Grande produced considerable quantities of wheat for export to Minas and Rio de Janeiro in the 1790s and early 1800s. But there were also forces at work which stimulated the ranching economy and culture. After the wild herds had been depleted, the cattle-raising estancias became increasingly important. The demand for dried beef (*charque*, originally a Quechua and then a Spanish term) in coastal cities, mines, and on plantations brought about at the same time the growth of the cattle industry and a decrease in agriculture. By 1826 the number of cattle increased to three times that of 1790, and by the former date Rio Grande was importing grain rather than exporting it. Along with this change, the culture of the ranch came to predominate. The horse, barbecued beef, and mate tea became the pillars of rural life, which was now increasingly oriented around the estancias. There was little to differentiate Rio Grande from the Banda Oriental (Uruguay), and ranchers often traded, raided, or smuggled across the frontier. In fact, in many ways life in southern Brazil was constantly overshadowed by the continuous Luso-Spanish struggle over these "debatable lands." Rio Grande was both a ranching and a military frontier, and to some extent the militarization of Rio Grande increased the importance of the gauchos, who could in time of war serve as cavalrymen.

The Pombaline reforms

The decade of the 1750s marked a significant turning point in the Luso-Brazilian economy and in the history of colonial Brazil. It was in these years that Brazilian gold production crested and then began its decline, and it was also at this time that Sebastião José de Carvalho e Mello (usually called simply the Marquis of Pombal, the title he received in 1770) rose to power within the Portuguese government. Pombal was a man who combined the principles of regalism and political despotism with a profound desire for economic reform and a deep sense of nationalism. He was often a pragmatist and sometimes his programs were confused or contradictory, but during the more than twenty-five years of his strong rule (1750–77), Portugal instituted a series of reforms that in many ways paralleled and often preceded those carried out by the Bourbon reformers in Spain and its empire. Unlike Spain, Portugal's empire in the eighteenth century still included major territories in Africa and Asia, but for our purposes we will concentrate on the Pombaline reforms and policies in Brazil, which was by this time the cornerstone of the empire. The motivation and content of these reforms were often much the same in Portugal as in Spain, but given the different historical, diplomatic, and economic conditions of the two empires, the results could not but differ.

As with the Bourbon reforms in Spanish America and Spain, Pombal's policies can probably be best understood as a matter of defensive reform. Pombal had risen to power as the confidant of Dom José I, a frivolous monarch who lacked both the talent and the interest to govern and who was willing to entrust the business of state to another. As prime minister, Pombal ruled Portugal and its colonies as a dictator with virtually no constraints. Although his intelligence and ruthlessness have made him a controversial character, there is no doubt that his administration marked a major turning point in the history of Portugal and Brazil. His earlier diplomatic experience in Vienna and especially London had made him aware of the general trends of European politics and economy and of Portugal's weakness and domination by Great Britain. Pombal had learned the lessons of England's commercial success and preeminence at first hand. The Methuen Treaty made Portugal and its colonies great consumers of English goods and created a trade imbalance that was paid for with Brazilian gold. Through both legal and contraband trade, English merchant houses in Portugal and factories in Brazil carried out a brisk commerce in English manufactures and Brazilian gold. Their superior access to capital and credit allowed the English penetration of the internal commercial lines of the Portuguese colonial economy and the domination of the trade of Portugal itself.

Pombal understood this situation and realized that the colonies and especially Brazil were the keys to Portugal's regeneration. Consolidating his powers during his rebuilding of Lisbon after a devastating earthquake in 1755, Pombal launched a series of measures designed to lessen Portugal's dependence on England by using the commercial, fiscal, and when possible even industrial techniques that the English themselves had developed. Within this program was a general attempt to restructure the political and economic shape of Brazil. Much of this sounds quite similar to what took place in Spain under the Bourbons, but there is an important difference to keep in mind. Portugal in the eighteenth century was not only an economic dependency of England but a political ally or client as well. Since the seventeenth century, an alliance between Portugal and England had been a foundation of Portuguese foreign policy in the face of the often hostile relationship with its neighbor, Spain, and Spain's ally, France. Thus Pombal's reforms and desire to break out of a harmful economic dependence were always constrained by political and military realities. What he sought was reciprocity, not the elimination of British trade or the British alliance.

Although many of Pombal's reform measures were quite in keeping with the general trend of regalism and royal despotism found in most contemporary European courts, more remarkable is the energy with which he pursued this policy in all areas of life. Not surprisingly, the battle of church and state was fought out in Pombal's Portugal. Although not abolished, the Inquisition was considerably reduced in power. The church hierarchy was brought under tighter royal control in the 1760s. The University of Coimbra, long under church and especially Jesuit influence, was reformed along modern lines, becoming in the process a center of regalist doctrine. Groups favoring the crown's reforms, like the Oratorian Fathers, received support, while those who opposed these measures, like the Jesuits, were hounded or suppressed. The nobility with its traditional rights and prerogatives also came under attack. Using an assassination attempt on the king as an excuse, Pombal eliminated some of the most important noble families. He created a school for the youth of the nobility to instill in them the principles of regalism. Access to noble status was made easier for those who contributed money or talent to favored projects.

There was a good deal of social tinkering as well. Pombal prohibited the traditional persecution and discrimination against the New Christians (1773), hoping to gain their investment in his economic projects. Slavery was abolished in Portugal, not because Pombal was an abolitionist but because he wanted to create jobs and stimulate artisan development in the mother country and assure a large supply of African slaves to the Brazilian colonies. There was hardly an area of life Pombal left untouched; he even legislated against the traditional mourning and seclusion of widows. But as a pragmatist, he realized that Portugal's only hope was its empire.

The 1750s witnessed a flurry of measures designed to eliminate the most flagrant ills of the empire. Vigorous anticontraband measures were introduced in Minas Gerais and in Portugal, and a new system for collecting the royal fifth in the mining zone brought increased revenues. To stimulate and protect the chief colonial agricultural products of sugar and tobacco, boards of inspection were established in the four main Brazilian ports to control the quality and price of these commodities. Neither Brazilian planters nor merchants were pleased with this arrangement, but the boards were maintained. Since 1711 the commerce of Brazil had been carried in fleets which visited the four major ports each year.

Pombal now moved to stimulate Brazilian trade by recourse to that typical institution for developing peripheral areas, the monopoly company. In 1755 the Company of Grão Pará e Maranhão was created, with a twenty-year privilege of exclusive rights to the slave trade and other commerce with Brazil's vast northern half. Although anyone could invest, the company was specifically designed to allow Portuguese nationals to compete successfully with foreign merchants. What could be done for undeveloped areas could also be tried to resuscitate old ones. In 1759 the Company of Pernambuco and Paraíba was created to stimulate the economy of the coastal northeast. These companies brought an end to the annual fleets to São Luiz and Recife, and in 1765 the fleets to Rio and Salvador were also ended. Opposition to these companies and to the port wine monopoly established in Portugal itself brought swift and unsparing government repression. Complaints against the company of Grão Pará by the merchant guild of Lisbon led to abolition of that body by Pombal in 1755 and the creation of a new Board of Trade directly under royal control. That the Jesuits had also voiced their complaints against the company would not be forgotten, as we shall see.

Pombal realized that commerce represented only a part of the problem and its solution. In the 1750s Brazil was entering a long period of depression caused by a decline in the production of gold and other colonial commodities and lower prices for these goods on the European market. At the very time that the increasingly heated military rivalry with Spain in South America called for more expenditures, royal revenues were falling. Although much of what Pombal did can be seen as the continuation of trends or policies of the previous decades, it is also true that his innovations must be viewed against the backdrop of this difficult financial situation. Like the

Bourbons in Spain, Pombal sought to innovate in the colonies in order to strengthen them economically and thus militarily. In both cases there was a realization that the ultimate position of the mother country depended on the success of colonial reform.

The improvement of administration and increased royal control were central elements of reform. The powers of the Conselho Ultramarino, the old colonial council, were reduced and strong colonial ministers, the first of whom was Pombal's own brother, took control in Lisbon. In Brazil the remaining private captaincies were abolished. The royal judicial system was reformed and expanded by the creation of a second High Court of Appeal in Rio de Janeiro (1751). That city also replaced Bahia as the colonial capital in 1763, in response to both the shift of population to the south caused by gold and the military conflict on the southern frontier. The status of the senior royal official in the colony had been elevated from governor-general to viceroy in 1720, and Pombal now established the viceregal residence in Rio de Janeiro, although little was done to increase the power of that officer. Pombal's conception of centralization resulted in his taking the reins of control ever more firmly in his own hands. The Brazilian viceroy had little control over the governors of the other captaincies, who were encouraged to communicate directly with Lisbon. In many ways each captaincy remained a separate colony, and centralization as such did little to sponsor Brazilian unity. Pombal was too shrewd to expect that organizational reform alone would bring the desired results, and he made a special effort to appoint vigorous colonial officers who were moved by the same principles of enlightened but forceful government. Men like the Marquês of Lavradio (viceroy, 1769–79) and the Morgado de Mateus (governor of São Paulo, 1765–75) set the tone of the new state activism in Brazil. Almost all the governors appointed in this period were nobles and high-ranking military men accustomed to obedience and command.

The heart of the reforms was necessarily fiscal. With falling revenues and rising debts, the decline of gold output in Minas Gerais, the decadence of mining in Goiás and Mato Grosso, and the failing economy of the northeastern coast, new ways of generating funds had to be found. Portugal's system of revenue collection was completely reformed. A central accounting office (*real erario*) headed by Pombal himself was created in Lisbon; in each captaincy of Brazil fiscal procedures were reformed and a whole new series of accounting offices created, although many taxes were still collected by private individuals who bid for the concession. The contracts so awarded tended to be large, thereby simplifying their administration. Such measures, although necessary, were unable to resolve the fundamental problems. The amount of money shipped from Rio de Janeiro to Lisbon in 1774 was only half the total sent in 1749. Not until the late 1770s did the Luso-Brazilian economy begin to experience some revival.

Portugal's expensive strategic concern in America was the vast interior frontier from the Amazon to the mouth of the Río de la Plata. Over the centuries the Portuguese had pushed well beyond the agreed line of division of Tordesillas, and conflict with Spain, especially in the Plata region, had become endemic. Matters became more complicated in the eighteenth century with the close alliance of France and Spain and the league of England and Portugal. In times of European conflict the English might raid Cartagena or Havana, and in return the French would strike at Rio de Janeiro, as they did in 1711. To end the threat of conflict, Portugal and Spain arranged an exchange of claims in 1750. Portugal was to cede its outpost at Colonia on the Plata in return for areas in the Amazon and the region of Jesuit missions on the Uruguay River. However, the Treaty of Madrid (1750) never went into effect. It was opposed by many, including Pombal, and faced violent opposition from the Jesuits and their Guaraní mission Indians, who rose in rebellion to stop the transfer of territory. The treaty was rescinded and was soon followed by military actions in 1762–3 and 1767–8. In fact, the Spanish-Portuguese struggle over the southern borderlands persisted into the early independence period and was not finally settled until the creation of Uruguay in 1828. From the Brazilian viewpoint this festering struggle consumed men, money, and energy throughout the second half of the eighteenth century. The defense of Portuguese America's frontiers became a central component of royal policy, and those elements which limited or opposed these efforts were special targets for attack by the crown.

Pombaline Brazil

Thus far we have examined the Pombaline period from the viewpoint of Lisbon and through the prisms of policy and reform. It is now appropriate to examine the effects of these measures on Brazil and its people. Just as in Spanish America, the regions that experienced the most change in the period of reform were formerly neglected fringes like the Amazon basin. The vast northern region of Brazil had, in fact, been a separate territory, the State of Maranhão, since 1621. Its contact and communication with Lisbon had been far more regular than with the rest of Brazil, because of the difficulty of the voyage to Bahia, and because it suited the crown politically. Symbolic of the separation was the subordination of the bishops of the area's two major cities, Belém and São Luiz, to the archbishop of Lisbon, not Bahia. This vast and mostly neglected area became a prime target for development under Pombal, who viewed it as a cornerstone in his defensive network and a region of potential colonial wealth. The creation of the Company of Grão Pará e Maranhão, with its monopoly rights to trade and its obligation to develop the area, was only part of Pombal's strategy. His brother Francisco Xavier de Mendonça Furtado was sent to Pará as governor with specific orders to stimulate the economy and to examine the activities and wealth of the Jesuits. What Pombal hoped to do was alter the old Amazonian structure in which missionary-controlled Indians extracted the wild fruits and products of the forest, and replace it with a replica of the settled plantation colonies.

Faced with the small population of Portugal itself and realizing that Portugal's claims in the Amazon and on other frontiers were indefensible as long as these areas were unoccupied, Pombal inaugurated a policy designed to foster miscegenation between Indians and Portuguese and thereby enlarge the population on the frontiers. Indians would no longer suffer discrimination, and unions between Indians and others would be encouraged by the state. The Indian was to become a full subject of the crown, acculturated, working for wages, and available to work or perform military duty. Portuguese laymen would assume roles of leadership and control in the Indian villages, where acculturation was to be enforced by prohibiting the use of the lingua geral (indigenous lingua franca), requiring the Indians to work for wages, fostering contact with whites, and establishing schools for Indian youth. All of this smacks of metropolitan lack of realism; if there was anything that proved resistant to legislation all over Latin America, it was the world of everyday social interaction, including ethnic relations and language. But the program was accompanied by more concrete measures which doubtless had some effects, if not exactly those intended. In 1757 the regular orders were deprived of their control of the Indian villages. Their rule was supplanted by the "Directorate of Indians," a lay group empowered to govern the Indian population.

Pombal was no social reformer interested in the plight of the Indian. His goal was strategic and economic benefit for Portugal. Undoubtedly, the next half century saw a considerable weakening of the indigenous element in the Amazon and the interior regions of

Brazil. The population remained mestizo in the majority, but the little river towns, outposts, and villages became thoroughly Europeanized, at least in outward forms. For the Indians, the directory system was a disaster. The laymen in the villages often simply assisted the colonists in their exploitation of Indian labor. Indians fled from forced acculturation and the resettlement of their villages. More contact with Europeans also meant more epidemic disease. By 1799, when the crown finally abolished the directory system, there were fewer than twenty thousand Indians under Portuguese control in the Amazon basin. The crucial factor was the simple entry of more Europeans into the area, which everywhere resulted in the displacement, destruction, and drastic diminution of nonsedentary Indian societies.

In truth, the Pombaline program for northern Brazil had mixed results. The area was really composed of two regions: the Amazon basin of Pará and Rio Negro with its capital at Belém and the territory of Maranhão centered on São Luiz. These two regions developed quite differently under the Pombaline policies and the stimulus of the Company of Grão Pará e Maranhão. Although the company exported great quantities of cacao from Pará, little success was achieved in any other endeavor. Because Amazonian cacao was still a wild plant, gathered by Indian laborers, it could be exploited with little alteration of Pará's economic structure, and plantations like those of Venezuela were never developed. The Pombaline policies did destroy missionary control of the population and tended to force acculturation, but aside from cacao, there was little else that the colony offered to Portugal. Pará remained an area of Indian labor and extractive forest products. Its population around 1800 was about 60 percent white and mestizo, 20 percent Indian, and 20 percent slave. Rather than becoming a replica of the Brazilian sugar and gold regions, it remained essentially a fringe.

Maranhão was a quite different story. Conditions around São Luiz and along the major rivers were suitable for newer plantation crops, such as cotton and rice, and the company was willing to sell slaves to planters on credit against these crops. Large numbers of slaves, mostly from Cacheu and Bissau in Portuguese Guinea, were imported to São Luiz. A coastal plantation economy flourished in Maranhão, supported by the cattle ranches of Piauí and the sertão. "White cotton turned the Maranhão black" went the expression, for by 1800 almost 65 percent of its 79,000 inhabitants were Black or mulatto, and 46 percent were slaves. Maranhão underlines the point we made earlier about the way in which a fringe area could be transformed by connection to the export sector and that the presence of a large Black population in an area usually rests on this connection.

It should be clear by now that for a variety of reasons the confrontation between the Portuguese state and the Jesuits was building to a climax. Their independence, power, wealth, control of education, and ties to Rome made the Jesuits obvious targets for Pombal's brand of extreme regalism. In this, the Jesuits might seem little different from other religious orders or the nobility, whom Pombal was also trying to bring fully under state control. But there were other reasons as well. Many colonists had long resented the particularly powerful position of the Jesuits in Brazil. Pombal came to view them as a group with vested interests directly opposed to his economic and demographic plans for Brazil. Their opposition to the Treaty of Madrid, their complaints against the Company of Grão Pará, their control of numerous Indian villages in the interior and hence of Indian laborers, all gave Pombal reason for action against them. Then too, the Jesuits were by far the wealthiest religious order in Brazil. Their holdings included urban properties, sugar plantations, cattle ranches, and farms. They were the largest institutional slaveowners in Brazil, listing thousands of slaves among their assets. On the single island of Marajó at the mouth of the Amazon the Jesuits ran over 100,000 head of livestock. On all these properties they had consistently refused to pay the tithe to the crown, claiming a papal exemption. Confiscation of Jesuit property and resale by the crown thus seemed to offer considerable economic benefits to Portuguese policy makers intent on generating more income from Brazil.

After a campaign of vilification and some unfounded charges that the Jesuits were accomplices to a plot against the king, the order of expulsion of the Jesuits and confiscation of their properties came in 1759. The reasons were many, and regalism was surely important (as it was in Jesuit expulsions from France in 1764 and Spain in 1767), but the strategic and economic considerations in Brazil also weighed heavily in the Portuguese case.

Although there may have been many who mourned the persecution of the Jesuits by Pombal but were afraid to speak out, there were others who benefited from the acquisition of their properties and the elimination of the Jesuits as creditors or commercial rivals. Here we must underline an aspect of the Pombaline reforms that stands in marked contrast to the Bourbon measures in Spanish America. In Brazil, certain individual reforms went against the interests of certain groups; for example, planters did not like the boards of inspection, and some merchants did not appreciate the monopoly companies. But Pombal's measures seemed to lack the peculiarly anti-creole tenor of the Gálvez efforts in Spanish America. Although specific groups might object to specific programs or laws, these measures as a whole did not represent an attack on the Brazilian oligarchy. Pombal was trying to make Brazil more profitable for Portugal, but Brazilians were not excluded from the process. Wealthy Brazilians invested in the Company of Grão Pará, and 10 percent of the stock of the Company of Pernambunco was owned by colonials. Confiscated Jesuit properties went into the hands of Brazilian planters and ranchers, who welcomed the opportunity to acquire some of the best-managed estates in the colony.

Nor did Pombal make Brazilian officeholders a specific target for reform. In fact, within the general lines of his reorganization, Pombal created new opportunities for Brazilians. The newly created boards of inspection, the new accounting offices, an expanded bureaucracy, and a reformed and expanded militia all invited the participation of colonials in government. Even in the mineral-producing regions where metropolitan interests were sometimes imposed with a heavy hand, opportunities for colonials were expanded. The junta created in Minas Gerais in the 1770s to collect taxes and arrange the tithe included local participants, and even in the diamond-mining district colonials were selected to serve as treasurers of the royal board of control. The new opportunities and the reward of office, title, and military commission all served to maintain the ties between the Brazilian elite and the Portuguese crown. Although this did little for the vast majority of the population in Brazil, it did allow some role in the operation of colonial government for those families who controlled the colony's economic resources. The Pombaline reforms did not exclude Brazilian upper groups from government but in fact tended to expand their role. So long as the colonial elite perceived a commonality of interest between themselves and Portugal, there was little reason to think of new political arrangements.

To be sure, the advantages may have been more apparent than real. The underlying goal of royal policy was to have the colonies serve the mother country ever more efficiently. Although Brazilian-born Portuguese were allowed to serve in the government and sometimes even rose to high office in Portugal itself, there was no doubt that Brazil would remain in a colonial status. No printing press was allowed to operate in the colony, nor was a university ever established in colonial Brazil. The sons of the Brazilian elite still had to seek their education at Coimbra or at some university in

France or Spain. In contrast to Spanish America, Brazil's intellectual life did not develop its own institutional centers. Just as the lines of governmental communication ran from each captaincy back to Lisbon, so too in cultural and intellectual life Portugal remained the center. In this regard Pombal was simply respecting a long-established tradition.

Finally, it should be noted that by allowing the Brazilian oligarchy to participate in, and in some cases benefit from, the reforms, Pombal had recognized the dominant role played by the great Brazilian families in the colony. In each captaincy a small group of extended and interrelated family clans had come to dominate social and economic life; through municipal and provincial office they dominated political life as well. The cattle barons and sugar planters often exercised considerable control over the rural population and were the means by which that population could be mobilized or controlled by the state. In eighteenth-century São Paulo, for example, dominant clusters of clans existed in each rural district. The heads of these clans were usually appointed to the leadership roles in the militia and thus when the state wished to mobilize the populace or tax them, it occurred through the cooperation and prestige of the leading families. Had the state attempted to rule in conflict with the prominent families, the result would have been at best uncertain. Brazil demonstrates how kinship and family politics could be wedded to a large system of imperial government.

Why these differences between the Spanish and the Portuguese reforms? One might say that they can be attributed to Pombal's astuteness in recognizing the limits within which his reforms had to operate. Or one can look for differences in the two situations. If the Portuguese government was less determined to replace the native-born with the peninsular-born in high places, surely that was partly because in Brazil the position of the native-born was not so well consolidated. In Brazil, for example, though locals often sat on the royal high courts, they never constituted a majority, whereas in Spanish America creoles were on the verge of displacing peninsulars entirely on some of the most prestigious Audiencias before the royal government took truly consistent counteraction. And on the other side of the coin, it seems that first-generation Portuguese may have still played a larger part in Brazilian society generally than peninsulars did in Spanish American society, especially in the expanding southern area of Brazil. Also, Spain's eagerness to fill more posts with peninsulars and take a more direct hand in the Spanish American economy was fueled partly by economic and demographic growth in several areas of peninsular Spain, a resurgence without any full equivalent in Portugal.

In general, Brazil and Portugal had remained in closer contact with, and less distinguished from, each other than had Spanish America and Spain. Because of their multiplicity, variety, and in some cases inaccessibility, the Spanish American territories could not nestle at the mother country's bosom but turned instead toward centers located in each territory. Brazil, however, was not only closer to Iberia than most of Spanish America, but the most populous parts of it faced out to sea, inclined for considerations of transport and the economy to look to Portugal as much as to the other parts of Brazil. Whereas Spain and Spanish America had grown apart, Portugal and Brazil had grown in some ways into an ever closer symbiosis, the mother country relying more and more on its giant colony.

In truth, the times had not been kind to Pombal and his reforms. Throughout this period Brazil faced an economic depression, the result of declining gold production and low prices for its agricultural products, which fiscal measures could not overcome. Despite all Pombal could do, Brazilian exports in 1776 were only 40 percent of what they had been in 1760. This decline was all the more serious because of Portugal's increasing military expenses resulting from involvement in European wars and conflicts with Spain. Although the Pombaline measures failed to bring the desired short-term economic results, they did sow some of the seeds of the future. In the next twenty years great international events – including the revolutions in North America (1776), France (1789), and Haiti (1791) – changed the patterns of supply and demand and the prices of many Brazilian products, some of which had been inaugurated during the Pombaline period. Except for one or two years, the prices of Brazilian agricultural exports rose from 1780 to 1800. New crops such as indigo and rice in Rio de Janeiro and Maranhão and cotton in Maranhão and Pernambuco provided new sources of revenue. By the end of the century Brazil was exporting large quantities of rice abroad. Cultivation of coffee also began in earnest in this period, although its real expansion lay in the following century. At the same time, sugar production revived because of the rapid rise in the price of that product after the revolution in Haiti and its elimination as a sugar producer. Note that the new Brazilian products are the same ones being developed in the Spanish circum-Caribbean at the end of the colonial period and that the recovery of Brazilian sugar was contemporaneous with its expansion in Cuba.

Along with Maranhão, the greatest beneficiary of both the Pombaline era and the subsequent agricultural growth was the captaincy of Rio de Janeiro and its capital city of the same name. Because of its proximity to Minas Gerais, Rio's importance had grown with the mining boom of the first half of the century. Its designation as the Brazilian capital in 1763 simply capped a process that had been taking place for half a century: the shift of population and economic power from north to south. With the stimulus of an expanded bureaucracy, and after 1776 a growing commerce, especially in the new crops like indigo and rice (as well as sugar), the population of Rio de Janeiro doubled in the last quarter of the century, to about 45,000. In the next twenty years that figure would reach a total of 112,000.

The city and the captaincy were transformed in this period. No longer simply an outlet for Minas gold and a supplier of subsistence crops to the mines, Rio was increasingly pulled into the export economy. The growth of the captaincy's agricultural sector meant increasing importation of slaves, in this case mostly from Angola. In addition, merchants, most of them commission agents of European firms, gained an increasingly powerful and dominant role in the port city as it was drawn into the world market. Because of its location, Rio de Janeiro became the hub of a network of an intercoastal trade linking southern Brazil with the Portuguese imperial system. In short, it was during this period that Rio de Janeiro rose to a dominant position in Brazil. But we must keep in mind that if Rio de Janeiro was booming, it was still a colonial city. Imported slave labor tended to depress wages and limit the rise of a tradesman class. The capital accumulated through commerce went into commercial agriculture, slaves, or luxury items, not into manufacturing. In fact, in 1785 Portugal had prohibited the manufacture of cloth in Brazil in an effort to protect the growing Portuguese textile industry. Such legislation and the continuing commercial nature of a city like Rio de Janeiro underline the limitations under which Brazil labored.

In many ways Pombal and his officers were both the products and the agents of changes that were taking place throughout Europe. Portugal, like Spain, was in touch with the intellectual currents of the Age of Reason; English, French, and Italian books on political economy, science, law, and philosophy could be found on the bookshelves of learned men in both Portugal and Brazil. The leaders in introducing these new ideas were often cosmopolitan diplomats, merchants, or intellectuals who in their experience abroad had witnessed firsthand the transformation of other nations. Some of these *estrangeirados* (the foreignized) ran afoul of the Inquisition for their heretical ideas, but that was not always the case. Pombal himself could fit into this category as a man who through his foreign experience had learned the new principles of political economy and wished to apply them, but who did not hesitate to ban books which contained ideas contrary to his own. The motto of these individuals, drawn from a book of the period, was "the man of letters has the whole world as his fatherland." The Portuguese king during the first half of the eighteenth century, Dom João V, greatly desired to emulate the brilliance of the court of his French contemporary, Louis XIV, and followed the French example in sponsoring royal academies of history and science. A periodical press began to operate in Portugal, and private libraries were filled with an increasing number of foreign books in the original or in Portuguese translations.

In Brazil groups of intellectuals began to meet in little clubs similar to the *amigos del país* in Spanish America, but tending more toward history and poetry than to science. In the course of the eighteenth century, six such groups operated in Salvador and Rio on a formal basis; the first, "the Society of the Forgotten" (Esquecidos), was established in Salvador in 1724. Probably just as important were small groups which gathered in Minas Gerais, Pernambuco, or other towns in salons and drawing rooms to discuss matters of common interest. In truth, the formal academies were relatively unimportant. Their membership was small, usually forty to fifty persons, their meetings were intermittent, and most lasted only a few years. Some idea of their composition can be gained from the members of the Academy of the Reborn (Renascidos), which met in Salvador in 1759. Its forty members included twenty-one priests, five military men, a merchant, and thirteen government bureaucrats. It is important to note that most members of these groups were European-born, not Brazilians. Such groups were not the platforms for launching radical political or social doctrines. Their small number, limited membership, and esoteric focus reduced their effect on Brazilian society as a whole, but the academies did demonstrate the existence of a certain intellectual ferment.

This ferment could be seen in other aspects of life as well. Educational reform based on Luís Antônio Verney's proscientific *True Method for Study* (1742) was in vogue by midcentury. Many of Verney's ideas helped shape Pombal's reform of the University of Coimbra. The expulsion of the Jesuits from Brazil left a wide gap in the colony's educational system, which both the state and other religious institutions moved to fill. Pombal levied a new tax, the literary subsidy, to pay for royally supported schools. Teachers of rhetoric, grammar, and philosophy came on contract from Portugal. Laymen in former Jesuit Indian villages of the backlands instructed children in first letters, lace-making, and weaving. In 1776 the Franciscans of Rio de Janeiro updated their curriculum to include physics, geometry, and natural history. The bishop of Pernambuco established a seminary in Olinda based on the principles of the reform of Coimbra, in which science received strong emphasis. In 1771 public education was placed under the direction of the Royal Board of Censorship, an arrangement reflecting the somewhat uneasy relationship between the new ideas and the traditional order.

The transformation of elite mentality, attitude, and interest came slowly, not all at once. As in Spanish America, although to a somewhat lesser degree, much attention was given to scientific and practical matters. Alexandre Rodrigues Ferreira, a Bahian trained at Coimbra, carried out ten years of scientific collecting and exploration in the Amazon (1783–93). Another Bahian, Joaquim de Amorim Castro, a royal official, proposed measures to improve the tobacco industry and made other useful proposals. Often it was clerics and bureaucrats who were most affected by the new intellectual trends. Not surprisingly, such men usually tended to be politically and socially conservative. Within the Brazilian context, Enlightenment ideas took on a peculiar colonial cast. We can use as an example here José Joaquim de Azeredo Coutinho (1742–1821), the reforming bishop of Pernambuco. Azeredo Coutinho was the son of a planter family of Rio. Educated and intelligent, he applied the lessons of Adam Smith, J. B. Say, and others to a defense of colonial, especially planter, interests. An advocate of slavery and the slave trade, he criticized those who espoused the "chimerical rights of liberty and humanity." As a staunch defender of religion and monarchy, Azeredo Coutinho reflected in his writings the inner tension of the Enlightenment within the colonial context. How could the ideals of individual freedom, property rights, and free trade be reconciled with a society based on an unequal hierarchy and an economy founded on slavery?

Population, family, and society

Brazil experienced a general trend of population increase over the last half of the eighteenth century. The late-developing favorable economic conditions created by increasing demand for Brazilian products, with consequent renewed European immigration, must have contributed to the overall growth, as did the very high levels of slave importation to Maranhão, Pernambuco, and Bahia, especially after 1790; by 1800 slaves were about one-third of the total population. These factors seem a less than entirely adequate explanation, however, especially since both came so late in time; at any rate, Brazil participated in the population increase that affected nearly all Latin American areas from about 1750 forward, whether they were especially flourishing or not. In the Brazilian case it is also important to note the way in which the population was now distributed (see Table 6). By 1808 Brazil had a total population of possibly 2.5 million, of which some 47 percent lived in the traditional areas of the northeast from Piauí to Bahia, concentrated around the towns and plantations of the coast. Rio de Janeiro, its neighboring areas, and Minas Gerais now contained a significant 27 percent, and the newly growing south held another 13.5 percent. The northern areas of Pará and Maranhão had grown to almost 9 percent of the population, and the scattered mining camps and ranches of the western captaincies of Mato Grosso and Goiás contained the remaining 3.5 percent.

Like most populations until recently, that of late colonial Brazil was characterized by both high fertility and high mortality rates. Studies of Minas Gerais and São Paulo indicate that the population was a young and, therefore, a rapidly growing one. Women married early, at about age twenty or twenty-one, and men married in their late twenties on the average. Only the upper class seemed able to come close to the Iberian ideal of an extended patriarchal family with any regularity. Even at the upper level extended families with more than two generations living together were never a majority; we should keep in mind that families and households were not static, but went through cycles as children married, parents died, and economic conditions changed. Brazilian households did contain some peculiar features. Their average size tended to be large because of the presence of slaves even in humble homes. Also, as so frequently occurred all over Latin America, *agregados* (attached people), who might be relatives, renters, former slaves, or employees, could often be found in the household along with foundlings who were reared with the children.

The family and household structure displayed a great variety. Studies of southern Brazil reveal that many households were headed by women, a probable result of the considerable mobility of men in search of mines or off on expeditions. Brazilian family life was also characterized by consistently high levels of illegitimacy, not only among slaves but among the free population as well. In São Paulo in the late period, almost 40 percent of the children born were illegiti-

Table 6. *Distribution of the Brazilian population, ca. 1800*

	Estimated population	Subtotal	percentage of total population	
Amazon and far north				
Rio Negro & Pará	80,000		3.8	
Maranhão	78,860		3.8	
Piauí	51,721		2.5	
		210,581		10.1
Greater northeast				
Ceará	125,764		6.1	
Rio Grande do Norte	49,391		2.4	
Paraíba	79,424		3.8	
Pernambuco	391,986		19.0	
Bahia	247,000		11.9	
		893,565		43.2
South-center				
Minas Gerais	407,004		19.7	
Rio de Janeiro	249,883		12.1	
São Paulo	158,450		7.5	
		815,337		39.3
South				
Santa Catarina	23,865		1.2	
Rio Grande do Sul	38,418		1.8	
		62,283		3.0
Far interior				
Goiás	52,076		2.5	
Mato Grosso	27,690		1.3	
		79,766		3.8
		2,061,532		99.4

Source: Dauril Alden, chapter on late colonial Brazil in the forthcoming *Cambridge History of Latin America.*

mate. As a rule of thumb, one can take illegitimacy as a measure of marginality or newness on the scene, and thus whites had the lowest rates, then pardos, free Blacks, and finally slaves.

The rapid growth of the Brazilian population was the underlying reason for some of the administrative and political changes that we have discussed. Certainly, to some extent, the expansion of bureaucracy was designed to tax, mobilize, and control an increasing population. Between 1700 and 1820 some 162 new towns and cities were founded in Brazil, compared with only 56 in the preceding two centuries. Ecclesiastical administration did not keep pace, since at the end of the colonial era Brazil had only one archbishopric at Salvador and six episcopal seats. But governmental concern with controlling the population was constant. The later eighteenth century in Brazil was characterized by increasing attempts to establish fixed settlements, to eliminate vagrancy and banditry, and to control in various ways a population that seemed to threaten the social order of the colony. Elite observers fretted about an "insolent, uppity and ungrateful" tide of mixed-blood pardos that seemed to swell out of the ground. Here was another result of the demographic growth of the colony.

The free colored population, the result of miscegenation and manumission, appears to have been the fastest growing group of the post-1750 period. Although the natural growth rate of the slave population seems to have been negative, and thus dependent on constant supply from Africa to maintain its numbers, the free population of color grew at a rapid rate (see Table 7). The reasons for the difference in growth between these two segments of the population are not clear. The slaves' rate of natural increase was probably depressed by the conditions of slavery, which produced higher mortality rates, and the sexual imbalance created by the tendency to import more men than women. Moreover, studies of manumission patterns indicate that masters tended to free women and children, thereby depleting the reproductive potential of the slave force and increasing that of the free colored population. In areas as different as Salvador, where pardos constituted more than half the population, and the Mato Grosso frontier, where they were 45 percent of the inhabitants, the free colored element had grown rapidly. Some vision of the social composition of Brazil can be seen in these figures from Minas Gerais in 1814: 84,000 whites, 143,000 free people of color, 150,000 slaves. Little wonder, then, that the social and racial fears of the Brazilian elites were intensified during the period.

The social hierarchies of Brazilian society were, in fact, not much changed from those of the seventeenth century. Depending on the region, planters, ranchers, or miners still dominated local government and exercised considerable control in the countryside. Interlocking families controlled the social and economic resources of each region. Needless to say, these clans were of European origin. Merchants, of course, had been in the colony since the beginning, but the increasing commercialization of Brazil through its ties to Euro-

Table 7. *Composition of the Brazilian population by ethnicity and legal status, late colonial period*

	% White	% Mulatto and Black			% Indian
		Free	Slave	Total	
Amazon and far north					
Pará	?[a]	?	20.0+	20.0	20.0
Maranhão	31.0	17.3	46.0	63.3	5.0
Piauí	21.8	18.4	36.2	54.6	23.6
Northeast					
Pernambuco	28.5	42.0	26.2	68.2	3.2
Bahia	19.8	31.6	47.0	78.6	1.5
South-center					
Minas Gerais	23.6	33.7	40.9	74.6	1.8
Rio de Janeiro	33.6	18.4	45.9	64.3	2.0
São Paulo	50.8	22.9	14.9	37.8	2.6
South					
Rio Grande do Sul	40.4	21.0	5.5	26.5	34.0
Far interior					
Goiás	12.5	36.2	46.2	82.4	5.2
Mato Grosso	15.8	legal status unknown[b]		80.4	3.8
All jurisdictions	29.4	31.4	34.5	65.9	4.6

[a]Estimated free: 57% including both white and persons of color.
[b]Mulatto: 27.2%; preto("dark"): 53.2%
Source: Dauril Alden, chapter on late colonial Brazil in the forthcoming *Cambridge History of Latin America.*

pean markets had altered their position somewhat. Often Portuguese-born, merchants gained increasing status in the eighteenth century and were able to attain high office and arrange marriages into the landowning aristocracy. The process is strongly reminiscent of developments in Mexico at the same time. Rather than the replacement of one leading group by another, the main trend seems to have been a fusion of the two, although over specific economic issues merchant–planter rivalry could be ardent. In addition to these groups, royal judges, other high-ranking officials, military professionals, and high-level ecclesiastics also enjoyed elite status.

The middling occupations, functionaries, artisans, shopkeepers and others, were composed of a variety of racial categories. Young men emigrating from Portugal without capital or family ties might end up here at least until fortune smiled and a suitable marriage or partnership could be found. For the free colored population such occupations were, in general, the best they could hope for. In the countryside the lavradores de cana continued for the most part to be whites hoping to own a plantation someday. Almost invariably Brazilian-born by this period, owning a few slaves yet lacking secure tenure, living very much at the whim of the plantation owners, they were a class in decline. Independent tobacco growers were also for the most part whites, although at the very end of the century more mulattoes and free Blacks seem to have entered this branch of agriculture.

Within the family, relationships were still based on Iberian models. Society was clearly male oriented and male dominated. In theory, women were to be secluded and protected. Even as independence approached, foreign travelers never failed to comment on the seclusion of upper-class Brazilian women. As always, virginity before marriage was closely associated with family honor. A man could kill an unfaithful wife with legal impunity, but the reverse was surely not true. Disobedient daughters and wives still might be placed in a retirement house or nunnery with little they could do about it. But these principles of male dominance were less characteristic of poorer and darker families, where women by necessity played a more active economic role. The small commerce of street vendors and neighborhood markets was often in the hands of free colored women. In fact, mounting evidence of large numbers of female-headed households, women in small commerce, and women who owned and managed rural properties, indicates that despite law and received ideals women played a more active role in family and economic matters than we have been led to believe.

In terms of social structure the major change of the century was the growth of a free rural population of humble people who were for the most part of mixed racial origin. Such people had always existed in the countryside, but after 1750, just as in Spanish America, demographic and economic forces rapidly swelled their numbers. In São Paulo and the south they were often small, independent subsistence farmers, living a rustic life in tiny villages. In the northeast they were more often *moradores*, a new rural category, juridically free but usually attached to a plantation or ranch. Often they would be allowed to farm a plot in return for labor and other services to the landowners. Although slaves still predominated in the countryside, the moradores constituted a majority of the free rural population. Impoverished, landless, and politically insecure, the moradores, who were in the main pardos, free Blacks, and caboclos, were socially well below the cane growers, who tended to be whites. Droughts periodically drove many of these people into the coastal cities, where they swelled the ranks of the urban poor. In either city or countryside this group had benefited little from the economic boom of the late colonial period. Increasingly, the merchant-planter elite and its spokesmen perceived this class as a threat to the existing social order. As was to be expected in a society constituted as this one was, definitions of social conflict were often perceived in terms of color rather than economic class. And as in parts of the Spanish Caribbean where the Indian element was negligible, the polarization was along Black–white lines, ignoring the Indian. One observer wrote in 1822, the year of Brazilian independence, that "white Europeans, white Brazilians, Blacks and mixed-bloods, some free, others slave, constitute so many classes that have sworn eternal enmity."

Finally, as we have already observed, the eighteenth century was a period of the growth and intensification of slavery. In Minas Gerais, Maranhão, and the area around Rio de Janeiro, new economic activity stimulated the demand for more slaves. Brazil received about 1.7 million African slaves across the century. The elimination of Haiti as a major sugar producer after 1793 caused a sugar boom in Bahia and Pernambuco, accompanied by large-scale importation of Africans. Most came from the Mina coast, many being Yoruba speakers, and thus right at the end of the century large numbers of Africans of similar cultural background were flooding into Bahia. Such human concentrations allowed for the maintenance and preservation of African cultural patterns in religion, music, language, and other aspects of life. Little wonder that much of Afro-Brazilian culture today has Yoruba origins and seems to date from this period. The arrival of large numbers of Africans of similar background in a short time also promoted a certain solidarity and cohesion that was lost when slave origins were mixed. This solidarity seems to underlie a series of serious slave revolts in the northeast and principally Bahia from 1807 to 1835. Although the basic conditions of slavery in eighteenth-century Brazil do not seem to have changed from those of the preceding century, the slave population itself was larger and more African in origin.

Late colonial Brazil, then, experienced some form of almost every process observed earlier for Spanish America during the same time period, from governmental reforms to demographic changes to the development of new crops. Even the blurring of ethnic lines and the increased prominence of the racially mixed were common to late colonial Spanish and Portuguese America, though in the latter case the mixture was mainly European-African, and Brazil, lacking the solid sedentary Indian base of much of Spanish America, had never developed the complex three-dimensional ethnic terminology of Mexico, Peru, or New Granada – but neither, for example, had the Argentine littoral. Yet if the elements were the same, the chronology and emphasis were different, in large part because of characteristics specific to the gold deposits and the sugar industry; also, the ease of communications between Brazil and Portugal and the mother country's growing reliance on the colony slowed trends toward polarization. Brazil's closest analogy to the Spanish American late eighteenth century, as a time of general economic upswing and quick social evolution in a framework of political stability under ancien régime auspices, was to come after independence, when coffee flourished and peace reigned under the traditional Portuguese royal dynasty, even if now separate from Portugal itself.

11

Epilogue: the coming of independence

In the preceding chapters we have been very conscious of the underlying historiography, but have felt that the purpose of the book precluded extensive historiographical discussion. On approaching the independence period, however, we must speak for a moment of the sources and the historical literature, for they illuminate and even almost determine our procedure. It has been said often and truly that the division between colonial and national periods is an artificial one, especially in the social, economic, and cultural domains where so much current scholarly interest lies. Yet at the level of documentary sources and historical approaches, the political independence of Latin America coincides with some gaps and sharp breaks which are not easily bridged.

Wherever armed struggle broke out in Latin America, the production of records suffered. More specifically, the orderly process of sending scattered locally written petitions, litigation, reports, and other documents to central repositories came to a halt. Record-keeping agencies as important as the high courts, the treasury offices, the viceregal secretariats, the merchant guilds, and the Inquisition tribunals ceased to function, to be replaced after an interval by different recording systems or, often, by nothing at all. As a result, many kinds of historical investigation must stop in their tracks at independence. Scholars doing careful work on the extensive late Bourbon censuses find no equivalent in the early national period. In Mexico, the rich vein of Nahuatl documents from hinterland towns, sent to Mexico City in connection with lawsuits on appeal, dries up entirely with the early nineteenth century.

Partly because of the sharp documentary break, partly because of differing kinds of interest in the two subjects, the independence and colonial periods have been studied mainly as two separate fields by separate sets of scholars who are not very deeply involved with each other's work. As a field, independence studies have all in all remained at a relatively early stage, concentrating on military events, well-known individuals, surface politics, and the like, most often within the framework of only one or two of the Latin American nations. Recently some studies that are more analytical and, in certain cases, cross-national have begun to appear, but they are few and inevitably based on sketchy data. Some pioneers have discovered that for various regions, the most local records – notarial, parish, and land documentation – which for many purposes are also the most informative, march past independence and on into the nineteenth century nearly as though nothing had happened. Highly suggestive local studies based on such records have appeared, dealing not so much with independence as with social-economic continuities between colonial and national periods. Yet once again, works of this type are scarce; in general, nineteenth-century society is still far less studied than that of preceding centuries, making comparisons difficult or impossible. Scholarly traditions of social, ethnic, economic, and institutional analysis in the colonial field seem to be spilling over now into the nineteenth century in a major way, and the historiographical picture is likely to change drastically in a very few years. For the moment, however, the best course seems to be a broad and highly abbreviated treatment of the independence movements and their implications, in the expectation that in the near future a truly integrated account of the colonial, independence, and national periods will become more feasible.

Preindependence stirrings

The decades before the launching of full-scale independence movements in Latin America witnessed various kinds of disturbances and dissent, some of a very serious nature. To what extent were these unprecedented, and to what degree can they be considered forerunners of independence? The overall stability of the region through the colonial centuries did not imply universal peace and order; certain types of conflict and protest were endemic, standard phenomena bringing on standard responses, not representing a true threat to the general system. On the far periphery, wars with essentially unconquered nonsedentary peoples had continued intermittently over the whole period with little effect on the more populated areas. Wherever Africans were concentrated in large numbers – in Brazil, the Antilles, all along the Caribbean coast – communities of runaway Blacks, sometimes predatory on other elements of society, had continued to exist in some form from the sixteenth century forward. We have spoken of the frequent limited, localized uprisings among sedentary Indians, best studied for Mexico but apparently little different in the central Andes. In more isolated regions, uprisings among quite sedentary peoples occasionally had a messianic flavor and spread through a broader countryside, leading to much bloodshed and the organization of a strong military response by authorities, as in the 1712 Tzeltal rebellion in the Mayan region of Chiapas. Large urban riots, if not exactly frequent, were surely not unknown; in the major centers they were often related to poor harvests and in mining towns to changes in working conditions. Nor did all dissent come from humble people or subordinate ethnic groups. Throughout the colonial period, especially but not exclusively in isolated regions, when the basic interests of local Spanish settlers were threatened, they had not hesitated to depose royally appointed governors, repeal new taxes, or eject ecclesiastics. Such episodes stretch from the conquest period, when the encomenderos of Peru deposed and killed a viceroy in the course of a major rebellion, on into the eighteenth century. One well-known example, the Comunero revolt of Paraguay (1732–5), involved ejection of a governor, struggle with the neighboring Jesuits, and open defiance of the viceroy of Peru. In Venezuela, resentment of the Caracas Company's monopoly over the country's growing export economy led to an unsuccessful revolt in 1749.

Except for the border wars and the runaway communities, which in a sense were outside the system altogether, protests usually occurred within the existing framework, for the accomplishment of specific, limited goals. The protesters usually put all blame on the officials immediately confronting them, proclaiming their loyalty to crown and church, appealing to higher authorities for different measures, and even affirming that their demands represented the king's true will. The response as well was usually a measured one, with severe punishment for only a figurehead or two; and although the crown never let its authority be questioned in principle, substantive concessions usually followed pacification – recall of the offending officials, moderation of the new taxes, and the like.

In 1780–1 two serious manifestations occurred in Spanish South America which, although unusually large in scale, had much in common with the now traditional types of manageable unrest; doubtless they remained alive in the minds of the generation which achieved Spanish American independence. First came the Tupac Amaru revolt in the Peruvian highlands, coinciding roughly with the activity of a Bourbon tax-reforming inspector general in the viceroyalty; it coincided also with bad economic conditions, partly related to the loss of Upper Peru and much of its silver to the new viceroyalty of the Río de la Plata. In contrast to the Indians of central Mexico, their more isolated counterparts in the central Andes retained some memory of imperial Inca rule and even of the royal dynasty as a rallying point. Leaders of indigenous uprisings in the Andean region often laid claim to Inca descent (as did even a renegade Spanish immigrant named Bohorques who operated in the Tucumán region). Thus in the 1770s as a cacique of Tinta, south of Cuzco, began to develop reformist political ambitions, he changed his surname from Condorcanqui to "Tupac Amaru" after the last Inca to hold out against the Spaniards in the sixteenth century and claimed, perhaps legitimately, to be directly descended from the rebel emperor. As Tupac Amaru he led a group which in November 1780 executed the local corregidor for abuse of the Indian populace, recruited a vast, largely indigenous army, fought battles against Spanish armed resistance, threatened Cuzco, and for some time dominated large stretches of the highland area, until forces were organized to defeat and execute him in May 1781. But if the revolt was indigenous at the base, it was largely creole and mestizo in its leadership – people from the middle levels of provincial society. Tupac Amaru himself was of partly Spanish descent, was well educated in Spanish, and had a Spanish wife. And if on the one hand he emphasized Inca patriotism among the Indians, among non-Indians he spoke of lower and fairer taxes, better courts, and a more open interregional economy. Nor did all Indians support the movement; age-old local ethnic rivalries played a role, and many of the most powerful caciques considered Tupac Amaru a dynastic upstart. To the end he consistently proclaimed loyalty to God and king. After his death the revolt spread into Upper Peru (the city of La Paz was under siege), becoming more violent, extreme, and hostile to non-Indians. Not until 1783 were the highlands pacified, and smaller disturbances associated with Tupac Amaru's name flared up far to the north and south in the greater Andean region. The overall effect of the revolt, despite the early participation in it of some highland creoles, seems to have been to retard any impetus toward independence that might have existed in Peru and what was to become Bolivia. The cross-ethnic leadership and the limited goals of the movement were overshadowed by the memory of what was perceived as an uncontrolled lashing out against all who were not Indians, something all such persons, whether native-born or not, whether of the Spanish, Black, or mixed groupings, wished never to see repeated.

Coming in April 1781, on the heels of the Tupac Amaru uprising, the Comunero revolt in New Granada (Colombia) was apparently parallel to it rather than inspired by it. New Granada had received its own inspector general, who was busily raising taxes and expanding royal monopolies amid widespread resentment. The highland town of Socorro, north of Bogotá, a textile and tobacco-growing center, took the lead in resistance. A spontaneous movement involving all sectors of the local populace took shape; as it spread, whole townships under their constituted municipal councils gave their adherence. The principal leaders emerging from the confusion were prominent local creoles. Immediately the rebels took forceful action against agents of the treasury and government monopolies, and before long they were marching in their thousands against Bogotá, the viceregal capital. After a rebel victory over the few royal troops who had not been sent to the distant coast to ward off the British threat, the government ceded to the dissidents' demands concerning taxes and monopolies. Rebel forces then began to disband, whereupon royal officials refused to honor the capitulations and in the end regained the upper hand, partly by taking advantage of regional and social tensions among the dissidents. Related uprisings occurred in several other parts of the country but never took on the same proportions as the Socorro movement. Although officials used military force and carried out some exemplary executions, the contrast with the aftermath of the Tupac Amaru rebellion is marked. After a general amnesty, many of the highest leaders of the Comunero revolt lived out normal lives, and there was no noticeable revulsion on the part of the general non-Indian population against dissent. Though some actions by Indians against non-Indians did occur, the Indian component was less than in the Peruvian rebellion, just as Indians were a smaller proportion of the population generally. Even at the height of the revolt, rebel leaders insisted that they remained loyal subjects of the crown and limited their opposition to certain specific bad laws. More even than the Tupac Amaru revolt, the Comunero uprising fits well into the older pattern of limited action in defense of regional interests and relative autonomy. Its most noticeable effect locally was a stiffening and reorganization of the New Granadan military by royal officials, carried out in a spirit of mistrust of the area's creoles, who were held back from the sometimes predominant military role and influence they possessed in regions never threatened by a serious general revolt.

A third major uprising in the preindependence period occurred outside the areas of Iberian dominance but nevertheless had a strong impact. In 1791 the Black slave population of French-ruled Saint Domingue, or Haiti, rebelled on a grand scale, destroyed the dominant group of plantation owners, brought the sugar industry to a halt, and started political maneuverings which finally led to Haitian independence. The effect was felt on the other Antilles and all around the edges of the Caribbean, wherever there was a substantial African element in the population. Although the Black, mulatto, and pardo component was a much smaller proportion of the total population in the Iberian areas than in Haiti, and was far more integrated into society generally, nevertheless no one failed to see the implications. Those of African descent might be tempted to emulate the Haitian example. Such was apparently part of the motivation of the Blacks and mulattoes, both slave and free, who carried out a rebellion in 1795 in the province of Coro, on the western Venezuelan coast, aiming not only to abolish slavery and excessive taxes but to destroy the dominant groups and rule for themselves. After some manifestations of violence the revolt was crushed, in good part by forces which were themselves pardo. Thereafter, Coro remained pacific and loyal to the Spanish crown even as other Venezuelan provinces went over to the cause of independence. Fear of another Haitian revolution did not deter independence movements in the general Venezuelan-New Granadan area, but it was a factor constantly on the minds of all concerned.

In Brazil as in Spanish America, ferment was apparent by the last decades of the eighteenth century. In the Brazilian case the early manifestations were abortive, never reaching the scale or intensity of Tupac Amaru's rebellion or the Comunero revolt. The most famous of the early Brazilian movements was the Minas conspiracy of 1788–9. It is perhaps not surprising that such activity arose in Minas Gerais, the briefly wealthy captaincy which had developed a distinctive culture in art, architecture, and music but had subsequently fallen on hard times. In Ouro Preto a small group of intellectuals, including priests, judges, royal officials, and men of property, began to meet to discuss political and cultural matters. In these interests and in their acquaintance with the major Enlightenment authors, they were like groups we have discussed earlier, but they went further, stimulated by the example of the American Revolution, to plot a rising against Portuguese rule. Here too the tax factor was important; what apparently pushed the group to active conspiracy was a new government attempt to collect arrears of the royal fifth on gold, an issue sure to meet widespread resistance and aid their cause. The plot was uncovered, the leaders arrested and tried. Most were exiled but spared because of their station in life. Only one man, José Joaquim da Silva Xavier, called Tiradentes ("Tooth-puller"), was executed. A minor army officer of no particular wealth or status, Tiradentes became a scapegoat.

The genteel conspirators of the rebellion in Minas Gerais envisioned no major changes in the social order. Very different were the participants of the Bahian plot of 1798, sometimes called the Revolt of the Tailors. Not unlike the Coro rebels, the Bahians were Black or mulatto artisans, soldiers, and workers, including some slaves. Influenced by the rhetoric of the French Revolution, they wanted to abolish slavery, extinguish all differences based on color, disallow monasteries, and establish maritime free trade. Their movement was crushed without having really begun; four of the leaders were executed and many others punished. It does not seem that the conspirators had the Haitian example in mind, but the planters and merchants who so resolutely opposed them apparently did. In any case, they saw where their self-interest lay, so that the social and ethnic context put sharp limits on their otherwise strong drive toward autonomy in relation to a mother country which Brazil threatened to overshadow.

In Spanish America too, small seditious conspiracies began to crop up with increasing frequency in the last decade of the eighteenth century and the first decade of the next. Most often they were of the same general type as the Minas Gerais plot, hatched in the framework of a club or clique of creole intellectuals who were modest professionals and lower officials. The improvement societies which came to exist everywhere in the late Bourbon period could easily be turned to such purposes. In these circles the mood, in many areas at least, turned from one of constructive promotion to a spirit of lampooning the constituted authorities. The examples of the American and especially the French revolutions could give quite a different slant to the Enlightenment doctrines by now so standard among Ibero-American intellectuals; one conspirator secretly printed the French *Declaration of the Rights of Man*, and others called for a vaguely defined liberty or even for political independence and popular sovereignty. Faster transportation, freer trade policies, and the economic upswing of late Bourbon times had resulted in larger numbers of Spanish Americans going abroad to study and travel, not only to Spain but to France, Italy, and England. Abroad some of the exiles became open revolutionaries, and even those who returned had at the least been directly exposed to Europe in a time of revolutionary change. Nevertheless, seditious plots among intellectuals and professionals, though sometimes going as far as detailed plans for local coups, were generally discovered in the talking stage, then crushed without using the most severe punishments or causing great public outcry. An invasion of Venezuela by exile Francisco de Miranda with a couple hundred men organized in North America, although it took place on the very eve of the independence movements in 1806, attracted no local support and failed utterly.

It can hardly be said, then, that by the beginning of the nineteenth century Ibero-America was seething with uncontainable movements to gain political independence from the mother countries. There had been some major uprisings, and the notion of complete independence had surfaced in some circles. But the two phenomena were not in conjunction. The larger movements were quite traditional in kind, for limited ends, even if they were exceptional in scope, and the ultimate effect appears to have been to stiffen the resolve of those opposed to a major change. Political radicalism, on the other hand, had as yet only a small minority of advocates, even among the intellectuals most prone to such ideas. One can point to many tensions in the overall society and economy, some of them relatively new, as we have seen in the two immediately preceding chapters. Given the existence of reasons for widespread dissatisfaction and the strongly localized subcultures which had grown up over centuries of semiautonomy, it is perhaps legitimate to say that political independence movements were inevitable in the long run, but the internal situation alone would hardly have suggested their imminence and relatively quick success. To explain the timing of Latin American independence, we must turn to the international context.

International developments

We have seen that over the middle and later colonial period basic changes had been occurring which had the potential, though for a long time not always the actual effect, of loosening the ties between Ibero-America and Iberia. Despite moments of revival, the Iberian powers fell ever further behind England and France at sea; hostilities, and they were frequent, were likely to leave parts of Ibero-America either out of touch or being supplied by foreign ships. Increasingly, the bulk of Ibero-America's market was in northern Europe, and the same countries were supplying ever more of its imports as well, especially manufactures, even though channeled through Iberian ports. It is true that the export of Spanish goods to America had not become so negligible as scholars once tended to think; in the time after the enactment of imperial free trade, nationally produced exports increased markedly not only in volume but as a proportion of the total, regularly surpassing exports of foreign origin in the mid-1790s. But even had Iberia's portion of the trade and its seapower sunk much lower, there would have been little threat to the tie in peacetime, or when powerful maritime allies were available, so that the Iberian countries could continue to be the channels through which trade would flow. Portugal had such an ally in Britain, easily the world's leading naval power. For eighteenth-century Spain, usually allied with France against Britain and its power at sea, the situation was more precarious, resulting repeatedly in mother country and colonies being quite out of touch. The preindependence decades especially were such a time; Spain was at war with Britain from 1796 to 1808, with only two intervening years of peace in which its transatlantic maritime traffic could proceed normally. The Spanish crown was forced to allow neutral ships to supply the colonies, carry the latter's exports, and even convey Indies revenues to Spain by means of a series of drafts and letters of credit in which the actual bullion leaving America went to countries other than Spain itself. Multinational consortia including North American, Dutch, and other interests ran this neutral trade, but ultimately the British themselves were dominant, sometimes openly so. Some areas of Spanish America, notably Cuba and Venezuela, had become so dependent on ships and traders of other nations that even when the Spanish crown ordered a halt to neutral trade at certain times, local officials refused to let the orders go into effect. Commerce with neutrals suffered from difficulties and irregularities, and apparently it was less efficient than supply through Spain in those years when direct trade was possible. Yet in a very real sense Spanish America had already acquired commercial independence from Spain in advance of any moves toward political separation.

Events of 1807–9, leaving Napoleonic France in direct control of almost the entire Iberian peninsula, had an even stronger impact than the years of British blockade. Not only did British trade with many parts of Latin America now expand vastly and regularize; the political implications were even more enormous. Portugal and Brazil were affected first. In 1807 Napoleon, no longer prepared to tolerate Portuguese collaboration with the British, invaded Portugal. But by the time French forces entered Lisbon, the Portuguese king João VI, his court, his government, and perhaps fifteen thousand of his subjects had put to sea in British-escorted ships, their destination Rio de Janeiro. That capital now began a quick transformation as its relatively weak set of institutions, traditionally dependent on easily reachable Portugal, was strengthened in many directions as Rio acquired a military academy, medical school, printing press, financial institutions, a reorganized judicial system, and much more. Revenues were no longer exported to Portugal, and there was no reason not to throw international trade entirely open (as was immediately done), even if the now indispensable British had not insisted upon it. Thus Brazil had attained much of the substance of independence by the mere transfer of some personnel. As accidental as the episode was, yet it was in line with the long tradition of close ties and easy movement between Portugal and Brazil and also with the shifting balance between the two. Aside from bringing a de facto independence, the move of the court also set the stage for the next step. Having once enjoyed the advantage of being governed from within their own borders, the Brazilians were not likely to give it up lightly when the Portuguese king with the changing fortunes of war inevitably would be returning to the homeland. And the sudden influx of such a large number of peninsular Portuguese, many of them naturally in high positions, for the first time brought on problems of displacement, resentment, and polarization between native-born and peninsular-born Iberians, comparable to what had been developing in Spanish America with the major Bourbon reforms from the 1770s forward.

Events in Spain for a time gave that country's dependencies a de facto autonomy as in Brazil but not under such clearly legitimate and uncontestable leadership. Napoleonic France had gained access to Spain in order to carry out the Portuguese invasion. Increasing French pressure indirectly caused the abdication of King Charles IV, and then in May 1808 Napoleon forced Charles's son Ferdinand VII to abdicate as well, in favor of Napoleon's brother Joseph. Resistance broke out all over Spain, but the French army gained ever greater ascendancy. Local resistance committees or juntas from all parts of the country formed a central junta in Seville, which was forced two years later to take refuge in Cádiz under British protection. A regency in the name of the absent Ferdinand replaced the junta, and a parliament (cortes) was convened. During this time, then, Spanish Americans faced the situation of choosing between a legal but unobeyed French-backed monarch and a popular, though not legal, replacement regime. The French-supported regime controlled much of Spain, whereas the junta and regency had hardly a toehold; on the other hand, the Bonaparte regime was blocked from contact with America, whereas its opponent had partial access to the colonies but was nearly powerless at home. The cortes, as a liberal splinter group, passed the Constitution of 1812, establishing a severely limited monarchy and removing many of the basic institutions and distinctions of the Spanish system as it had existed. All this was bound to antagonize the moderates and conservatives who were in charge in the Indies, whether they were peninsular officials or ranking creoles. And for all its liberalism, the cortes adamantly aimed at strong Spanish dominance over the colonies despite the transformed situation, thereby antagonizing the creoles even further (though a certain number of cortes seats were allotted to Spanish Americans).

Meanwhile, British-Spanish forces were retaking much of Spain from the French, until in 1814 the general victory of anti-French powers in Europe allowed Ferdinand VII to reoccupy his throne. No sooner had he done so than he proceeded to annul the Constitution of 1812 and reestablish, at least in theory, all aspects of the older regime, including some features not seen since the wave of Bourbon reform (such as readmission of the Jesuits). Now, for the first time in years, there was a Spanish government strong enough to send troops to the Indies and assert itself there. Many of the gains independence had made in the interim were now temporarily canceled. But Spain had not reached a true equilibrium. In 1820 forces about to be sent to the Indies mutinied, rendering strong Spanish military action in the Western Hemisphere impossible after that date. Spanish instability and relative impotence outside its peninsular borders continued to be the normal situation thereafter. Although the 1820 insurrection forced Ferdinand to restore the liberal Constitution of 1812, in 1823 absolute monarchy returned. By this time, however, the British had developed a vested interest in trade with Latin America and would no longer permit Spain to intervene in the Western Hemisphere to recoup its losses.

Thus Spanish America's ties of trade and communication with the homeland were cut off for most of the time between 1796 and 1808. From 1808 to 1814 Spain had no clearly authoritative rulership, and the competing, shifting partial regimes lacked power as much as they did stability. After 1814, with the restoration, a unified, if weak and indecisive, regime was somewhat able to take action in the Indies, but from 1820 Spain was once again unable to send troops or carry on large-scale trade.

The independence movements

The steps of the process leading to political independence in Spanish America correspond closely to the just outlined stages in international events. The last years of the wars with Britain brought one notable set of developments, connected with the 1806 British invasion of Buenos Aires. Within a brief time local forces, mainly creole, expelled the invaders, and in the meantime deposed their own ruling viceroy in favor of a leader deemed more competent militarily. Everything had been done in a loyalist spirit and soon received specific crown blessing, but local Platine patriotism had been enhanced, and it was seen that a viceroy could be overturned. When the 1808 Napoleonic take-over of Spain set the Spanish American regions so entirely on their own, most local sentiment, whether among high peninsular officials or prominent creoles, favored loyalty to Ferdinand, but under this banner actions of many types could be taken. In some places cliques of peninsulars overthrew existing authorities, claiming they were too weak, and replaced them with candidates they themselves preferred; the most egregious example was the forced removal of a viceroy of New Spain. Other such coups had creole participation. These seizures of power often maintained a tenuous legality through employment of emergency Audiencia powers and the like. Similar subterfuges for similar action had precedent going back as far as the conquest period, but under the present conditions, in which such steps divided an already fragmented loyalist sector and disturbed an already questionable legitimacy, they were extremely dangerous to the stability of the system.

An even more direct challenge were the juntas that began to spring up everywhere in the Indies, proclaiming loyalty to Ferdinand but independence from the weak and dubious junta in Spain; municipal councils of important cities were often the vehicle and basis of the juntas. Royal authorities in America interpreted these movements as rebellions and quickly put down the several organized in 1809. But in 1810, when the central junta fled Seville for Cádiz and seemed doomed, the Spanish American juntas could no longer be contained so easily. In Buenos Aires, Chile, Venezuela, and New Granada juntas or collections of juntas took over, leading in some cases to the declaration of independent republics, in others only to autonomy under loyalist auspices. Counterattacks soon took shape, however, either from inside the areas affected or, more often, from unaffected regions such as central Peru and Cuba. At this point sizable military actions became part of the usual scenario. From 1814 forward Spain began, as we saw earlier, to send substantial numbers of troops to the Indies to quell rebellions, so that by early 1817 the only independence movement still in control of the local situation was that in Buenos Aires, far removed from centers of imperial strength in Peru, Mexico, and the Caribbean.

Events of 1810 in Mexico had a quite distinct profile. As in Peru, no cabildo-based junta emerged. Instead, an intellectual-professional plot, of the type characteristic of earlier phases elsewhere, spread out of control among humble people of the countryside. The leader, Miguel Hidalgo, a modest secular priest stationed in a rural parish, was originally concerned with such standard creole interests as more access to office, promotion of the interregional economy, and perhaps political independence, but his Indian and casta followers, numbering in the thousands, were soon destroying haciendas, shutting down silver mines, and killing and robbing wealthy Spaniards, especially the peninsular-born. The movement thus invites comparison with the Tupac Amaru revolt in Peru a generation earlier. But whereas the Andean rebellion was centered in the heartland of the sedentary Indians, with the Indians as its base, the Mexican uprising started in the Bajío, an area quite centrally located, with rich mining and farming but without the corporate Indian towns of central Mexico proper. From the Bajío the movement spread west and north, again away from the lands of the sedentaries, and when the "hordes," as they are so often called, invaded those lands in a bold move toward the capital, they were defeated. Hidalgo was executed in 1811, to be succeeded by another secular priest, José María Morelos, who shifted the focus of the movement geographically to the southern periphery of central Mexico and intellectually toward the drafting of a liberal constitution and the establishment of a shadow regime independent of Spain. He attracted some support from other professionals, though not leading ones; after continuing the war for a time with diminishing success, he, like Hidalgo, was captured and executed. Only scattered guerrilla bands kept up the struggle. For the most part, the immediate effect of the Hidalgo-Morelos revolution was the same as that of the Tupac Amaru revolt: the creation, through revulsion, of a coalition of all upper elements to maintain the colonial regime in the already existing form.

In 1817 a second major phase of the independence movements began in Spanish South America. By now the aim of total separation from Spain had become general. These are the conflicts that one usually thinks of as the independence wars per se; large-scale and long-term campaigns stretched thousands of miles across the continent, bringing decisive battles and final independence. From Argentina forces under José de San Martín conquered Chile in 1817, proceeding in 1820 by sea to Peru; in 1821 they took Lima, though royalists still dominated the highlands. Major reinforcements from Spain were cut off once and for all, as we have seen, by the 1820 Spanish mutiny and insurrection. By this time Simón Bolívar, campaigning simultaneously with San Martín from a Venezuelan base, had won much of Venezuela and New Granada for the revolutionary movement, and after the events of 1820 in Spain he proceeded to bring most of the rest of the area, now Gran Colombia, under revolutionary control. Moving south with many of his followers, Bolívar was in Lima by 1823, replacing San Martín in the enterprise of leading a reluctant Peru to independence. A series of highland battles brought final victory in both Peru and the new Bolivia by 1825.

Mexico again stood apart. After the Hidalgo revolt the country had regained a certain stability, deterred like Peru from further initiatives in the direction of independence by the memory of a major insurrection from below, but unlike Peru outside the sweep of the transcontinental South American pincer movement. Nevertheless, much sentiment for independence existed, stronger by all appearances than in Peru, and the Spanish events of 1820 precipitated a definitive move, in this case not only because Spain could no longer send troops but because the restored liberal Spanish regime and constitution threatened the measures through which ranking creoles were attempting to rule the country, so that they were now willing to join those already pressing for independence, if only it could be done under a socially and politically conservative banner. In 1821 Agustín de Iturbide, the leader of royal forces against the only remaining sizable guerrilla concentration, combined with the rebel leader to pronounce in favor of Mexican independence as (theoretically) a monarchy. Within the year and with practically no resistance, this movement gained general acquiescence, even from a newly arriving viceroy, and in 1822 Iturbide was declared emperor of an independent Mexico. With this, Mexico had attained sovereignty once and for all, though both the emperor and the empire proved unable to maintain themselves for long.

We have noted earlier the direction developments were taking in Brazil. Ruled since 1808 by the Portuguese monarch in situ, Brazil too was set on a new path by the Iberian events of 1820. In that year Portugal as well as Spain saw a liberal revolt, leading to the establishment of a constitution and the Portuguese demand that the king return home. He did so, leaving his son Pedro as regent for Brazil. Soon thereafter the Portuguese parliament rescinded Brazil's equal status as a kingdom, abolished the new institutions it had gained, and demanded that the prince also return. Inevitably, the Brazilians urged Pedro to remain. He made his decision in 1822, and in the same year declared Brazil's independence with himself as monarch. Brazil thus freed itself from the mother country with less bloodshed, ferment, or concerted political campaigns than did Spanish America. Lest we think that this falls too far outside the general Latin American pattern, let us remember that accident and external factors played a great role in the timing and manner of independence in all the Ibero-American countries. Spanish Central America too attained independence peacefully, presided over by the local Spanish authorities themselves, as a reflex of the independence of Mexico. And the Spanish Caribbean island regions neither fought for, nor attained, independence at this time.

Some perspectives on the independence movements

In the preceding discussion we by no means intend to imply that the entire independence process was accidental or externally motivated. Rather, the movements strongly reflected Latin America's history and social-ethnic-economic makeup. Note the direction the drive for independence took in Spanish South America, rigorously retracing in reverse the path of the sixteenth-century conquest (see Map 16; compare Map 3). The areas conquered last were the first to rise and themselves aided actively in taking the others, converging on Peru in a mirror image of the sixteenth-century movement outward from that base. The parallel is so exact that the very first area taken by the Spaniards in America, the large Caribbean islands, was the last to be lost, waiting until the end of the nineteenth century for independence to come. (Of course, the proximity of the islands to Spain and the mere fact of their being islands may have been crucial to their long retention.) The neat reversal of path is matched by a close correspondence to the regional typology of the Indies. The revolutionary movement spread from former fringe areas to transitional areas and finally to the old central area; in terms of indigenous population, from lands of the nonsedentaries to those of semisedentaries and finally to those of fully sedentary peoples. Looked at in another way, complementary rather than contradictory, the drive was from east coast areas with explosively growing economies to areas of moderate growth less fortunately placed to areas isolated from the new kinds of economic development and hence in decline or on the verge of it. The rising Atlantic seaboard regions had, apparently, both greater incentives to act and a greater possibility of doing so. The latter aspect had partly to do with their more Hispan-

Map 16. Trajectory of the independence movements in Spanish South America.

ized and mobile populations, which were less inertia-bound, fragmented, and complex than those of the central Andes. It was also important that despite any relative decline (and we have seen that Peru's trade still surpassed that of the Plata region in the late eighteenth century), the old viceroyalties were still the center of imperial institutional and military development, with far the greatest concentrations of regular troops and organized militia.

Do Mexican events fit these patterns? Not neatly, perhaps, but there are some strong parallels. Ever since the conquest period, as we have noted in earlier chapters, greater Middle America had been a separate system comparable in many ways to the entire Spanish South American complex, with its own capital and trunk line, its own center and periphery. The near north and west of Mexico, cradle of the Hidalgo revolt, had many similarities with Venezuela and Argentina as an area outside the main centers of sedentary

Indian life, with largely Hispanized inhabitants, an area caught up in a major economic upswing, at least until the end of the eighteenth century. Thus here too a flourishing former periphery rose up and moved on a reluctant center which in the end was liberated more by external than by internal pressures.

As to the armies that fought the independence wars, they too reflected the general constitution of Spanish American society. Although in a few cases significant troop contingents arrived fresh from Spain, in general the combatants on both loyalist and insurgent sides were a great deal like the regular and militia units already existing in the Indies in the late colonial period and in fact, were often those selfsame units. Even on the loyalist side most of the men and some of the officers were native-born. The makeup of the forces, whether already existing or newly raised, remained much the same as before, with the locally prominent or socially high ranking as officers and humble Hispanized people, whether creole, mestizo, Black, mulatto, or urban-acculturated Indians, as the ordinary soldiers. As before, few of the less acculturated Indians living in their own corporations took part. And as before, units were closely attached to their own regions, reluctant to move very far from home. It is true that several leading figures in South America, seeing the necessity of cross-continental campaigns to assure permanent independence, moved thousands of miles in the direction of Peru, taking many of their followers with them. But their presence in regions other than their own was bound to be ephemeral, as were any vast new political entities arising from the campaigns. Major battles went on over a period of years with much loss of life and destruction of property in some places, but the effect on the overall organization of society was not correspondingly great. The entire conflict essentially took place within the Spanish world. Even there, the bulk of the combatants were defending their own region, obeying orders of social superiors in the customary way, or at most looking for personal advancement. Under these circumstances it becomes understandable how prisoners taken in combat could often be integrated into the ranks of the enemy without protest.

The independence wars did sometimes bring quite modest people to the fore. In Mexico the priest Morelos is reputed to have been of mixed descent and without connections, but had things taken a somewhat different turn, he might well have become the first head of government of independent Mexico. In Venezuela the plainsman José Antonio Páez, originally in relative terms a small holder, with little or no education, came through military leadership to the highest political office and ownership of vast cattle estates. Less well known and less spectacular cases abound in widely spread regions. In the end, however, this process was not a great departure for Spanish American society; the individuals affected merely entered into the upper circles as certain able, newly wealthy, or lucky people had always done, with no implication that the general station of persons of their category was to change. The formerly humble beneficiaries of independence can be compared to some sixteenth-century plebeians who were raised to encomenderos, town councilmen, and occasionally governors by virtue of participation in extraordinary events of the conquest.

Perhaps the problem of the overflowing middle, discussed earlier as a primary characteristic of late colonial Spanish American society, was the nearest thing to large-scale social pressure for change connected with independence. It was between the fully established prominent Spanish-creole families at the top and the corporate Indians, who in at least some senses occupied the bottom, that snowballing, massive growth was taking place, ultimately the product of ethnic and cultural mixture. The proportional change in the makeup of society, bringing overcrowding in the intermediary positions, affected not only the mestizos and mulattoes who once predominated in that sphere but also the humble Spanish-creoles who competed with them and the ever larger component of Hispanized Indians. As persons of mixed descent advanced increasingly into the lower levels of the professions, that malaise was felt there too, all alike suffering from the general oversupply of candidates and lack of opportunities of the kind desired. Thus a common element in the independence movements, not quite universal but seen in a wide assortment of regions and from the earliest manifestations to the latest, was the prominent participation of lower professionals – parish priests and minor officials as well as majordomos, small estate owners, artisans, muleteers, and the like. (The same was true in Brazil, as the two plots we outlined earlier demonstrate very well.)

Venezuela, with its population weighted so heavily toward pardos, was a case in which the aspirations of persons of mixed descent and culture, and also the resistance to those aspirations, played an especially large part in the independence struggles. The first serious movement in the direction of Venezuelan independence was visibly conservative, calculated to discourage pardo social ascent. Peninsular-led opposition to the movement was then able to draw successfully on pardo resentment. Bolívar and his allies finally changed their tack and allied themselves with the largely pardo plainsmen, rewarding the leaders handsomely and at the same time treading gingerly and constantly complaining of the pardo danger. That the conflicts in Venezuela were so bloody and destructive seems at least partly related to the size and distinctive ethnic profile of the intermediary group in that country. In just what ways independence may have changed the general status of the Venezuelan pardo grouping, the historiography hardly permits us to say.

Another social aspect of the age of independence was the alteration and deterioration of the "creole-peninsular" relationship. We have seen that in line with general social trends the distinction between native-born and European-born Spaniards was made more sharply and openly in late colonial times than in earlier times, but this in itself made no crucial difference in the allocation of roles and the mechanisms of gradual absorption of most peninsulars into local life. Then as independence approached, attitudes on both sides changed. The nascent independence movements, inevitably largely creole-dominated, needed a scapegoat and near-at-hand enemy, and the peninsular was admirably suited. The peninsulars began to feel more isolated and insecure and consequently developed considerable group cohesion, something which had been notably absent for most of the colonial period. The peninsular coups we mentioned earlier are one example of strong group action. The constant international wars of the preindependence and independence periods may have contributed to the alienation of the peninsular-born, disrupting standard routes of transatlantic migration and communication. In the years after 1808 especially, peninsulars began to abandon their normal identification with the new country, repatriating much capital and expecting to return to Spain rather than settle permanently in the Indies. In some places the wars brought mob attacks on peninsular life and property, blanket executions, and finally decrees of expulsion by some of the new governments. Thus a lifeline of colonial society was nearly cut, and one of its basic constituent parts was severely reduced in size and importance. Yet even after independence many peninsulars remained, and new Spanish immigration never entirely ceased in some areas, not to speak of the non-Iberian European immigration which replaced it and often fell into familiar patterns, from mercantile activity as the immigrants' favorite occupation, to drawing in nephews from home, to marrying the daughters of prominent local citizens, sometimes one's business partners and compatriots.

Postindependence continuities

All in all, the degree of continuity in the social, economic, and cultural realms between pre- and postindependence Latin America is obvious and overwhelming. Not only did cities, estates, ethnic groups, and regions retain their long-standing characteristics, but much of the change which occurred followed already established trends or repeated long familiar processes. For example, in the area of León in Mexico's Bajío, late colonial tendencies of rising land values and incipient estate fragmentation carried right on into the decades after independence. In chapter 9 we saw how in the Plata area Buenos Aires, on the basis of major new economic assets, had begun to grow and consolidate in late colonial times, a process which continued in the early national period as mercantile families acquired and developed land, producing the pattern known in Lima and Mexico City since the sixteenth century: a tightly intermarried group prominent in urban political and economic life and at the same time dominating much of the countryside through large well-organized, commercially oriented rural estates. Finally, by the third quarter of the nineteenth century, Buenos Aires reached out to take surrounding towns and regions into its orbit, forming a single network like those centered on the old viceregal capitals from centuries earlier.

General social evolution continued on the same lines as before. In Mexico and probably other areas, the slow increase in the role of permanent as compared to temporary labor continued as before, leaving temporary labor still largely predominant until the latter part of the nineteenth century, when, with increased markets, profit, investment, and mechanization, the balance finally turned. The newly independent governments typically abolished ethnic distinctions in the eyes of the law, a measure which has often been criticized as superficial or hypocritical. Surely it did not make all citizens equal or identical, but it did respond to the fact that the late colonial ethnic classificatory system had grown unrealistic and unworkable, and thus it was an attempt to adjust to the reality of social evolution. If the Spanish regime had survived, it probably would have done the same thing at much the same time.

One could go to great length detailing continuing trends. But there were some important breaks in continuity as well, especially in politics. Until independence, ultimate legitimacy, sovereignty, and jurisdiction rested in a monarch based across the sea invulnerable to attack, yet too distant to assert himself very forcefully in America, so that overall continuity and the free movement of people and organizations through the whole vast complex were assured, and yet local interests and regional variations could find expression. This system collapsed, presenting Latin America with large problems of establishing viable units and defining legitimate authority. In Spanish America, concepts of the optimum political entities varied from projected great confederations like Bolívar's Gran Colombia of Venezuela, Colombia, and Ecuador, to the opposite, atomization down to the municipality level, as actually occurred in the Plata region during the first half of the nineteenth century; one of the greatest issues in early nineteenth-century politics was how tightly the units were to be bound together (i.e., centralism vs. federalism). Even here, continuities abound. "Federalism," or the push toward regional autonomy, was the same force that had surfaced in the late colonial period with the creation of the intendancies; the states wanting self-rule were frequently identical in boundaries to the colonial intendancies (themselves mainly earlier bishoprics, as we have noted). In the end, neither general unification nor utter fragmentation won out; the effective functioning units in the colonial period, most often Audiencia districts, dictated the borders of the great majority of the independent states. The older situation thus reasserted itself, greatly altered it is true by separate sovereignties inside each unit instead of a single common sovereignty based outside.

Spanish America first abandoned rule by Spain, then by the Spanish monarch, and finally by any monarch. Several prominent leaders of independence favored monarchical government, possibly under princes of the Bourbon line, but no eligible dynasts were available, and monarchy without a monarch of the established dynasty proved ephemeral, as the Mexican case shows. The lack of monarchs, together with a natural revulsion against Spain and everything Spanish and a corresponding appreciation of France and the United States, soon impelled Spanish America into republicanism, a form of government not easy to adapt to its needs, habits, and social-ethnic variety. Neither the autonomous branches of the church nor the still half-separate Indian corporations could survive unchanged in the new setup; but we must remember that they were already undergoing various kinds of attack and quick change in the late colonial period. Working out viable sovereign entities and new forms of government at the same time was by itself enough to ensure a period of instability, even if there had not been other factors, such as the destruction left by the wars and the problems of transition to dealing directly with the North Europeans, now fully and frankly dominant in the transatlantic economy. Many aspects of postindependence life were normal enough, but it was not until a generation and more had passed that most of Spanish America began to enjoy a conventional political stability.

Portuguese America went quite a different route, retaining a monarch of the traditional dynasty for most of the nineteenth century and keeping its territorial-jurisdictional unity definitively. A prince of the royal line, so lacking in Spanish America, was available, willing, and already living in Brazil. The result was a long period of stability, with slow and gradual changes in laws and institutions. Having a monarch of unquestioned legitimacy helped Brazil preserve its unity, but there were many other factors as well. Huge though it was, Brazil was smaller, less populous, and far more compact than far-flung Spanish America. Most of the inhabitants lived near the coast, able to communicate with each other readily, and the former tight maritime ties between colony and motherland had not allowed relatively self-contained centers to proliferate as in Spanish America. There were strong regional feelings in Brazil, but only in the 1830s, when the monarch's legitimacy was diminished during a regency period, did regionalism produce bloody civil struggles at all comparable to those in Spanish America. All in all, Portuguese America could be compared to one large segment of Spanish America. Although the sequence and chronology of events in Portuguese and Spanish America differed markedly, there is little reason to think that the differences in their political development in the early national period go back to intrinsic propensities of Spaniards and Portuguese.

In both spheres of Ibero-America the events and trends of the "colonial period" continued to reverberate throughout the nineteenth century and still do today, not, we feel, as something necessarily negative. Rather than "colonial," the first three hundred years of Latin America's existence as a mixed Indian and non-Indian configuration may deserve, it seems to us, the nomenclature of "formative period," formative of the succeeding nations. Since the Iberians occupied such a large proportion of the area so early, the indigenous population was so numerous and highly organized, and the elapsed time was so substantial, the Ibero-American colonial period naturally looms into the national period far more massively than its equivalent does in North America. In any case, at the deepest level, there are only two periods in the history of the Western Hemisphere, preconquest and postconquest, with the entire span since the arrival of the Europeans a single, unbroken continuum in most respects.

Bibliography

Since our principal aim in preparing an annotated bibliography is to provide additional reading for newcomers to the field, we have tried to emphasize broad-ranging and readable books in English; at the same time, wishing to achieve a minimal comprehensiveness and in some way acknowledge important contributions to our thinking, we have also included some articles and highly specialized publications, as well as a certain number of particularly essential works in Spanish, Portuguese, and French. And since today not all excellent new scholarship is speedily published, we have listed several important doctoral dissertations, which after all are located in academic libraries and can be acquired for no greater expense than most books published by university presses. Finally, though most of the selections are by modern scholars, a certain number of exceptionally informative or representative writings dating from the colonial period are also included.

Although the body of writing on early Latin American history is copious and does not lack distinction, the field is not one (if in fact there are any such) where every theme and area is equally well covered, or research on all topics is frequently updated and synthesized. Consequently, the student, whether neophyte or experienced professional historian, must read both older work and new on a miscellany of often fragmentary topics, gradually obtaining an overview. One sort of perspective needed by the reader in such an enterprise is substantive: a knowledge of the characteristics of certain time periods and types of areas, the role of certain economic activities or ethnic groups, and the like. We hope that the present volume supplies the reader with a preliminary sense of such things. But the student also needs another type of perspective, on the historiography itself. It may be that one cannot properly speak of progress in the field of history, but in early Latin American history there has surely been a progression over time from one type of work to another; the reader needs to know something of where a given piece of writing stands in relation to others and what he can reasonably expect of it.

The first histories of the New World were written by close contemporaries of the early conquests, usually eyewitnesses. Many of the writings were bare military chronicles, others were more, but none give anything like the entire picture, usually misrepresenting the indigenous world and ignoring crucial social and economic aspects of Iberian action. Later came ecclesiastical chroniclers, at times somewhat broader in subject matter but still fiercely partisan in their views and conventional in their topics. By the eighteenth century one begins to find extensive accounts of travelers and scientists, highly informative to be sure but also full of the outsider's stereotypes.

In the nineteenth century a new cycle of historiography started, with epic or narrative treatments of the conquests long dominant. The old militarizing chronicles were the main source, all their biases faithfully reproduced, with the addition of romantic flights, nineteenth-century notions of the role of the prominent individual or great man, and new stereotypes about national character. Still, the brute facts reported are usually reasonably accurate. During the same time period much effort went into the collection and publication of archival documents, but since this resulted in fewer items which the neophyte is likely to see, it concerns us less here.

Next, beginning primarily in the years after World War I, scholars turned to institutional studies, usually taking one ecclesiastical or governmental agency at a time, using as a source mainly the reports that officials sent to the crown. This procedure revealed more structure and pattern than the narrative approach but also tended to make the various institutions look extremely powerful and the metropolitan crowns in very close control, especially since there was still little comprehension of either Iberian society in the Indies or the indigenous element.

With time, institutional work began to evolve in the direction of the study of internal records and statistical series produced by the various agencies studied, going beyond the reports they sent to the outside. The most important development, occurring after World War II, was demography on the basis of tribute records. There is little apparent inherent bias in the documents on which this kind of work is based, but since it is done in a relative vacuum, the problem of tying it in with other historical phenomena is a complex one. Demographic work continues to be produced, evolving ever more from concern with aggregate trends to more intense concentration on material, usually censuses and parish registers, concerning smaller entities.

From about the mid-1960s a new kind of study has made up a large part of the field's production. Social-economic in orientation, these works use a variety of locally produced sources, often including notarial and trial records, as well as the more traditional kinds of documentation. Rather than accepting reports as to how things were, writers in this vein follow the careers of actual individuals of the time, or the trajectory of individual businesses or organizations in a local setting, build up a number of examples, and analyze or generalize from there. To be feasible, such studies have to limit themselves to a quite restricted time and space, but usually their authors do not intend them as research on a specific region; they are investigations of wide-spread, long-lasting processes not visible to other approaches and must be read with that in mind.

Along with social history came ethnohistory, or study of the indigenous population, related to the former branch not only in its concern with ordinary people and subterranean processes but in its use of difficult localized sources. Works in Latin American history done before the 1960s rarely show much sophistication about Indians. The first ethnohistories tended to be quite institutional; gradually they have become more social and at the same time oriented toward other disciplines which have studied indigenous people, including anthropology and linguistics.

As each new phase has succeeded, work in older veins has continued, at least to some extent, though it is often affected by subsequent techniques and outlooks. By the later 1970s a kind of eclecticism was almost the rule, a combination of institutional and noninstitutional focus and sources, of statistical and career-pattern methods. One prevalent type of study fastens on one or more formal institutions but subjects them to a primarily socially oriented analysis. Eclectic studies are a particular challenge to the reader; some achieve an admirable balance and comprehensiveness, whereas others are unintegrated and, despite the appearances, as narrow and superficial as the work of a much earlier time.

Certain topics of great importance to the field have hardly been touched. Cultural and intellectual history have not been much practiced, and when they have, it has often been by people in other disciplines (literature, art history) who were not conversant with the main developments in Latin American history proper. Studies of the independence period, until the last few years, lagged behind at the narrative and naïve institutional stages, out of touch with trends in the historiography of the immediately preceding centuries (see Epilogue). Nor has the field concerned itself much with its vital Iberian and indigenous background. Iberian history has been a thing apart, until very recently occupied mainly with dynastic, political, or at most institutional matters, although some studies of the more recent types have begun to appear since the mid-1960s, with work on Seville leading the way. The Indian background has remained the province of anthropologists, who despite an increasingly ethnohistorical orientation remain in many cases archaeologists at heart, and the reader must not expect their works to mesh easily with studies of the postconquest period.

The following selections are listed under our own chapter headings, with the exception of some general works and others of long chronological span, but the correspondences are only approximate, and many items contain material relevant to other chapters as well.

General

Leslie Bethell (ed.), *The Cambridge History of Latin America* (Cambridge, forthcoming); a multivolume, multiauthor set, the earlier volumes of which contain substantial articles on many aspects of colonial Latin American history by outstanding present-day authorities.

C.R. Boxer, *The Portuguese Seaborne Empire, 1415–1825* (London, 1969); a readable general survey integrating Brazil into the wider history of Portuguese expansion on several continents.

Sérgio Buarque de Holanda (ed.), *História geral da civilização brasileira*, 9 vols. (São Paulo, 1960–77); the first two volumes contain a series of articles on the Brazilian colonial period by prominent historians.

Guillermo Céspedes, *Latin America: the Early Years* (New York, 1974); a brief general survey of Latin American history until about 1650, using much research then recently published.

Howard F. Cline (ed.), *Latin American History: Essays on Its Study and Teaching*, 2 vols. (Austin, Texas, 1967); deals with the development of the field in the United States, contains both historiographical and substantive articles written by several generations of scholars.

J. H. Elliott, *The Old World and the New, 1492–1650* (Cambridge, 1970); a study of the impact of the New World on Europe, especially in intellectual aspects.

Charles Gibson, *Spain in America* (New York, 1966); in the United States, the standard history of colonial Spanish America.

(ed.), *The Black Legend: Anti-Spanish Attitudes in the Old World and the New* (New York, 1971); an anthology of writings of various epochs on a topic we have construed as largely extraneous to early Latin American history proper.

Mario Góngora, *Studies in the Colonial History of Spanish America* (Cambridge, 1975); essays on a variety of broad topics, mainly intellectual and institutional.

C. H. Haring, *The Spanish Empire in America* (New York, 1947); the classic general study of Spanish American formal institutions from a Hispanocentric viewpoint.

Franklin W. Knight, *The Caribbean: The Genesis of a Fragmented Nationalism* (New York, 1978); treats both Spanish and non-Spanish island areas of the Caribbean up to the present; much of the book is concerned with the colonial period.

Magnus Mörner, *Race Mixture in the History of Latin America* (Boston, 1967); nearly tantamount to a history of society; a broad but concise synthesis of the literature on the topic to the date of publication.

J. H. Parry, *The Spanish Seaborne Empire* (New York, 1966); a survey of colonial Spanish American history with considerable attention to imperial, international, and maritime aspects.

Mariano Picón-Salas, *A Cultural History of Spanish America from Conquest to Independence* (Berkeley and Los Angeles, 1963; Spanish original 1944); a survey of intellectual currents across the colonial period as expressed in published books and other formal writings of the time; extraordinarily out of touch with the social, economic, and ethnic history of early Spanish America.

Caio Prado Júnior, *The Colonial Background of Modern Brazil* (Berkeley and Los Angeles, 1967; Portuguese original 1945); a well-known interpretation from a Marxist perspective based primarily on materials from the late colonial era.

Nicolás Sánchez-Albornoz, *The Population of Latin America: A History* (Berkeley and Los Angeles, 1974); a demographic study spanning the time from conquest to the present.

Works crossing the colonial period (or large portions of it) chronologically

Dauril Alden (ed.), *Colonial Roots of Modern Brazil: Papers of the Newberry Library Conference* (Berkeley and Los Angeles, 1973); a collection of research articles on various political and social-economic aspects of Brazil in the mature and late colonial periods.

Ward Barrett, *The Sugar Hacienda of the Marqueses del Valle* (Minneapolis, 1970); a study in historical geography on one important Mexican sugar estate throughout the colonial period.

Victoria Reifler Bricker, *The Indian Christ, the Indian King: The Historical Substrate of Maya Myth and Ritual* (Austin, Texas, 1981); uses historical sources including Indian-language ones, as well as surviving myths and ceremonies, to trace Indian cultural resistance in Chiapas and Yucatan from the conquest to the Caste War of the nineteenth century.

Huguette Chaunu and Pierre Chaunu, *Seville et l'Atlantique (1504–1650)*, 8 vols. (Paris, 1955–9); transatlantic shipping statistics and analysis thereof.

Germán Colmenares, *Historia económica y social de Colombia (1537–1719)* (Cali, 1973); statistically and institutionally oriented.

Sherburne F. Cook and Woodrow Borah, *Essays in Population History*, 3 vols. (Berkeley and Los Angeles, 1971–9); discusses both methodology and substance of Latin American demography, ranging widely in time and space but concentrating on colonial Mexico.

Charles Gibson, *The Aztecs Under Spanish Rule: A History of the Indians of the Valley of Mexico, 1519–1810* (Stanford, Calif., 1964); a massive study of the colonial Indian corporation and its points of contact with the Spanish world, using the example of Mexico's heartland.

Jacobo Gorender, *O escravismo colonial* (São Paulo, 1978); a sweeping, controversial Marxist interpretation of Brazilian slavery and its impact on the economy.

Richard E. Greenleaf (ed.), *The Roman Catholic Church in Colonial Latin America* (New York, 1971); an anthology of previously published studies, many of them by ecclesiastics, on institutional, intellectual, and cultural aspects of the church.

Clarence Henry Haring, *Trade and Navigation Between Spain and the Indies in the Time of the Hapsburgs* (Cambridge, Mass., 1918); a broad institutionally oriented study, covering the time to 1700.

Frances Karttunen and James Lockhart, *Nahuatl in the Middle Years: Language Contact Phenomena in Texts of the Colonial Period*, University of California Publications in Linguistics 85 (Berkeley and Los Angeles, 1976); a linguistic study showing the nature, pattern, and timing of changes taking place in central Mexico's principal indigenous language as it adapted to the influence of Spanish.

Herbert S. Klein, *The Middle Passage: Comparative Studies of the Atlantic Slave Trade* (Princeton, N.J., 1978); half the book deals with the slave trade to Brazil and Cuba.

Jacques Lafaye, *Quetzalcoatl and Guadalupe: The Formation of Mexican National Consciousness, 1531–1813* (Chicago, 1976; French original 1974); traces the surprisingly late evolution of the Guadalupe legend, mainly as expressed by intellectuals, and touches on a great many facets of colonial Mexican intellectual history.

Serafim Leite, S.J., *História da Companhia de Jesus no Brasil*, 10 vols. (Lisbon, 1938–50); a monumental history of the Jesuits in Brazil, sticking close to Jesuit correspondence, and hence giving much attention to missionary, educational, and cultural activities but little to economic ones.

Colin M. MacLachlan and Jaime E. Rodríguez O., *The Forging of the Cosmic Race: A Reinterpretation of Colonial Mexico* (Berkeley and Los Angeles, 1980); a survey of Mexican colonial history with the general reader in mind.

Rolando Mellafe, *A Brief History of Negro Slavery in Latin America* (Berkeley and Los Angeles, 1975; Spanish original 1973); summarizes the historical literature, including that for Brazil, to the date of publication, just before the appearance of Frederick Bowser's study on Blacks in Peru.

David J. Robinson (ed.), *Social Fabric and Spatial Structure in Colonial Latin America* (Ann Arbor, Mich., 1979); a collection of original pieces, mainly in historical geography and demography, on topics related to different areas across Latin America at different times in the colonial period (with the late eighteenth century predominant).

William Lytle Schurz, *The Manila Galleon* (New York, 1939); covers many aspects of the Pacific trade in which the Indies sent silver to the Philippines in return for Chinese silks.

Karen Spalding, "Indian Rural Society in Colonial Peru: The Example of Huarochirí," (Ph.D. diss., University of California, Berkeley, 1967); a socially and anthropologically oriented study of indigenous groups in a highland area near Lima throughout the colonial period.

Robert Stevenson, *Music in Aztec and Inca Territories* (Berkeley and Los Angeles, 1968); deals with preconquest, colonial-period, and later music in the two central areas of indigenous and early colonial development.

Manuel Toussaint, *Colonial Art in Mexico* (Austin, Texas, 1967; Spanish original 1949); a colorfully written compendium by a Mexican art historian active in the first half of the twentieth century and responsible for much of the revival of interest in the colonial art of his country.

Robert C. West, *Colonial Placer Mining in Colombia* (Baton Rouge, La., 1952); a study in historical geography covering the entire colonial period, with attention to social aspects as well as technical mining lore.

Harold E. Wethey, *Colonial architecture and sculpture in Peru* (Cambridge, Mass., 1949); a comprehensive study and inventory covering a wide area and the whole colonial period.

1. Iberian ways

Ida Altman, "Emigrants, Returnees and Society in Sixteenth-Century Cáceres," Ph.D. diss., Johns Hopkins University, 1981; at present the only existing career-pattern social history of an early modern Spanish region; also studies patterns of migration to and from the Indies at the level of the family and the individual.

Bailey W. Diffie and George Winius, *Foundations of the Portuguese Empire, 1415–1580* (Minneapolis, 1977); brings the results of Diffie's lifetime of research on early expansion into this collaboration with a specialist on Portuguese Asia.

J. H. Elliott, *Imperial Spain, 1469–1716* (London, 1963); a general survey including considerable social and cultural as well as political and dynastic discussion.

H.B. Johnson, Jr. (ed.), *From Reconquest to Empire: The Iberian Background to Latin American History* (New York, 1970); an anthology of extracts from well-known authors representing various, mainly older, points of view.

Richard L. Kagan, *Students and Society in Early Modern Spain* (Baltimore, 1974); a prosopographical and institutional study of higher education.

John Lynch, *Spain under the Hapsburgs,* 2 vols. (New York, 1964–9); a general survey of Spanish history, 1516–1700.

Vitorino Magalhães Godinho, *Os descobrimentos e a economia mundial,* 2 vols. (Lisbon, 1965); a lavishly produced book with extended analysis of the economic aspects of the Portuguese discoveries, including the sugar industry, in the Atlantic islands prior to the development of Brazil.

António de Oliveira Marques, *History of Portugal,* 2 vols. (New York, 1972); a general history of Portugal giving considerable space to the Portuguese empire.

J. H. Parry, *The Age of Reconnaissance* (London, 1963); covers early modern European expansion generally, with emphasis on maritime aspects.

Stanley G. Payne, *A History of Spain and Portugal,* 2 vols. (Madison, Wis., 1973); a relatively brief work covering the entire span of Iberian history.

Ruth Pike, *Aristocrats and Traders: Sevillian Society in the Sixteenth Century* (Ithaca, N.Y., 1972); a study of various segments of society in the city from which emigrants and fleets left Spain for the Indies.

Enterprise and Adventure: The Genoese in Seville and the Opening of the New World (Ithaca, N.Y., 1966); a detailed picture of Genoese-Sevillian individuals, families, and firms based in part on notarial records.

A. J. R. Russell-Wood, "Iberian Expansion and the Issue of Black Slavery," *American Historical Review* 83 (1978): 16–42; deals with moral and ideological issues.

A. C. de C. M. Saunders, *A Social History of Black Slaves and Freedmen in Portugal, 1441–1555* (Cambridge, 1982); a detailed monograph.

Jaime Vicens Vives (ed.), *Historia de España y América,* 5 vols. (Barcelona, 1961); a multiauthor work attempting to emphasize social and economic aspects across many centuries and both hemispheres; the earlier volumes and the sections on Spain proper are the ones of special interest here.

2. Indigenous ways

Frances F. Berdan, *The Aztecs of Central Mexico: An Imperial Society* (New York, 1982); contains much more social, economic, and political analysis than other surveys by anthropologists.

Woodrow Borah and Sherburne F. Cook, *The Aboriginal Population of Central Mexico on the Eve of the Spanish Conquest,* Ibero-Americana 45 (Berkeley and Los Angeles, 1963); on the method and substance of estimating the size of the indigenous population.

Pedro Carrasco, Johanna Broda et al., *Estratificación social en la Mesoamérica prehispánica* (México, 1976); an anthology of original articles on the social and political organization of various indigenous Mexican peoples around the time of the conquest.

Pedro de Cieza de Leon, *The Incas* (Norman, Okla, 1959); those portions relating to indigenous people from the extensive writings of Cieza, the most astute of the chroniclers of the Peruvian conquest period; Spanish original written ca. 1550.

Michael D. Coe, *The Maya,* rev. ed. (New York, 1980; original ed., 1966); an anthropological survey of Mayan civilization from earliest times to the conquest.

George A. Collier, Renato I. Rosaldo, and John D. Wirth (eds.), *The Inca and Aztec States, 1400–1800: Anthropology and History* (New York, 1982); a set of original essays by well-known scholars on a variety of ethnohistorical topics, both preconquest and postconquest, concerning the central areas.

William M. Denevan (ed.), *The Native Population of the Americas in 1492* (Madison, Wis., 1976); a collection of original pieces on aspects of indigenous demography, touching on several geographic regions.

Garci Díez de San Miguel, *Visita hecha a la provincia de Chucuito por Garci Díez de San Miguel en el año 1567* (Lima, 1964); records of an inspection tour carried out in a highland Andean area, including voluminous specific testimony by indigenous individuals; contains an analysis by John Murra of the records' contribution to our knowledge of Andean local and provincial organization.

Friedrich Katz, *The Ancient American Civilizations* (New York, 1972); a broad and comprehensive treatment based on the classic sources, concentrating especially on the Aztecs and Incas.

Edward P. Lanning, *Peru Before the Incas* (Englewood Cliffs, N.J., 1967); an anthropological survey emphasizing how much of Andean civilization far antedated the Incas.

Alfred Métraux, *A religião dos tupinambás e as suas relações com a das demais tribus tupi-guaranís,* 2nd ed., (São Paulo, 1979; originally published in French, 1928); a classic that uses modern ethnography and historical materials to analyze the culture of the Tupinambá at contact.

John V. Murra, *La organización económica del estado inca* (México, 1978); emphasizes the difference between Andean organization, with its regional and ethnic variety and adaptation to special climates, and modern welfare or totalitarian states; English edition expected.

Fray Bernardino de Sahagún, *Florentine Codex: General History of the Things of New Spain,* 12 vols., trans. Arthur J. O. Anderson and Charles E. Dibble (Salt Lake City, Utah, and Santa Fe, N.M., 1950–82); an encyclopedic presentation of Nahua or Aztec civilization just before the Spanish conquest of Mexico, organized by a Franciscan friar. The basic texts, written before 1570 by Indians in Nahuatl, are translated here into English. (Sahagún's own Spanish paraphrase and commentary also exists, and is of interest in its own right.)

Julian H. Steward and Louis C. Faron, *Native Peoples of South America* (New York, 1959); a summary of the multivolume anthropological reference work *Handbook of South American Indians.*

Robert Wauchope (ed.), *The Indian Background of Latin American History: The Maya, Aztec, Inca, and Their Predecessors* (New York, 1970); an anthology of previously published pieces and extracts by anthropologists and historians on widely varying topics.

3. From islands to mainland: the Caribbean phase and subsequent conquests

Arthur J. O. Anderson and Charles E. Dibble (eds.), *The War of Conquest: How It Was Waged Here in Mexico. The Aztecs' Own Story As Given to Fray Bernardino de Sahagún* (Salt Lake City, Utah, 1978); a section of the *Florentine Codex* (see listing under Chapter 2) edited for the general reader.

Herbert E. Bolton, *Coronado, Knight of Pueblos and Plains* (Albuquerque, N.M., 1949); a novelistic, chronicle-based account of a famous expedition north from central Mexico into the present southwestern United States.

Robert S. Chamberlain, *The Conquest and Colonization of Yucatán* (Washington, D.C., 1948); a scholarly account going considerably beyond pure narrative.

Hernando Cortés, *Letters to the Emperor* (various English editions); reports, written 1519–26, to the crown on the conquest of Mexico, eloquently magnifying Cortés himself and presenting everything as done in the service of God and king.

Bernal Díaz del Castillo, *True History of the Conquest of New Spain* (various English editions); a nostalgic, colorful account written in the 1560s by one of the conquerors in his old age, partially in reaction to overemphasis on Cortés as leader.

C. Harvey Gardiner, *Naval Power in the Conquest of Mexico* (Austin, Texas, 1956); an account of the role played by the brigantines the Spaniards built on Lake Texcoco during the siege of the Aztec capital Tenochtitlan.

Mario Góngora, *Los grupos de conquistadores en Tierra Firme (1509–1530)* (Santiago, Chile, 1962); an analysis of the social composition and organization of the conquerors of the Panama region.

John Hemming, *The Conquest of the Incas* (New York, 1970); a colorful narrative of the older style, with addition of more attention to the indigenous role.

F. A. Kirkpatrick, *The Spanish Conquistadores* (London, 1934); a mainly military narrative; covers the entire sweep of Spanish conquest in the Western Hemisphere.

Miguel León-Portilla, *The Broken Spears: The Aztec Account of the Conquest of Mexico* (Boston, 1962; Spanish original 1959); an anthology of pieces written in the first generation or two after the conquest by indigenous people.

James Lockhart, *The Men of Cajamarca: A Social and Biographical Study of the First Conquerors of Peru* (Austin, Texas, 1972); a detailed analysis of origins, careers, and patterns of interaction of the 168 Spaniards who captured the Inca ruler at Cajamarca in 1532.

Samuel Eliot Morison, *Admiral of the Ocean Sea: A Life of Christopher Colombus,*

2 vols. (Boston, 1942); an extensive biography, including a full picture of Columbus's crucial Italian and Portuguese background.

Enrique Otte, *Las perlas del Caribe: Nueva Cádiz de Cubagua* (Caracas, 1977); a full-scale treatment of the social, economic, and political aspects of the pearl boom on the islands off Venezuela in the second quarter of the sixteenth century.

William H. Prescott, *History of the Conquest of Mexico* and *History of the Conquest of Peru* (New York, 1931, and other editions; originally published 1843 and 1846); famous narratives, novelistic in approach, still entertaining and enlightening in some respects, thoroughly superseded in others.

Carl Ortwin Sauer, *The Early Spanish Main* (Berkeley and Los Angeles, 1966); a panorama of Spanish action in the Caribbean phase, mainly based on chronicles but with additional social, anthropological, and geographical insights.

4. Conquest society: central areas

Arthur Scott Aiton, *Antonio de Mendoza: First Viceroy of New Spain* (Durham, N.C., 1927); the biography of a famous viceroy of Mexico (1535–50), on the basis of his official correspondence, making him appear the bringer of Spanish civilization and main force for constructive colonization, opposed by a malevolent Audiencia. It is a shame that the author omitted from the title the "don" which was so essential a part of the viceroy's name.

Peter Boyd-Bowman, "Patterns of Spanish Emigration to the Indies until 1600," *Hispanic American Historical Review* 56 (1976):580–604; a statistical analysis based mainly on emigration permissions issued in Seville.

S. L. Cline, "Culhuacan, 1572–1599: An Investigation Through Mexican Indian Testaments," Ph.D. diss., University of California, Los Angeles, 1981; uses Nahuatl documents as the basis for an intimate portrait of an Indian town around 1580.

Noble David Cook, *Demographic Collapse: Indian Peru, 1520–1620* (Cambridge, 1981); historical demography; covers the area of the present republic of Peru.

George M. Foster, *Culture and Conquest: America's Spanish Heritage* (Chicago, 1960); a study by an anthropologist relying greatly on present-day ethnography and a Ricardian view of the conquest, nevertheless containing some acute observations about the formation of new and transplanted societies.

Charles Gibson, *Tlaxcala in the Sixteenth Century* (New Haven, Conn., 1952); shows how a large Indian corporation achieved a mixture of the Spanish and the indigenous in its postconquest local institutions.

Richard E. Greenleaf, *The Mexican Inquisition of the Sixteenth Century* (Albuquerque, N.M., 1969); contains political, social, and intellectual interpretation pulled from close study of inquisitorial cases.

Lewis Hanke, *The Spanish Struggle for Justice in the Conquest of America* (Philadelphia, 1949); a famous work presenting the main legal, religious, and humanitarian controversies surrounding the Spanish conquest and occupation, with emphasis on the Dominican fray Bartolomé de las Casas.

Robert G. Keith, *Conquest and Agrarian Change: The Emergence of the Hacienda System on the Peruvian Coast* (Cambridge, Mass., 1976); a study of the transition from the encomienda estates of the conquest period by way of relatively modest rural properties to the consolidation of haciendas by the early seventeenth century.

George Kubler, *Mexican Architecture of the Sixteenth Century*, 2 vols. (New Haven, Conn., 1948); concentrates on monastery construction by the mendicant orders; done as art history, but nevertheless represents an attempt to incorporate other scholarly approaches, including demography and ecclesiastical-cultural history à la Robert Ricard.

Peggy K. Liss, *Mexico Under Spain, 1521–1556: Society and the Origins of Nationality* (Chicago, 1975); a picture of the conquest period from the point of view of high officials in Spain and Mexico.

James Lockhart, *Spanish Peru, 1532–1560* (Madison, Wis., 1968); presents the standard types and patterns of Spanish society in the central areas during the conquest period on the basis of study of a large number of individual lives.

James Lockhart and Enrique Otte (eds.), *Letters and People of the Spanish Indies, Sixteenth Century* (Cambridge, 1976); letters written in the Indies by persons high and low to relatives, friends, and superiors, usually in Spain, with extensive commentary to each letter.

John McAndrew, *The Open-Air Churches of Sixteenth-Century Mexico: Atrios, Posas, Open Chapels, and Other Studies* (Cambridge, Mass., 1965); an exhaustive art-historical study of the specifically Mexican monastery complex.

J. H. Parry, *The Audiencia of New Galicia in the Sixteenth Century* (Cambridge, 1948); a study of a secondary Audiencia, basically institutional but with much narrative concerning the principal officials involved.

John Leddy Phelan, *The Millennial Kingdom of the Franciscans in the New World: A Study of the Writings of Gerónimo de Mendieta* (Berkeley and Los Angeles, 1956); a study in intellectual history detailing the Franciscan rationale for the conquest and for their own role therein, with emphasis on the Spanish and medieval background of the ideas.

Robert Ricard, *The Spiritual Conquest of Mexico: An Essay on the Apostolate and the Evangelizing Methods of the Mendicant Orders in New Spain, 1523–1572* (Berkeley and Los Angeles, 1966; French original, 1933); a classic, influential résumé of the activity of the mendicant orders and its rationale, based on the writings and reports of the mendicants.

G. Micheal Riley, *Fernando Cortés and the Marquesado in Morelos, 1522–1547: A Case Study in the Socioeconomic Development of Sixteenth-Century Mexico* (Albuquerque, N.M., 1973); shows the business activities of Cortés, which, though on a grand scale, were not different in kind from those of ordinary encomenderos.

William L. Sherman, *Forced Native Labor in Sixteenth-Century Central America* (Lincoln, Neb., 1979); a mainly institutional study of Indian slavery, encomienda labor, and repartimiento in Guatemala and environs.

Ronald Spores, *The Mixtec Kings and Their People* (Norman, Okla., 1967); an anthropological work resting partly on archaeology and ethnography, but its core, based on succession litigation, shows a set of indigenous principalities in south-central Mexico retaining the same rulers and rules of dynastic succession after the conquest as before.

Steve J. Stern, *Peru's Indian Peoples and the Challenge of Spanish Conquest: Huamanga to 1640* (Madison, Wis., 1982); a study of Spanish-Indian relations in a highland Andean area, showing the ability of each side to manipulate the other in certain respects.

Nathan Wachtel, *The Vision of the Vanquished: The Spanish Conquest of Peru through Indian Eyes, 1530–1570* (New York, 1977; French original, 1971); applies ideas of Claude Lévi-Strauss and John Murra to the sixteenth-century Andean indigenous world; also contains sections on conflicts between Spaniards and Indians in fringe areas.

Silvio A. Zavala, *La encomienda indiana* (Madrid, 1935); a classic study of the juridical aspects of the early development of the encomienda in the Spanish Indies.

5. Maturity in the Spanish Indies: central areas

Ida Altman and James Lockhart (eds.), *Provinces of Early Mexico: Variants of Spanish American Regional Evolution* (Los Angeles, 1976); an anthology of original pieces, mainly based on books and dissertations, portraying society in a selection of Mexican regions at various times in the mature and late colonial periods.

Arthur J. O. Anderson, Frances Berdan, and James Lockhart, *Beyond the Codices* (Berkeley and Los Angeles, 1976); a collection of Nahuatl documents with translations, illustrating both the kinds of things indigenous people of central Mexico wrote during the colonial period and various aspects of their ordinary lives.

P. J. Bakewell, *Silver Mining and Society in Colonial Mexico: Zacatecas, 1546–1700* (Cambridge, 1971); a thorough study of the technical, social, economic, and institutional aspects of Mexico's premier silver mining district in the sixteenth and seventeenth centuries.

Woodrow Borah, *New Spain's Century of Depression*, Ibero-Americana 35 (Berkeley and Los Angeles, 1951); a synthesis of the aggregate demographic trends of colonial Mexico and a preliminary attempt to correlate the demographic curve with other historical developments.

Frederick P. Bowser, *The African Slave in Colonial Peru, 1524–1650* (Stanford, Calif., 1974); a massive study of the role of the African in

Spanish America, combining institutional, statistical, and career-pattern approaches.

Fred Bronner, "Peruvian Encomenderos in 1630: Elite Circulation and Consolidation," *Hispanic American Historical Review* 57 (1977):633–58; a statistical analysis of the composition and interrelatedness of Peruvian upper groups, with emphasis on the weakness of encomienda-holding as a central characteristic of prominence by the early seventeenth century.

François Chevalier, *Land and Society in Colonial Mexico: The Great Hacienda* (Berkeley and Los Angeles, 1966; French original, 1952); a generalizing study of Mexican haciendas in the seventeenth and eighteenth centuries, concentrating on north Mexico and using French medieval models as the basis for much of the interpretation; point of departure for recent studies of Spanish American rural estates, which often reach very different conclusions.

Keith A. Davies, a book on rural estates and society in the Arequipa region from the conquest to about 1650, presently without definitive title (Austin, Texas, forthcoming); exhaustively traces individual families and estates of the region over generations, shows in detail the organization of local society and the commercial-agrarian economy, as well as their close intertwining, and depicts with great clarity the evolution from encomienda estates to emphasis on viticulture.

Pierre Duviols, *La lutte contre les religions autochtones dans le Pérou colonial ("L'extirpation de l'idolatrie" entre 1532 et 1660)* (Lima and Paris, 1971; also in Spanish); an institutional study of the ecclesiastical campaigns to uncover and combat survivals of indigenous Andean religion in the early mature period.

Thomas Gage, *Thomas Gage's Travels in the New World*, ed. J. Eric Thompson (Norman, Okla., 1958; originally published, 1648); a colorful journal of an Englishman who spent years in Mexico and Guatemala in the early seventeenth century as a Dominican friar.

Paul B. Ganster, "A Social History of the Secular Clergy of Lima during the Middle Decades of the Eighteenth Century," Ph.D. diss., University of California, Los Angeles, 1974; provides individual lives, career patterns, and statistics on the social composition and activity of the Peruvian secular clergy in the late mature colonial period.

Garcilaso de la Vega el Inca, *Royal Commentaries* (Austin, Texas, 1966; Spanish original, 1609–17); an account of the Inca empire and the Spanish conquest by a noble Peruvian mestizo, extolling both sides of his ancestry; more notable for its author's attitudes and style than for its reporting of the facts.

Lewis Hanke, *The Imperial City of Potosí* (The Hague, 1956); brief impressions of South America's greatest silver mining town, emphasizing its magnitude and encouraging research on the topic.

C. H. Haring, *The Buccaneers in the West Indies in the Seventeenth Century*

(London, 1910); a narrative staying close to the original accounts produced by the North European interlopers themselves.

Louisa Schell Hoberman, "Merchants in Seventeenth-Century Mexico City: A Preliminary Portrait," *Hispanic American Historical Review* 57 (1977): 479–503; helps to fill a near void in the historical literature.

Roland D. Hussey, *The Caracas Company, 1728–1784* (Cambridge, Mass., 1934); an institutionalizing study of the only major commercial monopoly company of the Spanish Indies.

Jorge Juan and Antonio de Ulloa, *A Voyage to South America* (abridged ed. New York, 1964; other editions available; Spanish original, 1748); a quasi-official report containing descriptions of society, economy, buildings, and even occasionally landscapes in various parts of South America, as well as latitudes, longitudes, and other semiscientific data.

Pál Keleman, *Baroque and Rococo in Latin America* (New York, 1951); gives examples of two prominent and closely related styles in Spanish American colonial art and architecture.

Herman W. Konrad, *A Jesuit Hacienda in Colonial Mexico: Santa Lucía, 1576–1767* (Stanford, Calif., 1980); a detailed study of all aspects of a large central-area hacienda complex, especially rich in information on staff and labor.

Asunción Lavrin and Edith Couturier, "Dowries and Wills: A View of Women's Socioeconomic Role in Colonial Guadalajara and Puebla, 1640–1790," *Hispanic American Historical Review* 59 (1979):280–304; uses both full examples from notarial records and a statistical sampling of data from them to elucidate general patterns and range of variation.

Irving A. Leonard, *Baroque Times in Old Mexico: Seventeenth-Century Persons, Places, and Practices* (Ann Arbor, Mich., 1959); a panorama of upper-level cultural and intellectual phenomena of seventeenth-century Mexico.

Murdo J. MacLeod, *Spanish Central America: A Socioeconomic History, 1520–1720* (Berkeley and Los Angeles, 1973); a massive, largely macroeconomic study of the Guatemala region, using administrative sources.

Luis Martín, *The Intellectual Conquest of Peru: The Jesuit College of San Pablo, 1568–1767* (New York, 1968); an institutional study of the central Jesuit establishment in Spanish South America, from a Jesuit viewpoint and using exclusively Jesuit sources.

Peter Marzahl, *Town in the Empire: Government, Politics, and Society in Seventeenth-Century Popayán* (Austin, Texas, 1978); studies local institutions in action in an important provincial city within a fleshed-out social context.

John Preston Moore, *The Cabildo in Peru Under the Hapsburgs: A Study in the Origins and Powers of the Town Council in the Viceroyalty of Peru, 1530–1700* (Durham, N.C., 1954); a strictly institutional study of the cabildo.

John Leddy Phelan, *The Kingdom of Quito in the Seventeenth Century: Bureaucratic Politics in the Spanish Empire* (Madison, Wis., 1967); centered on Quito's Audiencia, with special attention to the career of its president;

also covers other aspects of the area's political, intellectual, economic, and general development.

Hernando Ruiz de Alarcón, *Treatise on the Heathen Superstitions and Customs that Today Live among the Indians Native to this New Spain, 1629*, ed. J. Richard Andrews and Ross Hassig (Norman, Okla., forthcoming); a seventeenth-century ecclesiastic's account of indigenous religious beliefs and practices surviving into his day in the area south of the Valley of Mexico; especially interesting are the Nahuatl incantations reproduced and translated in the text.

William B. Taylor, *Drinking, Homicide and Rebellion in Colonial Mexican Villages* (Stanford, Calif., 1979); shows Mexican Indian towns retaining basic equilibrium through the colonial period, though more changed in their ways where more Spaniards were present.

William B. Taylor, *Landlord and Peasant in Colonial Oaxaca* (Stanford, Calif., 1972); a detailed land tenure study covering mature and late colonial periods; shows a high degree of Indian land retention and low degree of consolidation of Spanish estates in an area distant from the capital and silver mines.

A. C. van Oss, "Comparing Colonial Bishoprics in Spanish South America," *Boletín de Estudios Latinoamericanos y del Caribe* (Amsterdam), No. 24 (June 1978):27–65; categorizes the Hispanic South American bishoprics as to the timing of developments and the relative elaboration of staff and edifices; also shows cross-regional ecclesiastical career movements.

6. Brazilian beginnings

João Capistrano de Abreu, *Caminhos antigos e povoamento do Brasil* (Rio de Janeiro, 1930); a classic which has had a profound impact on the Brazilians' interpretation of their past.

Francis A. Dutra, "Duarte Coelho Pereira, Lord Proprietor of Pernambuco: The Beginning of a Dynasty," *The Americas* 29 (1973):415–41; a detailed study of the most successful captaincy.

John Hemming, *Red Gold: The Conquest of the Brazilian Indians* (Cambridge, Mass., 1978); an examination of Indian-Portuguese relations on the basis of printed documents and other existing literature.

H. B. Johnson, Jr., "The Donatary Captaincy in Perspective: Portuguese Backgrounds to Settlement in Brazil," *Hispanic American Historical Review* 52 (1972):203–14; deals with the origins and operation of the captaincy system, examining the concept of lordship (senhorio).

Serafim Leite, S.J. (ed.), *Monumenta Brasiliae*, 5 vols. (Rome, 1956–60); a minutely edited collection of the early Jesuit letters.

Pero de Magalhães de Gandavo, *The Histories of Brazil*, 2 vols. (New York, 1922; Portuguese original, 1578); one of the first chronicles of Brazil, promotional in nature but full of insights and information.

Alexander Marchant, "Feudal and Capitalistic Elements in the Portuguese Settlement of Brazil," *Hispanic American Historical Review* 22 (1942):493–512; focuses on the nature of the donatary captaincy.

From Barter to Slavery: The Economic Relations of Portuguese and Indians in the Settlement of Brazil, 1500–1580 (Baltimore, 1942); in effect, a brief economic history of Brazil in the pre-sugar period.

Charles E. Nowell, "The French in Sixteenth Century Brazil," *The Americas* 5 (1949):381–93; an able examination, emphasizing the secular nature of the French colony.

Stuart B. Schwartz, "Indian Labor and New World Plantations: European Demands and Indian Response in Northeastern Brazil," *American Historical Review* 83 (1978):43–79; concentrates on the transition from Indian to African slavery and questions some of Marchant's hypotheses.

Sonia A. Siqueira, *A inquisição portuguesa e a sociedade colonial* (São Paulo, 1978); an attempt to write a partial history of sixteenth-century Brazil using Inquisition records as a prism.

7. Brazil in the sugar age

André João Antonil [Giovanni Antonio Andreoni], *Cultura e opulência do Brasil por suas drogas e minas*, ed. André Mansuy (Paris, 1968; originally published, 1711); a penetrating discussion of the Brazilian economy and a revealing document on social interaction by an Italian Jesuit who saw long service in Brazil; this Portuguese and French edition contains valuable notes and supplementary documents.

João Lucio d'Azevedo, *História de Antonio Vieira*, 2 vols. (Lisbon, 1918); a biography of the prominent seventeenth-century Jesuit.

C. R. Boxer, *The Dutch in Brazil, 1624–1654* (Oxford, 1957); a copious general treatment of the period of Dutch occupation of Pernambuco.

Portuguese Society in the Tropics: The Municipal Councils of Goa, Macao, Bahia, and Luanda (Madison, Wis., 1965); studies the câmara as a municipal institution within a Portuguese imperial perspective, but also gives special attention to who served in municipal offices and why.

Salvador de Sá and the Struggle for Brazil and Angola, 1602–1686 (London, 1952); the biography of a governor of Rio de Janeiro whose transcontinental career illustrates the intertwining of Portugal, Brazil, and Portuguese Africa.

José Aderaldo Castello, *Manifestações literárias do período colonial* (São Paulo, 1975); a succinct overview of the little developed field of Brazilian colonial intellectual history, highlighting the major works and authors.

Rae Flory, "Bahian Society in the Mid-Colonial Period: The Sugar Planters, Tobacco Growers, Merchants, and Artisans of Salvador and the Recôncavo, 1680–1725," Ph.D. diss., University of Texas, Austin, 1978; an extensive study of northeast Brazilian social types and structures in the mature colonial period, based on notarial and other local records.

Rae Flory and David Grant Smith, "Bahian Merchants and Planters in the Seventeenth and Early Eighteenth Centuries," *Hispanic American Historical Review* 58 (1978):571–94; using copious individual examples as well as a statistical overview of the groups' characteristics, shows extensive merchant-planter interpenetration.

Gilberto Freyre, *The Masters and the Slaves: A Study in the Development of Brazilian Civilization* (New York, 1956, and other editions; Portuguese original, 1933); a famous book in a cultural-anthropological and literary vein on the society that grew up around the northeastern sugar industry; directed historians' attention away from politics and institutions toward matters of ethnicity, culture, and social organization, a trend which continues today, although very little of the work's specific analysis is still viable.

José António Gonsalves de Mello, *Tempo dos flamengos: Influência da ocupação holandesa na vida e na cultura do Brasil* (Rio de Janeiro, 1947); a well-known regional social history.

Juan Lopes Sierra, *A Governor and His Image in Baroque Brazil: The Funereal Eulogy of Afonso Furtado de Castro do Rio de Mendonça*, ed. Stuart B. Schwartz, trans. Ruth E. Jones (Minneapolis, 1979; Spanish original, 1676); a colorful account by a contemporary of aspects of the life and official activity of a governor of late seventeenth-century Brazil with a comprehensive introduction setting the scene.

Frédéric Mauro, *Le Portugal et l'Atlantique au xviie siècle (1570–1670)* (Paris, 1960); a fundamental macroeconomic study of the sugar trade and Brazil's role in the Atlantic economy.

Richard M. Morse, "Brazil's Urban Development: Colony and Empire," in A. J. R. Russell-Wood (ed.), *From Colony to Nation: Essays on the Independence of Brazil* (Baltimore, 1975), pp. 151–81; deals with the nature of Brazil's urban network and its social implications.

Wanderley Pinho, *História de um engenho do Recôncavo* (Rio de Janeiro, 1942); a study of an individual sugar mill and the family that owned it for three centuries.

Katia M. de Queiros Mattoso, *Être esclave au Bresil, xvie–xixe siècle* (Paris, 1979); an introduction to the topic for a general audience but incorporating very recent research.

A. J. R. Russell-Wood, "Colonial Brazil," in David W. Cohen and Jack P. Greene (eds.), *Neither Slave nor Free: The Freedmen of African Descent in the Slave Societies of the New World* (Baltimore, 1972), pp. 84–133; deals with free Blacks and pardos.

Fidalgos and Philanthropists: The Santa Casa da Misericórdia of Bahia, 1550–1755 (Berkeley and Los Angeles, 1968); a thorough study of a Bahian charitable organization, providing important insights into the social complexities of the Brazilian city and the northeast generally.

Stuart B. Schwartz, "Free Farmers in a Slave Economy: The *Lavradores de Cana* in Colonial Bahia," in Dauril Alden (ed.), *Colonial Roots of Modern*

Brazil (Berkeley and Los Angeles, 1973), pp. 147–97; a systematic study of the crucial role of the lavradores in engenho structure and their varied, changing relationship with millowners, using specific examples from internal mill records.

Sovereignty and Society in Colonial Brazil: The High Court of Bahia and its Judges, 1609–1751 (Berkeley and Los Angeles, 1973); a social-institutional study showing the members of the capital's high court as part of an imperial bureaucracy including both Portugal and its possessions, and at the same time becoming closely enmeshed in local Bahian society.

David Grant Smith, "The Mercantile Class of Portugal and Brazil in the Seventeenth Century: A Socio-Economic Study of the Merchants of Lisbon and Bahia, 1620–1690," Ph.D. diss., University of Texas, Austin, 1975; an extensive study of career patterns, social composition, and modes of operation of the merchant class.

Susan A. Soeiro, "The Social and Economic Role of the Convent: Women and Nuns in Colonial Bahia, 1677–1800," *Hispanic American Historical Review* 54 (1974): 209–32; examines the place of upper-class women in society and the financial role of convents in economic life, based on an extensive doctoral dissertation.

Arnold Wiznitzer, *The Jews of Colonial Brazil* (New York, 1960); studies the New Christians' role in society as well as the usual religious aspects.

8. The fringes

José de Alcântara Machado, *Vida e morte do bandeirante* (São Paulo, 1930); a picture of life in early São Paulo and the interior based on a multivolume series of published testaments.

Eduardo Arcila Farías, *El régimen de la encomienda en Venezuela* (Seville, 1957); presents a full example of the slow-developing, long-lasting, labor-oriented encomienda of fringe areas.

John Francis Bannon, S.J. (ed.), *Bolton and the Spanish Borderlands* (Norman, Okla., 1964); a selection of writings on institutions and people of the north Mexican frontier by Herbert Bolton, a well-known historian of the earlier part of the twentieth century who specialized on the Mexican north.

Peter Masten Dunne, S.J., *Black Robes in Lower California* (Berkeley and Los Angeles, 1952); the tale of Jesuit activity on an extreme periphery in the eighteenth century, told by a Jesuit and based on Jesuit accounts.

Florestan Fernandes, "São Paulo no século XVI," in his *Mudanças sociais no Brasil* (São Paulo, 1960), pp. 179–233; a suggestive essay on the development of Paulista society.

Robert J. Ferry, "Encomienda, African Slavery, and Agriculture in Seventeenth-Century Caracas," *Hispanic American Historical Review* 61 (1981):

609–35; elucidates the transition from the encomienda toward more intensive estates as Venezuela finds an exportable crop.

Maynard Geiger, O.F.M., *Franciscan Missionaries in Hispanic California, 1769–1848: A Biographical Dictionary* (San Marino, Calif., 1969); gives unsynthesized but systematic and at times colorful information on the friars who were sent to one of the farthest peripheries of Hispanic America.

Mario Góngora, *Encomenderos y estancieros: Estudios acerca de la constitución social aristocrática de Chile después de la Conquista, 1580–1660* (Santiago, Chile, 1971); Through study of numerous individual holdings, shows the gradual evolution from encomienda estates to greater reliance on landowning and more intensive use of labor.

"Urban Social Stratification in Colonial Chile," *Hispanic American Historical Review* 55 (1975): 421–48; a thorough, if brief, presentation of the constituent groups of urban society in Chile, with emphasis on the sixteenth and seventeenth centuries.

Alistair Hennessy, *The Frontier in Latin American History* (Albuquerque, N.M., 1978); comparative essay giving considerable attention to some of the peripheral areas and presenting a typology of frontiers.

Evelyn Hu-De Hart, *Missionaries, Miners, and Indians: Spanish Contact with the Yaqui Nation of Northwestern New Spain, 1533–1820* (Tucson, Ariz., 1981); history of a semisedentary indigenous group on the north Mexican frontier during the colonial period.

Alvaro Jara, *Guerra y sociedad en Chile* (Santiago, Chile, 1971); demonstrates how Chile's continual frontier wars drained men and resources from the country and influenced its subsequent social organization.

Oakah H. Jones, Jr., *Los Paisanos: Spanish Settlers of the Northern Frontier of New Spain* (Norman, Okla., 1979); filled with demographic and other information on the civil population; a start toward a social history of the area.

Mathias C. Kieman, O.F.M., *The Indian Policy of Portugal in the Amazon Region, 1614–1693* (Washington, D.C., 1954); a detailed description of laws, policies, and missionary efforts in the Amazonian fringe area, with emphasis on the Franciscans.

Eugene H. Korth, S.J., *Spanish Policy in Colonial Chile: The Struggle for Social Justice, 1535–1700* (Stanford, Calif., 1968); deals with missions and Indian wars on the Araucanian frontier, and more especially with the surrounding controversies.

Colin M. MacLachlan, "The Indian Labor Structure in the Portuguese Amazon, 1700–1800," in Dauril Alden (ed.), *Colonial Roots of Modern Brazil* (Berkeley and Los Angeles, 1973), pp. 199–230; treats the formal aspects of labor systems devised by the Portuguese in the Amazon on the basis of high-level official correspondence.

Carlos A. Mayo, "Los pobleros del Tucumán colonial," *Revista de Historia de América* (Jan.–June 1978), pp. 27–57; contains much information on the social and economic aspects of encomienda estates in the interior of the Plata region.

Magnus Mörner, *The Political and Economic Activities of the Jesuits in the La Plata Region: The Hapsburg Era* (Stockholm, 1953); a balanced portrayal showing how much the Jesuits shared with other Spaniards in their goals and procedures.

Max L. Moorhead, *The Presidio: Bastion of the Spanish Borderlands* (Norman, Okla., 1975); an in-depth study of a crucial institution of the north Mexican frontier.

Richard M. Morse (ed.), *The Bandeirantes: The Historical Role of the Brazilian Pathfinders* (New York, 1965); an anthology of previously published pieces of varying persuasion, with a substantial introduction.

Robert C. Padden, "Cultural Change and Military Resistance in Araucanian Chile, 1550–1730," *Southwestern Journal of Anthropology* (1957):103–21; an analysis of the impact of fighting against the Spaniards on Araucanian organization and culture.

Philip Wayne Powell, *Soldiers, Indians, and Silver: The Northward Advance of New Spain, 1550–1600* (Berkeley and Los Angeles, 1952); a classic study of the formation of the standard institutions of the north Mexican frontier, including the mission and presidio.

Elman R. Service, "The Encomienda in Paraguay," *Hispanic American Historical Review* 31 (1951):230–52; an exemplary account of the development of the encomienda in a fringe area, placed in the context of a semisedentary indigenous people.

Spanish-Guaraní Relations in Early Colonial Paraguay (Ann Arbor, Mich., 1954); expands on the immediately preceding item.

Edward H. Spicer, *Cycles of Conquest: The Impact of Spain, Mexico, and the United States on the Indians of the Southwest, 1533–1960* (Tucson, Ariz., 1962); an anthropologically oriented study which places the experiences of the colonial period on the north Mexican frontier in a longer chronological perspective.

David G. Sweet, "A Rich Realm of Nature Destroyed: The Middle Amazon Valley, 1640–1750," Ph.D. diss., University of Wisconsin, 1975; a study of Amazonian society based on intensive archival research.

David Werlich, "Colonization and Settlement in the Peruvian Montaña," Ph.D. diss., University of Minnesota, 1968; contains much information on society and missions in the western Amazon basin from discovery to modern times.

9. Late colonial times in the Spanish Indies

Christon I. Archer, *The Army in Bourbon Mexico, 1760–1810* (Albuquerque, N.M., 1977); within the limits imposed by military-institutional sources, a well-rounded treatment covering policy, execution, and social composition of the forces.

Jacques A. Barbier, *Reform and Politics in Bourbon Chile, 1755–1796* (Ottawa,

1980); an unusually broad study of institutional politics in a specific region, including all the more important governmental agencies, with attention to individual careers which cross institutions and a strong awareness of social and economic ties.

D. A. Brading, *Haciendas and Ranchos in the Mexican Bajío: León, 1700–1860* (Cambridge, 1978); a detailed, many-faceted, eclectic study of agricultural development in the Léon region in response to Guanajuato's silver mining boom.

Miners and Merchants in Bourbon Mexico, 1763–1810 (Cambridge, 1971); a massive study consisting of large sections on government, international commerce, silver mining, and Guanajuato specifically as the late period's greatest mining center; uses institutional and statistical approaches but especially the tracing of individuals.

Mark A. Burkholder and D. S. Chandler, *From Impotence to Authority: The Spanish Crown and the American Audiencias, 1687–1808* (Columbia, Mo., 1977); based on a statistical survey of judges' employment dossiers for all the Spanish American Audiencias; shows changing regional origins of the membership, transimperial career patterns, and policy toward recruitment.

Leon G. Campbell, *The Military and Society in Colonial Peru, 1750–1810* (Philadelphia, 1978); covers changing military policy, social composition of the forces, and performance in the Tupac Amaru revolt.

John K. Chance, *Race and Class in Colonial Oaxaca* (Stanford, Calif., 1978); an aggregate statistical study of urban demography and social stratification in a provincial city, using parish and census records of various times but in particular the census of 1792.

Javier Cuenca Esteban, "Statistics of Spain's Colonial Trade, 1792–1820: Consular Duties, Cargo Inventories, and Balances of Trade," *Hispanic American Historical Review* 61 (1981):381–428; measures the impact of international wars and the first decade of the independence movements on the volume of Spanish trade with the Indies.

N. M. Farriss, *Crown and Clergy in Colonial Mexico, 1759–1821* (London, 1968); an institutional study of attempted ecclesiastical reforms and the reaction to them.

J. R. Fisher, *Government and Society in Colonial Peru: The Intendant System, 1784–1814* (London, 1970); modeled on John Lynch's study for the viceroyalty of Río de la Plata.

"Imperial 'Free Trade' and the Hispanic Economy, 1778–1796," *Journal of Latin American Studies* 13 (1981):21–56; measures the impact of free trade on Spanish exports to America, the proportion of exports of Spanish origin, and the proportions received by the various destinations in the Indies.

Silver Mines and Silver Miners in Colonial Peru, 1776–1824 (Liverpool, 1977); gives figures demonstrating and measuring the late colonial Peruvian mining boom.

Enrique Florescano, *Precios del maíz y crisis agrícolas en México (1708–1810)* (México, 1969); uses public granary figures to establish trends in the price of maize in New Spain's capital in the late colonial period.

Brian R. Hamnett, *Politics and Trade in Southern Mexico, 1750–1821* (Cambridge, 1971); using local official correspondence, studies a variety of political, institutional, and economic topics relating to late colonial Oaxaca, of which the collaboration of merchants and alcaldes mayores in exploiting indigenous cochineal production stands out.

Alexander von Humboldt, *Political Essay on the Kingdom of New Spain*, 4 vols. (London, 1811); an encyclopedic, multiregional, often statistical description of economy, government, and to some extent society at the beginning of the nineteenth century by an officially sponsored German traveler.

John E. Kicza, "Business and Society in Late Colonial Mexico City," Ph.D. diss., University of California, Los Angeles, 1979; a large-scale study of social and economic organization in the Indies' largest city at the end of the colonial period, from the highest levels of commerce and the professions to humble traders and producers, using both career-pattern research and aggregate statistics. The first volume of an expanded version has been published as *Colonial Entrepreneurs: Families and Business in Bourbon Mexico City* (Albuquerque, N.M., 1983), and a second volume is to follow.

Herbert S. Klein, "The Structure of the Hacendado Class in Late Eighteenth-Century Alto Peru: The Intendencia de la Paz," *Hispanic American Historical Review* 60 (1980):191–212; a statistical study showing the proportion of multiple estate owners and the number of permanent employees per estate for an area of the Andean highlands in the late colonial period.

Allan J. Kuethe, *Military Reform and Society in New Granada, 1773–1808* (Gainesville, Fla., 1978); comparable to the study by Leon Campbell cited earlier, with evidence for the regional variation of the late colonial military.

Doris M. Ladd, *The Mexican Nobility at Independence, 1780–1826* (Austin, Texas, 1976); a thorough study, using both statistics and some individual examples, of the holdings, life-style, and interrelatedness of that portion of the upper group which bore titles of high nobility.

John Tate Lanning, *The Eighteenth-Century Enlightenment in the University of San Carlos de Guatemala* (Ithaca, N.Y., 1956); an institutional and intellectual study showing a provincial Spanish American university up to date with current trends of European Enlightenment thought, though in structure little changed from earlier days.

John V. Lombardi, *People and and Places in Colonial Venezuela* (Bloomington, Ind., 1976); a demographic study showing the ethnic composition of the population and the relatively high degree of consolidation of the capital and its hinterland in the late colonial period.

John Lynch, *Spanish Colonial Administration, 1782–1810: The Intendant System in the Viceroyalty of the Río de la Plata* (London, 1958); an institutional study of the activities of the newly established intendants in one viceroyalty, as reported by themselves to the crown.

Lyle N. McAlister, *The "Fuero Militar" in New Spain, 1764–1800* (Gainesville, Fla., 1952); a pioneering study, institutional with social implications, which made the field aware at how late a time a professional and well-organized military was established, and that it was composed primarily of Hispanics rather than Indians.

Magnus Mörner, *Perfil de la sociedad rural del Cuzco a fines de la colonia* (Lima, 1978); statistical studies of estates and demography in the central Andean countryside in the late colonial period.

(ed.), *The Expulsion of the Jesuits from Latin America* (New York, 1965); selections from the highly polemical literature on the topic, with a substantial introduction on the expulsion and the activities of the Jesuits in general.

John Preston Moore, *The Cabildo in Peru under the Bourbons: A Study in the Decline and Resurgence of Local Government in the Audiencia of Lima, 1700–1824* (Durham, N.C., 1966); like its companion volume for the Hapsburg period, a strictly institutional study.

Susan Migden Socolow, *The Merchants of Buenos Aires, 1778–1810: Family and Commerce* (Cambridge, 1978); a social-statistical study of the merchant community of a primary growth area of the late colonial period, with some examples of individuals.

Eric Van Young, *Hacienda and Market in Eighteenth-Century Mexico: The Rural Economy of the Guadalajara Region, 1675–1820;* (Berkeley and Los Angeles, 1981) a large-scale, broadly based study of many aspects of agrarian response to growth in the local urban market.

10. Brazil in the age of gold and absolutism

Dauril Alden, "The Population of Brazil in the Late Eighteenth Century: A Preliminary Survey," *Hispanic American Historical Review* 43 (1963):173–205; still a useful statement of the main demographic facts for the English reader.

Royal Government in Colonial Brazil, with Special Reference to the Administration of the Marquis of Lavadrio, Viceroy, 1769–1779 (Berkeley and Los Angeles, 1968); the career of a viceroy of Brazil, including many administrative, military, and demographic matters.

C.R. Boxer, *The Golden Age of Brazil, 1695–1750* (Berkeley and Los Angeles, 1962); although based largely on officials' and travelers' reports, gives social-economic surveys of the major Brazilian regions in the time of the gold boom.

E. Bradford Burns, "The Intellectuals as Agents of Change and the Independence of Brazil, 1724–1822," in A. J. R. Russell-Wood (ed.), *From Colony to Nation* (Baltimore, 1975), pp. 211–46; a broad survey of Brazilian intellectual movements and the impact of the Enlightenment.

Manoel Cardozo, "Azeredo Coutinho and the Intellectual Ferment of His Times," in Henry Keith and S. F. Edward (eds.), *Conflict and Continuity in Brazilian Society* (Columbia, S.C., 1969), pp. 72–103; traces the career and social-political thought of this intelligent but reactionary ecclesiastic.

"The Brazilian Gold Rush," *The Americas* 3 (1946):137–60; overview of the opening of Minas Gerais based on an extensive Stanford University doctoral dissertation of 1947.

José Ferreira Carrato, *Igreja, iluminismo, e escolas mineiras coloniais* (São Paulo, 1968); a monograph on the educational system of Minas and its impact on political thought.

José Jobson de A. Arruda, *O Brasil no comércio colonial* (São Paulo, 1980); an exhaustive quantitative study of foreign trade, which documents Brazil's emergence as the dominant partner in the Portuguese colonial system.

John Norman Kennedy, "Bahian Elites, 1750–1822," *Hispanic American Historical Review* 53 (1973):415–39; on the interlocking of upper social elements, both those with mercantile and landed wealth and those prominent in institutions, including the military.

Elizabeth Anne Kuznesof, "Household Composition and Economy in an Urbanizing Economy: São Paulo, 1765–1836" Ph.D. diss., University of California, Berkeley, 1976; uses the materials of the Paulista captaincy to study the interaction of societal and sexual roles in that complex society.

Maria Luiza Marcilio, *A cidade de São Paulo: Povoamento e população (1750–1850)* (São Paulo, 1968); uses demographic methods to trace São Paulo's transformation from fringe to core in the eighteenth and nineteenth centuries.

Kenneth R. Maxwell, *Conflicts and Conspiracies: Brazil and Portugal, 1750–1808* (Cambridge, 1973); essentially concerned with the Minas conspiracy of 1788, this study also provides a general examination of the Pombaline period and its aftermath.

Luiz R. B. Mott, "Estructura demográfica das fazendas de gado do Piauí colonial: Um caso de povoamento rural centrífugo," *Ciência e Cultura* 30 (1978):1196–210; discussion of the ranching society of the northeastern interior, demonstrating the large number of slaves and free farmers; one of several microstudies of northeastern regions by this anthropologist.

Iraci del Nero da Costa, *Populações mineiras* (São Paulo, 1981); a demographic study based on census and tribute records.

Fernando A. Novais, *Portugal e Brasil na crise do antigo sistema colonial (1777–1808)* (São Paulo, 1979); concentrates on the changing concepts of mercantilism and the ideology of the colonial compact.

Donald Ramos, "A Social History of Ouro Preto: Stresses of Dynamic Urbanization in Colonial Brazil, 1695–1726," Ph.D. diss., University of

Florida, 1972; contains a wealth of information on Mineiro society, with close attention to demographic factors of the area's growth.

A. J. R. Russell-Wood, "Local Government in Portuguese America: A Study in Cultural Divergence," *Comparative Studies in Society and History* 16 (1974):187–231; deals with the institutions of municipal government in Minas Gerais and their relationship to society.

Luís dos Santos Vilhena, *A Bahia no século XVIII*, 3 vols. (Bahia, 1969); a modern edition of *Recopilação de notícias soteropolitanas e brasílicas*, 1802, written by a Portuguese schoolmaster with perceptive eyes and an acid pen who lived in Bahia.

Pierre Verger, *Flux et reflux de la traite des nègres entre le golfe de Bénin et Bahia de Todos os Santos* (Paris, 1968); a detailed study reaching beyond the slave trade to the life of slaves in Brazil.

Francisco Vidal Luna, *Minas Gerais: Escravos e senhores* (São Paulo, 1981); draws unsuspected patterns in the distribution of slaveholding in Minas from census and tribute records.

Emilio Willems, "Social Differentiation in Colonial Brazil," *Comparative Studies in Society and History* 12 (1970):31–49; demonstrates the increasing complexity of rural life and the existence of a numerous rural peasantry.

11. Epilogue: the coming of independence

Patria Aufderheide, "Order and Violence: Social Deviance and Social Control in Brazil, 1786–1840," Ph.D. diss., University of Minnesota, 1976; examines the impact of independence on society, finding considerable continuity but also some striking changes, especially for the free colored population.

Diana Balmori and Robert Oppenheimer, "Family Clusters: Generational Nucleation in Nineteenth-Century Argentina and Chile," *Comparative Studies in Society and History* 21 (1979):231–61; shows the two areas and their capitals undergoing consolidation in response to economic upswing, comparable to the experience of other regions centuries earlier.

Nettie Lee Benson (ed.), *Mexico and the Spanish Cortes, 1810–1822: Eight Essays* (Austin, Texas, 1966); a collection of original pieces on the topic.

Simon Collier, *Ideas and Politics of Chilean Independence, 1808–1833* (Cambridge, 1967); a survey of formal political ideas of the independence period in Chile as expressed in newspapers, public forums, and correspondence.

Jorge I. Domínguez, *Insurrection or Loyalty: The Breakdown of the Spanish American Empire* (Cambridge, Mass., 1980); social-scientific analysis of the existing historical literature on the independence period in Chile, Cuba, Mexico, and Venezuela.

Richard Graham, *Independence in Latin America* (New York, 1972); a brief analytical survey, including Brazil as well as Spanish America.

Charles C. Griffin, "Economic and Social Aspects of the Era of Spanish American Independence," *Hispanic American Historical Review* 29

(1949):170–87; a classic article on a topic still not well covered by the historical literature.

Tulio Halperín-Donghi, *Politics, Economics, and Society in Argentina in the Revolutionary Period* (Cambridge, 1975); a principally political study, on a large scale, with some social and economic background.

Hugh M. Hamill, Jr., *The Hidalgo Revolt: Prelude to Mexican Independence* (Gainesville, Fla., 1966); a narrative of the revolt of 1810, deepened by attention to the social characteristics of the populace in the area where it broke out and to the nature of the propaganda campaigns waged by the opposing sides.

Brian R. Hamnett, *Revolución y contrarrevolución en México y el Perú (Liberalismo, realeza y separatismo, 1800–1824)* (México, 1978); follows high-level political manueverings in the struggles betwen loyalists and revolutionaries in the two oldest viceroyalties, with considerable attention to financial and economic aspects.

R. A. Humphreys and John Lynch (eds.), *The Origins of the Latin American Revolutions, 1808–1826* (New York, 1966); a broad, well-chosen selection of previously published pieces on intellectual, political, economic, and other factors; includes Brazil.

Jay Kinsbruner, *The Spanish American Independence Movement* (Hinsdale, Ill., 1973); a brief analytical survey covering all of Spanish America.

John Lynch, *The Spanish American Revolutions, 1808–1826* (New York, 1973); narrative of political and military events for all of Spanish America.

Carlos Guilherme Mota, *Nordeste 1817* (São Paulo, 1972); depicts the republican movement in Pernambuco and its suppression, and discusses the social limitations of the movement's ideology.

Manoel de Oliveira Lima, *Dom João no Brasil (1808–1821)*, 2nd ed., 3 vols., (Rio de Janeiro, 1945; published originally, 1909); a highly readable political and biographical account.

John Leddy Phelan, *The People and the King: The Comunero Revolution in Colombia, 1781* (Madison, Wis., 1978); a fleshed-out narrative combined with portraits of many leaders and extended analysis of the rationale of the participants in the Comunero revolt.

Jaime E. Rodríguez O., *The emergence of Spanish America: Vincente Rocafuerte and Spanish Americanism, 1808–1832* (Berkeley and Los Angeles, 1975); a study in political-intellectual history focusing on one significant personage of the age of independence.

José Honório Rodrigues, *Independência: Revolução e contra-revolução*, 5 vols., (Rio de Janeiro, 1976); a comprehensive study full of bibliographical references and suggestions for further research.

A. J. R. Russell-Wood (ed.), *From Colony to Nation: Essays on the Independence of Brazil* (Baltimore, 1975); an anthology of original pieces on the background and process of Brazilian independence.

Index

Haiti, 403, 410; *see also* Hispaniola, Saint Domingue

Cambridge Latin American studies

1 Simon Collier. *Ideas and Politics of Chilean Independence, 1808–1833*
2 Michael P. Costeloe. *Church Wealth in Mexico: A Study of the Juzgado de Capellanías in the Archbishopric of Mexico, 1800–1856*
3 Peter Calvert. *The Mexican Revolution 1910–1914: The Diplomacy of Anglo-American Conflict*
4 Richard Graham. *Britain and the Onset of Modernization in Brazil, 1850–1914*
5 Herbert S. Klein. *Parties and Political Change in Bolivia, 1880–1952*
6 Leslie Bethell. *The Abolition of the Brazilian Slave Trade: Britain, Brazil and the Slave Trade Question, 1807–1869*
7 David Barkin and Timothy King. *Regional Economic Development: The River Basin Approach in Mexico*
8 Celso Furtado. *Economic Development of Latin America: Historical Background and Contemporary Problems* (second edition)
9 William Paul McGreevey. *An Economic History of Colombia, 1845–1930*
10 D. A. Brading. *Miners and Merchants in Bourbon Mexico, 1763–1810*
11 Jan Bazant. *Alienation of Church Wealth in Mexico: Social and Economic Aspects of the Liberal Revolution, 1856–1875*
12 Brian R. Hamnett. *Politics and Trade in Southern Mexico, 1750–1821*
13 J. Valerie Fifer. *Bolivia: Land, Location, and Politics since 1825*
14 Peter Gerhard. *A Guide to the Historical Geography of New Spain*
15 P. J. Bakewell. *Silver Mining and Society in Colonial Mexico, Zacatecas 1564–1700*
16 Kenneth R. Maxwell. *Conflicts and Conspiracies: Brazil and Portugal, 1750–1808*
17 Verena Martínez-Alier. *Marriage, Class and Colour in Nineteenth-Century Cuba: A Study of Racial Attitudes and Sexual Values in a Slave Society*
18 Tulio Halperín-Donghi. *Politics, Economics and Society in Argentina in the Revolutionary Period*
19 David Rock. *Politics in Argentina 1890–1930: The Rise and Fall of Radicalism*
20 Mario Góngora. *Studies in the Colonial History of Spanish America*
21 Arnold J. Bauer. *Chilean Rural Society from the Spanish Conquest to 1930*

22 James Lockhart and Enrique Otte. *Letters and People of the Spanish Indies, Sixteenth Century*
23 Leslie B. Rout, Jr. *The African Experience in Spanish America: 1502 to the Present Day*
24 Jean A Meyer. *The Cristero Rebellion: The Mexican People between Church and State, 1926–1929*
25 Stefan De Vylder. *Allende's Chile: The Political Economy of the Rise and Fall of the Unidad Popular*
26 Kenneth Duncan and Ian Rutledge, with the collaboration of Colin Harding. *Land and Labour in Latin America: Essays on the Development of Agrarian Capitalism in the Nineteenth and Twentieth Centuries*
27 Guillermo Lora, edited by Laurence Whitehead. *A History of the Bolivian Labour Movement, 1848–1971*
28 Victor Nunes Leal, translated by June Henfrey. *Coronelismo: The Municipality and Representative Government in Brazil*
29 Anthony Hall. *Drought and Irrigation in North-east Brazil*
30 S. M. Socolow. *The Merchants of Buenos Aires 1778–1810: Family and Commerce*
31 Charles F. Nunn. *Foreign Immigrants in Early Bourbon Mexico, 1700–1760*
32 D. A. Brading. *Haciendas and Ranchos in the Mexican Bajio*
33 Billie R. DeWalt. *Modernization in a Mexican Ejido: A Study in Economic Adaptation*
34 David Nicholls. *From Dessalines to Duvalier: Race, Colour and National Independence in Haiti*
35 Jonathan C. Brown. *A Socioeconomic History of Argentina, 1776–1860*
36 Marco Palacios. *Coffee in Colombia 1850–1970: An Economic, Social and Political History*
37 David Murray. *Odious Commerce: Britain, Spain and the Abolition of the Cuban Slave Trade*
38 David Brading (ed.), *Caudillo and Peasant in the Mexican Revolution*
39 Joe Foweraker. *The Struggle for Land: A Political Economy of the Pioneer Frontier in Brazil from 1930 to the Present Day*
40 George Philip. *Oil and Politics in Latin America: Nationalist Movements and State Companies*
41 Noble David Cook. *Demographic Collapse: Indian Peru, 1520–1620*
42 Gilbert Joseph. *Revolution from Without: Yucatan, Mexico and the United States, 1880–1924.*
43 B. S. McBeth. *Juan Vicente Gómez and the Oil Companies in Venezuela, 1908–1975*
44 Jerome A. Offner. *Law and Politics in Aztec Texcoco*
45 Thomas J. Terbot. *Brazil's State-owned Enterprises: A Case Study of the State as Entrepreneur*
46 James Lockhart and Stuart B. Schwartz. *Early Latin America*

TERRA LINDA H.S. LIB.
T 64463